HONG KONG'S COURT OF FINAL APPEAL

In the years since it was established on 1 July, 1997, Hong Kong's Court of Final Appeal has developed a distinctive body of new law and doctrine with the help of eminent foreign common law judges. Under the leadership of Chief Justice Andrew Li, it has also remained independent under Chinese sovereignty and become a model for other Asian final courts working to maintain the rule of law, judicial independence and professionalism in challenging political environments.

In this book, leading practitioners, jurists and academics examine the Court's history, operation and jurisprudence, and provide a comparative analysis with European courts and China's other autonomous final court in Macau. It also makes use of extensive empirical data compiled from the jurisprudence to illuminate the Court's decision-making processes and identify the relative impacts of the foreign and local judges.

SIMON N. M. YOUNG is a Professor at the Faculty of Law, The University of Hong Kong and was Director of the Centre for Comparative and Public Law from 2007 to 2013.

YASH GHAI is an Emeritus Professor at the Faculty of Law, The University of Hong Kong, where in the past he has held the Sir Y. K. Pao Chair in Public Law.

HONG KONG'S COURT OF FINAL APPEAL

The Development of the Law in China's Hong Kong

SIMON N. M. YOUNG AND YASH GHAI

CAMBRIDGE
UNIVERSITY PRESS

CAMBRIDGE
UNIVERSITY PRESS

University Printing House, Cambridge CB2 8BS, United Kingdom

Published in the United States of America by Cambridge University Press, New York

Cambridge University Press is part of the University of Cambridge.

It furthers the University's mission by disseminating knowledge in the pursuit of education, learning and research at the highest international levels of excellence.

www.cambridge.org
Information on this title: www.cambridge.org/9781107011212

© Cambridge University Press 2014

First published 2014

Printed in the United Kingdom by Bell and Bain Ltd

A catalogue record for this publication is available from the British Library

Library of Congress Cataloguing in Publication data
Hong Kong's Court of Final Appeal : the development of the law in China's Hong Kong /
[edited by] Simon N. M. Young, Yash Ghai.
pages   cm
Includes index.
ISBN 978-1-107-01121-2 (hardback)
1. Hong Kong (China). Court of Final Appeal.   2. Appellate procedure – China – Hong Kong.
3. Judicial process – China – Hong Kong.   4. Courts of last resort – China – Hong Kong –
History.   5. Courts – China – Hong Kong – History.   6. Law – China – Hong Kong –
History.   7. Courts of last resort – China – Macau (Special Administrative Region)
I. Young, Simon N. M.   II. Ghai, Yash P., 1938–
KNQ9335.2.H54H665   2014
347.5125′035 – dc23   2013013119

ISBN 978-1-107-01121-2 Hardback

CONTENTS

v

FIGURES

TABLES

CONTRIBUTORS

PAULO CARDINAL, Chief Legal Adviser, Macau Legislative Assembly; Guest Lecturer, Faculty of Law, University of Macau

JOHANNES CHAN SC (Hon), Professor and Dean, Faculty of Law, The University of Hong Kong

ALBERT H. Y. CHEN SBS, JP, Chan Professor of Constitutional Law, Faculty of Law, The University of Hong Kong

JILL COTTRELL, formerly Senior Lecturer, Faculty of Law, The University of Hong Kong

ANTONIO DA ROZA, Research Assistant Professor, Faculty of Law, The University of Hong Kong; Barrister, New Chambers

MARK DALY, Partner, Daly & Associates, Hong Kong

YASH P. GHAI, Emeritus Professor, The University of Hong Kong

RICK GLOFCHESKI, Professor, Faculty of Law, The University of Hong Kong; Editor, *Hong Kong Law Journal*

JORGE GODINHO, Associate Professor, Faculty of Law, University of Macau

OLIVER JONES, Barrister, Seven Wentworth, Chambers of D F Jackson AM QC, Sydney

P. Y. LO, Barrister-at-law (England & Wales and Hong Kong); PhD, The University of Hong Kong

JOSEF MARKO, Professor and Dean, Faculty of Law, University of Graz, Austria; former international judge and Vice President of the Constitutional Court of Bosnia-Herzegovina;

SIR ANTHONY MASON AC, KBE, non-permanent judge, Court of Final Appeal, Hong Kong; Chief Justice of Australia, 1987 to 1995

GARY MEGGITT, Assistant Professor, Faculty of Law, The University of Hong Kong; Barrister and Solicitor Advocate (England & Wales), ACII, MCIArb, CEDR Accredited Mediator

MALCOLM MERRY, Associate Professor and Head, Department of Professional Legal Education, Faculty of Law, The University of Hong Kong; Barrister, Hong Kong

MICHAEL THOMAS CMG, QC, SC, Temple Chambers, Hong Kong; Essex Court Chambers, London; Attorney-General of Hong Kong, 1983 to 1988

WILLIAM WAUNG, formerly Justice of the Court of First Instance, High Court, Hong Kong

NANCY XIAONAN YANG, Lecturer, Law School, Dalian Maritime University

SIMON N. M. YOUNG, Professor, Faculty of Law, The University of Hong Kong; Director, Centre for Comparative and Public Law, 2007 to 2013

TRIBUTE TO THE
HONOURABLE ANDREW LI KWOK NANG

The Hon Andrew Li Kwok Nang was born in Hong Kong on 12 December 1948. He received his education in Hong Kong at St. Paul's Co-Educational Primary School and St. Paul's Co-Educational College until the completion of Form 3. He finished his secondary education in England and attended Cambridge University. He holds the degrees of Master of Arts and Master of Laws from that University. He was called to the English Bar in 1970 and the Hong Kong Bar in 1973.

Mr Li was appointed as the Chief Justice of the Court of Final Appeal, Hong Kong Special Administrative Region on 1 July 1997. Before his appointment, Mr Li practised at the Hong Kong Bar. In 1988 he was appointed Queen's Counsel.

Mr Li has a long record of public service. He was a member of the Executive Council and Steward of the Hong Kong Jockey Club. He had served as Chairman of the University and Polytechnic Grants Committee and the Land Development Corporation. He had served as Vice Chairman of the Council of the HK University of Science and Technology, Deputy Chairman of the Board of Review of Inland Revenue and as member of the Law Reform Commission, the Securities Commission, the Standing Committee on Company Law Reform, the Banking Advisory Committee and Judicial Service Commission. He is Vice Chairman of the Council of St. Paul's Co-Educational College. He is a trustee of the Friends of Tsinghua University Law School Charitable Trust and a Guest Professor of the Tsinghua University. He is Honorary Professor of Law at the University of Hong Kong, the Chinese University of Hong Kong, City University of Hong Kong, and Shue Yan University.

Mr Li's awards include Honorary Degrees awarded by the HK University of Science & Technology (1993); the Baptist University (1994); the Open University of Hong Kong (1997); the University of Hong Kong (2001); the Griffith University (2001); the University of New South Wales (2002), the University of Technology, Sydney (2005); the Chinese University of Hong Kong (2006); the Shue Yan University (2009); Lingnan University (2010); City University of Hong Kong (2010); and Oxford University (2013). He was made an Honorary Bencher of the Middle Temple in 1997 and an Honorary Fellow of Fitzwilliam College Cambridge in 1999. He was awarded the Grand Bauhinia Medal by the Hong Kong Government in 2008.

Mr Li is married with two daughters.

Secretary for Justice, Mr Wong Yan Lung, SC, 16 July 2010

Chief Justice, when your decision to take early retirement was announced last September, although everyone regretted your early departure from the bench, the applause for your outstanding achievement over your 13 years of tenure was in complete accord. You were praised by both the local and the overseas press. And the standing ovation after your speech at this year's opening of the legal year was a moving testimony to the respect you command in this community. It has been said the role of a judge is to bring about the realisation of the rule of law. As the first Chief Justice of the Hong Kong Special Administrative Region, you have shouldered the monumental task of bringing about the legal realisation of the innovative 'one country, two systems' principle. And 13 years on, the verdict is unanimous: The mission has been accomplished with resounding success. . . . The Chief Justice I know is more than a giant in the administration of justice, he is an exemplar of excellence with a soul. He is above all a man of compassion whose first concern is for the people of Hong Kong. In and out of this court room are individuals, among them members of the judiciary, legal practitioners in particular your pupils (with me included), also 11 batches of Bar Scholars, the staff of the CFA and judiciary, and many more whose hearts have been inspired by your example and whose lives have been touched by your generosity. That's why many legal practitioners have been happy to give up a lucrative private practice in exchange for the one-way ticket to join the judiciary. They see at its pinnacle an inspiring figure who truly lives out what he preaches.

Russell Coleman SC, Chairman of the Hong Kong Bar Association, 16 July 2010

It is, of course, no secret that Hong Kong has benefited enormously from the accident of timing that allowed the then Andrew Li QC to become the first Chief Justice of Hong Kong in the new era following the resumption of Chinese sovereignty. If we did not know it then, we now know what an inspired appointment it was. It is not just those of us in the law who think that way. In February 2010, the Chief Justice achieved the highest score ever recorded in a University of Hong Kong public opinion poll. His approval ratings would be the envy of any President, Prime Minister, Chief Executive, or indeed – to be closer to my home –any member of the Bar turned politician. . . . By my count, by 31 August 2010, the Chief

Justice will have been in post for 4,810 days. I wonder if it is simply a coincidence that the digits of that number, 4-8-1-0, add up to 13, the number of complete years of his tenure.... Justice is not fragile in Hong Kong, but it requires constant vigilance; such vigilance is the duty of all those in the legal profession, but perhaps particularly the duty of the judiciary and its head, the Chief Justice. As was once said by another Chief Justice: 'Justice is like oxygen: there is no reason to notice it if you have it in abundance. However, as you constrict the flow, it becomes more and more important until the point is reached where nothing else matters at all.' Under the Chief Justice's tenure, we have breathed rather easily.

Huen Wong, President of the Law Society of Hong Kong, August 2010

It was my honour and privilege to have the opportunity to attend and say a few words as President of the Law Society at the farewell sitting for Chief Justice Andrew Li on 16 July. The occasion was a testimony to the high regard in which the retiring Chief Justice is held. Over 100 guests gathered at the courtroom of the Court of Final Appeal to bid farewell to him. It was a moving occasion that, I am sure, will remain as one of the most memorable court sittings in the history of the Judiciary. Chief Justice Li took over the reins of the judiciary in an era of uncertainty when the unprecedented constitutional concept of 'one country, two systems' was implemented in Hong Kong. The judiciary plays a critical role in the building up of public confidence in this innovative concept. As stated in its mission statement, the judiciary is: 'To maintain an independent and competent judicial system which upholds the rule of law, safeguards the rights and freedoms of the individual, and commands confidence within and outside Hong Kong.' Throughout his tenure, Chief Justice Li has advanced the mission of the judiciary faithfully and fearlessly. The huge turnout at his farewell sitting and the recognition of his achievements both by the legal and judicial circles and the general public is proof beyond reasonable doubt of the high regard in which Chief Justice Li is held and that his mission has been accomplished.

The Honourable Dr Margaret Ng, Legislative Council, 9 June 2010

Deputy President, this is the first occasion for the elected legislature of the HKSAR to endorse the appointment of a Chief Justice. I would like to take this opportunity to pay tribute to Mr. Andrew Li, the outgoing Chief

Justice. He has served in that office for the most crucial first 13 years of the Hong Kong Court of Final Appeal with distinction, and our record will not be complete without acknowledgement.

By upholding fundamental rights and freedoms in his judgments right from the beginning, when the world wondered if 'two systems' can prevail under 'one country', he has boosted confidence in the rule of law in Hong Kong and made an essential contribution to Hong Kong stability. He has taken as his chief mission to build up a court of final appeal of stature and prestige. Among our non-permanent judges from overseas jurisdictions are former Chief Justices of Australia, a Lord Chief Justice of England and Wales, several Law Lords, former judges of the Supreme Court of New Zealand – judges who are household names to serious practitioners of the law. He has persuaded an unprecedented number of the best and brightest of Hong Kong's legal practitioners to abandon their lucrative practice to join the bench. He has established regular and fruitful exchanges with the judiciary on the Mainland and overseas. But above all, he has kept in touch with the sentiments of the ordinary men and women of our community and taken every appropriate occasion to address their concerns. As Chief Justice, he will leave an indelible mark in the annals of the history of the HKSAR.

ACKNOWLEDGEMENTS

Our project on Hong Kong's Court of Final Appeal (CFA) began in 2007, after we succeeded in obtaining a research grant from the Research Grants Council (RGC) of the Hong Kong Special Administrative Region (HKSAR) (Project No. HKU 7467/06H). Originally, we were to study the first decade of the CFA, but when the Chief Justice unexpectedly announced in September 2009 his retirement at the end of August 2010, we decided to extend the time frame to cover the CFA's first 13 years to coincide with the term of office of its first Chief Justice.

The initial research results were disseminated at a public conference organised by the Centre for Comparative and Public Law, held at the University of Hong Kong (HKU) on 5–6 March 2010. All the contributors to this volume and Kevin Zervos SC (now Justice Zervos of the High Court) presented papers at the conference, which was attended by the Chief Justice, the three permanent judges of the CFA, and non-permanent judges Lord Hoffmann and Justice Litton. The event was a success and increased public awareness of the CFA and its impact.

We begin by thanking the RGC for funding the project. We thank all of the contributors, especially our two keynote speakers, Sir Anthony Mason NPJ and Professor Josef Marko, all the Hong Kong judges who attended the conference, the Dean of the HKU Faculty of Law (Johannes Chan) and our colleagues in the Faculty who worked tirelessly to organise the event: Flora Leung, Sharron Fast, Raymond Lam, Eddie Leung and Jessica Cheng. We are also indebted to the many researchers who have contributed to our study. They include senior researchers Antonio Da Roza (who contributed enormously) and Kate Egan, and student researchers Bryan Chan, Ernest Ng, Ruby Ho, Chris Chan, Ivy Chen and Gary Lam. We also thank the many people who took an interest in our project and provided us with valuable information: District Judge Simon Kwang in the CFA Registry, Annie Tang, Kevin Zervos SC, Gerard McCoy SC, Clive Grossman SC, Michael Blanchflower SC, Matthew Groves, Mohammed

Talib and our many HKU colleagues and students who took an interest. We thank those who allowed us to reproduce their tribute to the former Chief Justice, and we acknowledge the HKSAR Government's copyright in the tribute from the former Secretary for Justice. We also thank Finola O'Sullivan (and her colleagues at Cambridge University Press) for her support and constant encouragement, Jill Cottrell for her editorial assistance right up until publication, and the current Chief Justice, Geoffrey Ma, and his colleagues in the judiciary for their continuous support.

Above all we are most grateful for all of Chief Justice Andrew Li's assistance.

TABLE OF CASES

TABLE OF LEGISLATION

LIST OF ABBREVIATIONS

ADR	Alternative Dispute Resolution
BiH	Bosnia-Herzegovina
BL	Basic Law of the Hong Kong Special Administrative Region of the People's Republic of China
BLC	Committee for the Basic Law of the Hong Kong Special Administrative Region under the Standing Committee of the National People's Congress
BLDC	Drafting Committee for the Basic Law of the Hong Kong Special Administrative Region
BMO	Building Management Ordinance (Cap. 344)
BOR	Hong Kong Bill of Rights
BORO	Hong Kong Bill of Rights Ordinance (Cap. 383)
CA	Court of Appeal
CCP	Chinese Communist Party
CFA	Court of Final Appeal of the Hong Kong Special Administrative Region of the People's Republic of China
CFA AC	Appeal Committee of the Court of Final Appeal
CFI	Court of First Instance of the High Court of the Hong Kong Special Administrative Region of the People's Republic of China
CJ	Chief Justice
CJR	Civil Justice Reform
CPC	Communist Party of China
CPG	Central People's Government of the PRC
CPR	English Civil Procedure Rules
ECtHR	European Court of Human Rights
ECJ	European Court of Justice
ECO	Employees' Compensation Ordinance (Cap. 282)
ECHR	European Convention on Human Rights
GDP	gross domestic product
HK	Hong Kong
HKCFAO	Hong Kong Court of Final Appeal Ordinance (Cap. 484)
HKLJ	Hong Kong Law Journal

HKSAR	Hong Kong Special Administrative Region of the People's Republic of China
HR	High Representative for Bosnia-Herzegovina
ICCPR	International Covenant on Civil and Political Rights
ICESCR	International Covenant on Economic, Social and Cultural Rights
JA	Justice of Appeal
JD	Joint Declaration of the Government of the United Kingdom of Great Britain and Northern Ireland and the Government of the People's Republic of China on the Question of Hong Kong
JORC	Judicial Officers Recommendation Commission
LAC	Legislative Affairs Commission of the Standing Committee of the National People's Congress
LegCo	Legislative Council of the Hong Kong Special Administrative Region of the People's Republic of China
LQR	Law Quarterly Review
MLO	Money Lenders Ordinance (Cap. 163)
NPC	National People's Congress
NPCSC	Standing Committee of the National People's Congress
NPJ	non-permanent judge of the Court of Final Appeal
NSW	New South Wales
OJLS	Oxford Journal of Legal Studies
PC	Judicial Committee of the Privy Council
PJ	permanent judge of the Court of Final Appeal
PLC	Provisional Legislative Council
PRC	People's Republic of China
RDC	The Rules of the District Court (Cap. 336, sub. leg. H)
RHC	The Rules of the High Court (Cap 4, sub. leg. A)
SAR	special administrative region
SPC	Supreme People's Court
SPP	Supreme People's Procuratorate
TSI	*Tribunal de Segunda Instância* or Court of Second Instance of the Macau SAR
TSJ	*Tribunal Superior de Justiça*
TUI	*Tribunal de Última Instância* or Court of Last Instance of the Macau SAR
UKSC	Supreme Court of the United Kingdom
UN	United Nations
US	United States of America

Themes and arguments

YASH GHAI

Origin and importance of the Court of Final Appeal

This book is a study of the Court of Final Appeal (CFA) of the Hong Kong Special Administrative Region of the People's Republic of China (HKSAR). It traces the first 13 years of the work of its judges and their jurisprudence. The CFA came into being on the transfer of Hong Kong's sovereignty to China on 1 July 1997, marking the end of British rule of more than a century. It marked both a departure and a continuation, with continuation the more significant role. Its primary role is the preservation of the rule of law, widely perceived to be the most important innovation and legacy of British rule,[1] promoting both its market economy and human rights.[2] Its unique characteristics as a judicial body in China are the membership of foreign judges, the application of the common law, and total separation from the Mainland Chinese judicial system – the elements of continuity.

In some respects, the CFA is regarded as the successor to the Privy Council (PC), whose jurisdiction over Hong Kong ended just as that of the CFA began. But the challenges it faced are significantly different from those of the PC. The PC was the court of the imperial authority, embedded securely within the traditions of the common law, its legitimacy challenged in neither Britain nor Hong Kong. The new sovereign, China,

---

[1] See e.g. Steve Tsang, *A Modern History of Hong Kong* (Hong Kong: Hong Kong University Press, 2004); Steve Tsang (ed.), *Judicial Independence and the Rule of Law in Hong Kong* (Hong Kong: Hong Kong University Press, 2001).

[2] The assumption that Hong Kong's robust legal system was responsible for its economic system is somewhat exaggerated; many other factors contributed (e.g. cheap labour, forms of patronage, preferential position of key companies, low tax, lack of regulation of competition); see Yash Ghai, 'The rule of law and capitalism: reflections on the Basic Law' in R. Wacks (ed.), *Hong Kong, China and 1997: Essays in Legal Theory* (Hong Kong: University of Hong Kong Press, l993) 342–66.

did not understand the common law or respect the independence of the judiciary. China had agreed to an institution such as the CFA to maintain confidence of the local and international community as investors in Hong Kong, before it fully understood the implications of the CFA. Negotiations on the details of the CFA, its composition and jurisdiction, were among the most difficult and protracted of any provisions of the Sino–British Joint Declaration and the drafting of the Basic Law (BL).[3] In the process, the composition as well as the jurisdiction of the CFA was modified. So unlike the PC, the CFA is not ultimately the final court for Hong Kong because in important ways, the CFA is subject to the overriding powers of the Standing Committee of the National People's Congress (NPCSC, the supreme state authority of China). Any account of the CFA has to take into consideration the impact of the NPCSC, even sometimes of its silences.

Hong Kong's legal system, based on the common law, often appears to be impenetrable to the Chinese authorities, who are not tuned in to the niceties of Western procedures and are more at home with the more flexible standards of Chinese law. The two legal systems have very different traditions, styles of interpretation, and capacity for accommodation to political pressures. The presence of a strong legal system in Hong Kong and the absence of a fully democratic system tend to convert contentious political, and sometimes social, matters into legal issues, but China prefers legal issues to be treated as political matters in which it has the upper hand. Courts thus often find themselves in the front line in the defence of the BL.

The scheme of the BL of the HKSAR, Hong Kong's constitution enacted by the National People's Congress (NPC), essentially subordinates Hong Kong's executive and legislature to the Mainland's authorities (see Chapter 2). The CFA's mandate to protect Hong Kong's autonomy and its people's rights is thus likely to bring the judiciary into conflict with other public authorities in the HKSAR. It is also likely to bring it into conflict with the Central Authorities, especially if common law assumptions of judicial review extend to the entire scheme of the BL. The law is deliberated on by the courts in an open process. Unlike the executive, the courts

---

[3] See M. Lee and W. Szeto, *The Basic Law: Some Basic Flaws* (Hong Kong: the Authors, 1988); Jonathan Dimbleby, *The Last Governor: Chris Patten and the Handover of Hong Kong* (London: Little, Brown and Co., 1997); and Chapters 5 (Young and Da Roza) and 8 (Thomas) in this volume.

cannot fudge issues; they have to decide disputes that are presented to them, and they have to do so in public and provide reasons and justifications for their decisions. Unlike secret political negotiations, awkward issues cannot so easily be ducked or fudged in a court (as is well illustrated by the sequence of events that led to the rights of abode cases, discussed in several chapters).

Perhaps the fundamental difficulty in the exercise of the jurisdiction of the CFA lies in differing concepts of the role of the courts on the Mainland and Hong Kong. In Hong Kong, courts are separate from and independent of the executive and the legislature. It is their responsibility to review the validity of legislation and executive acts. A judgment adverse to the government is not regarded as a challenge to its legitimacy or the right to rule. In China, courts follow Chinese Communist Party directives in appropriate cases and cannot refuse to enforce a law because it might be considered to contravene the constitution. There seems to be insufficient appreciation among Mainland officials and lawyers as to the bounds within which Hong Kong courts have to make decisions. The courts have little choice about what is litigated and are compelled by the generally accepted notions of the responsibilities of common law judges to adjudicate disputes brought before them in accordance with the law, albeit that the law is frequently flexible.

In its first 13 years, the CFA had to decide weighty matters such as the legality of the Provisional Legislative Council, the relationship of the BL to the People's Republic of China (PRC) Constitution, the scope of the application of Mainland legislation in Hong Kong, the validity of rules governing disciplinary and other aspects of public service, the right of abode in Hong Kong of certain Mainland residents, the fate of thousands of refugees from Vietnam, complex issues of land law, and the regime for the protection of rights and freedoms of Hong Kong residents. These issues have raised central questions about the autonomy of the HKSAR and the competence of the Central Authorities of the PRC over Hong Kong.

They have also major consequences for the social and economic future of Hong Kong, particularly the decisions on the right of abode, which affect the flow of migrants from the Mainland, the right to public housing, and the reach of the defamation law. More specifically, the litigation on the BL has raised questions about the place of law and legality in the mediation of the relationship between Hong Kong and the Mainland, and the role of the courts in defining or sustaining that relationship. These are momentous matters in a largely uncharted territory. Consequently, it is not surprising that the constitutional role of the courts, especially the CFA, has given rise to great controversy.[4]

But the CFA's jurisdiction goes beyond the constitution, covering all areas of the law. The foundation of its jurisdiction, in addition to the BL, is the common law, but not the common law as at the time of the resumption of Chinese sovereignty because it is freed from the English common law. Instead, it is free to choose from the common law of any particular country. This has given the CFA enormous flexibility in moulding the common law to the changing circumstances of Hong Kong. The membership of judges from other jurisdictions has enabled the CFA to understand developments in other common law countries and to assess their relevance for Hong Kong. This factor is equally, if not more, important in constitutional law, a field where Hong Kong had little experience, especially as regards human rights.

In the first 13 years of the resumption of sovereignty, Andrew Li was the Chief Justice (CJ) of Hong Kong and in that capacity presided over the CFA. The CFA must have five judges to constitute the bench. But the number of permanent judges (including the CJ) has not exceeded four (perhaps as a matter of policy) so that the CFA always had to sit with a non-permanent judge (NPJ) – in the majority of the cases with an overseas judge and occasionally with one overseas and one local NPJ. The procedures for the appointment and dismissal of judges are broadly in line with generally accepted standards (although in recent times the fairness with which the process is followed has been criticised, both for undue dominance of the influence of the executive and the lack of any public explanation as to the reasons and merits of overseas judges; see Chapter 9).

Li's role as CJ and as chair of the Judicial Officers Recommendation Commission was crucial to the fashioning of the HKSAR's legal and judicial system and ethos. Li had a brilliant legal and political career but had no judicial experience. His experience was largely in commercial and business law – and in what passed for politics in those days (as member of the Governor's Council). But these factors turned out to be no handicap, and his experience of the political and administrative system of Hong Kong was a great asset in dealing with the government and the wider

---

[4] The first major controversy, about the right of abode of Mainland children with links to Hong Kong, is documented at length in J. Chan, H.L. Fu, and Y. Ghai (eds.), *Hong Kong's Constitutional Debate: Conflict Over Interpretation* (Hong Kong: Hong Kong University Press, 2001).

public. He played a decisive role in the appointment of the other CFA judges, particularly the foreign judges. In that sense, as well as in other ways, for the first 13 years, the CFA was very much Li's court. But Li as CJ developed a very collegial style of administration and decision making. He assembled a remarkable bench of outstanding talent and openness, local as well as foreign. There are three categories of judges of the CFA: permanent (PJ), non-permanent overseas (NPJ overseas), and non-permanent local (NPJ local) – contrary to the provision in the Joint Declaration (JD) and BL, which provided for only the first two categories (see Chapter 11).

This book examines how the Court discharged its responsibilities in its first 13 years and how a very special set of judges put their imprint on the court and its jurisprudence.

Note on contributors

Contributors to this volume have achieved distinction in several fields and bring to their chapters the benefits of considerable scholarship and practical experience of autonomy systems, leading to differences in perspectives. Some of them have been deeply involved in the operation of autonomy systems: Sir Anthony Mason, the longest serving foreign judge; Michael Thomas, attorney general of Hong Kong during the formative years when the Sino–British Joint Declaration took shape and the long process for its implementation began; Albert Chen, the longest serving Hong Kong member of the Committee of the BL; Paulo Cardinal, the senior legal adviser to the Macau Legislative Assembly; William Waung, a former member of Hong Kong's Court of First Instance; Josef Marko, who served on the Constitutional Court (CC) of Bosnia-Herzegovina (BiH) as a foreign judge in which he played a critical role in the jurisprudence of that country; and Ghai, who has advised in a number of countries on autonomy or federal arrangements. Others have litigated or submitted legal opinions in litigation on the BL: Johannes Chan, Thomas, P. Y. Lo, Mark Daly, Ghai, Oliver Jones, Simon Young, and Antonio Da Roza. Among the authors are also the leading scholars of the BL and Hong Kong's, as well as China's, legal systems: Chen, Ghai, Jill Cottrell, Jones, Rick Glofcheski, Young, Mason, Gary Meggitt, Xiaonan Yang, and Malcolm Merry. Many authorities bring comparative perspectives to bear on the BL: Ghai, Marko, Cardinal, Cottrell, Jorge Godinho, and Yang. And most have, in different ways, contributed to education about the BL.

Hong Kong's autonomy in comparative perspective

The historical and comparative dimensions of Hong Kong's system are subthemes of the book. Ghai (see Chapter 2) locates the HKSAR within the system of autonomies and shows the distinct ways in which it differs from most autonomy systems – a rapidly growing constitutional phenomenon that has been adopted in many countries in the past few decades. He uses the comparative dimensions to assess the strengths and mostly the weaknesses of Hong Kong's autonomy, its lack of effective entrenchment, the subordination of the executive to the Chinese government, a less than democratic legislature in Hong Kong that fails fully to reflect the concerns of its residents, and the absence of a tradition of legality on the Mainland.

Autonomy connotes self-government, the ability of a region or community to organise its affairs without interference from the central government, neighbouring regions, or neighbouring communities. The foundations of most autonomies lie in constitutional and sometimes international arrangements, entrenched and based on traditions of the rule of law. Unlike most autonomies where ethnic differences dominate, Hong Kong's autonomy is characterised by different economic and social systems and the unusual detail with which the division of powers between Hong Kong and China are specified – a testimony perhaps to fundamental differences between ideologies and systems between the two entities. At the same time, this restricts policy options for Hong Kong.

On its own, the HKSAR cannot alter the main institutions of its government; the electoral laws; or, significantly, its rather laissez-faire economic system. But the NPC can change the BL on its own, subject to certain restrictions. But these restrictions have been overcome, with dubious legality, by some interpretations by the NPCSC. Another aspect of the institutional arrangements, centring on the office and powers of the Chief Executive, was Beijing's plan to acquire ultimate control over Hong Kong's affairs.

Other ways in which Hong Kong's autonomy differs from other autonomies lie in its origins and mode of negotiations (Sino–British negotiations within a framework established by China, with no participation by Hong Kong people). Institutions and procedures internal to Hong Kong are not democratic, so they do not always reflect people's choice nor do they set up a framework for free and vibrant politics. There is no really independent mechanism for adjudication of relations between the Central Authorities and Hong Kong. The absence of the rule of law in the relations between the two is a major weakness of Hong Kong's autonomy.

The ambiguity of what happens to Hong Kong's political, social, and economic system a few decades down the line (the autonomy is granted only for 50 years) – a matter for China to decide – is a further element in the unequal relations between the two entities. On the other hand, the divisions of powers are clearer than in other federal or autonomy systems – and they are overwhelmingly in Hong Kong's favour. Ghai argues Hong Kong's relationship with China is best understood as autonomy with the existence of two separate economic and politico-legal systems but with the HKSAR firmly under the ultimate direction of Beijing. The tensions that this creates are reflected in public law.

The Court of Final Appeal's role

The CFA's role and jurisdiction have to be understood in the context of Hong Kong's autonomy. The judiciary has played and plays a crucial role in maintaining the framework of autonomy and resolving disputes between the national government and the autonomous region. This task is normally performed by national courts, but that solution was not possible in Hong Kong because of weaknesses of the judicial system in China, including the absence of judicial independence. The legal and judicial system in Hong Kong was capable of this task, but as a regional court, its authority over national institutions and laws was limited. This has produced a lacuna, which the BL seeks to fill by the political role of the NPC through its Standing Committee. Thus, the legality approach of the CFA comes into clash with the political sovereignty and role of the NPCSC. This, reinforced by the rulings of the NPCSC, has rendered the CFA impotent in dealing with legal issues that touch on the constitutional and political relationships between the HKSAR and the national government. And gradually, it has reduced and weakened the CFA's role in the interpretation of the BL, blurred the distinction between the interpretation and the amendment of the BL, and marginalised the CFA's role in the protection of Hong Kong's autonomy against onslaughts from the national government. The CFA has, however, been robust in dealing with constitutional and other legal issues 'internal' to Hong Kong.

Privy Council and the Court of Final Appeal

Historically, the obvious comparison of the CFA is with the PC, which it replaced. Jones (Chapter 4) provides an historical introduction to the PC, emphasising its imperial origins and with the judiciary for the most part drawn from English courts. He notes a change with the independence of colonies because whereas in the early days its role was to establish a uniform understanding of the common law, after independence it made attempts to relate the law to the circumstances of the country from which the appeal had emanated (although in Chapter 13, Mason finds little evidence of this approach in respect of Hong Kong). And if in the earlier phase there might have been a tendency to favour imperial interests, later it asserted its role as the supreme court of the country concerned – and found a role for certain judges from the commonwealth. Jones notes that it is not easy to compare the PC with the CFA because one has a history of more than 150 years and the other just 13 (at the time of writing). One had appellate functions in respect of numerous jurisdictions, the other of only one. And the constitutional frameworks with which the two operated are fundamentally different (making public law a major component of the CFA's docket in comparison with the PC). Nevertheless, the history and decisions of the PC covering numerous jurisdictions might well be of interest to scholars of emerging regional and international tribunals. And a number of authors in this volume do compare the approach of the PC and the CFA, their workload, accessibility to court, principal areas of appeal, and styles of decisions.

Given that the justification for inclusion of foreign judges on the CFA was maintaining confidence in the quality and independence of Hong Kong's judiciary, it was perhaps more than coincidence that some of the foreign judges in its early years were members of the PC, such as Lords Hoffmann, Cooke, and Woolf. The diversity of the home jurisdictions of judges in the CFA is broader, although restricted to 'white' jurisdictions, with the curious exclusion of Canada. If the PC was a multijurisdictional court, the CFA is single jurisdictional but with judges from multiple jurisdictions. And unlike the PC, the CFA now looks to the precedents from several common law countries (allowing for a more flexible approach and openness to wider sources of ideas).

If the role of the PC was to preserve the interests of the empire, that of the CFA might be said to preserve the powers and authority of the HKSAR. That brings us to another point of (imperial) comparison. The CFA is not the final appeal court in the way the PC was. In one sense, the NPCSC is more like the PC – external to Hong Kong, which has no role in its composition, more concerned with the Mainland interests than Hong Kong's, able to overrule the CFA – but with the important distinction that the PC applied the common law, NPCSC Chinese law. And if the origins of the PC lay in a citizen's right to appeal a decision to the sovereign, outside the regular court system, might one regard the NPC as the supreme authority in similar although not identical terms? And if territorial courts might have been influenced by the possibility of an appeal to the PC, how far is the CFA influenced by the presence of the NPCSC?

Although Jones focuses on the history of the PC, Young and Da Roza (Chapter 6) compare the functions, work, and impact of the CFA with those of the PC, with a wealth of statistical analyses. They say (and several other contributors say) that the intention of structuring the CFA to maintain the authority and reassurance provided by the PC to investors has been amply achieved. They imply that the CFA has been even more efficient and successful than the PC. Its caseload is considerably heavier than that of the PC (in respect of Hong Kong cases). It turns a case around more speedily than the PC used to; it deals with a much larger variety of legal issues, particularly in public law; it is more innovative and willing to look at common law developments in many more jurisdictions than the PC; and its location in Hong Kong has greatly increased access to the final court. One could also say, as Young and Da Rosa imply, that the CFA has generally played a greater role in moulding people's thinking about justice.

Of course, one must not read these necessarily as criticisms of the PC. Many of the differences are the result of the changed context of Hong Kong. For most of the period of the jurisdiction of the PC, Hong Kong had no constitution to speak of, no entrenched guarantees of human rights, and no delicate balance between the colony or autonomy and the sovereign that the CFA has to manage. Most importantly, the PC did not have to play the role that has fallen to the CFA: bringing into operation and sustaining a constitutional order, shaping it by interpretations of the founding document, the BL. That is what final courts do in most democratic states.

Standing Committee of the National People's Congress and the Court of Final Appeal

This discussion appropriately brings us to the comparison between the NPCSC and the CFA. Comparisons can be drawn with regard to their function of interpretation, where their jurisdiction, style, and authority differ. Several chapters touch on these matters and the relationship between them, but the most systematic analysis is provided by Yang (Chapter 3). Her chapter is important to understand the role, influence, and orientation of the NPCSC. Its role is varied, although the greatest attention has been paid to interpretation under BL Article 158, which has been exercised relatively sparingly but significantly.

Yang examines the different traditions of and approaches to legality in China and Hong Kong and the constraints under which the NPCSC and the CFA operate. She draws connections between the common law and capitalism and between common law and the rule of law (the two, of course, are connected in bourgeoisie ideology). She analyses the institutional settings of the two interpreters and argues that different institutional concerns and missions inevitably bring the two interpreters to different interpretations of the BL. In China, the power to interpret belongs to the same organ as makes the law. Law is seen as the will of the ruling class, and the principles of checks and balances and the separation of powers are not applicable.

Yang points to the different roles that the NPCSC plays in Hong Kong and China as regards interpretation. On the Mainland, the ideal function of legislative interpretation is to achieve a compromise between conflicting state organs. In respect of Hong Kong, the NPCSC does not passively adapt itself to political, legal, and historical settings but strategically adjusts behaviour to achieve individual or institutional goals. Yang identifies its three key political missions as an interpreter of the Hong Kong BL: to maintain the prosperity and stability of the HKSAR, to maintain the authority of 'one country' as a state representative, and to behave as a self-restrained interpreter. She argues that the main concern of China regarding Hong Kong, from the time that it began to consider the resumption of sovereignty, has been to maintain the economic prosperity of Hong Kong. These active strategies are reflected in a change of interpretative styles and approaches in respect of Hong Kong.

The two bodies operate under different theories and conceptions of law and functions of interpretation – the CFA places importance on the role of law as limiting power and promoting predictability through it, and the NPC on the task to safeguard the supremacy of political power. Theoretically, the NPC's authority is derived from the will and power of the people, which therefore brooks no checks and balances and no separation of power and justifies the legislature's authority to interpret laws. In practice, the NPC is a creature of the Chinese Communist Party. Yang considers that for the NPCSC, 'the interpretation of the Basic Law is the most powerful and effective tool to exercise the powers of sovereignty'. Comparing approaches of the CFA and the NPCSC to interpretation – purposive, reasoning, asserting, differences in background materials, admissibility of evidence – in no other system is there such a huge divergence in the modes of interpretation.

Hong Kong and Macau

The interesting study of Macau by Cardinal and Godinho (Chapter 23) provides another type of comparison: between two special administrative areas under the same autonomy system but one with its legal foundations in the common law and the other in civil law (a comparative element built into the greater PRC system). There are also similarities and differences in history: just as the common law links Hong Kong to legal systems derived from Britain, so is Macau linked to Portuguese legal traditions and those of its former colonies. The authors notice a number of features that distinguish Macau's experience from Hong Kong's. There is only one dissenting judicial opinion in Macau, delivered in 2010. A total of 350 decisions of the final court were unanimous – despite the 'variety, legal complexity and political sensitivity of the broad range of issues upon which the [Court] was called to decide'. The authors notice the trend to rely on Chinese law even when the matter is internal to Macau, fearing that it would lead to the 'gradual dilution of Macau's own legal system identity and, at the end of the day, its own autonomy'. They point to the lack of a foreign judge in the final court, noting the many jurisdictions from which they could have been appointed and comment on the absence of commitment of the judiciary, unlike in Hong Kong, to freedoms.

These concerns raise interesting questions: is the greater assertion of Chinese authority in Macau due to the more robust character of the common law compared with the civil law? Is the presence of foreign judges conducive to dissents and to the protection of rights? These questions are not easy to answer because there are many other factors that could explain dissimilar influence of China: the smaller size of Macau, closer contact between Macau and China during respective colonial periods, an even less developed political system than in Hong Kong, Hong Kong's greater integration in the international economy, a more passive legal profession in Macau, the less active role by the Portuguese to protect rights and autonomy than the British, and the presence of highly talented and influential foreign judges (as indeed was the case in BiH). However, as Cottrell and Ghai (Chapter 12) show, foreign judges in Hong Kong tend not to dissent much. There may be other factors as well to explain differences between the two Chinese autonomies: the dominance in public life of lawyers, influence of clients (which in Hong Kong include powerful corporations), and strength of civil society. Thomas (Chapter 8) shows the strong role played by lawyers in Hong Kong in fighting for the common law and the rule of law – although perhaps as time went on, solicitors became careful not to offend the Chinese as they realised the work that would come their way. Nor should one rule out the traditional resistance of the common law to the invasion of other legal systems through the type of legal reasoning, grounding in facts, the specificity of doctrine, and the theory and practice of precedent.

Hong Kong and Bosnia-Herzegovina

The comparison of Hong Kong's experience with Macau is a comparison between 'likes' but that with BiH is between 'unlikes', each yielding specific kinds of insights. In a masterly essay, Marko (Chapter 24) discusses the experience of the Constitutional Court (CC) of BiH, and through subtle references to the CFA's relationship with the Central Authorities, gives us novel insights into the predicament of the CFA. He suggests a methodology for comparative analysis based not on comparison of institutions according to superficial similarities and differences but on an analysis of functions and structures. Interested in the intersection and mixing of legal systems, he examines a genuine mixing of and clash between civil and common law, which throws light on the disingenuous explanation by Chinese officials of differences of approach in China and Hong Kong solely on grounds of the differences between civil law in China and common law in Hong Kong.

The attempt in BiH is to get the best of both rather than the dominance of one. Marko demonstrates that there is no sharp distinction between common law and civil law and that within the civil law family, there are considerable variations. In both Hong Kong and BiH, there was the coming together of communist and civil law with emerging global 'constitutional' law, but in BiH, unlike Hong Kong, it fell to the same court to harmonise divergent strands of laws. (The more liberal-minded foreign judges and the more communist-oriented local judges sat in the same court.) Both courts tried to expand jurisdiction, resolving ambiguities in their favour, the CC with more success than the CFA, perhaps because the greater 'rule of law' ambience in Europe. And the CC is truly a national court, with jurisdiction throughout the country, unlike the CFA. In Hong Kong, additionally, there is little possibility of harmonisation because two critical institutions have different jurisdictions, different bodies of legal doctrine, and different political orientations (the expectation that some had that the BL Committee would play this role was dissipated with the first issue referred to it).

Marko examines the obligations and rules for reference by one court to another court (which also helps to place the system for reference by the CFA to the NPCSC in a comparative perspective, contrasting a more legal approach in BiH to a predominantly political approach of China). He points to the value of the functional (and comparative) approach to interpretation in constitutional and human rights cases to 'avoid the pitfalls or even ideological misuse of the strictly literal reading so common in continental European legal positivism' (areas where the CFA has richly reaped the rewards of the comparative approach; see Chapter 14 by Chen and Lo and Chapter 15 by Young). His account of the CC shows that it worked much like the CFA (especially in establishing jurisdiction and principles of interpretation).

However, there are important differences in the context of the two tribunals. In BiH, the court's role is the integration of the various parts of the country, deeply divided historically but loosely put together by the Dayton Accord, and the CFA's role is to maintain Hong Kong's separation from the Mainland. The CFA does not have any jurisdiction over Mainland affairs, but the CC has the responsibility to supervise relations between Entities (i.e. autonomous parts) *inter se* as well as between an Entity and the Centre (which go to the heart of the constitution). Nor is the CC constrained by considerations of a 'higher authority' as in Hong Kong; it is in a sense that higher authority but hardly comparable to the more political NPCSC. The status and role of foreign judges in BiH are considerably greater, as discussed in a later section.

The Court of Final Appeal's jurisprudence

In its first 13 years, the CFA built up a considerable body of case law, most of it of exceptionally high quality. The major challenge to it was to build the foundations of judicial review based on the common law in face of the overarching authority of the NPCSC, bound by no particular practice of law, to interpret any part of the BL. This constraint is essential to understanding the CFA's strategies and jurisprudence (as illustrated in considerable detail by Chen and Lo in Chapter 14). This consideration has been less important as far as the framework and structure of private law was concerned (where the theme is continuity) than in public and criminal laws as a new political order is established. We start with the impact of the BL, which sets up the framework for the new order and for Hong Kong's relationship with the Mainland.

Interpreting the Basic Law

Almost all chapters say something about the interpretations of the BL, but the most extensive discussion is that by Chen and Lo (Chapter 14), who periodise the interpretations into three stages: the first *foundational* phase between 1997 and 2002 when the CFA laid out the parameters of its constitutional jurisdiction; the *consolidation* phase between 2002 and 2006 during which it articulated the ingredients of the regime of human rights protection; and the third *innovation* phase between 2005 and 2009 when the CFA made major progress in defining and exercising constitutional jurisdiction. In a very detailed analysis of its case law (covering most leading authorities), Chen and Lo point out the considerable achievements of the CFA in establishing the courts' constitutional jurisdiction in the face of uncertain provisions of the BL, leaving no doubt about the superior constitutional status of the BL and drawing freely on common law and comparative jurisprudence of other countries.

Common law

The common law is Hong Kong's underlying law. Mason (Chapter 13) places special emphasis on the common law rules of interpretation for the vital role they have played in the development of Hong Kong's constitutional law. He emphasises the primacy of the legal text, although context and purpose are not otherwise unimportant (but that also reflects a strategy to deal with the NPCSC's suspicions of the engagement of the judiciary with policy issues – regardless of its own freewheeling interpretations). He also shows that reference to legislative materials has not proved to be a practical problem for the courts, but the CFA has also defined with care what materials are relevant, excluding, with considerable emphasis, many post-BL statements that the Mainland wished to use to justify its preferred interpretation. Mason notes that of all the legitimate influences on the development of Hong Kong's common law, the BL is the most important and gives as an example the well-known libel case of *Cheng* v. *Tse* (discussed in many chapters) of how the common law was developed to accord with constitutional values.

Mason also shows the independence of the CFA as a common law court, declining in many cases to follow PC or House of Lords judgments since July 1997 while respectful of them. The CFA has sometimes looked to jurisprudence of other common law countries (mostly 'white') to depart from English authorities (as to the extent to which the Court of Appeal is bound by its own decisions or directions to a jury as to character of the accused).

The CFA's approach is that the common law is dynamic and that it is its responsibility to develop, not merely apply, it (perhaps one of the most eminent courts to take this position so openly). The CFA has also been innovative in public law as regards remedies, suspension of invalidity of legislation for a reasonable period to enable the government to rectify the deficiency, or reading down a statute to maintain its validity (the relevant cases are discussed in detail in Chan's Chapter 16 and criticised in Young's Chapter 15).

Mason points to the difficulties facing a court that tries to be innovative, relying on comparative law or charting new approaches and compares it with the other branches of the government that can initiate policies and reforms, unlike courts that have to deal with such cases as appear before it. And in the Hong Kong context, there remains the possibility of conflict between interpretations by the NPCSC and the CFA, although he says that such instances are rare (a statement made before the *Congo* case[5]).

Private law

As mentioned previously, the CFA has faced few fundamental challenges in the adjudication of private law issues as the major theme of the BL is continuity in Hong Kong's economic system that has largely shaped its private law. However, to some extent the values of the BL, particularly human rights (less social justice), have influenced the development of private law. This is not to say that the CFA has not developed private law in interesting and innovative ways.

Commercial law

Waung (Chapter 18), surveying the decisions in laws on contract, shipping, arbitration, banking, money lending, and company law, notes the great expertise in commercial law among the CFA judges. He refers to

---

[5] *Democratic Republic of the Congo* v. *FG Hemisphere Associates LLC* (2011) 14 HKCFAR 95 (reference) and 395 (disposition).

the large number of commercial appeals the CFA has to decide (especially for a final appeal court) irrespective of whether there is any important point of law at issue, because of the financial threshold of the right to appeal (a matter discussed in several other chapters). From this large number, Waung selects the most interesting and legally significant. He comments favourably on the quality of judgments and says that the high reliability of the CFA in commercial appeals contributes to the high regard for Hong Kong held by the international business community.

Tort

Developments in the law of torts are discussed by Glofcheski (Chapter 20), who says that the BL has opened up possibilities of development in tort law, releasing it from its bondage to the PC. There have been more tort appeal cases than in a much longer period of the PC. In terms of the general body of tort case law, he comments on a few groundbreaking decisions – in particular in defamation, vicarious liability, and public nuisance. This, he notes, is important in an environment in which the administration has shown little or no inclination for statutory tort reform. But he does not see much progress in negligence.

On the whole, he commends the CFA for its boldness, innovation, and concern with the disadvantaged. The worker–plaintiff is almost always successful at the end of the appeal process, usually because of the court's sympathetic interpretation of the facts or in some cases because of the court's flexible interpretation or incremental development of the law. Through its decisions in the work injury tort cases, the court has improved the lot of the worker–plaintiff in Hong Kong in two ways: in the development of more flexible conditions for the proof of employee status (and hence, the law's coverage) and in the development of a more rigorous standard that employers must follow in providing safe working conditions for their employees.

Glofcheski says that without acknowledging it, Bokhary PJ arguably expanded the reach of the *res ipsa loquitur* principle beyond its previously understood boundaries, a ruling that is very pro-plaintiff, whether in the workplace or otherwise. Bokhary PJ's generosity did not end there, as he took the occasion to state, albeit in *obiter*, that *res ipsa loquitur* had application beyond negligence cases to cases of breach of statutory duty and occupiers' liability.

Land

Cases on land are discussed in several chapters – not surprising given the centrality of land to Hong Kong's economy and to state revenues.

The most detailed discussion is in Chapter 19 by Merry, who begins with a brief note on the complexity of land in Hong Kong and follows by discussing its many uses, speculation, and transactions around land, government-sponsored subsidised housing for the poor, land as security for loans, and the sensitivity of land values to general market conditions. The last factor in particular, he notes, tends to 'result in outbreaks of litigation. The amounts at stake usually justify pursuit of the litigation to the highest level'. So there were 50 appeals in the first 13 years, concerning largely agreements for sale and purchase, title, and conveyancing. Merry sets the legal issues in the context of Hong Kong's social and economic context and enables those not familiar with the intricacies of land law to follow the significance of the arguments before the CFA and its decisions.

Merry's verdict on the record of the CFA is broadly positive, noting changes and clarifications of the law in a difficult area. He is impressed by the erudition and experience of the judges and the confidence that consequently they bring to their decisions. But he also notes that the CFA has few law-creating judgments and has perhaps a tendency not to disturb the law – an attitude that he regards as inconsistent with the function of a final court to correct errors at lower levels. He is critical of a few judgments in which he considers that the CFA did not take the opportunity to adjust the law to Hong Kong's circumstances and practice. He is particularly critical of the *Polyset* case (which also features in other chapters, including Cottrell and Ghai in Chapter 12). In at least two cases, the CFA has departed from English precedents, in one instance through the lead judgment of Lord Millet NPJ disregarding a House of Lord's decision. His opinion is that the court has been fairly even handed, although with a slight bias in favour of the government in cases when the issue has been revenue to the state (and perhaps the propertied and business communities as well?).

Civil procedure

Meggitt (Chapter 21) says that there is not much to report on the CFA's decisions on civil procedure even if approximately 80 CFA judgments between 1997 and 2010 touched upon civil procedure. A quarter of them concerned the CFA's own procedures (i.e. when leave to appeal will be granted), and almost as many dealt with costs. Far fewer, he writes, addressed weightier matters such as pleadings or evidence. Only one case concerned a BL provision guaranteeing right of access to courts (Article 35) (*Solicitor (23/2005)* v. *The Law Society of Hong Kong*[6]). Meggitt notes

---

[6] (2006) 9 HKCFAR 175.

that relatively few cases in the CFA have dealt with issues of 'pure' civil procedure and that when a pure procedural matter has reached the CFA, the eventual decision 'has usually been a pragmatic one based on the facts of the case before it, with only an occasional thought-provoking judgment'. Consequently, 'it is difficult to identify or analyse any "philosophy" or "policy" towards civil procedure other than, perhaps, the desire to "do justice"'.

Meggitt suggests that the reason may well have been the review of civil procedure mandated by the CJ on more effective rules for civil justice (CJR), which covered the period 2000 to 2009. He says that the review gave CFA members on the committee more scope to influence civil procedure than they had through the usual channels of litigation, and decisions before the new rules would be rendered less relevant.

Public law

The most substantial and significant part of the workload of the CFA has been public law. This is not surprising for a final court; in most common law countries, this is the case. Moreover, public law represents a major change in Hong Kong's political and legal system – under the ever-watchful eye of the Mainland authorities. A centrepiece of the BL is the protection of human rights, on which there was limited case law. The CFA has been inclined to readily take constitutional cases in view of the lack of law reform by the government and the lack of democracy, increasing resort to courts (although towards the end of his tenure, Li CJ used to warn against too ready a resort to courts in essentially political questions; see Chapter 10). The CFA has devoted more time and pages to write public law judgments than in any other area.

Criminal law

Young (Chapter 17) reminds us that criminal law cases alone came to 111 (one-third of all the cases). This large number represents the CFA's concern with justice. Indeed, Young points out that a significant number of cases did not raise questions of law but whether the trial and subsequent appeals had delivered justice (a task not usually undertaken by final courts). Even when points of law are certified, the CFA has claimed 'jurisdiction to review findings of fact in exceptional cases when those findings are related to the certified points' and discretionary orders to stay a proceeding will be reviewed if the judge mistakes the facts or fails to give weight or sufficient weight to considerations relevant to a central matter. It has also taken a generous approach to its receipt of fresh evidence on appeal subject to certain conditions. The CFA has come under criticism for becoming too interventionist and not giving enough deference to findings of fact by lower courts, but Young thinks by statute the CFA cannot ignore its 'injustice' jurisdiction, and that the injustice cases demonstrated improved access to justice post-1997.

The CFA's approach to criminal law has been greatly influenced by the human rights provisions of the BL, subjecting criminal offences to the test of rights and other protective provisions of the BL. Young says that it has also adopted a robust approach to common law fair trial standards and police power and held law enforcement agencies to an exacting standard, chipping away at coercive powers even without constitutional challenge. In the few cases on sentencing, it has generally shown a tendency to favour human liberty and keep restrictions to a minimum.

But the CFA has also been conscious of the public interest in law enforcement and has not been unsympathetic to the challenges faced by the prosecution and law enforcement agencies in tackling serious fraud and corruption (as in the temporary suspension of the declaration of invalidity in the case concerning electronic surveillance, a case discussed in several chapters).

Human rights

The sharpest distinction between the political and constitutional systems of Hong Kong and the Mainland lies in their approach to human rights. Few countries in Asia match Hong Kong's record of respect for and protection of human rights – and few have such contempt for rights as China, although this is slowly changing. The exercise of human rights has given great vibrancy to politics and policies in Hong Kong under considerable resistance from the Mainland. It is to the great credit of the CFA that it has strenuously and often eloquently protected human rights. A number of chapters discuss the human rights jurisprudence of the CFA, but the specific focus on the subject is in chapters by two contributors deeply engaged in human rights litigation, Young and Daly – although from somewhat different perspectives.

Young (Chapter 15) notes that although human rights cases comprised only 17 per cent of the CFA judgments, they probably attracted the greatest attention in the local community (perhaps the same is also true of the international community). Rights that were most frequently considered by the CFA were the right of abode, presumption of innocence, arbitrary detention and imprisonment (including review for legal certainty), and right to a fair hearing. The rights of various groups were involved, but more than half concerned immigrants and those charged with criminal offences. And significantly, nearly half of the cases were supported by government-funded legal aid (although Daly notes a tendency towards decreased support for judicial review cases based perhaps on the former CJ's concern about too frequent a resort to courts on administrative decisions).

Not surprisingly the major crisis that has faced the CFA was in respect of human rights as applied to Hong Kong's relations with China. Young claims that the crisis changed the CFA's approach to subsequent right of abode cases. Only Bokhary PJ remained an unwavering supporter of freedoms and liberties; others became more pragmatic, conscious of the possible consequences of their decisions. The purposive approach yielded to some extent to the textual. Courts have sometimes upheld laws by reading them down or temporarily keeping in effect laws violative of rights – approaches criticised by Young (Chapter 15) as the triumph of pragmatism over principle (a view similar to those of Johannes Chan[7]).

Daly (Chapter 9) writes from the perspectives of a human rights practitioner, with perhaps the longest and largest engagement of any practitioner with litigation in this area. He writes within the broad framework of justice; he says he prefers the term 'justice system' as opposed to 'legal system' or 'court system' and believes that the difference is one of substance, going to the 'core of the role of the justice system in our community'. His vision of human rights is that of transforming unjust and authoritarian systems into just and humane societies. Judged from this perspective, he finds many failings in the approach of the CFA. He places the CFA in a broad political and economic context, which he considers is influenced by approaches drawn from the West that do not correspond to the political and economic circumstances of Hong Kong, with state authorities suffering from serious deficit. Among these he singles out what he calls 'misplaced margin' (the concept of the 'appreciation of margin' introduced into Hong Kong by Woolf in his days on the PC and now propagated by Lord Hoffmann, with its overtones of 'cultural relativism').

Related is his concern at what he considers the misplaced reliance by the CFA on deference to legislative and executive authorities, which he believes are devoid of legitimacy and operate within a political system that stresses social harmony and can, at times, demonise those critical of the government. He worries about the increased threshold test for leave, the

---

[7] Johannes Chan, 'Some Reflections on Remedies in Administrative Law' (2009) 39 *Hong Kong Law Journal* 321.

difficulty of getting cases to court, and tests for legal aid dependent on the stricter approach of the CFA. He suspects the judiciary of self-censorship and the continuing fallout from the 'reinterpretation' of the NPCSC and worries about the state of judicial independence.

It will be obvious that this critical stance is shared by few others. Glofcheski noted the concern of the CFA for the workers, its decision on strengthening the right to free speech, and what he calls a clear 'agenda of reform'. Daly, we might say, works at the coal face and sees a different reality. However, even he is not totally critical and acknowledges that Li CJ 'steered us capably through unique and difficult times when, because of the post-handover political uncertainty, perhaps a more conservative approach was deemed important when it came to human rights'. He is mindful of the progressive decisions of the court but points to the increasing difficulty of getting that far. He warns that serious human rights problems remain, and 'for the future court, a more rights-conscious public is not going to be satisfied with a legal system that does not deliver practical justice'.

Administrative law

The principal discussion of the CFA's engagement with administrative law is that by Chan (Chapter 16). He describes how the nature and purposes of judicial review (at the heart of administrative law) have so significantly changed under the impact of BL and human rights. The CFA has engaged in the most wide-ranging issues in administrative law and has delivered a number of major judgments which have far-reaching implications for, or that have steered, the development of common law and that blurred the distinction between constitutional and administrative law. He quotes the view of Li CJ that the availability and use of judicial review has had a significant impact on the conduct of the business of the government and has exercised considerable influence on public debate on many issues.

Chan notes the increase in number of judicial review appeals, which he attributes in considerable part to the ineffectiveness of legislative and political processes. The success rate of appeals is high, which suggests that the courts have had to shoulder the burden of a less than effective political system. The CFA raised the threshold for leave applications, perhaps to discourage the legalisation of political issues – a development that worried Li CJ towards the end of his office (see Chapter 10).

On the other hand, the CFA is prepared to grant leave even when the issue in the case has become academic if it involves matters of public interest. Chan discusses in detail a number of CFA decisions in which it has shown considerable willingness to innovate: on legitimate expectations, burden of proof in disciplinary proceedings, the definition of what is a 'court', prospective overruling and safeguarding previous decisions when the relevant law is declared invalid (dealing with 'the burden of the past' and 'the lacuna in the future' as Li CJ put it), and the nature of public interest litigation. The CFA indicated that it would, as a matter of statutory interpretation or common law principle of fairness, be prepared to assume a duty on a decision maker to give reasons unless there is contrary intention in the statute or it is otherwise inappropriate.

International law dimensions

The CFA has been very open to the case law from some other common law jurisdictions (although for the most part, it and the counsel before it, have paid little attention to numerous others, such as India, Singapore, and Malaysia, and only reluctantly to Canada). In human rights cases, the CFA has looked additionally to authorities from international and regional courts but also non-common law jurisdictions (driven in part by the common international human rights that apply in Hong Kong). They have been assisted by counsel, foreign and Hong Kong, knowledgeable about comparative and international cases (especially of countries from where the CFA's overseas judges come). The law faculties in Hong Kong have been highly cosmopolitan, and their research or participation in litigation also brings to the attention of Hong Kong courts foreign developments in the relevant fields. The influence of international and comparative law is discussed in various chapters (particularly by Mason, Chan, Young, Chen, and Lo).

The Court of Final Appeal's influence abroad

If the CFA has borrowed from or been influenced by foreign jurisprudence, it has also contributed to the jurisprudence of other jurisdictions. Lo (Chapter 22) traces citations of CFA decisions by courts and tribunals of numerous common law jurisdictions 'far and wide, from England and Wales, Scotland, Australia, Canada and New Zealand to Malaysia, Singapore, the Eastern Caribbean territories, the Cayman Islands, Trinidad and Tobago, the Fiji Islands and Tonga' (and Taiwan). The most influential CFA decision is the defamation case of *Cheng* v. *Tse*[8]

---

[8] *Albert Cheng* v. *Tse Wai Chun* (2000) 3 HKCFAR 339.

(discussed also in Glofcheski's Chapter 20), delivered as it turns out by a foreign judge, Lord Nicholls NPJ. A case that featured significantly in the new Supreme Court in the United Kingdom is *Koo Sze Yiu* v. *Chief Executive of the HKSAR*[9] (discussed also in Chan's Chapter 16) on the temporary suspension of a declaration of unconstitutionality of a law.

The CFA influence is also attributable to the impact of scholarship and law reporting. Lo notes the attention paid by foreign scholars to the litigation on the BL, documenting their scholarship extensively. The publicisation of CFA judgments abroad, particularly in England ('hub of legal exchange'), by publishers and practitioners has increased access to them. They were often first reported, noted, discussed, or cited in a specialist series of law reports, a practitioners' text, or a judgment before being referred to elsewhere in the common law world. Other factors are the familiarity of foreign lawyers who appear in Hong Kong courts with the Hong Kong cases as well as the weight given to CFA decisions by overseas judges in their home jurisdictions. The participation of distinguished foreign judges also helps to secure the wider attention to CFA decisions. However, Lo says that the knowledge of CFA decisions in Malaysia and Singapore is more likely caused by geographical proximity and cultural linkages.

Lo concludes that the CFA has by now been recognised as a 'regular supplier' of common law jurisprudence of good analytical quality for others to take constant and careful notice. This is testament not only to the contributions made by the NPJs from common law jurisdictions outside Hong Kong but also of the maturing indigenous judicial and legal human resources.

Judges and judging

The book contains a great deal of information and statistics on and analysis of judges and judging (especially in chapters authored and co-authored by Da Roza) and the background to Li CJ (Chapter 10) and other judges (Chapter 11). It is generally acknowledged that Andrew Li put together a formidable team of both local and foreign judges. He gave a great deal of thought and attention to the qualities needed in both categories of judges. The local judges, most of them with very distinguished records as barristers, showed great versatility and were able to sit in cases covering a range of subjects – just as well because the authorities were quite parsimonious

---

[9] *Koo Sze Yiu* v. *Chief Executive of the HKSAR* (2006) 9 HKCFAR 441.

in appointments of local judges. The load on the CJ and PJs was extremely heavy.

The scheme of local judges, overseas NPJs, and local NPJs provided considerable flexibility as to the composition of the bench, and at least for the last two categories, fitting expertise to the issue, except for the practice that an overseas NPJ would come for a month at a time and do two cases or so. A small core of overseas NPJs as well as local NPJs heard many appeals, but the others had minimal involvement, including some who did not sit even once. When compared with overseas NPJs, local NPJs sat on slightly fewer appeals on average. Most of the local NPJs appointed in 1997 did not reside in Hong Kong after retirement, thus limiting the flexibility to call upon them on short notice.

Despite the eminence of overseas judges, local judges have been the dominant influence, due to the clear and firm leadership of Li CJ and the intellectual calibre and industry of local judges, especially Bokhary and Ribeiro PJJ. Among overseas judges, Sir Anthony Mason NPJ has been a major influence – and much acclaimed.

But in this day and age, no room has been found for a female judge. This is a great pity. There has been no shortage of excellent female judges in common law jurisdictions or of outstanding female counsel in Hong Kong.

Overseas judges

Considerable attention is paid in this book to the role of overseas judges (sometimes called 'foreign judges' – not by reference to nationality as to the jurisdiction where they primarily sit or sat). Outside judges are unusual but not unique. During most of its colonial history, Hong Kong in a sense had 'foreign' judges in accordance with the imperial practice of shunting judges (and other legal officers) from colony to colony. Even when close to 1997, the majority of judges of senior courts were non–Hong Kong people. The BL allows the appointment of judges from other common law jurisdictions (BL Article 92) and legal practitioners from outside (BL Article 94). The only restriction is for two judicial posts (CJ of the CFA and Chief Judge of the High Court): they must be permanent residents of Hong Kong and Chinese citizens without a right of abode abroad (BL Article 90).

Reasons for having foreign judges have varied. In small countries in the Caribbean and the South Pacific, foreign itinerant judges often sit on appellate courts because the courts are essentially part-time and senior lawyers are in short supply. (Botswana, Lesotho, and Namibia also fall into this category.) A number of the CFA's overseas judges have also served on supreme courts of South Pacific countries (as noted by Mason in Chapter 13), and some Hong Kong judges have served in Brunei and in the Caribbean. Consequently, the intellectual capability of courts in small jurisdictions is generally formidable.[10]

The need for overseas judges in countries not lacking in local talent or experience derives from the lack of trust of local judges among the people because of ethnic conflict (and the imposition of the international community). The independence constitution of Cyprus (1960), negotiated after bitter conflict between Cypriot Greeks and Turks, disqualified any citizen of Cyprus but also of states closely connected with its politics – Greece, Turkey, or Great Britain – from the presidency of the High Court and the Constitutional Court. Foreign judges in BiH (the subject of Marko's Chapter 24) and Kosovo are appointed for similar reasons – and to help develop jurisprudence on international standards of human rights. Occasionally, foreign judges are appointed on national courts for trial of crimes against humanity, constituting a kind of hybrid court with registrars, prosecutors, and investigators from outside (Cambodia and Sierra Leone). And now many countries are getting used to judicial decisions enforceable domestically made by 'foreign' judges in regional and international tribunals in whose appointment they may have had no say.

Most chapters say something about the role and influence of overseas judges (with Young and Da Roza, Chapter 11, providing a detailed account of their background). The general verdict is very positive: at their learning, knowledge of law, not domineering, and engaging constructively with local judges to innovate and adapt the law to Hong Kong's circumstances. They are credited with positive development of the law, as well as their technical skills. The longest serving among them, Mason NPJ, has played a significant role in shaping the CFA's jurisprudence. Their very presence on the CFA has led to international attention to its jurisprudence. Because there is no retiring age for NPJs (65 for others), they bring another kind of benefit: of experience, wisdom, and historical perspective – although no chapter discusses this element.

Although no one questions foreign judges' knowledge of the common law, Daly (Chapter 9) wonders whether they have enough understanding of Hong Kong's social conditions, so not only are they unlikely to relate the

[10] I once appeared before the Samoa Court of Appeal, which included New Zealanders Robin Cooke and Professor Ken Keith, now on the International Court of Justice.

development of the law to them but are also likely to be unduly deferential to local judges. And their working well together with local judges, mutual respect, common values, and attitudes may be attributed to a similar background: the 'same stables', privileged background, top schools, and similar (if not the same) universities, and having, in their practices, served well off clients. Apart from Daly, indirectly, few address this sociological question.

At a doctrinal level, the diversity of jurisdictions from where the foreign judges come has had a beneficial effect, with earnest exploration of options, and freeing the CFA from the dominant and conservative influence of the English law, even if, as Young (Chapter 17) notes, that where the common law differed among jurisdictions, the foreign judge appeared to influence the majority to adopt the legal position of his home jurisdiction.

Court of Final Appeal foreign judges in a comparative perspective: Bosnia-Herzegovina

Because Macau has no foreign judge on its final court, comparative perspectives are restricted to the experience in BiH, drawing on Marko's chapter. The status and role of the foreign judges of the CC is much greater than in Hong Kong. The foreign judges are part of a wider set of arrangements for international intervention and participation, so their role is not queried or unusual and is supported by the European Union (EU) with the approval of the United States. Foreign judges are appointed by the Council of Europe on the nomination of its member states (thus potentially from a larger number of jurisdictions than in Hong Kong). They sit in a court that nationally is the most important (unlike the CFA). They sit for a term of five years, so there are periodic changes in the personnel, leading occasionally to shifts in jurisprudential approach contrasted with the effectively longer tenure in Hong Kong (perhaps at the cost of new ideas?).

Three foreign judges sit in a nine-member Constitutional Court (CC), compared with one in Hong Kong, although they are a minority in both. Local judges, elected by parliaments of respective Entities, are often deeply divided ethnically, and it falls to the foreign judges to avoid deadlocks and ensure that the law is fairly interpreted and applied (so cosy relations between foreign and local judges, as in Hong Kong, are not assured). The foreign judges sit in all the cases, not picked for particular cases as in Hong Kong.

Under the influence of foreign judges, the CC has helped to develop constitutional norms and established a purposive, progressive jurisprudence on human rights despite several conservative, communist judges, while in Hong Kong local and foreign judges have had no problems in agreeing on similar approaches. But unlike in BiH, foreign judges in Hong Kong have no opportunity to joust with Mainland judges but are under considerable pressure from Mainland politicians, who have the last say.

But foreign judges in both Hong Kong and BiH have discharged their diverse responsibilities and function well. The main role in Hong Kong was to maintain confidence in the effectiveness and impartiality of the legal system, particularly for foreign investors but also to protect rights and freedoms (not particularly valued in the Mainland). The jurisprudential impact of foreign judges in both jurisdictions has been similar: broadening the source of authorities, drawing on comparative and international law – but with some preference for doctrines from the home country. But because the Hong Kong judiciary in 1997 was competent, independent, and on the whole favoured the rule of law, foreign judges have merely strengthened rather than generated new approaches (indeed, the most human rights-oriented judge has been local). The challenge for foreign judges in BiH was greater; Marko says that 'foreign judges and the comparative law perspective which they bring with them are eye openers against cultural–national limitations in terms of interpretative approach or traditional constitutional doctrines. . . . Taken altogether, it becomes clear that this strong international presence in BiH was seen as a necessary element to support the institutional, political and economic reconstruction of the country after four years of terrible warfare'.

Judging

Several chapters, together, provide a great deal of statistical information on the CFA judgments (on volume; time taken to dispose of cases; reliance on overseas authorities; breaking away from the influence of English precedents; principal areas of the law covered; confirming or overturning appeals; joint, concurring, and dissenting judgments; lengths of judgments; leave applications for appeal granted or denied; and comparisons with the PC on some of these factors). This information provides an excellent basis for understanding the dynamics of the CFA.

On a more qualitative basis, Li CJ often referred to the court as 'collegial' because decision-making involved extensive discussion of the case amongst the judges during the hearing and in the deliberations afterwards. He chose the bench carefully to ensure the right expertise for the case and spent much time trying to get a consensus. Mason considers that the authority of the CFA's decisions has almost certainly been enhanced by its adoption of a collegial approach of joint rather than single judgments. Li CJ also worked hard to ensure the timely delivery of judgments.

Cottrell and Ghai (Chapter 12) analyse the styles of judgments, by considering the incidence of concurring and dissenting judgments. The rate of concurrence is not very high and the rate of dissent lower, considering the fact that most of the dissents are the work of one judge (Bokhary PJ). Indeed, the same judge has been the principal concurrer as well. The majority of cases are decided unanimously, particularly in criminal cases, where 78.8 per cent were decided without dissent or concurrence, with dissents in only four. Unless unanimous, the most common pattern is one majority with one concurring opinion. A number of cases involved 'judgments of the court'. Although most of these were straightforward criminal cases, a few were 'right of abode' cases, and in several of these there was a single judgment of the rest of the court – other than Bokhary PJ, who was in dissent.

Cottrell and Ghai consider whether foreign judges concur or dissent to a greater or lesser extent than the local judges. NPJs give judgments less often than they probably would in their own jurisdictions. Only one delivered any sort of judgment in more than half the cases in which he was involved: Lord Hoffmann NPJ; Sir Anthony Mason NPJ came next in terms of proportion but was top in terms of absolute number. The former's 18 of 32 equates to a judgment-giving rate of 56 per cent, and the latter's 31 of 88 for the latter to 35 per cent. Dissent by foreign NPJs is very rare, with only two instances.

Cottrell and Ghai argue that given the sensitivity about the presence of foreign judges, it would not be surprising if they and the local judges considered that they would be most effective if their influence was behind the scenes. Lord Cooke described that a function of an overseas judge is to 'give particular consideration to whether a proposed decision of this Court is in accord with generally accepted principles of the common law'. Ironically, the only case that seems to have provoked 'pro-Mainland' wrath with a foreign judge, in a defamation case by Lord Nicholls NPJ, has been followed in various other jurisdictions.

On joint judgments, they say that this phenomenon is perhaps explained by a greater cooperation and division of labour in judgment writing that comes with a heavy and ever-increasing caseload. It may also be explained by the increased complexity of cases, particularly those in the administrative and constitutional law areas.

The future...

The CFA has received many accolades and considerable recognition abroad. Thomas, with prolific appearances before the CFA and a former attorney general, says, 'The universal view of practitioners is that the Court has been an outstanding success. I have heard not a word to the contrary' (Chapter 9). The assessment by academics has not been so fulsome, especially when the CFA had to confront an issue in which China had an interest, although it has on the whole been positive. Its judges, for the most part, have shown little pomposity. They have worked hard to develop a jurisprudence that recognises the pre-eminent constitutional status of the BL, critical to Hong Kong's autonomy. They have delivered judgments without undue delay. Rightly, Li CJ's leadership has been widely admired. He had a clear vision of where he wanted to take the CFA and worked hard and intelligently to achieve that vision.

As the Li period comes to an end and that of Chief Justice Geoffrey Ma begins, one may ask how long Andrew Li's legacy will survive. Some think the omens are not promising. I conclude with observations on a judgment widely criticised by the academic and professional communities and the changing composition (and character?) of the CFA.[11]

The judgment is *Democratic Republic of the Congo v. FG Hemisphere Associates.*[12] It has cast doubts about the robustness of Hong Kong's legal system. Although theoretically contentious, until this case, few instances of the conflict between Mainland laws and the BL or the Hong Kong laws have arisen in courts. The principal issue was whether the immunity of foreign states in the Hong Kong courts was absolute – that is, it covered all their acts – or whether it was restricted to 'sovereign' governmental acts, excluding commercial transactions (as was the law in Hong Kong before the resumption of Chinese authority).

China had a clear interest because its state corporations were involved in the litigation, and the outcome would impact on its relations with the government of the mineral-rich Congo. China attempted quite openly to influence the CFA, assisted by the Hong Kong administration. China asserted that the rule of absolute immunity applied in China, and because

---

[11] See e.g. articles in volume 41(2) (2011) of the *HKLJ* and C. Chan, 'State immunity: reassessing the boundaries of judicial autonomy in Hong Kong' [2012] *Public Law* 601.

[12] *Democratic Republic of the Congo*, note 5 above.

this was an aspect of China's international relations, it was also the law in Hong Kong.

A first instance judge gave judgment for the defendants, which was reversed by the Court of Appeal by two judges to one.[13] The CFA (composed of judges from the Li court) reversed the CA by three judges in a single judgment (Chan, Ribeiro PJJ, and Mason NPJ) after seeking an interpretation from the NPCSC under Article 158(3) – the first such judicial reference. The majority judgment lacked conviction, dismissed casually Chinese signing of the New York Convention on Arbitration based on restrictive rule of state immunity, and was clearly against the commercial interests of Hong Kong.

The decision raises a number of troubling questions about the role of the Mainland government and legislature in relation to Hong Kong's law, which the CFA had hitherto been able to avoid. It is too early to say what effect the case will have on Hong Kong's laws and legal system, but there are fears that the gate against Chinese intrusion into Hong Kong's legal values and system, carefully locked, has now been opened. There were two dissents, one particularly robust and learned by Bokhary PJ and another carefully argued by Mortimer NPJ.

The second major concern about the CFA is whether what one commentator has called the 'change of guard', with the resignation of Li CJ and the retirement or imminent retirement of all CFA judges[14] (see Chapter 9), will be as committed to its independence as under Li and whether there will be increasing influence of the executive in judicial appointments. Since then the surprising decision not to grant Bokhary PJ (often described as the 'conscience of the CFA') an extension beyond his retirement as allowed under the law (which could have provided much needed continuity) has confirmed the anxieties of many.[15]

So although Andrew Li's achievements and those of the CFA under his watch were truly remarkable, it is less than clear that in the post-Li era the CFA will be able or choose to maintain their high standards – and commitments. Only time will tell.

---

[13] *FG Hemisphere Associates LLC* v. *Democratic Republic of the Congo* [2010] 2 HKLRD 66 (CA), rev'g [2009] 1 HKLRD 410 (CFI).

[14] Danny Gittings, 'Hong Kong's courts are learning to live with China' (July 2010) 19 *Hong Kong Journal*, accessible at www.hkjournal.org/archive/2010_fall/2.htm.

[15] Austin Chiu, 'Age crisis prompts fears for judiciary', *South China Morning Post*, 9 April 2012; Albert Cheng, 'Retirement of liberal judge raises fears for our core values', *South China Morning Post*, 4 April 2012; Austin Chiu and Adrian Wan, 'New judge older than retiree he's replacing', *South China Morning Post*, 29 March 2012.

PART I

Final appeals

Setting the context

.

Autonomy and the Court of Final Appeal

The constitutional framework

YASH GHAI

Introduction

This chapter sets out the constitutional, political, and economic frame-work within which the Court of Final Appeal (CFA) and other courts in Hong Kong operate. An evaluation of Hong Kong courts must take this framework into account, particularly of the CFA as it mediates between the Hong Kong judicial system and the political order in the People's Republic of China (Mainland), especially with the National People's Congress (NPC) in its role as the final interpreter of the Basic Law (BL). For this purpose, it is necessary to understand not only the political and legal system in Hong Kong but also that on the Mainland and the relations between the two systems. This would help to clarify the precise role of the Hong Kong judiciary in the broader framework of the relations between Hong Kong and the Mainland and give an idea not only of the responsibilities of the judiciary but also the opportunities and constraints to discharge them. Although the CFA's responsibilities are restricted to Hong Kong's legal system, various aspects of the CFA's jurisdiction are tied to the broader relationship between Hong Kong and the Mainland. So it may be that some issues within its jurisdiction concerning the relationship could or should, at least in the first instance, be handled through bureaucratic or political mechanisms. This chapter examines the effectiveness of these mechanisms and the consequences for the judiciary.

The constitutional concept that is used to describe the status of Hong Kong in China is 'autonomy' (Article 2 of the BL promises Hong Kong 'a high degree of autonomy'). The framework of autonomy is valuable in understanding the relationship between Hong Kong and the Mainland, the kind of tensions the system is likely to generate, the dynamics of politics and institutions, and the appropriate modes of dispute resolution.

Insights into a particular system of autonomy can be derived from a general, comparative analysis of the purposes, foundations, and institutions of autonomy. 'Autonomy' is not, as I argue in this chapter, a correct categorisation of Hong Kong's status, but it is officially described as such and does have many features associated with autonomy. Consequently, to a considerable extent, the fundamental principles of autonomy and the institutions through which it is exercised are critical to understanding the role of the CFA.

There is growing literature on autonomy systems.[1] Well before Deng Xiaoping's statement about the utility of the concept of autonomy (and 'one country, two systems') to solve the world's problems,[2] autonomy had been adopted in a number of countries (partly as strategy for decolonisation to grant forms of self-government characterised by special powers to regions inhabited by minorities, sometimes as the basis for the redesign of the state to resolve internal conflicts, particularly ethnic; and sometimes to facilitate the merger of an independent entity with another, larger, state). Many of these autonomies define the relationship between a small territorial, ethnic unit with a big state (e.g. Kashmir–India, Puerto Rico–United States, Québec–Canada, Åland–Finland, New Caledonia–France, Southern Sudan–Sudan, Zanzibar–Tanzania); their experience may be of particular significance for our purposes.

Nevertheless, the distinctiveness of Hong Kong's autonomy – in its objectives, relationships between the centre and autonomous region, institutions, and procedures – limits the value of the comparative method.

The framework of autonomy

I first set out, in general, some features of autonomy as a constitutional concept and then explore the specificity of autonomy in Hong Kong. The comparative study of autonomy systems shows that although each system is distinctive, specific to its context and circumstances, there are certain approaches, institutions, and procedures that have a considerable bearing on the prospects of autonomy.

---

[1] E.g. Markku Suksi, *Sub-State Governance Through Territorial Autonomy: A Comparative Study in Constitutional Law of Powers, Procedures and Institutions* (Heidelberg: Springer, 2011); Yash Ghai (ed.), *Autonomy and Ethnicity: Negotiating Competing Claims in Multi-Ethnic States* (Cambridge: Cambridge University Press, 2000); Yash Ghai and Sophia Woodman (eds.), *Practising Self-Government: A Comparative Study of Autonomous Regions* (Cambridge: Cambridge University Press, 2013).

[2] Deng Xiaoping, *On the Question of Hong Kong* (Hong Kong: New Horizon Press, 1993) 9, 13.

Autonomy connotes self-government, the ability of a region or community to organise its affairs without interference from the central government, neighbouring regions, or neighbouring communities. It is a device to allow ethnic or other groups claiming a distinct identity to exercise direct control over affairs of special concern to them while allowing the larger entity to exercise powers that cover interests common to both.[3] When negotiations on the oldest surviving autonomy, Åland,[4] were underway, the Finnish government defined the purpose of that autonomy in the following way: 'to secure for the Åland islanders the possibility of arranging their existence as freely as possible for a territory which does not itself constitute a state'. The inhabitants of the autonomous region make policy and organise and run the government without interference or direction from the centre. They can freely express their identity and pursue objectives for which there may not be much appetite in other parts of the country. Although in many respects autonomy resembles federalism, including constitutional entrenchment, unlike federalism, which provides a uniform system of dividing powers among different levels of government throughout the country, autonomy is restricted to one or a few parts of the country, largely to protect its culture, which is distinctive from other, more dominant communities, or to overcome problems of geographical distance.

Although Hong Kong is always described as autonomous, it can be argued that this categorisation is invalid because constitutional arrangements in Hong Kong do not fully conform to the principal purpose of autonomy – self-government. In the 1984 Sino-British Joint Declaration (JD), China undertook to establish, under Article 31 of the Chinese Constitution, a Hong Kong Special Administrative Region (HKSAR) 'which will enjoy a high degree of autonomy, except in foreign and defence affairs which are the responsibilities of the Central People's Government' (Article 3). Article 31 is very flexible; it gives the NPC authority to set up special administrative regions with such powers that it considers necessary.[5] In the BL of the HKSAR, the NPC 'authorises the Hong Kong

---

[3] Yash Ghai, 'Ethnicity and Autonomy: A Framework for Analysis' in Ghai, *Autonomy and Ethnicity*, note 1 above, 8–11.

[4] This claim is often made for Åland, but depending on how one defines autonomy, Québec can justifiably make that claim.

[5] Article 31 reads, 'The state may establish special administrative regions when necessary. The systems to be instituted in special administrative regions shall be prescribed by law enacted by the National People's Congress in the light of specific conditions'. Although the regions are described as administrative, it is clear that Hong Kong and Macau are more political than administrative.

Administrative Region to exercise a high degree of autonomy and enjoy executive, legislative and independent judicial power, including that of final adjudication, in accordance with the provisions of this Law' (Article 2). A more accurate description appears in the Preamble of the BL: 'under the principle of "one country, two systems", the socialist system and policies will not be practised in Hong Kong'. Instead, the BL prescribes the 'systems to be practised' in the HKSAR, as stated in the JD. Article 5 states that 'the previous capitalist system and way of life shall remain unchanged for 50 years'.[6] The BL describes in great detail the 'systems' to be followed in the HKSAR for its administration and the conduct of its economy, greatly restricting the policy choices for the people and government of Hong Kong.

Thus, the principal purpose of the BL is to separate off the economic systems of the Mainland and the HKSAR from the logic of which followed institutions to support Hong Kong's capitalism as understood by Beijing (with some instruction from Britain).[7] When presenting the BL to the NPC for its approval, Pengfei explained that the structure of government 'must facilitate the development of the capitalist economy in the Region'. Moreover, the HKSAR does not have the authority to alter the 'systems'. Consequently, Hong Kong people have to make laws and policies within the interstices of the 'systems'. In some respects, there is considerable scope for policy and law making, but the essential framework (and often the details) cannot be changed. The HKSAR cannot alter the main institutions of its government on its own, the electoral laws, or significantly a rather laissez-faire economic system. Another aspect of the institutional arrangements, centring on the office and powers of the Chief Executive, was Beijing's plan to acquire ultimate control over Hong Kong affairs. Hong Kong's institutions of governance are not fully democratic

---

[6] Article 3(12) of the JD has a promise from China that its policies regarding Hong Kong would 'remain unchanged for 50 years'. There is nothing to prevent China from extending it for a further period. As far as I know, no other autonomy is time bound; a time limit acts to weaken autonomy. Some autonomies provide for the termination of the autonomy, not through full re-integration with the state, but secession from it if the people of the autonomous region vote for it after a specified number of years (New Caledonia, South Sudan and Bougainville). South Sudan has already exercised this right and is now an independent state. The other two have yet to decide.

[7] The British government prepared detailed notes on the Hong Kong system to enable the Chinese negotiators to understand its dynamics (the focus was on the economy and on institutions, principally on the legal system, with little on the political arrangements). Some of these notes found their way into the Joint Declaration and the Basic Law. See Robert Cottrell, *The End of Hong Kong: The Secret Diplomacy of Imperial Retreat* (London: John Murray, 1993).

or independent of the Mainland; therefore, the people are not able to make decisions on policy, which is an essential component of autonomy. The judiciary is the most independent institution of all – and hence liable to deal with issues that other institutions cannot, or fail, to resolve.

However, I do not intend to pursue here the issue whether Hong Kong has a high degree of autonomy.[8] The BL does indeed confer upon Hong Kong many indicia of semi-sovereignty. It allows Hong Kong the right to determine its own immigration policies and to issue its own passports. Hong Kong has its own flag, currency, and stamps. It has also, in the form of 'the permanent resident of Hong Kong', its own quasi-citizenship, to which are attached important rights denied to other Chinese citizens. Its availability to non-Chinese, in the recognition of Hong Kong's cosmopolitanism, is a remarkable acknowledgement of the identity and distinctiveness of Hong Kong. Hong Kong is granted the common law, the use of the English language, and a comprehensive set of rights and freedoms. It is also granted very considerable powers of external affairs.

More than symbols, these provisions are the foundations of and sup-ported by an extraordinary range of substantive powers.[9] They include almost total control of the economy, monetary and tax affairs, trans-port (including aviation and shipping), social policies, education, health, sports, and so on. Only foreign and defence have been retained by the Central Authorities (Articles 13 and 14). On the other hand, the details in the BL on how Hong Kong institutions must exercise their powers (implicit in the requirement of 'preservation') severely limit Hong Kong discretion as regards policy. Detailed provisions on the conduct of econ-omy (particularly in Chapter V of the BL) impose many restrictions. Of the institutions, the most important is the executive, which, by the nature of the appointment of the Chief Executive and the discharge of his or her functions, is beholden and subordinated to the Mainland authorities. Nor does Hong Kong have the power to determine the structure or reform of its political and administrative systems, and severe restrictions have been placed on further democratisation.

---

[8] I have discussed this matter in detail in my book, Yash Ghai, *Hong Kong's New Constitutional Order: The Resumption of Chinese Sovereignty and the Basic Law*, 2nd edn. (Hong Kong: Hong Kong University Press, 1999) ch. 7.

[9] Unlike most autonomies, Hong Kong starts off with the big advantage that it had a well-established system of laws and administrative mechanisms covering the powers granted to it in the BL, so that there was no need for constant (and debilitating) negotiations with the Mainland on the transfer of these powers. But the institutions of governance were to be established afresh, neither democratic nor accountable, and dependent on the Central Authorities.

Nevertheless, a comparison of Hong Kong's system with other autonomy systems will enhance our understanding of its system. I examine
in this chapter key features of an autonomy system, pointing first to the
importance of the feature and then examining how it operates in Hong
Kong.

Negotiating and entrenching autonomy

Most states resist the grant of autonomy; in most countries, autonomy
has been achieved only after a long struggle, frequently through violence
or civil war. Because of the intensity of internal conflict, the international
community (regional or global) often becomes involved in facilitating
a settlement. Autonomy provides the basis for settlement because it is
midway between two competing claims, state sovereignty and secession.
Although state sovereignty remains the foundation of international law
and practice, a number of legal norms have emerged, principally under
international treaties or practice, which justify autonomy (and controver-
sially even secession) if the group seeking separation has been oppressed.
One of these is the principle of self-determination, which played a critical role in the decolonisation of territories under foreign rule after the
establishment of the United Nations (UN).[10]

China ruled out the application of the principle of self-determination
to Hong Kong when it joined the UN, persuading it that Hong Kong
was a matter left over from history to be negotiated between China and
Britain, thus turning the issue into a bilateral matter.[11] The decision on
Hong Kong's future status and system was made by China; Hong Kong
people had no choice in the matter.[12] Chinese proposals on the future
of Hong Kong to Britain formed the foundation of the JD and the BL.
On the surface, China offered a generous deal to Hong Kong without a
struggle of its people. But the lack of their participation and engagement
in the negotiations on the future of Hong Kong, particularly the disregard
of the principle of universal and equal franchise for election of the Chief
Executive and the Legislative Council, damaged the legitimacy of the
new system. And the element of solidarity among the people that comes
from a struggle was missing. The reception of the Sino–British agreement

---

[10] See *Reference re Secession of Québec* [1998] 2 SCR 217.
[11] Nihal Jayawickrama, 'The Right to Self-Determination' in Wesley-Smith, Peter (ed.), *Hong Kong's Basic Law: Problems and Prospects* (Hong Kong: Faculty of Law, University of Hong Kong, 1990) 85.
[12] Ghai, note 8 above, 41–4.

(essentially a conservative document except for provisions on human rights) was much more enthusiastic among the business community than the working class or supporters of democracy. In this way, the BL became a source of conflict among the Hong Kong people, which continues to retard progress towards constitutional reform.

A critical issue in the negotiations on autonomy is the manner in which it is to be protected against interference or abolition by the national government. Autonomous arrangements that are easy to remove put autonomy constantly at risk and deter the autonomous region from its full exercise. Autonomy that can be diminished or removed without the consent of the autonomous region is neither secure nor effective. Historically, great emphasis was placed on international guarantees (the League of Nations guaranteed several autonomy arrangements after the First World War). There are examples in contemporary times, in which the European Union or North Atlantic Treaty Organization (NATO) has played a prominent part (particularly in the arrangements in the Balkans following the collapse of the Yugoslav federation, especially Bosnia-Herzegovina and Kosovo). The example of an autonomy that depended entirely on enforcement by outside powers (United States, United Kingdom, and France) is that of the Kurdish regions of Iraq during the later part of Saddam's regime by the control of airspace over these regions.[13] In other instances, the principal or only protection is national, mainly through constitutional entrenchment enforced by the judiciary. Some autonomies enjoy the benefit of both.

As is well known, the genesis of Hong Kong's autonomy is the Sino-British JD, a treaty that was registered at the UN under which Britain agreed to return Hong Kong to China in return for the latter's undertaking to maintain the previous economic and social system and to democratise the political system. Britain agreed to transfer Hong Kong to China on the basis of China undertaking that the rights of the people and their way of life would be guaranteed, thereby assuming responsibility to ensure compliance by China. Although no formal mechanism for this purpose was agreed, various possibilities are open to Britain should it wish to intercede with China whenever the JD or BL is breached. But there is little evidence that Britain intended to take any action for the enforcement of the JD; its principal concern seems to have been the protection of British

---

[13] See 'Law for Autonomy in the Area of Kurdistan' in Hussein Tahiri, *The Structure of Kurdish Society and the Struggle for a Kurdish State* (Costa Mesa: Mazda Publishers, 2007) 358.

commercial interests. Britain did little to ensure that the BL faithfully carried out China's commitment in the JD.[14] The most that the British government did was to present six monthly reports to Parliament on the implementation of the BL (which continues to this day, although they are of little value). Under a US law, the United States-Hong Kong Policy Act, passed in 1992 under pressure from some groups in Hong Kong, the president has the power to suspend privileges and concessions given to Hong Kong if China no longer observes its obligations under the JD (including Hong Kong's special status under which US relations on trade and extradition with Hong Kong are based). However, the growing economic importance of China meant effectively that neither the United Kingdom nor the United States would really take any meaningful action for violations of the JD – any more than international organisations to whom China had declared the grant of autonomy to persuade them to continue Hong Kong's membership and status. Hong Kong courts do occasionally look at the JD as an aid to the interpretation of the BL but have not used it as an independent source of authority.

Effectively, therefore, we have to turn to the BL for guarantees of autonomy. Realising that the second of the 'two systems' could not be accommodated within the People's Republic of China's (PRC's) constitutional and political system driven by a command economy and the rule of the Communist Party, Article 31 as a General Principle, was adopted in the 1984 Constitution to establish special administrative regions outside the basic framework of the Constitution. General and brief, Article 31 was intended to be used for differing circumstances of territories identified for reunification (Taiwan being the principal target). It authorises the NPC to make arrangements for a special region to be specified 'in the light of specific conditions'. It can thus be argued that to examine the constitutional status and arrangements for a special administrative region, one turns primarily not to the PRC Constitution but to the BL. Support for this approach is to be found in the BL with its frequent statements that the institutions and powers of Hong Kong and its relationship with the Central Authorities are to be 'in accordance with the provisions of this Law', meaning the BL (Articles 2, 3, 6, 11, 12, and so on). Additional support is to be found in Article 11, which in its last paragraph prescribes that 'No law enacted by the legislature of the Hong Kong Special Administrative Region shall contravene' the BL. Nor could the NPC contravene the BL because the only Mainland laws that can be extended to Hong Kong are

---

[14] For deviations of the BL from the JD, see Ghai, note 8 above, 67–9.

'confined to those matters relating to defence and foreign affairs as well as other matters outside the autonomy of the Region as specified by this law' (Article 18(3)). Even this could only be done after consulting the Committee for the BL and the Hong Kong government.

Even more dramatically, the proviso in Article 159, dealing with the NPC's power to amend the BL, states: 'No amendment to this Law shall contravene the established policies of the People's Republic of China regarding Hong Kong' (which were formulated in the Sino-British JD). The Chinese Constitution itself imposes no restrictions on the power of the NPC to amend the Constitution. The BLs of Hong Kong and Macau are the only Chinese laws that provide for their own mode of amendment and do restrict the power of the NPC.

Article 31 has therefore to be read as providing a mechanism for opting out of portions of the Chinese Constitution in relation to special administrative regions and thus enabling great flexibility in the design of their philosophies, powers, and institutions. A decision of the NPC at the time of the adoption of the BL expressly affirms the constitutionality of the BL and quotes Article 31 as authority. Confirming the validity of a law that it has passed may seem odd but the NPC must have realised that many sections of the BL were incompatible with the Chinese Constitution and wanted to put beyond doubt the integrity and validity of the BL. It said: 'The systems, policies and laws to be instituted after the establishment of Hong Kong Special Administrative Region shall be based on the Basic Law of the Hong Kong Special Administrative Region'. This injunction is not restricted to the acts of the HKSAR. This can only be read as giving an especially high status to the BL and implying that when there is a conflict between the BL and the Constitution, the former is to prevail. Instead of reading the Constitution into the BL, the BL has to be read into the Constitution for the latter's application in Hong Kong.[15] This is also a better approach as regards the style of drafting because it obviates the necessity of going through the entire Constitution and expressly disapplying parts of the Constitution.

'One country, two systems' rests therefore on a remarkable sharing and diffusing of the internal sovereignty of the PRC (Ji Pengfei's speech

---

[15] To establish a secure constitutional basis for the autonomy of Scotland (in the face of parliamentary sovereignty), the British constitutional system is moving towards the notion of a special status for relevant legislation as an organic constitutional act superior to ordinary legislation. To some extent, Britain deals with this kind of situation through conventions (understandings of how political powers will be exercised). See C. M. G. Himsworth and C. M. O'Neill, *Scotland's Constitution: Law and Practice* (London: LexisNexis, 2003).

to the NPC when introducing the draft BL explicates clearly the reach of the sovereignty of the Central Authorities over Hong Kong, necessary only to maintain the 'one country', which leaves ample room for genuine and effective autonomy). Essential therefore to the true autonomy of Hong Kong was the 'self-contained' nature of the BL. However, this form of high guarantee is problematic. The guarantee is stated in the BL, not the Constitution, which stands at the top of the hierarchy of laws. Beijing was not persuaded by those who wanted the guarantee stated in the Constitution, perhaps even a separate chapter on Hong Kong. Moreover, the scheme for the enforcement of the BL poses various difficulties, particularly provisions dealing with the relationship between Beijing and the HKSAR, where the final word is with the NPC. Beijing has armed itself with various points of intervention in Hong Kong under the BL itself that undermine autonomous decision-making in Hong Kong. And most fundamentally, this kind of constitutional pluralism is antithetical to the Chinese communist mode of government and administration, which brooks no limit on the power of the Chinese Communist Party (CCP) and its principal state agencies, the NPC and the Central People's Government.

Constitution of the autonomous region

A closely connected factor fostering the scope and security of autonomy is that the autonomous region has its own constitution. A separate constitution cannot derogate from the national constitution applying to it (which would normally only contain provisions governing the actual powers of the region and its relationship with the national institutions). But it gives the region the power to organise institutions and procedures for the exercise of powers given to it (e.g. the system of government, determining the system of voting) and to amend the constitution when necessary. If it does, it is more likely to have full internal democracy, and the security of a substantial part of its autonomy. The power to organise internal affairs through its constitution is much valued by regions in federations and those enjoying autonomy.

However, in Hong Kong's case, although there is a separate constitution, it is not enacted by the region but by the NPC. Nor is it concerned only with Hong Kong's 'internal' matters. In some autonomies, there are two instruments, one for the relationship between the centre and the region, including division of powers, and the other for the constitution of the region (Puerto Rico–United States, Åland–Finland, Bougainville–Papua New Guinea). The constitution for the autonomous region is drawn up and adopted by the region itself and can be amended by itself. The constitutional law on the relationship between it and the central authorities can be changed by the national government only by a special procedure, which in some states requires the approval also of the region.

But in respect of Hong Kong, the BL defines both the powers and institutions of the region and its relationship with the Mainland Central Authorities. So the overall security of the autonomy depends on how and who can amend the BL. The amendment is enacted by the NPC, but the process for amendment can be initiated by its own Standing Committee, the State Council (i.e. the Mainland government), or the HKSAR (Article 159). It appears that in the first two cases, the HKSAR will have no role (except indirectly through the BL Committee (BLC), a joint committee of Mainland and Hong Kong members, which has to submit its views before the proposed amendment can be placed on the NPC's agenda). It also seems unlikely that an initiative for amendment from Hong Kong will be easy because it has to have the approval of two-thirds of the Hong Kong deputies of the NPC, two-thirds of the members of Hong Kong's Legislative Council, and Hong Kong's Chief Executive. For those who think that any amendment is likely to diminish autonomy, the veto-ridden procedure within Hong Kong would be welcome (although if the NPC delegates or the Chief Executive want amendment, they are more likely to approach the State Council, bypassing the local process). But the real safeguard against amendment is the last paragraph of the article that specifies that no amendment 'shall contravene the established basic policies of the People's Republic of China regarding Hong Kong' – in other words, most of the BL. To my knowledge, no other Chinese law (apart from the Macau Basic Law) seeks to restrict the powers of the NPC in this way. But because only the NPC can amend the BL, this severe restriction is unlikely to be a barrier, for no one is likely to or can challenge the NPC. And in all probability, if the Mainland authorities want an amendment, they would choose the powers of interpretation under Article 158 (as it has in relation to the provisions about democratisation).

Thus, there is no effective entrenchment of the BL. Even if the guarantee of the BL had been placed in the Chinese Constitution, it is doubtful if it would have achieved much. And this for at least two reasons, one political (the real basis of power is the Communist Party) and the other constitutional (the ultimate power of the NPC and its Standing Committee to interpret the constitution and laws). On the Mainland, the power of constitutional review has been of little significance unlike in Hong Kong, where the power is placed in the BL, which is embedded in the common law and subject to the scrutiny of judges and lawyers trained in the traditions of that law. From my perspective, the critical provision of the BL is Article 158 on which there are now several commentaries and judicial pronouncements (discussed briefly later).

Moreover, the very specific concept of sovereignty used by the Central Chinese authorities is inhospitable to autonomy (e.g. in its denial of residual powers). There is a conflation of the internal and external aspects of sovereignty, and in both of these aspects, the concept allows the centre extensive powers and vast jurisdiction. Yet the reach of the Chinese conception of sovereignty is unclear. At one level, it potentially negates the whole of the BL; indeed, opinion in high political and academic places leans in favour of the proposition that the NPC can make any law for Hong Kong even if it violates the BL.[16] This view was upheld by the Court of Appeal in the case of *HKSAR* v. *Ma Wai Kwan David*,[17] arising immediately after 1997, in which the legality of the provisional legislature was challenged.[18] The court held in *Ma* that as the establishment of the provisional legislature was authorised or ratified by the NPC, the Hong Kong courts could not question it because it was the act of the sovereign. One way to resolve the ambiguity between 'one country' and 'two systems' that arises from this overarching concept of sovereignty would have been to clarify the relationship between the Chinese Constitution and the BL, particularly given the rather insecure foundations of the scope of the BL in the Chinese constitutional system. This option was urged on China by some Hong Kong members of the BL Drafting Committee. But it was rejected by China. The *Na Ka Ling* case, in which the CFA reversed lower courts and gave a high constitutional status to the BL, provoked a ferocious attack from Beijing and forced the CFA into a sort of retraction. The result is continuing uncertainty about the precise application of the Chinese Constitution in Hong Kong (see later discussion). This difficulty is compounded by the system of interpretation and enforcement, which gives the final powers not to the judiciary but to the Standing Committee of the National People's Congress (NPCSC), essentially a political body, and effectively the agency of the CCP. In these circumstances, the

---

[16] E.g. Albert Chen, 'The Provisional Legislative Council of the SAR' (1997) 27 *HKLJ* 1. Chen argues, drawing upon Kelsen's legal theory, that with the transfer of sovereignty, Hong Kong is under a new political order whose *grundnorm* is the supremacy of the NPC with untrammelled powers over all of China.

[17] [1997] HKLRD 761.

[18] This was set up by the Beijing appointed Preparatory Committee to replace the Legislative Council elected under the 1994 election law that broadened the franchise in a way the Chinese government found unacceptable. The NPCSC declared the law void for incompatibility with the Basic Law. See Ghai, note 8 above, 260–2.

autonomy of Hong Kong depended greatly or solely on Article 31 – but it was unlikely to hold back political and administrative forces devoted to whims of the 'sovereign' (I discuss later the 'demise of Article 31').

Citizenship

Often an aspect of autonomy is the special status and rights of people or citizens living in the region that are denied to non-citizens or citizens from other parts of the country, at least until they have been residents for a specified period (especially when the population of the region is small and there is a threat of significant migration from other parts of the country). In Puerto Rico, US citizens cannot vote in local elections until resident for three years, and in Åland, non-resident citizens of less than 5 years cannot buy land, engage in business, or vote. In Hong Kong, two objectives are achieved by rules as to who benefits fully or substantially from autonomy: keeping Mainlanders out and maintaining the cosmopolitan nature of Hong Kong and Hong Kong identity. Chinese citizens who are not long-term residents are not entitled to various rights, including the right migrate to Hong Kong, but non-citizens who have been residents for seven years or more enjoy most rights given to Hong Kong Chinese citizens (under the concept of right of abode). A major reason for this rule is to control migration from China. But in effect, it is the Chinese government rather than Hong Kong that would decide on migration from the Mainland (as is demonstrated by the right of abode cases).[19] Even before the establishment of the HKSAR, China had manipulated the conditions for the right of abode in favour of those who had left the territory to take up residence and citizenship abroad, fearing communist rule in Hong Kong but later wished to return seeing that their worries were unjustified.[20]

Regional citizenship plays an important role in defining and sustaining local identity (as in Åland, Puerto Rico, Italian regions, Kashmir), and in promoting regional solidarity. Hong Kong identity has developed over a long period, when it was separated from the Mainland, constituted by Western influences and migration (resulting in a unique combination of Chinese and cosmopolitan culture and values).[21] Perhaps China has not

---

[19] E.g. Ghai, note 8 above, 72–3; Chapters 14 (Chen and Lo) and 15 (Young) in this volume.

[20] Ghai, note 8 above, 169–71. This was done effectively by interpretation of the BL by Mainland officials.

[21] See S. K. Lau, *Hongkongese or Chinese: the problem of identity on the eve of resumption of Chinese sovereignty over Hong Kong* (Hong Kong: Hong Kong Institute of Asia-Pacific Studies, 1997). Deng misread this when he talked of horse races and dancing.

been happy with this culture and has frequently emphasised the importance of 'patriotism'. On the whole, the BL provides ample recognition
and protection of Hong Kong identity (particularly in the Bill of Rights
and Chapter VI of the BL on education, science, culture, sports, religion,
labour, and social services) and in the rights given to non-Chinese permanent residents (although there is some clawing back in their rights to
stand for elections).[22] Identity is influenced by the law but is, more fundamentally, the product of many other influences. Despite the attempts
by Mainland authorities to downplay Hong Kong identity in favour of
'Chinese' identity, the former has much greater appeal in Hong Kong than
the latter.

Division of powers and responsibilities and entitlement to resources

The powers and responsibilities given to the autonomous region are at the
core of autonomy. A key motive for seeking autonomy is the authority to
make policies and laws on matters that are important to the group for one
reason or another, the most common being the preservation of its culture
or protection of the group against discrimination. Sometimes the group
may want to exert control over natural resources found within its region
for revenue or ecology. In some societies, land is tied to many aspects
of culture or history, which the group would want to control. None of
these motives is important in the case of Hong Kong; as we have seen, the
motive is to preserve Hong Kong's economic and social system.

There are many different methods, relying on separate and concurrent
legislative lists, by which powers are divided. Today within each list there
are many requirements to consult the other level of government or the
building of consensus. The manner in which powers are divided between
the centre and the region also impacts on autonomy. Autonomous regions
prefer a clear division of powers, to minimise legal controversies, and to
be able to pursue regional policies on their own without having constantly
to worry about legal challenges or negotiations with the centre. They also
want to be left alone to do their own thing. They want a distancing from
the centre. They therefore want to avoid significant areas of concurrent
powers, which the centre tends to dominate.

At an early stage of the drafting of the BL, an attempt was made to
develop a list of powers to be given to Hong Kong, but because of its
length (and no doubt the near impossibility of including all the powers it
would exercise), it was abandoned in favour of specifying the powers of the

---

[22] See BL, Article 67.

Central Authorities. The assumption then would be that everything else (i.e. 'residual matters') is within Hong Kong's powers. But BL introduced two ambiguous concepts – of 'other matters outside the competence of the Region' and 'relations between Hong Kong and China'– in a manner that contrasts sharply with the legal niceties of Hong Kong's own internal system but rendered powerless in this instance. It is not easy to give meaning to these concepts; this can perhaps be done only by going through the BL article by article.

Even with this difficulty 'residual powers' could be with Hong Kong, but some Chinese scholars maintain that residual matters cannot belong to an autonomous region.[23] There is no theoretical reason why not. (Globally, we find much variation, and there are examples of residue lying with the regions, especially when territories with established government join another entity in forming a larger state such as the reunification of Hong Kong with China.) Many disputes in federations and autonomy are about which government has which power, resolved ultimately by the courts. At one time it seemed that this would not be a problem in Hong Kong because under the BL all powers, except defence and foreign powers, would be with Hong Kong. Now this is not clear, and a particular difficulty is that disputes will essentially be decided by one interested party, the Mainland government. The BL contains a helpful rule that only laws (on defence and foreign affairs or otherwise outside the limits of Hong Kong's autonomy) that are expressly extended to Hong Kong by the Mainland authorities after consultation with the Hong Kong government and listed in Annex III of the BL are applicable in Hong Kong (Article 18). However, Hong Kong does not have to consult the Mainland before it introduces or passes a law. But the scheme of introducing or enacting law in Hong Kong gives considerable power to the Chief Executive and restricts that of the legislature in respect of critical areas (Arts. 74 and 76). It is unlikely, give the nature of the subservient political relationship of the Hong Kong executive, that a local bill that did not have the approval of the Mainland would be introduced or passed. And the Mainland does have the power to invalidate a Hong Kong law if it considers that it violates the BL (Art. 17).

During the first thirteen years of the HKSAR (the period covered by this book), no issue of power over the division of competences arose, but

---

[23] Ghai, note 8 above, 148–9. See also 'Final Report on Residual Power', Special Group on the Relationship between the Central Government and the SAR, Consultative Committee for the Basic Law, 10 Feb 1987, Hong Kong, accessible on Basic Law Drafting History Online, ebook.lib.hku.hk/bldho/books/B35911694.pdf.

in 2010 there was an issue whether a commercial corporation of a foreign state enjoyed legal immunity before the Hong Kong courts.[24] Under Hong Kong common law, it would not, but China (with the support of the Hong Kong government) argued that the issue, being a matter of foreign affairs, fell to be resolved by Chinese law, which confers absolute immunity on such corporations.[25] Because a considerable range of foreign and external affairs are within powers given to Hong Kong, the case sets a bad precedent in leaving the matter to be decided by the Mainland authorities even in the absence of the formal extension of the relevant law.[26]

On the other hand, Hong Kong and the Mainland do not have to quarrel over tax issues or the allocation of national or Hong Kong revenue or, for the most part, how these revenues might be spent. And although land belongs to the national government, its administration has been vested in the HKSAR.

National and regional institutions and relationships between them

A democratic system in the autonomous region is another pre-requisite for autonomy. If the regional government is elected by and accountable to the people of the region, it is more likely to stand up for the interests of the region and to negotiate vigorously with the national authorities. A regional democratic system also helps to articulate local aspirations and interests and define regional identity, which is now widely recognised as critical to the safeguarding of autonomy. Democracy changes the nature of dispute settlement. As the experience of Puerto Rico and Åland shows, regional democracy does not diminish state sovereignty but makes it hard for the central authorities to go against the wishes of the majority

---

[24] Normally, China shows little interest in commercial law cases and seems to be content on the whole with Hong Kong's economic policies. In this case, the Chinese government had its own interests, both because Chinese state corporations were defendants and Chinese strategy for securing raw materials from Africa could be at risk if transactions with corporations of African states were to be examined by courts.

[25] *Democratic Republic of the Congo* v. *FG Hemisphere Associates LLC* (2011) 14 HKCFAR 95 (reference) and 395 (disposition).

[26] It was argued by the majority in the CFA that because the rule of immunity in the Mainland is a general but not codified principle of Chinese foreign relations, it was not possible to extend it through the Annex III mechanism. Presumably, one obvious reason for the rule was that the people of Hong Kong (including lawyers and judges) were not familiar with Chinese law (long treated as foreign law). The approach taken by the majority (in the face of powerful dissents) now opens up difficulties of establishing in the absence of litigation which Chinese 'rules' are applicable in Hong Kong.

of the region. So democracy can turn weak legal provisions into strong guarantees. But without regional democracy, strong legal guarantees can be rendered ineffective. This effect arises not only from the fact that regional democracy helps to promote regional identity but also that well-accepted values require that democratically arrived at views should be respected. Also, in a system where there is commitment to democracy, the central authorities know that they cannot push the region too much because it might force it into an escalation of its demands for a higher form of autonomy or even secession.[27]

Autonomy operates through institutions at the level both of the autonomous region and the national. At both levels there are legislatures and executives, each with some responsibility for affairs of the autonomous region. As discussed, the Mainland has limited direct authority in Hong Kong as regards policies or laws, and there are few institutions for this purpose. However, it makes key decisions for Hong Kong, including the appointment of the Chief Executive and other senior officers. It also exercises considerable supervisory authority. Some of this is done through legal powers and procedures in the BL, and some is done informally.

The representative and democratic nature of institutions is important for another reason. Inevitably, there are differences and even tensions between authorities at the two levels. Differences can be resolved by various methods, including bureaucratic, political, and judicial. In a democracy, the political process is important, especially if political parties at the autonomous level also have a national character or, if regional, play some role in national institutions. This option is not available in respect of Hong Kong for obvious reasons, including that China is effectively a one-party state, and Hong Kong's institutions do not have sufficient clout in the Mainland to secure a political solution. So the burden falls on the judiciary, especially if private litigants are able to invoke its jurisdiction.

Another factor is the nature and degree of the representation of the autonomous region in national institutions and vice versa. If significant, the autonomous region will be able to exercise a measure of political influence at the national level (Québec and Catalonia are examples and so is India in which today no national party can form government

---

[27] The Canadian Supreme Court has ruled that if a province of Canada is unhappy in Canada and wishes to secede, provided that it has the support of a majority of the people, the national government has to negotiate with the provincial authorities to resolve the causes of unhappiness or allow secession. This ruling is based squarely on principles of democracy (see footnote 10 for citation).

without coalition with one or more regional parties). Hong Kong has but miniscule representation in the NPC and People's Consultative Assembly, and even that is susceptible to Mainland control. The Mainland has less of a presence in Hong Kong, where it has few direct functions but is bigger proportionately. That presence is critical to the exercise of Mainland influence, if not control. Furthermore, the Mainland has significant formal influence on Hong Kong's institutions, particularly the Chief Executive and his or her government. All of these minimise the potential of a political process in which all relevant groups in Hong Kong can participate, again a factor tending resort to courts.

Relationship between different levels of government and mechanisms to handle them

Given the increasing complexity of intergovernmental relations, many federal and autonomy systems now incorporate formal mechanisms to deal with relationships between governments at different levels to promote co-operation and coordination, agree on fiscal transfers, and resolve differences. (The South African constitution prohibits reference to courts unless mediation has been tried first.) These mechanisms are singularly absent in respect of Hong Kong. One reason could be that Hong Kong and the Mainland are supposed to be separate in many respects ('one country, two systems'), and the greater the contacts, the more Hong Kong's autonomy would be undermined. But it is also possible that China regards it as demeaning that it should be seen as other than the 'sovereign', negotiating with a mere special administrative region. Looking at the scheme of the BL, China seems to prefer informal and confidential discussions. The one exception is the BLC, consisting of an equal number of Mainland and Hong Kong nominees, which has a consultative role in the determination of the validity of Hong Kong legislation, extension of Mainland law to Hong Kong, and formal interpretation of the BL by the NPCSC. It is well known that the BLC has been very ineffective, and its Hong Kong members have been given little hearing but are expected to rubber stamp decisions made in advance by the Chinese authorities. An interim assessment must be that the BLC has not played (or has not been called upon to play) the role of a body that provides a bridge between the two legal systems and assists in the interface between them. Instead, the BLC has become another tool of the Mainland. The experience of the BLC shows just how reluctant the Mainland is to accept a truly independent body operating in its own discretion – and transparently.

The lack of intergovernmental mechanisms may reflect two features: one the lack of tradition in the Communist Party of negotiations and consultation with others and the other the overweaning sovereignty of the PRC that gives it the power to make any type of decision or imposition on the HKSAR.

The weakness of institutions

The political structure of federal or autonomy systems consists of two components: its internal institutions and their relationship with central authorities. China's primary preoccupations for Hong Kong's internal institutions were to ensure there was an executive-dominated system (in Hong Kong parlance, 'executive led'), which implied a weak legislature, and to ensure that the chosen form of parliamentary representation would privilege business and professional groups and minimise the role of political parties. The foundations for such a system were well and truly laid by the British; China built upon these to create the present political edifice of Hong Kong. Rules regarding the Chief Executive draw their inspiration from those for the office of the colonial governor. He or she is appointed by the central government after a process of consultation or nomination in Hong Kong; the prevalent view is that China is free to veto a nomination that emerges from the local process, although no provision is made for fresh nominations (Article 45). The process is designed to minimise the role of political parties and indeed to some extent to favour 'independents'.[28] The powers of the government are vested in the Chief Executive, who is assisted by senior officials, whose appointments are subject to the approval of the central government, and an executive council that the Chief Executive appoints and that has a largely advisory role. The Chief Executive has no power to appoint the members of the legislature nor are senior officials any longer ex-officio members, as they were during the colonial era. Nevertheless, as discussed later, the provisions for parliamentary representation are intended to secure a legislature that is supportive of and friendly to the Chief Executive.

The Chief Executive cannot be removed by the legislature on a vote of no confidence, although he or she can be impeached through a complicated procedure weighted in favour of the Chief Executive. Even then, the

---

[28] The Chief Executive cannot be a member of a political party. See Chief Executive Election Ordinance (Cap. 569), s. 31; Simon N. M. Young and Richard Cullen, *Electing Hong Kong's Chief Executive* (Hong Kong: Hong Kong University Press, 2010) 85, 89, 101.

decision whether or not to accept the impeachment lies with the Central People's Government (CPG) (Article 45). On the other hand, the Chief Executive may dismiss a recalcitrant legislature, although only once in a term of office. It is clear that the goal of having an 'executive-led' system is secured in part by the weakening of the legislature.

There are several additional ways in which this result is achieved. First, the principles and rules for election to the legislature are designed to ensure that the majority of members will be drawn from groups sympathetic to the Chief Executive, assuming that the Chief Executive will in effect be a representative of the business community. China has built on the system of functional constituencies, from which half of the members of the legislature are returned, under which, in general, candidates and electors are restricted to a particular industry or profession. In some cases, voting is corporate, which means that effectively one or more individuals with majority equity in a number of companies can control the outcome. Second, the influence of popularly elected members, who now constitute half the membership since September 2004, is diminished by voting rules that require all bills, motions, and amendments by members to be submitted to separate voting by functional constituency members and other categories of members.[29] Third, there are severe restrictions on the power of members to introduce legislative bills, rendering their role in law making subsidiary to that of the executive.[30] All of these provisions detract from the legislature's legitimacy. A political system that is dominated by the executive and representatives of the business community lends itself to influence, if not control, by the central government.

This brings us to the second aspect of the political structure, the relationship of the central authorities with Hong Kong's institutions. By controlling the appointment of the Chief Executive and to some extent his or her tenure, the central government can influence the policies and conduct of the Hong Kong government. The CPG is also authorised to give directions to the Chief Executive on matters for which it retains responsibility (Article 43), and because this concept is not free from ambiguity, the Chief Executive could find him- or herself caught between his or her

---

[29] BL, Annex II. For a detailed study of the origins, operation, and consequences of functional constituencies, see Simon N. M. Young and A. O. K. Law, 'Privileged to Vote: Inequalities and Anomalies of the FC System' in Christine Loh and Civic Exchange (eds.), *Functional Constituencies: A Unique Feature of the Hong Kong Legislative Council* (Hong Kong: Hong Kong University Press, 2006) 59–110.

[30] BL, Article 74.

responsibility to the CPG and the LegCo. It is clear that in such a system, the Chief Executive would show greater deference to the CPG than to the LegCo.[31]

The method of election for legislative councillors also gives the central government considerable leverage over the work of the legislature, particularly in the election of functional constituency members. Nor is the Mainland reluctant to interfere in general elections by advising and funding political parties of its choice. The NPCSC is authorised to scrutinise legislation passed in Hong Kong for compatibility with those provisions of the BL that concern the responsibilities of the central authorities or the relationship between them and Hong Kong (Article 17(3)). In addition, China exercises considerable control over the 'elections' of Hong Kong's representatives to the NPC, retaining the right to make the law for these elections, and can use this control to influence Hong Kong politics with the substance and style of national politics, giving eminence to its supporters.[32] Hong Kong members to national institutions are effectively handpicked by Mainland authorities and their allies in Hong Kong. Their role, especially in respect of Hong Kong's autonomy, is unclear, but they are widely acknowledged as spokespersons for Beijing, as are most members of the BLC.

The members of the BLC, both from Hong Kong and the Mainland, have been quite outspoken in their criticism of judicial decisions, including those of the CFA, and doubts have been expressed about their impartiality and thus the qualifications to provide independent advice to the NPCSC.

Thus, although the BL gives considerable responsibilities to Hong Kong's institutions for policy and administration over Hong Kong, the weak institutional autonomy means that the Hong Kong people may not be the primary influence on the discharge of these responsibilities. At the least, no policy to which the central government is opposed is likely to be adopted in Hong Kong. In that sense, one can regard the constitutional

---

[31] In the HKSAR, where the Central Authorities appoint and can in practice dismiss the Chief Executive, there are likely to be fewer (if any) conflicts between the region and the centre than in other autonomy systems but more conflicts between other Hong Kong institutions and the centre than in other systems.

[32] Hualing Fu and D. W. Choy, 'Of Iron or Rubber? People's Deputies of Hong Kong to the National People's Congress' in Hualing Fu, Lison Harris, and Simon Young (eds.), *Interpreting Hong Kong's Basic Law: the Struggle for Coherence* (New York: Palgrave Macmillan, 2007) 201–29.

arrangements in Hong Kong more as a shell to pursue a different system from that on the Mainland than as a site for a separate, much less an alternative, source of power.

Nor does the business community provide much support to Hong Kong's autonomy even though the rationale for the autonomy is its market economy. But the truth is that the Hong Kong economy has always depended on political patronage and favours. Key business people are now tied in various ways to the Mainland leadership and have major investments on the Mainland. Cultivating those leaders is more fruitful than promoting autonomy, which would in fact limit the powers of these very leaders.

Judiciary and legal systems

Disconnected legal system

It is within the above framework of governance that I examine the Hong Kong judiciary. In federal and autonomy systems, the judiciary is the most integrated of state institutions; even when the national and subnational units have separate courts, the training, values, and techniques of judges are the same. Normally, the final court (whether a supreme or constitutional court) monitors constitutional obligations of the various governments and holds them to their respective spheres of authority or norms of cooperation. This type of court is best (and is generally) considered not the court of the central government but the national court, even where appointments may be made by the central authorities. It achieves this status for several reasons: its judges are drawn from different parts of the country; many of its members may have previously served in regional courts; and most importantly, they subscribe to a common set of values about justice, share a common technique of analysis, and see their mission as the maintenance of the rule of law and the safeguarding of the constitution.

But in Hong Kong, there is a remarkable discontinuity between the legal and judicial systems of Hong Kong and the Mainland. In many respects, the CFA is the 'final court' for Hong Kong, in practice if not in law. The judiciary is the most sharply 'separated' of all Hong Kong institutions from the Mainland in terms of the appointment or dismissal of judges (which, at least formally, require no reference to Beijing); the principal source of law (the common law) that it applies is unknown in the Mainland; there are no appeals from Hong Kong to judicial authorities on the Mainland; and foreigners may, and in the case of the CFA must, be appointed to Hong Kong courts. The judiciary, in particular the CFA, is the custodian of the common law, as a live, developing jurisprudence. It has independent links to the wider world of the common law and law more generally. It cites numerous authorities from other jurisdictions, not only from common law countries on common law issues but none from the Mainland (not even on human rights where, for the most part, Hong Kong and the Mainland are part of the same international regime of rights).

Although the CFA is the highest court for the application of the common law, it has little responsibility for the application of Chinese law other than that expressly extended to Hong Kong. The rules governing interpretation and the doctrine of precedence are quite different from those on the Mainland, where no provision of the national Constitution is justiciable.[33] But in common law and now in other systems, the constitution is the supreme law. When the CFA encounters a Mainland institution, the NPCSC, it is a political, not a judicial, body and as a superior authority applying very different set of values and modes of decision-making.

The major reasons and the constituent elements responsible for this discontinuity are, of course, well known and understandable. At the heart of it are fundamentally divergent political values, the legitimacy of institutions, and ways of governing a society, manifested in a myriad of ways. The vortex at the apex of the judicial system is thus hard to manage and inherently prone to disharmony not only of method but, more fundamentally, of objectives.

Judicial review as a safeguard of the constitution

Just as in a federation, autonomous systems need overriding judicial authority to adjudicate and sustain the delicate and yet changing relationship of the autonomous region with the national government, especially as autonomous regions tend to have less clout than regions in a federation which are able to work together to exert pressure on the centre. The maintenance of political and economic boundaries between the centre and the region, central to autonomy, should be the responsibility of bodies that are disinterested in the question, not of a body that is interested in the

---

[33]   See Albert H. Y. Chen, *An Introduction to the Legal System of the People's Republic*, 4th edn. (Hong Kong: LexisNexis, 2011).

outcome, and that have both professional competence and moral courage for this difficult, politicised task.

Federations or autonomy systems in which there is an integrated (even if not single) judiciary have found the judicial role critical to dispute settlement and the sustaining of the overall political system and a measure of consensus building and community mobilisation around the degree of separation and integration, with all its tensions. Perhaps the best example comes from Canada, where the courts ever since the foundation of that state have settled differences, elaborating the principles that must govern relations between regions and communities, and where the civil French law and the English common law have blended to produce a public law that is sensitive to the concerns of all and built on a core of common values. Among the many reasons the judiciary can play this role is its legitimacy, considerable measure of transparency, common vocabulary and discourse among the key players in legal process, and the ability to identity with some precision differences among the parties and possible ways of resolving them with the help of an authoritative text.

Even before civil law countries started to establish constitutional courts, an exception in favour of judicial review, by domestic or international courts, was made in respect of autonomy arrangements. An interesting example is the Finnish autonomous Ålands Islands, where the Supreme Court was given an advisory role in settling legal disputes between the Islands and Helsinki; this was, as far as I know, the first European instance of judicial jurisdiction over constitutional matters. Such was the success of this mechanism, that 50 years later, in a major review of the Finnish constitution, that specific and limited jurisdiction was generalised across the entire constitution without resorting to a new constitutional court.

It seems at one point that China was headed in this direction when it first enunciated the ingenious policy of 'one country, two systems'. In particular, there was the reference to the Scandinavian model – the Åland solution having been adopted in Denmark in relation to autonomies of the Faroe Islands and Greenland. The Scandinavian model consists of two elements, political negotiations, failing which judicial settlement. The first are conducted through a joint committee of the autonomous and national government.[34] As the idea of the Committee on the BL was flagged by the Mainland, it seemed as if China had really bought into the Scandinavian

---

[34] I have discussed the systems of dispute resolution in Åland and Puerto Rico and compared them with the Hong Kong system in Yash Ghai, 'Resolution of Disputes between the Central and Regional Governments: Models in Autonomous Regions' (2001) 5 *Journal of*

model. But as the details of the BLC emerged, it became clear that what China had in mind was something quite different.

There were several hurdles in the adoption of the Scandinavian model in both its political and judicial aspects. Foremost was that the Chinese political and constitutional model is based on the total domination of the CCP. China is not, in that sense, a 'constitutional' state. There was also, what China claimed was its legal tradition, the civil law that did not provide for judicial review (although, ironically, the reason for that approach in Europe was the strict adherence to the separation of power, an anathema to the CCP). In other federal or autonomous systems, differing legal traditions have not been a major problem to the eminence of the judicial function (United States–Puerto Rico and Canada–Québec). Equally problematic was the Chinese conception of sovereignty, which was as much concerned with internal relations within China as with China's relations with the outside world (ruling out in Beijing's eyes the possibility that Mainland officials would sit with Hong Kong officials to settle, on a basis of equality, political difficulties between the two governments and people).

Differing conceptions of law

A major difficulty in the accommodation of Hong Kong's autonomy to Chinese sovereignty lies in the differing systems of law. Hong Kong's common law tradition suggests that the foundation of its public policy and jurisdiction must be the law. Indeed, it is hard to think of any effective or meaningful system of autonomy that is not founded on fundamental laws, reinforced by a regime of legality. China, despite its commendable and in some instances far-reaching legal reforms since 1979, operates with a very different concept of legality, subordinated as it still is to policy or administrative convenience. In recent years, both pre- and post-transfer of sovereignty, there has developed a tendency in Hong Kong to turn political issues into legal issues, principally because Hong Kong does not have an effective democratic system but does have a good legal regime of rights.[35] But the practice in China is to turn legal questions into political questions. It is significant that the Standing Committee has made several

---

Chinese and Comparative Law 1–20. For an authoritative discussion of the Ålands system, see Suksi, note 1 above.
[35] Yash Ghai, 'Sentinels of Liberty or Sheep in Wolf's Clothing? Judicial Politics and the Hong Kong Bill of Rights' (1997) 60 *The Modern Law Review* 459–80.

interpretations of the BL in the short time since it was adopted, but fewer interpretations have been made of the PRC Constitution or other laws for the larger and more complex Mainland.

Nothing better illustrates the differences between the two legal traditions than the system for the interpretation of laws, in this case the BL. The key to the autonomy of Hong Kong lies in the system of interpretation: it hangs precariously on the structure and exigencies of the interpretation of the BL. The BL provides many points at which an act of interpretation by the NPCSC is required[36] or permitted.[37] Its formulations are frequently vague, there are different understandings of various provisions, and the relationship of the BL to the PRC Constitution and laws is unclear. The power to interpret the BL thus becomes critical to Hong Kong's relationship to the Central Authorities and to its autonomy. Here is the Achilles heel of autonomy: the ultimate responsibility for the interpretation of the BL lies with the NPCSC.[38] The assumption underlying the BL is that the responsibility for policing the boundaries between Hong Kong's institutions lies with the HKSAR courts, but the policing of boundaries between them and the central authorities is with the NPCSC.[39] In doctrine and practice, however, there is no restriction on the NPCSC's powers of interpretation.

In the common law, the function of interpretation is to bring coherence to the constitution, to explicate its underlying principles, and to harmonise other laws with it. The very rules for interpretation are designed to increase the predictability of the outcome of legal disputes.[40] In China, on the other hand, the rules for interpretation allow the NPCSC to extend the reach of pre-existing law and to add to the law. There are no rules that facilitate predictability, especially because no reasons are given for decisions reached by the NPCSC. Interpretations of law are influenced more by policy changes than by the letter of the law.[41]

Perhaps China thought that the version of the rule of law based on the common law was essential to capitalism and was prepared to accept a very considerable entrenchment of the common law. Several provisions

---

[36] BL, Articles 17, 18, 158, 159, and 160.   [37] BL, Article 158.   [38] *Ibid.*

[39] Many provisions are based on it such as the powers of law making in Article 17 and the formulation in Article 11.

[40] Although it does not always work like this; judges are, especially in the common law, often a law unto themselves.

[41] Kong Xiaohong, 'Legal Interpretation in China' (1991) 6 *Connecticut Journal of International Law* 491–506.

provide for the application of the common law and the continuation of the previous legal and judicial systems (Articles 8, 18, 19, 80–96, and 160). There is provision for judges from other common law countries to sit on the CFA, and in practice, there is always one such judge, chosen from a list of some of the most distinguished common law judges (Article 82). Permanent judges at all levels of court may be recruited from other common law jurisdictions (Article 92), a broader authorisation to recruit foreigners than is permitted in respect of other officials. HKSAR may make provision for lawyers from outside Hong Kong to practice ('on the basis of the previous system', presumably from prescribed common law countries; Article 94). Courts are free to refer to precedents of other common law jurisdictions (Article 84). The jury system has been preserved, although the jury does not play an important role in Hong Kong (Article 86).

The scope of the jurisdiction of Hong Kong courts is very wide and includes the interpretation and enforcement of the BL itself, including an impressive range of human rights. Importantly, the judiciary enjoys a high degree of independence, 'free from any interference' (Article 85) in their appointment and dismissal.[42] The Hong Kong judiciary is the custodian of constitutionalism; it has to safeguard the BL as the supreme law in Hong Kong. The BL defines with particularity the respective spheres of power and authority of the Mainland and the HKSAR. As the custodian of the BL, it should ensure that the Mainland's acts applying in Hong Kong are also in conformity with the BL. The BL is a special (organic) law of the NPC, the highest legislative (and indeed state) authority in the PRC. The BL is not addressed only to Hong Kong institutions but also to the Mainland authorities. Article 11 is quite explicit that all laws and policies in Hong Kong must be based on the BL. It is true that the second paragraph of Article 11 expressly forbids only the Hong Kong legislature from enacting a law in contravention of the BL. But this must not be read as excluding the Mainland authorities (including the NPC itself in its ordinary legislative authority) from the application of this article.

However, despite Hong Kong courts' comprehensive jurisdiction over BL questions, its ability to protect autonomy is severely restricted by the powers of the NPCSC. As far as the BL is concerned, the final authority for its interpretation is the NPCSC. The competencies of the Hong Kong

---

[42] The rules governing the status, appointment, and removal of judges are discussed in Chapter 11 (Young and Da Roza) in this volume.

courts and the NPCSC are dealt with in Article 158, which has proved a most contentious provision.[43]

Mechanisms of dispute settlement

Disputes about the respective jurisdictions of national and autonomous governments and differences on the scope of constitutional or legal provisions are endemic to systems of divided authority. In Hong Kong, there is often great anxiety when differences with the CPG are aired in public or a case is made for the rights of Hong Kong. This anxiety may be rooted in the Confucian value of harmony, or it may stem from fear of offending the all-powerful CPG (in my view, the latter). In most systems, the response is not to hide one's head in the sand but to argue the case for one's interpretation of the law or the merits of policies and search for the resolution of differences. A fair and successful resolution of disputes generally contributes more to the strengthening of national unity and the legitimacy of autonomous arrangements than dispute avoidance. Almost all autonomous – and federal – systems have provisions for the resolution of disputes. Most provide, either formally or informally, a mechanism for negotiations, with mediation or conciliation as a first step. Only if these mechanisms fail is the dispute turned over to the judiciary, which makes authoritative rulings of law and hopefully brings the matter to closure.[44] What is crucial is that the body that makes the final determination should have both legal competence and legitimacy. The latter is derived from the independence and impartiality of the court and its status as a neutral umpire between the national and autonomous governments. In general, the final court is the national supreme or constitutional court. Some may see it as allied to the national government, but in most democratic countries operating on the principle of separation of powers, national courts are accepted as independent. No threat to autonomy is perceived in vesting them with the final authority to adjudicate and interpret.

The problem in Hong Kong, as discussed earlier, is that there are no formal or informal intergovernmental institutions to tackle differences between China and Hong Kong. Although the Chief Executive is indirectly cast in that role, being responsible to both the CPG and the LegCo,

---

[43] Hualing Fu, Lison Harris, and Simon Young (eds.), *Interpreting Hong Kong's Basic Law: the Struggle for Coherence* (New York: Palgrave Macmillan, 2007).

[44] South Africa and some other systems require the exhaustion of mediation procedures before resort to courts (for South Africa, see sections 41(3) and (4) of its constitution).

he or she is grossly incapacitated from performing this function. Nor are there competent bodies with legitimacy that can serve as neutral adjudicators and interpreters between Hong Kong and China. The final powers of interpretation are vested in the NPCSC, which takes its instructions from the CPG and ultimately the CCP. Because the latter two institutions are frequently a protagonist in differences and disputes, there is no independent authority to resolve them, and Hong Kong has no choice but to follow what are widely perceived as biased interpretations. These problems are rooted in the political system of the PRC, particularly its Leninist lineage and conception of sovereignty. Proposals for institutional solutions are generally condemned as denying or challenging the authority of the PRC, and thus discussion is stifled.

The power of interpretation

Although much of the discussion on interpretation has focussed on Article 158, it is necessary to note that other parts of the BL also provide for an interpretative role by Beijing authorities. The NPCSC had to decide at the birth of the HKSAR which colonial laws would be repealed for inconsistency with the BL (Article 160). When a Mainland law is extended to Hong Kong, there must be a determination that the law relates to defence or foreign affairs or other matters outside the autonomy of Hong Kong (Article 18). Law passed by Hong Kong's legislature may be reviewed by the NPCSC for consistency with the BL and declared invalid if inconsistent (Article 17). Questions of interpretation would also arise in relation to the last paragraph of Article 159, dealing with amendments of the BL, because no amendment may contravene the 'established basic policies of the People's Republic of China'. In this case, the final power of interpretation would be that of the NPC itself. Thus, the power of interpretation is intertwined deeply in the relationship between Beijing and Hong Kong; it is not simply about the meaning of laws but about power relationships.[45]

---

[45] Some eminent Chinese scholars involved in the drafting of the BL have long argued that Hong Kong courts have no authority to review Mainland laws or to review Hong Kong legislation by reference to the BL (see Xiao Weiyun and others, 'Why the Court of Final Appeal Was Wrong: Comments of the Mainland Scholars on the Judgment of the Court of Final Appeal' in Johannes Chan, Hualing Fu, and Yash Ghai (eds.), *Hong Kong's Constitutional Debate: Conflict Over Interpretation* (Hong Kong: Hong Kong University Press, 2000) 53–60), but on the whole, the Mainland authorities have not adopted this position.

Under Article 158, the responsibility for interpretation is divided between the NPCSC and the Hong Kong courts. Given this, there are at least two major issues about interpretation that fundamentally affect the authority of the CFA. The first, on which the BL is silent, is the actual function of interpretation. In the common law, it is to give meaning to the text of the law, using the plain meaning of the words, and when there is ambiguity, take into account the purpose and context of the law.[46] In the Mainland, interpretation, particularly by the NPCSC, is used for broader purposes, including amendment of the law.[47] Which rule do the Hong Kong courts apply, particularly when they have to apply Mainland legislation?

Hong Kong courts apply the common law approach, using the well-established rules on constitutional interpretation where the text of the constitution is fundamental. The NPCSC adopts a broader approach that encompasses amendments through interpretation.[48] An illustration of these contrasting approaches is to be found in the right of abode cases, particularly the *Ng Ka Ling* decision by the CFA and the NPCSC inter-pretation of Article 22. Soon after the coming into force of the BL, the CFI and CA were inclined to dismiss challenges to any acts (including legislation) of the Mainland authorities ('the sovereign') at the urging of the HKSAR government. However, on appeal, the CFA asserted the juris-diction and the duty of the HKSAR courts to review any legislative acts of the NPC or NPCSC for violation of the BL. The CFA reached its decision, first, by a declaration of a general constitutional principle (supremacy of the constitution), and second, by reference to specific provisions of the

---

[46] It is fair to point out that within the common law, there are different approaches to interpretation, some more literal than purposive and some more restrictive than others, and sometimes but rarely relying on the background materials that can be used as aid to interpretation.

[47] Hongshi Wen, 'Interpretation of Law by the Standing Committee of the National People's Congress' in Johannes Chan, Hualing Fu, and Yash Ghai (eds.), *Hong Kong's Constitutional Debate: Conflict Over Interpretation* (Hong Kong: Hong Kong University Press, 2000) 194.

[48] When the Hong Kong government wanted to exclude from entry into Hong Kong children born on the Mainland but with a parent with the right of abode in Hong Kong, it weighed the advantages of either an interpretation by the NPCSC or an amendment of the BL. But because the NPC (which alone could amend the BL) was not to meet for several months, it decided on interpretation! At the end of 2011, some saw a similar dilemma – wanting to overrule a first instance decision that would give numerous maids from other countries the right of abode, some people were discussing the relative merits of pursuing an appeal or asking the NPCSC to interpret the first instance decision: 'Abode Issue is Strictly HK's Affair', *South China Morning Post*, 6 August 2011.

BL. The CFA designated the BL as 'an entrenched constitutional instrument to implement the unique principle of "one country, two systems"'. More specifically, it held that the HKSAR judiciary has been given the responsibility for interpretation of provisions within the autonomy of the HKSAR (Articles 19(1) and 80), and for the review of acts of both the NPC and its Standing Committee. Having assumed jurisdiction, the CFA decided that the right of abode under Article 24(3) was not qualified by Article 22, which applied only to Mainlanders who did not have the right of abode, thus disregarding as unconstitutional the Chinese law requiring exit permits for those with the right of abode in Hong Kong and the Hong Kong legislation that applied that restriction. This robust statement of its jurisdiction got the CFA into trouble with Hong Kong deputies to the NPC, Hong Kong and Mainland members of the BLC, and some leading Chinese lawyers. In a most unusual procedure, the government asked, and the Court agreed, to 'clarify' the part of its judgment that related to the NPC and its Standing Committee, stating that the NPCSC had authority to interpret the constitution binding the regional court and that the CFA could not question the authority of the NPC or its Standing Committee 'to do any act which is in accordance with the provisions of the Basic Law and the procedure therein'.[49]

In Hong Kong, the 'clarification' was generally seen as necessary to placate the Mainland authorities rather than as an exercise in elucidation,[50] but it did not detract from the court's conclusions in the original judgment. Nevertheless, it did mark the demise of Article 31, and it is now unlikely that any Hong Kong court would find an act of the Central Authorities unconstitutional for any reason, including violation of the BL. Article 158(1) rather than Article 158(3) is the likely route to the disregard of the BL (Article 158(1) dealing with the original rather than the appellate jurisdiction of the NPCSC).

The interpretation of Article 22(4) of the BL made by the NPCSC under Article 158(1) merely stated that Article 22(4) covers children born of parents who have residency status under Articles 24(1) or 24(2) require Mainland permission to enter Hong Kong even though as permanent residents they would be entitled to enter and stay in Hong Kong. No reasoning

---

[49] *Ng Ka Ling* v. *Director of Immigration (No 2)* (1999) 2 HKCFAR 141, 142. It is possible to read this statement as a paraphrase of its original judgment but it was expedient for both the Mainland and the Hong Kong governments to read it as a retraction of the original decision.

[50] Yash Ghai, 'A Play in Two Acts: Reflections on the Theatre of the Law' (1999) 29 *HKLJ* 5–7.

is provided for the conclusion of the NPCSC (merely that this was the intention). So this interpretation amounts to an amendment of the BL. Whatever the general law or practice is in China on interpretation powers of the NPCSC, it must be restricted to genuine interpretation because the BL provides a separate article for amendment, which is intended to provide protection for Hong Kong against violations of the JD and the BL.

Another way in which the CFA tried to obtain some purchase over the jurisdictional issues was to enunciate rules for reference to the NPCSC. In *Ng Ka Ling*, the CFA was quite emphatic that it was up to it, and not the NPCSC, to decide whether a matter fell within the autonomy of Hong Kong or not (classifying an article), and if not, whether it affected the decision in the case and so had to be referred to the NPCSC (determining the 'necessity' for reference). In its own interpretation (under Article 158(1) and not Article 158(3)), the NPCSC chided the CFA for not referring Article 22(4) to it but did not directly comment on the doctrine of the 'predominant' article test. It was clear that it did not approve of it. The matter has stood thus.[51]

Another way in which the CFA had tried to limit the influence of the NPCSC was by restricting the admissibility of documents as an aid to interpretation to those documents which existed before the BL came into existence – and then only if they are in the public domain. Thus, documents that the NPCSC has used (and urged others to use) are disregarded by the CFA, giving it greater latitude in interpretation.[52]

The other jurisdiction of the NPCSC

This broader jurisdiction of the NPCSC to make interpretations of the BL can be invoked by other authorities, directly (by the Mainland authorities) or indirectly (by the HKSAR government requesting the Mainland authorities). This is not the place for a detailed analysis of the procedure and substance of the interpretations so far given by the Standing Committee.[53] The interpretations have been highly politically motivated,

---

[51] But made somewhat palatable to the Mainland by the majority decision of the CFA in the *Congo* case when a reference was in fact made in 2011 – for the first time (see *Congo*, note 25 above). For more on the case, see Chapter 1 (Ghai) in this volume.

[52] See Yash Ghai, 'The Intersection of Chinese Law and the Common Law in the Hong Kong Special Administrative Law: Question of Technique or Politics' (2007) 37 *HKLJ* 363–406, fn 52.

[53] For this purpose, see Ghai, *ibid.*; Albert H. Y. Chen, 'Constitutional Adjudication in Post-1997 Hong Kong' (2006) 15 *Pacific Rim Law and Policy Journal* 627.

whether those relating to the adoption of previous laws under Article 160; the Chinese Nationality Law as it affects Article 24 of the BL; the right of children of permanent residents of Hong Kong to enter Hong Kong; and perhaps most importantly, the scope of political and constitutional reform under Annexes I and II of the BL.

The first point is that the interpretations were initiated either by the Hong Kong government or the CPG. If one examines the circumstances in which the NPCSC has made its interpretations, it is obvious that interpretations have been made to impose the will of Beijing on Hong Kong or to assist the Hong Kong government to overcome local difficulties, including real or potentially inconvenient decisions of courts. Sometimes the Hong Kong government uses the NPCSC to undermine the CFA or to pre-empt discussions on critical political issues (e.g. term of the Chief Executive after the premature resignation of the predecessor or, more importantly, the form and pace of political and constitutional reform). The framework for decisions of the interpretations of the NPCSC envisaged in the BL has been hijacked, and decisions are effectively made by the CCP and the CPG. There are suspicions of collusion between the Hong Kong administration and the CPG. No public consultations have been conducted. The role of the BLC has been to rubber stamp decisions made by the Chinese authorities before its meetings. The Standing Committee has in no case undertaken a detailed and careful analysis of the nature of Hong Kong's autonomy or the specific provisions interpreted.[54] No reasons are given that might guide individuals and institutions in future understanding or interpretations of the BL or Hong Kong's relationship with the Central Authorities.[55] Often, on the contrary, waters are muddied, as reports of other bodies endorsed by or even presented to the Standing Committee become in themselves sources of the BL.[56]

This introduces further indiscipline in interpretation when the precise provisions of the BL are glossed over or disregarded by vague formulations that have no place in the text of the BL such as 'executive-led'

---

[54] A closely reasoned decision of the Court of Final Appeal (*Ng Ka Ling* v. *Director of Immigration*), running to a typescript of nearly 100 pages, was overturned in a couple of paragraphs.

[55] In many respects, the rulings of the NPCSC on reference from the CPG (whether on its own initiative or that of the Hong Kong government) suffer from the weaknesses as advisory opinions in the common law – abstract in the lack of a factual situation and often without adequate presentation of legal arguments by interested parties.

[56] E.g. the reports of the Preparatory Committee in the run up to the transition of sovereignty and the reports of the Chief Executive and the Task Force on Constitutional Reform have the potential to become such 'sources'.

system, 'stability and prosperity', or 'the sovereign', interpreted to mean what suits the Mainland authorities or their supporters in Hong Kong.[57] The power to interpret has been used as a 'hands-on' device for the CPG to intervene in Hong Kong affairs as the indirect method of control and influence through the Hong Kong administration has faltered. Future use of interpretation in this way would also effectively bring about further amendments of the BL, bypassing the formal procedures of Article 159, which are directed to the preservation of the autonomy of Hong Kong, thereby threatening considerable confusion in its legal system.[58] Do these interpretations affect other provisions in which these concepts and procedures apply, such as Article 17 dealing with fundamental questions of the legislative authority of the LegCo and the role of the NPCSC? Questions like this point to the ad hoc nature of the PRC approach to law. And they point to how in some crucial constitutional areas, the CFA is marginalised and has little influence on political issues even when compared with courts in the twilight of colonialism. The diverse forms of jurisdiction of the NPCSC tend to blur the boundary between the legal and the political (and the decisions of the highest tribunal form little basis for precedent).

The fact that differences between Hong Kong people and Mainland authorities as to jurisdiction or decisions arise only in relation to 'political issues' and not for the most part commercial or economic issues (the *Congo* case had elements of both) shows how fast and far the convergence of interests between the Chinese communist leaders and Hong Kong's capitalist leaders has emerged. When differences arise between sections of the Hong Kong people and China, these capitalist leaders are on China's side – or sometimes, more accurately, China is on their side. China seems comfortable with a capitalist Hong Kong without political rights. In the end, it was not capitalism but democracy that threatened the Mainland system and the authority of its self-appointed 'leadership', a 'socialist'

---

[57] Examples are the reports of the Task Force on Constitutional Reform and Chief Executive Tung Chee-hwa's famous 'nine points' in support of the government's approach to political reform. See Chee-hwa Tung, 'Report on Whether There is a Need to Amend the Methods for Selecting the Chief Executive of the Hong Kong Special Administrative Region in 2007 and for Forming the Legislative Council of the Hong Kong Special Administrative Region in 2008', 15 April 2004, accessible at www.cmab.gov.hk/en/issues/electoral4.htm.

[58] For example, the NPCSC has decided that there is no difference in law between a matter being referred to the CPG for 'approval' in Annex I and 'for record' in Annex II – both require the consent of the CPG – nor between procedures requiring the initial engagement of the Central Authorities.

regime more afraid of democracy than of capitalism. The sharp distinction between the public and private spheres is to some extent reflected in the fragmentation of law into the public and 'private' spheres. In private, Hong Kong mostly triumphs; in public, Beijing does.

Conclusion

This chapter has shown the context in which the Hong Kong courts, particularly the CFA, operate, including opportunities as well as difficulties. The Hong Kong courts are completely separated from the Mainland courts, and the principal law it administers is the common law, tied to several key jurisdictions, and the law is flexible. The provenance of human rights applicable in Hong Kong, again connected to the wider world, allow the courts to search for solutions from many jurisdictions and tribunals. Of all the public institutions in Hong Kong, the legal system is the most autonomous, enjoys much greater prestige and legitimacy than the courts on the Mainland, and is able to fashion the law to the circumstances of the region. But with prestige come problems: the courts are looked to to solve problems that Hong Kong's insufficiently representative and democratic institutions cannot cope with, and the lack of dispute resolution mechanisms between Hong Kong and the Mainland cannot easily resolve differences between the region and the Mainland. On two major occasions, the former Chief Justice Li stated that the burden placed on the courts is that they are forced into dealing with problems that are best solved through the political process.

The focus of the chapter has been mostly on the politico-technical difficulties the courts have had in the exercise of their jurisdiction. It is necessary, however, to point out that the Hong Kong judiciary faces difficulties only or mostly when an element of public law applies. This is particularly the case when there is actually an intersection between the two systems – that is, between the independent legal system of Hong Kong and the political system of the Mainland (under the formal auspices of the NPCSC). Major differences between the systems then appear. These include the clash of values and principles, the differences in the functions and rules of interpretation, the admissibility of evidence and the sources of law, and the nature and styles of decisions compounding political difficulties, the lack of understanding of the technique of the other, and the different ways of articulating issues. Consequently there is no effective engagement between the courts and regional or Mainland authorities, illustrated, for example, by the long-running saga of right of abode cases. The absence of a consensus on the status of the BL and its relationship to the national constitution compounds these difficulties. Sir Anthony Mason, a non-permanent member of the CFA who has played a critical and constructive role in moulding the approach of the CFA, notes the inherent tension in the BL and examines the ability of Article 158 to manage it. He realises that when the two key institutions charged with the interpretation of the BL use such different approaches and principles of interpretation and espouse different values, they may arrive at different conclusions to the same question. And for this reason, 'there is an inherent difficulty in ascertaining what the final answer to that legal question will be'. Because the finality of the answer may depend on whether an interpretation by the NPCSC under Article 158 will be necessary, 'the operation of the Basic Law involves a novel element of unpredictability'.[59]

Working in a situation where judges know that the 'sovereign' does not place much value on their role and status and that they do not have the support of the Hong Kong government at critical points must serve to demoralise them. Given these difficulties, the verdict that the Hong Kong courts, under the leadership of the CFA, have strengthened the protections of the law, particularly through a robust jurisprudence on human rights, and retained the reputation of learned and impartial decision-making, the results are somewhat surprising – and greatly to be welcomed.

---

[59] Anthony Mason, 'The Role of the Common Law in Hong Kong' in Jessica Young and Rebecca Lee (eds.), *The Common Law Lecture Series 2005* (Hong Kong: Faculty of Law, University of Hong Kong, 2006) 1.

Two interpreters of the Basic Law

The Court of Final Appeal and the Standing Committee of the National People's Congress

XIAONAN YANG

The Hong Kong Basic Law (BL), the fundamental law of the Hong Kong Special Administrative Region of the People's Republic of China (HKSAR), plays a significant role in its legal system, providing for the institutional framework of all branches of government and determining the validity of all laws within this system. The Court of Final Appeal (CFA), as the final court of appeal in this jurisdiction, is vested with the power to interpret and enforce the BL. However, this highest court of the HKSAR – a common law court – does not enjoy the final, unchallengeable authority to decide on the interpretation of the BL. Instead, the Standing Committee of the National People's Congress (NPCSC) shares the power to interpret the BL with the CFA. Without doubt, the NPCSC functions as a crucial constraint on Hong Kong's autonomy and inevitably generates interaction between the legal systems of Mainland China and Hong Kong. This chapter analyses the institutional settings of the two interpreters and argues that different institutional concerns and missions inevitably bring the two interpreters to different interpretations of the BL.

The institutional role of the Standing Committee of the National People's Congress and its missions

According to Article 158(1) of the BL, the NPCSC has a general power to interpret the BL. In the 13 years from 1997 to 2010, the NPCSC issued three formal interpretations of the BL, one of which overruled an interpretation by the CFA. The NPCSC is also a legislative interpreter in Mainland China.[1] The interpretation of the BL by the NPCSC is usually compared with legislative interpretation in the Mainland. However, this chapter

---

[1] See generally, Hualing Fu, Lison Harris, and Simon N. M. Young (eds.), *Interpreting Hong Kong's Basic Law* (New York: Palgrave Macmillan, 2007).

takes the view that, institutionally, these two kinds of interpretations function differently.

In Mainland China, as a matter of form, the power to interpret laws is not formally affiliated with any governmental power (i.e. legislative power or judicial power) but listed as an independent power by the Constitution of the People's Republic of China (PRC) in 1982.[2] Nevertheless, Professor Zhang Zhiming observes 'this power is closely related to the legislative power shared by the same state organ'.[3] Chinese legal theory takes the Marxist view that 'law in nature is the will of the ruling class'.[4] The legislature (the National People's Congress [NPC] in China) is the ideal interpreter of the popular will that is reflected in laws. The principles of checks and balances and the separation of powers are not applicable within the regime of Mainland China. The judiciary plays a much less important role in China's system of legal interpretation than in the United States or Hong Kong. Besides the NPCSC, the Supreme People's Court (SPC) shares the power of legal interpretation with the Supreme People's Procuratorate (SPP) and the State Council. Only the SPC of China, not all levels of courts, has the power to issue an authoritative judicial interpretation. Although selected sample cases published by the SPC are usually instructive or persuasive to lower courts, they are not legally binding like common law precedents.[5] In practice, conflicts among different levels of courts or between two governmental branches have usually been resolved via internal reports and communications. Moreover, the SPC, the SPP, and some branches of the State Council usually issue legal interpretations jointly. When two state organs do not concur with each other, the NPCSC

---

[2] The Constitution of the PRC 1982, Articles 67(1) and (4).

[3] Zhiming Zhang, *Fa Lu Jie Shi Cao Zuo Fen Xi (An Analysis of Legal Interpretation)* (Beijing: Zhong Guo Zheng Fa Da Xue Chu Ban She, 1999) 220.

[4] Karl Marx and Frederick Engels, *The Communist Manifesto* (London: Electric Book Company, 2001) 32. The original texts in chapter 2, 'Proletarians and Communists', read: 'Your very ideas are but the outgrowth of the conditions of your bourgeois production and bourgeois property, just as your jurisprudence is but *the will of your class* made into a law for all, a will whose essential character and direction are determined by the economical conditions of existence of your class' (emphasis added by this author).

[5] Since 1985, the SPC has been publishing the *Gazette of the SPC,* which includes selected judgments. In Chinese legal theory, the precedents are not legally binding, (i.e. the courts cannot try cases according to previous judgments cited as authorities). In the early issues of the *Gazette* (1985–1986), the SPC added some comments to the judgments and clearly instructed that the other courts refer to them in trials. However, this kind of declaration was deleted in the later issues. Thus, although the lower courts usually studied these selected judgments and refer to them when applying laws in trials, they cannot cite them directly as legal authorities. See Jieping She, Zaizai Huang, and Quan Jin, 'From Normal Judgments to Precedents' (2003) 9 *Fa Lu Shi Yong (The Application of Laws)* 41.

may issue a legislative interpretation to clarify the meaning or application of controversial provisions. Several instances of legislative interpretation by the NPCSC were made in such circumstances.[6]

The NPCSC faced much fewer political challenges in rendering legislative interpretations in Mainland China than the interpretation of the BL. Other authoritative interpreters – the State Council, the SPP, and the SPC – are all accountable and subject to the NPC. The NPCSC, as the standing organ of the NPC, is politically stronger and more confident to make powerful legislative interpretations because the ideal function of legislative interpretation is partly to achieve a compromise between the conflicting state organs, especially the SPC and the SPP. The NPCSC has never been openly challenged on its legitimacy and authority in making such interpretations. It is accepted by almost all that legislative interpretations by the NPCSC have the status of legislation, normative instead of specific. Although the NPCSC has not declared that its power is ultimate, the NPCSC *de facto* exercises its power of legislative interpretation in this manner. On most occasions, the NPCSC, having vested some of its powers to the SPP, the SPC, and even the State Council, expects these institutions to exercise these powers in accordance with its authorisation and prefers to leave questions of interpretation to them.

The NPCSC, however, undertakes quite different missions in Hong Kong.[7] This chapter explores this issue from a new institutionalism perspective (i.e. interpreters do not passively adapt themselves to political, legal, and historical settings but strategically adjust behaviour to achieve individual or institutional goals).[8] These active strategies are reflected in a change of interpretative styles, approaches, or even outcomes of interpretation. The chapter begins with a review of the key institutional factors of the NPCSC and then examines its three key political missions as an interpreter of the Hong Kong BL: to maintain the prosperity and stability of the HKSAR, to maintain the authority of 'one country' as a state representative, and to behave as a self-restrained interpreter.

---

[6] See Xiaonan Yang, 'Legislative Interpretations by the Standing Committee of the National People's Congress in China' (2008) 38 *HKLJ* 255–86.

[7] The term 'mission' here means the self-recognised identity of an organisation in the given institutional settings.

[8] Professor Gillman noted that 'there is little reason to think that Supreme Court justices are frequently forced by circumstance to back away from their position on the substantive merits of a case'. See Howard Gillman, 'The Court as An Idea, Not a Building (or a Game): Interpretive Institutionalism and The Analysis of Supreme Court Decision-Making' in Cornell W. Clayton and Howard Gillman (eds.), *Supreme Court Decision-Making: New Institutionalist Approaches* (Chicago and London: The University of Chicago Press, 1999) 69–70.

From an economic perspective: to maintain the prosperity and stability of the HKSAR

The economic role that Hong Kong played in the transition and post-handover periods is seldom examined by legal scholars approaching legal issues about the BL. This chapter, however, suggests that the economic concerns may be significant, even determinative of the missions of the NPCSC in interpreting the BL. By the time of the Sino-British negotiations and during the transition period, Hong Kong had no doubt become one of the most attractive Asian cities in an economic and financial sense. In the 1980s, there was a vast economic imbalance between Hong Kong and the Mainland. In 1985, the gross domestic product (GDP) of Hong Kong was about 11.6 per cent of the GDP of the Mainland.[9] In 1997 (the end of the transition period), the per capita GDP of Hong Kong was 22.2 times that of the richest Chinese metropolitan city (Shanghai) and 35.5 times Hong Kong's neighbouring province (Guangdong).[10] Furthermore, economic development had been the primary task of the Chinese government since 1978 – 'Third Plenum of the 11th CPC Congress', which led China to a 'Reforms and Opening up to the Outside World' period. Foreign investment then played a very important role in Chinese economic development. Nevertheless, foreign investors did not have enough confidence in a socialist system (in terms of its economic and legal systems) in the 1970s. At the early time of the Reforms and Opening up to the Outside World period, Hong Kong served as a platform for foreign investments to the Mainland (see the Direct Investment to the Mainland in the Annex to this chapter).

Not surprisingly, maintaining the prosperity and stability of the HKSAR is one of the most important missions of the NPCSC in interpreting the BL. This goal is provided in the preambles of the BL and the Sino-British Joint Declaration (JD). It is also reflected in the later proposed 'through train' policy. It was first stressed by Mr Deng Xiaoping in three important statements on 'one country, two systems'.[11] In a significant speech, Deng expressed his two major concerns regarding Hong

---

[9] This percentage is calculated after considering the exchange rate between RMB and HKD.
[10] This percentage is calculated after considering the exchange rate between RMB and HKD.
[11] Deng Xiaoping's Speech in the Meeting with the Visiting Group of Hong Kong Industrial and Commercial Representatives, 22–3 June 1984; Deng Xiaoping's Speech in the Meeting with the Group of Hong Kong and Macao Ceremony Attendants, 3 October 1984; and Deng Xiaoping's Speech in the Meeting with the Members of the Drafting Committee of the BL, 16 April 1987.

Kong's transition: 'the withdrawal of British investments' and 'a great fluctuation of Hong Kong currency'.[12] As a psychological matter, almost 100 years after the British government took over the governance of Hong Kong, local citizens lacked a sense of belonging to the PRC then. When the economic development of Hong Kong was influenced by the transition, the real stability of local society would be at risk. Subsequent leaders have also held the same mission. When the former Deputy President (and later the President), Mr Hu Jintao, first expressed his concern about the interpretation of the BL, he said that the starting point of the NPCSC's interpretation of the BL was to 'ensure the correct implementation of the BL and to maintain the prosperity and stability of the HKSAR'.[13] Mr Qiao Xiaoyang, a key person in the interpretation of the BL by the NPCSC, similarly reiterated that 'the starting point and goals of the NPCSC in interpreting the BL are to ensure the implementation of "one country, two systems" and the BL and maintain the prosperity and stability of Hong Kong'.[14]

For a political purpose: to ensure the implementation of 'one country, two systems' and especially to maintain the authority of 'one country'

The NPCSC is a purely political institution. No doubt, a political mission has crucial influences on its behaviour. The NPCSC is one of the Central Authorities mentioned in the BL. According to the BL, the NPCSC has the following powers: to review the constitutionality of enactments passed by the Legislative Council (LegCo) (Article 17(3)), to add or remove national laws applied to the HKSAR in Annex III (Article 18(3)), to declare a state of war or state of emergency (Article 18(4)), to interpret the BL (Article 158), to propose amendments to the BL (Article 159(2)), and to adopt the pre-existing laws as the laws of the HKSAR (Article 160(1)). In most other countries, the powers of constitutional review and constitutional interpretation are closely related, but here the NPCSC's powers of constitutional interpretation and review are separately provided for in the BL.

---

[12] Deng Xiaoping's Speech in the Meeting with the Members of the BLDC on 16 April 1987.
[13] 'Hu Jintao States that the NPCSC's Interpretation Maintains the Rule of Law in Hong Kong, when Meeting with the Officials, Members of the Executive Council and the LegCo and Persons in Charge of the Judiciary', *Ta Kung Pao*, 1 July 1999, K1. English translation is given by this author.
[14] 'In light of "One Country, Two Systems", Statements on the Necessity and Legitimacy of the NPCSC's Interpretation', *Ta Kung Pao*, 9 April 2004, A4. English translation is by this author.

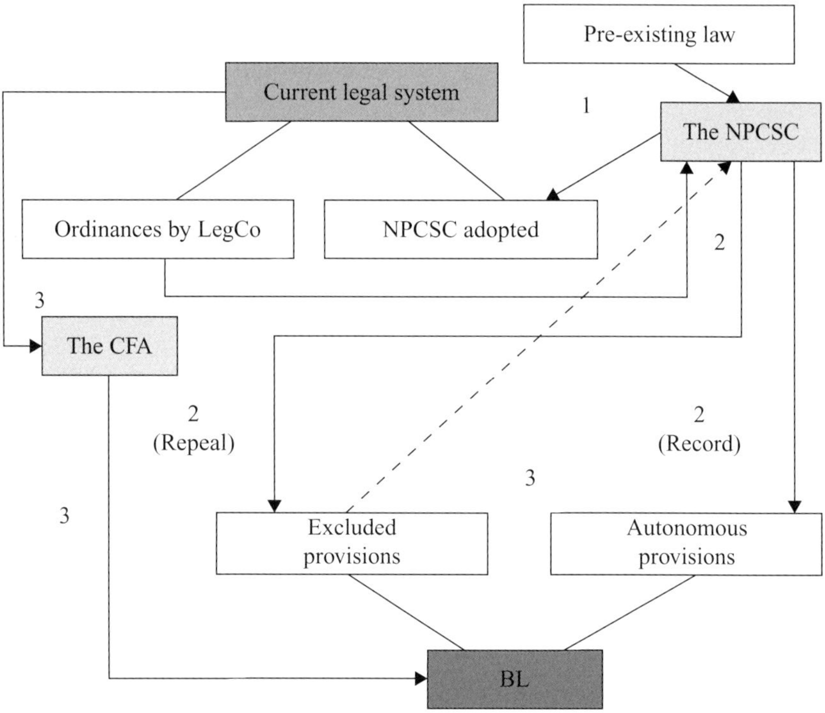

Figure 3.1   Constitutional review in the Hong Kong Special Administrative Region of the People's Republic of China.[a]

[a] This figure illuminates the mechanism of constitutional review of the current legal system. The CFA and NPCSC are the reviewers of laws. The BL is the standard of substantial review. The current legal system is composed of laws enacted by the LegCo and those adopted by the NPCSC. Upon the establishment of the HKSAR, the NPCSC reviewed the constitutionality of the pre-existing laws and adopted the laws consistent with the BL as laws of the HKSAR. This review is presented by Line 1. Line 2 shows the review by the NPCSC of the laws passed by the LegCo. As regards laws that are not consistent with the two kinds of excluded provisions: non-autonomous provisions and the provisions involving the Central Authorities of the BL, the NPCSC returns them without amendment. As regards the other laws only involving autonomous provisions, the NPCSC only records them. Line 3 explains that the CFA reviews the constitutionality of the whole system when needed in litigation. When the CFA interprets the excluded provisions of the BL, a referral may be needed.

Nevertheless, constitutional review and constitutional interpretation are the two most effective mechanisms under the BL for the NPCSC to determine local affairs involving the Central Authorities. The NPCSC's power to review the constitutionality of local enactments is limited (Figure 3.1).

First, the NPCSC has no power to review the pre-existing laws after 1997. According to the provision of Article 160, the NPCSC reviewed the pre-existing laws and adopted those that were consistent with the BL as laws of the special administrative region (SAR) at the time of the handover. This power could only be executed on one occasion upon the establishment of the HKSAR. Even if the NPCSC later thinks that more provisions of the pre-existing laws are in contravention of the BL, the NPCSC cannot execute the power under Article 160. Pursuant to Article 17, the NPCSC can only review laws enacted by the LegCo of the HKSAR because the BL assumes that the NPCSC has already finished the review of pre-existing laws. Second, the NPCSC cannot review the common law. Under Article 8, the pre-existing laws include 'the common law, rules of equity, ordinances, subordinate legislation and customary law'.[15] When the NPCSC reviewed the pre-existing laws, it did not substantively review the common law. The NPCSC did not actively adopt laws that are consistent with the BL but repealed selected ordinances. After the transition, the NPCSC has no power to review the non-written laws.

Third, according to Article 17, all laws passed by the LegCo shall be reported to the NPCSC for the record. However, the NPCSC only substantively reviews those repugnant to the non-autonomous provisions and the provisions involving the Central Authorities. Furthermore, the NPCSC does not have the power to change the substance of the law in question but merely returns the law with no amendment. Fourth, there are some procedural deficiencies in this mechanism. The scope of provisions involving the Central Authorities is vague. The BL does not provide for clear procedural rules on the exercise of the review power of the NPCSC. Although the law returned is invalid, the invalidation is not retrospective. In the meantime, the BL does not provide any time limit or procedural limitation. Considering this restriction, the NPCSC thus has to act in a very cautious manner in constitutional review because a decision of returning a law possibly causes a legal vacuum. Therefore, the NPCSC may not easily exercise supervision over local legal affairs involving the Central Authorities under this mechanism. The implementation of this power may cause great political controversies.

As regards amending the BL, the NPC instead of the (NPCSC) has the power to pass amendments. The NPCSC can only propose bills for amendments on its own according to Article 159(2). Before putting bills on the agenda, the NPC shall request views from the Committee for the BL

---

[15] BL, Article 8.

of the HKSAR under the NPCSC (BLC). The NPCSC's power regarding amendment is limited and not so determinative.

In contrast with the above powers, the NPCSC's power to interpret the BL (authorised by Article 158(1)) is general and free- standing. Undoubtedly, it is more effective and less controversial than constitutional review and amending the BL. Therefore, the interpretation of the BL becomes a useful tool for the NPCSC to influence local affairs relevant to the BL.

However, Article 158 does not suggest an active power explicitly. The NPCSC is not a judicial organ or a special tribunal. Rather, it is a purely political institution. The power of the NPCSC is normative rather than specific, similar to its power of legislative interpretation. A judicial reference is required only before a non-appealable judgment is made. The request for the interpretation by the NPCSC can only be brought by the CFA and not other courts. Possibly, judgments by lower courts may involve an interpretation of an excluded provision. This interpretation becomes legally effective when the required period of appeal expires. Article 158 does not concern such cases, and this is similar to legislative interpretation in the Mainland. The interpretation by the NPCSC cannot affect judgments previously rendered by the courts but binds the courts prospectively. Article 158(3) aims to guarantee the sovereignty of 'one country' but with the least intrusion into the independence of the judiciary in the HKSAR.

In addition, the NPCSC treats 'one country, two systems' in a different way from the CFA. Although the commitments in the JD bind the Chinese government ('because of good faith'),[16] the Chinese government does not think that the legitimacy of its sovereignty in Hong Kong is based on this bilateral international treaty. For most Mainland people, Hong Kong always legitimately belonged to China even though the British government had governed Hong Kong for almost 100 years. For them, the 1997 transition is merely a reunification instead of diplomatically taking over the sovereignty over Hong Kong from the British government. This is also the reason why some Mainland scholars posit that '"one country" is the prerequisite and foundation of "two systems"'.[17] It is on the same ground that the NPCSC deals with the legal issues concerning Hong Kong and Macao.

---

[16] Deng Xiaoping's Speech in the Meeting with the Group of Hong Kong and Macao Ceremony Attendants, 3 October 1984.

[17] Yong Xia, '"One Country" Is the Prerequisite and Foundation of "Two Systems"', *Wen Wei Po*, 23 February 2004, A 1.

For the Central Authorities and Mainland officials and scholars, 'two systems' is by all means designed to achieve 'one country'. The Chinese government has practised various autonomous policies in Mainland China since the establishment of the PRC. For example, on the Agreement of the Central People's Government and the Local Government of Tibet on Measures for the Peaceful Liberation of Tibet ('17 Points Agreement'), the PRC government had thought in 1955 to establish an autonomous government of Tibet over a period.[18] Later, according to the 1982 Constitution of the PRC, the central government authorised the governments of the autonomous regions of minority nationalities to deal with autonomous affairs. Since the implementation of the policy of Reforms and Opening up to the Outside World, the Central Authorities have established several economic autonomous regions where the local governments can practice flexible and preferential economic policies.[19] Comparatively, the Hong Kong and Macao SARs have broader autonomous powers than the autonomous regions of minority nationalities and economic autonomous cities. Within 'one country', the powers of the HKSAR are considered to be authorised by the Central Authorities.[20] The autonomy of the SAR is thus not unlimited. The judiciary is the local organ upon which the least limitations have been imposed (only the limitations on their jurisdiction regarding acts of state in Article 19 and the limitation on the CFA provided in Article 158(3)).

Moreover, the basic policies of the Central Authorities regarding the HKSAR are somehow patriarchal. Deng thought that the criterion for interference was 'whether interference is in favour of the interests of Hong Kong people and the prosperity and stability of Hong Kong'.[21] Qiao included three principles for the exercise of the power of the Central Authorities: (1) 'concerning state sovereignty, such as defence, foreign affairs',[22] (2) 'concerning the relationship between the central authorities and the SAR',[23] and (3) concerning the declaration that the SAR is in a state of emergency according to Article 18(4). The first two principles are provided in Articles 17 and 158. For the NPCSC, the interpretation of

---

[18] The central government prepared to establish a government with certain autonomous powers between 1955 and 1959. This plan later failed for other political reasons.

[19] They are called Jing Ji Te Qu (經濟特區) in Chinese, including Shenzhen, Zhuhai, Shantou, Xiamen, and Hainan Province.

[20] 'In light of "One Country, Two Systems"', note 14 above.

[21] Deng's speech on 3 October 1984, note 17 above. English translation is given by this author.

[22] 'In light of "One Country, Two Systems"', note 14 above.   [23] *Ibid.*

the BL is the most powerful and effective tool to exercise the powers of sovereignty.

From a legally professional perspective: to behave as a self-restrained interpreter

To achieve the primary mission – maintaining the prosperity and stability of Hong Kong – the interference from the Central Authorities needs to be modest and cautious. According to the principles of 'Hong Kong People Governing Hong Kong' and a high degree of autonomy, the HKSAR has the power to deal with autonomous affairs. These principles are also reflected in Article 158(2) of the BL. The courts are authorised to interpret laws on their own in adjudicating cases. Although the power of the NPCSC to interpret the BL is not restricted by the BL, the NPCSC takes a *self-restrained* attitude towards the interpretation of the BL. Otherwise, a high degree of autonomy and the idea of 'two systems' would not be achieved. The secretary general of the NPCSC, Mr He Chunlin, once promised that 'the NPCSC interprets laws or the BL in a very cautious manner'.[24] Premier Wen Jiabao also expressed similar opinions when he met with the British Minister.[25] Qiao also stated that 'the NPCSC exercises the power [to interpret the BL] very seriously and cautiously. It does not exercise the power if there are alternatives'.[26]

However, the NPCSC has to be restrained by *itself* rather than by any local organ (e.g. the CFA) because constraints from local authorities are not in accord with the NPCSC's second mission – the exercise of sovereignty. Hence, as regards the question whether the NPCSC only has residual power (which means that the NPCSC can only interpret the non-autonomous provisions and the provisions involving the Central Authorities), the NPCSC considers its power to interpret the BL as general and free-standing. The CFA also agreed with this view of the NPCSC's power in the *Lau Kong Yung* judgment.[27]

As regards its three BL interpretations, the first was made on fears that the economic and social stability of the HKSAR might be affected

---

[24] 'Secretary General of the NPCSC: The NPCSC's Interpretation Will Not Be Easily Issued', *Ming Pao Daily News*, 24 June 1999, A10. English translation is given by this author.

[25] See 'Minister Wen: Wish Hong Kong People to Understand the Interpretation, Trust the Central Authorities, Follow the Rule of Law, Hang Together and Improve Themselves', *Ta Kung Pao*, 12 May 2004, A2.

[26] 'In light of "One Country, Two Systems"', note 14 above. English translation is given by this author.

[27] *Lau Kong Yung and Others* v. *Director of Immigration* (1999) 2 HKCFAR 300.

by the new arrivals resulting from the *Ng Ka Ling*[28] and *Chan Kam Nga*[29] decisions. Furthermore, the *Ng Ka Ling* decision challenged the NPCSC's sovereignty in the HKSAR. Thus, the first interpretation can also be seen as serving to maintain the authority of 'one country'. In the second interpretation, the NPCSC had to make an active interpretation to maintain political stability, at a price of sacrificing the third mission (of being self-restrained).[30] The NPCSC may have found that the adverse public reaction to the second interpretation influenced the fulfilment of its primary mission (of maintaining Hong Kong's stability). Local criticism and distrust arose from this active interference. Thus, the NPCSC adjusted its strategies; it provided a rationale for the third interpretation (which came shortly after the second one) in the body text.[31] Political discontent is always the major concern of the NPCSC. In a complex political setting, the NPCSC has to adjust its strategies to achieve its missions to the maximum extent. Although the NPCSC might take a different view from the CFA or even the HKSAR in the 'two-year versus five-year debate' leading to the third interpretation, the NPCSC's interpretative approaches are more theoretically tenable.

The Court of Final Appeal's political relationship with the Standing Committee of the National People's Congress and its missions

The BL grants the CFA the power of final adjudication but without a detailed description of its political functions in the new constitutional order. The BL provides for the separation of powers at the local level but does not provide a corresponding system of checks and balances. Although the BL provides some rules of the vertical distribution of powers between the central government and the autonomous region, learned jurists hardly reach an agreement on the question of whether specific arrangements in the BL aim to mainly serve 'one country' or 'two systems'.

---

[28] *Ng Ka Ling* v. *Director of Immigration* (1999) 2 HKCFAR 4.

[29] *Chan Kam Nga* v. *Director of Immigration* (1999) 2 HKCFAR 82. These two cases and the NPCSC interpretation are discussed in Chapters 3 (Ghai) and 14 (Chen and Lo) in this book.

[30] The second interpretation adopted on 6 April 2004 concerned the process for reforming the electoral systems for the Chief Executive and LegCo beyond 2007; see generally *Interpreting Hong Kong's Basic Law*, note 1 above.

[31] The third interpretation adopted on 27 April 2005 provided that when the office of Chief Executive became vacant, the new Chief Executive must as his or her first term serve out the remainder of the previous Chief Executive's term.

The relationships between local organs and the Central Authorities are complex. The Central Authorities explicitly mentioned in the BL include the Ministry of Foreign Affairs of the PRC (responsible for foreign affairs regarding Hong Kong), military forces (responsible for defence), State Council (probably equated with the Central People's Government), NPCSC, and NPC. According to Articles 13 and 14, defence and foreign affairs are the only two issues that are exclusively the responsibility of the central government. The relationships between the central government and local institutions are outlined mainly in Chapters IV and VIII of the BL. The Chief Executive is appointed by the Central People's Government in accordance with Article 45. Some BL observers argue that the power to appoint the Chief Executive 'is a substantial power, which means that the Central Government can appoint a Chief Executive, or not if the Central Government thinks the appointment inappropriate'.[32] According to Article 48(8), the Chief Executive has the function 'to implement the directives issued by the Central People's Government in respect of the relevant matters provided for in this Law'.[33] The Chief Executive is directly accountable to the State Council on matters connected to the powers of the Central Authorities but in practice on all matters. The relationship between the Chief Executive and the NPCSC regarding the interpretation of the BL is implicit and indirect. In the case of the first two BL interpretations by the NPCSC, the then Chief Executive made a request to the State Council for an NPCSC's interpretation. The Chief Executive made the enquiries according to Article 48(2).[34]

Within the local political organisations, the judiciary has the least limitations imposed by the Central Authorities. The legal system of the PRC is quite different from that of Hong Kong. The CFA exclusively has the power of final adjudication in Hong Kong and is completely independent from the judicial system of the PRC. Compared with other local institutions, the judiciary is more independent from the Central Authorities and best reflects the principle of a high degree of autonomy. The jurisdiction of the courts is only limited in issues regarding acts of state such as defence and foreign affairs and restrictions imposed by the previous legal systems according to Article 19. The NPCSC is the only organ that is directly related with the judiciary under Article 90

---

[32] Nai Keung Lau, 'The Appointment of the Chief Executive: A Reflection of the Sovereignty', *Wen Wei Po*, 11 June 2007, A18. English translation is by this author.

[33] BL, Article 48(8).

[34] It provides for the Chief Executive's responsibility 'for the implementation of this Law and other laws which, in accordance with this Law, apply in the [HKSAR]'.

(concerning the appointment of judges) and Article 158 (concerning the interpretation of the BL). Although the appointment and removal of CFA judges and the Chief Judge of the High Court is to be reported to the NPCSC for the record (Article 90), no evidence suggests that such a report mechanism has any substantive impact on appointments or removals.

In comparison with the LegCo, there are fewer restrictions by the executive branch on the power of the judiciary. An independent judiciary is said to be the greatest achievement of the rule of law in the HKSAR. The judges of the CFA are appointed by the Chief Executive on the recommendation of the Judicial Officers Recommendation Commission (JORC), which was established in accordance with the Judicial Officers Recommendation Commission Ordinance[35] according to the BL.[36] The Chief Secretary for Administration replied to a written question by a LegCo member concerning the selection criteria of members of the JORC: 'in appointing a person to serve on the JORC, consideration would be given to the candidate's integrity, standing in the community, judgment, and ability in carrying out the statutory functions of the Commission independently and impartially'.[37] In the Chief Justice's speech at the ceremonial opening of the legal year 2010, he said that '[i]n our jurisdiction, [the judicial appointment process] has not been politicised and I trust that it will never be'.[38] Moreover, it is also worth noting that the CFA is uniquely composed of permanent judges, local non-permanent judges, and overseas non-permanent judges. There are only a few jurisdictions worldwide where the court of final appeal invites foreign judges.[39]

Under the arrangements in Article 158(3), the CFA is not only an autonomous organ but is also a bridge both between the NPCSC and the lower courts and between the legal system of Mainland China and the common law system in Hong Kong because the Court seeks the interpretation by the NPCSC when necessary as it did in June 2011.[40] Consistent with the principle of 'one country, two systems', Article 158

---

[35] Judicial Officers Recommendation Commission Ordinance (Cap. 92).

[36] BL, Article 88.

[37] *Hong Kong Hansard*, 19 May 1999, cited from The Process of Appointment of Judges in Hong Kong Since 1976, accessible at www.legco.gov.hk/yr00-01/english/library/0001rp_7.pdf.

[38] 'CJ's speech at Ceremonial Opening of the Legal Year 2010', accessible at www.info.gov.hk/gia/general/201001/11/P201001110174.htm.

[39] Other parts of this book discuss the appointment and composition of the CFA in more detail. See Chapters 10 (Young, Da Roza, and Ghai) and 11 (Young and Da Roza).

[40] *Democratic Republic of the Congo* v. *FG Hemisphere Associates LLC* [2011] 4 HKC 151; [2011] 5 HKC 395 (CFA).

restrains the CFA's power to interpret the BL. The CFA only needs to seek the NPCSC's interpretation regarding two categories of provisions of the BL: 'concerning affairs which are the responsibility of the Central People's Government' (the non-autonomous provisions) or 'concerning the relationship between the Central Authorities and the Region' (the provisions involving the Central Authorities).[41]

Two problems arise from this prescription. First, except using similar terms in Article 17,[42] nowhere in the BL are these two categories defined exhaustively. According to Annex I (section III) of the JD and Article 18 of the BL, foreign affairs and defence are the responsibilities of the Central Government. Chapter II of the BL, 'Relationship between the Central Authorities and the Hong Kong Special Administrative Region', also seems to fall into these two categories. However, other provisions in the BL that belong to these two categories are not readily apparent. Second, the BL does not provide detailed procedures regarding the reference issue. The open texture of Article 158(3) provides great room for the CFA's strategic behaviour.

The CFA's missions are the identifiable purposes, goals, and professional expectations perceived by the judges that are determined by external pressures or impetus. Although an individual judge of the CFA may hold different personal goals, judges of the CFA (an identifiable institution) have certain common values and collective goals in a given period. Besides this observation, the institutional factors of the CFA are unique and complex: some disputes over the BL remain from the period of drafting the BL; some common values are entrenched in this regional constitution; the long-time common law tradition exists in the local legal system; the status of the Hong Kong Bill of Rights Ordinance (BORO)[43] (before and after the transition) and constitutional judicial review under the BORO in the colonial period (much of it challenged by the Chinese government); a powerful executive branch exists in the local political regime; the local legislature is undemocratic and relatively weak, to some extent with a dearth of leading political parties; and the powers of

---

[41] BL, Article 158.

[42] Article 17 uses slightly different words, namely, 'the provisions of this Law regarding affairs within the responsibility of *the Central Authorities* or regarding the relationship between the Central Authorities and the Region' (emphasis by this author). Arguably, the Central People's Government means the State Council. However, no study has attempted to define the boundaries between 'the responsibility of the Central Authorities' and 'the responsibility of the Central People's Government' in Hong Kong's contexts. Thus, I ignore the slight difference between them here.

[43] Cap. 383.

the Central Authorities are very influential in the local political regime without clear boundaries. This complex setting determines the multiplicity and complexity of the missions of the CFA. The CFA's missions are thus multifaceted, hierarchical, and dynamic.

In his first address at the opening of the legal year in 1998, Chief Justice Li said that 'the community expect and have a right to expect that their judiciary has the supreme qualities of independence with integrity and professional competence'.[44] Maintaining the independence of the judiciary and the supreme quality of professional competence may be the main professional expectation and goals of the CFA (i.e. the two major missions conceived at the early period of its establishment).[45]

The independence of the judiciary is a core value of the rule of law in the common law tradition. This principle reflects the political role of the judiciary in a given regime. It is said to be the common goal of all common law judges. However, in different institutional settings, the independence of the judiciary may have different implications. The CFA's understandings of the requirements of the independence of the judiciary are reflected as its primary mission when interpreting the BL. The CFA is a new organisation under the new constitutional order. Article 85 provides for the independent judicial power 'free from any interference'.[46] The CFA is embedded in the local regime and has to deal with the relationship between the HKSAR and the Central Authorities. As the leading local court, the CFA considers the independence of the judiciary as including independence from both the HKSAR authorities and the Central Authorities.

In the local political regime, Chief Justice Li considered that the principle of judicial independence shall include 'checks and balance between the Executive, the Legislative and the Judiciary'.[47] Hence, the courts should 'ensure that the acts of the Executive and the Legislature comply fully with the [BL] and the law, and that our fundamental rights and freedoms, which represent enduring values of our society, are fully protected'.[48] In his last speech at the opening of the legal year, Chief Justice Li used almost the same words to emphasise this primary concern of his court: '[T]he independent Judiciary has a vital constitutional role to ensure that the acts of the Executive and the Legislature comply fully with the [BL] and the law and that our fundamental rights and freedoms, which are at the heart of

---

[44] 'The Chief Justice's Address at the Opening of the Legal Year 1998', accessible at www.judiciary.gov.hk/en/other_info/speeches/legal_yr_cj.htm.

[45] The observation of the missions is usually positive and descriptive, albeit these missions more or less reflect the normative side of judicial responsibility. This is one assumption of institutional analysis in this essay.

[46] BL, Article 85.   [47] CJ's speech 1998, note 45 above.   [48] *Ibid.*

Hong Kong's system, are fully safeguarded'.[49] Obviously, the CFA believes that real independence of the judiciary requires that judges conduct the appropriate review of the acts of the executive and legislative branches and protect human rights.

At a vertical level, the independence from the NPCSC is very important to the CFA. First, Mainland China applies a different legal system from that in Hong Kong. Although the PRC signed the International Covenant on Civil and Political Rights (ICCPR) in 1998, it has yet to ratify the treaty.[50] The PRC has signed and ratified the International Covenant on Economic, Social and Cultural Rights (ICESCR) and other international human rights conventions and submitted its reports to the United Nations.[51] However, the government implements these international human rights conventions in a top down manner by issuing or amending criminal, civil, and administrative statutes and policies instead of putting specific administrative behaviour and legislation under the review of the judiciary or other special tribunals according to these international human rights conventions.[52] The 1982 Constitution of the PRC includes some protection of basic rights and freedoms, especially with an amendment (passed in 2004) that 'the state respects and protects human rights'.[53] However, this constitution is not justiciable. There is no effective mechanism of constitutional review in Mainland China. Therefore, China's mechanism of the protection of human rights is questioned on the effectiveness of its remedies. To protect human rights, the CFA must be independent of the legal system of the PRC and free from any interference of the Central Authorities. After all, the NPCSC has the

---

[49] CJ's speech 2010, note 39 above.

[50] When the Chief Justice issued his first speech, the PRC had signed only the ICESCR. Neither Chinese mechanism of human rights nor the attitudes of the CFA towards the Chinese mechanism of the protection of human rights have changed clearly in the past ten years. Therefore, I stress this issue here despite the possibility of confusing the chronological order.

[51] By August 2008, China had submitted six periodic reports (covering thirteen reporting periods) under the International Convention on the Elimination of All Forms of Racial Discrimination (CERD), four periodic reports (covering six reporting periods) under the International Convention on the Elimination of All Forms of Discrimination against Women (CEDAW), four periodic reports (covering five reporting periods) under the International Convention against Torture and Other Cruel, Inhuman or Degrading Treatment or Punishment (CAT), two reports under the Convention on the Rights of the Child (CRC), and one report under the ICESCR. See China's National Report Submitted in Accordance With Paragraph 15 (A) Of The Annex To Human Rights Council Resolution 5/1, February 2009, accessible at www.ohchr.org/EN/HRBodies/UPR/PAGES/CNSession4.aspx.

[52] Ibid.   [53] The Constitution of the PRC 1982, Article 33(3).

final power to interpret the BL. Although the judgments before the interpretation by the NPCSC are not affected, its interpretation binds future decisions. Neither the procedure of decision-making nor the interpretative methodologies of the NPCSC are clear to the CFA. If the CFA is readily subject to the NPCSC, public confidence in the continuity of the common law system and a high degree of autonomy will hardly be maintained.

Real independence demands the CFA to exercise the checks on the local branches and keep itself free from the interference of the Central Authorities. Both in the local regime and in the relationship with the Central Authorities, the CFA considers itself a better protector of rights and freedoms of Hong Kong residents (not only minority rights but also majority rights). Maintaining a high quality of professional competence is seen as the key to achieving the primary mission – the real independence of the judiciary. Chief Justice Li considered a high quality of professional competence as having three aspects:

> First, judges must know the law and appreciate the law's purpose and spirit . . . They should assist in developing the law to meet the fast changing needs of our society. Secondly, judges should have the balanced temperament to operate the judicial process . . . Judges must function courteously but firmly, deeply conscious that they are servants of the people . . . If public confidence in the courts is to be maintained, it is of vital importance that win or lose, litigants and their lawyers feel that they have had their day in court and they go away from the door of the court with an enhanced respect for the judicial process. Thirdly, judges in any modern judiciary must function with efficiency.[54]

Some judges in the CFA are invited from other common law jurisdictions. This arrangement is consistent with one core value of the BL (the continuity of the common law after the transition) but brings up some problems, which is that foreign judges may lack the necessary knowledge of local circumstances and the sense of belonging to Hong Kong's community. In this context, it is more important to stress professional competence. Furthermore, a high quality of professional competence is also the main reason why the judiciary has such high public support. If public confidence in the courts is maintained, the authority of the courts in constitutional review will be enhanced. With public support, the executive and legislative branches are less likely to ignore or distort the rulings in constitutional review cases.

In brief, missions reflect organisational identity. Judicial review is the last resort for the protection of rights and freedoms. In an executive-led

---

[54] CJ's speech 1998, note 45 above.

regime with limited democracy, the assertion of the protection of rights is particularly important. The CFA identifies itself in Hong Kong's regime with this most important mission. The CFA can develop its interpretative methodologies step by step. It is common for other judiciaries worldwide to revise their own methods, principles, or standards established earlier. However, if judicial independence from political organs (especially the Central Authorities) cannot be maintained, neither 'one country, two systems' nor the authority of the BL can be fully realised. This dynamic image reflects the hierarchy of political goals and missions of the CFA in the early period after the transition.

As regards the relationships between the central and regional powers, the US Supreme Court experienced a hard time when faced with a vertical distribution of powers. Comparatively, the CFA is only a regional court. Whereas the CFA identifies itself as an autonomous organ, the US Supreme Court, whether conservative or liberal, is a national organ. Thus, the CFA's competence is more limited. It hardly balances the competitive interests between the Central Authorities and the region because it is neither a centralised court nor a political organ. From the standpoint of the CFA, the NPCSC is a political organ, and some of the NPCSC's interpretative methods may seem incompatible with the rule of law. Not surprisingly, judges of the CFA may perceive the history of Hong Kong's transition differently from the NPCSC. Chief Justice Li and Justices Bokhary, Ribeiro, Chan, and Sir Anthony Mason are the five judges who heard the most BL cases. With the exception of Sir Anthony, these judges were born or raised in colonial Hong Kong. In addition, all of the previous and current permanent judges of the CFA, except Justice Patrick Chan (who graduated from the University of Hong Kong), were educated and obtained law degrees in the United Kingdom. They were not only educated in the British common law but also affected by British social tradition. Liberal constitutionalism and the relevant conceptions about the rule of law and limited governments are at the core of Western constitutional values. For these judges, Hong Kong's transition is based on the international treaty (the JD) and relevant legal arrangements. 'One country, two systems' is understood more legally than politically even in adjudicating BL cases. Considering these differences between the NPCSC and the CFA, it is not surprising that the CFA experienced a difficult time when interacting with the NPCSC.

In its interaction with the NPCSC in *Ng Ka Ling,* the CFA ambitiously asserted constitutional jurisdiction over the local and central governments to affirm the independence of the judiciary. The unpredictable sequel to this ruling (the NPCSC's overruling of the judgment) greatly attacked the authority of the CFA and the public confidence in 'one country, two systems' and the continuity of the common law. Therefore, the CFA had to retreat from an ambitious stance, to a position described by Pojen Yap as '[w]here decisions implicate the validity of PRC laws or NPCSC decisions, the courts would always defer to the central government'.[55] Although the CFA's retreat in the clarification and *Lau Kong Yung* to a certain degree went against part of its missions (professional competence), the CFA had to pay a price for the ambitious judgments that were aimed at achieving its primary mission. At the same time, it tried to make the smallest possible political retreat. The CFA did not revise the test for referring cases for interpretation in *Lau Kong Yung*. Neither did the CFA explicitly reject its jurisdiction over the acts of the NPCSC or the NPC in the clarification. As the chicken game theory suggests, a rational actor retreats from his ideal stance to the minimum extent, provided that a destructive reaction will not be provoked.[56]

Brief review of the Hong Kong Basic Law Committee: does the bridge work well?

Particular attention must be given to a committee within the NPCSC (i.e. the BLC) when discussing the political relationship between the NPCSC and local institutions. The BLC could potentially bridge the two systems, making the interaction between the CFA and NPCSC proceed more smoothly. However, under the arrangements since 1997, its neutrality and effectiveness are far from clear. In the limited space remaining, only a brief review of the BLC will be conducted.

The BLC is established according to the BL. It is composed of 12 members, half from each side. Hong Kong members shall be 'Chinese citizens who are permanent residents of [the HKSAR] with no right of abode in any foreign country and shall be nominated jointly by the Chief Executive, President of the Legislative Council and Chief Justice of [the

---

[55] Pojen Yap, '10 Years of the Basic Law: The Rise, Retreat and Resurgence of Judicial Power in Hong Kong' (2007) 36 *Common Law World Review* 180.

[56] The chicken model is a model of game theory, similar to the prisoner's dilemma. Its name is from 'a game reportedly played by prestige and status in juvenile gangs'. Its principle is that 'while each player prefers not to yield to the other, the outcome where neither player yields is the worst possible one for both players'. This economic model is also used in political science and law as part of game theory. See Glenn H. Snyder, '"Prisoner's Dilemma" and "Chicken" Models in International Politics' (1971) 15 *International Studies Quarterly* 66, 82 (fn 12).

CFA] of the Region for appointment by [the NPCSC]'.[57] In the three terms of the BLC, half of the Hong Kong members were from the legal profession: law professors, barristers, and solicitors. Mainland members were usually officials in other relevant state organs, including the deputy secretary of the NPCSC, the deputy head of the NPCSC's Legislative Affairs Commission (LAC), the deputy minister of foreign affairs (later replaced by the deputy head of the Liaison Office of the Central People's Government in the HKSAR), the deputy head of Hong Kong and Macao Affairs Office of the State Council, and one or two constitutional law professors.

As regards the interpretation of the BL, scholars with official or quasi-official affiliation have received inadequate attention. In the first constitutional crisis in Hong Kong, four scholars criticised the *Ng Ka Ling* ruling concerning the relationship between the Central Authorities and the HKSAR.[58] They were called 'guardians of the BL' by some Hong Kong journalists. They had all been members of the BL Drafting Committee (BLDC). Among them, Professor Xiao Weiyun was the convener of the BLDC's subgroup on the political system; Professors Shao Tian-ren (the convener) and Wu Jianfan were members of the subgroup on the relationship between the HKSAR and the Central Authorities; and Professor Xu Chongde was a member of the subgroup on education, science, technology, culture, sports, and religions. They know the work of the drafting process well. Xu even participated in the drafting and the amendment of the 1954 Constitution of the PRC and the 1982 Constitution of the PRC. The traditional 'Progressive Living Confucian' lifestyle influences most Mainland scholars.[59] These scholars were educated in the socialist legal system. (Two of them studied law in the Soviet Union.) Not surprisingly, these scholars would like to make more contributions to or have more influences on political affairs of the state. As councilors or members of a think tank (the Institute of Hong Kong and Macao Research under the State Council), 'the scholars

---

[57] Decision of the NPC Approving the Proposal by the BLDC on the Establishment of the Committee for the BL of the HKSAR under the NPCSC, adopted by the 7th NPC at its 3rd Session on 4 April 1990 [4].

[58] See their statement in Johannes Chan, HL Fu, and Yash Ghai (eds.), *Hong Kong's Constitutional Debate: Conflict over Interpretation* (Hong Kong: Hong Kong University Press, 2000) 53–60.

[59] It means 'Ru Shi Tai Du' (入世態度) in Chinese, which is one of the Confucian political attitudes, meaning active political participation.

hope that their opinions are adopted [by the government]'.[60] Opinions of these scholars (especially the drafters of the BL) are unquestionably valuable to the NPCSC. Their comments are usually put under the spotlight of the Hong Kong media. Although their comments sometimes reflect the attitudes of the NPCSC to a notable degree, it is inappropriate to equate the missions or decisions of the NPCSC with the comments of the scholars.

The BLC's functions are stipulated in the BL, as follows:

1. According to Article 17, the NPCSC needs to consult the BLC before reviewing laws enacted by the LegCo.
2. To add or delete from the list of laws in Annex III, the NPCSC needs to consult the BLC in accordance with Article 18.[61]
3. Pursuant to Article 158, the NPCSC shall consult the BLC before giving an interpretation of the BL.
4. Article 159 stipulates that before a bill for amendment to the BL is put on the agenda of the NPC, the BLC shall study it and submit its views.

According to these provisions, the NPCSC has to consult this special working committee about the crucial decisions concerning the HKSAR. However, this committee is an advisory body only instead of a decision maker or supervisor. Although some members of this committee (e.g. Qiao Xiaoyang) have influence over the LAC and the NPCSC regarding legal issues, the BLC is only one of many working organs subordinate to the NPCSC within the organisational structure of the NPCSC.

The BL does not provide working procedures according to which the members conduct the above-mentioned functions. Because the BL treats the BLC's advice as a mandatory requirement, a clear and transparent procedure would be preferable. The working documents of the BLC are also inaccessible to the public. Having accessible records and formal minutes of meetings or seminars are necessary to establish a complete reference system. Most Mainland members are officials. Therefore, political neutrality of the BLC is sometimes problematic. However, the role of the BLC in coordinating the conflicts of the two systems always draws the attention of scholars and politicians. After its working procedures are legally

---

[60] 'What are the Relations with Vice President Zeng Qinghong? Hong Kong People Over-imagined the Reality', *Sing Tao Daily*, 24 April 2004, A10. English translation by this author.
[61] Possibly a form of indirect lawmaking, although the NPCSC will not legislate for the HKSAR; according to Article 18, the local legislators have the responsibility to make laws to implement the laws in Annex III.

formalised and brought into the public, its function as a bridge between the two systems can be realised.

Conclusion

This chapter argues that the missions of actors reflect their organisational identity. These missions have significant influence on legal interpreters. On most occasions, judges make a decision not because of economic interests, political pressures, or collegial strategies but because of their beliefs in the ideal judicial function. Political bodies, on the other hand, make decisions based on broader considerations.

The missions of the two interpreters are partially determined by their own legal rules and conventions because they are doing legal work. However, the legal factor is not the only determinant. Judges in the CFA distinguish themselves from other officials, legislators, and private legal practitioners because the judges believe that the CFA plays specific functions in a given regime. The NPCSC has peculiar missions in interpreting the BL, different from those missions in legislative interpretation, because the NPCSC plays different roles in the HKSAR from its role in Mainland China.

'One country, two systems' was brought up by Deng as an innovative concept. However, there exist theoretically inherent conflicts between the two parts of this concept. Where 'one country' is overstressed, there is a weaker version of 'two systems' and *vice versa*. No provision in the BL, the JD, or other legally binding instruments explicitly and clearly explains the relationships between 'one country' and 'two systems' and between the 'two systems'. The discussions on whether the Central Authorities shall only have the residual power and whether the NPCSC's active interpretations and decisions diminish the legitimate powers of the SAR's government originates from the above-mentioned paradox. These arguments are naturally political, historical, and ideological. If 'one country' is considered as absolute and superior to 'two systems', the priority will then be given to the Mainland system.

On the one hand, Mainland China lacks the mechanism of constitutional review and the related culture of the protection of human rights and liberal constitutionalism. For the NPCSC, the BL is just an ordinary national law, not superior to the other laws enacted by the NPC. Judicial review of the acts by the NPCSC or the NPC is incompatible with the Chinese theory of the people's democratic dictatorship. Therefore, it is understandable why the CFA's (a regional court) assertion about its jurisdiction over the acts of the NPC or the NPCSC was so acutely criticised by Mainland scholars and officials. However, the NPCSC's primary mission is to maintain the prosperity and stability of the HKSAR. For political reasons, the NPC is not willing to amend the BL casually. The NPCSC treats itself as a significant guarantee of the Central Authorities to supervise a free regional judiciary. Nevertheless, the NPCSC does not suppose itself able to enforce the BL in an active way. Its role in Hong Kong is a self-restrained supervisor. Its active acts may trigger the fears that the high degree of autonomy is being threatened.

On the other hand, the CFA tries to maintain supreme qualities of judicial independence and professional competence in judicial review. In the local regime, the CFA is not the primary executor of policies and laws. The CFA's function is remedial, as the final protector of human rights. Sometimes the CFA cannot realise its own judgments directly. After a statute is overruled by the CFA, it is the executive and legislative branches' responsibility to propose and pass a new bill or amendment. In an executive-led political system without a fully democratic mechanism, the CFA's mission is to ensure independence of the judiciary and active protection of human rights and provide an effective check on the executive and legislative branches. In Hong Kong's unique context, the CFA recognised that its independence from the Central Authorities is also very important. The CFA's interpretation of the BL is subject to the NPCSC's interpretation, but the NPCSC usually uses different approaches to interpret the BL. Furthermore, the Chief Executive has sought the NPCSC's interpretation via the State Council twice. This act may affect judicial independence in the local political regime. If the CFA too readily seeks an NPCSC interpretation, the CFA's authority in the political and legal systems will be weakened, and its checks on the executive and legislature will fail eventually.

In one word, the relationship between the CFA and the NPCSC is much more complex than the relationship between an ordinary regional court and a central authority. Judicial independence from the NPCSC reflects the value of 'two systems'. As noted earlier, one of the NPCSC's missions in interpreting the BL is to supervise the implementation of the BL as one of the representatives of 'one country'. This is the political divergence between the CFA and the NPCSC. On the one hand, the CFA attempts to minimise the influence of the NPCSC in the interpretation of the BL; on the other hand, the NPCSC has to interpret the BL if an interpretation is politically necessary. This tension between the CFA and the NPCSC can be reduced to the inherent ideological tension between 'one country' and 'two systems' as mentioned. This is in nature ideological and political.

Annex

Table 3.1 Economic comparison among Hong Kong (HK), the People's Republic of China (PRC), Guangdong (GD), and Shanghai (SH)[a]

Year	HK GDP HK$ Billion	HK per capita GDP HK$	HK Inward Direct Investment HK$ Billion	HK Direct Investment to Mainland HK$ Billion	PRC GDP RMB Billion	PRC per capita GDP RMB	GD per capita GDP RMB	SH per capita GDP RMB	Exchange Rate of RMB and HK$
1983	216	40,482	—	—	599	585	675	2,963	
1984	261	48,308	—	—	724	699	827	3,259	
1985	279	50,735	—	—	904	860	1,026	3,855	37.57
1986	319	57,784	—	—	1,027	963	1,164	4,008	44.22
1987	394	70,521	—	—	1,205	1,111	1,443	4,396	47.74
1988	465	82,672	—	—	1,504	1,366	1,926	5,162	47.7
1989	536	94,310	—	—	1,700	1,520	2,251	5,487	48.28
1990	599	104,996	—	—	1,872	1,648	2,484	6,107	61.39
1991	690	120,015	—	—	2,183	1,897	2,941	6,954	68.45
1992	805	138,795	—	—	2,694	2,312	3,699	8,650	71.24
1993	928	157,261	—	—	3,526	2,992	5,085	10,729	74.41
1994	1,047	173,554	—	—	4,811	4,036	6,530	13,870	111.53
1995	1,116	181,241	—	—	5,981	4,964	8,129	17,022	107.96
1996	1,229	191,047	—	—	7,014	5,761	9,139	19,779	107.51

Year								
1997	1,365	210,350	—	—	7,806	6,346	10,130	22,583	107.09
1998	1,293	197,559	1,744	548	8,302	6,685	10,819	24,513	106.88
1999	1,267	191,731	3,149	621	8,848	7,063	11,415	26,527	106.66
2000	1,318	197,697	3,551	1,012	9,800	7,762	12,736	29,671	106.18
2001	1,299	193,500	3,270	844	10,807	8,497	13,849	32,201	106.08
2002	1,277	189,397	2,622	843	11,910	9,301	15,361	35,329	106.07
2003	1,235	183,449	2,960	931	13,517	10,492	17,795	39,128	106.24
2004	1,292	190,451	3,522	1,212	15,959	12,314	20,870	46,338	106.23
2005	1,383	202,928	4,056	1,477	18,409	14,120	24,435	51,529	105.3

GDP = gross domestic product; RMB = renminbi.

[a] Data from the websites of Census and Statistics Department of the HKSAR, accessible at www.censtatd.gov.hk/home/index.jsp and the Department of Statistics of the PRC, accessible at www.stats.gov.cn/english/statisticaldata. The exchange rate means the amount of RMB exchanged with 100 HKD.

4

A worthy predecessor? The Privy Council on appeal from Hong Kong, 1853 to 1997

OLIVER JONES

Introduction

Analysing the work of the Privy Council (PC) on appeal from Hong Kong, rather than that of the Court of Final Appeal (CFA), presents a dilemma. There is almost 150 years of case law, as opposed to nearly 15 years. The decisions involve everything from the mercifully historical, such as a case on 'marketable opium',[1] to the almost vogue, being the reception in Hong Kong of customary international law.[2] Nearly every area of law is represented, with a sharp uptake in appeals immediately before the handover.[3] How can one tackle such wide-ranging jurisprudence succinctly?

It would be possible simply to trawl through all of the Hong Kong appeals, discussing those with titillating facts or influential rulings. However, this would be piecemeal and parochial. There is another way. The imperial role of the PC has long been discussed, especially as the Empire became a Commonwealth. There has been praise and criticism of decision-making by the PC on appeal from other jurisdictions. It has been accused of incompetence in constitutional law, as well as ignorance and inconsistency in criminal law. However, it has been feted as a protector of minorities and can even be regarded as a bastion of independence.

---

[1] *Tronson* v. *Dent* (1853) 14 ER 159, 175.

[2] *Chung Chi Cheung* v. *R* [1939] AC 160, 167–8, 175–6. The question of such reception has been explored in *C* v. *Director of Immigration* [2011] 5 HKC 118 (CA; unreported FACV18/2011, 25 March 2013 (CFA) and (CA); (2011) 14 HKCFAR 395. *FG Hemisphere Associates LLC* v. *Democratic Republic of Congo* [2010] 2 HKLRD 66 (CA; (2011) 14 HKCFAR 395).

[3] Two appeals were determined before the handover with reasons being delivered after the handover: *Cheng Yuen* v. *Royal Hong Kong Golf Club* [1997] HKLRD 1132 and *Commissioner for Inland Revenue* v. *Cosmotron Manufacturing Co Ltd* [1997] 1 WLR 1288. The last appeals to be determined before the handover were, in the criminal sphere, *Thongjai* v. *R* [1998] AC 54 and, on the civil side, *Sze To Chun Keung* v. *Kung Kwok Wai David* [1997] 1 WLR 1232.

The work of the PC in relation to Hong Kong has rarely been discussed at a general level.[4] This chapter provides a special opportunity to place that work into the wider international discourse. Did the role of the PC change with the advent of the Commonwealth? What did the PC decide for Hong Kong in the field of constitutional law? Are there any noticeable tendencies in its consideration of criminal law? Was it a guardian of the minorities and judicial independence of Hong Kong? Or, alternatively, is the story of the Board in relation to Hong Kong respectable but almost humdrum compared with the often electric atmosphere of the Andrew Li Court?

The imperial role of the Privy Council

Foundations and independence

The PC is an unlikely source of judicial decisions. It grew out of the right of a litigant dissatisfied with a decision of a colonial court to petition his or her Majesty in Council for prerogative relief.[5] However, the determination of those petitions became curial. In particular, the Judicial Committee Act 1833 (Imp) (1833 Act) delegated the work to a Judicial Committee, constituted for each case by senior judges collectively known as 'the Board'. The Board had the procedural powers of a court.[6] It delivered its reasons for judgment in open court.[7] It considered itself independent, whether from imperial or colonial authorities.[8] While the judgments of the Board were under section 3 of the 1833 Act a report to the monarch, it was 'unknown and unthinkable that [the monarch] should not give effect to them'.[9]

---

[4] See e.g. W. S. Clarke, 'The Privy Council, Politics and Precedent in the Asia-Pacific' (1990) 39 ICLQ 741.

[5] See e.g. *British Coal Corp.* v. *R* [1935] AC 500; *Attorney-General of St Christopher and Nevis* v. *Rodionov* [2004] 1 WLR 2796; P. Howell, *Judicial Committee of the Privy Council 1833–1876: Its Origins, Structure and Development* (Cambridge: Cambridge University Press, 1979); D. Swinfen, *Imperial Appeal: the Debate on the Appeal to the Privy Council 1833–1986* (Manchester: Manchester University Press, 1986) ch. 1.

[6] Swinfen, note 5 above, 7, 55; Howell, note 5 above, 31–2, 39–40, 58, 155–6.

[7] Howell, note 5 above, 38–9.

[8] *Ibralebbe* v. *R* [1964] AC 900, 919–21 (Viscount Radcliffe, for the Board); *Independent Jamaica Council for Human Rights (1998) Ltd* v. *Marshall-Burnett* [2005] 2 AC 356, 371 (Lord Bingham, for the Board).

[9] *British Coal Corp.*, 510–11 (Viscount Sankey LC, for the Board). See also *Hull* v. *M'Kenna* [1926] IR 402, 403 (Viscount Haldane LC, for the Board) and V. Lowe and J. Young, 'An Attempt to Rewrite a Judgment' (1978) 94 LQR 255.

The 1833 Act also dealt with the circumstances in which appeals to the Board would lie. Section 24 enabled Orders in Council to regulate appeals from a particular jurisdiction. This must be read with the Judicial Committee Act 1844 (Imp) (1844 Act), which supplemented any law by which the Board already heard appeals with appeals by special leave from any colonial court, including one at first instance.[10] This statutory framework superseded the prerogative basis for the work of the Board.[11] It was recognised and effected in Hong Kong by two Orders in Council, which provided that 'appeals from Hong Kong would lie (1) as of right, from any final judgment of the Court of Appeal where the matter in dispute amounted to more than a specified monetary amount, or at the discretion of the Court of Appeal; or (2) by special leave of the Privy Council'.[12]

Board's desire for uniformity

Despite its strident assertions of independence, it has long been suggested that the Board was an 'integral part of the system of imperial government'.[13] In other words, the Board was believed to uphold imperial unity by providing legal uniformity and even by protecting imperial interests, whether governmental or commercial.[14] Let us begin with legal uniformity. The desire of the Board to pursue such uniformity has been proclaimed by several of its most prominent members, Lord Atkin,[15] Lord Westbury LC,[16] and Viscount Haldane LC. Viscount Haldane went so far as to say that uniformity was pursued even across the various systems of law administered by the Board:

> We administer Roman-Dutch law from South Africa or from Ceylon, or French law from Quebec, or the common law of England for Ontario . . . [We] try to look for the common principle underlying systems of jurisprudence of differing kinds.[17]

---

[10] *Campbell* v. *R* [2010] UKPC 26, [6] (Lord Mance, for the Board).
[11] *Rodionov*, 2800 (Lord Bingham, for the Board).
[12] *A Solicitor* v. *Law Society of Hong Kong* (2003) 6 HKCFAR 570, [15].
[13] Swinfen, note 5 above, 14.   [14] *Ibid.*, vi, 28, 61.
[15] Lord Atkin, 'Appeal in English law' (1927) 3 CLJ 1, 7.
[16] Hansard, HL, vol. 202, col. 1284, 1 July 1870, cited in Swinfen, note 5 above, 63.
[17] Viscount Haldane, 'Address to the Ontario Bar Association', 23 May 1924, quoted in J. Hall and D. Martin, *Haldane – Statesman, Lawyer, Philosopher* (Chichester: B. Rose, 1996) 175.

This was hardly controversial for its time. The Board simply wished to achieve consistency across the British Empire, including consistency of values.

Dilution of uniformity after decolonisation

Unsurprisingly, though, the Board retreated from its quest for uniformity as the Empire evolved into the Commonwealth of Nations. In *Australia Consolidated Press* v. *Uren*,[18] the Board said:

> There are doubtless advantages if within those parts of the Commonwealth (or indeed of the English-speaking world) where the law is built upon a common foundation development proceeds along similar lines. But development may gain its impetus from any one and not from one only of those parts. The law may be influenced from any one direction. The gain that uniformity of approach may yield is however far less marked in some branches of the law than in others.[19]

Accordingly, on this and subsequent occasions, the Board deferred to the views of lower courts.[20] A New Zealand judge went so far as to say that in such cases, the Board 'effectively denied the appellants ... their right of appeal'.[21] However, the Board reserved the right to disagree with lower courts, including those of New Zealand, where there were principles 'having general application throughout all jurisdictions based on the common law [which did] not depend on local considerations'.[22]

Approach taken to Hong Kong

It is debatable how far this development reached Hong Kong. The Board certainly seemed to pursue uniformity until late in the day. It seems to have overruled English authority on only a handful of occasions, each

---

[18] [1969] 1 AC 590.   [19] *Ibid.*, 641 (Lord Morris, for the Board).

[20] *Ibid.*, 644. See also *Geelong Harbour Trust Commissioners* v. *Gibbs Bright & Co Ltd* [1974] AC 810, 820–1 (Lord Diplock, for the Board); *Baker* v. *R* [1975] AC 774, 788 (Lord Diplock, for the Board); *Jamil bin Harun* v. *Yang Kamsiah* [1984] AC 529, 535 (Lord Scarman, for the Board); *Bell* v. *DPP* [1985] AC 937, 953 (Lord Templeman, for the Board); *Attorney-General (HK)* v. *Reid* [1994] 1 AC 324, 338–9 (Lord Templeman, for the Board); and *Lange* v. *Atkinson* [2000] 1 NZLR 257 (CA).

[21] See Sir Kenneth Keith, 'The Interplay with the Judicial Committee of the Privy Council' in L. Blom-Cooper, G. Drewry, and B. Dickson (eds.), *Judicial House of Lords: 1876–2009* (Oxford: Oxford University Press, 2009) 326 and additional authorities cited therein.

[22] *Hart* v. *O'Connor* [1985] AC 1000, 1017 (Lord Brightman, for the Board).

occurring as late as the 1990s.[23] Furthermore, when in the late 1980s the Hong Kong Court of Appeal refused to follow a decision of the House of Lords, it was quite quickly overruled by the Board, ushering the decision of the House into the law of Hong Kong.[24] This must have been discouraging for Hong Kong courts in forging a distinctive path for Hong Kong law. It may well have meant that, in subsequent cases, Hong Kong courts eschewed innovation with respect to or departure from English authority for fear of reversal by the Board.[25]

On the other hand, the Board expressed its desire to apply the common law so as to 'meet the changing circumstances and patterns of [Hong Kong] society'.[26] It also claimed to be 'always willing and anxious to give full weight'[27] to the local knowledge of Hong Kong judges. The fact that it did so has been recognised by the CFA.[28] On one occasion, the Board did so 'to such a great extent that they simply adopted the reasons of the [Hong Kong Court of Appeal] without providing reasons of their own!'.[29] Yet at the very time it made some of these pronouncements, the Board also insisted certain rules 'must be the same in any common law jurisdiction'[30] and that at least some decisions by the House of Lords were effectively binding on Hong Kong courts.[31]

Lesser treatment?

Where does the truth lie? Did Hong Kong have the benefit of a post-imperial Board? Or, as some scholars have concluded, did the Board persist with paternalism toward Hong Kong, partly because it was a colony,

---

[23]   *Liangsiriprasert* v. *United States* [1991] 1 AC 225; *Wai Yu Tsang* v. *R* [1992] 1 AC 269; *Siu Yin Kwan* v. *Eastern Insurance Co Ltd* [1994] 2 AC 199; *Take Harvest Ltd* v. *Liu* [1993] AC 552; *Mercedes Benz AG* v. *Leiduck* [1996] AC 284; and *Cosmotron Manufacturing*.

[24]   *Red Sea Insurance Co. Ltd* v. *Bouygues* [1995] 1 AC 190, *overruling Adhiguna Meranti* [1988] 1 Lloyd's Rep 384 in favour of *Boys* v. *Chaplin* [1971] AC 356.

[25]   E. Veitch, 'The Many Facets of *Cook* v. *Lewis*' (2010) 61 *University of New Brunswick Law Journal* 287, 288.

[26]   *de Lasala* v. *de Lasala* [1980] AC 546, 557 (Lord Diplock, for the Board).

[27]   *R* v. *Chan Hak-So* [1988] 1 HKLR 332, 334 (Lord Bridge, for the Board).

[28]   *China Field Ltd* v. *Appeal Tribunal (Buildings)* (2009) 12 HKCFAR 342, [76] (Lord Millett NPJ for the Court).

[29]   O. Jones, 'After the Decennial: The New Doctrine of Precedent in the Hong Kong Court of Appeal' [2010] *Law Lectures for Practitioners* 107, 149, citing *Asia Television Ltd* v. *Television Broadcasts Ltd* [1988] UKPC 12.

[30]   *Chan Hak-So*, 334.

[31]   *de Lasala*, 558. See also the more extreme *Tai Hing Cotton Mill Ltd* v. *Liu Chong Hing Bank Ltd* [1986] AC 80, 108 (Lord Scarman, for the Board), which was effectively overruled in *Attorney-General (Jersey)* v. *Holley* [2005] 2 AC 580, discussed in Jones, note 29 above, 154–5.

not worthy of the more *laissez-faire* treatment accorded jurisdictions that had become independent?[32] There is evidence that the Board drew a distinction in this respect. In *Lim Yam Tek* v. *Public Prosecutor*,[33] it suggested that, in ascertaining the extent of its criminal jurisdiction, there was a relevant difference between determining appeals from 'an independent sovereign state' and having the 'oversight of the legal administration of subordinate parts of the Empire'.[34]

Furthermore, the Law Lords have recognised, albeit in a different context, that an imperial approach persists for the few remaining dependencies of the United Kingdom. In *R (Bancoult)* v. *Secretary of State for Foreign and Commonwealth Affairs*,[35] the House of Lords held that prerogative powers with respect to a jurisdiction that remained a colony could be exercised in the interests of the United Kingdom as a whole without being confined to the interests of the colony itself.[36]

Lastly, there is a discernible difference between the dilution of the Board's quest for uniformity in relation to independent sovereign states and its attitude towards Hong Kong. Of course, in relation to such states, the Board still sometimes insisted upon uniformity. Furthermore, the Board displayed some deference to Hong Kong judges and society. On balance, though, the Board seems to have had a greater willingness to intervene in the Hong Kong judicial landscape and a lesser tolerance for originality there.

Sympathy for imperial interests?

This leaves the more sinister question of whether the Board advanced the interests of imperial government or commerce. The latter should not be exaggerated. It is probably true that at the height of the Empire, British businesspeople preferred retaining the Board to being solely at the mercy of colonial courts. However, it does not follow that the Board subtly or blatantly favoured their interests. The Board was, on one occasion, accused by an Australian judge in a merchant shipping case of acting 'in the interests of great fleet-owning nations'.[37] However, at least ordinarily,

---

[32] Clarke, 'The Privy Council', note 4 above. [33] [1972] 2 *Malayan Law Journal* 41.
[34] *Ibid.*, 41 (Lord Kilbrandon, for the Board). [35] [2009] 1 AC 453.
[36] *Ibid.*, 487–8 (Lord Hoffmann), 508 (Lord Rodger), 509 (Lord Carswell).
[37] *Port Jackson Stevedoring Pty Ltd* v. *Salmond & Spraggon (Aust) Pty Ltd* (1978) 139 CLR 231, 258 (Stephen J). The judgment of which these reasons formed part was reversed by the Privy Council: *Port Jackson Stevedoring Pty Ltd* v. *Salmond & Spraggon (Aust) Pty Ltd* [1981] 1 WLR 138.

British businesspeople simply preferred the established to 'new chums'[38] and the certain or uniform to the unpredictable or diverse.[39] Similar sentiments probably motivate the modern presence of non-permanent judges on the CFA[40] and preference for international investment arbitration.[41]

What of imperial government? Was the Board more sympathetic to Westminster or Whitehall than more far-flung legislators, administrators, or peoples? Did it resist challenges to the legitimacy of Empire? This is more difficult to gauge. There is no doubt that British politicians wanted the Board's 'power over colonial courts [used] to enforce obedience to imperial policies'.[42] However, at least after the passage of the 1833 Act, it is unclear whether their desires were met. It is true that Viscount Haldane, in a judgment of the Board, once stated that '[w]e sit as an Imperial Court which represents the Empire, and not any particular part of it'.[43] Furthermore, there were arguable traces of imperialism in the assumption by the Board of power to strike down colonial legislation. However, this occurred infrequently.[44]

Of course, the Board summarily rejected challenges to the scope of imperial boundaries. If the British government stated that certain territory formed part of the British Empire, the Board would apply that statement without assessing its correctness as a matter of international law. In *Christian* v. *R*,[45] defendants in criminal proceedings arising out of events in Pitcairn challenged the very existence of British rule over the island. The Board ruled:

> For over 100 years Pitcairn has been administered by the Crown as a British possession and whatever its history or the inclinations of its people may have been, it is unthinkable that the Judicial Committee of Her Majesty's Privy Council would not accept an executive statement affirming it to be part of the territory of the Crown.[46]

---

[38] Sir Garfield Barwick, Chief Justice of Australia, quoted in D. Marr, *Barwick* (Sydney: Allen and Unwin, 2005) 125.

[39] M. Gleeson, 'The influence of the Privy Council on Australia', 31 May 2007, accessible at www.highcourt.gov.au/speeches/cj/cj_31may07.pdf, 13–14.

[40] Y. Ghai, *Hong Kong's New Constitutional Order*, 2nd edn (Hong Kong: Hong Kong University Press, 1999) 323.

[41] C. Dugan, D. Wallace, N. Roberts, and B. Sabahi, *Investor-State Arbitration* (Oxford: Oxford University Press, 2008).

[42] Howell, note 5 above, 24.   [43] *Hull* v. *M'Kenna*, 404.

[44] Swinfen, note 5 above, 14–15.   [45] [2007] 2 AC 400.

[46] *Ibid.*, 408–9 (Lord Hoffmann, for the Board).

This may have had the consequence of facilitating imperial acquisition. However, it does not follow that this outcome has been pursued by the Board. Acceptance of executive statements regarding international boundaries comes down to the 'one voice' doctrine, namely that steps or pronouncements by the executive in international relations should not be contradicted in the courts. The reason is not because the courts support specific steps or pronouncements, including the acquisition of territory. Instead, it is a general area where the courts do not think it appropriate to prejudice the executive, whether or not the latter acts wisely.[47]

In addition, the Board seems to have been even handed in cases when it had to consider the validity of attempts by former British colonies to abolish its jurisdiction, exhibiting no clear desire to preserve or revive its jurisdiction.[48] As Empire gave way to Commonwealth, the Board even emphasised that it was not an imperial but a jurisdictionally specific court.[49] The high watermark of these sentiments occurred in 2005. On appeal from Jamaica, the Board said that it was 'sitting as the final court of appeal of Jamaica [and] exists in this capacity to serve the interests of the people of Jamaica'.[50] Of course, by analogy from *Lim* and *Bancoult*, it is possible that this thinking did not extend to jurisdictions that remained colonies.

It is probably impossible to settle the debate over the imperial tendencies of the Board. However, it surely cannot be said those tendencies were pronounced, let alone inconsistent with the judicial character of the Board. This was certainly the case in Hong Kong. While there is one decision by the Board arguably benefiting imperial interests, it did not involve the Board actively favouring those interests. In *Winfat Enterprise (HK) Co Ltd* v. *Attorney-General*,[51] the Board refused to enforce protections of indigenous inhabitants by the Second Peking Convention, under which the United Kingdom had leased the New Territories from Mainland China.

---

[47] L. Collins, 'Foreign Relations and the Judiciary' (2002) 51 ICLQ 485, 487.

[48] See e.g. *Nadan* v. *R* [1926] AC 482; *Moore* v. *Attorney-General (Irish Free State)* [1935] AC 484; *British Coal Corp* v. *R* [1935] AC 500; *Attorney-General (Ont.)* v. *Attorney-General (Canada)* [1947] AC 127; *Madzimbamuto* v. *Lardner Burke* [1969] 1 AC 645; *Kitano* v. *Commonwealth* [1976] AC 99; *Dow Jones Publishing Co* v. *Attorney-General of Singapore* [1989] 1 WLR 1308; *De Margon* v. *Director-General of Social Welfare* [1998] AC 275; and *Marshall-Burnett*. See also Gleeson, note 39 above, 15. Compare J. Krikorian, 'British Imperial Politics and Judicial Independence: The Judicial Committee's Decision in the Canadian Case *Nadan* v. *The King*' (2000) 33 *Canadian Journal of Political Science* 291.

[49] *Ibralebbe*, 921–2 (Viscount Radcliffe, for the Board).

[50] *Marshall-Burnett*, 363 (Lord Bingham, for the Board).　　[51] [1985] AC 733.

This arguably strengthened the hand of the imperial or colonial occupiers in relation to the conquered peoples.[52] However, the reason for the decision was separate. In the absence of incorporating legislation, the provisions of a treaty were not enforceable, lest the executive acquire the capacity to make law simply by concluding the treaty. This approach is taken in all cases of unincorporated treaties irrespective of the substance of those treaties.

Inherent imperialism

Still, perhaps this is not the relevant line of inquiry. Whether it favoured imperialism or not, the fact is that the very existence of the Board often represented imperialism to those under its jurisdiction. Funnily enough, this was something the Board once denied. In *Ibralebbe* v. *R*,[53] on appeal from a newly independent Ceylon, the Board stated:

> it seems . . . a misleading simplification to speak of the continuance of the Privy Council appeal as being inherently inconsistent with Ceylon's status as an independent territory or as being bound up with a relationship between Her Majesty and colonial subjects . . . . [T]rue independence is not in any way compromised by the continuance of that appeal, unless and until the sovereign legislative body decides to end it.[54]

In a sense, the Board is right. If an independent jurisdiction could at any time abolish those appeals, there is no threat to its independence. However, the point is that many jurisdictions ultimately pursue abolition because appeals are regarded as inconsistent with independence.[55]

As the Attorney-General of Kenya, Charles Njonjo, once said:

> Although the Judicial Committee of the Privy Council is a court of very high legal standing, it is not our court . . . it is my personal view that continuing appeals to the Judicial Committee of the Privy Council would not be in keeping with the dignity of our Republic.[56]

The seriousness of this view is best demonstrated by New Zealand. In that jurisdiction, very few decisions by the Board aroused hostility.[57] Yet in

---

[52] Ghai, note 40 above, 8–9.   [53] [1964] AC 900.   [54] *Ibid.*, 925.

[55] See e.g. Swinfen, note 5 above, 169–72; J. Eddy, 'India and the Privy Council: the last appeal' (1950) 66 LQR 206, 214; D. O'Brien, 'The Caribbean Court of Justice: a difficult birth' [2006] *Public Law* 344, 352–4.

[56] Kenya National Assembly Official Record (Hansard), 24 March 1965, p. 747.

[57] *Wallis* v. *Solicitor-General (NZ)* [1903] AC 173, discussed in Keith, note 21 above, 327–8 and M. Richardson, 'The Privy Council and New Zealand' (1997) 46 ICLQ 908, 908. See also *Lesa* v. *Attorney-General (NZ)* [1983] 2 AC 20, reversed by the New Zealand Citizenship and Western Samoa Act 1982 (NZ).

the 1970s, a New Zealand judge, Sir Thaddeus McCarthy, remarked, '[I]t is only a matter of time when the link with the Privy Council will go'.[58] Several decades later, the Board was replaced with the Supreme Court of New Zealand. Many argued for its retention.[59] Yet the desire for judicial, as well as legislative and executive, independence ultimately prevailed.[60]

Hong Kong can be considered in the same vein. Of course, Hong Kong was not achieving independence. Rather, it was becoming an autonomous part of the People's Republic of China (PRC). So there was no question of whether the retention of appeals to the Board after the handover would be incompatible with the independence of Hong Kong. However, the abolition of appeals was 'inevitable' because it was 'not acceptable' to the PRC.[61] This must have been because the Board represented imperialism to the PRC and was regarded as inherently incompatible with the resumption of sovereignty.

The Privy Council and constitutional law

Controversy in Canada

The Board has aroused the greatest opposition in the field of constitutional law. On appeal from Canada, the Board's principal task was to interpret the balance of power between federal and provincial governments under the Canadian Constitution, then called the British North America Act 1867 (Imp) (1867 Act). The Board consistently favoured the provincial governments. This aroused the ire of people desiring broader national powers. They roundly criticised the Board for overlooking the drafting history of the 1867 Act and being ignorant of Canadian circumstances.[62]

---

[58] Richardson, note 57 above, 918.

[59] N. Cox, 'The Abolition or Retention of the Privy Council as the Final Court of Appeal for New Zealand: Conflict Between National Identity and Legal Pragmatism' (2002) 20 NZULR 220.

[60] C. Thompson-Barrow, *Bringing Justice Home: the Road to Final Appellate and Regional Court Establishment* (London: Commonwealth Secretariat, 2008) 14–20. See also Richardson, note 57 above, 915–17. Those in favour of the Supreme Court also cited practical reasons.

[61] Ghai, note 40 above, 303.

[62] Swinfen, note 5 above, ch. 2, esp. 45–8; P. Hogg, 'Canada: From Privy Council to Supreme Court' in J. Goldsworthy (ed.), *Interpreting Constitutions: A Comparative Study* (Oxford: Oxford University Press, 2006) 75–6 and J. de P Wright, 'The Judicial Committee of the Privy Council' (2007) 10 *Green Bag* (2d) 363, 368. See also J. Saywell, *The Lawmakers: Judicial Power and the Shaping of Canadian Federalism* (Toronto: University of Toronto Press, 2002) ch. 4.

The Board gave traction to such allegations when it referred in one judgment to the 'Province of Montreal'.[63]

Criticism justified?

However, one of the dominant figures on the Board in Canadian cases, Viscount Haldane, considered its approach to the federal–provincial balance to be one of its greatest achievements.[64] Perhaps the criticism of the Board was unfair. A Chief Justice of Australia, the Hon Murray Gleeson, has plausibly suggested in relation to Canada that

> any decision affecting the distribution of power between the constituent units of a federation is bound to be declared, by supporters of the losing side, to be contrary to the original intentions of the framers. It is an inescapable part of the rhetoric of political, and sometimes of legal, argument in a federal system.[65]

Furthermore, Prime Minister Trudeau would ultimately praise their Lordships as farsighted. Without the Board's provincial inclination, he felt, Québec would have left the Confederation.[66]

Lastly, in the field of individual rights, one constitutional decision by the Board on appeal from Canada clearly had a positive legacy. In *Edwards* v. *Canada*,[67] the Board reversed the Supreme Court of Canada by deciding that women were 'persons' within the meaning of section 24 of the 1867 Act, with the result that they were eligible to be members of the Senate of Canada. The appropriateness of this decision in modern times is undoubted. Moreover, the Board famously articulated the 'living tree' doctrine, by which the Canadian Constitution became amenable to contemporary development.[68] It was described by the Supreme Court of Canada in 2004 as 'one of the most fundamental principles of Canadian constitutional interpretation'.[69]

---

[63] *Attorney-General (Quebec)* v. *Queen Insurance Co* (1878) LR 3 App Case 1090, 1096 (Sir George Jessel MR, for the Board). Montreal is, of course, merely a city in the province of Québec.

[64] Swinfen, note 5 above, 47. See also F. Vaughan, *Viscount Haldane: The Wicked Stepfather of the Canadian Constitution* (Toronto: University of Toronto Press, 2010).

[65] Gleeson, note 39 above, 6. See also Swinfen, note 5 above, 48.

[66] Hogg, note 62 above, 76. Note, though, that Hogg sees this as the Board's accident rather than its design.

[67] [1930] AC 124.   [68] *Ibid.*, 136.

[69] *Re: Same Sex Marriage* [2004] 3 SCR 698, [22].

Impact on Australia

Yet, rightly or wrongly, the perception that the Board was ill equipped to decide federal constitutional disputes took root. The High Court of Australia stated that when the Australian Constitution was being drafted, it was 'common knowledge' in Australia that 'the decisions of the Judicial Committee in Canadian cases had not given widespread satisfaction'.[70] The reason was that the typical members of the Board were 'entirely unfamiliar' with the relevant constitutional law.[71] Nor did their Lordships know 'the history or conditions of the remoter portions of the Empire'.[72]

As a result, when the Imperial Parliament enacted the Australian Constitution, it contained a provision restricting appeals to the Board in cases concerning the federal division of powers. In early disagreements between the Board and the High Court over the scope of the restriction, the latter was scathing:

> In our opinion, the intention of the British legislature was to substitute for a distant Court, of uncertain composition, imperfectly acquainted with Australian conditions, unlikely to be assisted by counsel familiar with those conditions, and whose decisions would be rendered many months, perhaps years, after its judgment has been invoked, an Australia Court immediately available, constant in its composition, well versed in Australian history and conditions [and] Australian in its sympathies.[73]

The High Court would repeat such sentiments on several subsequent occasions.[74] In the result, the Board had little impact on Australian federal constitutional law. For this reason, Gleeson CJ has suggested that in Australia, there was never 'the same intensity of feeling about the role of the Privy Council as there was in Canada'.[75]

Broader significance?

One could perhaps look to other common law federal states to see whether Canadian opposition to the approach taken by the Board was also

---

[70] *Baxter* v. *Commissioner of Taxation (NSW)* (1907) 4 CLR 1087, 1111 (Griffith CJ, Barton and O'Connor JJ). This judgment is said to have been written by the Chief Justice: see Gleeson, note 39 above, 4.

[71] *Baxter, ibid.*   [72] *Ibid.*   [73] *Ibid.*, 1118.

[74] See e.g. *Nelungaloo Pty Ltd* v. *Cth* (1952) 85 CLR 545, 570 (Dixon J) (Fullagar J agreeing); *O'Sullivan* v. *Noarlunga Meat Ltd (No 2)* (1956) 94 CLR 367, 375–6 (Dixon CJ, Williams, Webb and Fullagar JJ); and *Kirmani* v. *Captain Cook Cruises (No 2)* (1985) 159 CLR 461, 464 (Gibbs CJ, Mason, Wilson, Brennan, Deane and Dawson JJ).

[75] Gleeson, note 39 above, 12.

influential there. However, it is perhaps better to focus on another aspect of the Canadian experience at the hands of the Board: individual rights. It was the one clear positive for the Board in Canada. Does this reflect a broader pattern of decisions regarding individual rights under constitutional law? Ghai has suggested that, in this context, the Board has been 'undistinguished, when not actually negative ... few of its decisions are memorable'.[76]

Another commentator, Zander, has been positively gushing, claiming that the Board exhibited a 'strong concern for fundamental rights and a willingness to defy legislative or Government authority'.[77] A recent and detailed study by Roberts has suggested the truth may lie between a 'wholly pessimistic assessment' and 'unbridled enthusiasm'. The Board's approach to individual rights gives 'cause for optimism' but hardly involves a consistently robust approach to individual rights.[78] Perhaps this is the best one could hope for, namely that the Board is balanced, even in the field of individual rights.

Relevance to Hong Kong

The status of the Board in the field of constitutional law is of marginal relevance to Hong Kong. One reason for this is that there were very few cases concerning imperial or colonial constitutional law. The most prominent of these cases – *Winfat* – was mentioned earlier. Although it doubtless involved disappointment for the litigants concerned, it does not seem to have aroused consternation in Hong Kong. Another reason that constitutional law was in the minor key on appeal from Hong Kong is that the colony lacked even statutory protection of fundamental rights until the enactment of the Hong Kong Bill of Rights Ordinance (Cap 483) (BORO) in 1991.

The Board would give several decisions regarding BORO. As Roberts would have predicted, the Board did not display a clear tendency to strike down Hong Kong legislation under BORO. Rather, it was somewhat more likely to uphold such legislation.[79] Furthermore, it urged balance in the

---

[76] Ghai, note 40 above, 323.

[77] M. Zander, *A Bill of Rights*, 3rd edn (London: Sweet and Maxwell, 1985) 64.

[78] N. Roberts, 'The Law Lords and Human Rights: The Experience of the Privy Council in Interpreting Bills of Rights' [2000] *European Human Rights Law Review* 147, 180.

[79] For instances of striking down legislation, see *Attorney-General* v. *Lee Kwong Kut* [1993] AC 951 and *Tan Te Lam* v. *Superintendent of Tai A Chau Detention Centre* [1997] AC 97. For instances of upholding legislation, see *Chan Chi Hung* v. *R* [1996] AC 442; *Ming*

application of BORO. In *Attorney-General (HK)* v. *Lee Kwong Kut*, the Board said:

> While the Hong Kong judiciary should be zealous in upholding an individual's rights under the Hong Kong Bill, it is also necessary to ensure that disputes as to the effect of the Bill are not allowed to get out of hand. The issues involving the Hong Kong Bill should be approached with realism and good sense, and kept in proportion. If this is not done the Bill will become a source of injustice rather than justice and it will be debased in the eyes of the public. In order to maintain the balance between the individual and the society as a whole, rigid and inflexible standards should not be imposed on the legislature's attempts . . . It must be remembered that questions of policy remain primarily the responsibility of the legislature.[80]

The Privy Council and criminal law

A Caribbean storm

The difficulties encountered by the Board in the field of criminal law principally arose in one region subject to the Board's jurisdiction, the Commonwealth Caribbean. Roberts has considered the Board's work on the death penalty in Caribbean cases as part of its approach to fundamental rights.[81] However, this work repays more specific consideration. In the famous case of *Pratt* v. *Attorney-General (Jamaica)*,[82] the Board, departing from some of its own jurisprudence,[83] ruled that delay in carrying out the death penalty could render it inhuman and degrading treatment or punishment, contrary to typical Caribbean constitutional guarantees. The Board effectively imposed a time limit of five years on Caribbean governments, after which the death penalty fell to be commuted to a life sentence.

Pratt led to widespread criticism in the Caribbean, where, in a developing region with high crime rates, the death penalty remained popular.[84] There was a sense that local circumstances were not fully appreciated by

---

Pao Newspapers Ltd v. *Attorney-General* [1996] AC 907; and *Fok Lai Ying* v. *Governor in Council* [1997] HKLRD 810.

[80] *Lee Kwong Kut*, 975 (Lord Woolf, for the Board). Compare Y. Ghai, 'Sentinels of Liberty or Sheep in Woolf's Clothing? Judicial Politics and the Hong Kong Bill of Rights' (1997) 60 *Modern Law Review* 459.

[81] Roberts, note 78 above, 153–60.   [82] [1994] 2 AC 1.

[83] See, in particular, *Abbott* v. *Attorney-General (Trinidad and Tobago)* [1979] 1 WLR 1342 and *Riley* v. *Attorney-General (Jamaica)* [1983] 1 AC 719.

[84] O'Brien, note 55 above, 350.

the Board.[85] The decision was also difficult to implement. It was accepted that a person could not be executed while he or she appealed to an international human rights body such as the United Nations Human Rights Committee. However, appeals to those bodies typically resulted in the five-year period being exceeded.

A request to the Board in a subsequent case for the period to be extended or, alternatively, for the overseas bodies to be excluded when calculating the period was refused.[86] Indeed, the period seems to have been reduced.[87] This coincided with a tendency for the Board to overrule itself in Caribbean criminal cases generally.[88] Approaches by Caribbean governments to the overseas bodies to expedite matters were also held unconstitutional.[89] However, those governments had some success in defending the death penalty in later cases, albeit with the Board again departing from its own decisions.[90] In the result, significant numbers of criminals sentenced to death had instead to receive life sentences.[91]

The Board's work in criminal appeals from the Caribbean was so controversial that it was undoubtedly one factor in the move to replace the Board with the Caribbean Court of Justice (CCJ). So prominent was criminal law in the debate over the creation of the CCJ that some asked whether it would become a 'hanging court' determined to reverse the work of the Board.[92] Even so, opposition to the Board and support for the CCJ arguably should not be overstated. Although all the relevant Caribbean states have agreed by treaty to establish the CCJ, very few, including Jamaica, have successfully reformed their domestic law so as to enable appeals.[93] At the very least, some in the Caribbean may still prefer the Board as the 'devil you know'.

---

[85]　Thompson-Barrow, note 60 above, 30.

[86]　*Bradshaw* v. *Attorney-General (Barbados)* [1995] 1 WLR 936.

[87]　*Guerra* v. *Baptiste* [1996] 1 AC 397; *Henfield & Farrington* v. *Minister of Public Safety* [1997] AC 413.

[88]　*Lewis* v. *Attorney-General (Jamaica)* [2001] 2 AC 50; *Gibson* v. *United States* [2007] 1 WLR 2367. See, generally, D. O'Brien, 'The Privy Council Overrules Itself – Again!' [2008] *Public Law* 28.

[89]　*Thomas* v. *Baptiste* [2000] 2 AC.

[90]　*Matthew* v. *Trinidad and Tobago* [2005] 1 AC 433; *Boyce* v. *R* [2005] 1 AC 400.

[91]　O'Brien, note 55 above, 351.

[92]　This scenario seems to have been avoided; see D. O'Brien, 'The Caribbean Court of Justice Answers its Critics' [2007] *Public Law* 189.

[93]　See, generally, O. Jones and C. Ononaiwu, 'Smoothing the way: the Privy Council and Jamaica's Accession to the Caribbean Court of Justice' (2008) 16 *Caribbean Law Review* 183–97. Since that article, Belize has joined Guyana and Barbados in abolishing appeals to the Board and submitting the same to the CCJ; see Awich A. C. J, 'Speech

Evaluation

It would, of course, be possible to deflect opposition in the Caribbean to the Board's decisions in much the same way as in Canada and Australia. In other words, what was arguably mere disagreement with the valid preferences of the Board wrongly became a challenge to its competence and legitimacy. However, at the very least, the Board should be criticised for its frequent reversal of its own precedents. Another criticism can be made. One could accept the Board's resistance to delay in death penalty cases as a matter involving universal values rather than local considerations. Still, it could perhaps have been more sensitive to the practicalities of the administration of its rulings in a developing region.

The reason for this arguable insensitivity may well lie in the Board's 'dislocation'[94] from the Caribbean. The point is captured by Geoffrey Robertson QC, who has described his regular appearances in Caribbean cases before the Board sitting in London:

> The parade of black taxis and red buses passing Big Ben reminds the visitor that he or she is located precisely at the epicenter of what was once the British Empire. What is bizarre, however, is that the concentrated legal minds in this room must all imagine they are in another country. If they look out this window they must see the pitted roads and slum housing of downtown Kingston, or the open sewers of Belize. . . . This is a court which is jurisprudentially orbiting in space, landing one day in Antigua, another in Trinidad.[95]

Of course, this does not render the Board's task impossible, as its wise decisions in many areas demonstrate. However, in Caribbean criminal appeals, separation from the governments and societies subject to its decisions was arguably damaging.

---

at the Opening of the 2011 Court Year of the Supreme Court of Belize', [2], accessible at http://belizelaw.org/supreme_court/judgements/2011/Annual%20Address%20-%20Ceremonial%20Opening%202011.pdf.

94 O'Brien, note 55 above, 344.

95 G. Robertson, *The Justice Game* (London: Vintage, 1998) 85. The Board has, on a handful of occasions, sat outside of London, in the Bahamas and Mauritius; see *Alexiou* v. *Campbell* [2007] UKPC 11; *Knight* v. *Attorney-General (Cayman Islands)* [2008] UKPC 14; *Todd* v. *R* [2008] UKPC 22; *Callachand* v. *Mauritius* [2008] UKPC 49; *Icebird Ltd* v. *Winegardner* [2009] UKPC 24; *Parsooramen* v. *Nahaboo* [2010] UKPC 10; *Hurnam* v. *Bholah* [2010] UKPC 12; *Aubeeluck* v. *Mauritius* [2010] UKPC 13; and *Mirbel* v. *Mauritius* [2010] UKPC 16.

The Board and crime in Hong Kong

There was little chance that the Board's work in criminal cases from Hong Kong would resemble its work in the Caribbean. Hong Kong has generally existed without serious challenges to public order. Furthermore, the death penalty, while technically mandatory until 1993, had been automatically commuted to a life sentence since 1966.[96] Thus, death penalty cases were never embraced by BORO, which largely recognised that penalty, in any event.[97] It is unsurprising, then, that, on most occasions when the Board was considering a pre-1966 conviction of murder with sentence of death, it affirmed the conviction, leaving scope for the death penalty to proceed.[98]

In the absence of cases involving both criminal law and fundamental rights, the Board fell back on its traditional reluctance to act as a court of criminal appeal. Since *Ibrahim* v. *R*,[99] the Board has insisted that it does not 'sit as a Court of Criminal Appeal'.[100] For the Board to interfere with a criminal conviction, 'there must be something so irregular or so outrageous as to shake the very basis of justice'.[101] However, the Board later remarked, by reference to appeals from Hong Kong:

> these principles are not necessarily to be applied with the most extreme rigidity. Where an important point of law of general application is raised by an appeal, and the decision in question is capable, if not reversed, of constituting a precedent not conducive to the public interest in the proper administration of justice, the appeal may be capable of being accommodated within the intendment of the principles.[102]

This typical reticence of the Board in criminal cases not involving fundamental rights may help explain why its work in this field was uncontroversial on appeal from Hong Kong.

---

[96] M. Jackson, *Criminal Law in Hong Kong* (Hong Kong: Hong Kong University Press, 2003) 489. Although Jackson states that the practice of automatically commuting life sentences began in 1965, the last execution in Hong Kong is said to have occurred in 1966; see Correctional Services Department website, accessible at www.csd.gov.hk/english/abt/abt_his/abt_his_1950.html.

[97] Hong Kong Bill of Rights Ordinance (Cap 383), s. 8, Article 2(2).

[98] *Ibrahim* v. *R* [1914] AC 599; *Chan Kau* v. *R* [1955] AC 206; *Lee Chun Chuen* v. *R* [1963] AC 220; *Khan* v. *R* [1967] 1 AC 454; and *Chan Wei Keung* v. *R* [1967] 2 AC 160. Compare *Chung Chi Cheung*.

[99] *Ibid.*

[100] Practice Direction (1932) 48 TLR 300, cited with approval in *Badry* v. *Director of Public Prosecutions* [1983] 2 AC 297, 303 (Lord Hailsham of St Marylebone LC, for the Board).

[101] *Ibid.* See also *Lee Chun-Chuen* v. *R* [1963] AC 220 and *Attorney-General* v. *Wai Bun* [1994] 1 AC 1, 5 (Lord Woolf, for the Board).

[102] *Buxoo* v. *R* [1988] 1 WLR 820, 824 (Lord Keith of Kinkel, for the Board).

The only question that remains is whether the Board had a noticeable tendency to allow or dismiss Hong Kong criminal appeals. It has been said that because of the above principles, criminal appeals from other jurisdictions 'rarely succeeded'.[103] Yet in criminal proceedings emanating from Hong Kong, the Board allowed 28 appeals and dismissed the same number.[104] In other words, it was as likely to allow as it was to dismiss a criminal appeal. If this truly represents a higher rate of reversal than for other jurisdictions, it would mean that, at least at certain points in Hong Kong history, its criminal courts were more prone to serious errors than such courts elsewhere.

The Privy Council and minorities

The Board has been perceived to be supportive of minorities, principally on appeal from New Zealand. Some Maori were so convinced of the Board's sympathies that they opposed its replacement by the Supreme Court of New Zealand.[105] It is true the Board had some history of supporting Maori rights over the objections of the New Zealand courts.[106] However, in more recent times, the picture was mixed. On one prominent occasion, the Board affirmed a decision by the New Zealand Court of Appeal against the Maori.[107] On another such occasion, the Board became popular with traditional Maori for overruling an attempt by the New Zealand Court of Appeal to extend certain rights to urban Maori.[108]

If one were looking for further evidence of the Board's support for minorities in New Zealand appeals, one could cite a decision by the Board that allowed the people of Western Samoa to gain New Zealand citizenship.[109] That decision was reversed by legislation.[110] Perhaps one could weave the Board's support for minorities into a broader discussion of the imperial tendencies of the Board, arguing that it formed part of a Caesarean strategy of *divide et impera*. The evidence for all of this is

---

[103] Keith, note 21 above, 336.
[104] These figures have been compiled using the reported decisions available on www.westlaw.co.uk.
[105] Richardson, note 57 above, 910.
[106] See J. Tate, 'Hohepa Wineera: Native Title and the Privy Council Challenge' (2004) 35 VUWLR 73.
[107] *New Zealand Maori Council* v. *Attorney-General* [1994] 1 AC 466.
[108] *Treaty Tribes Coalition* v. *Urban Maori Authorities* [1997] 1 NZLR 513.
[109] *Lesa* v. *Attorney-General (NZ)* [1983] 2 AC 20.
[110] New Zealand Citizenship and Western Samoa Act 1982 (NZ).

thin. The Maori may have enjoyed success before the Board on some occasions and the Western Samoans on one occasion. However, this does not provide a compelling case that the Board typically chose to favour minorities, let alone for imperial motives.

Much the same can be said in relation to Hong Kong. A famous decision by the Board on appeal from Hong Kong was *Tan Te Lam* v. *Superintendent of Tai A Chau Detention Centre*.[111] Hong Kong experienced a large influx of illegal immigrants from Vietnam from the 1970s. Many were placed in detention, which sometimes ran for many years. The High Court granted habeas corpus. The Court of Appeal allowed an appeal. The Board restored the trial judge's decision. The issues of law are complex and beyond the scope of this chapter. It is enough to say that *Tan Te Lam* is an instance when the Board protected a minority without necessarily establishing a tendency to that effect.

The Privy Council and judicial independence

The problem of proof

A more concrete case can be made that the Board sometimes provided a source of judicial independence that was lacking in the courts of the jurisdictions providing appeals. At first blush, the Board is not an obvious source of judicial independence because it is merely a committee within a monarchical body and delivers judgments merely in the form of advice to the monarch. However, as indicated, the Board considered itself an independent court, and there is little evidence to the contrary. Even the regular presence of the Lord Chancellor on the Board, as one of his many other roles, 'more or less worked'.[112]

On the other hand, allegations of a lack of judicial independence in lower courts subject to the Board should not be lightly made. Leaving aside flagrant cases, one is attempting to draw inferences as to the unstated motives for judicial decisions. Detailed reasoning and cautious conclusions are therefore required. Under this standard, there were two instances when the Board arguably displayed independence that had been lacking below. Both of these instances emanated from Asia on appeal from Ceylon (now Sri Lanka) and Singapore.

---

[111] [1997] AC 97.
[112] D. Oliver, 'The Lord Chancellor as Head of the Judiciary' in Blom-Cooper, note 21 above, 97.

Upheaval in Sri Lanka

Ceylon supplied the famous case of *Liyanage* v. *R.*[113] The circumstances were extraordinary. There had been an attempted *coup d'état* in Ceylon. The alleged conspirators were apprehended and kept in 'very rigorous custody'.[114] The government resolved that a 'deterrent punishment of a severe character must be imposed'.[115] It pursued this result in an unusual way. Parliament enacted retrospective legislation clearly directed toward the alleged conspirators.[116]

In the words of their Lordships, the legislation did the following:

- 'legalised *ex post facto* the detention for 60 days of any person suspected of having committed offences against the State';[117]
- 'altered the mode of trial for the offences in question [such that] the Minister could direct that the appellants should be tried by three judges without a jury';[118]
- required that those three judges 'be nominated by the Minister';[119]
- 'provided for the addition of two more judges to the Supreme Court, such provision to come into operation on such date as the Minister might appoint';[120]
- inserted a minimum term of imprisonment as punishment for certain offences, while also adding 'a new offence . . . *ex post facto* to meet the circumstances of the abortive *coup*';[121]
- altered the law of evidence for the trial of the relevant offences so far as it included 'protections to an accused person'. It 'swept these protections away',[122] including a 'vital and age old protective rule of evidence';[123]
- provided for most of the foregoing 'to end when the proceedings based on the *coup* come to an end'.[124]

Their Lordships drily noted that this 'would appear to be the fulfilment of the promise'[125] to deal with the alleged offenders harshly. It was, in truth, an extraordinary *ad hominem* interference with the judicial process. It should have fallen foul of any constitution respecting judicial independence. To their credit, several judges of the Supreme Court of Ceylon allowed a preliminary objection by striking down the provision that enabled the Minister to nominate three judges to try the accused.[126] However, after some amendments to the legislative scheme in response

---

[113] [1967] 1 AC 259.   [114] *Ibid.*, 278 (Lord Pearce, for the Board).   [115] *Ibid.*
[116] *Ibid.*   [117] *Ibid.*, 279.   [118] *Ibid.*   [119] *Ibid.*   [120] *Ibid.*   [121] *Ibid.*, 280.
[122] *Ibid.*   [123] *Ibid.*, 281.   [124] *Ibid.*   [125] *Ibid.*, 282.   [126] *Ibid.*

to this ruling, a trial in the Supreme Court proceeded, and the appellants were convicted and sentenced.[127]

The response of the Board

The Board had no hesitation in striking down the whole of the legislative scheme and quashing the convictions. Their Lordships held that 'there exists a separate power in the judicature which under the Constitution as it stands cannot be usurped or infringed by the executive or the legislature'.[128] So much had occurred in the present case. The legislative scheme was a 'grave and deliberate incursion into the judicial sphere'.[129]

The significance of *Liyanage* should not be overstated. In reaching its conclusion, the Board praised the work of the Supreme Court and applied its reasoning so as to invalidate the entire legislative scheme.[130] However, one can at least speculate that the Supreme Court was reluctant to go so far in the context of institutional upheaval and threats to judicial independence. In faraway Whitehall, the Board had no such concerns.

Law and politics in Singapore

Similar issues arose in a famous Singaporean case: *Jeyaretnam* v. *Law Society of Singapore.*[131] The appellant was the sole opposition Member of Parliament (MP) in Singapore. He had been tried on several charges by the Senior Judge of the District Court in relation to the use of a cheque, payable to his political party, to discharge a debt owed by a third person, also a member of the party. The debt arose out of failed litigation against a government politician.[132] The charges had a particular significance for the appellant: if convicted and fined over a certain amount or sentenced to imprisonment for more than a certain period, he would be disqualified from Parliament under the Singapore Constitution.[133]

The appellant was convicted of one of the charges and acquitted of the remainder. Intentionally or otherwise, the trial judge imposed a penalty below the threshold for disqualification from Parliament.[134] Whether for this reason or otherwise, the trial judge was replaced as Senior Judge of

---

[127] *Ibid.*, 277, 283.   [128] *Ibid.*, 289.   [129] *Ibid.*, 290.   [130] *Ibid.*, 288–9.

[131] *Jeyaretnam* v. *Law Society of Singapore* [1989] AC 608.

[132] *Ibid.*, 617–21 (Lord Bridge, for the Board).

[133] Constitution of the Republic of Singapore, Article 145.   [134] *Jeyaretnam*, 621.

the District Court.[135] Both the appellant and the prosecutor appealed to the High Court. As one commentator put it, '[T]hat was when things started to go haywire'.[136] Such appeals are ordinarily heard by a single judge.[137] The Chief Justice heard the appeal. He dismissed the appeal against conviction by the appellant and sentence by the prosecutor while allowing the bulk of the appeals against acquittal by the prosecutor. In doing so, the Chief Justice, similar to the trial judge, imposed penalties that would not lead to disqualification.[138]

As to the remaining acquittal, the Chief Justice ordered a retrial. He also refused to reserve any points of law for consideration by the Court of Criminal Appeal, which, under the intricacies of Singaporean law, produced the result that there could be no appeal to the Board.[139] The appellant brought a motion before another judge of the High Court to have the retrial conducted by that court. Such a retrial, again under the intricacies of Singaporean law, would have produced scope for an appeal to the Board. The motion was dismissed as an abuse of process. Accordingly, the retrial took place before the new Senior Judge of the District Court. The appellant was convicted and sentenced to a term of imprisonment, yet again without leading to his disqualification.[140]

The appellant appealed against the conviction and sentence to the High Court. A judge of the High Court dismissed the appeal against conviction. However, he allowed the appeal against sentence by reducing the term of imprisonment and adding a fine. The Board memorably described the consequences:

> For the solicitor this was indeed a Pyrrhic victory, since a person sentenced to pay a fine of $5,000 or more on any single criminal charge is automatically disqualified for five years from membership of Parliament. The solicitor thus lost his seat as the single opposition member and was unable to stand at the next general election in 1988.[141]

The judge refused to reserve any questions of law for the Court of Criminal Appeal, again precluding any appeal to the Board.[142] This was not the end of the matter for the appellant. The appellant was a lawyer. Accordingly, the Attorney-General reported to the Law Society of Singapore that on the basis of his convictions, the appellant should be disciplined. This question

[135] *Ibid.*, 624.
[136] L. Sheridan, 'Professional Discipline, Procedure and the Privy Council: Singapore' [1989] *Public Law* 389, 391.
[137] *Jeyaretnam*, 621.   [138] *Ibid.*, 622.   [139] *Ibid.*, 621–4.
[140] *Ibid.*, 624.   [141] *Ibid.*, 624.   [142] *Ibid.*, 624–5.

fell to be decided by three members of the High Court, including the Chief Justice. The Chief Justice, on the basis of an apparently mandatory statutory provision, refused to recuse himself. The court ordered that the appellant be struck off the roll of advocates and solicitors.[143]

The reaction of the Board

At last, there was scope for an appeal to the Board. The Board held that it had been 'quite unacceptable' for the Chief Justice to sit, and the statutory provision relied upon in this respect was merely directory.[144] The Board then took the exceptional course, recognised by authority, of re-examining the correctness of the convictions of the appellant for the purposes of the disciplinary measures even though there was no appeal to their Lordships against those convictions.[145] The Board was fortified in this course by the fact that their Lordships found it 'difficult to understand' why questions had not been reserved for the Court of Criminal Appeal, thus enabling an appeal to the Board.[146]

The Board emphatically found the convictions to be erroneous. In particular, they confessed 'astonishment' that the application for the conduct of the retrial before the High Court had not been allowed. The judgment concluded in exceptionally strong terms:

> Their Lordships have to record their deep disquiet that by a series of misjudgments [the appellant has] suffered a grievous injustice. [He has] been fined, imprisoned and publicly disgraced for offences of which [he was] not guilty. [The appellant], in addition, has been deprived of his seat in Parliament and disqualified for a year from practising his profession. Their Lordships' order restores him to the roll of advocates and solicitors of the Supreme Court of Singapore, but, because of the course taken by the criminal proceedings, their Lordships have no power to right the other wrongs which [the appellant has] suffered. [His] only prospect of redress, their Lordships understand, will be by way of petition for pardon to the President of the Republic of Singapore.[147]

The president did not grant a pardon.[148] Rather, Singapore promptly abolished appeals to the Board in virtually all cases.[149] The little remaining

---

[143]   *Ibid.*, 625.   [144]   *Ibid.*, 626.   [145]   *Ibid.*, 627.   [146]   *Ibid.*   [147]   *Ibid.*, 631–2.

[148]   G. Robertson, 'Obituary: Joshua Jeyaretnam', *The Guardian*, 7 October 2008, accessible at www.guardian.co.uk/world/2008/oct/07/2.

[149]   Judicial Committee (Amendment) Act 1989 (Singapore).

scope for appeals was finally extinguished in 1994.[150] One of the last cases before the Board from Singapore was not a happy affair. The Court of Appeal had been asked to announce its decision first and deliver its reasons later, so that a party might take advantage of transitional provisions and appeal to the Board. The Court rejected this request. Their Lordships upheld the validity of the effective abolition of appeals. Given the approach of the Court of Appeal, the Board also had to refuse special leave to appeal under the transitional provisions. It seemed unimpressed.[151]

What conclusions can one draw? *Jayaretnam* certainly did not involve an orchestrated undermining of judicial independence as occurred in *Liyanage*. After all, the appellant in *Jeyaretnam* was only disqualified from Parliament as a result of his own decision to appeal against his retrial. Furthermore, the stinging rebuke to the Singaporean courts issued by the Board was enabled by the decision of the Singaporean government to pursue disciplinary proceedings against the appellant. However, one can certainly say that the litigation raises questions about the approach taken by the Singapore courts in politically controversial cases, arguably not for the last time.[152] One can add that in the same context the Board was manifestly and fearlessly independent.

Impact on Hong Kong

The difficulties that emerged in Ceylon and Singapore did not arise in Hong Kong. The colony was generally stable and, in the tradition of the British Empire, there was significant emphasis on the development of the rule of law. Ghai, while warning against 'rosy images',[153] describes the position as follows:

> Judges had substantial independence . . . senior judiciary enjoyed security of tenure . . . though not perfectly, the Hong Kong legal system was based on the essential principles of the common law. There was equality before the law. Individuals and groups aggrieved by a decision of a government official or public agency could go to courts for address. Courts could also review the legality of legislation and government policies.[154]

---

[150] Judicial Committee (Repeal) Act 1994 (Singapore).
[151] *Dow Jones Publishing Co* v. *Attorney-General of Singapore* [1989] 1 WLR 1308, 1312 (Lord Bridge, for the Board).
[152] See e.g. T. H. Tey, 'Judicial Internalising of Singapore's Supreme Political Ideology' (2010) 40 *HKLJ* 293.
[153] Ghai, note 40 above, 25.   [154] *Ibid.*, 24.

Conclusion

More than one appellate judge has characterised his or her work as a sometimes thankless treadmill.[155] This adequately describes much of the caseload of the Board on appeal from Hong Kong. A stable and ultimately prosperous jurisdiction generated a healthy but relatively bland diet of commercial and criminal appeals, which the Board dealt with competently and impartially.

Many of the great battlegrounds in the history of the Board simply bypassed Hong Kong. There were almost no heady constitutional cases. Tension between the colonial government and the Board in the intersection between fundamental rights and crime did not arise. Hong Kong, with its independent judiciary, did not fall to be supplemented in this respect by the Board.

Certain tendencies on the part of the Board could arguably be perceived on appeal from Hong Kong, such as support for imperial interests and protection of minorities, with the latter possibly also for imperial motives. However, there is simply not enough evidence to sustain such serious allegations against the Board. The most that can be said is that, at the height of Empire, the Board prized legal uniformity. This desire waned as the Commonwealth of Nations emerged. In Hong Kong, which remained a colony, the Board was less accommodating.

In short, while its work has been typically commendable and sometimes interesting, the Board on appeal from Hong Kong is uncontroversial.

---

[155] See e.g. F. Kitto, 'Why Write Judgments?' (1992) 66 ALJ 787; M. Kerr, *As Far As I Remember* (Oxford: Hart Publishing, 2006) 313.

PART II

The Hong Kong Court of Final Appeal

5

Genesis of Hong Kong's Court of Final Appeal

SIMON N. M. YOUNG, ANTONIO DA ROZA, AND YASH GHAI

Introduction

The genesis of Hong Kong's Court of Final Appeal (CFA) marked the end of the old avenue of appeal to the Judicial Committee of the Privy Council (PC) and the beginning of a new domestic final appellate court. This chapter tells the story of how the new court emerged from a highly charged political atmosphere of negotiating and compromising as part of a broader diplomatic setting concerning China's resumption of sovereignty over Hong Kong. There were widely divergent views on how a court of final appeal under Chinese sovereignty should be shaped after an extensive period of colonial rule and influence. In the end, no single vision for the court completely won out over others. Both the Chinese and British sides made compromises to reach an agreement that was strongly rejected by Hong Kong's legislators and legal community. Two years before the handover when the prospect that China might otherwise impose a final court on Hong Kong, a majority of legislators finally accepted the compromises made by the two sides.[1] Despite the divided opinions, all parties shared the aim of ensuring that Hong Kong's strong tradition of rule of law continue with the establishment of a world-class court of final appeal.

Sino–British negotiations

The resumption of sovereignty was preceded by lengthy negotiations between Britain and China as to the future of Hong Kong. One of the key issues was Hong Kong's judicial and legal systems, which had often been heralded as the key to Hong Kong's continuing economic success. Arrangements had to be made in respect of the power of final appeal,

---

[1] See further Chapter 8 (Thomas) in this volume.

which under British colonial rule was vested in the PC. In theory, it was possible that even with the resumption of sovereignty by China final appeals could continue, with the consent of the British government, to go to the PC, the possibility was never mooted; it was inconceivable that China would accept it.

It is difficult to pinpoint exactly when the idea that Hong Kong would establish its own final appeal court was first formed. It was unlikely to have been before 1982, the year when the Sino–British negotiations on the future of Hong Kong began after Prime Minister Margaret Thatcher's visit to China on 22 September 1982.[2] The idea probably originated with China before Thatcher's visit. In his personal account, Wong Man Fong, a former senior official of the Xinhua news agency, described how the 12 points representing China's policies regarding Hong Kong came to be drafted in January 1982 by a small policy task force (of which Wong was a member) set up in Beijing to 'work out concrete policies for Hong Kong'.[3] Wong wrote that these 12 points were the same ones that found their way into the Sino-British Joint Declaration (JD), which when concluded in 1984 stated the policy of vesting the Hong Kong Special Administrative Region of the People's Republic of China (HKSAR) with 'independent judicial power, including that of final adjudication.'[4] Wong's account suggests that China contemplated the end of appeals to the PC months before the Sino–British negotiations began, this being consistent with China's basic policy of 'Hong Kong people ruling Hong Kong'.[5]

Did China ever contemplate establishing the final court in Beijing? In an *Asiaweek* article published in 1983,[6] it was reported that a senior Chinese official insisted on having the court in Beijing.[7] But in response to the story, 'sources close to leftwing circles' rejected the report as being incorrect and stated that it was never Beijing's intention to establish such

---

[2] James T. H. Tang and Frank Ching, 'The MacLehose-Youde Years: Balancing the "Three-Legged Stool," 1971–86' in Ming K. Chan (ed.), *Precarious Balance: Hong Kong Between China and Britain, 1842–1992* (Hong Kong: Hong Kong University Press, 1994) 157–8.

[3] Wong Man Fong, *China's Resumption of Sovereignty over Hong Kong* (Hong Kong: The David C Lam Institute for East-West Studies, 1997) 17–18, 37.

[4] Joint Declaration of the Government of The United Kingdom of Great Britain and Northern Ireland and The Government of the People's Republic of China on the Question of Hong Kong, [3(3)]; Wong Man Fong, *ibid.*, 20.

[5] Wong Man Fong, *ibid.*, 40, 47–50.

[6] 'Watch That "British Link"' (1983) 9(44) *Asiaweek* 16.

[7] 'UK reveals its "bottom line" on future', *Hong Kong Standard*, 4 November 1983.

a court.[8] Even before the second round of Sino–British negotiations in July 1983, Deng Xiaoping had conveyed China's position that the final authority of adjudication would remain in Hong Kong.[9] And during the seventh round of talks held in December 1983, official and unofficial assurances were given by China that Beijing would not be the 'arbiter' of Hong Kong jurisprudence.[10] By the time of the eleventh round of negotiations, there was basic agreement that the final adjudication power had to be in Hong Kong and Mainland China could not veto or overrule the judgments of the Hong Kong courts.[11]

Views from within Hong Kong at the time were also in favour of maintaining the common law system and establishing a final court in Hong Kong. The then Chief Justice, Sir Denys Roberts, believed that Hong Kong could maintain its legal and judicial systems even if the link to the United Kingdom was severed.[12] He cited the merits of the common law system, including judicial independence, predictability, and accessibility in terms of comprehension for other countries.[13] In March 1983, an amendment bill to the Supreme Court Ordinance of Hong Kong proposed the creation of a five-judge panel in the Court of Appeal with the power to overrule the existing appeal court.[14] The bill would have enabled litigants to bring their appeals to the five-member Court of Appeal before further appeal to the PC.[15] But the bill was shelved permanently in November 1983, only after first reading, because of opposition from the Bar Association, which considered that it was unnecessary and because of concerns that it might prejudice the Sino–British negotiations.[16]

At a Legislative Council (LegCo) meeting in June 1984, John Swaine, LegCo member and barrister, called for British judges to join Hong Kong

[8] Staff reporters, 'Peking Won't Preside Over HK Courts', *South China Morning Post*, 5 November 1983. But cf. Zhong Shiyuan, *Xianggang hui gui li cheng: Zhong Shiyuan hui yi lu* (香港回歸歷程：鍾士元回憶錄) (Hong Kong: The Chinese University Press, 2001) 55.

[9] James Tang, 'Round Two on 1997 Opens Today', *Hong Kong Standard*, 12 July 1983.

[10] Staff reporters, '1997 Talks: The Word is "Progress" – At Last', *South China Morning Post*, 9 December 1983.

[11] Jiping Wu, *Zhong Ying hui tan feng yun lu* (中英會談風雲錄) (Hong Kong: *Sing Tao Daily*, 1997) 194.

[12] 'Legal System Could Be Kept', *South China Morning Post*, 22 October 1983.   [13] *Ibid.*

[14] Lindy Course, 'Super Court Plan "Loses to Politics"', *South China Morning Post*, 21 March 1984.

[15] *Ibid.*

[16] John McLean, 'A Bill Doomed to Stay Shelved', *South China Morning Post*, 20 October 1984.

courts to ensure that judicial decisions of the Hong Kong courts continued to command respect internationally.[17] In a speech given in October 1984, Justice of Appeal Yang Ti-liang (as he then was, later Chief Justice T. L. Yang) suggested establishing a final court with two to three judges appointed from the Court of Appeal; the other one or two sitting judges would be 'senior judges from common law countries such as the United Kingdom, Australia, New Zealand and Canada'.[18] In 1986, Yang JA drew parallels to the court system of Brunei, which had a system of visiting expatriate common law judges.[19] The issue of overseas judges (or more precisely, the number of such judges sitting) would in later years become a central controversy in the establishment of the CFA. Other views expressed in the 1980s concerned the need for a constitutional court in Hong Kong sitting with Hong Kong and Mainland judges to adjudicate conflicts concerning the Basic Law (BL)[20] and calls for the final court to be set up early to allow for a gradual change in the legal system.[21]

Joint Declaration and Basic Law

An independent final court established in Hong Kong was an essential feature of the Sino-British JD signed in December 1984.[22] In paragraph 3(3), it was declared: 'The Hong Kong Special Administrative Region will be vested with executive, legislative and independent judicial power, including that of final adjudication. The laws currently in force in Hong Kong will remain basically unchanged'. The elaboration in Annex I, section III, stated that:

> The power of final judgment of the Hong Kong Special Administrative Region shall be vested in the court of final appeal in the Hong Kong Special Administrative Region, which may as required invite judges from other common law jurisdictions to sit on the court of final appeal.

---

[17] 'UK Judges Needed for Local Courts', *South China Morning Post*, 28 June 1984.

[18] Stanley Leung, 'Final Appeals Must Be in HK', *South China Morning Post*, 19 October 1984.

[19] 'A Case for Expatriate Judges after "97"', *Hong Kong Standard*, 27 June 1986. See also Simon N. M. Young, 'The Hong Kong Multinational Judge in Hong Kong Criminal Appeals' (2008) 26 *Law in Context* 130, 133–4.

[20] Patricia Tse, 'Basic Law "Needs Own Court"', *South China Morning Post*, 4 June 1984.

[21] Chris Yeung, 'Final Appeal Court "Should Be Earlier"', *South China Morning Post*, 24 October 1984; Agnes Chen, 'Court of Final Appeal "Should Be Set Up Early"', *South China Morning Post*, 13 December 1984.

[22] Joint Declaration, Annex I, section III.

Thus, the idea of high-calibre foreign judges sitting on the final court was one of the JD's defining features in respect of the future judicial system.

The CFA was entrenched in the BL, the first draft of which was published in April 1988, and after a public consultation exercise, the second draft was published in February 1989 with another consultation exercise.[23] The wording of the main article concerning the CFA was not significantly altered from the wording in the JD.[24] The development of the court thereafter, however, was tumultuous and controversial.

Against the background of the Tiananmen Square massacre in June 1989, concerns were expressed over the continuation of the rule of law and the potential damage to business confidence and implications for fundamental rights and freedoms in Hong Kong.[25] The enactment of the Hong Kong Bill of Rights Ordinance in 1991,[26] intended as reassurance of the continued protection of fundamental rights in Hong Kong after 1997,[27] was met with objections from the Chinese government as the law was passed without China's approval.[28] The objections in turn caused some to question China's commitment to preserve Hong Kong's freedoms despite the entrenchment of international covenants on human rights by the JD and the BL.

Rejection of the Joint Liaison Group's 1991 agreement

The JD set up a Sino-British Joint Liaison Group (JLG) to 'ensure a smooth transfer of government in 1997' and for the 'effective implementation' of

---

[23] See Articles 80 and 81 of the two draft versions of the Basic Law, which can be found in Ming K. Chan and David J. Clark (eds.), *The Hong Kong Basic Law: Blueprint for 'Stability and Prosperity' Under Chinese Sovereignty?* (Hong Kong: Hong Kong University Press, 1991) 63–91, 145–61.

[24] Article 82 of the BL provides as follows: 'The power of final adjudication of the Hong Kong Special Administrative Region shall be vested in the Court of Final Appeal of the Region, which may as required invite judges from other common law jurisdictions to sit on the Court of Final Appeal.'

[25] 'Hong Kong: The Current Issues', Research Paper 95/52, International Affairs and Defence Section, Paul Bowers, 26 April 1995, House of Commons Library ('Hong Kong: The Current Issues').

[26] Hong Kong Bill of Rights Ordinance (Cap. 383), in force 8 June 1991.   [27] *Ibid.*

[28] The Association of the Bar of the City of New York: The Committee on International Human Rights, 'Preserving the Rule of Law in Hong Kong After July 1, 1997: A Report of a Mission of Inquiry' (1997) 18 *University of Pennsylvania Journal of International Economic Law* 367.

the JD.[29] One of the tasks of the JLG was to reach agreement on the setting up of the CFA. In 1991, the JLG reached its first such agreement.

Although the BL would not come into effect to establish formally the CFA before 1 July 1997, it was agreed on all sides that the CFA should be set up before then to enhance the transition process.[30] On 27 September 1991, a 'breakthrough' in negotiations during a JLG meeting was heralded in respect of the composition of the CFA.[31] The 1991 agreement specified that the CFA would be composed of a chief justice, three other Hong Kong judges, and one judge from a list of Hong Kong judges or senior judges from countries with a common law system.

The agreement was widely and heavily criticised. The primary bone of contention was the composition of the Court; in particular, the limit set on the number of overseas judges who could sit in any case appeared to contradict the unqualified number suggested by the word 'judges' in both the JD and BL.[32] LegCo member Martin Lee QC claimed that whilst he was a member of the Basic Law Drafting Committee in 1987, he had proposed (and Chinese government representatives agreed) that the majority of the CFA judges would consist of visiting judges who were not Chinese nationals.[33] The original British position in respect of the composition was said to have included two overseas judges,[34] but the 'poor political atmosphere'[35] and desire to establish the court before 1997 may have led to the compromise of the 1991 agreement. As such, the 1991 agreement is better viewed as a 'deal' rather than a strict interpretation of the treaty between Britain and China, justified by the diffusion of political tension following the Tiananmen Square massacre, as well as the practical issues of workability and benefits of having the Court set up before 1997.[36]

---

[29] Joint Declaration, [5] & annex II.

[30] 'Hong Kong: The Current Issues', note 25 above.

[31] David Wallen, 'Breakthrough in Court of Final Appeal row', *South China Morning Post*, 27 September 1991.

[32] Roda Mushkat, *One Country, Two International Legal Personalities – The Case of Hong Kong* (Hong Kong: Hong Kong University Press, 1997).

[33] 'Preserving the Rule of Law', note 28 above, 402 (fn 170).

[34] Lindy Course, 'Government "Misled by Law Bodies"', *South China Morning Post*, 4 November 1991, 1.

[35] David Wallen, 'Breakthrough in Court of Final Appeal row', *South China Morning Post*, 27 September 1991.

[36] See Mushkat, note 32 above.

This pragmatism was of little comfort. In a joint statement, the Bar Association and the Law Society objected to the agreement as a contravention of the spirit and letter of the JD and BL.[37] The restriction on overseas judges in particular was criticised for potentially limiting the development of the Court because of the 'small pool of judicial talent' in Hong Kong.[38]

Another issue was whether a court so composed would be sufficiently distinguished from the Court of Appeal, given the possibility that the court could sit without an overseas judge and with all five members of the court being current serving members of the judiciary. The agreement was also criticised in providing for matters, such as composition, which, it was said, ought to be left to the discretion of the court itself or to be determined by local legislation as contemplated by Article 83 of the BL.[39]

At its heart, the issue was not only the number of sitting foreign judges but also the judicial independence and autonomy promised under the JD and BL. The restriction upon matters that were thought to be left for the court's own determination led to some concerns about the courts of Hong Kong becoming no different than those of China, and the limitation on outside participation showed that Chinese authorities believed 'local' judges would be easier to control than judges from overseas.[40]

The legal profession was not alone in its criticism of the agreement; their criticisms were supported not only by local and professional groups but also by the English legal profession. The joint statement of the Bar Association and Law Society was also supported by a subsequently published legal opinion of Sir William Wade. A report by the International Commission of Jurists concluded:

> The agreement reached by the Joint Liaison Group on the composition of the Court of Final Appeal is contrary to the Joint Declaration and the Basic Law and is constitutionally invalid; the Court of Final Appeal itself should be allowed to determine the number and identity of foreign judges to sit as temporary members.[41]

---

[37] Johannes Chan, 'The Judiciary' in Johannes Chan and C. L. Lim (eds.), *Law of the Hong Kong Constitution* (Hong Kong: Sweet & Maxwell, 2011) 293.

[38] Alison W. Conner, 'Final Appeal Court Proposal Stirs Controversy in Hong Kong', *East Asian Executive Reports*, 15 November 1991.

[39] Article 83 provides that 'The structure, powers and functions of the courts of the Hong Kong Special Administrative Region at all levels shall be prescribed by law.'

[40] Conner, note 38 above.

[41] International Commission of Jurists (ICJ), *Countdown to 1997: Report of a Mission to Hong Kong* (Geneva: ICJ, 1992) 91.

Another issue that arose was the restriction upon the court's jurisdiction in respect of acts of state, such as defence and foreign affairs. Although this exclusion is entrenched in the BL under Article 19, the restriction was arguably inconsistent with the JD.[42]

The force with which these criticisms were levelled against the agreement was based on a widely held belief that a court of final appeal in Hong Kong after 1997 needed to be perceived as independent, impartial, and as prestigious as the PC. Statistics of the PC cited at that time showed that in almost half the appeals from Hong Kong to the PC, the lower court judgment was reversed. It was argued that this high rate of reversal signified the importance of the PC and the need for a court of very high stature and independence, not least of which was because of fears that commercial interests would lose confidence in the legal system of Hong Kong after the resumption of sovereignty.[43]

The response of the LegCo was unequivocal: at a closed in-house session on 25 October 1991, the 1991 agreement was rejected by a majority of 38 to 2 votes. Frank Ching remarked upon the significance of the vote: 'This was the first time in history that the Hong Kong legislature had stood up to oppose an agreement reached by Britain and China on the future of Hong Kong.'[44] The overwhelming view was in favour of setting up a court with greater flexibility to invite overseas judges. The two who voted against argued that the 1991 agreement did not breach the JD and the BL and that it was up to the National People's Congress (NPC) to interpret the BL.[45] The response by the Chinese government was equally strong, with Chinese officials making statements that LegCo had no authority to veto the agreement as it was merely an advisory body and not a representative one. It was suggested that the NPC could enact legislation to set the court up if the 1991 agreement was rejected, and one Chinese law expert expressed the opinion that the court should be set up under Chinese national laws rather than the laws of the special administrative region.[46]

---

[42] See Mushkat, note 32 above.   [43] Conner, note 38 above.

[44] Frank Ching, 'Toward Colonial Sunset: The Wilson Regime, 1987–92' in Ming K. Chan (ed.), *Precarious Balance: Hong Kong Between China and Britain, 1842–1992* (Hong Kong: Hong Kong University Press, 1994) 190.

[45] See Doreen Cheung, 'Call to Reconsider Court Agreement', *South China Morning Post*, 25 October 1991; *Hong Kong Hansard*, 4 December 1991.

[46] *Hong Kong Hansard*, 4 December 1991, 992, per Hon. James To referring to Mr. Wu Jianfan; Louis Ng, 'Beijing Floats Plan to Legislate on Final Court', *Hong Kong Standard*, 13 November 1991.

Simon Ip's Legislative Council motion

On 4 December 1991, after the rejection of the 1991 agreement, Simon Ip, then representative of the legal profession in the LegCo, moved the following motion:

> That when the Court of Final Appeal in Hong Kong is set up, it should have more flexibility to invite overseas judges to sit on it than has been agreed by the British and Chinese Governments, and such flexibility should be in accordance with the Joint Declaration and the Basic Law.

Against the motion, it was argued that the composition, although not ideal, was workable and consistent with the JD and the BL. Moreover, the best interests of Hong Kong would be served by having the statutory footing of the CFA well before 1997 in order for it to be established formally on 1 July 1997 without delay, surprise, or disruption. The importance of this early establishment was emphasised by the fact that the vesting of the power of final judgment to courts of a non-sovereign territory was untried. The confidence of the community, particularly the business community, would also be best served by setting up the court early even though not provided for under the JD and BL – the key factors at stake being certainty and continuity.

It was further argued that the four permanent judges to one non-permanent judge (NPJ) composition of the court would not prejudice its independence. A court composed of a majority of visiting judges was clearly not viable, and in interpreting the JD and BL in this context, it is clear that the discretion to invite judges from other common law jurisdictions was never intended to be unlimited. Because neither the JD nor the BL specified the number of judges, the matter was to be dealt with by way of legislation. Hence, the motion would effectively be a request that the JLG reopen talks on the composition of the Court – something that the Chinese government had already stated it was not prepared to do.

The then Chief Justice T. L. Yang was also cited during the LegCo debate as having expressed the opinion that the composition was 'acceptable', although he had been quoted in the news as acknowledging he would have preferred the flexibility of the court only having three permanent judges and having the discretion to invite overseas judges for the other seats, at least in its initial years.[47] Wu Jianfan, a member of the Basic Law Drafting

---

[47] L. Wong, L. Course, and C. Yeung, 'Final Appeal Court Accord Under Attack', *South China Morning Post*, 28 September 1991, 1.

Committee, was also quoted during the debate as suggesting that China would simply enact the laws for the establishment of the Court after the resumption of sovereignty if the agreement was not endorsed by LegCo.[48]

The arguments in favour of the motion began with objections and criticisms that LegCo should not function as a 'rubber stamp' for the JLG, particularly when it had not been consulted in respect of the agreement. The agreement raised some serious issues about the confidence the people of Hong Kong could have in the JD and the BL: the limitation in the agreement was not found anywhere in either the JD or the BL, and the agreement was said to alter the clear wording and meaning of the two documents. Approval of the agreement would also set a dangerous precedent, and the Chinese and British governments could agree upon other limitations in respect of the JD and the BL.

Of greater importance than the need to establish the court early was the need to sort out its composition – after all, there was still a right of appeal to the PC that would continue until 1 July 1997. Statistics provided by the Hong Kong government showed that from 1985 to 1989, of the 41 cases from Hong Kong heard by the PC, 23 were civil cases, with an overall success rate of 46 per cent. These figures were used to demonstrate the importance of final adjudication to the business community, and it was argued that under the agreement, the CFA would be the Court of Appeal in a different guise. Without distinguished jurists of comparable stature to the PC, the CFA would be incapable of securing the confidence of the business community.

In respect of local judicial talent, when compared with the Law Lords on the PC, it was argued that Hong Kong lacked judges of the quality and standing comparable to those of the PC. Moreover, of the nine serving Justices of Appeal, all were overseas nationals who were approaching the age of 64 years on average; with the judicial retirement age set at 65 years, it would be some time before judges of sufficient seniority could rise through the ranks to the CFA, making the CFA more reliant on overseas jurists, at least at first. It was anticipated that the need for overseas jurists would eventually diminish as the CFA gained recognition and stature.

Reservations were expressed even by those in support of the motion in respect of the deletion of the words 'by 1993', which had appeared in the draft version of the motion. The original British objective was to have the CFA operational by 1993, an idea that was supported by most LegCo

---

[48] See note 46 above.

members despite their opposition to the proposed structure.[49] During the in-house session, the idea that the CFA should be set up early was still present, but it was a point of contention as some who supported the motion did not agree with the position that no court (before 1997) was better than accepting the four-to-one ratio. However, despite this reservation, the motion was passed by a majority of 34 to 11 votes.

In the face of such opposition, the Hong Kong government did not proceed with the legislation for the court, although in one British report it was suggested that the Hong Kong government nevertheless submitted to China draft legislation that remained relatively close to the 1991 agreement in May 1994.[50] The report also suggested that Hong Kong's legal profession also came under pressure from Beijing, leading the Law Society to rescind its objections to the proposed composition of the court and the Law Society had caved in to pressure from law firms dependent on Chinese business.[51]

Preliminary Working Committee's eight-point proposal

Four years passed before the matter of the establishment of the court was again put before the LegCo. In 1995, the Preliminary Working Committee of the Preparatory Committee for the HKSAR studied the issue and developed an eight-point proposal on the establishment of the CFA.[52] The proposal was submitted to and was discussed by the JLG. The eight points were as follows:[53]

1. To abide by the Joint Declaration and the Basic Law, and to meet the principle that the Hong Kong Special Administrative Region should enjoy an independent judicial system and power of final adjudication to improve confidence in the maintenance of the rule of law in Hong Kong.

---

[49] Doreen Cheung, 'Call to Reconsider Court Agreement', *South China Morning Post*, 26 October 1991.

[50] Hong Kong: The Current Issues, note 25 above.   [51] *Ibid.*

[52] The Preparatory Committee for the HKSAR, established by the NPC, was responsible for preparing the establishment of the HKSAR, including various political bodies. See Decision of the National People's Congress on the Method for the Formation of the First Government and the First Legislative Council of the Hong Kong Special Administrative Region, adopted at the third Session of the seventh National People's Congress on 4 April 1990, [2].

[53] Minutes of the fifth and sixth plenary meetings of the NPCSC's HKSAR Preparatory Committee Preparatory Working Committee, translated by Ernest Ng.

2. The Court of Final Appeal should consist of the Chief Justice, 3 Permanent Judges, and Hong Kong and overseas non-permanent Judges, the total number of which should not exceed 30, though the total number of non-permanent Judges can be increased in accordance with need. The hearing panel should consist of 5 judges, in which all 4 permanent judges should participate. The Chief Justice shall choose a Hong Kong non-permanent Judges as a substitute where one of the permanent judges cannot participate. The final spot on the panel shall be a non-permanent Judge chosen by the Chief Justice in accordance with the need of the case.

3. Permanent judges shall be chosen from the High Court Judges of the Hong Kong Special Administrative Region or barristers having practised in Hong Kong for more than 10 years; however, during the formation of the Court of Final Appeal, the selection pool may be expanded to retired judges of the Hong Kong Supreme Court. Local non-permanent Judges shall be chosen from retired Chief Justices of the High Court, current or retired Justices of Appeal, retired Permanent Judges of the Court of Final Appeal, and barristers who have practised in Hong Kong for 10 or more years. Overseas non-permanent Judges must be current or retired judges from other common law jurisdictions outside Hong Kong. In accordance with the Basic Law, the Chief Justice must be a Hong Kong permanent resident, being a Chinese citizen without any right of abode in any foreign countries.

4. Court of Final Appeal judges are to be appointed by the Chief Executive of Hong Kong on the recommendation of an independent commission (the Judicial Officers Recommendation Commission) consisting of local judges, legal professionals and eminent persons from other sectors – appointed by the Chief Executive and chaired by the Chief Justice. The endorsement of LegCo is also needed and such appointments or removals are to be reported to the Standing Committee of the National People's Congress for records.

5. The retirement age of the permanent judges should be set at 65, but the Chief Executive can extend the terms of office no more than twice for 3 years each time. The Chief Executive may also appoint a person above the age of 65 to be a permanent judge for 3 years if manpower needs require. Non-permanent Judges are appointed on a term basis, each term being 3 years – the Chief Executive will make decisions about extensions of appointment based on the recommendation of the Chief Justice. The Chief Justice may only be disciplined by a tribunal

appointed by the Chief Executive consisting of not less than 5 judges. The Chief Justice may only be removed by the Chief Executive on the recommendation of that tribunal, with the endorsement of LegCo – and the matter should be reported to the Standing Committee of the National People's Congress. Judges of the Court of Final Appeal may resign by notifying the Chief Executive in writing.

6. Other than acts of state, the jurisdiction of the Court of Final Appeal is that of the highest adjudicatory body in Hong Kong. It has the power to maintain, reverse or alter the decision of a trial court under appeal or to remit the relevant matter to the trial court for disposal. Certificates must be obtained by the Court of Final Appeal from the Chief Executive in respect of acts of state, and in respect of the Basic Law, seek interpretation from the Standing Committee of the National People's Congress where it must rule on provisions concerning matters that are the responsibility of the Central People's Government or in respect of the relationship between the Central Authorities and the Region.

7. Trial procedure should be dealt with by way of legislation with reference to the present practice of Hong Kong.

8. The Court of Final Appeal shall be established on 1 July 1997 – the Chief Executive shall appoint the Judicial Officer's Recommendation Committee to recommend candidates for Court of Final Appeal judges, and the Chief Executive shall appoint such candidates with the consent of LegCo.

This eight-point proposal led to the second JLG agreement in respect of the CFA in 1995, which was followed by the preparation and revision of draft legislation to establish the CFA. The revised draft of the Hong Kong Court of Final Appeal Ordinance was then submitted to LegCo in the same year.

The Joint Liaison Group's 1995 agreement

The text of the JLG's 1995 agreement, dated 9 June 1995, was as follows:

> After full consultations, the two sides of the Sino-British Joint Liaison Group have reached the following agreement on the question of the Court of Final Appeal in Hong Kong:
>
> (1) The British side agrees to amend the Court of Final Appeal Bill on the basis of the eight suggestions published by the Political Affairs

Sub-group of the Preliminary Working Committee of the Preparatory Committee of the Hong Kong Special Administrative Region on 16 May 1995.

(2) The Chinese side agrees to the British side amending the Court of Final Appeal Bill to make it clear that section 83P of the Criminal Procedure Ordinance applies in a case where an appeal has been heard and determined by the Court of Final Appeal, and that there is therefore no need for further legislative or other provisions in relation to the power to inquire into the constitutionality of laws or to provide for post-verdict remedial mechanisms.

(3) The British side agrees to amend the Court of Final Appeal Bill to include the formulation of "acts of state" in Article 19 of the Basic Law and to provide that the Court of Final Appeal Ordinance shall not come into operation before 30 June 1997.

(4) The Chinese side agrees that, after the Chinese and British sides reach this agreement, the legislative procedures for the Court of Final Appeal Bill, on which the two sides have reached a consensus through consultation, will be taken forward immediately to enable them to be completed as soon as possible before the end of July 1995. The Chinese side will adopt a positive attitude in this regard.

(5) The Chinese and British sides agree that the team designate of the Hong Kong Special Administrative Region shall, with the British side (including relevant Hong Kong Government departments) participating in the process and providing its assistance, be responsible for the preparation for the establishment of the Court of Final Appeal on 1 July 1997 in accordance with the Basic Law and consistent with the provisions of the Court of Final Appeal Ordinance.[54]

Commentary on the 1991 and 1995 agreements

The importance of the JLG's agreements on the CFA was clear, but whether or not they were valid interpretations of the JD and BL, particularly with regard to international rules of treaty interpretation, was an issue that attracted much debate and criticisms.[55]

In her commentary on the two agreements, Roda Mushkat noted that the JD as an international treaty was to be interpreted in good faith in

---

[54] Agreement Between the British and Chinese Sides on the Question of the Court of Final Appeal in Hong Kong, dated 9 June 1995, reproduced at note 1 of Frankie Fook-Lun Leung, 'Hong Kong: The Hong Kong Court of Final Appeal Ordinance' (1996) 35 *International Legal Materials* 207.

[55] See Jonathan Dimbleby, *The Last Governor* (London: Little, Brown and Company, 1997) ch. 15, for the conflict between Governor Patten and ministers in London.

accordance with the ordinary meaning given to the terms of the treaty in the context of the treaty's object and purpose.[56] She thought it clear from the terms of the JD that the CFA was vested with the discretion to invite judges from other common law jurisdictions as needed. The object of the JD in this regard was to guarantee the independence of the CFA and a high standard of membership, with the ultimate goals of preserving stability and allowing for a high degree of autonomy to the HKSAR, particularly in respect of final adjudication. Weight could only be placed upon the two agreements if they could be construed as interpretive documents of sufficient authority to displace the ordinary meaning of the words of the JD that would otherwise be consistent with its object and purpose. Mushkat argued that the process to implement the JD should not be used to circumvent the obligation to perform the treaty in good faith. In denying the CFA flexibility in choosing overseas judges, its power to invite judges from other common law jurisdictions had been unduly inhibited and was not in compliance with the JD's promise of judicial autonomy.

Mushkat also expressed concern with the exclusion of 'acts of state' from the court's purview, opening the door to abuse because of its loose definition and lack of explicit reference to interpretive sources or determining authorities. Whilst acts of state under the common law were narrowly defined, the potential for expansion of the definition under an expression of executive policy would have serious implications for judicial independence (on which issue see the *Congo* case decided in 2011).[57]

The issue of the court's composition was subjected to further criticisms when the 1995 agreement was submitted to LegCo, for example, the four-to-one formula being described as nothing more than an enlarged version of the Court of Appeal and, more importantly, the criticism of the Hong Kong Human Rights Monitor that '[s]uch a court serves no useful purpose unless its judges are substantially more skilled and learned than those of the present Hong Kong Court of Appeal'.[58] Significantly, the standing of the two agreements was also raised before LegCo, with an argument that the JD and the BL were superior to the agreements reached by the

---

[56] See Mushkat, note 32 above, 158–60.
[57] See *Democratic Republic of the Congo* v. *FG Hemisphere Associates LLC* (2011) 14 HKCFAR 95 (reference) and 395 (disposition).
[58] *Hong Kong Hansard*, 26 July 1995, 5876, per Hon. Martin Lee.

JLG by virtue of the fact that the JD is an international treaty registered with the United Nations but the two agreements were not.[59]

The British government was not unaware of departures from the spirit, if not the letter of the JD or of its responsibilities to the people of Hong Kong (particularly on the issues of the acts of state and the number of foreign judges). But by then British interests in a broader and more positive relationship with China, as prospects of economic gain from China's shift to a new economic system, led to concessions on Hong Kong issues – much to the frustration of Chris Patten, the new governor. But Patten justified the delays in setting up the CFA on the ground that this would give Britain more say in the drafting of the legislation. He agreed to drop the demands against the exclusion of acts of state but to retain them as in the BL without further elaboration as China had wanted. In return, China agreed that the CFA could adjudicate on 'constitutionality of laws'.[60] According to Dimbleby, Patten was concerned that Britain was running out of time as sovereign power while China was worried by the low morale of civil servants 'for whom British standards of justice and law were a sine qua non of civil order and about the possible exodus of capital from Hong Kong that could so easily be precipitated by a failure to resolve such a crucial issue'.[61]

LegCo readings of the Court of Final Appeal Bill

The Hong Kong Court of Final Appeal Bill (to establish the CFA) was first read on 14 June 1995, and a little more than a month later, on 26 July 1995, the Bill underwent its second reading.[62] For the Bills Committee, the 'acts of state' exclusion was a contentious issue, as was the composition of the court (i.e. the four-to-one formula, which again was criticised by members of the Committee, as well as the Bar Association, for its inflexibility and apparent non-compliance with the JD and BL, although by this time the Law Society had changed its stance on the matter). It was also noted that the delayed setup of the court to 1 July 1997 was not in accordance with the original intentions of the Hong Kong government.

A motion to adjourn the reading was tabled; it was argued that there had been 'indecent haste' in pushing the bill through the Bills Committee

---

[59] *Ibid.*

[60] See Dimbleby, note 55 above, ch. 15, for the conflict between Patten and ministers in London and subsequent deals between Patten and the Chinese authorities (the chapter is titled 'A Matter of Decency').

[61] *Ibid.*, 280.   [62] *Hong Kong Hansard*, 26 July 1995, 5849.

stage in only three weeks.[63] Given that the ordinance would not come into effect until 1 July 1997, it was argued that more time to review the bill was desirable. The motion was defeated in light of the fact that such an adjournment would have led to further uncertainty over Hong Kong's court of final adjudication.[64]

A number of amendments were moved but defeated.[65] A motion to establish the court before 1 July 1997 was defeated because it would have been in breach of the 1995 agreement and raised issues about the continuing jurisdiction of the PC and potential confusion over two avenues of final appeal before 1 July 1997. Another motion to remove the distinction between permanent and non-permanent judges to allow NPJs to participate more fully was also defeated, as was a motion to allow overseas judges to sit on the Appeal Committee; in that regard, it was criticised that the overseas judges would not be treated as proper members of the court. A motion to allow overseas judges to take part in the Rules Committee was also defeated, with the Hong Kong government introducing the idea of a 'nucleus' of permanent judges to operate the CFA, including its Rules Committee. A motion to amend the precedence of judges to take into account the overseas judges' standing in their native jurisdictions was defeated. Motions to amend provisions concerning 'acts of state' or to define the term in accordance with the common law were also defeated. Motions to remove the limits on the number of judges and to limit the jurisdictions from which overseas judges may come were defeated. Motions to amend the composition of the court and to introduce flexibility on its composition were also defeated, although the issue of flexibility was defeated by the narrowest margin of the day of 32 to 25 votes. A motion to abolish as of right appeals was also defeated; it was argued that to abolish such appeals would be to restrict public access to the court. A motion to introduce a 'leapfrog' procedure was also inadvertently defeated as it was contained in the proposed amendments to the subsections concerning civil appeals to the court; when the motion to abolish appeals as of right was defeated, the leapfrog process could not be put. A motion to allow leave in criminal cases to be granted either by the Court of Appeal or the Appeal Committee of the CFA was defeated on the grounds that it would lead to an increase in the CFA's workload, although a view was expressed that if the CFA's workload was comparable to that of the PC's in respect of Hong Kong appeals (meaning the court would

---

[63] *Ibid.*, 5855.   [64] *Ibid.*, 5871–2, for the vote and the debate on uncertainty following.
[65] *Ibid.*, 5929–6055.

only be engaged for seven to nine weeks of the year), it could cope with such an increase in workload. Amendments to allow the Judicial Officers Recommendation Commission a say in extensions of the terms of the permanent judges and the appointment of the Registrar of the CFA were also defeated.

In the end, the bill passed on 26 July 1995 was not significantly different from the JLG's vision of the court when their first agreement was concluded in 1991.

Jurisdictional issue

This chapter deals principally with the controversies and agreements on the formation of the CFA, although it touches on some aspects of its jurisdiction (e.g. over acts of state). However, because the significance of the CFA cannot be understood without knowledge of its jurisdiction (nor fully the debates about the composition of the CFA), a brief account is provided here of the different approaches canvassed during the making of the BL. As noted earlier, the idea of an independent judicial system in the HKSAR came from the Chinese and was embodied in paragraph 3 of the JD. The annex to that document provided for the participation of overseas common law judges as 'may be required'.

The BL gave HK courts the 'judicial power' of the region. The general powers of the judiciary are defined by previous rules and practice. However, it is in Article 158 that its powers in relation to BL issues themselves are defined (as issues about its interpretation). It would seem that this point was not discussed, or resolved, in the Sino–British negotiations. However, it arose during the drafting of the BL (by a committee that had both Mainland and Hong Kong members, the former mostly officials and academics close to the Communist Party); the outcome was Article 158 of the BL. Martin Li has given an authoritative account of the negotiations in the Drafting Committee of which he was then a member (expelled after the Tiananmen killings).[66] These provisions were widely understood in Hong Kong as giving the HKSAR the powers of interpretation of the BL (even if Chinese interests or executive acts were concerned) just as the Hong Kong courts were then free to interpret the Letters Patent and the

---

[66] See Martin Lee, 'A Tale of Two Articles' in Albert Chen and Peter Wesley-Smith (eds.), *The Basic Law and Hong Kong's Future* (Hong Kong: Butterworths, 1988) 309 and Yash Ghai, *Hong Kong's New Constitutional Order: Basic Law and the Resumption of Sovereignty*, 2nd edn (Hong Kong: Hong Kong University Press, 1999) ch. 5.

Royal Instructions – constitutional instruments for colonial Hong Kong. This view was reinforced by another provision in the JD that the current laws would remain basically unchanged (paragraph 3(3) and section II, paragraph 1 of Annex I), including the common law under which courts would interpret constitutional instruments.

In the early drafts of the BL, the powers of the HKSAR courts were largely restricted to adjudication, but those of the NPCSC were confined to interpretation. The HKSAR courts were to have no general powers of interpretation but were allowed a limited competence for this in the context of actual litigation. The 1988 draft stated that the HKSAR courts might, 'in adjudicating cases' interpret a provision of the BL unless it concerned 'defence, foreign affairs and other affairs which are the responsibility of the Central Government'. When an article concerned such cases, the courts would have had to seek an interpretation from the NPCSC before making their final judgement (draft Article 169). It is unnecessary to go through the different permutations of this article; an interesting history is provided by Martin Lee (1988), who played a key but only partially successful role in its amendment.[67] Suffice it to say that the initial proposals met with considerable opposition from Hong Kong drafters as well as members of the legal profession, principally on the ground that such arrangements threatened the rule of law and the integrity of the BL because the NPCSC was not a judicial body. The draft provisions were partially amended in response, giving all the powers of adjudication to the Hong Kong courts and dividing the responsibility for interpretation. It is unnecessary to go into that history or the way in which the CFA's interpretation of the BL and its relationship to the NPCSC has worked out; the latter is the subject of various chapters in this volume (particularly Chapter 14 by Chen and Lo). But it is important to note the point that the restriction on the CFA's jurisdiction when a Mainland law or interest is involved meant that the CFA (and indeed, lower HKSAR courts) had not been given all previous jurisdictions because the Hong Kong courts as well as the PC could consider cases against the British colonial and imperial governments for violation of the constitution or law.

Appointment of Chief Justice Andrew Li

With the statutory footing in place, the next step in the genesis of the CFA was the appointment of the first Chief Justice of the HKSAR. On

---

[67] Lee, *ibid.*

12 April 1997, Chief Executive–elect Tung Chee Hwa named the first members of the Judicial Officers Recommendation Commission (JORC):[68] Dr Edgar Cheng (chairman of the Hong Kong Stock Exchange) and Chan Wing Kee (of the Yangtzekiang garment and aluminium group), both also members of the Preparatory and Selection Committees.[69] Also named to the commission were members of the former Judicial Service Commission: Nazareth JA, Patrick Chan J, Secretary for Justice–elect Elsie Leung, Gladys Li (barrister), Roderick Woo (solicitor), and Victor Fung (Trade Development Council chairman). The first task of the JORC was to name the new Chief Justice.

Two candidates were mentioned as being the main contenders for the position: Executive Councilor Andrew Li QC and Benjamin Liu JA, with Chief Executive–elect Tung Chee Hwa reportedly preferring Andrew Li and the Xinhua news agency preferring Benjamin Liu.

Liu JA, then 66 years old, was described as Hong Kong's 'most overtly political judge',[70] who had gained publicity over his extra-judicial comments, including his criticism of the passage of the Bill of Rights Ordinance, and there had been calls for him to resign over his controversies in the political sphere. One senior judge was said to have threatened to resign if Liu JA was appointed Chief Justice.[71] Liu JA was called to the Bar in England in 1957 before returning to Hong Kong and being called to the bar locally in 1959 and was subsequently called to the Inner Bar in 1973. He then took up his first judicial post at the District Court not long after being called to the Inner Bar. It was reported as being 'well known that Mr. Justice Liu did not get on well with former Chief Justice Ti Liang Yang'.[72] Liu JA's links to China were forged through his position as chairman of the Judicial Officers' Association, which had been accused of being a political animal that blurred the distinction between the judiciary and the executive. Liu JA was reportedly described by a 'top lawyer' as 'an intellectual lightweight'.[73]

By contrast, Andrew Li QC, then 49 years old, was described as a specialist in commercial law and had chaired the University and Polytechnic Grants Committee, campaigning for an independent research council. He

---

[68] Wang Hui Ling, 'Tung Names Judicial Commission', *The Straits Times* (Singapore), 12 April 1997.

[69] The Preparatory Committee for the HKSAR and the Selection Committee for the First Government of the HKSAR are referred to in the NPC's Decision of 4 April 1990, note 52 above.

[70] Cliff Buddle, 'A Legal Imperative', *South China Morning Post*, 21 April 1997.

[71] *Ibid.*   [72] *Ibid.*   [73] *Ibid.*

had also served on the Judicial Service Commission. He was appointed to the Executive Council in 1992, at the same time as Tung Chee Hwa, and was regarded as 'an excellent lawyer' who would have 'the total support of most members of the Bar'.[74] However, two factors that weighed against Andrew Li QC were his lack of judicial experience and the fact that he was a candidate from outside the judiciary with close ties to the executive.

Also in contention was former Chief Justice Sir T. L. Yang, who resigned from the post of Chief Justice to contend for the office of Chief Executive. After his loss to C. H. Tung, he reported that Tung had offered the post back to him.[75] Sir T. L. Yang turned down the offer because the position of Chief Justice was not 'something you could return to', accepting a seat on the post-1997 Executive Council instead.

On 21 May 1997, by a unanimous decision, the JORC recommended Andrew Li QC as the first Chief Justice. The move was hailed as one that would boost confidence in the post-handover era.[76] This was followed by the approval of his appointment by LegCo.[77] The claim that LegCo 'rubber stamped' the appointment of Li CJ was dismissed by Secretary for Justice–elect Elsie Leung, who said that LegCo had a constitutional duty to endorse the candidate for the post of Chief Justice unless the JORC had acted irrationally.[78] It was her view that attempts by LegCo to vet appointees would have the effect of politicising judicial appointments and subjugating the judiciary to the legislature.[79]

As Chief Justice, Li CJ chaired the JORC, which had to consider the other appointees to the CFA. On 24 July 1997, the Provisional Legislative Council endorsed the appointment of the first NPJs of the CFA. The appointments were hailed as 'a good selection', although concern was expressed with the appointment of local NPJs who were no longer residing in Hong Kong.[80]

Reflections in retrospect

The establishment of the CFA was a tumultuous process consumed by politics and negotiations between the Chinese and British governments

---

[74] *Ibid.*   [75] *Ibid.*

[76] Chris Yeung, 'Andrew Li named as Top Judge', *South China Morning Post*, 21 May 1997.

[77] See *Hong Kong Hansard*, 24 May 1997 (Chinese only available from Hong Kong Legislative Council; English translation by University of Pennsylvania Linguistic Data Consortium).

[78] Angela Li, 'Top Judge Choice Wins Full Support', *South China Morning Post*, 25 May 1997.

[79] *Ibid.*

[80] Angel Lau and Priscilla Cheung, 'Judges at Highest Court Approved', *Hong Kong Standard*, 24 July 1997.

as well as the legislature of Hong Kong. It highlighted how much Hong Kong people at that time valued the importance of having distinguished overseas judges sitting on the final court. It also highlighted the mistrust that Hong Kong people felt about China, especially after the events of 4 June 1989. In the end, the shape of the CFA reflected much Chinese thinking, probably more so than British or Hong Kong aspirations for the Court. Having such a stake in its genesis, China surely wanted to see that it succeed after 1997. This may help to explain why Chinese intervention in the judicial processes of Hong Kong has been minimal since 1997.[81]

With the benefit of more than 14 years of hindsight, it is of some interest to reflect on some of the issues raised during the heated debates on the CFA's establishment. The debate over the four-to-one ratio of judges largely died down after the resumption of sovereignty and the commencement of CFA appeal hearings. Indeed, in the early days of the court, the overseas NPJs were subject to criticisms to the effect that they were insufficiently familiar with local circumstances[82]; these criticisms too, would die down. One wonders whether the criticisms would have been more pronounced and persistent had the Court been established with discretion to invite two or more overseas judges to sit in any case.

As a matter of the Court's operations, the four to one ratio has proven effective and workable.[83] Overseas judges are invited to sit for periods of approximately one month, hearing cases in the first two weeks and concentrating on judgment writing in the latter part of their stay, greatly enhancing the Court's efficiency as the imminent departure of the visiting judge prompts speedy decision-making and judgment writing. The Court was able to have two serving English Law Lords and several retired Australian and New Zealand judges on its panel of overseas judges. Had the ratio of overseas judges been greater, there would have been administrative difficulties in arranging the increased number of visits by these eminent and busy jurists, particularly the serving Law Lords.

---

[81] There have only been two NPCSC BL interpretations in relation to litigation. The first was sought by the government in response to the CFA's decision on the right of abode in *Ng Ka Ling* v. *Director of Immigration* (1999) 2 HKCFAR 4. The second was sought by the CFA in the decision concerning state immunity, see *Congo* v. *FG Hemisphere*, note 57 above.

[82] Cliff Buddle, 'Judges Who "Drop In"', *South China Morning Post*, 9 March 2001 and Angela Li, 'Beijing "Fearful of Judicial Activism"', *South China Morning Post*, 21 February 2001.

[83] See further Chapter 11 (Young and Da Roza) in this volume.

The overseas judge amongst four Hong Kong judges is placed in a unique position to influence the outcome of the case. That they rarely write dissenting judgments reflects their consistent contribution to forming the majority viewpoint. But had there been more than one such judge sitting in any case, there probably would be a greater likelihood of dissent or separate opinions from these judges, for example, if two overseas judges from different jurisdictions were unable to form a common view with the other members of the court.[84] The dynamics of the relationship between the permanent judges and the overseas judges might also have been different. For example, there could have been a greater shift to relying upon the overseas judge(s) to write the majority opinion or a shift in the other direction of more dominant decision making by permanent judges to emphasise the importance of having a localised jurisprudence.

The exclusion of the overseas judges from leave hearings and the Rules Committee of the CFA, criticised when the CFA Bill was debated, was a wise decision. Inviting eminent jurists from outside of Hong Kong to sit and hear cases undoubtedly involves some degree of diplomacy, including assurances that the time of such eminent jurists would be well spent on deciding cases of importance. Leave application and rules committee work is drudgery best left for the local judiciary to determine. This has meant that much of the workload of the Court has been born by the permanent judges (including the Chief Justice), as was envisioned by then-Attorney General Jeremy Mathews in LegCo.[85]

Once described as the 'worst situation' in LegCo,[86] the Court has on a number of rare occasions sat with a five to zero ratio – that is, with the Chief Justice, the three permanent judges and a local NPJ. The cases have attracted little attention or criticism, an indication perhaps that the court itself is viewed with sufficient respect locally that even without a judge from another common law jurisdiction, the quality and independence of the court are not in question. This happy state of affairs also owes a great deal to the calibre and self-confidence of local judges and the excellent professional relationships that they developed with overseas judges.

The thought that the court would not be very busy, based on the previous workload of the PC, proved far off the mark. As detailed in other chapters in this volume, the workload of the court significantly increased from that of the PC from the start, and that workload continued along

---

[84] See similar view in Chapter 8 (Thomas) in this volume.
[85] *Hong Kong Hansard*, 26 July 1995, 5949.   [86] *Ibid.*, 5895.

an increasing trend.[87] The increased workload of the court illustrates an improved access to final justice (something that would have been unachievable had the court been located elsewhere, such as Beijing) and, given the slight decreasing trend in the workload of the Court of Appeal in the same period, highlights the confidence litigants have had in the CFA.

Since its establishment, the procedure of the court has undergone few changes. One major change introduced after three years of operation was the 'leapfrog' procedure, which again was the subject of an amendment proposed but rejected when the CFA Bill was debated. Although the procedure has only been used twice, its adoption signalled an evolution along the path of other common law supreme courts (which have a similar procedure) and away from the previous PC appeal channel (which did not).

One issue that was raised during the debates and still lingers is the justification for civil appeals as of right in the tradition of the PC. During the LegCo debates, the proposal to delete this avenue of appeal was rejected in order not to reduce access to the court. However, since the establishment of the court, there has been an increasing amount of grumbling from both Chief Justices and other members of the court that the procedure takes away valuable judicial resources which could be better spent on more worthy issues.[88] It appears likely that the executive will respond favourably to these pleas for reform in the coming years.

---

[87] Chapter 6 (Young and Da Roza) in this volume.
[88] See Chapter 10 (Young, Da Roza, and Ghai) in this volume.

6

Final appeals then and now

SIMON N. M. YOUNG AND ANTONIO DA ROZA

Introduction

Before and after 1997, Hong Kong's economic success can be attributed
to its proximity to China and its robust common law legal system. When
the Judicial Committee of the Privy Council (PC) sat as Hong Kong's
highest appellate court, it kept Hong Kong connected to the rest of
the common law world while ensuring that appeals would be decided
by high-calibre judges who were truly independent of the executive
branch.

The importance of the legal system to Hong Kong's economic success
meant that at its inception, there were concerns about the future quality
of the Court of Final Appeal (CFA): Would the local judiciary be capable
of taking up the duties of a court of final adjudication? Would the CFA be
accorded the same stature that its predecessor had? Would its independence (and the independence of the judiciary in Hong Kong by extension)
be vigorously defended and sufficiently safeguarded? The doubts those
questions represented before and at the time of the handover can be contrasted with the recognition the Hong Kong judiciary has achieved since
1997.[1]

One way to understand the impact of the CFA in Hong Kong is to
compare the current system of final appeals with the previous one. This
chapter examines how the conditions of final justice in Hong Kong have
shifted and developed in the 20-year period that spans the last decade
of appeals to the PC and the first decade of appeals to the CFA. It uses
quantitative data gathered from a statistical study of the jurisprudence
of the two courts to provide a comprehensive description of change and
development.

---

[1] See e.g. the Political and Economic Risk Consultancy business survey (which rated Hong
Kong's judicial system as the best in Asia), Agence France-Presse, 'Hong Kong Has Best Judicial System in Asia: Business Survey' (15 September 2008), accessible at www.abs-cbnnews.
com/world/09/15/08/hong-kong-has-best-judicial-system-asia-business-survey.

The study finds three significant changes in the conditions for final justice. First, in response to the substantial increase in appeal applications (which was inevitable with the establishment of a local final court), the CFA applied jurisdictional measures to control its docket, having the effect of turning away a substantial number of applications. At the same time, it decided 226 per cent more appeals than its predecessor. Second, the change in the system of judges substantially affected the process of decision-making. For example, post-1997, there was a greater diversity of legal opinions emanating from the final court, although dissent remained infrequent. Third, there was a change in how the final court treated public law (i.e. administrative and constitutional law) cases. The CFA paid more attention than the PC to these types of appeals relative to others. This chapter provides empirical evidence of these changes and discusses their possible causes and significance for Hong Kong.

Dealing with an influx of applications

In its design and jurisdiction, the CFA was meant to provide continuity in final appeals after 1997. Continuity, however, did not mean 'business as usual'. One of the challenges immediately confronting the CFA was a significant number of litigants wanting to be heard.

Hearing and deciding more appeals

In the decade preceding 1 July 1997, the PC decided 108 substantive appeals. In the decade following, the CFA decided 244 substantive appeals.[2] These figures reflect the substantial increase in the number of cases going before the final court after 1997. The caseload appears on a year-on-year basis in Figure 6.1.

Ignoring the anomalous rise in decided appeals in 1996 and 1997, likely attributable to the uncertain future of Hong Kong's legal system, the PC decided about seven to ten cases annually in its last decade of Hong Kong appeals. By contrast, the CFA delivered two or three times as many judgments annually in the following decade.

---

[2] A comparison with data available from the Hong Kong judiciary may reflect some discrepancy because of the difference in method of counting: although the judiciary prefers counting by file number, some cases may have more than one file number, and for the purposes of this study, the count of cases for which judgment was printed and published was preferred. When statistics from the judiciary sources are relied upon, they will be noted.

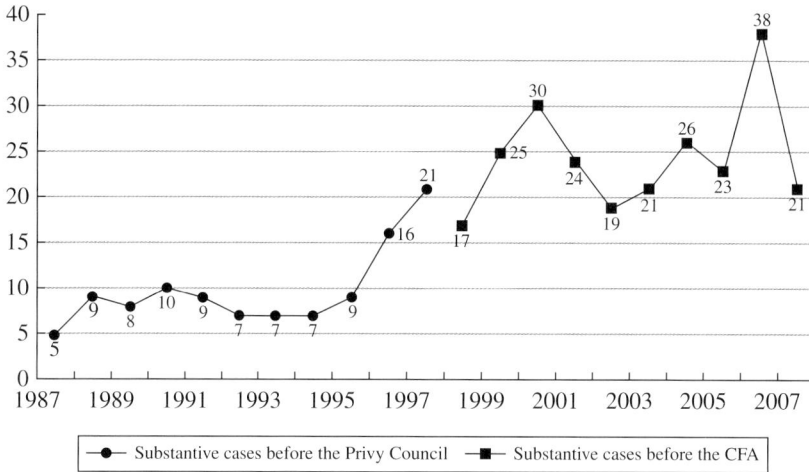

Figure 6.1 Number of substantive cases by year for the Court of Final Appeal (CFA) versus the Privy Council (PC).

The sharp rise in caseload in its early years led the CFA to begin to apply the Rule 7 procedure that allows cases to be filtered out without a hearing. With the deployment of Rule 7 in 2001, a decrease was recorded in the number of leave application hearings (see later discussion), which resulted in a fall in the number of substantive appeals in 2001 and 2002. After 2002, however, another increasing trend began, reaching a high watermark of 38 decided appeals in 2006.[3] The CFA's burgeoning caseload was a foreseeable consequence of relocating the final court to Hong Kong, thereby reducing costs and other barriers to accessing the court.

As with the PC, the CFA grants leave to appeal primarily on points of law of great and general importance. Each CFA decision is read carefully by the legal community because it has the potential to depart or reaffirm previous Hong Kong and English authorities and provides guidance on how the law should be applied. The CFA's more rapid rate of rendering judgments meant that over the same duration of time, the CFA had a greater potential than the PC to develop and change the law in Hong Kong.

---

[3] The figure for 2007 represents appeals only up to 1 July 2007.

Leave filter

The requirement of obtaining leave serves as an important bar by which unmeritorious cases are filtered out, ensuring that the court's resources are not wasted. There are many appeal routes from lower courts to the final appellate court, whether PC or CFA. Not all the data in respect of these routes are readily available;[4] however, when applications for leave are made to the final appellate court itself, the study was able to collect this data on the basis of reported decisions and other accessible data. This enabled a comparison of leave applications being made to the PC and CFA.

The normal procedure for obtaining leave before the PC was broadly similar to obtaining leave in the CFA – an oral hearing before the leave committee consisting of three judges.

The data that follow show that there was a sharp rise in leave applications made to the final court after 1997 and that the CFA granted leave in a significantly smaller proportion of cases than the PC.

Granting leave

From Figure 6.2, it can be seen that the total number of reported leave decisions before the CFA (386) was significantly higher than the number of leave decisions before the PC (149). The most likely reason for this difference was the significantly greater expense of seeking leave from the PC, which required not only Hong Kong legal services but also payment for a London solicitor's firm (known as the London agent) and (typically) English barrister instructed to argue the leave petition.

The proportion of leave applications granted after hearing at the CFA (22 per cent) was slightly lower than that of the PC (26 per cent). The proportion becomes even lower when the cases dismissed by way of the Rule 7 procedure are taken into account.

Rule 7 procedure

One rule under the Hong Kong CFA Rules that has no exact parallel in the Judicial Committee Rules (as they were when applicable to Hong Kong),[5]

---

[4] Data for all leave applications are not readily available; of particular note are cases that are withdrawn by consent and leave granted at the CFA by way of an oral decision without a printed or published judgment. Data made available by the Hong Kong judiciary for the period 2001 to 2008 in respect of the CFA reflect broadly consistent trends.

[5] Rule 52 of The Judicial Committee (General Appellate Jurisdiction) Rules Order 1982, S.I. 1982 No. 1676 empowered the Registrar to refuse to receive a petition on the ground that it disclosed no reasonable cause of appeal, was frivolous, or contained scandalous matter

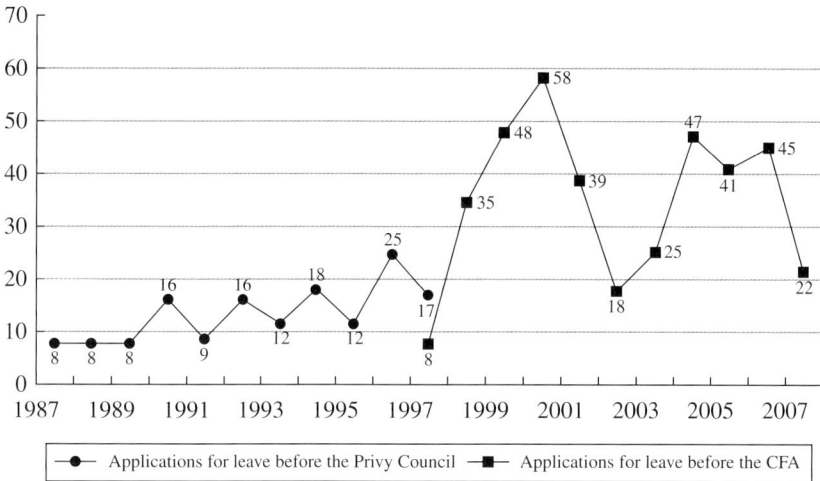

Figure 6.2 Number of leave applications by year for the Privy Council (PC) versus the Court of Final Appeal.

is Rule 7 ('Application that discloses no reasonable grounds, is frivolous or fails to comply with Rules').[6]

Rule 7 allows applications for leave to be dismissed by the CFA Appeal Committee without holding an oral hearing. Although the rule existed in 1997, the procedure was not used until 2001, presumably in response to the rising number of applications. Although Rule 7 decisions are generally not made public, data on the procedure can be found in the Judiciary's Annual Reports.

In the years 2001 to 2008, the CFA dismissed a total of 675 leave applications, representing some 80 per cent of the total number for that period. Rule 7 accounted for 471 of those dismissals or 70 per cent of all dismissed leave applications. Criminal cases tended to be dismissed more often than civil ones. In the first 10-year period, the CFA dismissed

---

or failed to comply with the provisions of Rule 3. However, Rule 52 also provided that the Registrar's decision could be appealed by way of motion to the Judicial Committee. It appears that an oral hearing would normally be held for such appeals; see *Ogilvy* v. *Minister of Legal Affairs (St Lucia)* [2002] UKPC 7; *Ramdeen* v. *The State (Trinidad and Tobago)* [2000] UKPC 10.

[6] Hong Kong Court of Final Appeal Rules (Cap. 484, sub. leg. A), Rule 7. Unlike Rule 52 of the Judicial Committee (General Appellate Jurisdiction), Rules Order 1982, *ibid.*, Rule 7 only empowers the Registrar to summons the applicant to show cause before the Appeal Committee why the application should not be dismissed. Rule 7(2) empowers the Appeal Committee to dismiss the leave application without an oral hearing but may direct such a hearing if the justice of the case requires it.

a total of 723 applications for leave under the Rule 7 and normal leave procedures combined. The percentage of leave applications granted by the CFA (taking into account the Rule 7 procedure) was 10.5 per cent from 1997 to 2007. This is compared with the 26 per cent rate of granting leave in the PC. Hence, although the CFA was dealing with a much larger number of applications for leave than the PC, it granted leave in a proportionately fewer number of cases.

Increasingly more litigants wanting to be heard

One noteworthy trend is the significant rise in leave being sought from the CFA (see Figure 6.2). As noted earlier, the increasing trend of leave sought from the CFA shows a slight upward trend from the years 1987 to 1997 in the PC and then a significantly steeper upward trend in the CFA for the years 1997 to 2000. In 2001, with the deployment of the Rule 7 procedure, the number of leave hearings at the CFA fell for a period of two years and then rose again for two years before levelling out, with a steadily growing number of leave applications dismissed under Rule 7.[7]

The increasing trend of cases before the CFA, however, is not reflected in the caseload trends of the lower courts and must be attributed to the characteristics of the CFA itself.[8] The reasons for the rise in applications to the CFA are not entirely clear. It may reflect an increasing dissatisfaction with decisions obtained in the courts below. But it may also reflect a greater awareness on the part of unrepresented litigants of their right to apply for leave and the ease by which that right can be exercised.[9]

Implications of the Rule 7 practice

With the steep and steady increase in applications for leave, there appears to be a belief in a higher level of access to final justice on the part of applicants than previously existed in respect of the PC despite the proportionately lower number of applications being granted by the CFA (Table 6.1).

---

[7] The trend is reflected in the judiciary's statistics on leave file disposal from 2001 to 2008, which includes leave granted after hearing (150), applications dismissed after hearing or by Rule 7 (675), and cases that were withdrawn by consent (20).

[8] Our data on cases filed in the High Court from 2000 to 2008 do not show a similar increasing trend in the caseload.

[9] Data provided by the Acting Registrar of the CFA in July 2009 shows that in 2008, 65 per cent of all applications disposed of by Rule 7 were made by unrepresented persons.

Table 6.1 *Disposition of leave applications in the Court of Final Appeal, 1997–2007*

Year	1997	1998	1999	2000	2001	2002	2003	2004	2005	2006	2007
Allowed (%)	25	11	21	10	10	13	6	14	13	10	6
Dismissed after hearing (%)	75	89	79	90	44	16	24	44	27	30	10
Dismissed by Rule 7 (%)	0	0	0	0	46	71	70	42	60	60	84

Table 6.2 *Disposition of leave files in the Court of Final Appeal, 2001–2008*

Year	2001	2002	2003	2004	2005	2006	2007	2008
Files granted leave after hearing (%)	12	16	16	26	20	14	19	18
Applications dismissed after hearing (%)	53	15	22	32	23	27	21	12
Applications dismissed by Rule 7 or Rule 7 summons (%)	30	68	62	41	54	56	58	67
Withdrawn (%)	5	1	0	1	3	3	2	3

Table 6.1 shows the CFA decides more than half of its leave applications on the papers without a hearing. This is largely consistent with the statistics provided by the judiciary in respect of disposal of leave files from 2001 to 2008 (Table 6.2).

The increasing reliance on the Rule 7 procedure for dismissing leave applications raises the issue of whether or not greater transparency is required for the procedure. At present, neither reasons are given nor is an oral hearing normally held before applications are decided.[10] In 2003, the Appeal Committee of the CFA found the Rule 7 procedure to be constitutionally compliant with the right to a fair hearing under the Hong Kong Bill of Rights.[11] The availability of oral and public hearings in the lower courts, the further opportunity to 'show cause', albeit in the form of

---

[10] In the years 2001 to 2008, only eight per cent of all Rule 7 matters led to an oral hearing before the Appeal Committee. Forty-four per cent of these oral hearings resulted in leave being granted.

[11] *Chow Shun Yung* v. *Wei Pih and Another* (2003) 6 HKCFAR 299 (CFA AC).

Table 6.3 *Disposition of leave applications in the Privy Council, 1987–1997*

Year	1987	1988	1989	1990	1991	1992	1993	1994	1995	1996	1997
Allowed (%)	25	13	63	38	22	19	25	17	17	24	29
Dismissed (%)	75	87	37	62	78	81	75	83	83	76	71

written submissions, and the procedure to allow members of the public to access file documents were the main reasons for finding compliance with the Bill of Rights.[12]

Greater consistency in the rate of granting leave

Despite its lower rate of granting leave, the CFA has managed to achieve greater consistency in its rate of granting leave. The standard deviation of the CFA's rate of allowing leave applications (see Table 6.1) from 1997 to 2007 was 5.5, and, from 2001 to 2007, when the Rule 7 procedure was applied, it was only 3.1. In comparison, the standard deviation of the PC's rate of allowing leave applications (Table 6.3) from 1987 to 1997 was 13.2.

The greater consistency in determining leave applications is most likely attributable to the CFA's concentration of decision making in a small handful of permanent judges (PJs). In the PC, the composition of the leave committees was largely varied. From 1987 to 1997, the PC assembled 79 distinct panels to decide leave petitions from Hong Kong. Lords Lloyd, Steyn, and Hoffmann sat together most frequently, hearing eight petitions for leave together.

By contrast, because of the smaller pool of PJs at the CFA, there were only 17 distinct panels deciding leave applications in the first decade. From 1997 to 2000, 66 of 108 leave hearings before the CFA were heard by the panel consisting of Litton, Ching, and Bokhary PJJ, and from 2000 to 2007, 158 leave hearings were heard by the panel consisting of Bokhary, Chan, and Ribeiro PJJ. The panel consisting of the Chief Justice and Bokhary and Chan PJJ heard 53 leave hearings in this period.

Achieving greater efficiency

Despite a substantial and increasing number of applications for leave, the CFA has maintained a high level of efficiency in its decision-making role.

---

[12] *Ibid.*, [38]–[39].

Table 6.4 *Waiting time from the issuance of notice to hearing by the Court of Final Appeal, 1997–2007*

	Overall average (2000–07)	1997	1998	1999	2000	2001	2002	2003	2004	2005	2006	2007*
Civil cases (days)	43.4	N/A	N/A	44	32	32	52	46	45	62	38	40
Criminal cases (days)	41.6	N/A	N/A	37	40	36	40	46	44	49	46	37

* Counting the whole year.
N/A = not applicable.

Table 6.5 *Number of days of hearing before the Privy Council (for Hong Kong cases), 1987–1997*

	1 day	2 days	3 days	4 days	5 days	7 days	9 days	11 days	12 days
Cases	45	34	18	6	1	1	1	1	1

The CFA's efficiency exceeds that seen with the Hong Kong appeals to the PC; however, one should bear in mind in making this comparison that the PC heard appeals from many jurisdictions and had a correspondingly greater judicial capacity to hear such appeals.

Table 6.4 shows how well the CFA has maintained an average waiting time of less than 1.5 months from issuance of notice to the actual hearing date.[13]

As for the time spent hearing appeals, the modal number of hearing days for both final courts was one day, but for the PC, two days was almost as likely (Tables 6.5 and 6.6).

By contrast, more than half of the CFA substantive appeals were heard within one day hearings, leading to a lower average: the average time for hearing at the PC being 2.19 days, but before the CFA, the average was 1.91 days.

---

[13] Unfortunately, corresponding data for the PC were not available.

Table 6.6 *Number of days of hearing before the Court of Final Appeal,*
1997–2007

	1 day	2 days	3 days	4 days	5 days	6 days	10 days	11 days
Cases	138	48	28	16	8	2	2	1

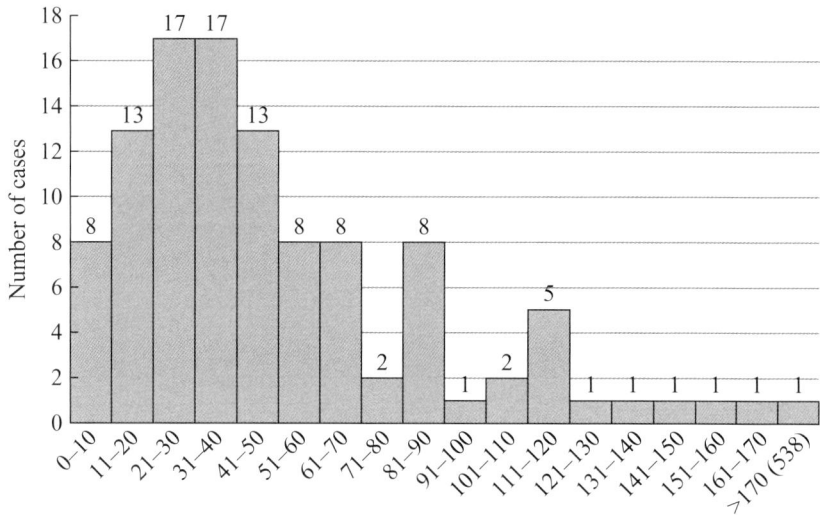

Number of days to render judgment by the Privy Council, 1987–1997

Figure 6.3 Number of days to render judgment by the Privy Council (PC) (for Hong Kong cases) from 1987–1997.

A more striking contrast may be seen in respect to the time taken to deliver judgments. There is a substantial difference in the time taken to render judgment. In the PC, the mean was 53 days, skewed considerably by one case that took 538 days, but the normal range was between zero and 200 days (Figure 6.3).

A modal analysis showed that 33 days was the highest repeated number of days taken to deliver judgment, and the range with the highest number of cases was 30 to 39 days.

The mathematical mean of the CFA was 24 days, again, an average skewed by one case that took 262 days and five cases in the 100- to 150-day range; the normal range was between zero and 150 days (see Figure 6.4).

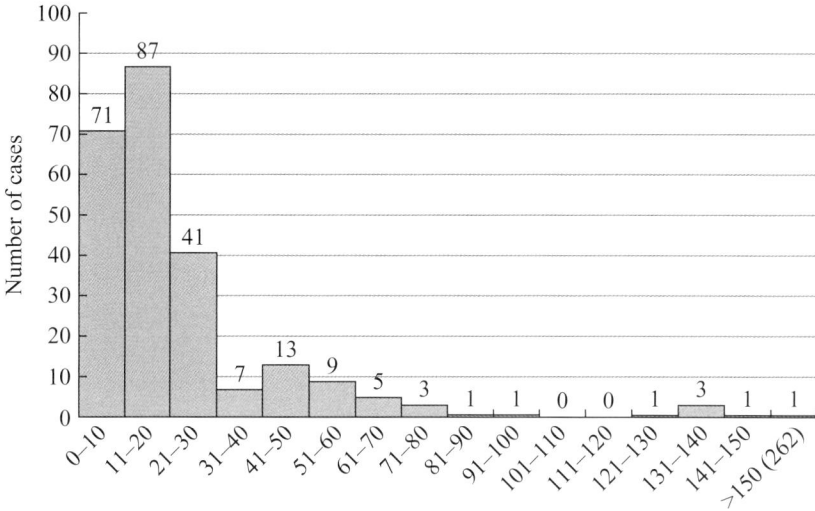

Number of days to render judgment by the CFA, 1997–2007

Figure 6.4 Number of days to render judgment by the Court of Final Appeal (CFA) from 1997–2007.

However, the modal number of days to deliver judgment was only seven at the CFA, and the modal range was 11 to 20 days. It is clear that the CFA took considerably less, almost only half, the time it took the PC to deliver judgment. The efficiency was achieved even with an increased multiplicity of judgments and longer judgments (see later discussion).

One possible explanation for the expeditious judgments in the CFA is the use of target times by the judiciary for the management of its caseload (as is reflected in the Judiciary's annual reports). More importantly, however, the presence of the visiting judges may necessitate such efficiency – the visiting judges might typically be in Hong Kong for only two weeks, during which time hearings must take place. Although the proportion of separate judgments has increased, the majority of appeals before the CFA still led to a single judgment from the court, necessitating judgments to be written before the visiting judge departs as a matter of convenience for the facilitation of discussion and circulation of draft judgments in addition to the visiting judge's access to the case materials.[14]

---

[14] See Sir Anthony Mason, 'Reflections of an Itinerant Judge in the Asia-Pacific Region' (2000) 28 *International Journal of Legal Information* 311, 318 and Simon N. M. Young,

Although the visiting judge phenomenon may explain fast judgments, it is argued that the overall efficiency of the CFA largely results as a consequence of the court's strict exercise of control over its jurisdiction. Limiting the number of cases admitted to appeal helps to ensure that those cases that are admitted are heard and disposed of as soon as possible. As the saying goes, 'justice delayed is justice denied', and so the efficiency of the CFA is one of its applauded achievements. It also serves as an example for all the other courts and tribunals in Hong Kong. Having achieved and sustained this standard of efficiency at the CFA, it is worth asking, however, whether there is room to relax the CFA's controls over its jurisdictions to enable more cases to be heard without compromising efficiency too greatly but with a net benefit for final justice.

New system of final judges

Having considered how localizing the final court has affected caseload and efficiency, we turn to a consideration of the relationship between the system of judges and the court's decision-making function.

Permanent judges bearing the brunt of judicial work

The establishment and composition of the CFA in Hong Kong substantially narrowed the pool of judges available to hear final appeals. The intention was to invest the power of adjudication within a core team of PJs. Tables 6.7 and 6.8, respectively, show the frequency of involvement by individual judges in the PC and CFA cases. One readily observes in Table 6.8 the concentration of involvement by the Chief Justice and other PJs on the CFA. Non-permanent judge (NPJ) Sir Anthony Mason stands out by his exceptionally greater involvement (79 appeals, i.e. 40 more than the NPJ hearing the second greatest number of cases). The impact of concentrating decision making within a smaller group of judges is also reflected in the frequency of authorship of majority judgments by individual judges.

The same high degree of concentration of cases being heard by a small number of judges is not seen with the PC (Table 6.7). The number of cases heard by Law Lords of the PC is more evenly distributed.

'The Hong Kong Multinational Judge in Criminal Appeals' (2008) 26 *Law in Context* 130, 137.

Table 6.7 *Number of Hong Kong cases heard by the judges of the Privy Council*

Law Lord	Cases heard	Majority judgments
Goff	39	7
Jauncey	31	7
Bridge	31	5
Keith	29	5
Ackner	29	8
Oliver	28	5
Browne-Wilkinson	28	8
Lloyd	25	6
Griffiths	23	7
Templeman	22	6
Steyn	22	1
Hoffmann	22	6
Slynn	21	6
Mustill	20	6
Lowry	18	3
Nicholls	16	3
Brandon	14	2
Woolf	10	4
Nolan	10	2
Hope	10	1
Hutton	9	2
Roskill	7	2
Slade	7	1
Clyde	7	1
Cooke	6	1
Stephenson	4	0
Elwyn-Jones	3	0
May	3	2
Mackay	2	0
Brightman	2	0
Eveleigh	2	0
Fraser	2	0
Kerr	2	0
Eichelbaum	2	0
Hardie Boys	2	0
Gibson	2	0

(*cont.*)

Table 6.7 (cont.)

Law Lord	Cases heard	Majority judgments
Megarry	1	0
McMullin	1	0
Hailsham	1	0
Bisson	1	0
Telford Georges	1	0
Casey	1	1
Lane	1	0
Balcombe	1	0

Writing duties at the PC were generally evenly spread over the authoring judges, with a range of one to eight judgments per judge and a modal number of judgments at six, although clearly evident was a division between judges who wrote fewer judgments (i.e. one or two) and those who wrote more (e.g. six to eight).

This contrasts sharply with judgment writing at the CFA, attributable to the combination of the small pool of permanently appointed judges and the relatively larger pool of non-local judges, with a high concentration of the judgments being written by the Chief Justice and PJs but a much lower number of judgments written by the NPJs, with the exception being Sir Anthony Mason NPJ.

Changing tendencies in judgment writing

The historical role of the PC, to advise the king (or queen) of England, gave rise to a tradition that the PC would only give a single judgment in respect of any appeal heard by its judicial committee.[15] This judgment constituted the advice given to the king, who would give effect to it by an Order in Council. The tradition was abolished in 1966, allowing for dissenting judgments in the PC, but the practice of the Judicial Committee was such that often only a single judgment continued to be given.[16] This tradition, however, was not carried on by the CFA.

[15] See Chapter 4 (Jones) in this volume.
[16] See David B. Swinfen, *Imperial Appeal: the Debate on the Appeal to the Privy Council, 1833–1986* (Manchester: Manchester University Press, 1987) ch. 8.

Table 6.8 *Number of cases heard by the judges of the Court of Final Appeal*

Justice	Cases heard	Majority judgments	Concurring judgments
Bokhary PJ	231	55 (6 joint)	46 (3 joint)
Chan PJ	182	33 (10 joint)	16 (3 joint)
Li CJ	157	37 (8 joint)	6
Ribeiro PJ	154	36 (8 joint)	8
Litton PJ/NPJ	89	26 (2 joint)	23
Mason NPJ (Au)	79	22 (5 joint)	7
Ching PJ	52	8	5
Millett NPJ (UK)	39	9 (1 joint)	4
Nazareth NPJ	36	4 (1 joint)	2
Hoffmann NPJ (UK)	27	9	5
Mortimer NPJ	26	3 (1 joint)	3
Scott NPJ (UK)	17	6 (1 joint)	2
Cooke NPJ (NZ)	16	2	2
Brennan NPJ (Au)	16	4 (1 joint)	1
Power NPJ	15	3	1
Silke NPJ	15	3	2
Nicholls NPJ (UK)	10	2	0
Richardson NPJ (NZ)	10	1	1
Fuad NPJ	8	1	0
Eichelbaum NPJ (NZ)	8	2	0
Woolf NPJ (UK)	7	1	0
Clough NPJ	6	1	0
Huggins NPJ	4	1	1
Roberts NPJ	4	0	0
Cons NPJ	4	1	1
Dawson NPJ (Au)	4	0	1
McHugh NPJ (Au)	3	1	0
Somers NPJ (NZ)	1	0	0

The CFA is truly a supreme court in that it is not bound by the decisions of any court, including itself.[17] Although in theory this was also true of the PC, the common presence of Law Lords in both the PC and the House of Lords ensured the dominance of English law. This explains why in the PC cases from Hong Kong considered in this study, the PC expressly

---

[17] Explained in *A Solicitor* v. *Law Society of Hong Kong* (2008) 11 HKCFAR 117.

Table 6.9 *Comparison of the proportion of cases with one judgment and two or more judgments*

Number of cases with	1 judgment	2 judgments	3 judgments	4 judgments	5 judgments
Privy Council	100	8	0	0	0
Court of Final Appeal	147	62	20	9	6

departed from English case law on only two occasions and never overruled itself.[18] The CFA, on the other hand, has shown a greater willingness to depart from English authorities, including authorities from the House of Lords.[19] There is now a greater presence of local Hong Kong counsel appearing before the courts. This influence together with the influence of non-English visiting NPJs contribute to the changes described more fully below in the final court's decision-making function.

More diversity of legal opinions

Of the 108 substantive PC appeals examined in our study, 100 spoke in a single judgment, and eight had a dissenting judgment. By contrast, of the 244 CFA cases studied, one finds 90 separate concurring judgments and 13 dissenting judgments. Table 6.9 shows the increased plurality of judgments given in individual cases after 1997.

---

[18] The first case was *Owners of Cargo on Board the "K.H. Enterprise"* v. *Owners of the Ship or Vessel "Pioneer Container"* [1994] 2 HKLR 134; [1994] 2 AC 324; [1994] 3 WLR 1, departing from *Johnson Matthey* v. *Constantine Terminals* [1976] 2 Lloyd's Rep 215. Note, however, that the PC held that English law would follow the same departure. The second case was *Red Sea Insurance Company Ltd* v. *Buoygues S.A. and 22 Others* [1995] 1 HKLR 224; [1995] 1 AC 190; [1994] 3 WLR 926, not following *The Adhiguna Meranti* [1998] 1 Lloyd's Rep 384 (CA).

[19] See *Tang Siu Man* v. *HKSAR* (1997–1998) 1 HKCFAR 107, not following *R* v. *Vye* [1993] 1 WLR 471 (HL); *Kwan Siu Man* v. *Yaacov Ozer* (1997–1998) 1 HKCFAR 343; *The Bank of East Asia Ltd* v. *Tsien Wui Marble Factory Ltd and Others* (1999) 2 HKCFAR 349, not following *Murphy* v. *Brentwood District Council* [1991] 1 AC 398; *HKSAR* v. *Wong Sau Ming* (2003) 6 HKCFAR 135, not following *R* v. *Edwards (John)* [1991] 1 WLR 207); *Lee Fuk Hing* v. *HKSAR* (2004) 7 HKCFAR 600, not following *R* v. *Ryan* (1966) 50 Cr App R 144); *Tam Kin Hon* v. *HKSAR* (2006) 9 HKCFAR 206, not following *R* v. *Watson and Others* [1988] 1 QB 690 and *R* v. *Atlan* [2004] EWCA Crim 1798. See also Chapter 13 (Mason) in this volume.

Before the PC, 92.6 per cent of cases had only one judgment, with the remaining 7.4 per cent representing cases in which there were two judgments. There were no separate concurring judgments in the PC cases. By contrast, only in 60.3 per cent of the substantive appeals before the CFA was a single judgment delivered – although still a majority, the proportion of single opinions being given by the final appellate court has fallen significantly. A further 25.4 per cent of substantive appeals before the CFA gave rise to two judgments; in 8.2 per cent of cases, there were three judgments. In 3.7 per cent of the cases, there were four judgments, and in 2.5 per cent of the cases, all five members of the court wrote separate judgments.

Length of judgments and the rise in separate opinions

With more judgments being written per case, naturally the length of written decisions as measured by word count has grown. The average number of words per case from the PC was 4,758 words, an average that drops slightly to 4,436 words when the average per judgment instead of per case is taken. The average number of words written per case before the CFA, however, was 7,673 words, an average that drops to 4,716, closer to the PC average, when the average is taken per judgment. Thus, the CFA appears to be producing an average of almost two judgments' worth of words in each substantive appeal.

Falling dissent

The significant increase in separate judgments can be contrasted with the proportion of judgments that contain dissent. In the PC, 7.3 per cent of the cases had a dissenting judgment. In absolute terms, there has been more dissent in the CFA, but in relative terms, the overall proportion of dissent (based on the total number of cases) has fallen to 5.3 per cent in the CFA. Thus, although more separate views are being expressed, disagreement on the outcome of cases is less so in the CFA than in the PC. For a young final court in a new constitutional order, this should be considered a virtue. Different judicial voices are being expressed, a phenomenon that can contribute to the long-term development of the law, but the results of cases have been unequivocally certain, and a clear majority view of the law is stated.

The pool of judges who dissented was also considerably larger in the PC: Lords Brandon and Bisson, Bridge and Jauncey, Goff and Hoffmann, Goff and Nicholls, and Mustill and Slynn, all jointly dissented in five cases.

Lords Hoffmann and Nicholls each respectively dissented in two further cases.

By contrast, in the CFA, the majority of dissenting judgments are attributable to Bokhary PJ (nine dissenting judgments). Litton NPJ dissented twice (once as a PJ and once after he became a local NPJ),[20] and Ribeiro PJ, Cooke NPJ and Nicholls NPJ dissented once each, the latter two being the only two visiting NPJs who have dissented in the first decade.[21] Lord Nicholls wrote his own separate dissenting opinion but also agreed with Bokhary PJ's dissenting opinion.[22] In regards to Lord Cooke's dissent,[23] Bokhary PJ agreed with Lord Cooke's judgment without writing his own.

Joint judgments

Another distinct phenomenon that may be observed in the CFA is that of joint judgments, when a single judgment is attributed to two judges as co-authors or when a judgment is written in two or more parts dealing with separate issues but must be read together as a single judgment. Previously, such judgments were only seen in PC dissents, but in the CFA, joint judgments have become common in majority and concurring judgments and less so with dissenting opinions. This phenomenon is perhaps explained by a greater cooperation and division of labour in judgment writing that comes with a heavy and ever-increasing caseload. It may also be explained by the increased complexity of cases, particularly those in the administrative and constitutional law areas.

Increased reversals?

In terms of disposal of appeals, the PC dismissed 65 substantive appeals from 1987 to 1997 and allowed 43. The CFA dismissed 112 substantive appeals from 1997 to 2007 but allowed 132. *Prima facie*, the CFA appears to allow a significantly higher number of substantive appeals (54 per cent) compared with the PC (38 per cent). This high proportion of appeals allowed must, however, be looked at in the context of the earlier discussion in respect of leave applications. The 132 appeals allowed by the CFA must be considered in the context of the 301 leave applications dismissed by the

[20] *Bewise Motors Co. Ltd* v. *Hoi Kong Container Services Ltd* (1998) 1 HKCFAR 256 and *Polyset Ltd* v. *Panhandat Ltd* (2002) 5 HKCFAR 234, respectively.
[21] See further Chapter 12 (Cottrell and Ghai) in this volume.
[22] *The Bank of East Asia Ltd* v. *Tsien Wui Marble Factory Ltd and Others* (1999) 2 HKCFAR 349.
[23] *Next Magazine Publishing Ltd and Others* v. *Ma Ching Fat* (2003) 6 HKCFAR 63.

CFA at the leave stage and the 723 leave applications dismissed by way of the Rule 7 procedure. Taking the leave hurdle into account, the odds of an appeal succeeding at the CFA may be expressed as slightly more than one in ten, or 10.4 per cent. Although only 42 appeals were finally allowed by the PC, the odds of those appeals being allowed were in fact almost one in five, or 19 per cent, when taking into consideration the petitions for leave dismissed.

Having regard to the entire filtering process that appeals must undergo before reaching the full court of the CFA, the higher proportion of substantive appeals allowed is not surprising. By contrast, some of the barriers to the PC, such as the cost and difficulties of overcoming geographical accessibility and case management and administration from Hong Kong to London, may have contributed to the filtering out of cases with less chance of success on appeal.

Government wins and losses

Given public concerns about the judiciary's independence even before the CFA's creation and during such controversies as the right of abode cases from 1999 to 2001,[24] the success of the government as litigant before the final court is important to track. Between 1987 and 1997, government parties won 34 cases and lost 19 cases before the PC. By contrast, between 1997 and 2007, the government won 55 cases but lost 68 cases before the CFA.

The government appears to have won proportionately more cases before the PC than the CFA, but these figures must be put in proper perspective that takes into consideration the previous discussion of the leave application filtering process. Data are unavailable at this time in respect to the government's win–loss record in cases denied leave to appeal.

Giving greater attention to public law cases

Various indicators suggest that the CFA, compared with the PC, has given more attention and deliberation to constitutional and administrative law ('public law') cases, more so than other types of cases, particularly criminal law cases. This is another important change in the conditions for final justice since 1997.

---

[24] See further Chapter 14 (Chen and Lo) in this volume.

Table 6.10 *Number and proportion of substantive cases by subject, 1987–2007*

	Privy Council cases, n (%)	Court of Final Appeal cases, n (%)
Constitutional law	5 (4.6)	45 (18)
Administrative law	22 (20)	24 (9.8)
Criminal law and procedure	28 (26)	68 (28)
Civil procedure	6 (5.6)	19 (7.8)
Commercial law	19 (18)	22 (9)
Land law	14 (13)	28 (11)
Tort law	5 (4.6)	15 (6.1)
Miscellaneous	9 (8.3)	23 (9.4)
Total	108 (100)	244 (100)

Types of cases

The types of cases heard by the final appellate courts can be broken down by subject classifications. For the purposes of this study, substantive cases were divided into eight mutually exclusive subject classifications: constitutional law, administrative law, criminal law and procedure, civil procedure, commercial law, land law, tort law, and miscellaneous cases.[25] The proportions of substantive cases by subject classifications are shown in Table 6.10.

---

[25] Constitutional law cases were defined as any case that concerned the BL or the Hong Kong Bill of Rights Ordinance (BORO). Administrative law cases were cases that involved an appeal or review of governmental action that did not involve BL or BORO issues; examples include taxation cases and environmental law cases. Criminal law and procedure cases were all appeals in criminal matters that did not involve BL or BORO issues. Civil procedure cases included all civil cases concerning points of evidence, procedure, and process in non-administrative law proceedings. Again, cases that were predominantly concerned with BL or BORO issues were excluded. Commercial law cases included non-land transactional cases, including contract disputes and arbitration issues. Non-land equity cases fell under this category, but company law and insolvency cases were excluded. Land law cases included all conveyancing and landlord and tenant cases, as well as equity cases that concerned interests in land. Tort law cases included all cases dealing with torts, including defamation. Miscellaneous cases collected together all cases that did not fall within any of the other categories, including non-transactional company law cases, wills and probate, conflicts of law, family law, and so on.

Although the CFA dealt with a considerably lower proportion of administrative law cases (9.8 per cent) than the PC (20 per cent), one must take note of the CFA's new constitutional law jurisdiction, which accounted for 18 per cent of its substantive caseload from 1997 to 2007 as opposed to only 4.6 per cent in the PC. Thus, there has been a small increase in the proportion of public law cases from 25 per cent before the PC to 28 per cent before the CFA. The proportion of criminal law and procedure cases rose slightly from 26 per cent in the PC to 28 per cent before the CFA.[26]

Civil procedure cases also increased slightly from 5.6 per cent before the PC to 7.8 per cent in the CFA. This may possibly be attributed to better access, leading to litigants being more prepared to take procedural issues to final appeal. It remains to be seen whether or not the enhanced requirements for civil appeals to the Court of Appeal (particularly in respect of interlocutory appeals) under the 2009 civil justice reforms will eventually manifest as a reduction of this type of case in the CFA's caseload.

The proportion of commercial law cases fell dramatically, from 18 per cent before the PC to only 9 per cent in the CFA. This may be attributable to the shift in the local economy from secondary to tertiary industries and to the doubling of the amount threshold to HK$1 million for appeals as of right.[27] Whereas land law cases fell slightly from 13 per cent in the PC to 11 per cent before the CFA, the proportion of tort law cases increased slightly from the PC to the CFA at 4.6 per cent and 6.2 per cent, respectively.

Changing character of 'public law' cases

As noted earlier, the public law caseload of the final court has increased slightly from the PC to the CFA. The increase in cases that incorporate a constitutional law point represents the single biggest change. Although the proportion of administrative law cases has fallen, a new breed of constitutional law cases involving issues concerning the BL has arisen as

---

[26] Note that a substantial number of criminal cases are counted within the constitutional law category. The criminal law and procedure category does not count criminal appeals that predominantly involve a constitutional issue.

[27] The CFA has interpreted this avenue of appeal strictly to include only liquidated sums (and not unliquidated damages) or, in the case of disputes concerning property or civil rights, clearly quantifiable claims that have immediate financial impact in the quantified amount. For discussion, see Chapter 7 (Da Roza) in this volume and Peter So, 'Final Appeal Criteria for Civil Appeals involving Damages Claims' [2009] 7 *Hong Kong Lawyer* 59.

part of an increasing trend of public law litigation.[28] Taking into account criminal appeals, there was a 5.2 per cent increase in appeals involving the government.

Although there has been an increase in public law cases generally, the proportion of appeals from judicial reviews has fallen slightly. Before the PC, 23 of the 27 constitutional and administrative law cases were civil cases involving government departments or regulatory or statutory bodies, that is, appeals arising out of a judicial review. The 23 cases accounted for 20.9 per cent of all substantive appeals heard by the PC. By contrast, before the CFA, of the 69 public law cases, 47 were civil cases that involved government departments or regulatory or statutory bodies. The total number of appeals to the CFA from judicial review increased in absolute terms but only accounted for 19.3 per cent of all substantive appeals heard by the CFA.

Special treatment of public law cases

A number of indicators suggest that the CFA, compared with the PC, gave special treatment and attention to its public law cases by reference to the time spent hearing such cases, the time spent deliberating before delivery of reasons for judgment, the involvement of NPJs in judgment writing, and the number and length of judgments.

More 'air time' for public law litigants

Whereas the mean number of hearing days for constitutional and administrative law cases before the PC was 2.22 days, the mean for the CFA was slightly higher at 2.64.[29] Although both courts spent more time on average hearing public law cases (compared with their respective mean hearing time for all cases), the differential is noticeably greater for the CFA.[30] In other words, litigants in public law cases before the CFA, compared with corresponding figures for the PC, have been given considerably more 'air time' relative to the average litigants appearing in the final court.

---

[28] Hong Kong Government Press Release, *CJ's Speech at Conference on Effective Judicial Review: A Cornerstone of Good Governance* (10 December 2008), accessible at www.info. gov.hk/gia/general/200812/10/P200812100125.htm. See also Chapter 14 (Chen and Lo) in this volume.

[29] However, the modal numbers of hearings days before the PC and CFA were two and one, respectively.

[30] The differential for the CFA being 0.73 days and only 0.03 days for the PC.

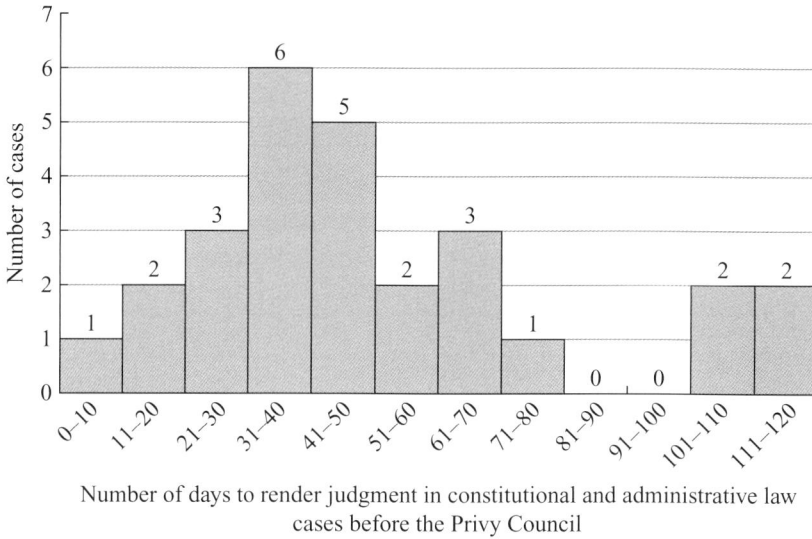

Number of days to render judgment in constitutional and administrative law cases before the Privy Council

Figure 6.5 Number of days to render reasons in constitutional and administrative law cases in the Privy Council (PC) from 1987–1997.

Taking relatively more time to deliberate public law issues

The contrast is furthered by the number of days taken to render the reasons for judgment (Figures 6.5 and 6.6). For the PC, the mean for public law cases was 51 days compared with the 53 days for the overall mean in the PC. For the CFA, however, the mean for public law cases was 31 days in contrast to its general mean of 24 days. These averages were not skewed significantly by outlying statistics, although for both courts, there was a small cluster of cases at the far extreme.

The CFA appears to have had greater difficulty adhering to its efficient standards when it comes to delivering reasons for judgment in public law cases. The CFA judges are taking more time to mull over and deliberate the issues, which often involve questions of first impression having potentially significant consequences for Hong Kong society.

Writing more public law

We have said that the CFA produced relatively more and longer judgments than the PC, and this is no less true with public law cases. In respect of public law cases in the CFA, the mean number of words written per case was 10,018, in sharp contrast with only 5,044 per case before the PC. The mean number of words *per judgment* for public law cases before the CFA

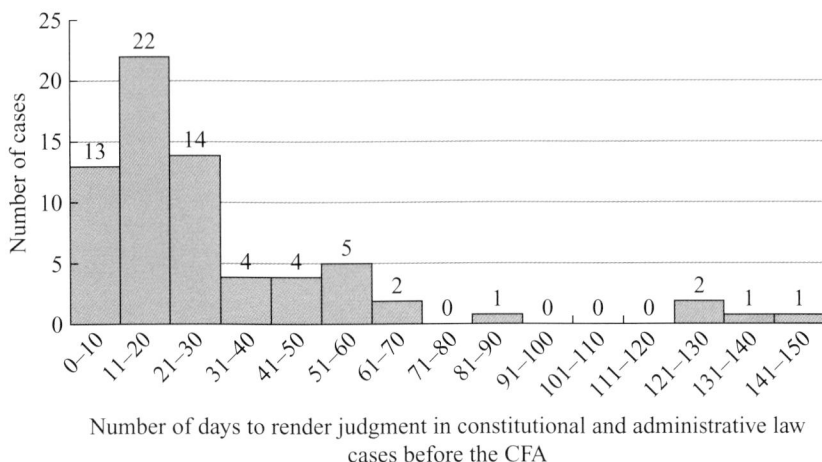

Number of days to render judgment in constitutional and administrative law cases before the CFA

Figure 6.6 Number of days to render reasons in constitutional and administrative law cases in the Court of Final Appeal (CFA) from 1997–2007.

was 5,530, contrasted with the 4,697 mean words per judgment in the PC. This again illustrates the increased word count before the CFA largely being taken up by the additional judgments that are being written. But when compared with the CFA's per judgment average of 4,716, it is clear that the CFA is writing relatively more when it comes to public law cases.

Authorship of majority and dissenting opinions in public law

Although the pool of authors and spread of judgment writing duties was generally even in the PC, the same observation of concentration of judgment writing in the PJs of the CFA can be observed in the context of public law cases. The visiting NPJs, particularly Sir Anthony Mason NPJ and Lord Millett NPJ, have played a significant role in writing the CFA's public law jurisprudence (Figure 6.7).

The visiting NPJs have either written or co-authored 39.1 per cent of all majority judgments in public law cases before the CFA.

In respect of dissent, there were a total of seven dissents in public law cases before the CFA, six written by Bokhary PJ and one by Ribeiro PJ. This amounted to a relatively high proportion of cases in which there was dissent: 10.1 per cent of public law cases before the CFA had a dissenting opinion, contrasted with 5.3 per cent of cases before the CFA generally. The proportion of dissent was also high in the PC, where 11.1 per cent of the public law cases had at least one dissenting opinion compared with 7.3 per cent of cases before the PC generally.

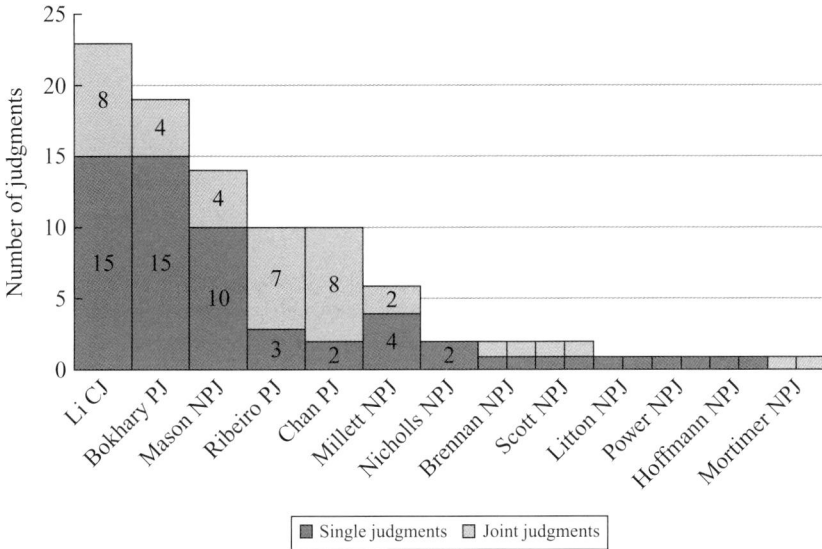

Figure 6.7 Authorship of Court of Final Appeal majority judgments in constitutional and administrative law cases. NPJ = non-permanent judge; PJ = permanent judge.

Disposal of substantive matters in the public law context

The disposal data in public law cases by the two courts does not differ significantly from the general statistics. Before the PC, 63 per cent of public law cases were dismissed, similar to the 60 per cent of all cases being dismissed. In the CFA, 52.2 per cent of public law cases were allowed, similar to the 54 per cent of all substantive appeals being allowed by the CFA.

Although the CFA may be paying more attention to its public law docket, this has not translated into any significantly higher likelihood of winning against the government. The government's win–loss record in public law cases before the two courts is also similar (16 winning cases or 62 per cent before the PC and 32 winning cases or 55 per cent before the CFA), although the government tends to lose more often in the CFA than in the PC.

New constitutional jurisdiction

The CFA's special treatment of public law cases can be largely explained by its new constitutional law jurisdiction. Since 1 July 1997, the final court has had a jurisdiction to interpret Hong Kong's Basic Law (BL) to determine constitutional violations and to devise constitutional remedies when there has been a violation. There is no special avenue of appeal or reference for constitutional questions, but given the novelty and significance of BL issues, these cases often engage the great and general importance limb for granting leave.

In the spirit of *Marbury* v. *Madison*, the CFA has applied its constitutional jurisdiction in a robust manner, recognizing and adhering to its duty to declare invalid (i.e. to strike down) laws and executive actions that are in breach of the BL.[31] To a much more limited extent, the PC had a constitutional jurisdiction insofar as to determine whether the 1991 Hong Kong Bill of Rights Ordinance and Letters Patent had repealed any inconsistent laws. Since 1997, cases that involve the Hong Kong Bill of Rights are also treated by the courts (and by this study) as constitutional cases. Rights provisions in the BL together with those in the Hong Kong Bill of Rights have provided a very robust and comprehensive regime of constitutional protection.[32]

The CFA has recognized that the BL mandates a separation of powers that did not previously exist when Hong Kong was a British colony. However, the BL also states that China's Standing Committee of the National People's Congress (NPCSC) is the final interpreter of the constitution, and the CFA enjoys only delegated authority to interpret those provisions of the BL that are within the high degree of autonomy of Hong Kong. When asked to interpret provisions concerning affairs that are the responsibility of the Central People's Government or concern the relationship between the Central Authorities and Hong Kong, the CFA has a duty to refer the interpretive point to the NPCSC for an interpretation. In upholding Hong Kong's autonomy and judicial independence, the CFA has resisted the few attempts made by the government to have questions referred to the NPCSC.[33]

Under this new constitutional order, it becomes readily apparent why the CFA had taken relatively more time to hear, consider, and deliberate upon public law cases in its first decade. Not only have the BL issues been unique but they have also been of great importance to many people outside the litigation and have at times involved sensitivities between

---

[31] The first constitutional rights case was *Ng Ka Ling and Others* v. *Director of Immigration* (1999) 2 HKCFAR 4.

[32] See Chapter 15 (Young) in this volume.

[33] P. Y. Lo, 'Rethinking Judicial Reference: Barricades at the Gateway?' in H. L. Fu, L. Harris, and S. N. M. Young (eds.), *Interpreting Hong Kong's BL: The Struggle for Coherence* (New York: Palgrave Macmillan, 2007). The CFA made its first Article 158 reference in June 2011 in a case concerning state immunity; see *Democratic Republic of the Congo* v. *FG Hemisphere Associates LLC* (2011) 14 HKCFAR 95 (reference) and 395 (disposition).

the Hong Kong and Central Authorities. The high incidence of multiple judgments (including dissenting ones) is a way for the judges to respond to and reflect the different views that exist on these difficult issues.

There are two other important influencing factors that help to explain the court's behaviour. First, there appears to be a greater awareness of rights with the Hong Kong public generally and amongst litigants specifically. Rights are often invoked in litigation along with a growing body of supportive comparative constitutional law and international human rights law. Proper consideration of comparative and international law is challenging and time consuming. The CFA judges struggle to declare the appropriate legal position for Hong Kong, notwithstanding authorities that may hold a different position for another country.[34]

Second, many have written about the problems of governance that the Hong Kong government has experienced since the 1997 transition.[35] Signs of these problems are plentiful. They range from mass demonstrations in the streets, the resignation of the first Chief Executive, generally low public approval ratings for various government officials, the difficulties of passing legislation in the legislature, the fractured politics of pan-democratic and pro-establishment lawmakers, and frequently criticized public policies and policy-making processes. Most critics attribute the governance problems to the lack of democracy in Hong Kong and to the government's unwillingness to fight for a quicker pace of democratization. In this climate, the courts have become an often used means to try to achieve various political and social goals that litigants perceive are unachievable via the usual political process. Thus, the CFA has been responsive to these litigants, although not necessarily agreeing with their arguments, by providing a full hearing and taking more time than usual to decide and provide (multiple) reasons for their decisions.

Conclusion

After the enactment of the Hong Kong CFA Ordinance[36] in July 1995, very little was known or predictable about the CFA and its future performance. The enactment of Rule 7 indicated that some may have anticipated a heavy caseload, but this did not appear to be of great concern then.

---

[34] See e.g. the CFA's decision not to follow the US Supreme Court's decisions in *Texas* v. *Johnson* 491 US 397 (1989) and *United States* v. *Eichman* 496 US 310 (1990) on flag desecration; see *HKSAR* v. *Ng Kung Siu* (1999) 2 HKCFAR 442.

[35] See e.g. Joseph Y. S. Cheng (ed.), *The July 1 Protest Rally: Interpreting a Historic Event* (Hong Kong: City University Press, 2005) chs. 1, 2, and 7.

[36] Cap. 484.

The preoccupations were more with protecting the court from post-1997 executive or Mainland interference and the decision to allow only one overseas judge to sit in individual cases. We now know that the concerns behind these preoccupations have not (or rarely) materialized.

Rather, as this chapter has revealed, there have been many other more important issues that have confronted the CFA as a result of the changes in the conditions for final justice. In response to the increasing number of leave applications, the CFA took steps to control its docket and maintain its high standards of operational efficiency. This led to many (and an increasing number of) applicants being turned away without being given an oral hearing. Many of them were unrepresented, raising a concern of whether the CFA has turned away meritorious cases that simply were not properly presented because of a lack of legal representation.

The findings that shed light on the CFA's special treatment of public law cases reflect society's many discontents with the government and increased resort to rights litigation. The CFA's response has been to hear these disputes fully and decide them conscientiously. One might debate that given the increased public interest in constitutional litigation that there should be new avenues to bring constitutional questions before the CFA. However, in the early days of a constitution, there is value in having constitutional questions tested first in the lower courts before reaching the final court and to insist on such questions arising only in the context of a contentious dispute rather than being raised in the abstract.

Having established within its first decade certain practices in the treatment of public law cases, there may be a public expectation now that these practices continue, at least for the short to medium term. Given the amount of public interest in such cases, the CFA should begin or continue to track its performance in this area (by reference to quantitative indicators such as those used in this study) to avoid reverting to a practice like that of the PC, which treated these cases like average appeals.

It is now clear that final justice in Hong Kong is no longer a rare opportunity enjoyed only by those who could then afford the cost of accessing the PC in London. But with the increased ease of reaching the final court, there is a reduced likelihood of obtaining a hearing of the full court. Once inside the doors, however, the litigants are greeted with a new set of conditions for final justice that guarantee the same independence, quality, and international influence that characterized the work of the Judicial Committee of the PC.

7

Jurisdiction and procedure

ANTONIO DA ROZA

Introduction

In accordance with the Basic Law (BL),[1] after the resumption of sovereignty by China over Hong Kong in 1997, the power of final adjudication was vested in the Court of Final Appeal (CFA). The role of the CFA being at the apex of the hierarchy of courts in Hong Kong has been described as being similar to that of the Privy Council (PC) under British colonial rule.[2]

The role of a final appellate court is not merely to review decisions of the intermediate appellate court but also to decide points of law of public significance. This role is very much reflected in the CFA's requirements for appeal, particularly at the leave stage. These requirements are used as much to control its docket as they are to ensure the merit of the cases before it. Although much of the jurisdiction and procedure of the CFA is derived from its predecessor, it is more accurate to state that the procedure and jurisdiction of the CFA reflect extensive development from that of the PC, including a number of significant evolutionary changes necessary for local conditions. The evolutionary steps taken by the CFA give rise to the issue of whether it should continue to be thought of as a substitute body for the PC or whether it should be regarded as being in the same league as other supreme courts in common law jurisdictions. As argued in this chapter, the CFA appears to be progressing along this latter evolutionary path.

Gatekeeping

In respect to appeals to the PC, leave applications in civil cases were made to the Court of Appeal of the Supreme Court of Hong Kong or the PC

---

[1] Basic Law, Articles 82 and 158.
[2] *A Solicitor* v. *The Law Society of Hong Kong & Anor* (2003) 6 HKCFAR 570, [28], per Li CJ.

itself. The grounds for appeals could be found in section 2 of the Order in Council regulating appeals from the Supreme Court or Court of Appeal for Hong Kong to His Majesty in Council. Under the Order in Council, an appeal would lie as of right from any final judgment when the matter in dispute amounted to a value of $5,000 or more; this figure would increase over time. An appeal would also lie at the discretion of the Court of Appeal or PC from any judgment involving an issue that ought to be submitted to His Majesty in Council for decision because of its great and general or public importance or otherwise. In criminal cases, there was no appeal as of right, and leave from the PC was always required as a pre-condition.

Appeals as of right

Similar to the pre-handover practice, the right to appeal after 1997 did not extend to a right of final appeal.[3] The sole exception is found under section 22(1)(a) of the Hong Kong Court of Final Appeal Ordinance (HKCFAO),[4] under which appeals may be made as of right from final judgments of the Court of Appeal when

> the matter in dispute on the appeal amounts to or is of the value of $1000000 or more, or where the appeal involves, directly or indirectly, some claim or question to or respecting property or some civil right amounting to or of the value of $1000000 or more.

The wording of this section is based on section 2 of the Order in Council regulating appeals from Hong Kong to the PC before the resumption of sovereignty in 1997.

When a party wishes to access the CFA as of right, a process has been adopted that requires an application for conditional leave from the Court of Appeal or CFA to determine if the section 22(1)(a) criteria have been met.[5] When the parties agree to the entitlement to a final appeal as of right, it is unnecessary to apply for conditional leave; instead, the notice of motion for conditional leave is simply endorsed with the consent of the parties, and the application is dealt with by a single judge of the Court of Appeal without the need to fix a date for hearing.[6]

Figure 7.1 illustrates the significant proportion of cases that reach the CFA as of right. In most years from 2001 to 2010, appeals as of right

---

[3] *Sun Honest Development Ltd* v. *Appeal Tribunal (Buildings) & Anor* (2009) 12 HKCFAR 68.
[4] Cap. 484.   [5] HKCFAO, sections 23(3) and 25.
[6] Practice Direction 2.1, 'Civil Appeals to the Court of Final Appeal', 15 Feb 1998, accessible at legalref.judiciary.gov.hk/lrs/common/pd/pdcontent.jsp?pdn=PD2.1.htm&lang=EN.

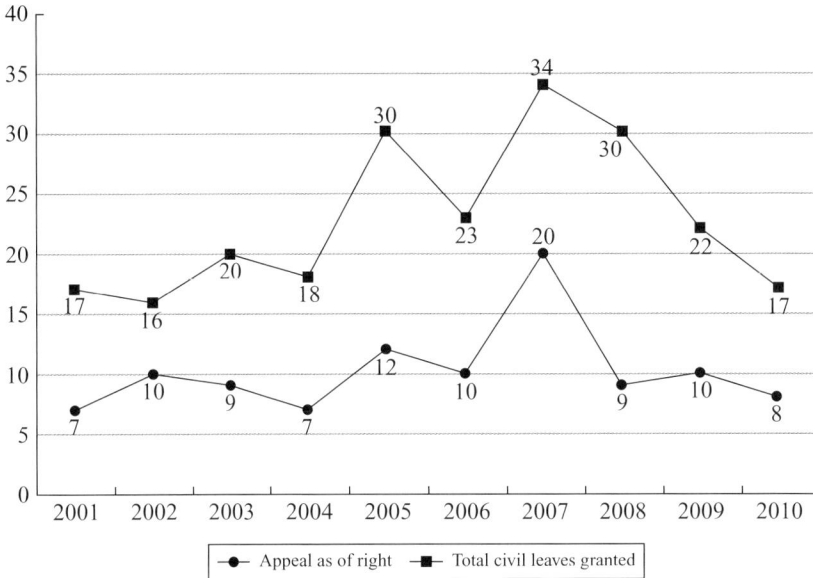

Figure 7.1   Appeals as of right and total civil leaves, 2001–2010.

accounted for close to half of the CFA civil appeals heard. Ribeiro PJ has stated that '[i]t is exceptional for courts of final appeal to entertain appeals as of right and we do not consider that there should be any enlargement to the existing classes of cases falling within that category'.[7] This message was repeated in *Sun Honest Development Ltd* v. *Appeal Tribunal (Buildings)*,[8] in which he noted that the considerations of the need for consistency at the PC in respect to its widespread and disparate jurisdiction, which led to a policy of conferring a right to approach the final appellate court, no longer applied to Hong Kong. Noting (as Li CJ did[9]) the increase in the number of applications to the CFA and the fact that 'an appeal to the [CFA] as of right is in principle oppressive to the party who has won in the Court of Appeal where the further appeal is without substance'. Ribeiro PJ

[7] *Bill Chao Keh Lung* v. *Don Xia* (2004) 7 HKCFAR 260, [8] (CFA AC).
[8] *Sun Honest Development Ltd* [13].
[9] See 'The Chief Justice's Address at the Opening of the Legal Year', 11 January 1999, accessible at www.judiciary.gov.hk/en/other_info/speeches/legal_yr_cj99.htm; 'The Chief Justice's Address at the Opening of the Legal Year', 15 January 2001, accessible at www.judiciary. gov.hk/en/other_info/speeches/legal_yr_cj01.htm; and Chapter 10 (Young, Da Roza, and Ghai) in this volume.

found that these considerations strongly favoured a narrow construction of the provisions on appeals as of right.[10]

Accordingly, the court has continued to deploy the 'applications test' previously used by the PC in deciding whether or not an order of the Court of Appeal is a final or interlocutory order,[11] and when an order is only interlocutory, leave will be refused. The amount in section 22(1)(a) has been held to (1) refer to the amount liable by a respondent to a claimant, not the total potential liability;[12] (2) include only liquidated claims;[13] and (3) exclude costs.[14] All of these measures have been adopted by the CFA to serve the aim of narrowing the ambit of appeals as of right.

However, the narrowing of this right to appeal has not been without controversy. Although it is well established that the first limb, 'where the matter in dispute on the appeal amounts to or is of the value of $1000000 or more', has been consistently confined to claims for liquidated sums of money, the second limb, concerning 'some claim or question to or respecting property or some civil right' has been the subject of recent jurisprudence.

In *China Field Ltd* v. *Appeal Tribunal (Buildings)(No 1)*,[15] it was argued that this second limb concerned the value of the property, not the value of the claim or question, following the PC case of *Meghji Lakhamshi & Brothers* v. *Furniture Workshop*.[16] The CFA, however, declined to follow this approach, finding that the language of the statute was focused on the value of the claim, not on the property or right that has some connection to the claim. Thus, the requirement under the second limb was that on the evidence, the relevant value must be quantifiable as $1 million or more, and the court's order in disposing of the appeal would immediately confer or impose a financial benefit or detriment in the quantified amount.

---

[10] *Sun Honest Development Ltd*, [17].

[11] *B+B Construction Ltd* v. *Sun Alliance and London Insurance plc* (2000) 3 HKCFAR 503.

[12] *Re UDL Argos Engineering & Heavy Industries Co. Ltd,* unreported, FAMV12/2001, 4 May 2001, CFA AC.

[13] *Cheng Lai Kwan* v. *Nan Fung Textiles Ltd* (1997–1998) 1 HKCFAR 204 (CFA AC), applying *Zuilani* v. *Veira* [1994] 1 WLR 1149 (PC).

[14] *Peter PF Chan* v. *Hong Kong Society of Accountants* (2001) 4 HKCFAR 197 (CFA AC). An amount slightly less than $1000000 does not entitle an appeal as of right but has been found by the Court of Appeal to be a factor that, in conjunction with good grounds for granting leave under s 22(1)(b), made the court more readily disposed towards the grant of leave; see *Ting Kwok Keung* v. *Tam Dick Yuen* (2002) 5 HKCFAR 336.

[15] *China Field Ltd* v. *Appeal Tribunal (Buildings)* (2009) 12 HKCFAR 68 (CFA AC).

[16] [1954] AC 80.

This judgment was criticised for 'inadvertently relax(ing) the criteria for civil appeals involving damages claims' because the requirement of a liquidated claim is not present in this formulation of the criteria for the second limb.[17]

Subsequently, in *WLK* v. *TMC*, the Appeal Committee stated that 'for a claim to fall within the second limb, it must be a claim to some particular property or to a proprietary right of the requisite value'.[18] The judgment was criticised by the same commentator for confining the term 'civil right' to proprietary rights only, which was argued to be in conflict with the literal meaning of the statute.[19] But as argued later, a more natural reading of the provision may give rise to three rather than two limbs of appeal.[20]

Three limbs to appeals 'as of right'?

Table 7.1 charts the three possible limbs of the 'as of right' avenue of appeal.

Although the judgment of the Appeal Committee in *WLK* v. *TMC* spoke of only two limbs, discussion was restricted to 'some particular property or to a proprietary right'. To interpret 'some civil right' as being limited to 'proprietary rights' only would indeed be a gross distortion of the natural language used in section 22(1)(a). It would be preferable to consider that the 'second limb' of section 22(1)(a) is made up of two sub-limbs, one concerning 'property or to a proprietary right' (which would be a natural extension of the word 'property') and another dealing with civil rights.

The PC continues to hear 'as of right' appeals, but the ground has not been maintained by other courts of final adjudication in jurisdictions that have ended appeals to the PC.[21] Li CJ thought it would be reasonably proportionate to limit access 'not only by increasing the monetary threshold for civil appeals as of right from final judgments of the Court of Appeal but even by abolishing such appeals as of right altogether'.[22]

---

[17] Peter So, 'Final Appeal Criteria for Civil Appeals Involving Damages Claims', *Hong Kong Lawyer*, June 2009, accessible at www.hk-lawyer.com.

[18] (2009) 12 HKCFAR 473, [10].

[19] Peter So, 'Final Appeal Criteria for Civil Appeals: Part II', *Hong Kong Lawyer*, January 2010, accessible at www.hk-lawyer.com.

[20] HKCFAO, section 22(1)(a) provides as follows: '(1) An appeal shall lie to the Court – (a) as of right, from any final judgment of the Court of Appeal in any civil cause or matter, where the matter in dispute on the appeal amounts to or is of the value of $1000000 or more, or where the appeal involves, directly or indirectly, some claim or question to or respecting property or some civil right amounting to or of the value of $1000000 or more'.

[21] For example, Supreme Court of New Zealand, but cf Caribbean Court of Justice.

[22] *A Solicitor* (2003), [36].

Table 7.1 *Appeals as of right*

Any final judgment of the Court of Appeal in any civil cause or matter	(i) Where the <u>matter in dispute</u> on appeal amounts to or is of the value of $1,000,000 or more
	or
	(ii) Where the appeal involves, directly or indirectly, some claim or question to or respecting <u>property</u> . . . amounting to or of the value of $1,000,000 or more
	or
	(iii) Where the appeal involves, directly or indirectly, some claim or question to or respecting . . . some <u>civil right</u> amounting to or of the value of $1,000,000 or more

Others have also supported the expedient route to reducing the number of 'as of right' appeals by raising the monetary threshold.[23] It remains to be seen whether such reform may take place in the future.[24]

Court of Final Appeal judges continue to make statements in judgments advocating the abolition of as of right appeals. Ribeiro PJ expressed for the Appeal Committee in *Chinachem Charitable Foundation Ltd* v. *Chan Chun Chuen* that the as of right basis for appeals to the CFA should be reconsidered, citing the fact that all major Commonwealth jurisdictions had already abandoned it.[25] Bokhary PJ, in his concurring judgment in *Wealth Duke Ltd* v. *Bank of China (Hong Kong) Ltd*, noted that other courts of last resort had already abolished such appeals.[26] He found that such appeals were both incompatible with the CFA's role and a source of vexation when the appeals are devoid of merit; the abolition of such appeals would not, in his opinion, prevent any meritorious case reaching the CFA. Both Litton and Scott NPJJ agreed not only with Chan PJ's

---

[23] See So, 'Final Appeal Criteria for Civil Appeals: Part II', note 19 above.
[24] The Hong Kong Bar Association's position paper of 10 August 2012, 'Rights of Appeal to the Court of Final Appeal in Civil Matters' also favoured abolishing the as of right basis of appeal, accessible at www.hkba.org.
[25] Unreported, FAMV20/2011, 28 October 2011, CFA AC, [16]–[19].
[26] Unreported, FACV2/2011, 23 November 2011, CFA, [1].

majority judgment in that case but also with the words of Bokhary PJ in respect to appeals as of right.

In his speech at the Ceremonial Opening of the Legal Year 2012, Ma CJ stated that the time had come 'to give serious consideration to abolishing the automatic right of litigants in a civil dispute to appeal from the Court of Appeal to the Court of Final Appeal based solely on monetary value'.[27] Ma CJ in particular criticised the right as being an anachronism of colonial practice, which was maintained in very few other common law jurisdictions. More significantly, Ma CJ also criticised appeals that come by this route because of the waste of judicial resources, stating that 'the majority of appeals that have been heard by the Court of Final Appeal by this route, have been totally unmeritorious', and concluded that he would be pressing for legislative changes in this regard.

Rule 7 procedure

Rule 7 of the Hong Kong Court of Final Appeal Rules (HKCFAR)[28] empowers the Registrar of the CFA to summon an appellant to show cause before the Appeal Committee of the CFA as to why his or her application for leave should not be dismissed. The grounds for so doing are where the Registrar is of the opinion that an application discloses no reasonable grounds for leave, is frivolous, or fails to comply with the HKCFAR.

The Rule 7 procedure is intended to prevent the waste of judicial resources on hopeless or abusive applications.[29] Examples of when this procedure will be deployed include the dressing up of an issue of fact as a point of law.[30] The usual course is for the Registrar to consider and determine the matter on the papers without an oral hearing.[31]

The legal and constitutional validity of the Rule 7 procedure was challenged in *Chow Shun Yung* v. *Wei Pih Stella* on the basis that it was unlawful for the Registrar to restrict an applicant to written submissions in response to a Rule 7 summons, that an applicant was entitled to an oral and public hearing for leave to appeal before the Appeal Committee and such a restrictive interpretation of Rule 7 was inconsistent with the other

---

[27] 'CJ's Speech at Ceremonial Opening of the Legal Year 2012', 9 January 2012, accessible at www.info.gov.hk/gia/general/201201/09/P201201090309.htm.

[28] Cap. 484A.

[29] *Chow Shun Yung* v. *Wei Pih Stella* (2003) 6 HKCFAR 299, [15.2] (CFA AC).

[30] *Choi Man Wai* v. *HKSAR*, unreported, FAMC23/2001, 28 September 2001, CFA AC, [1].

[31] *Chow Shun Yung*, [8].

rules, particularly Rules 9, 10, and 12, as well as sections 18(2) and 47(2) of the HKCFAO.[32] It was further contended that limitations on the right to a hearing must be prescribed by law in accordance with Article 39 of the BL, and Rule 7(2) was not sufficiently clear.

These challenges were rejected by the Appeal Committee, which found that the purpose of Rule 7 was clearly to prevent applicants from abusing the court's procedure by lodging leave applications that disclosed no reasonable grounds, were frivolous, or failed to comply with the rules. It would defeat the purpose of Rule 7 to waste the court's and the other party's resources if the showing of cause required an oral hearing and not merely written submissions. As to the issue of consistency, it was held that Rule 7 concerned a procedure in relation to a specific category of cases that were objectionable on their face and thus should not be allowed to proceed in accordance with the ordinary procedure.

As to the right to a hearing under Article 10 of the Hong Kong Bill of Rights, the Appeal Committee found that even in the jurisprudence of the European Court of Human Rights, at first instance the right to a hearing does not always require oral submissions. The right to a hearing is even less demanding in relation to applications for leave to a final appeal court. Furthermore, under Rule 72, the public is provided means to apply to the Registrar to obtain access to documents, including those dealt with under the Rule 7 procedure.

It should be noted that previously, under Rule 52 of the Judicial Committee Rules 1908, it was provided that 'The Registrar of the PC may refuse to receive a petition on the ground that it contains scandalous matter'. It should be noted, however, that a petitioner was given the right to appeal by way of motion to the Judicial Committee against such refusal.[33] The language of the rule has since modernised ('The Registrar may refuse to accept an application that contains no reasonable ground of appeal or is an abuse of process'[34]), and the right to appeal such refusals has now been replaced by a process whereby procedural questions are normally considered on the paper first, usually by the Registrar unless he or she refers the matter to the Judicial Committee with discretion to direct an oral hearing.[35]

---

[32] *Ibid.*   [33] Judicial Committee Rules 1908, r. 52.

[34] See r. 11(3) of the Judicial Committee (Appellate Jurisdiction) Rules 2009, being The Schedule to The Judicial Committee (Appellate Jurisdiction) Rules Order 2009, SI 2009 No 224.

[35] *Ibid.*, r. 9.

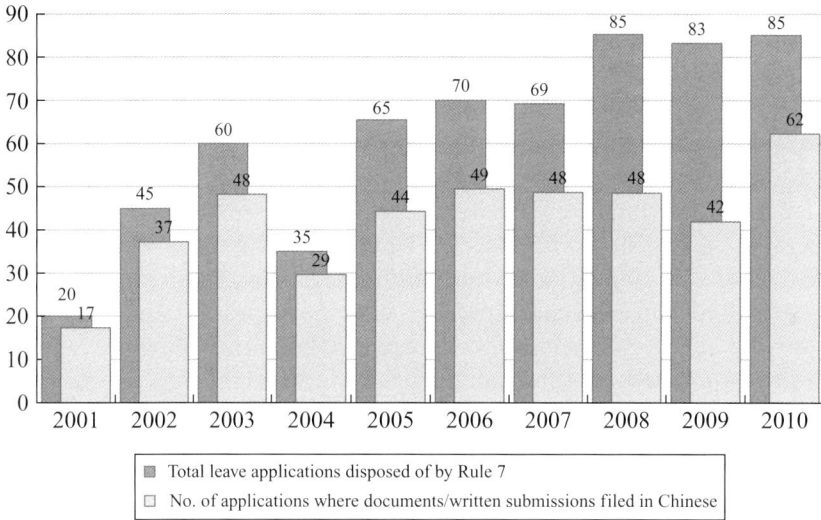

Figure 7.2 Use of Chinese in Rule 7 proceedings, 2001–2010.

Use of Chinese and the Rule 7 procedure

In contrast to lower courts, the CFA is the only court in Hong Kong where the Chinese language has not been integrated. This may be attributed to the presence of the non-permanent judges (NPJs) from other common law jurisdictions, and it remains to be seen whether it will ever be possible for proceedings at the CFA to take place in Chinese.

However, one part of CFA proceedings permits the filing and use of Chinese documents – under the Rule 7 procedure. As can be seen from Figure 7.2, since the use of the Rule 7 procedure began in 2001, well over half of those applications have involved documents or submissions filed in Chinese. This use of Chinese at the CFA is presumably for the benefit of applicants in person.

At present, the Registry of the CFA accepts the filing of leave applications written in Chinese. The Chinese applications are processed in the same way as those in English, such that the Registrar will decide whether to issue a Rule 7 summons or to direct a hearing; this would be the process not only for applicants acting in person, for example, but also when the matter had been dealt with in the High Court in Chinese such as in a magistracy appeal. In the event a Rule 7 summons is issued, applicants may file their written submissions in Chinese. When a hearing is directed, all of the documents filed and lodged by the parties written in Chinese will be translated into English for the purposes of holding the hearing.

For a hearing in criminal cases when the applicant is acting in person, the Registrar will direct the Court Language Section to translate the relevant documents into English, and the translated copies will be provided to all parties concerned and the Appeal Committee.

For the hearing of civil leave applications, when the applicant is in person, the Registrar will direct the Court Language Section to translate the lower courts' judgments into English. The translated copies will be provided to all parties concerned as well as the Appeal Committee. However, the applicants themselves are responsible for providing the English translation of written submissions to the court and the opposite party.

When such applicants are represented, whether in criminal or civil cases, the applicant's solicitors will be directed to carry out the translation work, and if the parties can agree upon the translation, then certification by the Court Language Section can be dispensed with.

Procedure for leave

The purpose for limiting access to the CFA is clear: to prevent waste of the Court's resources. As stated by Bokhary PJ in *A Solicitor* v. *The Law Society of Hong Kong*,

> A good illustration of the limits that can be constitutionally placed on access to a court of final appellate jurisdiction like this one is to be found in the discretionary criteria laid down by the [HKCFAO], for leave to appeal to this Court. Those criteria spare the Court from being overburdened, but do not seek to bar matters of high importance from the Court's purview.[36]

Thus, only matters of importance should be brought before the final appellate court.

Obtaining leave in civil cases

The CFA's civil jurisdiction is prescribed in section 22 of the HKCFAO. Under subsection (1)(a), the criteria for appeals as of right (as discussed above) are set out. Under subsection (1)(b), an appeal to the CFA shall lie at the discretion of either the Court of Appeal or the CFA itself from any judgment of the Court of Appeal, whether final or interlocutory, if in the opinion of either court, the question involved is one that ought to be

---

[36]   *A Solicitor* (2003), [45].

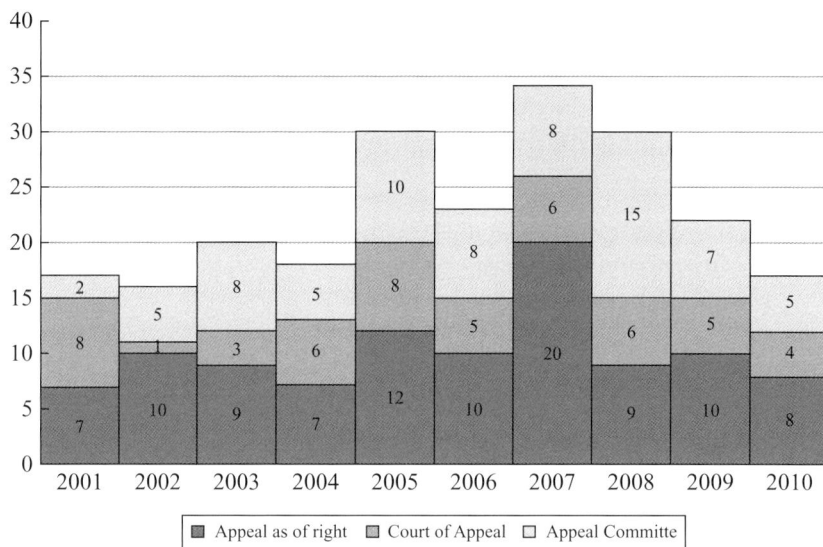

Figure 7.3 Types of civil appeals to the Court of Final Appeal, 2001–2010.

submitted to the CFA for decision because of its great general or public importance or otherwise.

Subsection (1)(c) contains a further limb, which is at the discretion of the CFA itself in respect of a determination by the Court of First Instance under section 37(1) of the Chief Executive Election Ordinance[37] or from a judicial review or any other proceedings that put in issue whether a candidate has been duly determined not to be returned by election under section 26A(4) or declared under section 28 of the Chief Executive Election Ordinance. To date, this limb of the CFA's civil jurisdiction has not been engaged.

Leave to appeal may be granted by either the Court of Appeal or the CFA itself. A division of the Court of Appeal consists of three justices of appeal, and leave to appeal is to be determined by a panel of three. Leave hearings before the CFA take place before an Appeal Committee, which is made up of either the CJ and two permanent judges of the CFA or three permanent judges of the CFA, and when there is an insufficient number of permanent judges, a local NPJ of the CFA may be nominated by the CJ to sit in the place of a permanent judge.[38] Overseas NPJs do not partake in leave application decisions. Figure 7.3 shows how the numbers of the

[37] Cap. 569.   [38] HKCFAO, section 18.

three types of civil appeals (as of right, leave granted by the CA, and leave granted by the CFA) have fluctuated from 2001 to 2010.

There is no provision in the HKCFAO that allows the CFA to refuse to hear the case when the Court of Appeal has granted leave. This is not to say that the hands of the CFA are entirely bound by the Court of Appeal because as Bokhary PJ has stated:

> Neither are the Court's hands tied in the more usual case where the applicant is content to argue the appeal on the grounds upon which leave was granted by the Court of Appeal. The Court can and often does, inform the parties in advance that it will require certain points not mentioned by the Court of Appeal (or indeed not mentioned by the Appeal Committee) to be dealt with at the hearing. . . . Accordingly, while the appeal is centred on the questions or other grounds on which leave was given, the Court will decide any issue requiring resolution for the proper disposal of the appeal (obviously bearing in mind the needs of procedural fairness).[39]

The CFA has given the precondition of absence or refusal of leave from the Court of Appeal a broad interpretation.[40] When appellants are dissatisfied with the grounds on which the Court of Appeal granted leave or are dissatisfied with any conditions imposed by the Court of Appeal on the grant of leave, they may apply afresh before the Appeal Committee.[41] However, the application is treated as a fresh application, and the Appeal Committee maintains its full discretionary powers to deal with it, including the power to reject the entire application after hearing or pursuant to the Rule 7 procedure.[42] Hence, appellants risk losing their right to appeal to the CFA, including leave to appeal as granted by the Court of Appeal, if they so apply.

What constitutes great general or public importance must include some practical impact, according to Ribeiro PJ in *Deacons (a firm) v. White & Case LLP*.[43] The CFA will not engage its jurisdiction on academic questions of law. In that case, the Appeal Committee found that not only would the appeal, which was interlocutory in nature, have no wider impact on persons other than the parties (thus already failing in the requirement of great general or public importance), there would have been no impact on any procedural or substantive aspect of the underlying action. The

---

[39] *Hong Kong Island Development Ltd* v. *The World Food Fair Ltd & Anor* (2006) 9 HKCFAR 162, [22]–[23].

[40] HKCFAO, section 23.   [41] *Hong Kong Island Development Ltd*, [15].

[42] *Cathay Pacific Airways Ltd* v. *Wong Sau Lai* (2006) 9 HKCFAR 45, [5] (CFA AC), applying *Hunt & Winterbotham (West of England) Ltd* v. *BRS (Parcels) Ltd* [1962] 1 QB 617 (CA).

[43] *Deacons (a firm)* v. *White & Case LLP* (2003) 6 HKCFAR 322, [35] (CFA AC).

case again illustrates not only the restrictive approach to giving access to the CFA but also reflects the fundamental need of the CFA's resources to be appropriately engaged.

The restrictive approach of the CFA in respect of appeals against interlocutory orders or judgments has been noted earlier in the as of right discussion; such appeals are statutorily excluded by section 22(1)(a) of the HKCFAO. To bring such appeals under section 22(1)(b), not only must such an appeal genuinely raise a question of law of great general or public importance, but the result of the appeal must also be shown to turn on how that question is answered, and the result must be likely to make a significant contribution to the just disposal of the litigation.[44] The reason for such a restrictive approach to interlocutory appeals is the policy of the court that, 'interlocutory appeals merely delay the determination of the real issues'.[45] No doubt this restrictive approach in respect of interlocutory appeals will continue to be applied actively in the post civil justice reform era.

Even more restricted is the 'or otherwise' ground.[46] In *Incorporated Owners of Hip Wo House* v. *Gallant King Development Limited*, the Court of Appeal's policy in respect of this ground was not to grant leave save in 'very exceptional circumstances' because the 'or otherwise' ground was viewed as a matter reserved for the CFA. In this context, the often-cited brief comment made by the Appeal Committee on this ground for leave is that 'leave to appeal under the "or otherwise" limb is an exceptional course'.[47]

It has been noted earlier in respect of the 'as of right' limb that an amount in dispute slightly under the threshold may, in combination with questions of great general or public importance, be taken into consideration in the grant of leave; this approach was taken by the Court of Appeal in *Ting Kwok Keung* v. *Tam Dick Yuen & Ors*[48] and was cited by the CFA.[49] In respect of cross-appeals, it was held in *Thanakharn Kasikorn Thai Chamkat* v. *Akai Holdings Limited (In Liquidation)* that a respondent seeking to bring a cross-appeal must also seek leave to do so.[50]

---

[44] *CSAV Group (Hong Kong) Ltd* v. *Jamshed Safdar* (2007) 10 HKCFAR 629, [1] (CFA AC).

[45] *Chan Kam Chuen* v. *Tsuen Wan Adventist Hospital*, unreported, FAMV23/1998, 25 February 1999, CFA AC, [3].

[46] HKCFAO, section 22(1)(b).

[47] *Hui Yiu Wing* v. *Regional Council*, unreported, FAMV16/2002, 24 September 2002, CFA AC, [1].

[48] Unreported, CACV751/2000, 14 September 2001, CA.   [49] *Ting Kwok Keung.*

[50] (2010) 13 HKCFAR 283.

The leapfrog procedure

Another innovation in the HKCFAO is the existence of the 'leapfrog' procedure under Division 3 of Part II, which deals with appeals from the Court of First Instance to the CFA.

The procedure was proposed by the Hong Kong Bar Association in 1995 during the consultation in respect of the Hong Kong Court of Final Appeal Bill. The Administration at the time did not agree with the proposal but agreed to revisit the issue after the CFA became established. The procedure was modelled on Part II of the Administration of Justice Act 1969 (United Kingdom) for appeals from the High Court directly to the House of Lords, bypassing the Court of Appeal. In 2002, an amending ordinance was enacted to add the procedure to the civil jurisdiction of the CFA.[51]

The advantage of the leapfrog procedure is that it spares appellants the need to first appeal to the Court of Appeal. The procedure itself was intended to be rarely used and only for the purposes of cutting out unnecessary tedium and expense when a point in issue has been fully argued and considered. The disadvantage of the procedure is that the CFA is deprived of the expository judgments of the Court of Appeal, and it may not be easy at first instance to identify cases suitable to go straight to the CFA – even in England, the procedure is applied only in restricted circumstances.[52] In Hong Kong, a restriction in the leapfrog procedure is in respect of issues concerning the BL. BL points are generally excluded from the leapfrog procedure unless they are points that have been previously considered, so as not to deprive the CFA the benefit of the Court of Appeal's judgment.

For an application to leapfrog to the CFA, the trial judge must first certify the issue for appeal and must be satisfied that there is a sufficient case for an appeal to the CFA and that the parties consent to the certification. Most importantly, the trial judge must be satisfied that the point of law (and it must be on law alone) is one of great general or public importance that relates wholly or mainly to legislation fully argued and considered, is one which the trial judge is bound by a decision of the Court of Appeal or the CFA itself and was fully considered by the Court of Appeal or CFA in

---

[51] Hong Kong Court of Final Appeal (Amendment) Ordinance 2002, Ord. No. 11 of 2002.

[52] See Legislative Council Secretariat, 'Report of the Bills Committee on the Hong Kong Court of Final Appeal (Amendment) Bill 2001', paper for the House Committee, LC Paper No. CB(2)1705/01–02, 25 April 2002, pp. 2–3, accessible at www.legco.gov.hk/yr01-02/english/hc/papers/hc0426cb2-1705.pdf ('Report of the Bills Committee').

that decision, or relates wholly or mainly to the construction of the BL on an issue that the trial judge is bound by a decision of the Court of Appeal or CFA in which the relevant part of the BL was fully considered in that decision.[53] The decision of the trial judge to certify or refuse to certify an issue for the leapfrog procedure is not open to appeal.

When the appeal being sought by way of the leapfrog procedure concerns a combination of issues that can and cannot be the subject of a leapfrog procedure, it is expected that the trial judge will have to exercise his or her judicial discretion, having regard to the grounds of appeal and the particular circumstances of the case.[54] The statutory provision of section 27C requires that the point of law 'relates wholly or mainly' to the construction of the BL or the construction of an Ordinance or subsidiary legislation; the trial judge must therefore still find that the issues put before the CFA can 'mainly' be brought. After the certificate has been issued, an application may be made to the Appeal Committee for leave.[55]

The leapfrog procedure was first used in *Town Planning Board* v. *Society for Protection of the Harbour Ltd* because of the urgent nature of the subject matter and indeed set out an expedited procedural timetable for the case;[56] such was the urgency of the matter that the Appeal Committee exercised its power to grant leave without an oral hearing and further directed an expedited procedural timetable. The case concerned the interpretation of the Protection of the Harbour Ordinance[57] and was considered to be of importance not only because it would affect decisions of the Town Planning Board, whose plans for reclamation were in question, but also applies to any reclamation proposal of Victoria Harbour. The procedure was subsequently used again in the case of *Secretary for Justice* v. *Michael Reid Scott*[58] when the Appeal Committee found that the same constitutional issues in *Lau Kwok Fai* v. *Secretary for Justice*[59] were being raised, making it desirable for the appeals to be heard together.

The existence of the leapfrog procedure and its basis coming from the practice of the House of Lords rather than the PC suggests that the CFA should be more comparatively regarded as a supreme court of the HKSAR rather than simply a substitute body for the PC.

---

[53] HKCFAO, section 27C. [54] Report of the Bills Committee, note 52 above.
[55] HKCFAO, section 27D. [56] Unreported, FAMV26/2003, 29 September 2003, CFA AC.
[57] Cap. 531. [58] Unreported, FAMV5/2005, 4 March 2005, CFA AC.
[59] [2004] 3 HKLRD 570 (CA).

Obtaining leave in criminal cases

The criminal jurisdiction of the CFA is set out in section 32 of the HKC-FAO. The criminal jurisdiction of the CFA has two limbs: points of law of great and general importance and when substantial and grave injustice has been done.

The process for obtaining leave in criminal cases differs from that of civil cases. When proceeding on the point of law limb, it is a prerequisite to obtaining leave for the point of law to be certified by either the Court of Appeal (or Court of First Instance in the case of magistracy appeals) or the CFA.[60] The usual practice is to seek certification from the court below first and if the court below has declined to certify, an application may be made to the CFA for both certification and leave to appeal.[61] Unlike civil appeals, where leave may be obtained either from the Court of Appeal or the Appeal Committee, criminal appeals face two hurdles: first, the point of law must be certified, either by the court below or CFA, and second, leave must be obtained from the Appeal Committee. The second hurdle is not a rubber stamp of any certification from the court below. The CFA has discretion and could exercise its discretion to refuse leave even if the court below certifies a point of law of great and general importance.[62] The position of the CFA was clarified in *Lau Suk-han* v. *HKSAR*, in which Li CJ stated:

> [E]ven where the lower court has certified a point of law, the Appeal Committee has a discretion whether to grant leave. It is clear on the plain wording of section 32 and also section 33 that the granting of leave in relation to its criminal jurisdiction is a matter only for the Court exercised by the Appeal Committee.[63]

Leave will not be granted when the point of law has been fully argued in the court below and the decision is plainly right.[64] Similarly, leave will not be granted on points of law when the law is already well settled and there is no dispute as to what the law is.[65] The point of law on which the appeal rests must be reasonably arguable before leave will be granted.[66]

---

[60] HKCFAO, section 32(2).   [61] *Ibid.*, section 32(3).
[62] See e.g. *Tang Siu Man* v. *HKSAR* (1997–1998) 1 HKCFAR 4.
[63] *Lau Suk-han* v. *HKSAR* (1997–1998) 1 HKCFAR 150, [12].   [64] *Ibid.*, [13].
[65] *Chim Pui-chung* v. *HKSAR* [1999] HKLRD 836.
[66] In *Lee Kin-pong* v. *HKSAR* [1998] 1 HKLRD 182, the CFA AC refused certification and leave as the point was not reasonably arguable.

As to the second limb of criminal jurisdiction, the CFA's approach to the substantial and grave injustice ground differs. The wording of the phrase was taken from the PC case *Re Dillet*.[67] In *Zeng Liang Xin* v. *HKSAR*, the Appeal Committee held that the requirement of certification only applied to the point of law limb.[68] When an applicant relies upon the substantial and grave injustice limb, there is no need for certification. This means the applicant applies directly to the CFA for leave.[69]

Li CJ observed in *Zeng* that it is not the role of the CFA to function as a second Court of Appeal.[70] Moreover, the substantial and grave injustice limb imposes a 'high hurdle' that would rarely be satisfied.[71] Bokhary PJ set out the test under this limb in *So Yiu Fung* v. *HKSAR* as 'it must be shown that there has been to the appellant's disadvantage a departure from accepted norms which departure is so serious as to constitute a substantial and grave injustice'.[72]

Evolution from the Privy Council

The clear demarcation of the civil[73] and criminal[74] jurisdiction under the HKCFAO, involving different tests for obtaining leave, is a clear evolution from the PC, which continues to rely strictly upon the common law tests for leave without explicitly separating its civil and criminal caseload.

Given this clear demarcation between civil and criminal, one question that may arise is whether or not it is satisfactory to have different leave processes and criteria for civil and criminal cases in the context of constitutional issues and thus whether it may be necessary for a third jurisdiction to be carved out by way of statute to create parity for all constitutional cases.

Substantive appeals

After leave has been granted by the Appeal Committee (or the Court of Appeal in civil matters) and in civil appeals as of right, the case will proceed to a substantive hearing before the full court of the CFA.

---

[67] (1887) 12 App Case 459. [68] (1997–1998) 1 HKCFAR 12. [69] *Ibid.*
[70] *Ibid.*, [37]. [71] *Ibid.* [72] (1999) 2 HKCFAR 539.
[73] HKCFAO, Part II. [74] *Ibid.*, Part III.

Composition of the Court of Final Appeal

Under section 16 of the HKCFAO, appeals are heard and determined by a panel of five judges: the CJ or a PJ designated to sit in the CJ's place, three PJs nominated by the CJ, and a non-permanent Hong Kong judge or an NPJ from another common law jurisdiction selected by the CJ.

As the CFA must sit with five judges, when a PJ sits in place of the CJ, the CJ must nominate a non-permanent Hong Kong judge to sit in the place of the permanent judge.[75] In the event that a hearing has commenced and a judge is absent before the determination of the appeal for any reason, the appeal may continue with the remaining judges with the consent of all the parties as long as the remaining judges number not less than four.[76]

Although the CFA is not required to sit with an NPJ from another common law jurisdiction, the general practice of the CFA is that it will sit with such an NPJ.[77] Only on rare occasions has the CFA been composed entirely of Hong Kong judges, permanent and non-permanent.

Judges may not sit as part of the CFA to hear or determine matters that arise from a judgment or order made by the relevant judge himself or by a court in which such a judge was sitting as a member or any appeal against a conviction or sentence by such a judge.[78] This provision is of particular importance with respect to sitting or recently retired Hong Kong judges newly appointed as CFA judges.

Although the CFA does not follow the previous tradition of the PC to give only a single judgment or, at most, a majority judgment and a dissenting judgment,[79] section 16 does require that there be a judgment or order from the majority of the judges sitting; otherwise, a rehearing is required.

Powers of the Court of Final Appeal

After a substantive hearing, the CFA may confirm, reverse, or vary the decision of the court below.[80] The CFA may also remit the matter to the court below with its opinion thereon or make such other order in the matter (including any order as to costs) as the CFA thinks fit.

For these purposes, the CFA may exercise any powers of the court below, including the power to order a retrial. In the exercise of its powers

---

75 *Ibid.*, section 16(2)–(4).   76 *Ibid.*, section 16(7).
77 See Chapter 11 (Young and Da Roza) in this volume.   78 HKCFAO, section 16(8).
79 See Chapter 6 (Young and Da Roza) in this volume.   80 HKCFAO, section 17.

to order a retrial in a criminal case, regard must be had by the CFA to the provisions of section 83E of the Criminal Procedure Ordinance (CPO),[81] which sets out the power of the Court of Appeal to order a retrial.[82]

One example of when the CFA exercised the powers of a court below can be found in *Re Resource 1*, in which Bokhary PJ stated, 'It would be worse than a waste of time and costs if, instead of ourselves determining the application for an extension on which we have already heard full argument, we were to remit the case to the Court of Appeal for it to entertain such an application' and thus granted an extension of time under Order 3, Rule 5 of the rules of the High Court. Similarly, in *HKSAR v. Hau Kin*, the CFA considered its power either to remit the matter back to the Court of Appeal or consider the question of the calculation of time under section 83W of the CPO itself. Section 83W(1) of the CPO allows the Court of Appeal to take into consideration the time that an appellant is in custody awaiting the determination of his appeal as part of the term of any sentence to which the appellant is subject. The CFA ultimately held that the Court of Appeal had been mistaken in ordering loss of time that was greater than the period from the time that an application for leave to appeal is filed and the determination of that appeal and reduced the period directly instead of remitting the matter back to the Court of Appeal.

In respect of criminal matters, when the CFA restores a conviction, it may also make an order for restitution of property that the trial court could have made or order such compensation as the trial court could have made under section 73 of the CPO.

Findings of fact

The approach of the CFA in disturbing concurrent findings of fact is set out in the judgment of Bokhary PJ in *Sky Heart* v. *Lee Hysan Estate Co. Ltd*, particularly that there must be some miscarriage of justice or violation of some principle of law or procedure.[83] A miscarriage of justice means such a departure from the rules that permeate all judicial procedure as to make what happened in the material case not proper judicial procedure at all.[84] The violation of some principle of law or procedure must be so

---

[81] Cap. 221.   [82] *Ting James Henry* v. *HKSAR* (2007) 10 HKCFAR 632.
[83] (1997–1998) 1 HKCFAR 318.
[84] *Ibid.*, 334, citing *Srimati Bibhabati Devi* v. *Kumar Ramendra Narayan Roy* [1946] AC 508 (PC).

erroneous that if the proposition were corrected, the finding could not stand or it may be the neglect of some principle of law or procedure whose application would have the same effect.[85] The question of whether there is evidence on which the courts could arrive at their finding is such a question of law.[86]

Admissibility of evidence is a proposition of law, but the question involved must materially affect the finding before it could be disturbed.[87] The question of the value of evidence is not a sufficient reason for departure from the practice.

Bokhary PJ stated in *Sky Heart* that the broad objectives are to reach an acceptable balance between due access to the courts and a reasonably early end to litigation and to properly distribute the functions of three court levels: first instance, intermediate appeal, and final appeal.[88] After a review of the relevant authorities from the PC, the House of Lords, and the High Court of Australia, the CFA concluded that it should follow the same approach as that of the PC without the latter's reluctance to disturb findings of fact for reason of lack of familiarity with local conditions.[89]

New points on appeal

The CFA adopted the position of the PC in *Ahamath* v. *Sariffa Umma*,[90] applied in *Attorney General* v. *Cheng Yick Chi*,[91] that '[i]t must only be under very exceptional circumstances that an issue dropped in the intermediate Court of Appeal and for that reason not dealt with or referred to by that Court can be revived before this Board'.[92]

As Li CJ stated in *Wong Tak Yue* v. *Kung Kwok Wai*, the 'Court as a court of final appeal should be very reluctant to consider an issue which was not duly raised and considered in the Court of Appeal'.[93] In that case, it was found that the circumstances were indeed exceptional and justified the reopening of an issue. In reaching the conclusion that the issue could be reopened, the CFA also took into account the fact that the question to be reopened was essentially one of law, that the other side had ample notice that the issue was being sought to be reopened, and that the other side had not suffered any prejudice that could not be compensated by costs.

Bokhary PJ further clarified in *Flywin Co Ltd* v. *Strong & Associates Ltd*: 'Clearly the foundational imperative of the "state of the evidence"

---

[85] *Ibid.* [86] *Ibid.* [87] *Ibid.* [88] *Ibid.*
[89] *Ibid.*, 337. [90] [1931] AC 799. [91] [1983] UKPC 19 (21 June 1983).
[92] *Wong Tak Yue* v. *Kung Kwok Wai* (1997–1998) 1 HKCFAR 55, 66. [93] *Ibid.*

bar . . . is fairness. Even where a new point is not barred on that basis, there is still a hurdle facing a party who seeks to raise in the final appellate court a point which was not pursued in the intermediate appellate court'.[94] Citing *Wong Tak Yue*, it was held that the need for exceptional circumstances was even greater

> when entertaining the new point and accepting it would constitute a major development of the law. In such an exercise, it is to be expected that having the intermediate appellate court's view on the point of law involved would be of assistance to the final appellate court. Therefore where the question of a major development of the law is involved, the foundational consideration underlying the 'not considered on intermediate appeal' hurdle, as I propose to call it, is that when the courts develop the law, it is best that they do so with all their intellectual resources fully deployed.[95]

Finality

Although matters are generally brought to an end after the substantive hearing and delivery of judgment at the CFA, there may still be outstanding matters to be dealt with.

Costs

Costs are dealt with under section 43 of the HKCFAO, which empowers the CFA to make orders in respect of both the costs of its own proceedings as well as those of the courts below. Costs are taxed by the Registrar, and when parties are aggrieved by decisions in respect of taxation, they may appeal to the CFA under section 45. A single permanent judge may exercise the powers of the CFA to hear and determine such an appeal.

Clarification

The CFA has been asked to clarify its orders in the past.[96] It was noted in *Ng Ka Ling* v. *The Director of Immigration* that clarification is an exceptional course and an exercise of the CFA's inherent jurisdiction that must take place within the limits of the proper exercise of judicial power.[97] Typically,

---

[94] (2002) 5 HKCFAR 356, [39].   [95] *Ibid.*

[96] *Secretary for Justice* v. *To Kan Chi*, unreported, FACV8/2000, 4 August 2006, CFA; *Commissioner of Inland Revenue* v. *HIT Finance Limited*, unreported, FACV8/2007, 19 May 2008, CFA.

[97] *Ng Ka Ling* v. *The Director of Immigration* (1999) 2 HKCFAR 141.

the CFA deals with the clarification request on paper by delivering a brief judgment in response to the parties' application.

Reopening

The CFA has also been asked to reopen cases, such as in *Secretary for Justice* v. *Michael Reid Scott*,[98] in which after the delivery of the judgment in the substantive matter when the appeals by the secretary for justice were allowed, the respondent sought in writing to reopen the appeals on the basis of the CFA's inherent jurisdiction.[99] Li CJ noted that the CFA would only ever reopen an appeal for 'wholly exceptional reasons', which the respondent's application lacked, and the appeal was dismissed with costs if the appellant sought them.[100] In a subsequent murder case reopening, which the court found to be 'bereft of foundation', Bokhary PJ warned that future reopening applications may not even be accepted for filing if the Court was to so direct.[101]

Maintaining jurisdiction

The CFA has also had to maintain its jurisdiction over several years after the decision was rendered in *Ng Siu Tung* v. *Director of Immigration* to deal with the individual right of abode claims of many claimants who were part of the original litigation but not the representative applicants whose cases were determined in the original judgment.[102] The relevant matters were remitted to the Court of First Instance for determination and reporting, after which the CFA ultimately disposed of the cases.[103]

Constitutional jurisdiction

Of particular interest in respect of finality before the CFA is its constitutional jurisdiction. Article 158 vests the power of final interpretation of the BL in the Standing Committee of the National People's Congress.[104]

---

[98] (2005) 8 HKCFAR 304.

[99] As reported in local papers, the challenge was aimed at Sir Anthony Mason NPJ, who authored the judgment; see Jimmy Cheung and Martin Wong, 'Top Court Asked to Rethink Pay Cut Ruling', *South China Morning Post*, 17 February 2006.

[100] (2006) 9 HKCFAR 221.

[101] *Habib Ahmed* v. *HKSAR* (2010) 13 HKCFAR 449, refusing application to re-open (2010) 13 HKCFAR 305.

[102] *Ng Siu Tung* v. *The Director of Immigration* (2002) 5 HKCFAR 1.

[103] See *Ng Siu Tung* v. *The Director of Immigration*, unreported, FACV1/2001, various decisions dated 25 February 2002; 30 July 2002; 9 January 2004; 26 March 2004; 5 January 2006; 13 February 2006; 13 November 2006; 25 July 2007; and 18 March 2008, CFA.

[104] See also Chapters 2 (Ghai) and 3 (Yang) in this volume.

Thus, the CFA is not necessarily the final interpreter of the BL. The case of *Ng Ka Ling* and the interpretation of the BL sought by the HKSAR government after the delivery of the judgment has been the subject of much controversy and analysis and does not bear further discussion for these purposes except to note that it was stated in the clarification in that case that:

> The Court's judgment on 29 January 1999 did not question the authority of the Standing Committee to make an interpretation under Article 158 which would have to be followed by the courts of the Region. The Court accepts that it cannot question that authority. Nor did the Court's judgment question, and the Court accepts that it cannot question, the authority of the National People's Congress or the Standing Committee to do any act which is in accordance with the provisions of the [BL] and the procedure therein.[105]

The test for the CFA seeking such an interpretation is that the provision(s) of the BL being interpreted concern affairs that are the responsibility of the Central People's Government or concern the relationship between the Central Authorities and the HKSAR, and such interpretation will affect the judgment of the case before the CFA. In 2011, the CFA sought an interpretation in the case of *Democratic Republic of the Congo* v. *FG Hemisphere Associates LLC* by a majority of three to two judges.[106]

Conclusion

The difference between an appeal to the intermediate appeal court and a final appeal court has been discussed in some depth by the court itself. Bokhary PJ noted in *Ting Kwok Keung* v. *Tam Dick Yuen* that 'it is not for a final appellate court to function as an intermediate appellate court'.[107] Ribeiro PJ stated rather directly that '[l]itigants in Hong Kong have a right of appeal to the Court of Appeal in respect of final judgments generally. The role of the Court of Final Appeal is not to permit a third bite of the cherry to any litigant who wishes to have another go'.[108] In *A Solicitor* v. *The Law Society of Hong Kong*, Li CJ stated: 'It has to be recognized that most appeals to the Court of Appeal end there and do not proceed to the Court of Final Appeal. There is only a limited category of cases which enjoy the right of appeal and leave has to be obtained in other

---

[105] *Ng Ka Ling*.
[106] *Democratic Republic of the Congo* v. *FG Hemisphere Associates LLC* (2011) 14 HKCFAR 95 (reference) and 395 (disposition).
[107] *Ting Kwok Keung*, note 14 above. [108] *Sun Honest Development*.

cases'.[109] In respect of these limitations of access to the CFA, Li CJ has stated: 'The limitations serve a legitimate purpose namely, to prevent the Court at the apex of the judicial system from being unduly burdened with appeals so as to enable it to focus on appeals, the judgments on which will be of importance to the legal system'.[110] Although the procedure and jurisdiction of the CFA are largely based on the procedure and jurisdiction of its predecessor, the PC, evolutionary changes have been made to the procedure and jurisdiction of the CFA, and those changes have been informed by its role as the court of final adjudication in Hong Kong.

As has been noted elsewhere, particularly by Li CJ, 'Since the establishment of this Court on 1 July 1997, much greater use has been made of it, compared to the [PC] as Hong Kong's final appellate court before the resumption of the exercise of sovereignty'.[111] Ribeiro PJ further noted that the considerations of the widespread and disparate jurisdictions under its purview and the policy of the PC for uniformity in legal development no longer applied to the CFA.[112] Following on from that point, although the roots of the creation of the CFA in the PC are clear, certain elements of the predecessor court, such as appeals as of right, have proven potentially undesirable.

With the separation of the CFA's civil and criminal jurisdiction and the innovation of the leapfrog procedure, it is clear that the continued evolution of the CFA is less likely to be informed by its predecessor, the PC, and more by other supreme courts of common law jurisdictions.

---

[109] (2008) 11 HKCFAR 117.   [110] *A Solicitor* (2003).
[111] *A Solicitor* v. *The Law Society of Hong Kong* (2008) 11 HKCFAR 117.
[112] *Sun Honest Development.*

8

A practitioner's perspective

MICHAEL THOMAS

It is a privilege to be asked to contribute to this timely assessment of the work of the Court of Final Appeal (CFA) under the leadership of the first Chief Justice of the Hong Kong Special Administrative Region of the People's Republic of China (HKSAR). The universal view of practitioners is that the CFA has been an outstanding success. I have heard not a word to the contrary.

Its judges have earned a reputation for first class exposition of legal principles and sound analytical reasoning. They have already created an impressive body of Hong Kong jurisprudence. They are invariably well prepared for the arguments through study of the parties' written cases, the record, and the authorities cited. They are always both courteous and patient at hearings, never harassing counsel. They are also commendably quick in handing down their written judgments.

More than that, there is wide public recognition that the one outstanding feature of this special administrative region under the Basic Law (BL) has been the legal system, led from the top, conspicuously asserting the rule of law. People in Hong Kong as well as the wider international community have taken note of the way in which a self-confident judiciary has expounded and applied the law since 1997 fearlessly and impartially, serving the needs of traders and investors in their private commercial and property disputes as effectively as it has resolved the conflicts between government and individuals in the context of public administration. The work of Andrew Li and his personal and dedicated leadership of the judiciary needs to be recognised and applauded in that wider context.

Any assessment of the record and achievements of the CFA should be seen in perspective. It must be measured against the task that the CFA was set by the Hong Kong Court of Final Appeal Ordinance (HKCFAO)[1]

---

[1] Cap. 484.

enacted in 1995 following four years of fractious political wrangling and the reservations of many practitioners and legislators. It may be appropriate to remind ourselves of that history if only to emphasise just how far the CFA has come since those times to leave those controversies behind.

In 1983, as talks began between Britain and China over the future of Hong Kong and the end of British administration became certain, it was soon appreciated that if its judicial and legal system were to continue, appeals to the Privy Council (PC) would have to end. Because the People's Republic of China's Supreme People's Court in Beijing could not be expected to handle appeals from common law courts, Hong Kong would need to set up its own 'Court of Final Appeal' as it was and is still termed. That it should be a discrete third-tier court composed of five judges seems never to have been an issue. But the practical question loomed large: how to fill the new court so that it would have the stature to fill the shoes left vacant by the PC.

Informal conversations with the New China News Agency at an early stage produced an encouraging response. Chinese officials saw a need for overseas judges from other common law jurisdictions to sit in the future CFA to add judicial weight and experience and to keep Hong Kong in lockstep with developments in common law jurisprudence overseas. They were reported to have said that two or even more overseas judges might sit in any one appeal, depending upon the nature of the issues it raised.[2]

You may think that for any sovereign power to accept that a procession of foreigners might enter its territory to sit in final judgment upon local disputes is a remarkable constitutional concession. That such an anomaly was favoured for the HKSAR displayed pragmatic realism, recognising both the importance of the common law to an international and financial centre and the limited pool of local talent then thought available to staff the new court.

The Sino-British Joint Declaration (JD) signed in 1984, guaranteeing that Hong Kong's judicial and common law systems would continue, said in terms: 'The power of final judgment of the Hong Kong Special Administrative Region shall be vested in the court of final appeal in the Hong Kong Special Administrative Region, which may as required invite judges from other common law jurisdictions to sit on the court of final

---

[2] See statements of the Hon. Martin Lee in *Hong Kong Hansard*, 3 May 1995, p. 3539; 26 July 1995, p. 5939; 26 June 2008, p. 9570; L. F. So and C. Law, 'Pledge to Bar "Broken" – Judge Selection Row Grows', *South China Morning Post*, 1 November 1994.

appeal.'[3] These words were repeated in Article 81 of the 1990 BL. Note the use of 'judges', not 'a judge'.

As 1997 approached, legislation proposed by the outgoing colonial government for setting up the CFA was reviewed in the Joint Liaison Group. It transpired in September 1991 that the two sides had agreed that in any appeal, along with the CJ and its permanent local judges, the Court might sit with one, only one, visiting overseas judge and one former retired Hong Kong judge.

There was a strong reaction to this. LegCo debated the issue in December 1991. The Bar twice opposed the introduction into LegCo of a draft CFA bill. There were two special meetings of the Bar[4] and one of the Law Society.[5] The main focus of criticism was that a single overseas judge was a breach of the JD and the BL, which referred to 'judges', and that 'if required' promised flexibility. The 1983 informal assurances were cited as evidence of a promise reneged.

It was then fashionable to think that the BL could be read literally, a view since rejected by the CFA, as Sir Anthony Mason shows in Chapter 13. The BL provides a political landscape showing the great outlines of how powers are to be devolved and distributed; it is not meant to be an ordnance survey map precisely laying out details of the ground.[6]

Initial outright opposition to setting up the CFA eventually gave way to criticisms of details of the bill as practitioners began to accept the need for a CFA to be up and running on 1 July 1997, anticipating the novel constitutional and administrative disputes that would soon come its way.

The executive's introduction of the bill led to further debates in the Legislative Council. Several amendments were moved, debated, and rejected after divisions. On its third and last reading, it was still opposed by 17 members voting against 38 in favour. Thus, the HKCFAO was finally enacted to come into force on 1 July 1997.

A reader of *Hong Kong Hansard* today may find it difficult to understand each and every criticism then voiced by legislators and by practitioners, as well as the intransigence displayed. But it is easy to forget the fears and

---

[3] See Annex 1, Part III of the Sino-British Joint Declaration, accessible as Instrument A301 in the Department of Justice's Bilingual Law Information System, available at www.legislation. gov.hk.

[4] There was an open seminar and an Extraordinary AGM held on 8 December 1994.

[5] An EGM was convened, but 350 members turned up, too many for the Mandarin Oriental, and it was adjourned to the Queen Elizabeth stadium with 800 attending on 15 January 1995.

[6] See *Cheng Kar Shun* v. *Hon. Li Fung Ying* [2009] 4 HKC 204 at 246 (CFI).

apprehensions then aroused by the impending change of sovereignty and the anxiety to see the new constitutional order underpinned by the best possible legislative means.

Of course, no one could then have foreseen the ease with which the CFA would be able to settle into its role, fulfilling the needs that impelled its creation, and devising methods of working that would be fair and efficient. That is truly the measure of the achievement of Andrew Li and his judges.

The last formal public submission[7] of the Bar Council dated 3 July 1995 (as the bill was proceeding through LegCo) sets out five basic objections: (1) that the method of selection and appointment of the CJ and the judges undermined the rule of law and the independence of the judiciary, (2) that the bill did not match the JD and BL's provisions for overseas judges to sit, (3) that the Court's jurisdiction was insufficiently flexible, (4) that denial of jurisdiction over acts of state was inconsistent with current court practice, and (5) that administrative separation between the CFA and the lower courts was both desirable and insufficiently made clear. Let me comment on each one of these in the light of experience of the Court in operation.

First, the way in which CFA judges are selected under the HKCFAO simply reflects Articles 88 and 90 of the BL. They provide that the Chief Justice, if duly qualified, shall be appointed by the Chief Executive, on the recommendation of an independent commission,[8] who shall obtain the endorsement of LegCo and shall report the appointment to the NPCSC for the record.

One can see how this might be abused if local politicians or Mainland authorities wished to pick a quarrel with the selection process. But it is difficult to see why anyone by such conspicuous interference should want to undermine the constitutionally entrenched principle of judicial independence that counts for so much in this territory. The process was again tested when Andrew Li's successor, Geoffrey Ma, came to be appointed. The Chief Justice said in his last annual address:

> It is essential to judicial independence that the process of judicial appointment should never be politicised. In our jurisdiction, it has not been politicised and I trust that it will never be. This includes the endorsement process in the Legislative Council for the most senior judicial appointments.

[7] An earlier position paper of late 1994 cannot presently be found.
[8] See the Judicial Officers Recommendation Commission Ordinance (Cap. 92).

> I am glad to see that the Legislative Council has adopted a procedure
> for dealing with endorsement which ensures that whilst enabling it to
> discharge its duty, the process is not politicised. I am confident that the
> Council will continue to deal with the process of endorsement without
> politicising it.[9]

Second, on the role of an overseas single judge, I have seen for myself how
the court as a whole benefits from the participation of eminent jurists with
high intellectual skills and vast legal experience from the House of Lords,
the High Court of Australia, and the Supreme Court of New Zealand.
These jurists are famous throughout the common law world, and it flatters
Hong Kong that they are willing to come here to sit for a month at a time.
Although most of the current overseas judges on the list have retired from
office, Andrew Li was fortunate in persuading successive Lord Chancellors
to allow serving law lords to take leave of absence from Westminster. From
the bar table, one can sense the confidence each overseas judge brings to
our permanent judges in difficult cases and the influence they can bring
to bear as the judges confer among themselves.

The additional retired Hong Kong judge[10] will often make up the five
when either the Chief Justice or a permanent judge cannot sit because
of other commitments, ill health, or a disqualifying personal interest.
Because that list includes many with long experience in the Court of
Appeal and in one case a former permanent CFA judge, of course they
make excellent substitutes.

The overseas judge always sits on the extreme left of the presiding judge
in the 'junior' seat. He (and we have yet to see a she in this court) takes
care not to dominate the proceedings or to upstage the local members. By
questions put with an old world courtesy that hides devastating content,
the core of many a shaky argument is penetrated, essential weaknesses
of reasoning are exposed, verbosity is sweetly punctured, and the ill-
prepared advocate is pulled up in his tracks. That is all to the good. Apart
from anything else, it keeps every advocate up to the mark, and it provides
some amusement to everyone else in court.

But of one thing I feel sure. After 13 years of operation, I see no reason
to think that the Court has ever been handicapped by sitting with only
one overseas judge or that it would have been better off had it been sitting
with two or more.

---

[9] 'CJ's speech at Ceremonial Opening of the Legal Year 2010', *Hong Kong Government Press Release*, 11 January 2010.
[10] HKCFAO, section 8.

More extensive background knowledge is scarcely needed because the Court always welcomes materials of comparative law and practice, as well as textbooks and academic articles. The JD and BL provide that precedents from other common law jurisdictions can be referred to. And they are all too freely cited – relevant decisions of any court, eminent or obscure, that the internet researches of junior counsel have discovered. There is no blind loyalty to British precedents when there is cause to prefer the reasoning in Australian or New Zealand decisions, or less frequently, a Canadian case.

Very often the overseas judge sees no need to give a substantive judgment. It is rare for one to dissent. I recall only two cases – I was in both – in which the court divided three to two, with the overseas judge in the minority both times.[11] In any case, two overseas judges would not necessarily speak with one voice and would only add to the court's difficulties if they were violently to disagree.

Third, although the bill was criticised for the way in which the jurisdiction of the court was circumscribed, experience has thrown up little cause for amendment. Although the Bar argued for greater flexibility, the criteria for accepting appeals were modelled on the statutes of the PC. The Bar Council wanted provision for appeals directly from the Court of First Instance to save time and costs in suitable cases. So-called 'leap frog' appeals were later brought in by amendment in 2002, but strict conditions apply,[12] and few cases will ever qualify. Any court of last resort will ordinarily wish to have the benefit of the opinion of the Court of Appeal before making final pronouncements on important questions.

Fourth, there was criticism of section 4 that denies jurisdiction to the court over acts of state such as defence and foreign affairs. This necessarily reflects the express jurisdictional limitation in Article 19 of the BL and the limits on Hong Kong's autonomy. Not surprisingly, it was said to break with the previous judicial system. There was no matching precedent for limiting PC appeals, although of course a plea of 'act of state' has long been a common law defence. I am not aware of any case that has fallen foul of this limitation, although in a 2011 appeal, the concept of 'act of state' and the scope of 'foreign affairs' were considered for the first time.[13]

---

[11] *Bank of East Asia Ltd* v. *Tsien Wui Marble Factory* (1999) 2 HKCFAR 349 and *Next Magazine Publishing Ltd* v. *Ma Ching Fat* (2003) 6 HKCFAR 63. The first time for a local NPJ to dissent was in June 2011; see *Congo* case, note 13 below.

[12] HKCFAO, sections 27A to 27E.

[13] See *Democratic Republic of the Congo* v. *FG Hemisphere Associates LLC* (2011) 14 HKCFAR 95 (reference) and 395 (disposition).

Lastly, there was objection to what became section 6(2). It was argued that the Chief Justice should not be the head of the judiciary or charged with its administration; that should be left to the Chief Judge in the lower court. Presumably, it was sought to match the similar isolation of the House of Lords and PC.

Given the time and trouble that Andrew Li devoted to these important duties of his office – because he could only spare time to sit in about half the appeals – he might have been pleased if the Bar had had its way. But given the size and homogeneity of Hong Kong, it seemed pointless to separate the most senior judges from the rest because they all share the same concern for conditions of service, provision of resources, and best meeting the needs of the customers.

At the apex of the courts, the Chief Justice is in the best position to assess the strengths and weaknesses of those whose judgments are being scrutinised and to spot from members of the Bar the best candidates for judicial office. It is no secret that Andrew Li personally devoted a great deal of time and thought to judicial appointments, planning promotions to fill the vacancies created by retirement. He was personally responsible for persuading several outstanding barristers to apply to step up to the bench.

In this context of judicial administration, we should acknowledge the devoted service to Hong Kong of Sir Anthony Mason. His huge contribution to the court's jurisprudence in the landmark constitutional cases, many affecting public administration, is obvious from the reports. From the start he took pains to understand Hong Kong, its concerns, and its way of life. And he has also given invaluable advice and support to Andrew Li in relation to judicial administration. For example, he prepared an important paper for presentation to the government to expound and entrench the principle of judicial independence in the context of judicial remuneration and terms of service. Sir Anthony has given truly outstanding service to the court and the community of Hong Kong in many different ways.

In the remaining portion of this chapter, I will offer some personal reflections on how the court does its work and the ways in which it might change to make things better still. Every member of the Bar would wish me to record that for all the charm and splendour of the old French Mission chapel in which the court now sits, the acoustics are simply terrible. Those sitting can clamp the amplifying headphones over their wigs, but the advocate on his feet cannot. Some time ago, the interventions of one overseas judge baffled everybody, judges as well as counsel, handicapped by both a country accent and ill-fitting dentures. The voice of a judge sitting back in his chair with a hand near his mouth and musing aloud scarcely reaches the microphone on his desk, let alone the advocate below, straining to hear the pearls of wisdom. And I dare say, there are advocates who cannot easily be heard by the court.

The other professional whinge (apart from the lack of a coffee machine in the building) is that the bar table simply cannot accommodate the scores of bundles of documents and authorities that counsel need to handle in the complex cases. Deeper tables and shelves would help enormously. I am sure that when the court moves back to the old Supreme Court building, things will improve.

On less mundane matters, I have some ideas for reform. I see no real justification for preserving the old PC provision for appeals as of right if the amount at stake exceeds a certain amount (currently, 1 million Hong Kong dollars, not a large sum in today's commercial and real estate sectors). In setting up a new court, one can see why familiar precedents were adopted. But whatever fears the old Empire builders had for the fate of their colonial investments in remote courts, the amount of money at stake has no bearing on the significance of legal issues. Cases surely do not warrant a third hearing for this reason alone. An unjust result is no more tolerable measured in six figures than it is in seven figures.

Nor need so much argument and citation be devoted to the question whether a particular case fulfils the statutory rubric of section 22(1)(a) on which there are numerous relevant authorities.[14] They show that many a case does not qualify even though the impact of a decision is bound to be felt in millions of dollars (e.g. a decision on liability in which damages have not yet been assessed or a matrimonial determination in which family assets have yet to be distributed).

As in section 22(1)(b), no case should engage the valuable resources of the highest court in the territory unless either the Court of Appeal or the CFA rules that it should. They should be reserved for cases of true legal significance or putting right manifest injustice. The court already has wide discretion. In general, a point of great general or public importance

---

[14] Section 22(1)(a) of the HKCFAO provides an appeal as of right 'from any final judgment of the Court of Appeal in any civil cause or matter, where the matter in dispute on the appeal amounts to or is of the value of $1,000,000 or more, or where the appeal involves, directly or indirectly, some claim or question to or respecting property or some civil right amounting to or of the value of $1000000 or more'. See further Chapter 7 (Da Roza) in this volume.

needs to be identified. But the discretion can be exercised even if none can be found (the 'or otherwise' provision). This gives the court power to correct the occasional case where the Court of Appeal has rendered a manifestly bad or defective decision (yes, it does occasionally happen).

There is also much to be said for streamlining the procedures for obtaining leave to appeal. It should not be necessary to have an oral hearing in the Court of Appeal (unless the court calls for one). The question should be decided at the hearing of the appeal or on paper soon after the judgments are handed down when the issues are fresh in the memory. I had a case when we waited several months for a date before the three members of the court could all be reconvened to consider one morning whether we should have leave to appeal. Most applications to the CFA for leave to appeal could also be decided on paper. Presently, the hearings dictated by Part II of the rules are generally listed for half a day and often stray deeply into arguing the grounds of appeal. Oral applications to the House of Lords and PC on average used to take about 20 minutes, but most are now dealt with on paper.

I would also advocate a more realistic approach to the question of ordering security for costs. Presently, there is a limit of $400,000 and no power to order more.[15] This sum is far less than the likely costs of a successful respondent in a heavy case with leading and junior counsel. There may have been a desire not to restrict unduly access of a dissatisfied litigant in a colony to present his or her petition to the Queen in Council in London. But surely the power to order security for costs should not be limited for appellants wishing their case to be heard a third time by the CFA, when it is unlimited before the Court of Appeal hearing the case for the second time.

A recent case has also thrown up a lacuna in the court's power that may need attention.[16] The Court of Appeal had refused to order a stay of execution. An escrow agent was free to release monies previously in court as a consequence of allowing the appeal. The unsuccessful party intended to seek leave to appeal from the Court of Appeal but meanwhile sought a stay of execution, which was refused. It then applied to the CFA for a stay. It was refused by a single judge for want of jurisdiction. He held that until a formal application for leave had been filed, the CFA lacked power to order a stay.

---

[15] Section 25(3)(b) of the HKCFAO and *World Fuel Services (Singapore) Pte Ltd* v. *Forens Container Inc* (2007) 10 HKCFAR 252.

[16] *DLA Piper Hong Kong* v. *China Property Development Holdings Ltd* (2010) 13 HKCFAR 14.

There may or may not be an 'inherent jurisdiction' in a new statutory court (as against one taking over powers previously enjoyed by its predecessors),[17] but it might be thought to have implied power to do all things necessarily and reasonably incidental to the just and effective determination of appeals.

In any case, it was held that as a necessary prerequisite to the exercise of such a power, there must already be an application for leave to appeal (or an appeal) pending before the CFA. Until its process had been engaged, its inherent jurisdiction could not be invoked. This seems an unsatisfactory lacuna given the urgency of the matter because it is often the case that the release of money can render nugatory a successful appeal to the CFA should leave subsequently be given.[18]

A final thought from one who is sometimes champing at the bit in London, waiting to get my hands on Part B of the record to start working on a case. These bundles contain the relevant evidence at trial for reference in the course of argument. The registrar does valuable work to prevent solicitors from copying unnecessary, illegible, or duplicated documentation. But I would urge him to make sure that the bundles are ready at least four weeks before the hearing. That means getting the process towards agreement started early on to allow for the time that busy solicitors need to prepare and exchange lists and to exhaust their capacity to disagree about what should be included before going to the registrar to seek his approval.

With those few thoughts, I conclude by expressing the pleasure I have had in appearing before this court. It is always a forensic treat. In the CFA, I know I am before judges who are interested and ready, willing, and abundantly capable of sorting out the issues, however complex, convoluted, or strained the arguments might have become in the effort to succeed. I often feel that I have not really understood what the case is all about until the hearing is over. I am humbled to know that to be the case after reading their judgments.

---

[17]   As Bokhary PJ has held and Ribeiro PJ has confirmed; see *Secretary for Justice* v. *To Kan Chi* (2000) 3 HKCFAR 264; *Shanghai Tongji Science & Technology Industrial Co. Ltd* v. *Casil Clearing Ltd*, unreported, FAMP2/2003, 11 August 2003, CFA (Ribeiro PJ in Chambers); *Joint and Several Liquidators of Kong Wah Holdings Ltd* v. *Grande Holdings Ltd* (2006) 9 HKCFAR 795.

[18]   See also *Admiral Taverns (Cygnet) Ltd* v. *Daniel* [2009] 1 WLR 2192 (CA).

9

A human rights lawyer's perspective

MARK DALY

The retirement of Andrew Li CJ and this conference provide an opportunity to reflect on Hong Kong's Court of Final Appeal (CFA) and consider the future. My perspective is that of a human rights lawyer and practitioner before the court, and the cases that my firm has litigated have involved issues of constitutional importance and fundamental human rights. Because a number of our new cases seem to be headed towards the CFA, while realizing the significance of this occasion for commemoration, I cannot help 'working', in the sense of considering what may be the barriers to justice and, with lessons since 1997, consider the prospects for success in future cases.

Can we achieve justice in our courts and in the CFA? I prefer the term 'justice system' as opposed to 'legal system' or 'court system' and believe that the difference is one of substance going to the core of the role of the justice system in our community. Can we win? This seems to be the fundamental question, certainly for aggrieved applicants,[1] and before working towards an answer, I wish to make a few initial contextual observations.

Context

The Hong Kong CFA is an enormously important court, and developments here, including structural, political, and legal, can have worldwide significance. Various factors support this proposition. The first of these is the 'China factor' and the interaction, perhaps collision, with the legal

---

[1] I am reminded of a conversation with a prominent academic who queried whether we should consider not appealing in one of our cases because we had achieved a useful statement of principle in the judgment. He had to be reminded that we lost the case and that the clients/applicants would find little solace in the statement of principle.

system of Mainland China. How the justice system in China, as a rising global power, develops will have an impact on the world. The justice system of the Hong Kong Special Administrative Region (HKSAR) has a major role to play in the exportation of concepts of justice and the rule of law.[2] Legal exchanges at all levels between lawyers and judges of Hong Kong and the Mainland take place, although exchanges on human rights and judicial review are only in the nascent stages.

In addition to the unique position of Hong Kong's common law courts in China, the Hong Kong courts can have a major influence in the region because of their well-respected legal traditions and role in being a contributor to justice in a region where the traditional checks and balances in a modern functioning state do not exist or are not fully formed, international human rights conventions are not ratified or domesticated, and other avenues to achieving justice are significantly curtailed. An example of this regional impact is litigation in the refugee and Convention Against Torture (CAT) areas of law. This is followed closely by practitioners and non-governmental organisations in the region, which may be experiencing human rights problems that have to a large extent been solved in more developed jurisdictions.[3] The Hong Kong courts can also at times function as a forum where 'Asian values' and relativistic and universal values compete. I am fond of the quote from Yash Ghai in which he compares the roles of human rights in the West and in Asia:

> The role of human rights is to fine-tune the administrative and judicial system and fortify rights and freedoms that are largely uncontroversial. In Asia, on the other hand, human rights have a transformative potential.[4]

---

[2] If anything the system in China should be moving towards a system like that in Hong Kong. See prescription by Lin Feng, *Constitutional Law in China* (Hong Kong: Sweet & Maxwell Asia, 2000) 111. Justice Bokhary of the CFA stated after a trip by 15 HKSAR judges to Beijing: 'We are not there to learn about mainland law with a view to applying it' in Cliff Buddle, 'Judge Defends Independence of Judiciary', *South China Morning Post*, 27 April 2000. Journalist Tim Hamlett notes, 'The attraction of the "one country, two systems" principle, after all, is that it insulates us from the ramshackle structure which passes up there for a legal system. This is an attraction because what China is pleased to call its legal system fails to meet even the most exiguous international standards' in Tim Hamlett, 'City U Unimpressive in Defending Its Own', *South China Morning Post*, 6 August 2001, 12.
[3] Mark Daly, 'Refugee Law in Hong Kong: Building the Legal Infrastructure', *Hong Kong Lawyer*, September 2009, 14.
[4] 'Democracy, Development and Human Rights: Challenges for Lawyers', *Forum Asia and the Indonesian Legal Aid Foundation*, 1995.

Barriers to justice

I do not wish to play Darth Vader on this occasion, but the importance of justice trumps commemoration and calls for a dose of reality.[5] I worry about the direction the courts in the Hong Kong SAR are heading with the CFA's role in setting the agenda. I can identify some of the areas of concern. The first is 'misplaced margin' and the dangers and inappropriateness of importing such a concept into Hong Kong.[6] This is intertwined with a lack of political development. The second is the increased threshold test for leave and the difficulty of getting cases to court. The third is judicial self-censorship and the continuing fallout from the 'reinterpretation'. Last, we need to be serious about judicial independence.

Misplaced margin

Non-responsive and non-democratic governance invites judicial reviews often as the only means of achieving some form of remedy. On political development in the HKSAR, Johannes Chan, in an article that contains perhaps an overly glowing assessment (see the 'Reinterpretation fall-out' section later) of the judiciary, acknowledges the 'democratic deficit' and the unique circumstances in the HKSAR.[7] After restating the basics and the place of the judiciary in a functioning democracy, he states the following:

> In contrast, the functional constituency system in Hong Kong enables a powerful elite group to dominate the legislature, and the elected representatives of the people have only a weak voice. The Government is able to push through any legislation by engaging sufficient support from some elected representatives and the majority of the functional constituency representatives. On some occasions this was done irrespective of the merits or reasoning of the opposition. When the political process is no longer dictated by reasoning, and when opposite views are treated with ignorance or even contempt, those who are frustrated or disillusioned could

---

[5] At times appreciated! See C. J. S. Knight, 'Publication Review of "Effective Judicial Review: A Cornerstone of Good Governance"' (2010) 126 *Law Quarterly Review* 651–4.

[6] For an early criticism of the application of the margin of appreciation in Hong Kong, see Yash Ghai, 'Sentinels of Liberty or Sheep in Woolf's Clothing? Judicial Politics and the Hong Kong Bill of Rights' (1997) 60 *The Modern Law Review* 459.

[7] Johannes Chan, 'Basic Law and Constitutional Review' (2007) 37 *HKLJ* 407. See pp. 445–6, where Chan writes: 'It has restored its full vigour and confidence after the *Chong Fung Yuen* case' and 'by and large, fundamental rights have been upheld'.

only resort either to street politics or to the courts. Thus, when many cases of a political nature or with political overtone are brought before the Courts as attempts to change the system have led to nowhere in the political process, this is in a way a negative verdict and a sign of frustration of the political process. If the political forum remains ineffective, this trend of seeking judicial intervention will inevitably continue. In so doing, the integrity and independence of the judiciary will be subject to the most strenuous test. After all, the judiciary is not the appropriate forum to deal with difficult issues of distribution of resources or to formulate policies with far reaching consequences. So far, the verdict on the performance of the judiciary in adhering to its proper role and in withstanding political pressure is quite positive. However, if this trend continues unchecked, if the political process remains ineffective, and when the judiciary is unable to meet the expectations of the people, the rule of law will be undermined.[8]

Richard Cullen refers to the lack of democracy as well and states:

> It is for this reason that undue deference by the Hong Kong judiciary towards the executive and towards the legislature raises special concerns. In the HKSAR, freedom is something of a 'two-legged stool'. The judiciary and a free press provide two legs but the third, democracy, is at best only half a leg.[9]

And noting the importance of 'legitimacy', Yash Ghai writes,

> Courts are now more willing to take on jurisdiction, in part because other institutions often enjoy less legitimacy than courts. Sometimes it is only by court intervention that a modicum of legality can be preserved . . . In Hong Kong, this point is particularly pertinent since neither the Hong Kong executive or legislature is fully elected.[10]

Because of the 'two-legged stool', the rationales advanced for deference by the judiciary to the executive or the legislature in the Hong Kong SAR lose much of their force. On this point, when administrative law expert Christopher Forsyth visited Hong Kong and was asked by the author whether in the Hong Kong context there should be a more interventionist

---

[8] *Ibid.*, 446–7.
[9] Richard Cullen, 'Media Freedom in Chinese Hong Kong' (1998) 11 *Transnational Law* 383, 401.
[10] Yash Ghai, 'Litigating the Basic Law: Jurisdiction, Interpretation and Procedure' in Chen, Fu & Ghai (eds.), *Hong Kong's Constitutional Debate: Conflict over Interpretation* (Hong Kong: Hong Kong University Press, 2000), 23.

judiciary in light of the lack of proper political checks and balances, he replied that 'arguments for judicial deference weaken'.[11]

If deference is a pathogen infecting the judiciary in Hong Kong, then one of the vectors is the doctrine of 'margin of appreciation'. Hartmann J (who became a Justice of Appeal and remains a non-permanent judge [NPJ] of the CFA) in a 2007 paper entitled 'Judicial Review (The most striking Development in the Common Law Since the Second World War)' stated:

> The doctrine of proportionality is always accompanied by the recognition by the courts that they are not the primary decision-makers on matters of policy and a 'margin of appreciation' *must* be given to public authorities to enable them to make legitimate policy decisions.
>
> But how wide is this margin? The answer is that the margin increases or decreases depending on the subject matter.
>
> Particular deference is given in areas of economic and planning policy. Put another way in these areas, the courts will recognize a broader 'discretionary area of judgment' to which they will defer, on democratic grounds, to the considered opinion of the public authority.
>
> However, the greater the restriction on fundamental rights, the less margin of appreciation, especially in areas where the courts themselves have particular experience and expertise (e.g., restrictions going to the trial process) [emphasis mine].[12]

In the case of *C* v. *Director of Immigration*, a case with great implications for the development of international human rights law, Justice Hartmann also referred to Hong Kong as an 'open, democratic society'.[13] Ghai was an early critic of the doctrine of the margin of appreciation as applied by Lord Woolf in an appeal to the Privy Council from Hong Kong.[14] Writing on margin of appreciation, Sir Anthony Mason describes it as '[a]nother European importation' and 'an area of decision-making where

---

[11] Lecture/Discussion, Margaret Ng LegCo Offices, 28 September 2001. Note also W. S. Clarke, 'Judicial Review of the Discretionary Powers of the Attorney General of Hong Kong in the Conduct of Criminal Proceedings' (1983) 13 *HKLJ* 133, where he writes on p. 147, 'The status quo may well suit the needs of countries overseas. But in light of the peculiar circumstances of Hong Kong it is submitted that the scope of judicial review here needs to be broadened'.

[12] On file with the author.

[13] *C* v. *Director of Immigration* [2011] 5 HKC 118 (CA), aff'g [2008] 2 HKC 165, [183] (CFI), but ultimately reversed by the CFA in FACV18/2011, 25 March 2013.

[14] Yash Ghai, 'Sentinels of Liberty or *Sheep* in Woolf's Clothing? Judicial Politics and the Hong Kong Bill of Rights' 60 (1997) *Modern Law Review* 459–80.

other institutions enjoy a *unique legitimacy* and expertise which the courts lack' [emphasis mine].[15] Lord Lester, however, cautions that:

> The concept of 'margin of appreciation' has become as slippery and elusive as an eel. Again and again the court now appears to use margin of appreciation as a substitute for coherent legal analysis of the issues at stake . . . The danger of continuing to use the standardless doctrine of the margin of appreciation is that . . . it will become the source of a pernicious 'variable geometry' of human rights, eroding the 'acquis' of existing jurisprudence & giving undue deference to local conditions, and practices.[16]

It does not strengthen the rule of law or do the cause of justice any good to pretend that we live in a democracy in the HKSAR. Justice will not be the result if we start from a fictitious premise. If the institutions referred to are the executive and the legislature, then the reality is that their legitimacy is, at a minimum, questionable.

If local context is important, then the whole idea of margin, as a European concept, born of functioning democratic jurisdictions should not be incorporated into the 'two-legged stool' that is the HKSAR. And if imported, the special context and circumstances of the HKSAR would dictate that the pendulum of intervention is required to move in the opposite direction for justice to be done.[17] In his chapter in this volume, Mason NPJ refers to Lord Hoffmann's (also NPJ of our CFA) speech, 'The Universality of Human Rights'[18] and Hoffmann's criticism that the Strasbourg Court should allow a greater margin of appreciation for domestic courts before noting that these developments 'could be relevant to the use to be made by the CFA of the Strasbourg jurisprudence'. It would be a dangerous development to transpose the European debate into Hong Kong without understanding the structural circumstances and the

---

[15] Sir Anthony Mason, 'The Place of Comparative Law in Developing the Jurisprudence on the Rule of Law and Human Rights in Hong Kong' (2007) 37 *HKLJ* 299.

[16] Lord Lester of Herne Hill, 'The European Convention on Human Rights in the New Architecture of Europe: General Report' in 8th International Colloquy on the European Convention on Human Rights: proceedings organised by the Secretariat General of the Council of Europe in co-operation with the Ministry of Justice of Hungary and the Institute for Legal and Administrative Sciences of the Hungarian Academy of Sciences, Budapest, 20–23 September 1995 (Strasbourg: Council of Europe, 1996) 227.

[17] Perhaps a theoretical construct having aspects similar to the original intent of the Courts of Equity is necessary for justice to be done in jurisdictions such as the HKSAR.

[18] Judicial Studies Board Annual Lecture, 19 March 2009, published in (2009) 125 LQR 416. See also, 'Lord Hoffmann in All-Out Attack on European Court of Human Rights', *Solicitors Journal*, 7 April 2009, accessible at: www.solicitorsjournal.com/story.asp?sectioncode=2&storycode=14002&c=1&eclipse_action=getsession.

barriers to justice there. For one thing, although there may be legitimate 'fine-tuning' criticisms in Europe, in this region, we lack effective mechanisms to redress human rights violations.

With respect to conventions on human rights, Paul Mahoney refers to the concerns that the doctrine of margin of appreciation is 'an improper reading into the text of a pro-government restriction'.[19] He rejects criticisms that 'through the margin of appreciation, the [European] Court has emptied many of the strict conditions laid down in the Convention of their strength'.[20] Macdonald states:

> But perhaps the Convention system is now sufficiently mature to be able to move beyond the margin of appreciation and grapple more openly with the questions of appropriateness which that device obscures.[21]

Benvenisti sets out what is at stake when judges misuse margin:

> Margin of appreciation, with its principled recognition of moral relativism, is at odds with the concept of the universality of human rights. If applied liberally, this doctrine can undermine seriously the promise of international enforcement of human rights that overcomes national policies. Moreover, its use may compromise the credibility of the applying international organ. Inconsistent applications in seemingly similar cases due to different margins allowed by the court might raise concerns about judicial double standards. Even more importantly, the rhetoric supporting national margin of appreciation and the lack of corresponding emphasis on universal values and standards may lead national institutions to resist external review altogether, claiming that they are the better judges of their particular domestic constraints and hence the final arbiters of their appropriate margin. Thus, not only would universal standards be undermined, but also the very authority of international human rights bodies to develop such standards in the long run also may be compromised.[22]

It can become too easy for the courts to resort to the 'special circumstances' justification (in its various formulations) to depart from international human rights standards.[23] Another potential ideological

---

[19] Paul Mahoney, 'Judicial Activism and Judicial Self-Restraint in the European Court of Human Rights: Two Sides of the Same Coin' (1990) 11 *Hum. Rts L. J.* 57, 80.

[20] *Ibid.*, 81.

[21] 'The Margin of Appreciation' in R. St. J. Macdonald, F. Matscher, and H. Petzold (eds.), *The European System for the Protection of Human Rights* (Dordrecht: Kluwer Academic Publishers, 1993) 83, 122.

[22] Eyal Benvenisti, 'Margin of Appreciation, Consensus, and Universal Standards' (1999) 31 *International Law and Politics* 843.

[23] Mark Daly, 'International Human Rights Standards in Hong Kong Courts', Dissertation LLM (Human Rights) 2001, Department of Law: The University of Hong Kong. See for

threat to the international human rights regime is the overemphasis of cultural relativism. Much has been written on the topic in respect of Asia,[24] and there is the danger of resorting to a simplistic dismissal of international human rights standards without careful analysis as to whether the supposed differences really do justify denial of the fundamental human right at issue. Carol Jones writes:

> Like the rule of law, the appeal to a common 'Chineseness' is one means of uniting the rulers and the ruled, the elites and the masses, the Hong Kong people and the Mainland government. If this succeeds, sooner or later English rule of law may be seen as ill-suited to a Hong Kong which is now more Chinese in complexion.[25]

Leave test

Concern has been expressed in Hong Kong about the rise in the number of judicial reviews. In his speech at the opening of the new legal year on 8 January 2007, the former Chief Justice, Mr. Andrew Li Kwok-nang, talked about the 'phenomenon of judicial review' and said 'it should be seen as providing an essential foundation for good governance under the rule of law'.[26] However, he cautioned that judicial review cannot provide a 'panacea' for these problems:

> Within the limits of legality, the practical solutions to the complex and difficult political, economic and social problems faced by society must be discussed and found through the proper operation of the political system. Citizens have to look to the political process to deliver appropriate workable solutions to these problems.[27]

example, *Ng Kung Siu* v. *HKSAR* (1999) 2 HKCFAR 442 (the flag case) and the CFA's view that 'due weight' should be given to the HKSAR legislature and 'Hong Kong is at the early stage of the new order' as relevant factors in deviating from the dominant international trend. Any detailed rationale for deviating from the international perspective seems lacking.

24 Joanne R. Bauer and Daniel A. Bell (eds.), *The East Asian Challenge for Human Rights* (Cambridge: Cambridge University Press, 1999) Part I.

25 Carol Jones, 'Politics Postponed: Law As a Substitute for Politics in Hong Kong and China' in Kanishka Jayasuriya (ed.), *Law, Capitalism and Power in Asia: The Rule of Law and Legal Institution* (London: Taylor & Francis Ltd Routledge, 1998).

26 'CJ's speech at ceremonial opening of the legal year 2007', accessible at www.info.gov.hk/gia/general/200701/08/P200701080120.htm.

27 *Ibid.*

The message was toned down slightly from the same occasion in 2006, when he said:

> The courts could not possibly provide an answer to, let alone a panacea for, any of the various political, social and economic problems which confront society in modern times.[28]

Later in the same year, the CFA revisited the test for leave in the case of *Peter Po Fun Chan*, in which Chief Justice Li referred to the earlier 'potential arguability' test in the Court of Appeal case of *Ho Ming-sai*[29] and stated:

> Hartmann J, who has wide experience in this area of the law, whilst accepting that judges at first instance were bound by the test, expressed sympathy with the view that the test was too weak.[30]

Referring to the rise in the number of judicial reviews, the Chief Justice then continued:

> Whilst in a society governed by the rule of law, it is of fundamental importance for citizens to have access to the courts to challenge decisions made by public authorities on judicial review, the public interest in good public administration requires that public authorities should not have to face uncertainty as to the validity of their decisions as a result of unarguable claims. Nor should third parties affected by their decisions face such uncertainty.[31]

With a brief justification for the change, the test of arguability was then adopted to replace the potential arguability test, although it is recognised that 'more time may need to be spent by the judge in dealing with leave applications than previously'.[32]

The change was reported in a *South China Morning Post* article wherein I commented that 'the judgment might end up curtailing one of the few avenues Hong Kong people had for challenging the actions of their government'.[33] With the stricter test, I was concerned many human rights

---

[28] 'Chief Justice's speech at the ceremonial opening of the legal year 2006', accessible at www.info.gov.hk/gia/general/200601/09/P200601090137.htm.

[29] *Ho Ming-sai* v. *The Director of Immigration* [1994] 1 HKLR 21.

[30] *Peter Po Fun Chan* v. *Winnie C.W. Cheung* (2007) 10 HKCFAR 676, 684[10].

[31] *Ibid.*, 685[14].   [32] *Ibid.*, 686[17].

[33] 'Top Court Acts on Increase in Judicial Reviews', *South China Morning Post*, 1 December 2007, 1.

cases were 'not going to see the light of day' and legal aid was going to be more difficult to obtain because of the new standard.[34] The article noted that 'without legal aid, some people would be unable to take even the first step of seeking leave for a review'.[35] Within two weeks, the Legal Aid Department and a High Court Master referred to the new test in refusing to provide legal aid support in a case with human rights implications. Such cases may now have to be taken on a *pro bono* basis, and the applicant will have to consider potential adverse cost consequences if the putative respondent is going to be more routinely invited to an oral hearing at the leave stage.

Six weeks later, on the occasion of the opening of the legal year, it was reported that 'the Secretary for Justice reminded Hong Kongers that their right to have government decisions judicially reviewed is a limited one. . . . The comments by Wong Yan-lung seem to be aimed at stemming the rising tide of applications by members of the public to have government decisions reviewed'.[36] Two cases were referred to and the article reported that the

> use of judicial review over Queen's Pier was described by Martin Lee Chu-ming as performing the role of a proxy in place of fully representative and responsive government. Mr. Wong also used his speech to endorse a November decision by the Court of Final Appeal that raised the bar in terms of the test the courts will use in determining whether or not a review should proceed.[37]

In the same article, it was stated: 'The minister's comments come a week after the Court of Appeal warned against what it described as a growing *fashion* in Hong Kong for people in criminal cases to apply for judicial reviews of decisions relating to the conduct of those cases' [emphasis mine].[38]

The concern emanating from, *inter alia*, government officials and the judiciary has to be seen in the context of a political system that stresses social harmony and can, at times, demonise those critical of the government.

---

[34] *Ibid.*   [35] *Ibid.*
[36] 'Minister Lays Down the Law Over Right to Seek Judicial Reviews', *South China Morning Post*, 15 January 2008. See also the criticisms by Johannes M. M. Chan, 'A Retrograde Judgment', *Ming Pao*, 13 February 2008.
[37] 'Minister Lays Down the Law', *ibid.*   [38] *Ibid.*

Although the vehicle of judicial review may occasionally be hijacked and perhaps misused, one needs to look closely at each case and the overall spectrum of cases and probe the reasons for the judicial review in the first place. Often, it is only by initiating a judicial review that the hidden, non-transparent or absent policymaking will be exposed to some scrutiny. In the area of asylum seekers and CAT claimants, it is entirely the fault of the HKSAR government and may even be a preferred strategy, making the situation as difficult as possible for the claimants and only putting in place occasional incremental and piecemeal changes in reaction to litigation, thus forcing the courts into the role of leading the impetus for changes – a difficult role that they do not seem willing or able to play.[39]

Reinterpretation fallout

In describing the HKSAR context and some of the barriers to justice, one cannot fail to mention the spectre of interpretations by the Standing Committee of the National People's Congress (NPCSC) (or 'reinterpretations' from the perspective of many, realizing the damage it has inflicted on our legal system, demoting our CFA in the eyes of some to that of a 'Court of Semi Final Appeal'[40]). Being declaratory of the law *as it always has been* and at a stroke (and without open debate) dismissing the jurisprudential determinations of the courts, the threat of a possible NPCSC interpretation is quite unique to the HKSAR.

The only limitation on such an interpretation is that if it is made under the procedure provided for in Article 158 of the Basic Law (BL), it would preserve 'judgments previously rendered'. *Lau Kong Yung*[41] decided that this meant the judgment insofar as it determined the legal position of the parties to the proceedings and no further. The judgments in *Ng Ka Ling*[42] and *Chan Kam Nga*[43] were therefore stripped of any broader effect insofar as non-litigants were concerned.[44]

---

[39] See note 4 above.

[40] Resulting in a well-attended demonstration by traditionally conservative Hong Kong lawyers.

[41] *Lau Kong Yung* v. *The Director of Immigration* (1999) 2 HKCFAR 300.

[42] *Ng Ka Ling* v. *The Director of Immigration* (1999) 2 HKCFAR 4.

[43] *Chan Kam Nga* v. *The Director of Immigration* (1999) 2 HKCFAR 82.

[44] See Johannes Chan, Hualing Fu, and Yash Ghai (eds.), *Hong Kong's Constitutional Debate, Conflict Over Interpretation* (Hong Kong: Hong Kong University Press, 2000).

The prospect that a test case may ultimately be reduced to the narrow confines of its sealed orders is enough to radically alter the nature of advice given to clients when interpretations of the BL may be involved. It may never more be the advice of lawyers that persons in the same legal position need not launch their own proceedings but need only wait until the judgments in the proceedings in which they are interested are handed down. The applicants who after 1 July 1997 sought right of abode did precisely that (waited patiently) and were ultimately disentitled unless they fulfilled the random and unjust 'concession policy' promulgated by Hong Kong's Chief Executive as a palliative on the day the NPCSC announced its interpretation.

Even more dramatically, it may not be sufficient to launch proceedings, as these may not result in a 'judgment' to which protection might attach. The only safe course may be to advise the client not only to launch proceedings to raise the same issues but seek by joinder application to become a party to the test case. If it is too late for such an application because, for example, the test case has proceeded beyond first instance, then after judgment has been delivered, assuming it is favourable, an urgent hearing may have to be sought to ensure judgment is delivered in the 'coattails' action as soon as possible, lest there be an interpretation. This is not a practitioner or advocate's paranoia but the nature of the system in which we are operating.

The resistance by the HKSAR government to 'test cases' is well known to my firm. The HKSAR government is now extremely reluctant to acknowledge proceedings as test cases and to agree that persons other than the actual litigants might benefit. It, as well as everyone else, is hamstrung by history. It cannot give reassurance to non-parties, lest that be used against them in subsequent proceedings to found a 'legitimate expectation' of benefiting (as *some* fortunate right of abode litigants who had received letters telling them not to rush to courts before the CFA January 1999 rulings were able to argue successfully highlighting the 'anti rule of law' nature of all of this) in the subsequent January 2002 ruling in *Ng Siu Tung*.[45] At the same time, any general reassurance that the non-parties can rest easy on the basis of the doctrine of precedent rings hollow. The government is in no position to give such a reassurance in cases involving a BL interpretation and is unlikely to do so, wishing to 'keep its options open' lest an unfavourable and indigestible judgment be delivered

---

[45]   *Ng Siu Tung* v. *Director of Immigration* (2002) 5 HKCFAR 1.

again by the CFA. The prospects of 'prompting' another 'reinterpretation' undoubtedly factor into the thinking of lawyers and judges involved in the next big case.[46]

Judicial independence

Although one may be persuaded by arguments along the lines of Michael Mandel,[47] who is critical of the Charter of Rights and Freedom era in Canada, taking important questions on social issues and human rights out of the hands of elected politicians and putting them in the hands of an unelected judiciary, for the reasons set out earlier in this chapter, the arguments weaken in the HKSAR context.

There has been some muted criticism[48] of the process of judicial appointments, including the lack of transparency of the process, lack of adequate information being provided to the Legislative Council, the fact that a resolution could be carried even if there were two dissenting votes on the Judicial Service Commission (now the Judicial Officers Recommendation Commission [JORC]), the presence of the Secretary for Justice as a member of JORC, and concern about political appointments onto the JORC.

As recently as 7 November 2008, the public was informed in a brief press release on behalf of the judiciary that Mr Murray Gleeson AC, The Right Honourable the Lord Walker of Gestingthorpe, and The Right Honourable The Lord Neuberger of Abbotsbury were recommended as NPJs from other common law jurisdictions to the CFA. Given the important cases that they may hear on social and human rights questions, should the public not be entitled to know a little more about how they were selected?

Foreign judges sitting on the CFA have been criticized for their possible impact and importation of ideas wrongfully transplanted from

---

[46] See Chapter 3 (Yang) in this volume. Although appropriate, it does not inspire confidence thinking of the CFA judges playing a game of chicken with the NPCSC.

[47] Michael Mandel, *The Charter of Rights and the Legalization of Politics in Canada* (Toronto: Wall & Thompson, 1989).

[48] 'The Process of Appointment of Judges in Hong Kong Since 1976', Research and Library Services Division, Legislative Council Secretariat, 10 April 2001, accessible at www.legco.gov.hk/yr00-01/english/library/0001rp_7.pdf. See also Berry F.C. Hsu, 'In Colonial Hong Kong, the Concept of Separation of Powers Was Rather Murky. The HKSAR Inherits This Legacy' in 'Judicial Independence in Hong Kong: Apparent or Real?', *Hong Kong Lawyer*, October 2004.

Western countries, being referred to as 'parachute judges'.[49] The criticism is mainly that they would not have due regard to the social conditions in the HKSAR. But I would argue that it is equally likely that parachute judges would be overly deferential as would be any polite guest unfamiliar with his or her new surroundings. As discussed earlier, concepts of judicial restraint from the West can be wrongly imported into Asia. I recall Beverley McLachlin from Canada's Supreme Court speaking at the Commonwealth Law Conference in Malaysia in 1999 about judicial restraint precisely when the Malaysian judiciary (of questionable independence) needed to be emboldened because of the political pressures from the executive. For those advocating a robust, independent and rights-protecting judiciary in Malaysia, it was the wrong message at the wrong time.[50]

Conclusion

Chief Justice Andrew Li steered us capably through unique and difficult times when, because of the post-handover political uncertainty, perhaps a more conservative approach was deemed important when it came to human rights. But serious human rights problems remain, and for the future court, a more rights-conscious public is not going to be satisfied with a legal system that does not deliver practical justice. Concerns about the possibility of achieving justice are heightened when barriers to success in the courts are erected, such as the misuse of margin of appreciation

---

[49] Cliff Buddle, 'Judges Who "Drop In"', *South China Morning Post*, 9 March 2001 and Angela Li, 'Beijing "Fearful of Judicial Activism"', *South China Morning Post*, 21 February 2001. It seems to be a requirement that such judges hail from 'union jack' countries, namely the United Kingdom, Australia, and New Zealand.

[50] The author has attended, as international observer for Amnesty International, the trials of Anwar Ibrahim and Lim Guan Eng (both opposition leaders at the time). See Christine Sypnowich, 'Ruling or Overruled? The People, Rights and Democracy' (2007) 27 OJLS 757:

> Indeed, revulsion at the values of apartheid should entail an assessment of the judicial decisions that upheld those values not in terms of their faithfulness to the morality of the community, constitutional or otherwise. If it were, judges would be able to do nothing when facing sufficiently thorough-going wicked political orders. Rather, as David Dyzenhaus argues, the old South Africa's judiciary, by upholding the social order of apartheid instead of curtailing it by reference to fundamental rights, were guilty of a 'dereliction of duty'.

> David Dyzenhaus' remarks quoted here are contained in his book, *Judging the Judges, Judging Ourselves: Truth, Reconciliation and the Apartheid Legal Order* (Oxford: Hart Publishing, 1998) 60, 71.

and the increased threshold for leave. The pressure on the future court to find a remedy is exacerbated by the fact that in Hong Kong there exists a democratic deficit, and there is no 'Strasbourg'.

Although an aggrieved applicant has had a better chance of success in the CFA, it is very difficult to get there. The danger for the rule of law and justice in Hong Kong lies in the maintenance and installation of further barriers so that human rights victims consider it futile to use the courts.

PART III

Judges and judging

10

Role of the Chief Justice

SIMON N. M. YOUNG, ANTONIO DA ROZA, AND YASH GHAI

Introduction

The Chief Justice of the Hong Kong Special Administrative Region of the People's Republic of China (HKSAR) has many roles, not only as President of the Court of Final Appeal (CFA) and administrative head of the entire judiciary but also important representational and ceremonial roles.[1] Although much of this work is prescribed by law, the needs of Hong Kong's new constitutional order after the resumption of sovereignty required Chief Justice Andrew Li to take on much more in respect of both the setting up of the CFA as well as leading the Hong Kong judiciary. Some of the most important duties and powers relating to the legal system are conferred on the Chief Justice, including those that relate to the composition of the CFA, the recommended appointment of judges and magistrates, the nomination of members to the Basic Law Committee (BLC), law reform, and shaping public opinion about the rule of law and the judiciary. The Chief Justice is arguably the most important person charged with maintaining and upholding the rule of law in Hong Kong.

Colonial Chief Justices

The Hong Kong Letters Patent, from 1917 to 1997, made only insignificant reference to the position of a 'Chief Justice of the Supreme Court'. The first reference was to the duty of 'the Chief Justice or other Judge of the Supreme Court' to administer the oaths of office to newly appointed Governors.[2] The second and only other reference was to the retiring age

---

[1] 'The Chief Justice as Head of the Judiciary has a range of important and heavy responsibilities: judicial, administrative and representational'. See 'Chief Justice Andrew Li: Departing with No Regrets', *Hong Kong Lawyer*, August 2010, 15.

[2] Hong Kong Letters Patent 1917 to 1995, [3].

of 65 years in relation to the 'Chief Justice and any other judge of the Supreme Court'.[3] No reference was made to the Chief Justice in the Hong Kong Royal Instructions.

The Supreme Court Ordinance was more detailed in setting out the role of the colonial Chief Justice.[4] The Supreme Court consisted of the High Court and the Court of Appeal,[5] and the Chief Justice was made a member of both levels of court[6] and particularly the President of the Court of Appeal.[7] He was also a member of the Rules Committee.[8] The Chief Justice had power to appoint deputy judges of the High Court[9] and Vice Presidents of the Court of Appeal,[10] and to request High Court judges to sit as an additional judge of the Court of Appeal.[11] He also had authority to direct a High Court proceeding to be heard and determined by two or more judges of that court.[12]

Under the Judicial Service Commission Ordinance,[13] the Chief Justice chaired the Judicial Service Commission,[14] whose function was to advise the Governor in respect of the filling of vacancies in judicial offices, representations from judicial officers regarding their conditions of service, and any other matter affecting judicial officers prescribed or referred by the Governor to the Commission.[15]

From 1844 to 1997, Hong Kong had 16 Chief Justices.[16] The last Chief Justice, Sir Ti-liang Yang, was the first ethnic Chinese to hold the office and was remembered for introducing the Chinese language in the courts and resigning from office in 1996 to contest the first election for Chief Executive.[17]

Chief Justice under the Basic Law

The Sino-British Joint Declaration provided for the continuation of the courts and legal system after 1997, referring only once to the chief justice's position when reference was made to the 'tribunal appointed by the chief judge of the court of final appeal, consisting of not fewer than three local

---

[3] *Ibid.*, [16A].
[4] Supreme Court Ordinance (Cap. 4), originally Ord. 92 of 1975, in force 20 February 1976.
[5] *Ibid.*, section 3(1).   [6] *Ibid.*, sections 4(1) and 5(1).   [7] *Ibid.*, section 5(3).
[8] *Ibid.*, section 55(1).   [9] *Ibid.*, section 4(1)(c).
[10] *Ibid.*, section 5(1A), added by Ord. 52 of 1987, section 5.   [11] *Ibid.*, section 5(2).
[12] *Ibid.*, section 32(3).   [13] Cap. 92.   [14] *Ibid.*, section 3.   [15] *Ibid.*, section 6.
[16] Count excludes Sir Noel Power, who was acting Chief Justice from 1996 to 1997.
[17] 'Hong Kong Rumour Mill Starts to Spin as Chief Justice Stands for Patten's Job', *The Lawyer*, 10 September 1996.

judges', responsible for recommending to the Chief Executive the removal from office of a particular judge.[18]

After 1997, the Supreme Court became known as the High Court, consisting of the Court of First Instance and Court of Appeal.[19] In contrast to the Letters Patent, the Basic Law (BL) conferred distinct prominence to the role of Chief Justice. There is to be a 'Chief Justice of the Court of Final Appeal' and a 'Chief Judge of the High Court', both of whom must be Chinese citizens and permanent residents of Hong Kong with no right of abode in any foreign country.[20] The Chief Justice is appointed by the Chief Executive, on the recommendation of an 'independent commission composed of local judges, persons from the legal profession and eminent persons from other sectors',[21] which is known as the Judicial Officers Recommendation Commission.[22] For all appointments to the CFA and the appointment of the Chief Judge of the High Court, the Chief Executive must obtain the endorsement of the Legislative Council (LegCo) and report the appointments to the Standing Committee of the National People's Congress (NPCSC) for the record.[23] The other BL references to the Chief Justice are in relation to the accountability of the Chief Executive[24] and the removal of judges.[25]

Under the Reunification Ordinance,[26] all references in statute law to the Chief Justice of the Supreme Court of Hong Kong were to be read as references to the Chief Judge of the High Court of the HKSAR.[27] This confirmed that the previous office of 'Chief Justice of the Supreme Court' evolved into the new post of 'Chief Judge of the High Court', and the

---

[18] Sino-British Joint Declaration, Annex I, section III.   [19] Basic Law, Article 81.

[20] *Ibid.*, Article 90.   [21] *Ibid.*, Article 88.

[22] Judicial Officers Recommendation Commission Ordinance (Cap. 92).

[23] Basic Law, Article 89.

[24] The newly elected Chief Executive must declare his or her assets to the Chief Justice on record (*ibid.*, Article 47), and the Chief Justice may be given a mandate by the LegCo to form and chair an independent investigation committee investigating a charge against the Chief Executive of serious breach of law or dereliction of duty (*ibid.*, Article 73(9)).

[25] Judges may only be removed for inability to discharge their duty or for misbehaviour by the Chief Executive on the recommendation of a tribunal appointed by the Chief Justice and consisting of not fewer than three local judges (*ibid.*, Article 89). Removal of the Chief Justice by the Chief Executive must be on the recommendation of a tribunal consisting of no fewer than five local judges (*ibid.*), and such removal must have the endorsement of the LegCo and be reported to the NPCSC for the record (*ibid.*, Article 90).

[26] Cap. 2601.

[27] Reunification Ordinance, Ord. 110 of 1997, section 6, which added Sch. 8 of the Interpretation and General Clauses Ordinance (Cap. 1).

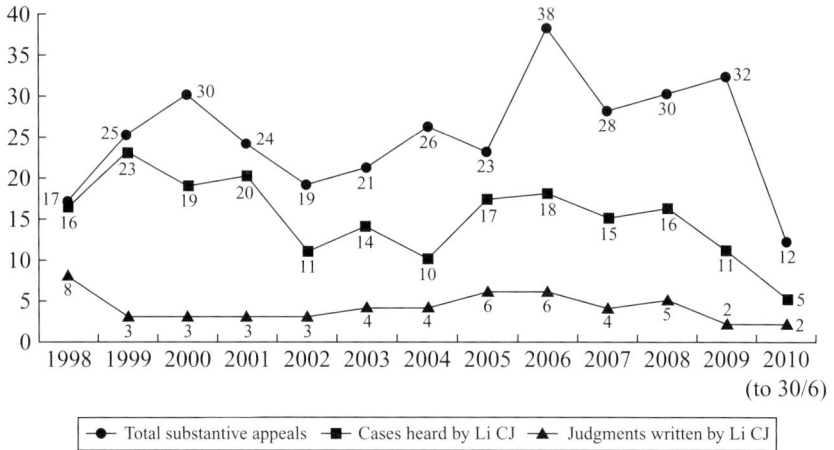

Figure 10.1   Judgments by Chief Justice (CJ) Li and cases heard by Li CJ and the Court of Final Appeal, 1998–2010.

post-1997 office of 'Chief Justice of the CFA' was a new creature established with the new CFA and Hong Kong Court of Final Appeal Ordinance.[28]

President of the court

The judges of the CFA consist of the Chief Justice, the permanent judges (PJs), and such non-permanent judges (NPJs) as may be required.[29] The Chief Justice is President of the CFA, and when he is unavailable to hear an appeal, he must designate a PJ to sit in his place and be President.[30] The Chief Justice may form part of the Appeal Committee that hears applications for leave.[31]

In the 13 years of Li CJ's tenure, he presided over 179 leave applications, or 36 per cent of all leave hearings, and 195 appeals, or 60 per cent of all substantive appeals. The workload for leave applications involved 183 days of hearings and authorship of 58 leave determinations. For substantive appeals, Li CJ sat approximately 370 hearing days and authored a total of 53 judgments. Cumulatively, the judicial work undoubtedly represented the largest proportion of Li CJ's work. Broken down by year, the number of cases heard by Li CJ showed a slight downward trend (Figure 10.1).

[28]   Hong Kong Court of Final Appeal Ordinance (Cap. 484) (HKCFAO), section 6.
[29]   *Ibid.*, section 5.   [30]   *Ibid.*, section 16(2).   [31]   *Ibid.*, section 18.

The number of judgments written remained relatively consistent and did not follow the pattern of number of cases heard (see Figure 10.1).

Although the balance of cases heard by Li CJ in respect of civil and criminal cases did not differ greatly from the court's overall balance (at around 65 per cent civil cases),[32] the proportion of constitutional and administrative law appeals heard by Li CJ was higher than the court's share. Of the 325 substantive appeals heard by the CFA in its first 13 years, 25 per cent of them primarily concerned constitutional or administrative law.[33] Of the 195 cases presided over by Li CJ, 31 per cent dealt with constitutional or administrative law,[34] a proportion that becomes higher if only judgments written by Li CJ were counted. Out of the 53 judgments authored by Li CJ, 19 were in respect of constitutional law cases and 10 concerned administrative law cases, representing almost 55 per cent of all judgments written by Li CJ.

This balance in the judicial work of Li CJ reflected the importance with which he viewed constitutional and administrative law cases. As he stated in his first Opening of the Legal Year address in 1998: 'the Judiciary has a vital constitutional role to ensure that the acts of the Executive and the Legislature comply fully with the BL and the law, and that our fundamental rights and freedoms, which represent enduring values of our society, are fully protected'.[35] The protection of fundamental rights under the concept of 'one country, two systems' was a topic that Li CJ mentioned again in his Opening of the Legal Year speeches in 2000, 2001, and 2003. And on the occasion of his retirement in 2010, he stated:

> The foundation of the new order is "one country, two systems" with each being part of the principle. Constitutional interpretation is a challenging task. The Basic Law is a living instrument intended to meet changing needs and circumstances. The court has laid down various principles for its interpretation: a purposive approach should be applied; a generous interpretation should be given to the guaranteed rights and freedoms;

[32] A total of 122 of the 195 substantive appeals heard by Li CJ (63 per cent) were civil cases; this may be compared with 214 civil cases of a total of 325 cases (66 per cent) for the CFA in its first 13 years.

[33] For the purposes of this study, 50 cases (15 per cent) were categorized as constitutional law cases, and 34 cases (10 per cent) were categorized as administrative law cases.

[34] A total of 39 of the cases heard by Li CJ (20 per cent) were categorized as constitutional law cases, and another 22 cases (11 per cent) were categorized as administrative law cases.

[35] 'The Chief Justice's Address at the Opening of the Legal Year', 12 January 1998, accessible at www.judiciary.gov.hk/en/other_info/speeches/legal_yr_cj.htm.

and a proportionality test should be applied in considering the validity of restrictions to rights and freedoms.[36]

In later years, the annual speech was used to bring attention to what Li CJ perceived to be an increasing tendency to use the courts to solve difficult political and social issues. The increase in rights cases by way of judicial review was referred to in 2005 (when the requirement of a reasonably arguable case was obliquely mentioned),[37] 2006 (when Li CJ considered the reasons for the increase in judicial reviews and gave statistics of the increase),[38] and 2007.[39] In *Winnie C. W. Cheung* v. *Peter Po Fun Chan*, the CFA (with Li CJ presiding) finally addressed the growing numbers of judicial review cases in Hong Kong by discarding the 'potential arguability' test for obtaining leave in judicial review at first instance for the arguability test (i.e. that the case must be reasonably arguable).[40] In his last Opening of the Legal Year speech, Li CJ highlighted the impact of the change when he noted (having considered that leaves granted for judicial review in 2008 and 2009 were 49 and 47 per cent, respectively):

> So, in the past two years, a substantial number of applications for judicial review were refused at the initial leave stage because they failed to meet the threshold test of a reasonably arguable case laid down by the Court of Final Appeal in November 2007. These figures provide food for thought and the community may consider it worthwhile to reflect on them.[41]

Administration of the Court of Final Appeal

In accordance with the Hong Kong Court of Final Appeal Ordinance, the Chief Justice is responsible for determining the composition of panels of judges that hear and decide leave applications and substantive appeals. The Chief Justice appoints the times and places where the court shall sit and directs the distribution of the court's business.[42] In short, the Chief

---

[36] 'Departing with No Regrets', note 1 above.
[37] 'Chief Justice's Speech at Ceremonial Opening of the Legal Year 2005', 17 February 2005, accessible at www.info.gov.hk/gia/general/200502/17/02170118.htm.
[38] 'Chief Justice's Speech at Ceremonial Opening of the Legal Year 2006', 9 January 2006, accessible at www.info.gov.hk/gia/general/200601/09/P200601090137.htm.
[39] 'CJ's Speech at Ceremonial Opening of the Legal Year 2007', 8 January 2007, accessible at www.info.gov.hk/gia/general/200701/08/P200701080120.htm.
[40] (2007) 10 HKCFAR 676.
[41] 'CJ's Speech at Ceremonial Opening of the Legal Year 2010', 11 January 2010, accessible at www.info.gov.hk/gia/general/201001/11/P201001110174.htm.
[42] HKCFAO, section 47.

Justice not only presides over the CFA but is also responsible for its overall administration.

Judges from other common law jurisdictions

Non-permanent judges are appointed by the Chief Executive in accordance with the recommendation of the Judicial Officers Recommendation Commission, which is chaired by the Chief Justice.[43] The total number of names on the list of non-permanent Hong Kong judges and list of judges from other common law jurisdictions is not to exceed 30 at any one time.[44]

The role of the Chief Justice in identifying and obtaining the consent of senior overseas jurists to become a member of the court is significant. At the beginning, Li CJ first reached an agreement with then Lord Chancellor, Lord Irvine, in September 1997 to have two serving Law Lords made available to the CFA as NPJs.[45] The arrangement was confirmed and continued with subsequent Lord Chancellors. As serving Law Lords retired, they continued to serve on the CFA. Australia and New Zealand have only been able to send retired jurists because sending serving judges would be too onerous on these relatively smaller jurisdictions. To date, judges from no other common law jurisdiction have been appointed, possibly because Hong Kong's legal system shares its closest affinity with Australia, New Zealand, and the United Kingdom.

Although statute provides that either a non-permanent Hong Kong judge or NPJ from another common law jurisdiction may be nominated to sit on an appeal,[46] in practice, an NPJ from another common law jurisdiction has sat on 97 per cent of all appeals heard by the CFA.[47] Thus, it could be said that the first Chief Justice established a convention of selecting a sitting overseas NPJ to form a member of the appeal panel except in the rarest of cases.

---

[43] Judicial Officers Recommendation Commission Ordinance (Cap. 92), section 3.

[44] HKCFAO, section 10.   [45] 'HK Judges Named', *The Lawyer*, 9 December 1997.

[46] HKCFAO, section 16.

[47] Of the 325 substantive appeals in the CFA's first 13 years, 172 cases were heard by a combination of the Chief Justice and two PJs or three PJs, together with a Hong Kong and overseas NPJ. A further 134 cases were heard by the Chief Justice together with the three PJs and an overseas NPJ, and on nine rare occasions, the CFA sat with two PJs, two Hong Kong NPJs and an overseas NPJ. In only 10 cases was the court made up of the Chief Justice, the three PJs, and a Hong Kong NPJ.

Establishing the reputation of the CFA soon after 1997 was obviously a priority for Li CJ. In the 1999 Opening of the Legal Year speech, he proudly stated, 'I believe that Hong Kong is fortunate to have as NPJs on the overseas panel distinguished jurists of the highest standing from Australia, New Zealand and the United Kingdom, in addition to the non-permanent Hong Kong judges'.[48] He referred again to the importance of having visiting common law judges in his 2001 speech:

> As to the participation of judges from other common law jurisdictions as one member of the Court, as the Secretary for Justice publicly stated recently, this "has received widespread support both locally and overseas". Indeed, the Hong Kong model in having a non-permanent judge from other common law jurisdictions is being seriously examined in a jurisdiction such as New Zealand which is considering establishing its own final appellate court to replace the Privy Council.[49]

In the end, of course, New Zealand did not choose to have visiting judges, notwithstanding strong support for the idea from Lord Cooke of Thorndon (an NPJ from 1997 to 2003).[50]

Managing the workload

As early as 1999, Li CJ commented on the increased workload of the CFA.[51] He would remark again on the increase in 2001, when he stated, 'In the last three and a half years, the Court has disposed of 85 appeals and over 190 applications for leave to appeal. This far exceeds the number of cases which went to the Privy Council from Hong Kong within a similar period before 1997'. This was followed by the following statement, which foretold the deployment of the Rule 7 procedure later that year:

> at present, leave applications are invariably the subject of oral hearings by the Appeal Committee. As with most final appellate courts including the Privy Council, the Appeal Committee should dispose of the straightforward applications without an oral hearing.[52]

---

[48] 'The Chief Justice's Address at the Opening of the Legal Year', 11 January 1999, accessible at www.judiciary.gov.hk/en/other_info/speeches/legal_yr_cj99.htm. See also CJ's 2007 Speech, note 39 above, where Li CJ would reflect: 'I have every reason to believe that in its first decade, the Court has made good progress in establishing its stature.'

[49] 'The Chief Justice's Address at the Opening of the Legal Year', 15 January 2001, accessible at www.judiciary.gov.hk/en/other_info/speeches/legal_yr_cj01.htm.

[50] See Report of the Justice and Electoral Committee on the Supreme Court Bill, New Zealand Parliament, 2003, accessible at legislation.knowledge-basket.co.nz/gpprint/docs/bills/20030162.txt.

[51] CJ's 1999 Speech, note 48 above.   [52] CJ's 2001 Speech, note 49 above.

Under the Rule 7 procedure, if the Registrar forms a view that there is no reasonable ground for leave to appeal or the application is frivolous or fails to comply with the rules, the applicant is given the opportunity to submit further materials and show cause why the application should not be dismissed. The Appeal Committee then considers the application on the papers and can decide to either dismiss it or order an oral hearing. In contrast with other final appellate courts, which can reject the application on the papers without giving the applicant a further opportunity to submit materials, the Rule 7 procedure gives an applicant such a further opportunity. In 2008, 18 per cent of the Rule 7 cases were given a hearing after consideration of the further materials submitted by applicants, and 9 per cent were eventually granted leave. If an order is made dismissing the application, the order is posted on the notice board in the CFA. No reasons are given beyond stating the limb in Rule 7 applied.

Other prescribed duties

Other statutory responsibilities of the Chief Justice in respect of the CFA include his role on the Court of Final Appeal Rules Committee,[53] which determines the rules of procedure for the CFA; the appointment of other officers of the court, including a replacement for the Registrar if the Registrar is absent;[54] to direct the use of the seal of the court, which must be affixed to all judgments, orders, documents, exemplifications or copies thereof;[55] directing the sittings of the CFA in vacation;[56] directing the days on which the court offices will be open;[57] and any matter not provided for under the Rules in respect of the practice and procedure of the CFA.[58]

Administration of the judiciary

The Hong Kong Court of Final Appeal Ordinance provides that the 'Chief Justice shall be the head of the Judiciary and shall be charged with the administration of the Judiciary and such other functions as may from time to time be lawfully conferred on him'.[59] This arrangement is rare in common law jurisdictions. For the courts of England and Wales, the Lord Chief Justice, who bears this administrative role, does not preside over the final appellate court; in Australia and Canada, the Chief Justice

---

[53] HKCFAO, section 40.   [54] *Ibid.*, section 42.   [55] *Ibid.*, section 48.
[56] Hong Kong Court of Final Appeal Rules (Cap. 484A), r. 62,   [57] *Ibid.*, r. 63.
[58] *Ibid.*, r. 78.   [59] *Ibid.*, section 6(2).

is only responsible for the administration of the final appellate court. Although an onerous responsibility, the Chief Justice is assisted by a team of administrators within the judiciary and a court leader (e.g. Chief Judge of the High Court) at each level of court.

Mission of the judiciary

One of the earliest accomplishments of Li CJ was to draft the mission statement of the HKSAR Judiciary, which reads as follows: 'To maintain an independent and effective judicial system which upholds the rule of law, safeguards the rights and freedoms of the individual, and commands confidence within and outside Hong Kong'.[60] The aim of commanding public confidence reflects the priority accorded by Li CJ to establishing a roster of distinguished overseas NPJs.

Appointment and extension of judges

The Chief Justice chairs the Judicial Officers Recommendation Commission (JORC), which is responsible for making recommendations to the Chief Executive in respect of the filling of vacancies in judicial offices, and advising on representations from judicial officers regarding conditions of service and any other matter affecting judicial officers as prescribed by the Chief Executive.[61] In respect of extension of terms of NPJs and extension beyond the retiring age of PJs, the Chief Justice alone makes the recommendation to the Chief Executive.[62]

Although the BL provides for the appointment of judges on the basis of their judicial and professional qualities, the collection of feedback in respect of candidates by the JORC is an important function given the wide range of views that can exist in the community about the suitability of a candidate.

At all levels of court (save the Court of Appeal and CFA), recruitment is conducted by open advertisement; the JORC does not consider candidates who have not applied. Thus, the Chief Justice may spend some time in consultation with the Chief Judges of the High Court and District Court

---

[60] See Hong Kong Judiciary Website, accessible at www.judiciary.gov.hk/en/others/mission. htm.
[61] Judicial Officers Recommendation Commission Ordinance (Cap. 92), section 6.
[62] HKCFAO, section 14(4).

and the Chief Magistrate to identify suitable candidates, who would be encouraged to apply.

The composition of the JORC (consisting of nine members) can be divided into three categories: three judges (the Chief Justice and two other judges), three lawyers (the Secretary for Justice, a barrister, and a solicitor), and three lay members.[63] In appointing the barrister and solicitor members, the Chief Executive will consult with the governing bodies of the respective branches of the profession.

When considering possible appointments, the barrister and solicitor members of the JORC consult with the respective branches of the profession (without breaching the confidentiality provisions) in respect of the applicants for appointment. Similarly, the Secretary for Justice will take into account the experience of the Department of Justice in respect of the applicants.

Upon receiving applications for each level of court, the judiciary sets up selection boards of judges for the relevant level of court. The members of the selection boards are expected to be familiar with the work of the candidates, and the selection boards give their views on the candidates to assist the JORC. The selection boards may include the judicial members of the JORC.

Judicial conduct

In 2004, Li CJ announced that a Working Party had been appointed in 2002 to advise on a guide to judicial conduct in keeping with developments in other jurisdictions.[64] The Working Party recommended and Li CJ accepted the recommendation in January 2003 that a Guide to Judicial Conduct should be drafted to provide judges with useful and practical guidelines on judicial conduct, including out-of-court activities. The guide was published in October 2004 and is available to the public on the judiciary's website.[65]

In May 2006, it was reported that a recorder of the Court of First Instance of the High Court and a deputy District Judge joined a local political party in Hong Kong as founding members, raising issues as to

---

[63] *Ibid.*, section 3.
[64] 'CJ's Speech at Ceremonial Opening of Legal Year 2004', 12 January 2004, accessible at www.info.gov.hk/gia/general/200401/12/0112136.htm.
[65] Hong Kong Judiciary, *Guide to Judicial Conduct* (Hong Kong: Hong Kong Judiciary, 2004), accessible at www.judiciary.gov.hk/en/publications/gjc_e.pdf.

whether or not the Guide to Judicial Conduct dealt with the issue of political affiliation and the terms of judicial appointment.[66] This prompted Li CJ to issue a guideline in relation to part-time Judges and participation in political activities in June 2006.[67]

Review of judicial performance

The Chief Justice meets once a month with the court leaders, the Chief Judges of the High Court and the District Court and the Chief Magistrate, individually to discuss issues that concern the courts of different levels.

There is a system of annual appraisal reports of judges and magistrates written by the various court leaders. In addition, after appeals from the magistrates' courts, tribunals and the District Court, there is a system whereby the intermediate court of appeal may complete an assessment form. The form is completed by a judge of the Court of First Instance for appeals from the magistracy court and tribunals, or the presiding judge of the Court of Appeal in respect of District Court appeals. The form is typically completed if the lower court's judgment was regarded as poor or exceptionally good; when the judgment appealed from was regarded as competent, comments may be made but are not necessary. For assessments that are poor or exceptionally good, the relevant court leader informs the judge or magistrate concerned.

Li CJ also set up a system to monitor the timely delivery of judgments after concerns over the issue were raised. He highlighted the issue in his 2009 Opening of the Legal Year speech:

> Having regard to the purpose which litigation serves and the stress which it can involve, it is important for cases to be resolved within a reasonable time. Where the hearing has concluded, the judge has a duty to ensure that judgment is delivered within a reasonable time. In a collegiate court, the duty rests not only on the presiding judge but also on its other members. Where appropriate, a judge would be allowed time off from other judicial work to clear outstanding judgments. Each Court Leader has the responsibility to operate the mechanism for monitoring outstanding judgments

---

[66] 'LegCo Question No. 10 (Written Reply)', 24 May 2006, LC Paper No. CB(2) 2517/05–06(05), Legislative Council Panel on Administration of Justice and Legal Services Year 2005–2006, accessible at legco.hk/yr05–06/english/panels/ajls/papers/aj0626cb2–2517-5e-scan.pdf.

[67] Li CJ, 'Guideline in Relation to Part-Time Judges and Participation in Political Activities', 16 June 2006, accessible www.judiciary.gov.hk/en/crt_services/pphlt/pdf/guideline_part_time_judge.pdf.

to seek to ensure that they are given within a reasonable time. Where necessary, the Court Leader will inform the Chief Justice who can deal with the matter where appropriate.[68]

Fortnightly returns are made to the Chief Justice, and the court leaders use a colour-coded system to indicate how long the judgment has been outstanding. In his monthly meetings with the court leaders, the Chief Justice discusses the current return and ensures that the court leader deals with the matter as appropriate (i.e. by discussing the situation with the relevant judge).

Complaints are typically handled by the relevant court leader, although complaints against judicial decisions are not entertained because the proper forum for airing such complaints is an appeal. The court leader handling the complaint will take into account all relevant materials, such as court documents and audio recordings of the proceeding, and give the judge or magistrate an opportunity to explain. The court leader then decides whether or not the complaint is justified, unjustified, or partially justified. When a complaint is justified or partially justified, the court leader will inform the complainant and inform and give appropriate advice to the judge or magistrate complained against.[69]

The Chief Justice is provided with a quarterly report of all complaints against judicial conduct at all levels of court, whatever their outcome. Justified or partially justified complaints are referred to by court leaders in writing annual appraisal reports, as well as views expressed in any appeal assessment forms. This information is also made available to the JORC.

Strategic projects

The first Chief Justice was involved in several strategic projects of the judiciary, including the use of Chinese in the courts, civil justice reform, the promotion of mediation and the use of technology in the courts.

The use of Chinese in the courts was originally initiated by Sir T. L. Yang CJ and was continued and expanded after the resumption of sovereignty.

---

[68] 'CJ's Speech at Ceremonial Opening of the Legal Year 2009 (with photos)', 12 January 2009, accessible at www.info.gov.hk/gia/general/200901/12/P200901120166.htm.
[69] Hong Kong Judiciary, *Complaints Against a Judge's Conduct* (Hong Kong: Hong Kong Judiciary, Nov 2010 (3rd edn)), accessible at www.judiciary.gov.hk/en/crt_services/pphlt/pdf/complaintsjjoleaflet.pdf.

Li CJ expressed a cautious note on furthering the use of Chinese in court proceedings:

> The use of Chinese in court proceedings is a complex subject and no other jurisdiction has the experience in the use of Chinese in a common law setting to help us. We have in fact built up substantial experience in the lower courts. We need to progress steadily but cautiously.[70]

Although the Chinese language has yet to be used (without translation) in the CFA, there was a significant expansion in the use of Chinese in other courts.[71]

To enhance the capacity to use technology in the courts, the Technology Court was developed early in his tenure. Li CJ described the special court in this way:

> Although located in the High Court, it will be made available for use by courts and tribunals at all levels. It offers many facilities including those for multi-media presentations and an electronic documentation and exhibits handling system and we will soon be demonstrating them to the profession. The Technology Court offers up to date modern technological facilities and I trust they will be extensively used.[72]

Li CJ also established the resource centre for unrepresented litigants in civil proceedings in the High Court and District Court.[73] The centre provides assistance to unrepresented litigants who are either parties to or about to commence civil proceedings in the High Court or District Court. Assistance from the centre relates only to procedural matters, such as guidance in filling in court forms, filing of court bundles, and provision of oaths and declaration services; staff will not provide legal advice or comment on the merits of a case. In the absence of a system of government-funded poverty legal clinics in Hong Kong, the centre is an important resource for unrepresented litigants.

---

[70] CJ's 1998 Speech, note 35 above.

[71] In 2010, the percentage of criminal cases heard in Chinese in the following courts was as follows: Court of Appeal, 42 per cent; Court of First Instance (Magistracy Appeal), 67 per cent; Court of First Instance (trial), 26 per cent; District Court, 46 per cent; and Magistrates' Court, 81 per cent. See Department of Justice, 'Use of Chinese in Court Proceedings', paper for LegCo Panel on Administration of Justice and Legal Services, LC Paper No CB(2)1353/11–12(01), Dec 2011, [5].

[72] 'CJ's Speech at Ceremonial Opening of the Legal Year', 13 January 2003, accessible at www.info.gov.hk/gia/general/200301/13/0113127.htm.

[73] 'Speech by the Chief Justice at Ceremonial Opening of the Legal Year 2002', 14 January 2002, accessible at www.info.gov.hk/gia/general/200201/14/0114101.htm.

The judicial initiatives that received the greatest attention were the introduction and implementation of the civil justice reform and the promotion of mediation. In 2000, Li CJ announced the appointment of a Working Party chaired by then-Chief Judge of the High Court, Mr. Justice Patrick Chan, to conduct a review of the civil rules and procedures of the High Court and District Court.[74] This review was aimed at ensuring and improving access to justice at reasonable cost and speed. The Working Party initiated a public consultation in November 2001,[75] which ended in July 2002.[76] In March 2004, the Working Party published its Final Report,[77] which was submitted to Li CJ, who accepted the recommendations in the report.[78] The implementation of the recommendations was dealt with by the Steering Committee on Civil Justice Reform, which issued a Consultation Paper on the necessary amendments to primary and subsidiary legislation in April 2006.[79] The amendments were introduced into the LegCo in April 2007[80] and, after enactment by the LegCo and a period of training for both the Judiciary and the legal profession, came into force on 2 April 2009.[81]

Although Li CJ was not directly involved in the implementation of Civil Justice Reform, his intervention was required when members of the Law Society raised concerns about the draft Practice Direction on Mediation. Li CJ was directly involved in the revision of the Practice Direction as well as the reaching of a consensus on its terms, resulting in its implementation being deferred until 1 January 2010.[82]

---

[74] 'Speech by the Chief Justice at Opening of the Legal Year', 17 January 2000, accessible at www.info.gov.hk/gia/general/200001/17/0117134.htm.

[75] 'Consultation on Civil Justice Reform Sets Off', Press release issued by the Judiciary, 29 November 2001, accessible at www.info.gov.hk/gia/general/200111/29/1129158.htm.

[76] 'Civil Justice Reform Consultation Ended', Press release issued by the Judiciary, 2 July 2002, accessible at www.info.gov.hk/gia/general/200207/02/0702231.htm.

[77] 'Final Report of the Working Party on Civil Justice Reform Released', Press release issued by the Judiciary, 3 March 2004, accessible at www.info.gov.hk/gia/general/200403/03/0303195.htm.

[78] 'Implementation of the Civil Justice Reform', Press release issued by the Judiciary, accessible at www.info.gov.hk/gia/general/200403/19/0319225.htm.

[79] 'Views sought on proposed legislative amendments for implementation of Civil Justice Reform', Press release, accessible at www.info.gov.hk/gia/general/200604/12/P200604120242.htm.

[80] 'Civil Justice (Miscellaneous Amendments) Bill to be Gazetted', Press release, accessible at www.info.gov.hk/gia/general/200703/28/P200703280249.htm.

[81] 'Civil Justice Reform to take effect on April 2', Press release issued by the Judiciary, accessible at www.info.gov.hk/gia/general/200904/01/P200904010181.htm.

[82] 'Mediation', Practice Direction 31, issued by Li CJ, 12 February 2009, accessible at legalref.judiciary.gov.hk/lrs/common/pd/pdcontent.jsp?pdn=PD31.htm&lang=EN.

Li CJ was active in promoting mediation, from as early as 2004 when he stated:

> Mediation is now gradually becoming established in many common law jurisdictions as an alternative method of dispute resolution to litigation. Mediation has certain advantages over litigation. Whereas adversarial litigation fought out to the end results in an all or nothing outcome, mediation may bring about a more satisfactory resolution of the dispute for the parties with less stress in the process. Further, where a dispute is successfully mediated, it is usually speedier and less costly compared to litigation.[83]

Mediation was a topic to which Li CJ returned in his Opening of the Legal Year speeches in 2005, 2007, 2008, 2009, and 2010.

Limited delegation

The Chief Justice bears a heavy administrative load and manages to off load some of the work to the PJs of the CFA. Examples of such delegation include Bokhary PJ chairing the committee on higher rights of audience for solicitors, Chan PJ's membership on the use of Chinese committees (chaired by Li CJ), and Ribeiro PJ chairing the committee on use of technology in the courts. In these instances, delegation allowed the Chief Justice to be apprised of the broad picture without the burdensome details.

The role of individual court leaders frees the Chief Justice from administering the day-to-day operation of the lower courts, but for important issues affecting the courts, the Chief Justice would be consulted and involved as appropriate.

In dealing with judiciary administration, the Chief Justice is assisted by a judiciary administrator, whose rank is equivalent to a permanent secretary in the civil service. The administrator represents the judiciary before the LegCo's committees. Media inquiries are also dealt with by the administrator; although sensitive media replies go through the Chief Justice.

Relations with the executive and legislature

In the administration of the judiciary, the Chief Justice is required to engage the executive and the legislature on a number of levels. Although the resources for the judiciary are largely committed (e.g. in respect of

---

[83]   CJ's 2004 Speech, note 64 above.

salaries), the judiciary is still subject to budgetary constraints. In 2003, Li CJ announced the freezing of judicial remuneration, and in 2004, he announced mergers of the Western, North Kowloon, and Tsuen Wan Magistracies to deal with budgetary constraints and achieve savings and economy of scale.[84] In 2005, Li CJ drew attention to the negative effects of budgetary constraints on waiting times and other operations:

> The Judiciary must cope with whatever may be the caseload from time to time. Even on the assumption of a stable caseload, it must be recognised by all concerned that the inevitable consequence of budgetary constraints over a period of time will be that the waiting times will be lengthened at all levels of court. It will take a longer time to obtain a hearing date. It is my duty to explain this plain fact frankly to the community. If there comes a point of time when the waiting times are considered to be unacceptable, the question of providing additional resources to the Judiciary will have to be raised and addressed by the Administration and the Legislature.[85]

The judiciary must also bid for additional resources. In 2008, it succeeded in bidding for additional judicial manpower in the form of a new Justice of Appeal post and five new Court of First Instance posts.

The Chief Justice also deals with draft legislation of two kinds: those that relate to the operation of the courts, initiated by the judiciary, such as civil justice reform, and those relating to the judiciary initiated by the executive, such as a proposal to set up a Competition Tribunal as part of the judiciary. This is all in addition to the Chief Justice's *ex-officio* membership on the Law Reform Commission of Hong Kong, which published 27 final reports from 1997 to 2010 on a wide range of topics.[86]

As a result of Hong Kong's political structure, which includes a legal functional constituency LegCo member, the legal profession has a direct voice on matters with which the legislature is concerned. Legislator and barrister, Ms Margaret Ng, held this seat for the entire time of Li CJ's tenure. When matters relating to the administration of justice are before LegCo, both branches of the legal profession are asked for their views, and the Chief Justice thus works with the stakeholders in the judicial system to achieve consensus. One example of working towards consensus was Civil

---

[84] CJ's 2003 and 2004 Speeches, notes 72 and 64, respectively, above.
[85] CJ's 2005 Speech, note 37 above.
[86] See Law Reform Commission of Hong Kong's website at www.hkreform.gov.hk for information on published reports.

Justice Reform, which involved a large working party closely working together with policymakers, legislators, members of the legal profession and judiciary. In the end, the entire process took nine years compared with five years in the United Kingdom with the Lord Woolf reforms.

Relations with the legal profession

The Chief Justice has a number of important statutory duties in respect to the legal profession under the Legal Practitioners Ordinance.[87] These include the power to make rules[88] (which take precedence over the rules made by the Bar Council);[89] to appoint members of the Bar Disciplinary Tribunal,[90] Solicitors Disciplinary Tribunal,[91] and Notaries Disciplinary Tribunal;[92] to appoint Senior Counsel;[93] and to prescribe the manner in which barristers[94] and solicitors[95] are admitted.

The Chief Justice also engaged the profession on issues for which the judiciary needed the support of the profession, such as civil justice reform or the promotion of mediation. Another such initiative was the topic of higher rights of audience for solicitors. In 2001, Li CJ described the proposal for solicitors to be accredited as advocates in the High Court as 'premature'.[96] In 2005, however, Li CJ announced the appointment of a Working Party chaired by Bokhary PJ to consider whether solicitors' rights of audience should be extended and, if so, the mechanism for granting such extension.[97] A consultation paper was issued in 2006 by the Working Party, and the final report was delivered in 2007. Legislation to implement the final recommendations was passed in 2010.[98] A Higher Rights Assessment Board was established to decide on the solicitors who should be granted higher rights of audience. It is chaired by a senior judge (Hartmann JA) and consists of judges, barristers, solicitors, a law officer, and a lay person. Applicants for higher rights must have five years post-qualification experience, and in the three years before applying, the applicant must have what the Board will consider sufficient litigation experience.

---

[87] Legal Practitioners Ordinance (Cap. 159).   [88] *Ibid.*, section 72.
[89] *Ibid.*, section 72AB.   [90] *Ibid.*, section 34.   [91] *Ibid.*, section 9.
[92] *Ibid.*, section 40G.   [93] *Ibid.*, section 31A.   [94] *Ibid.*, section 27.
[95] *Ibid.*, section 4.   [96] CJ's 2001 Speech, note 49 above.
[97] CJ's 2005 Speech, note 37 above.
[98] Legal Practitioners (Amendment) Ordinance 2010, Ord. 2 of 2010, in force 2 July 2010, L.N. 51 of 2010.

Engaging the public

Public, rule of law, and judges

In contrast to previous colonial chief justices, Li CJ was anxious to engage with the public and the academic community. The academic community warmly welcomed his appointment, and he reciprocated by showing considerable interest in our work (and attending an occasional seminar at law faculties when time permitted). His wish to engage with the public and academics was also driven by pragmatic considerations.

The rule of law has for long been valued for moral and pragmatic reasons in Hong Kong, and Li CJ no doubt realised that the public's understanding of the manifestations of and challenge to the rule of law (as well as the researches of academics) was crucial to its support of the judiciary. His public pronouncements were limited but always to the point. He chose the Chief Justice's annual lectures at the start of the legal year for his dialogue with the public.[99] In his 2002 speech, he articulated this thus:

> This important occasion hosted by the Judiciary focuses public attention on our legal system. Our legal system with the rule of law and an independent Judiciary is an invaluable community asset. It is universally accepted to be a cornerstone of our society and one of Hong Kong's main competitive advantages. This occasion provides an opportunity for us to speak about the exciting challenges which we face. And it enables the Judiciary, together with the Bar, the Law Society and government lawyers, to reaffirm our common purpose in serving the community by maintaining the rule of law.[100]

He explained the value of the independence of the judiciary in this way: 'It is not a privilege but is essential to enable judges to perform their constitutional role of adjudicating disputes between citizens and between citizen and government fairly and impartially'.[101] He emphasized more than once the community's 'common objective and indeed the shared responsibility of maintaining the rule of law'.[102] He believes that the rule of law has continued to thrive as the result of vigilance: 'Such vigilance must be exercised by all, by those who have been entrusted to govern as well as by the public, by lawyers who have a special role to play as well as by non-lawyers. And such vigilance must be exercised not only in relation

---

[99] His speeches can be found on the Hong Kong Judiciary website at www.judiciary.gov. hk/en/other_info/speeches.htm.

[100] CJ's 2002 Speech, note 73 above.   [101] CJ's 2004 Speech, note 64 above.

[102] CJ's 2003 Speech, note 72 above.

to the enforcement and interpretation of laws but also, in relation to the formulation and enactment of new laws'.[103]

He realized the importance of public debate. Seeing the value of public debates on judicial decisions as protection of judicial independence, he invited public scrutiny and criticism of the judgments of the court 'if necessary'.[104] He reminded the public that many issues concerning the rule of law are 'inevitably controversial, with diverse views held by different people of goodwill'.[105] Therefore, it was 'all the more important that there is a meaningful dialogue conducted on the basis of mutual respect'.[106] Additionally, he pointed out that because it would be inappropriate for 'judges to have to defend their judgments in the political arena', public and professional debates on judicial decisions should be conducted in 'an objective and rational manner'.[107] He emphasized this point several times. He urged that the debate be 'conducted calmly, rationally and thoroughly', whether about court judgments or the formulation of new laws. The debate is 'not and should not be regarded as a tussle of strength involving government and polarised sections of the community, with victories and defeats. . . . It is only through reasoned and vigorous debate that one can hope to find constructive solutions to difficult problems'.[108]

He included the government among the participants in the debate – and those with responsibility to promote the rule of law. In his 2000 speech (post if not proctor the attack on the court by the NPCSC), he said that 'where the courts come under unwarranted attack, it is the constitutional responsibility of the Government, that is, the executive authorities, to explain and defend the fundamental principle of judicial independence, whether or not the decision in question is in its favour. I am sure that the Government understands and accepts the importance of that responsibility'.[109]

In pursuance of his objective to promote public debates, he cautioned that there 'must be a will by all concerned to listen to, understand, and learn from other points of view. This applies to both Government and those who agree with it as well as to their critics'.[110] He came back to this theme again in 2002, when he said:

> The Court has dealt with and will continue to face challenging questions of law and principle in many interesting areas. As far as constitutional litigation is concerned, the Court's judgments will no doubt continue to

[103] *Ibid.*   [104] *Ibid.*   [105] *Ibid.*   [106] *Ibid.*
[107] CJ's 2000 Speech, note 74 above.   [108] CJ's 2003 Speech, note 72 above.
[109] CJ's 2000 Speech, note 74 above.   [110] CJ's 2003 Speech, note 72 above.

arouse controversial debate. In a free society, such debate is to be expected. Indeed, reasoned debate should be welcomed as it plays a constructive role in the development of jurisprudence in the new order. That development can only take place gradually with the passage of time.[111]

In 2008, he explained the role of the judge in sentencing, referring to criticism by the public of leniency or harshness, which he recognized as 'understandable'.[112] While recognizing the need for judges to retain the confidence of the public in judicial sentences, he said, 'In a society which values freedom of speech as a fundamental right, all court decisions, including sentencing decisions, are open to public discussion. Such discussion is most meaningful when it is well informed and well considered, taking into account the circumstances of the case in question and the reasons of the sentencing judge'.[113]

In 2009, the theme of his speech was again the judiciary, in this case on the question of whether serving judges should be appointed on commissions (e.g. on an enquiry) or other administrative tasks.[114] It was clear that he was not in favour of it but would defer to the legislature if it prescribed so or there was public demand. He noted that the 'Judiciary's approach in recent years has been to request the Administration to look for a suitable person who is not a serving judge and to agree to make a serving judge available only where no other suitable person is available' and noted the growing pool of retired judges and a pool of senior legal practitioners available for this task.[115] Such an approach is more consistent with the independence of the judiciary (as in Australia); Li CJ was trying to get away from the British practice.

Promise of an activist judiciary

An active judiciary, signalled in his first speech, was also a frequent theme. Chief Justice Li did not use the following *quid pro quo* terms: you support the independence of the judiciary and the rule of law, and I and my colleagues will actively protect your rights. But he did promise an activist judiciary. In his first speech in 1998, Li CJ talked at length about the importance of the independence of the judiciary, the smooth transition (from British to Chinese sovereignty), and his commitment to the rule of

---

[111] CJ's 2002 Speech, note 73 above.
[112] 'CJ's speech at Ceremonial Opening of the Legal Year 2008 (with photos)', 14 January 2008, accessible at www.info.gov.hk/gia/general/200801/14/P200801140146.htm.
[113] *Ibid.*   [114] CJ's 2009 Speech, note 68 above.   [115] *Ibid.*

law.[116] He emphasized the judiciary's vital constitutional role to ensure that the acts of the executive and the legislature complied fully with the law, particularly the BL. He signalled his own responsibility when he said that 'there is no place in a free society for a supine Judiciary'.[117] He also committed himself to the protection of 'our fundamental rights and freedoms, which represent enduring values of our society'.[118] In 2003, he said that 'central to the rule of law is the proper and effective protection of the individual rights and freedoms which are at the heart of Hong Kong's separate system'.[119]

In 2005, he said the 'constitutional role of judges is to adjudicate disputes between citizens and between citizen and government fairly and impartially'.[120] The community must understand, he said, that the judge does not function in the political arena where solutions to problems frequently involve a compromise of many factors and interests. 'The duty of a judge is always to administer justice according to law without fear or favour. A judge should not be deflected from this duty by considering what may be an expedient political solution'.[121] He explained, 'Everyone is equal before the law. Citizen and government, the powerful and the weak, the rich and the poor are all equal before the courts'.[122]

He recognized that to protect and enhance the judiciary's reputation, it is of fundamental importance that judges must at all times observe the highest standards of conduct and integrity. This is essential for the maintenance of public confidence in the judiciary and the administration of justice. Judges must do their utmost to uphold the independence and impartiality of the judiciary and to preserve the dignity and the standing of the judicial office.

Courts and social policy

In 2005, Andrew Li hinted that the courts were receiving many judicial review cases, explaining in terms of the complexity of life which increases the need for administrative regulation as well as the development of public law.[123] He might also have mentioned that the rise was caused by the failure of the political process (discussed in several chapters in this volume). Noting that many cases relate to the constitutional guarantees of rights and freedoms, he observed that citizens 'have a constitutional

---

[116] CJ's 1998 Speech, note 35 above.   [117] *Ibid.*   [118] *Ibid.*
[119] CJ's 2003 Speech, note 72 above.   [120] CJ's 2005 Speech, note 37 above.
[121] *Ibid.*   [122] *Ibid.*   [123] *Ibid.*

right of access to the courts and the courts must ensure that all parties have a fair opportunity of presenting their cases'.[124]

It was in 2006 that he fully explored the significance of this increase. He was at pains to explain the limited nature of the court's role, that the 'courts are concerned and only concerned with the legality of the decision in question, adjudged in accordance with common law principles and the relevant statutory and constitutional provisions' and could not provide a 'panacea for any of the various political, social and economic problems which confront society in modern times'.[125] These had to be resolved through the political process in which 'a suitable compromise may be found, reconciling the conflicting interests and considerations in question and balancing short term needs and long term goals. The responsibility for the proper functioning of the political process in the interests of the community rests with the Administration and the Legislature'.[126]

He returned to this theme again in 2007, when he noted:

> the availability and use of judicial review has had a significant impact on the conduct of the business of government and has exercised a considerable influence on public debate on many issues. It would not be right for judicial review to be viewed negatively as a hindrance to government. On the contrary, it should be seen as providing an essential foundation for good governance under the rule of law.[127]

But he did not say this without an element of ambiguity because he added, 'Within the limits of legality, the practical solutions to the complex and difficult political, economic and social problems faced by society must be discussed and found through the proper operation of the political system. Citizens have to look to the political process to deliver appropriate workable solutions to these problems'.[128] Did this represent some crisis in his belief in the problem-solving capability of the law or just coping with the pressures emanating from the lack of respect for the rule of law by the Chinese and Hong Kong administrative authorities, deemphasising the political dimensions of judicial decisions, to protect judicial autonomy, pretending that judges do less than they do?

Valedictory

In his final speech in 2010, he revisited some old, and introduced some new, themes. He noted that in the period since 1997, judicial

---

[124] *Ibid.*   [125] CJ's 2006 Speech, note 38 above.   [126] *Ibid.*
[127] CJ's 2007 Speech, note 39 above.   [128] *Ibid.*

independence had been universally recognized and accepted to be of 'pivotal importance' to Hong Kong.[129] He cautioned against the politicization of judicial appointments (which he had successfully managed to avoid). He emphasized the independence and impartiality of the judges in all cases, whether or not the government is involved. He emphasized again the fundamental nature of the BL, particularly provisions of human rights. He praised the judges for being 'deeply conscious of the community's high expectations of the Judiciary' and warned about the great importance of observing the highest standards of judicial conduct.[130]

And for the first time he referred to the Mainland, saying that under '"one country, two systems", it is of course important that Judges in the Mainland and Hong Kong have a mutual understanding of each other's system and the differences between them. In the last 12 years, we have made great efforts to develop this through conferences, visits, courses and the like'.[131] But as if to provide balance, he also reminded the public of Hong Kong's legacy of his beloved common law: 'As the only common law jurisdiction in China under "one country, two systems", it is equally important that Hong Kong continues to maintain its links with leading common law jurisdictions through similar activities'.[132] And, modestly as ever, his verdict on the CFA: 'Over the last 12 years, the Court of Final Appeal has been functioning smoothly'.[133]

Other roles

The Chief Justice also attends conferences, such as the Yale Constitutionalism Seminar and the Biennial Conference for Chief Justices of Asia and the Pacific, and receives distinguished visitors, such as judges from around the world, including the Mainland, and consuls general from major jurisdictions. The Chief Justice also attends ceremonial occasions such as National Day ceremonies on 1 October and presides over such events as the Ceremonial Opening of the Legal Year and the Admission of New Senior Counsels.

Another important role of the Chief Justice relates to the BLC established in 1990 as a working committee under the NPCSC. The BLC, composed of six Mainland members and six Hong Kong members, meets

---

[129] CJ's 2010 Speech, note 41 above.   [130] *Ibid.*   [131] *Ibid.*
[132] *Ibid.*   [133] *Ibid.*

about three times per year to discuss matters related to the implementation of certain BL provisions. Although the Chief Justice is not a member of the BLC, he has authority to nominate Hong Kong members for appointment by the NPCSC. Such nominations must be made jointly with the Chief Executive and President of LegCo, thereby ensuring that there is a consensus in the nomination.

Future challenges

In his extra-judicial statements, Li CJ expressed his views on some of the future challenges of the CFA and the judicial system in future.

New building

As early as 2002, Li CJ noted: 'The present building at Battery Path is inadequate for the Court's functioning. In particular, the Court room for all its charm is manifestly inadequate in various aspects: For the judges, for counsel and solicitors, for the parties, for the media and for the public'.[134] It was suggested that with plans to relocate the LegCo that the CFA should be given the existing LegCo building.

Li CJ would continue to make his case for the relocation in 2006 and 2007, stating:

> That building was built as and formerly housed Hong Kong's Supreme Court. It is a prestigious historic building on a prominent site. The location of the Court there would not only provide it with sufficient space but would be fitting, having regard to the Court's position at the apex of our judicial system.[135]

In his final Opening of the Legal Year speech in 2010, Li CJ announced that plans were underway to relocate the CFA to the LegCo Building. Although he suggested that he would be nostalgic for the French Mission Building that housed the CFA since its establishment, the considerably larger space, the character and history of the LegCo building would serve the court better, as well as provide the opportunity of establishing a public exhibition gallery about the judiciary and the historical heritage of the building.

---

[134] CJ's 2002 Speech, note 73 above.   [135] CJ's 2006 Speech, note 38 above.

Appeals as of right

Under section 22 of the Hong Kong Court of Final Appeal Ordinance, there lies, as a matter of right, an appeal to the CFA from any final judgment of the Court of Appeal in any civil cause or matter which is of the value of $1,000,000 or more. This avenue of appeal was derived historically from the Privy Council (PC). Other common law jurisdictions that abolished appeals to the PC also abolished this quantum-threshold basis for civil appeals as of right. For example, New Zealand did not abolish appeals to the PC until the end of 2003. When the Supreme Court of New Zealand was established, appeals as of right were not maintained, and all appeals to the Supreme Court must be by way of leave.[136]

Li CJ criticized the 'as of right' ground of appeal on the basis of fairness, as well as being out of line with the practice of final appellate courts of other jurisdictions and for the relatively low level at which the threshold was set:

> First, this is in contrast to judgments in criminal cases and other civil judgments where appeal is with leave on defined criteria. It could be argued that civil final judgments involving more than $1 million should not be in a different position. Secondly, having a category of judgments which are appealable as of right is unusual compared to final appellate courts in other jurisdictions; the norm is that the appeal must be with leave of the Court which would consider whether a point of law or principle is involved. The Privy Council is the exception probably because of history. Thirdly, the $1 million threshold is now far too low, having regard to the value of assets and the size of commercial transactions.[137]

He would have preferred to have been able to abolish the as of right basis for appeal. But the political and legal environment was perhaps not ripe for this whilst the CFA was establishing its reputation. This task is now left to another Chief Justice to address.

Fusing of the two branches of the legal profession?

With the grant of higher rights of audience for solicitors, the issue of whether or not an independent Bar continues to be necessary has been raised in some quarters, along with the suggestion that it may be beneficial

---

[136] 'How Cases Come to the Supreme Court', Courts of New Zealand website, accessible at www.courtsofnz.govt.nz/about/supreme/cases/intro.
[137] CJ's 2001 Speech, note 49 above.

to merge the two branches of the legal profession. Li CJ, however, was critical of the idea:

> The grant of higher rights of audience for solicitors through an assessment process is a significant development. I think the present structure of the profession has served the public quite well. I do not favour a fused profession.... I appreciate the market forces which have led to increasing commercialisation of the legal profession. But ultimately, the practice of law cannot be treated merely as a business. It is an honourable profession, with high ethical standards and ideals of service. This must not be compromised in the future development of the profession.[138]

Enhancing access to justice

Li CJ identified early on the greatest challenge for the judicial system, to ensure access to justice for all. In 1999, he spoke of the increased workload of the CFA as a sign that the final appellate court of Hong Kong had been made more accessible.[139] However, in 2000, it was pointed out that it must be a serious concern that the affordability of legal representation directly affects what is a constitutional right to have access to the courts for the resolution of disputes.[140]

In his final speech in 2010, Li CJ suggested that the problem cannot be completely solved and that all the judiciary could do is work on improving the situation by various measures:

> As we stand at the threshold of the second decade of the 21st century, our judicial system faces the major challenge of seeking to ensure access to justice for all. The rich and the big corporations may be able to afford to litigate. Those with low income are eligible for legal aid. But the bulk of the population, including small and medium enterprises, find it difficult to afford the legal fees involved in litigation.... There is no magic wand which can be waved to solve the problem. A number of measures are necessary to alleviate the situation, including making procedures less complex, the availability of pro bono services and the use of mediation.[141]

Conclusion

As shown in this all too brief overview of 13 years, the first Chief Justice of the HKSAR was a dynamic leader who wrote many memorable and defining judgments and set down a solid foundation for the judiciary,

---

[138] 'Departing with no regrets', note 1 above.   [139] CJ's 1999 Speech, note 48 above.
[140] CJ's 2000 Speech, note 74 above.   [141] CJ's 2010 Speech, note 41 above.

guaranteed to last much longer than the 50 years of continuity promised in the BL. Li CJ moulded the role of the Chief Justice from his own vision and showed us what was both necessary and possible in that role. His concerns with having the highest quality of CFA judges from within and outside of Hong Kong, ensuring the highest standards of integrity in the judiciary, and improving access to justice for all demonstrated the paramount role played by the Chief Justice in sustaining and enhancing the rule of law in Hong Kong. Nor was judicial work neglected. In addition to running the CFA efficiently, Li CJ showed us the importance of the Chief Justice presiding over landmark constitutional cases that define the legal characteristics of the HKSAR and its relationship to the central authorities. That he never once penned a dissenting opinion reflected the influence of his views in the deliberations and perhaps also a strong desire to reach consensus in decision making. Naturally, this was important in the early years of the court.

Generations will wonder how Li CJ was able to balance all of his different roles to achieve so much both inside and outside the courtroom. He faced great challenges inside the courtroom in establishing the jurisprudence of the new order as well as outside it; especially in piloting through major reforms in the legal system in the political arena and seeking to improve access to justice. Hong Kong is most fortunate to have a great Chief Justice as its first one and all future Chief Justices will have to be seen and judged in that light.

11

The judges

SIMON N. M. YOUNG AND ANTONIO DA ROZA

Introduction

The Hong Kong Court of Final Appeal (CFA) differentiates its judges by their permanency and place of origin. The classification goes beyond the distinction between a Chief Justice and other Justices. The Basic Law (BL) contemplates two categories of CFA judges: permanent ones and those invited 'from other common law jurisdictions to sit on the Court of Final Appeal'.[1] Legislation, however, creates three categories of CFA judges: permanent judges (PJs), non-permanent judges from Hong Kong (local NPJs), and NPJs from another common law jurisdiction (overseas NPJs).[2] Appointment qualifications, tenure and extension terms, precedence, and sitting arrangements differ according to the category of judge.

This chapter examines the contribution of CFA judges to the work of the court. It finds that the categorisation of judges systemically differentiates the contribution made by judges. For example, as one would expect, PJs contribute more to the work of the court than NPJs. Empirically the overseas NPJs have contributed more than the local NPJs, and this reflects the practice of having an overseas NPJ sit in each case. The Chief Justice has considerable influence over the composition and seating arrangements of the court. Brief biographies of all the judges can be found in the Annex to this chapter.

Appointment and removal

The BL provides that the judges of the courts of the Hong Kong Special Administrative Region of the People's Republic of China (HKSAR) '*shall be* appointed by the Chief Executive *on the recommendation of*

---

[1] Basic Law, Article 82.
[2] The office of Chief Justice is treated separately in legislation and is considered as neither a PJ nor an NPJ.

an independent commission composed of local judges, persons from the legal profession and eminent persons from other sectors' (italics added for emphasis).[3] The provision's plain meaning is that the commission's recommendation of the candidate is a prerequisite to that candidate's appointment. Whether the article has the narrower meaning of the Chief Executive being duty bound to appoint the commission's recommended candidate is unsettled, although the language used in the Sino-British Joint Declaration would tend to support this view.[4] CFA judges, similar to the Chief Justice of the CFA and Chief Judge of the High Court, must pass another level of scrutiny: the Chief Executive must 'obtain the endorsement of the Legislative Council and report such appointment . . . to the Standing Committee of the National's People's Congress for the record'.[5]

In practice, PJs and NPJs are appointed by the Chief Executive in accordance with recommendations of the Judicial Officers Recommendation Commission (JORC), previously known as the Judicial Service Commission, which operated under essentially the same statutory framework.[6] As chairman, the Chief Justice plays a critical role in the work of the JORC, as does the Secretary for Justice, who is the only other *ex-officio* member.[7] The remaining seven members are appointed by the Chief Executive and must include two judges, a practicing solicitor, a practicing barrister, and three persons not connected with the practice of law.[8] Legislation protects the confidentiality and integrity of JORC proceedings. JORC communications to the Chief Executive and Chief Justice are privileged.[9] It is an offence to provide false information to the JORC, to publish or disclose information that comes to one's knowledge in connection with the JORC Ordinance, and to influence or attempt to influence a decision of the JORC.[10]

---

[3]　Basic Law, Article 88.

[4]　See Sino-British Joint Declaration, Annex I, section III where it is stated, 'Judges of the [HKSAR] courts *shall* be appointed by the chief executive of the [HKSAR] *acting in accordance with* the recommendation of an independent commission composed of local judges, persons from the legal profession and other eminent persons' (emphasis added).

[5]　Basic Law, Article 90. Compare with the relevant language in the Sino-British Joint Declaration, Annex I, section III: '*the appointment* . . of principal judges (i.e. those of the highest rank) *shall be made* by the chief executive *with the endorsement* of the [HKSAR] legislature and reported to the Standing Committee of the National People's Congress for the record' (emphasis added). This suggests that the legislature's endorsement is a pre-requisite to a lawful appointment, but the report to the NPCSC occurs after the appointment is complete. Compare further with section 7A of the Hong Kong Court of Final Appeal Ordinance (Cap. 484) (HKCFAO), which contemplates LegCo endorsement after appointment.

[6]　Judicial Officers Recommendation Commission Ordinance (Cap. 92), sections 7, 8, and 9.

[7]　*Ibid.*, section 3.　　[8]　*Ibid.*　　[9]　*Ibid.*, section 9.　　[10]　*Ibid.*, section 12.

Li CJ made several notable public comments about the appointment-process:

> By statute, if there are three or more dissenting votes [in the JORC], there is no valid recommendation. . . . The Basic Law provides that judges and judicial officers shall be chosen on the basis of their judicial and professional qualities. I have never come across any instance where it was suggested that judges should be chosen on some other basis.[11]

He also expressed the view that the process of judicial appointments had not been and should never be politicised,[12] including the process of endorsement by the Legislative Council (LegCo) of senior judicial appointments.[13] Legislators have shared this view, and thus LegCo endorsements have been made with little fanfare or controversy.[14]

The Hong Kong Court of Final Appeal Ordinance (HKCFAO) sets out the professional qualifications of the different categories of CFA judges.[15] A person is eligible to be appointed as Chief Justice if he or she is a PJ, the Chief Judge of the High Court, a Justice of Appeal, judge of the Court of First Instance, or a barrister who has practised in Hong Kong for a period of at least 10 years. In addition, the Chief Justice must be a Chinese citizen and Hong Kong permanent resident with no right of abode in a foreign country.[16]

A person will be eligible to be appointed as a PJ if he or she is the Chief Judge of the High Court, a Justice of Appeal, a judge of the Court of First Instance, or a barrister who has practised in Hong Kong for a period of at least 10 years. There is no citizenship or residency requirement for PJs or NPJs.

Retired Chief Justices of the CFA, PJs, Chief Judges of the High Court (or Supreme Court, before 1 July 1997), serving or retired Justices of Appeal, and barristers who have practised in Hong Kong for a period of at least 10 years are eligible to be appointed as local NPJs. When the CFA

---

[11] 'Chief Justice Andrew Li: Departing with No Regrets', *Hong Kong Lawyer*, August 2010.

[12] See *ibid.*; 'CJ's Speech at Ceremonial Opening of the Legal Year 2010', 11 January 2010, accessible at www.info.gov.hk/gia/general/201001/11/P201001110174.htm.

[13] In respect of the endorsement process by LegCo, in most cases, a committee will be formed to consider the matter, although there was no committee formed for the endorsement of Lord Walker, Lord Neuberger, and Mr. Murray Gleeson.

[14] See e.g. minutes of the LegCo's Subcommittee on Proposed Senior Judicial Appointments' meeting on 21 April 2011 and minutes of the LegCo's Panel on Administration of Justice and Legal Services' meeting on 23 November 2009, accessible from the LegCo website at www.legco.gov.hk/english/index.htm.

[15] HKCFAO, section 12.　　[16] Basic Law, Article 90; *ibid.*, section 6(1A).

was first established in 1997, the local NPJs appointed were all serving or retired justices from the Court of Appeal.

Overseas NPJs must be judges or retired judges of a court of unlimited jurisdiction in civil or criminal matters in another common law jurisdiction, ordinarily resident outside of Hong Kong, and have never been a judge of the High Court (or Supreme Court before 1 July 1997), District Court, or a permanent magistrate in Hong Kong.[17] Note from these requirements that the invited jurist need not have been a judge of the final court in his or her respective jurisdiction, although in practice Hong Kong has generally appointed serving or former supreme court justices.

Even though the NPJs are likely to be older and have more judicial experience than the PJs, statute sets the order of precedence as follows: the Chief Justice, the PJs (ranked in accordance with the priority of their appointments), the local NPJs, and the overseas NPJs (respectively, ranked in accordance with the priority of their appointments to their respective lists).[18] All CFA judges are prohibited from practising as barristers or solicitors in Hong Kong whilst they hold office and after they cease to hold office.[19]

The BL provides that judges can only be removed 'by the Chief Executive on the recommendation of a tribunal appointed by the Chief Justice of the Court of Final Appeal and consisting of not fewer than three local judges',[20] and the reason for removal can only be for 'inability to discharge his or her duties, or for misbehaviour'.[21] With CFA judges, their removal must also be endorsed by LegCo and reported to the Standing Committee of the National People's Congress (NPCSC) for the record. Fortunately, in the first 15 years of the HKSAR, there has been no reason to activate the procedures for removing judges.

Tenure and retirement

Under the HKCFAO, the 'retiring age' for the Chief Justice and PJs is 65 years.[22] Their term of office can be extended by the Chief Executive but by not more than two periods of three years. Extension of the Chief Justice's term is made on the recommendation of the JORC; the terms of the PJs are extended on the recommendation of the Chief Justice.

By contrast, NPJs, whether local or overseas, have no retiring age. They are appointed for a term of three years, which may be extended an unlimited number of terms by the Chief Executive on the recommendation of

---

[17] HKCFAO, section 12(4).   [18] *Ibid.*, section 11.   [19] *Ibid.*, section 13.
[20] Basic Law, Article 89; *ibid.*, section 14.   [21] Basic Law, Article 89.
[22] HKCFAO, section 14.

the Chief Justice. Thus, the Chief Justice has an extremely influential role to play in deciding the continued tenure of CFA judges.

In the 13 years from 1997 to 2010, the Chief Executive appointed 5 PJs (not including the Chief Justice), 13 local NPJs,[23] and 17 overseas NPJs. There is no cap on the number of appointed PJs, but the practice has been to have no more than the three minimally required. The number of appointed NPJs is capped at 30 without apportioning this figure between local and overseas NPJs.[24] While it is mandatory to have a Chief Justice and PJs to constitute the court, appointed NPJs are not essential and are only invited by the court to sit 'as required'.[25] In practice, however, NPJs have made an indispensable contribution to the work of the court since 1997.

Table 11.1 below shows the number of cases heard by all CFA judges during the period of their tenure up to the end of August 2010. The Australian and United Kingdom NPJs tended to hear more cases than the New Zealand ones, and Sir Anthony Mason NPJ topped the list with 91 cases. The CFA started with 10 local NPJs in 1997, but their numbers have gradually diminished, reflecting their more limited role in standing in for a PJ or Chief Justice when necessary.

Judicial work

Judicial work in the CFA consists primarily of hearing and determining applications for leave to appeal and hearing and deciding substantive appeals. Overseas NPJs are only involved in substantive appeals.

Leave applications

Leave hearings are mostly heard and determined by a combination of the Chief Justice and PJs or three PJs. Of the 492 leave hearings in the CFA's first 13 years, there were only 23 instances when the Appeal Committee included a local NPJ. Many leave applications are filed in the Chinese language by unrepresented litigants. Thus, the Chinese-literate members of the CFA play an important role at the leave determination stage, especially where the Registrar applies the Rule 7 procedure for determining unmeritorious applications on the papers.[26]

---

[23] Ching PJ was appointed as a local NPJ as from 7 October 2000, but he passed away on 30 November 2000 without hearing a case in such capacity.

[24] HKCFAO, section 10.   [25] *Ibid.*, section 5(2) and (3).

[26] See further Chapter 7 (Da Roza) in this volume.

Table 11.1 *Tenure of Court of Final Appeal judges, 1997–2010 (number of appeals heard indicated in brackets)*

	97	98	99	00	01	02	03	04	05	06	07	08	09

CJ and PJs

Li CJ (195)
Bokhary PJ (311)
Litton PJ (56)   Litton NPJ (55)
Ching PJ (52)

Chan PJ (263)
Ribeiro PJ (233)
Mason NPJ (91)
Dawson NPJ (4)
Brennan NPJ (21)
McHugh NPJ (10)
Gleeson NPJ (2)
Hoffmann NPJ (36)
Nicholls NPJ (10)

Overseas NPJs

Millett NPJ (50)
Woolf NPJ (22)
Scott NPJ (22)
Walker NPJ (3)
Neuberger NPJ (0)
Cooke NPJ (16)
Somers NPJ (1)
Eichelbaum NPJ (8)
Richardson NPJ (10)
Gault NPJ (9)

Nazareth NPJ (41)
Mortimer NPJ (39)
Power NPJ (24)
Silke NPJ (15)
Fuad NPJ (8)
Clough NPJ (6)
Cons NPJ (4)

Local NPJs

Roberts NPJ (4)
Huggins NPJ (4)
McMullin NPJ (0)
MacDougall NPJ (0)

NPJ = non-permanent judge; PJ = permanent judge.

Table 11.2 *Frequency of seating arrangements in the Court of Final Appeal, 1997–2010*

Seat 4	Seat 2	Seat 1	Seat 3	Seat 5	Number and percentage of appeals
Local NPJ	PJ	CJ or PJ	PJ	Overseas NPJ	172 (53%)
PJ	PJ	CJ	PJ	Overseas NPJ	134 (41%)
PJ	PJ	CJ	PJ	Local NPJ	10 (3%)
Local NPJ	PJ	CJ or PJ	Local NPJ	Overseas NPJ	9 (3%)

NPJ = non-permanent judge; PJ = permanent judge.

Substantive appeals

The CFA sits with five judges to hear substantive appeals,[27] and the usual rule is that the Chief Justice and PJs will sit with one NPJ. If the Chief Justice cannot sit for any reason, the next most senior PJ will assume the president's chair, and another NPJ will be asked to sit. In the rare situation when both the Chief Justice and a PJ cannot sit, then there will be three NPJs sitting. Ultimately, the Chief Justice decides the final seating arrangements. Table 11.2 shows that its most frequent arrangement was to have one overseas NPJ and one local NPJ. Forty-one per cent of the cases were heard with the Chief Justice, three PJs, and an overseas NPJ. The rare situation of having three NPJs occurred in only 3 per cent of the cases.

The CFA can sit without an overseas NPJ, and there is a rule with controversial origins that limits the number of such NPJs to only one in each case.[28] Chief Justice Li instituted a practice of having an overseas NPJ in more than 90 per cent of the hearings. Only in 10 of 325 cases in the Court's first 13 years did the hearing panel not have an overseas NPJ (see Table 11.2).[29] One contributing factor to this practice was that most of the local NPJs in the first batch appointed in 1997 lived abroad after retiring from the Hong Kong judiciary. Thus, to arrange the sitting of a local NPJ was no more convenient than to arrange the visit of an

---

[27] If the appeal hearing commenced with five judges, it can continue with only four (but no less): HKCFAO, section 16(7).
[28] See Chapter 5 (Young, Da Roza, and Ghai) in this volume.
[29] Of those 10, half concerned criminal law and procedure, and the rest concerned administrative law, civil procedure, commercial law, land law, and tort law.

overseas NPJ, and clearly the preference was to have an overseas judge of international distinction to help develop the early jurisprudence of the court.

The new system of judges changed the conditions for final justice quite significantly from a court of final adjudication overseen by judges of primarily British nationality (and occasionally from other Commonwealth countries) sitting in a court in London to a court sitting in Hong Kong with primarily four Hong Kong judges and a judge from another common law jurisdiction. This new composition served to make the final court more indigenous, to give greater 'permanency' to decision making and judgment writing, and to maintain an international influence within the final court.

Insights into the roles of the different categories of judges can be gained by looking at the adjudicative practices of the CFA. In a calendar year, the CFA would usually schedule seven one-month stints for visits by overseas NPJs. Hearings were fixed for the first two weeks of the month, and the two remaining weeks were left vacant for judgment writing. Judges hearing a case would receive the papers well in advance of the hearing. Responsibility for writing the lead judgment was usually allocated by the Chief Justice, in consultation with the PJs, often also well before the hearing. This is done on a tentative basis, and the allocation may be changed after the judges have come to final views after the hearing. Li CJ once stated, 'The time taken to hear an appeal is the tip of the iceberg of the considerable time spent by the judges before and after the hearing on the case. Particularly time for preparation of the judgment since statements in them may have a far reaching impact'.[30]

The Chief Justice often referred to the court as a 'collegiate' one[31] because decision making involved extensive discussion of the case amongst the judges during the hearing, such as in the mid-morning break and lunch break. Discussion continued after the hearing without a practice of hearing first from the most junior member, a practice established in the United Kingdom Supreme Court and previously the House of Lords and the Privy Council (PC). By legislation, the judgment or order of the majority of the judges sitting is deemed to be the judgment

---

[30] 'The Chief Justice's Address at the Opening of the Legal Year', 11 January 1999, accessible at www.judiciary.gov.hk/en/other_info/speeches/legal_yr_cj99.htm.

[31] See CJ's 1999 Speech, *ibid.*; CJ's 2010 Speech, note 12 above; and 'The Chief Justice's Address at the Opening of the Legal Year', 15 January 2001, accessible at www.judiciary.gov.hk/en/other_info/speeches/legal_yr_cj01.htm.

Table 11.3 *Majority judgments by categories of Court of Final Appeal judges 1997–2010*

Author	Sole majority	Joint majority	Total majority	Total as percentage
CJ	36	10	46	14%
PJ	166	24	190	58%
Overseas NPJ	67	10	77	24%
Local NPJ	29	4	33	10%

NPJ = non-permanent judge; PJ = permanent judge.

or order of the CFA.[32] The court, however, is not required to reach a majority judgment; if there is no judgment or order formed by a majority of the judges sitting, a rehearing must be ordered.[33]

Table 11.3 shows that almost 60 per cent of the majority judgments were written by the PJs, and a quarter of all majority judgments were written by the overseas NPJs. The Chief Justice alone wrote substantially more majority judgments than all the local NPJs combined.

The collegial atmosphere of the CFA must have contributed to the significant number of jointly authored judgments as seen in Table 11.3. Joint judgments are probably of three types: (1) when there are separate judgments dealing with different issues that must be read together; (2) when as a result of extensive revisions to a judgment of one judge at the suggestion of another judge it becomes a joint judgment; and (3) those typically in the public law area when although it has been written by one judge, it is decided that it would be better to have it as a judgment of the court to provide it with greater authority as a matter of public perception. The relative proportion of these types of joint judgments is unknown.

Permanent judges

By design, the bulk of the CFA's work is taken up by the Chief Justice and PJs. During its first 13 years, there were a total of five PJs and no more than three at any one time: Litton, Ching, and Bokhary PJJ from 1997 to 2000 and Bokhary, Chan, and Ribeiro PJJ from 2000 to 2010. The issue of appointing a fourth PJ, although permissible by law, is controversial because the presence of four PJs and a Chief Justice may reduce the

---

[32] HKCFAO, section 16.   [33] *Ibid.*, section 16(6).

Table 11.4 *Appeals heard and judgments written by the Chief Justice and permanent judges, 1997–2010*

CJ or PJ	Total number of CFA appeals during tenure	Number of appeals heard	Appeals heard as percentage of total	Majority opinions	Concurring opinions	Dissenting opinions
Bokhary	325	311	96%	78 (including 10 joint)	62 (including 4 joint)	11
Chan	266	263	99%	49 (including 16 joint)	23 (including 4 joint)	0
Ribeiro	266	233	88%	56 (including 11 joint)	11	1
Li	325	195	60%	46 (including 10 joint)	7	0
Litton	59	56	95%	16 (including 1 joint)	13	1
Ching	59	52	88%	8	5	0

CFA = Court of Final Appeal; CJ = Chief Justice; PJ = permanent judge.

opportunity for NPJs, both overseas and local, to contribute to the work of the court.

From 1997 to 2010, the CJ sat with three PJs and a single NPJ in almost half of all appeals heard (i.e. 144 of the 325 cases, approximately 44 per cent of all cases) (see Table 11.2). This meant that in more than half of the cases, the CJ or a PJ was relieved from sitting by an additional NPJ, and in nine instances, there were only two PJs (or the CJ and a PJ) sitting (Table 11.2). On average, a PJ sat on 93 per cent of all appeals heard during their tenure, and the CJ sat on 60 per cent (Table 11.4). This indicates that it was the CJ who was more likely to be relieved from appellate work to allow him to carry out his many other duties (see Chapter 10 in this volume). But PJs could also be relieved if, for example, they were conflicted from sitting or needed time to discharge other judicial duties.

One sees from this data that the CFA's system of PJs and NPJs has conferred much flexibility to incorporate overseas talent and expertise, to maintain a core of local high-calibre PJs, and to relieve those PJs as and when needed. This flexibility is essential in a system that must sit with five judges in every appeal, unlike other supreme courts that sit with a flexible number of justices, e.g. ranging from five to nine, and deal with absences by reducing the size of the panel.

The flexibility is also apparent in judgment writing (see Table 11.4). The CJ and PJs wrote 253 of the 325 majority judgments (78 per cent), leaving NPJs (mostly the overseas ones) to write just under a quarter of all majority judgments. The CJ and PJs contributed concurring opinions, in over a third of the cases, and most of the dissenting opinions from the court (although the total number of those opinions were very few).

Overseas non-permanent judges

International attention is often paid to the CFA and its jurisprudence because of the repute of its overseas judges, which included leading retired or serving jurists of the United Kingdom Supreme Court, the former House of Lords, Australian High Court, and New Zealand Supreme Court and Court of Appeal. These judges were appointed for a three-year period and, when scheduled to do so, flew into Hong Kong to sit on a panel of five judges to hear and decide appeals usually in one-month stints.

The system of overseas judges, which was built into Hong Kong's constitution (BL, Article 82), was adopted not to ensure uniformity with English laws and legal principles but to have a continuity of international legal expertise of the highest calibre after the abolition of appeals to the PC in 1997. It was also partly motivated by the perceived lack of interest amongst leading Hong Kong barristers to join the judiciary at the time. Yash Ghai noted that the continuity was seen as being necessary to 'reassure the business community' and 'enhance the court's prospects of independence'.[34]

The overseas NPJs provide diversity in legal views and experience, leadership and innovation in tackling new legal problems, and additional strength in research and writing. The heavily weighted balance of local expertise on the court ensures that any initiatives of the overseas judge are kept in check with local laws, conventions, and culture. They are chosen

---

[34] Yash Ghai, *Hong Kong's New Constitutional Order: The Resumption of Chinese Sovereignty and the Basic Law*, 2nd edn. (Hong Kong: Hong Kong University Press, 1999) 323–4.

strategically to sit on cases based on their expertise. For example, Lord Millett NPJ would be sought for insolvency or property cases rather than criminal appeals.[35] Sir Anthony Mason NPJ has contributed the most of all the overseas judges to the jurisprudence and showed leadership and innovation particularly in constitutional and public law areas.

In interviews, CFA judges have reflected upon the distinct features of Hong Kong's overseas judge system. In 1999, Mortimer NPJ, a local NPJ, pointed out that:

> It means that there is international or inter-common law input into the Court. The Court, indeed all courts in Hong Kong, has an open door to listening to authorities from all other common law jurisdictions. While this is happening in other jurisdictions as well, it is perhaps more readily accepted here. That of itself means that Hong Kong is in the position of being able to develop not only its own law, but it is also open to the best developments in other common law jurisdictions as well. For that reason, I personally believe that in due course the Court of Final Appeal is likely to become one of the most respected courts in the common law world.[36]

Sir Anthony Mason NPJ spoke of how

> the participation of overseas judges who have an international reputation gives the Hong Kong Court of Final Appeal a degree of acceptability which it might not otherwise have. In saying that I'm not in any way suggesting that the quality of the judges on the Court falls short of the highest quality. What I'm saying is that, in the eyes of people elsewhere, particularly people who are looking at Hong Kong as an international financial centre, it probably gives a degree of reassurance that you have overseas judges of international reputation participating in the work of the Court.[37]

He also added: 'Although the differences in the jurisprudence of the various common law jurisdictions are minor rather than substantial, there are subtle points of difference, and NPJs from other jurisdictions can offer distinctive contributions and perspectives'.[38]

There is certainly great respect and appreciation for the contributions of the overseas NPJs from the PJs. Bokhary PJ once stated,

---

[35] A case in point is *Sun Honest Development Ltd* v. *Appeal Tribunal (Buildings)* (2009) 12 HKCFAR 342 which took advantage of Lord Millett NPJ's knowledge of the law of easements and lost modern grant.

[36] 'A Conversation with Justice Barry Mortimer', *Hong Kong Lawyer*, September 1999.

[37] 'One on One, Court of Final Appeal, Sir Anthony Mason', *Hong Kong Lawyer*, July 2001.

[38] 'Sir Anthony Mason: A Non-permanent Fixture on the CFA', *Hong Kong Lawyer*, August 2010.

Every single one of the overseas judges is a distinguished jurist in his own
jurisdiction. They are devoted to the law. Their willingness to come to
Hong Kong is greatly to their credit and greatly to our advantage. And I
believe that, as they become more familiar with Hong Kong and its people,
their devotion to the law becomes accompanied by a devotion to Hong
Kong as well. I think when the legal history of Hong Kong is written they
will enjoy a very notable place in it. Speaking personally it's a great honour
to serve with jurists of such standing.[39]

Ribeiro NPJ echoed these sentiments when he stated, 'It's a fantastic
advantage to be able to sit with some of the top jurists in the world
today'.[40]

There is no question of domination by the overseas judges, although
these judges write a fair share of judgments (Table 5). Mason NPJ highlighted Hong Kong's distinctive model in these terms:

It is different from the models in the other jurisdictions where I have
sat – Fiji and the Solomon Islands – where there's more dependence on the
visiting judges. Thus you have a bench either consisting wholly of visiting
judges or of a majority of visiting judges. In Hong Kong it's the other way
around and I think there's a lot to be said for that model. In other words,
the local judges form the majority.[41]

And after serving as a NPJ for about a year, Lord Millett NPJ noted,

My real disadvantage – and it's an area where I would defer to other members of the court – is that I'm not familiar with local conditions . . . there
are other aspects of Hong Kong which may be different from England.
There I would defer to the knowledge of my colleagues on the Bench.
That's why one has five of them after all.[42]

Moreover, Li CJ emphasised that 'as is well appreciated by the overseas
judges, when they sit on the Court, they function as and only as Hong
Kong judges in Hong Kong's own circumstances under "one country, two
systems"'.[43] This view was reinforced by Mason NPJ when he stated:

An NPJ, no matter where he comes from, needs to see himself primarily
as a Hong Kong judge, serving its community and seeing legal problems
through a Hong Kong lens. A legal solution fashioned in Australia or

---

[39] 'The Court of Final Appeal: Mr Justice Bokhary', *Hong Kong Lawyer*, February 2002.
[40] 'The Court of Final Appeal: Mr Justice Ribeiro', *Hong Kong Lawyer*, May 2002.
[41] 'One on One, Court of Final Appeal', note 37 above.
[42] 'The Court of Final Appeal: Lord Millett', *Hong Kong Lawyer*, December 2001.
[43] CJ's 2010 Speech, note 12 above.

Table 11.5 *Appeals heard and judgments written by overseas non-permanent judges, 1997–2010*

NPJ	Total number of CFA appeals during tenure	Number of appeals heard	Appeals heard as percentage of total	Majority opinions	Concurring opinions	Dissenting opinions
Mason (AU)	325	91	28%	25 (including 6 joint)	7	0
Millett (UK)	266	50	19%	12 (including 1 joint)	4	0
Hoffmann (UK)	324	36	11%	12	8	0
Scott (UK)	199	22	11%	7 (including 1 joint)	3	0
Woolf (UK)	199	22	11%	4	0	0
Brennan (AU)	266	21	8%	5 (including 1 joint)	2	0
Cooke (UK/NZ)	213	16	8%	2	2	1
McHugh (AU)	116	10	9%	1	2	0
Nicholls (UK)	136	10	7%	2	0	1
Richardson (NZ)	178	10	6%	1	1	0
Gault (NZ)	119	9	8%	2	0	0
Eichelbaum (NZ)	247	8	3%	2	0	0
Dawson (AU)	128	4	3%	0	1	0
Walker (UK)	38	3	8%	1	0	0
Gleeson (AU)	38	2	5%	1 joint	0	0
Somers (NZ)	213	1	0%	0	0	0

CFA = Court of Final Appeal; NPJ = non-permanent judge.

elsewhere, for that matter, may not be the best solution to a Hong Kong legal problem.[44]

The limit of one overseas NPJ per case and their tendency to defer to the local judges on local matters probably help to explain why the public

---

[44] 'Sir Anthony Mason', note 38 above.

criticisms of the overseas judges in the early years, mostly for failing to understand local conditions, never reached an audible or sustained level.[45]

Although Li CJ has emphasised in his tenure as Chief Justice the importance of efficiency and effective case management,[46] the system of visiting judges enhanced the efficiency of the CFA in delivering judgments, given the commonly understood need to discuss and complete the writing of the majority judgment before the departure of the overseas NPJ. The problem of delay in producing judgments has not been seen with Hong Kong's CFA, which has done well in adhering to a policy of publishing its judgments a reasonable time after the hearing.

As detailed in Table 11.5, a total of 16 overseas NPJs heard substantive appeals in the first 13 years of the court. As mentioned already (see Table 11.2), in all but 10 appeals there was a sitting overseas NPJ.

The degree of participation by overseas NPJs was not evenly distributed. There were a small handful of judges (from Australia and the United Kingdom) who contributed significantly to the court, while many others had less involvement, sitting in less than 10 per cent of cases heard during their tenure. This showed a practice of ensuring all appointed overseas NPJs had an opportunity to contribute, but reliance was placed on a core of three to five NPJs who visited more regularly. The three leading overseas NPJs were Sir Anthony Mason, who heard 91 appeals and authored either individually or jointly 25 majority judgments; Lord Millett, who heard 50 appeals and authored 12 majority judgments; and Lord Hoffmann, who heard 36 appeals and authored 12 majority judgments. Various factors can affect the degree of participation, including whether the jurisdiction allowed serving justices to be appointed (only the United Kingdom allowed this), the availability of jurists, their proximity to Hong Kong, the issues in the scheduled appeals and the expertise offered by jurists, and ultimately the interest of jurists to contribute.

Table 11.5 also reveals that the overseas NPJs rarely dissented; there were only two occasions when it happened, arising respectively in a tort and defamation case[47] and not in the sensitive constitutional or public law cases. Both cases had common characteristics in that Li CJ was not presiding, a local NPJ was also sitting, and Bokhary PJ also dissented in

---

[45] See Cliff Buddle, 'Judges Who "Drop in"', *South China Morning Post*, 9 March 2001; Chapter 9 (Daly) in this volume.

[46] 'The Chief Justice's Address at the Opening of the Legal Year', 12 January 1998, accessible at www.judiciary.gov.hk/en/other_info/speeches/legal_yr_cj.htm.

[47] *The Bank of East Asia Ltd* v. *Tsien Wui Marble Factory Ltd* (1999) 2 HKCFAR 349 and *Next Magazine Publishing* v. *Ma Ching Fat* (2003) 6 HKCFAR 63.

Table 11.6 *Appeals heard and judgments written by local non-permanent judges,*
1997–2010

NPJ	Total number of CFA appeals during tenure	Number of appeals heard	Appeals heard as percentage of total	Majority opinions	Concurring opinions	Dissenting opinions
Litton	266	55	21%	12 (including 1 joint)	14	2
Nazareth	325	41	13%	5 (including 2 joint)	2	0
Mortimer	325	39	12%	4 (including 1 joint)	3	0
Power	313	24	8%	4	2 (including 1 joint)	0
Silke	306	15	5%	3	2	0
Fuad	306	8	3%	1	0	0
Clough	213	6	3%	1	0	0
Cons	213	4	2%	1	1	0
Huggins	128	4	3%	1	1	0
Roberts	128	4	3%	1	0	0
McMullin	128	0	0%	0	0	0
MacDougall	128	0	0%	0	0	0

CFA = Court of Final Appeal; NPJ = non-permanent judge.

the decision. One can only speculate if the court would have been less
divided if Li CJ presided. One might also argue that it was easier for the
overseas NPJ to dissent when joined with a PJ, and the probability that an
overseas NPJ would dissent on his own in the Hong Kong system remains
extremely low.

Local non-permanent judges

The local NPJs are nominated by the Chief Justice to sit when either the
Chief Justice or a PJ cannot sit. From 1997 to 2010, these judges sat on
191 of the 325 substantive appeals (see Table 11.2). Table 11.6 shows the

breakdown of the appeals heard and judgments written by the 10 local NPJs in this time period.

As with overseas NPJs, a small core of local NPJs heard many appeals, but the others had minimal involvement, including some who did not sit even once. When compared with overseas NPJs, local NPJs sat on slightly fewer appeals on average. However, overseas NPJs were significantly more likely to contribute a majority judgment. With the exception of Litton NPJ, each of the local NPJs wrote less than six majority judgments; they contributed a few concurring judgments and no dissenting judgments (other than the two by Litton NPJ) (see Table 11.6).

Given the heavy workload of the CJ and PJs, one might ask whether more work could have been assigned to local NPJs to ease their load. But as mentioned already, most of the local NPJs appointed in 1997 did not reside in Hong Kong after retirement, thus limiting the flexibility to call upon them on short notice. By the end of Li CJ's tenure in 2010, only three local NPJs remained on the list of appointed NPJs (see Table 11.1). In April 2010, on the same day when the name of the next CJ was announced, three serving members of the Court of Appeal were also appointed to take office along with Chief Justice Geoffrey Ma on 1 September 2010.[48] These three justices, unlike previous local NPJs, would continue to reside in Hong Kong, particularly because they continued to serve in the High Court.

In June 2011, the issues of appointing serving Justices of Appeal as NPJs and judicial manpower at the CFA were discussed in the LegCo's Panel on Administration of Justice and Legal Services. It was noted that because of the possible appearance of bias, the new CJ did not hear appeals from cases on which his spouse, Justice of Appeal Maria Yuen, sat. Bokhary PJ was in a similar position because his spouse, Justice Verina Bokhary, sat as a justice in the Court of First Instance. Given the increased likelihood of needing a local NPJ to relieve the CJ or PJs, legislators queried whether and when it was appropriate for a serving Justice of Appeal to also sit on appeals in the CFA.

Legislation contemplates the appointment and concurrent service of Justices of Appeal as local NPJs.[49] Concerns were raised by legislators as to whether or not there may be a blurring of the distinction between the CFA and the Court of Appeal, particularly giving rise to the idea

---

[48] Press Release, 'Appointment of Non-Permanent Hong Kong Judges of the Court of Final Appeal', 8 April 2010, accessible at www.info.gov.hk/gia/general/201004/08/P201004080188.htm.

[49] HKCFAO, section 12(3)(d).

that appellants were denied a real appeal. The judiciary was of the view that there was no cause for concern because the local NPJ was only one of five judges hearing the substantive appeal. Serving Justices of Appeal were appointed local NPJs in the past (e.g. in July 1997); Justices Sir Noel Power, Nazareth, and Mortimer were all serving members of the Court of Appeal when they were appointed local NPJs and continued until 2000 as appointed judges of both courts.

In addition, the judiciary had formed a policy to continue to select local NPJs to sit who were retired judges rather than serving Justices of Appeal, who would also each be limited to sitting on no more than 10 appeals in total each year. Furthermore, as required by legislation, NPJs cannot hear appeals or applications from decisions made by a court in which he was sitting as a member.[50] To ensure even greater integrity, the judiciary stated a policy of not asking the serving Justice of Appeal to sit as a local NPJ when the CFA was asked to resolve conflicting decisions in previous cases of the Court of Appeal or if the judge in question had written a leading judgment in a previous case and the correctness of that case was before the CFA.[51] These restrictive conditions on the deployment of the three local NPJs appointed in 2010 naturally led legislators to query about the adequacy of judicial manpower in the CFA and generally in all courts. But it was only a short period of time before these three judges retired from the Court of Appeal, and given their continued residency in Hong Kong, they potentially will be used more frequently in hearing appeals than the previous batch of local NPJs.

Conclusion

It is often said that the composition of the court can make all the difference to the outcome of a case. Thus, those who study court behaviour pay close attention to the processes of judicial appointment, tenure, and to some extent removal. Beyond these processes, the only other weighty consideration that affects composition is the selection (typically done by the Chief Justice) of appointed justices to sit on smaller-sized panels to hear appeals or applications.[52]

---

[50] *Ibid.*, section 16(8).

[51] Judiciary Administration, 'Appointment of Serving Justices of Appeal as Non-permanent Judges of the Court of Final Appeal and Judicial Manpower Situation in the Court of Final Appeal and Other Levels of Court', paper for LegCo Panel on Administration of Justice and Legal Services, June 2011, [15], LC Paper No. CB(2)2154/10–11(03).

[52] See Benjamin Alarie and Andrew James Green, 'The Power of the Chief Justice: Choosing Panels on the Supreme Court of Canada', January 2012, unpublished paper, accessible on SSRN's LSN, papers.ssrn.com/sol3/papers.cfm?abstract_id=1884428.

With Hong Kong's CFA, there is a more complex array of considerations determining composition. With only the CJ and three PJs, at least one NPJ is selected to sit in each case from a list of up to 30 names of overseas or Hong Kong jurists. If the CJ and one or two PJs cannot sit, then further choices are made to determine the panel. Although ideally jurists are chosen for their needed expertise in a particular case, this is not always possible given the vagaries of arranging one-month visits by senior jurists. The ordinary residence in Hong Kong by local NPJs (which was unlikely before) may now increase the participation of this category of judges even perhaps at the risk of reducing the involvement of overseas NPJs. So the availability of the NPJ to sit (especially if on short notice) may also affect composition.

Another important characteristic of the Hong Kong system is the significant degree of influence of the Chief Justice over not only decisions of who sits on each panel but also decisions concerning appointment and tenure. These decisions are watched carefully by the public and just as they can be made to boost confidence in the administration of justice they can easily have the effect of raising concerns that lead to public mistrust and misunderstanding about the judiciary.

Annex: Biographies of the judges

Biographies of Chief Justice and permanent judges

Mr. Andrew Li Kwok-nang CJ

Li CJ was born in 1948 in Hong Kong and obtained his MA and LLM from Fitzwilliam College, Cambridge University. He was called to the Middle Temple in 1970 and subsequently called to the Hong Kong Bar in 1973. He was appointed a Deputy Judge of the District Court from 1982 to 1985 and was made a Queen's Counsel in 1988. He was appointed a deputy high court judge from 1991 to 1997, and upon the handover of sovereignty over Hong Kong from Britain to China, became the Chief Justice of Hong Kong.

Although the office of Chief Justice involves the administration and oversight of the entire Hong Kong Judiciary, Li CJ heard 195 substantive appeals (60 per cent of the total number heard in the CFA's first 13 years), writing a total of 53 judgments. Thirty-five per cent of these judgments were in the area of constitutional law, with a further 19 per cent in administrative law, with 26 per cent on criminal law and procedure. As the CJ sat on many controversial constitutional and public law cases, it is unsurprising to see that there was a dissenting opinion in 15 per cent of the cases in which Li CJ authored a majority or concurring judgment.

Mr. Syed Kemal Shah Bokhary PJ

Bokhary PJ was born in 1947 in Hong Kong. He obtained his legal education in London and was called to the Bar in England in 1970. He was called to the Bar in Hong Kong in 1971 and made a Queen's Counsel in 1983 and a justice of peace in 1984. He was appointed a judge of the High Court from 1989 to 1993 before being appointed to the Court of Appeal until 1997, when he became a PJ of the CFA.

Being the longest serving CFA judge along with the Chief Justice, Bokhary PJ sat on almost all of the substantive appeals heard (less 14) from 1997 to 2010. He is famous for his dissenting judgments, almost all on human rights grounds. From 1997 to 2010, there were only 17 dissenting judgments in total, and of those, Bokhary PJ authored 11 (or 65 per cent). By virtue of his long tenure and dedication, Bokhary PJ was the most prolific judge, having authored 78 majority judgments and 62 concurring judgments along with his famous dissents. Although the majority of cases heard by Bokhary PJ were in the area of criminal law and procedure, he wrote almost as many constitutional law judgments as he had criminal law judgments.

Mr. Henry Denis Litton PJ

Litton NPJ was born in 1934 in Hong Kong. He completed his education at King's College, Taunton, Somerset; and Merton College, Oxford University before being called to the English Bar in 1959. He was called to the Hong Kong Bar in 1960 and made a Queen's Counsel in 1970. He became a justice of appeal in 1992 and was appointed a vice president of the Court of Appeal in 1995, before being appointed a PJ of the CFA in 1997. He remained a PJ until his retirement in 2000 and continued to sit as a non-permanent Hong Kong judge of the CFA. He was also appointed a member of the Court of Appeal of Brunei in 2007, where he also continues to sit.

As a PJ, Litton PJ heard a total of 56 substantive appeals, and since his appointment as a NPJ, he heard a further 55 appeals to 2010. The majority of cases heard by Litton NPJ as both a PJ and an NPJ were in the area of criminal law and procedure, but the majority of his judgments as a PJ were written in the area of land law. This area of special interest was reflected in his judgment writing as an NPJ, having written only one less judgment in land law than in the area of commercial law.

Mr. Charles Arthur Ching PJ

Ching PJ was born in Hong Kong in 1935. He studied at King's College, Taunton, and University College, Oxford University and was called at Gray's Inn in 1959. He was called to the Hong Kong Bar in the same year and was made a Queen's Counsel in 1974. He served briefly as a justice of appeal from 1995 to 1997 before being appointed a PJ of the CFA. He retired in 2000 and passed away in the same year.

Ching PJ heard a total of 52 substantive appeals, the majority of which were in the area of criminal law and procedure. It appears, however, that tort law may also have been an area of interest because he wrote judgments in all three of the tort law cases he heard – the same number of criminal law and procedure judgments he authored.

Mr. Patrick Chan Siu-oi PJ

Chan PJ was born in Hong Kong in 1948 and obtained both the LLB and the PCLL from the University of Hong Kong. He was called to the Hong Kong Bar in 1976 and was appointed a District Court Judge in 1987. He subsequently became a Deputy Registrar of the Supreme Court in 1991 before becoming a Judge of the High Court in 1992. He became the first Chief Judge of the High Court in 1997, and was appointed a PJ of the CFA in 2000.

Similar to Bokhary PJ, the majority of the appeals heard by Chan PJ were in the area of criminal law and procedure, and this was reflected in his judgment writing. Although Chan and Bokhary PJJ were the most frequent co-authors of joint judgments, Chan PJ did not author a dissenting judgment in the period of study.[53]

Mr. Roberto Alexandre Vieira Ribeiro PJ

Ribeiro PJ was born in Hong Kong in 1949 and obtained both his LLB and LLM from the London School of Economics. He became a lecturer at the University of Hong Kong before being called at the Inner Temple and to the Hong Kong Bar in 1978. He was made a Queen's Counsel in 1990 and became an advocate and solicitor of Singapore in 1995. He was appointed a Deputy High Court Judge in 1992 and became a recorder of the High Court in 1997. He served briefly as a Judge of the Court of First Instance from 1999 to 2000, before becoming a Justice of Appeal in 2000. He was appointed a PJ of the CFA in the same year.

---

[53] Chan PJ wrote the dissenting judgment in *ML* v. *YJ* (2010) 13 HKCFAR 794 delivered on 13 December 2010, with which Bokhary PJ agreed.

Similar to Bokhary and Chan PJJ, the majority of appeals heard by Ribeiro PJ were in the area of criminal law and procedure. However, the vast majority of Ribeiro PJ's judgments were in the area of commercial law. Ribeiro PJ's judgments are easily distinguished from the judgments of other judges of the CFA because of their length. His judgments average some 10,190 words per judgment compared with the court's average of 4,935 words per judgment.

Biographies of overseas non-permanent judges

Sir Anthony Frank Mason NPJ

Sir Anthony Mason was born in Australia in 1925 and obtained his bachelor's degrees in arts and law from the University of Sydney. He was called to the New South Wales Bar in 1951 and was made a Queen's Counsel in 1964. He was the Commonwealth solicitor-general from 1964 to 1969 and became a judge of the Supreme Court of New South Wales (as a member of the Court of Appeal) in 1969. He then went to the High Court of Australia in 1972, becoming Chief Justice of the High Court of Australia in 1987, a position in which he remained until 1995. He was appointed an NPJ of the CFA in 1997.

Mason NPJ was by far the most active NPJ of the CFA, having heard a total of 91 substantive appeals in the first 13 years of the court's existence. A little over a third of the cases Mason NPJ heard and half of the judgments he wrote were in the area of constitutional law. Mason NPJ also heard and wrote judgments in all other areas of law considered by the court.

Lord Peter Julian Millett of St Marylebone in the City of Westminster NPJ

Lord Millett was born in 1932 in England and received his MA in classics and law from Trinity Hall, Cambridge. He was called to the Middle Temple in 1955 and admitted *ad eundum* to Lincoln's Inn in 1959. He was made a Queen's Counsel in 1973 and called to the Bar in Singapore and Hong Kong in 1976 and 1979, respectively. He was a Judge of the High Court from 1986 to 1994 and subsequently became a Lord Justice of Appeal. He served as a Lord of Appeal in Ordinary from 1998 to 2004 and was appointed an NPJ of the CFA in 2000.

Millett NPJ is the second most active NPJ of the CFA, having heard 50 substantive appeals in the 10 years he has been appointed. Some 90 per cent of the appeals he heard were civil cases, including several administrative law cases and none in the criminal law and procedure area.

Lord Leonard Hubert Hoffmann of Chedworth in the County of Gloucestershire NPJ

Lord Hoffmann was born in South Africa in 1934. He attended the University of Cape Town and Queen's College, Oxford University, and was called to Gray's Inn in 1964. He was made Queen's Counsel in 1977. He was appointed to the Courts of Appeal of Jersey and Guernsey from 1980 to 1985, a Judge of the Chancery Division from 1985 to 1992, and became a Lord Justice of Appeal in 1992. He was made a life peer and Lord of Appeal in Ordinary in 1995, a position he remained in until recently. He was appointed an NPJ of the CFA in 1998.

Thirty per cent of the cases heard by Hoffmann NPJ were in the area of criminal law and procedure, with another 30 per cent in the area of land law in which he also wrote 40 per cent of his judgments.

Lord Harry Kenneth Woolf of Barnes in the London Borough of Richmond NPJ

Appointed:	NPJ of the CFA (2003–present)
Other:	Queen's Bench Division (1979–1986); Lord Justice of Appeal (1986–1992); life peer and Law Lord (1992–1996); Master of the Rolls (1996–2000); Lord Chief Justice (2000–2005); President of the Qatar Financial Centre Civil and Commercial Court (2007–present)
Cases heard as NPJ:	22

Lord Richard Rashleigh Folliott Scott of Foscote in the County of Buckinghamshire NPJ

Appointed:	NPJ of the CFA (2003–present)
Other:	Chancery Division (1983–1991); Vice Chancellor of the County Palatine of Lancaster (1987–1991); Court of Appeal (1991–1994); Lord Justice of Appeal, PC; Vice Chancellor (1994–2000); Head of Civil Justice (1995–2000); life peer and Lord of Appeal in Ordinary (2000–2009)
Cases heard as NPJ:	22

Sir Francis Gerard Brennan NPJ

Appointed:	NPJ of the CFA (2000–present)
Other:	Australia Industrial Court (1976–1981); Additional Judge of the Supreme Court of ACT (1976–1981); Federal Court of Australia (1977–1981); High Court of Australia (1981–1995); Chief Justice of Australia (1995–1998); External Judge, Supreme Court of the Republic of Fiji (1999–2000);
Cases heard as NPJ:	21

Lord Robin Brunskill Cooke of Thorndon, of Wellington in New Zealand and of Cambridge in the County of Cambridgeshire NPJ

Appointed:	NPJ of the CFA (1997–2006)
Other:	Judge of the New Zealand Supreme Court (1972–1976); New Zealand Court of Appeal (1976–1996); President of the New Zealand Court of Appeal (1986–1996); Life peerage and Lord of Appeal (1996–2001); President of the Courts of Appeal of Samoa, Cook Islands, Kiribati; Judge of Supreme Court of Fiji
Cases heard as NPJ:	16

Lord Donald James Nicholls of Birkenhead, of Stoke d'Abernon in the County of Surrey NPJ

Appointed:	NPJ of the CFA (1998–2004)
Other:	High Court judge (1983–1986); Lord Justice of Appeal (1986–1991); Vice Chancellor of the Supreme Court (1991–1994); life peer and Lord of Appeal in Ordinary (1994–2007)
Cases heard as NPJ:	10

Sir Ivor Lloyd Morgan Richardson NPJ

Appointed:	NPJ of the CFA (2003–2009)
Other:	High Court of New Zealand (1977); Court of Appeal (1977–2002); PC (1978); President of the Court of Appeal (1996–2002)
Cases heard as NPJ:	10

Mr. Michael Hudson McHugh NPJ

Appointed:	NPJ of the CFA (2006–present)
Other:	Court of Appeal of the Supreme Court of New South Wales (1984–1989); Judge of the High Court (1989–2005)
Cases heard as NPJ:	10

Sir Thomas Munro Gault NPJ

Appointed:	NPJ of the CFA (2006–present)
Other:	Judge of the High Court (1987–1991); Court of Appeal (1991–2003); PC (1992); President of the Court of Appeal (2002–2003); Supreme Court of Fiji (2002); Supreme Court of New Zealand (2004–2006)
Cases heard as NPJ:	9

Sir Johann Thomas Eichelbaum NPJ

Appointed:	NPJ of the CFA (2000–2009)
Other:	High Court of New Zealand (1982–1988); Chief Justice of New Zealand (1989–1999); Fiji Court of Appeal (part-time)
Cases heard as NPJ:	8

Sir Daryl Michael Dawson NPJ

Appointed:	NPJ of the CFA (1997–2003)
Other:	Australian Motor Sport Appeal Court (1974–1986), Chairman (1987); High Court of Australia (1982–1997)
Cases heard as NPJ:	4

Lord Robert Walker of Gestingthorpe in the County of Essex NPJ

Appointed:	NPJ of the CFA (2009–present)
Other:	Deputy High Court Judge (1992–1994); High Court Judge, Chancery Division (1994–1997); Lord Justice of Appeal (1997–2002); life peerage and Lord of Appeal in Ordinary (2002–2009); Justice of the Supreme Court of England (2009–present)
Cases heard as NPJ:	3

Mr. Anthony Murray Gleeson NPJ

Appointed:	NPJ of the CFA (2009–present)
Other:	Chief justice of the Supreme Court of New South Wales (1988–1998); Chief Justice of the High Court of Australia (1998–2008)
Cases heard as NPJ:	2

Sir Edward Somers NPJ

Appointed:	NPJ of the CFA (1997–2002)
Other:	Judge of the Supreme Court of New Zealand (1974–1981); Court of Appeal, New Zealand (1981–1990)
Cases heard as NPJ:	1

Lord David Edmond Neuberger of Abbotsbury in the County of Dorset NPJ

Appointed:	NPJ of the CFA (2009–present)
Other:	Recorder (1990–1996); Chancery Division (1996–2004); Supervisory Chancery Judge (2001–2004); Lord Justice of Appeal and PC (2004–2007); life peer and Lord of Appeal in Ordinary (2007–2009); Master of the Rolls (2009–present)
Cases heard as NPJ:	0 (as of 31 August 2010)

Biographies of local non-permanent judges

Mr. Henry Denis Litton NPJ

Appointed:	NPJ of the CFA (2000–present)
Other:	Justice of Appeal (1992–1997); Vice-President, Court of Appeal (1995–1997); PJ of the CFA (1997–2000); Justice of the Court of Appeal of Brunei (1997–present)
Cases heard as NPJ:	55

Mr. Gerald Paul Nazareth NPJ

Appointed:	NPJ of the CFA (1997–present)
Other:	Judge of the High Court (1985–1991); Justice of Appeal (1991–2000); Vice President, Court

of Appeal (1994–2000); Justice of the Court of Appeal of Bermuda (2001–2010)

Cases heard as NPJ: 41

Mr. John Barry Mortimer NPJ

Appointed: NPJ of the CFA (1997–present)
Other: Recorder of the Crown Court (1971–1985); Chancellor of the Diocese of Ripon (1971–1985); Chairman, Mental Health Review Tribunal (1984–1985); Judge of the High Court (1985–1993); Justice of Appeal (1993–2000); Vice President of the Court of Appeal (1997–2000); Court of Appeal, Brunei (2007–present); president of the Court of Appeal, Brunei (2010–present)
Cases heard as NPJ: 39

Sir Noel Plunkett Power NPJ

Appointed: NPJ of the CFA (1997–2009)
Other: Magistrate, Lands Tribunal (1965–1969); Senior Magistrate, Lands Tribunal (1969–1976); President of Lands Tribunal (1976–1979); Puisne Judge, Supreme Court (1979–1987); Visiting Judge, Brunei Darussalam (1980); Chair, Broadcasting Review Board (1984); Justice of Appeal (1987–1999); Vice President of the Court of Appeal (1993–1999); Acting Chief Justice (1996–1997); Court of Appeal of Brunei Darussalam (2003–2009); President of the Court of Appeal of Brunei Darussalam (2007–2009)
Cases heard as NPJ: 24

Mr. William James Silke NPJ

Appointed: NPJ of the CFA (1997–2009)
Other: Magistrate, Borneo (1959); Stipendiary Magistrate, Sabah and Sarawak, Malaysia (1960–1965); Registrar, High Court in Borneo (1965–1966); Judicial Commissioner, Sabah

(1965–1966); Puisne Judge, High Court in Borneo (1966–1969); Magistrate, Hong Kong (1969–1971); President, Tenancy Tribunal (1971–1974); President, Lands Tribunal (1974–1975); District Judge (1975–1979); Judicial Commissioner, Brunei (1978); Judge of the High Court, Hong Kong (1979–1981); Justice of Appeal (1981–1995); Vice President of the Court of Appeal (1987–1995); Judicial Commissioner, Brunei Darussalam (1998)

Cases heard as NPJ: 15

Mr. Kutlu Tekin Fuad NPJ

Appointed: NPJ of the CFA (1997–2009)
Other: Magistrate, Cyprus (1953); Resident Magistrate, Uganda (1956); Judge of the High Court, Uganda (1963); Judge of the High Court, Hong Kong (1980–1982); Justice of Appeal (1982–1993); Vice President of the Court of Appeal (1988–1993); President, Court of Appeal, Brunei (1993)

Cases heard as NPJ: 8

Mr. Philip Gerard Clough NPJ

Appointed: NPJ of the CFA (1997–2006)
Other: District Judge, Hong Kong (1981–1983); Judge of the High Court (1983–1986); Justice of Appeal (1986–1992); Justice of Appeal, Gibraltar; Justice of Appeal, Bermuda (1998)

Cases heard as NPJ: 6

Sir Derek Cons NPJ

Appointed: NPJ of the CFA (1997–2006)
Other: Magistrate (1955–1962); Principal Magistrate (1962–1966); District Judge (1966–1972); Puisne Judge (1972–1976); Judge of the High Court (1976–1980); Justice of Appeal (1980–1993); Vice President of the Court of Appeal (1986–1993);

Commissioner of the Supreme Court of Brunei
(1993); Justice of the Court of Appeal, Bermuda
(1994–2002); President of the Court of Appeal of
Brunei (2003–2006)

Cases heard as NPJ: 4

Dato' Seri Paduka Sir Denys Tudor Emil Roberts NPJ

Appointed: NPJ of the CFA (1997–2003)
Other: Chief Justice of Hong Kong (1979–1988); Chief
Justice of Brunei Darussalam (1979–2001); Presi-
dent of Court of Appeal of Bermuda (1988–1994);
President of the Court of Appeal of Brunei Darus-
salam (2002–2003)

Cases heard as NPJ: 4

Sir Alan Armstrong Huggins NPJ

Appointed: NPJ of the CFA (1997–2003)
Other: Resident Magistrate, Uganda (1951–1953);
Stipendiary Magistrate (1953–1958); District
Judge (1958–1961); Puisne Judge (1961–1976);
Judicial Commissioner, Brunei Supreme Court
(1966–2000); Court of Appeal (1976–1987); Vice
President of the Court of Appeal (1980–1987);
President of the Court of Appeal of Brunei
(2000–2002); Justice of Appeal of the Falkland
Islands, the British Antarctic Territory, Gibraltar,
St Helena, the British Indian Ocean Territory, and
Bermuda

Cases heard as NPJ: 4

Mr. Art Michael McMullin NPJ

Appointed: NPJ of the CFA (1997–2003)
Other: Judiciary since 1950; Puisne Judge (1968–1976);
Judge of the High Court (1976–1979); Court of
Appeal (1979–1986); Vice President of the Court
of Appeal (1980–1986)

Cases heard as NPJ: 0

Mr. Neil MacDougall NPJ

Appointed:	NPJ of the CFA (1997–2003)
Other:	Judge of the High Court, Hong Kong Judiciary (1980–1989); Justice of Appeal (1989–1995); Vice President of the Court of Appeal (1993–1995)
Cases heard as NPJ:	0

12

Concurring and dissenting in the Hong Kong Court of Final Appeal

JILL COTTRELL AND YASH GHAI

Introduction

Justice Ruth Ginsburg tells of attending a conference where a French colleague expressed mystification:

> How can the law have more than one plausible meaning? Or, more accurately, how can a court judgment openly so acknowledge?... Isn't it the court's responsibility to identify by judgment *the* (one and only) correct interpretation?[1]

French courts, with their terse, almost cryptic, judgments, are perhaps at the opposite extreme to the US Supreme Court, where 'the dissent rate [for individual judges] sometimes reaches more than sixty per cent'.[2] Equally, practices about concurring judgments vary greatly from jurisdiction to jurisdiction, court to court, and even judge to judge. The first part of this chapter discusses those differences, reasons for them, and arguments for and against them, and the second part presents some exploration of practices in the Hong Kong Court of Final Appeal (CFA).

Courts of final appeal take various forms, although all have multiple judges, indeed, most more than four. Some sit essentially *en banc*, with all the members available sitting in every case (as in the US Supreme Court). A few sit in divisions, such as the Supreme Court of India, where a typical bench comprises five judges, and more than one bench may sit at a time.

The rules and the practice elsewhere

The tradition to which the CFA is heir was not the British tradition as applied in the United Kingdom but the colonial. However, especially

---

[1] Ruth Bader Ginsburg, 'Remarks on Writing Separately' (1990) 65 *Wash. L. Rev.* 133, 133.
[2] John Alder, 'Dissents in Courts of Last Resort: Tragic Choices?' (2000) 20 *OJLS* 221, 243.

within the common law tradition – and to some extent within the European – similar issues arise as to how to deal with the existence of multiple judges with multiple views in most countries, and practices are more varied than one might expect.

The British[3]

Reflecting, or creating, the nature of the common law as 'a maze and not a motorway', in the words of Diplock LJ,[4] the main tradition of English multi-judge courts has been for each judge to give a judgment. In some cases, each of several judges gives full consideration to the entire case as though they have no idea what the other judges are going to say. Historically, this was probably very often the case: judgments were given immediately, *ex tempore*, and orally. In the English Court of Appeal, there has been something of a trend towards composite judgments – 'judgments of the court' (i.e. a single judgment not attributable to any one judge), around 10 per cent of cases in the early part of the century.[5] And in around 40 per cent of cases, one judgment was concurred in by the other judges.[6] There is a long established practice in the court's Criminal Division (following the practice of the Court of Criminal Appeal) of having only one judgment,[7] and according to Lord Mance, there has only ever been one dissent in that division.[8]

It is surprising, perhaps, how much discussion there has been of single judgments. Lord Mansfield CJ pushed his judges towards agreed judgments,[9] although he said that, ultimately, whether or not to dissent was a matter of the judicial conscience.[10] Generally, however, unanimity has not been the practice since the sixteenth century.[11] However, there was discussion in the mid-nineteenth century of whether there should

---

[3]   Used rather than 'English' because, although there is no treatment of specifically Scottish courts, the House of Lords and the Privy Council are not just English.

[4]   In *Morris* v. *Martin* [1966] 1 QB 716, 730, quoted by Lord Mance in 'The Common Law and Europe: Differences of Style or Substance and Do They Matter?', The Holdsworth Address 2007, Birmingham UK, Holdsworth Club, 2007, at 13, accessible at www.birmingham.ac.uk/Documents/college-artslaw/law/holdsworth-address/holdsworth06-07-mance.pdf. Interestingly, during the Diplock period in the House of Lords, single judgments were common (at 7).

[5]   Roderick Munday, 'All for One and One for All: The Rise to Prominence of the Composite Judgment in the Civil Division of the Court of Appeal' (2002) 61 *CLJ* 321.

[6]   *Ibid.*, 323.   [7]   Supreme Court Act 1981 s. 59.   [8]   Mance, note 4 above, 6.

[9]   Alder, note 2 above, 222.

[10]   *Ibid.*, citing *Millar* v. *Taylor* (1769) 4 *Burrows* 2303, 2395.   [11]   *Ibid.*

be one judgment only in the House of Lords,[12] an idea that recurred in discussion about the setting up of the new Supreme Court in the United Kingdom.[13]

A practice in the House of Lords of having one judgment in criminal cases was abandoned after the much-criticised decision in *DPP* v. *Smith*.[14] Its general practice of multiple judgments, which might include dissents and concurrences, is followed by its successor, the Supreme Court. A commentator has observed:

> There are good reasons for thinking that the new UKSC ought to be more dissentient than the Judicial Committee of the House of Lords. More judgments [sc. cases] are heard by more judges, and research has shown that larger bench sizes tend to produce more dissenting opinions. The composition of the court is more consistent, and the circulation of draft opinions seems to be more extensive, both factors which could either promote consensus or, should a draft opinion strike a bum note, end up polarizing justices and creating clear lines of demarcation.[15]

Baroness Hale, now on the Supreme Court but with experience of the House of Lords, has written that in 20 of the first 57 cases decided by the Supreme Court, there was a 'judgment of the court', and 'in a further 11, there was either a single judgment (with which all the other Justices agreed), or a single majority judgment (with which all the Justices in the majority agreed), or an 'effectively' single or single majority judgment (because separate judgments were simply footnotes or observations)'.[16]

---

[12] *Ibid.*, 235 citing the Select Committee of the House of Lords on the Appellate Jurisdiction, *Parliamentary Papers, House of Lords*, (1856) 46 XXIV.

[13] Andrew Le Sueur, 'A Report on Six Seminars about the UK Supreme Court' (Queen Mary University of London, School of Law Legal Studies Research Paper No. 1/2008), accessible at papers.ssrn.com/sol3/papers.cfm?abstract_id=1324749. The judges of the court have not ceased to talk about it, not just as affects their own court; see Lord Neuberger, 'No Judgment – No Justice' (First annual BAILII Lecture) November 2012, accessible at www.supremecourt.gov.uk/docs/speech-121120.pdf, and Lord Kerr of Tonaghmore, 'Dissenting Judgments – Self Indulgence or Self Sacrifice?' (The Birkenhead Lecture) October 2012, accessible at www.supremecourt.gov.uk/docs/speech-121008.pdf.

[14] Alder, note 2 above, 245. The case was reported at [1961] AC 290; the object of criticism was their Lordships' endorsement of a partially objective test of intention in murder.

[15] Chris Hanretty, 'Dissenting Opinions in the UKSC', 19 August 2010, accessible at ukscblog.com/dissenting-opinons-in-the-uksc, but originally published on the author's blog. It includes comparative charts of unanimous judgments from the final appellate courts of the United States, Australia, Canada, South Africa, and the United Kingdom.

[16] Brenda Hall, 'Judgment Writing in the Supreme Court', accessible at ukscblog.com/judgment-writing-in-the-supreme-court-brenda-hale.

Hong Kong's final court until 1997, the Judicial Committee of the Privy Council (PC), has been the main site of single judgment giving. This used to be justified on the basis that formally the committee was giving 'advice' to Her or His Majesty, and the monarch ought not to be confused by being given varying or conflicting advice! A more recent justification was that, since appeals came there mostly from the colonies, the citizens of those countries (no doubt already bemused by the system of law imposed upon them) ought to be given a clear message about what the law was, since they were 'not attuned to the institutions and conventions of their Imperial masters'.[17] One 1901 argument against change was that unanimity was important because of 'half-educated Hindu lawyers'.[18]

Australian judges who sat on the committee chafed against this rule. Eventually, change came, and an Order in Council in 1966[19] provided that the Judicial Committee may have two opinions – one majority and one dissenting – '[p]ossibly the worst of both worlds'.[20]

United States

The US courts, of course, are also inheritors of the British tradition. But in the early days of the US Supreme Court, Chief Justice Marshall (not so far removed from the time of Mansfield[21]) tried to introduce the practice of single decisions.[22] Marshall sometimes wrote the majority opinion even when he disagreed with it,[23] although he was not rigid on this point and dissented several times, and he once gave a concurring judgment.[24] Alder links the Supreme Court approach both to natural law ideas and to the 'quasi-corporate' identity of the court as a branch of government in the 'separation of powers' model of the US constitution.[25] He also points out that Marshall was concerned to shore up the young court's authority. Justice Brennan said the practice 'consolidated the authority of the Court

[17] Ginsburg, note 1 above, 135 quoting L. Blom-Cooper and G. Drewry, *Final Appeal: A Study of the House of Lords in its Judicial Capacity* (Oxford: Clarendon Press, 1972) 82.

[18] Alder, note 2 above, 236, citing R. B. Stevens, *Law and Politics, The House of Lords as a Judicial Body* (London: Weidenfeld and Nicholson, 1978) 417.

[19] Judicial Committee (Dissenting Opinions) Order 1966, SI 1966, No. 1100.

[20] Alder, note 2 above, 35.   [21] Mansfield retired in 1788.

[22] Ginsburg, note 1 above, 138.

[23] Victoria Heine, 'Institutional Unity Vs Freedom of Expression: A Dissent Analysis of the Richardson Courts' [2002] 33 *VUWLR* 581.

[24] Ginsburg, note 1 above, 138.   [25] Alder, note 2, 238.

and aided in the general recognition of the Third Branch as co-equal partner with the other branches'.[26]

Similarly, in the 1920s, the court was under attack, which led its members to stick together.[27] Indeed, the American Bar Association Code of Judicial Ethics included, between 1924 and 1972, a provision discouraging dissent.[28] Now, however, dissents and concurrences are common. Justice Ginsburg describes the system: 'As in civilian systems, we have but one judgment, and we mark it the Court's. But in tune with the British tradition, we place no formal constraints on the prerogative of each judge to speak out separately'.[29]

Other jurisdictions

Multiple judgments are the norm in most common law jurisdictions, including in the apex courts of Australia, Canada,[30] and India; the Court of Appeal of New Zealand (although English practice in criminal cases applied in the last, until 2008[31]); and the New Zealand Supreme Court. This is not to say there has been no debate in those countries. In Canada, for example, academics and the profession debated in the 1950s whether the Supreme Court should adopt the one-judgment system.[32] And in Australia, various Chief Justices have tried to reduce the number of judgments given.[33] A cursory glance at the *Singapore Law Reports* indicates that the norm for the Court of Appeal is a 'judgment of the court'.

Occasionally, constitutional rules prescribe the practice. The Supreme Court of Ireland is required by the Constitution to give only one opinion when the constitutionality of a Bill passed by Parliament is in issue; neither concurrence nor dissent is permitted.[34] By contrast, the Constitution of Nigeria provides that '[e]ach Justice of the Supreme Court or of the Court of Appeal shall express and deliver his opinion in writing or may state

---

[26] William J. Brennan, Jr., '*In Defense of Dissents*' (1986) 37 *Hastings L.J.* 427, quoted by Kermit V. Lipez, 'Some Reflections on Dissenting' (2005) 57 *Maine L. Rev.* 313.

[27] *Ibid.*, 316.   [28] *Ibid.*, 315.   [29] Note 1 above, 138.

[30] Peter McCormick, 'The Choral Court: Separate Concurrence and the McLachlin Court, 2000–2004' (2005–2006) 37 *Ottawa L. Rev.* 1.

[31] Heine, note 23 above (until 2004, the final appellate court for New Zealand was the Judicial Committee of the Privy Council). See section 398(1) of the Crimes Act 1961 repealed in 2008.

[32] Maxwell Bruce, 'The 1953 Mid-Winter Meeting of Council' (1953) 31 *Canadian Bar Review* 178, 182, cited in Andrew Lynch, 'Is Judicial Dissent Constitutionally Protected?' (2004) 4 *Macquarie Law Journal* 81, 87.

[33] *Ibid.*, 86.   [34] Art. 26.2.2. See also Art. 35.5.

in writing that he adopts the opinion of any other Justice who delivers a written opinion' (Article 294(2)). This precludes a composite judgment of the court and requires judges to acknowledge that they disagree.

European and Scandinavian practices vary. The Supreme Court of Norway uses the 'English model' of separate judgments.[35] In Greece, dissents must be published, according to Article 93(3) of the Constitution.[36] In pre-revolutionary Spain, dissents were circulated among the judges but were not published.[37] In Germany since 1970, the Constitutional Court may publish concurring and dissenting judgments, although they are still not frequent.[38]

In China, no individual judgments are published, and there is no indication of concurrence or dissent. But in Japan, dissents and concurrences have been known since the Second World War.[39]

At one point, the former Permanent Court of International Justice followed the practice of circulating but not publishing dissents.[40] The Court of Justice of the European Union delivers only a unanimous judgment.[41] But the European Court of Human Rights and the International Court of Justice permit dissenting judgments.

Reasons for these practices include the origins of the courts, including the fact that the European Court of Justice came into existence before the United Kingdom joined the then European Economic Community. Among the original member countries were several that countenance no dissent in their courts, including Italy. It has also been pointed out that the judges have renewable terms, and it is perhaps in their interests not to be exposed as the authors of opinions that might not have favour in their own countries, which must support any renewal.[42] There is also the practical element of language – not all judges have equal ability to produce

---

[35] McCormick also uses the expression 'English model', at note 30 above, 4.

[36] Alder, note 2 above, 244.   [37] *Ibid.*, 245.

[38] Ginsburg, note 1 above, 146, citing Grementieri and Golden, 'The United Kingdom and the European Court of Justice: An Encounter Between Common and Civil Law Traditions' (1973) 21 *Am. J. Comp. L.* 664.

[39] Hiroshi Itoh, *The Japanese Supreme Court: Constitutional Policies* (New York: M. Wiener, 1989) 93.

[40] Alder, note 2 above, 245.

[41] 'One only has to look at some of the Judgments of the CJEU in Luxembourg to see how compulsory unanimity can result in decisions which (i) are incomprehensible, (ii) have internally inconsistent reasoning, (iii) do not answer the issue that has been referred, or (iv) manage to enjoy all these three regrettable characteristics.' Lord Neuberger, note 13 above.

[42] Ginsburg, note 1 above, 146.

a judgment in French.[43] In Germany, Constitutional Court judges' terms were changed to 12 years, non-renewable, at the same time as they were permitted to concur or dissent.

The different approach of many European countries is partly attributable to the very different nature of the judiciary.[44] In most of these countries, the judiciary is a career path. Judges are bureaucrats. But academics may be appointed to the German Constitutional Court. In common law countries, the common practice (less followed in colonies) was to appoint to the bench practising advocates: individuals who become the 'third side of an argumentative triangle'.[45]

Concurrence: pros and cons

Cons (reasons not to allow or to discourage)

It is sometimes said that concurring judgments do not produce clarity and that people will be confused; indeed, lawyers may be confused. It is sometimes hard enough to identify the *ratio decidendi* when there is one judgment only, but when there are several, it can be extremely elusive.[46] Justice Brennan (the American one) said: '[I]n most matters it is more important that the applicable rule of law be settled than that it be settled right. This is commonly true even where the error is a matter of serious concern, provided correction can be had by legislation'.[47]

Those in favour of unanimity argue that it does not necessarily imply suppression of minority views; there is an incentive to judges to discuss their differences, and this may well result in some judge modifying her views or the views of an otherwise concurring judge becoming part of the majority.[48] Desire for unanimity may be particularly strong in countries where judges come from political backgrounds but strive to be neutral. 'Italian politics are so conflictual that adding dissent would be like adding

---

[43] Mance, note 4 above, 7.   [44] Ginsburg, note 1 above, 137.

[45] Harry Lawson, 'Comparative Judicial Style' (1977) 20 *Am J Comp. L* 364, 365, quoted by Roderick Munday, 'Judicial Configurations' (2002) 61 *CLJ* 612, 639.

[46] Resembling Lewis Carroll, *Hunting of the Snark* (London: Constable, 1874) says Munday, *ibid.*, 641. Text accessible at www.literature.org/authors/carroll-lewis/the-hunting-of-the-snark/index.html.

[47] Brennan, note 26 above, cited in Ginsburg, note 1 above, 145.

[48] Mance, note 4 above, 7. See also the interesting discussion 'Global Constitutionalism Seminar Offers Students a Window to the World's "Greatest Legal Minds"' with comments on e.g. the practice in the German and Italian constitutional courts, accessible at www.law.yale.edu/intruders/12738.htm.

confusion to confusion', said Justice Sabino Cassese of the Constitutional Court of Italy.[49]

Even some common lawyers have argued that a judgment to which all the judges adhere has greater authority. In relation especially to a final court, one may say that 'a major function . . . is to provide legal certainty, to deliver authoritative statements of the law for the guidance of lower courts, to legitimate specific doctrinal interpretations and extrapolations of the law'.[50]

On a slightly different point, Munday says that judges have suggested to him that a composite judgment was preferable and carried more weight than one judgment followed by a chorus of 'I concur's' because there is some lack of credibility about the concurrences. And they have also said that an admittedly composite judgment means that all judges can be credited with the work rather than what may be the work of several minds being attributed to the judge who presents it.[51]

Pros

Turning to the defence of multiple judgments, one strain is a counterpart to the argument that combined judgments will represent the intellectual contributions of several judges – namely, that the very fact that another judge may write a concurring judgment, perhaps more convincingly, is an incentive to put one's judicial best into writing one's own.[52]

Justice Brennan's views on certainty may be applicable to commercial cases. It is less true of the accidental involvement situations, such as tort, criminal law, and the situation of a citizen faced with the public official (the latter may be able to shape her behaviour; the former has less choice, typically). Munday suggests that generally, cases are not just about outcomes but also about how decisions are reached and about the right principle.[53] And as with dissenting judgments, today's minority view may become tomorrow's orthodoxy.[54] Most English lawyers would feel their jurisprudence would have been poorer without Atkin's famous dissent in *Liversidge* v. *Anderson*[55] or Denning's in *Candler* v. *Crane, Christmas & Co.*[56]

Munday also suggests that appellants may have particular faith in the plurality of judicial brains that are to be focussed in their case[57] and that they might feel short changed, if they lose, if there is only one judgment.

---

[49] *Ibid.* [50] McCormick, note 30 above, 3. [51] Munday, note 44 above, 648.
[52] *Ibid.*, 640. [53] *Ibid.* [54] *Ibid.* [55] [1942] AC 206.
[56] [1951] 2 KB 164 – to become orthodoxy in *Hedley Byrne* v. *Heller* [1964] AC 465.
[57] Munday, note 44 above, 635–6.

Arguably, multiple judgments (dissenting or concurring) help keep the system transparent and more honest.[58] Certainly, in a system where judges regularly take bribes, the necessity for every judge to say where he or she stands, and – even more – personally expressed reasons would be some small safeguard. This, and a concern about 'coasting judges', probably lies behind the Nigerian Constitution provision quoted earlier. Thomas Jefferson castigated composite opinions as 'an opinion ... huddled up in conclave, perhaps by a majority of one, delivered as if unanimous and with the silent acquiescence of lazy or timid associates by a crafty chief justice'.[59]

Criticisms of the composite judgment as such include that as a compromise it may be less clear and less nuanced than when individual judges have to spell out their views in detail and thus less useful in future cases.[60] Munday says that a French judge tried an extra-judicial experiment and concluded that a judgment written by a single person was intellectually stronger than a joint effort and that the individual would think more deeply when working alone.[61] Lord Reid said:

> With the passage of time I have come more and more firmly to the conclusion that it is never wise to have only one speech in this House dealing with an important question of law. My main reason is that experience has shown that those who have to apply the decision to other cases and still more those who wish to criticise it seem to find it difficult to avoid treating sentences and phrases in a single speech as if they were provisions in an Act of Parliament. . . . When there are two or more speeches they must be read together and then it is generally much easier to see what are the principles involved and what are merely illustrations of it.[62]

Munday's particular focus was on composite judgments, and the thrust of his critique was on the lines that this goes contrary to the very nature of the common law approach, trading the extreme openness of that system, with the judges being candid about their disagreements,[63] for a 'smidgen of certainty'.[64] He suggested that this modern approach was more *dirigiste*,[65] very different from the English tradition.[66]

---

[58] *Ibid.*, 641.
[59] Paul Leicester Ford (ed.), *The Writings of Thomas Jefferson*, vol. 9 (1816 to 1899) (New York: G. P. Putnam's Sons, 1892 to 1899) 169–71, quoted in Alder, note 2 above, 238. Lord Mance also suggests that unanimity protects weak judges at note 4 above, 11.
[60] Mance, note 4 above, 10.   [61] Munday, note 45 above, 651–2.
[62] *Broome* v. *Cassell & Co. Ltd.* [1972] AC 1027, 1085–6.
[63] Munday, note 45 above, 631.   [64] *Ibid.*, 645.   [65] Munday, note 5 above, 348.
[66] Citing Macmillan in *Read* v. *Lyons* [1947] AC 156.

The very texture of the composite judgment is different, Munday suggests, including some risk of 'intellectual dilution':[67]

> Composite judgments, clipped numbered paragraphs,[68] indexes, moral lessons spelled out in *post scripta*, the subordination of fact to principle, all these features combine to create an impression that the law is coherent and readily intelligible even to those who dwell outside the legal conventicle.[69]

He suggests that all this is the result of managerialism and a desire to be 'relevant' and a response to complaints that judgments have been getting too long (perhaps justified). And he finds it no more convincing that all judges really agree with the composite judgment than that those who insist 'I concur' actually do agree with all the twists and turns of their colleague's (or colleagues') reasoning.

Dissent: pros and cons

Some arguments against dissent are on the same lines as those against concurring judgments. Displaying dissension may undermine confidence in the legal system[70] and creates uncertainty in the law. Judge Learned Hand of the US Supreme Court said that dissent 'cancels the impact of monolithic solidarity on which the authority of a bench of judges so largely depends'.[71] Dissenting may be viewed as judicial self-publicity at the expense of the public.[72] And it undermines the collegiality of the court.

Although some have suggested that if dissent is not permitted or is discouraged, the need to reach unanimity will lead to more vigorous discussion among the judges,[73] others suggest that, on the contrary, the possibility of dissent may improve the quality of the majority judgment.[74] Within the common law system, many would no doubt agree that 'there is no more dispiriting spectacle than a contrived unanimity reflected in a bland opinion designed to obscure differences and offend nobody'.[75]

More positively, writers and judges have proposed that, as with concurring judgments, but perhaps even more so, permitting dissent is

---

[67] Munday, note 5 above, 347, citing Patricia Wald, 'The Rhetoric of Results and the Results of Rhetoric: Judicial Writings' (1995) 62 *U. Chi. L. Rev.* 1371, 1377–8.

[68] For which he blames neutral citations, pioneered by AustLII (see www.austii.edu.au).

[69] Munday, note 45 above, 616.   [70] Alder, note 2 above, 242.

[71] Lipez, note 26 above, 317 quoting Learned Hand, *The Bill of Rights* (Cambridge: Harvard University Press, 1958) 72.

[72] Alder, note 2 above, 243.   [73] *Ibid.*   [74] Lipez, note 26 above, 322.   [75] *Ibid.*, 318.

democratic, a view shared even by Justice Brennan, and it compensates for the 'democratic deficit' that is lacking in the common law.[76] Some argue that it is a matter of freedom of judicial speech.[77] William O. Douglas is quoted as having said 'only fascists and Communist systems insist on certainty and unanimity in the law'.[78] Justice Michael Kirby has said:

> The demand by observers for unanimity amongst Judges is often infantile. If it is an insistence that judges hide their disagreements from the public they serve, it denies the ultimate sovereign, the people, the right to evaluate, and criticise, judicial choices. Pretending that everything is certain in the law, and that judges simply operate on automatic pilot, will deceive relatively few.[79]

Dissents are also said to help clarify the law, revealing weaknesses and highlighting difficult issues.[80] They play a part in ongoing debates on the law and may highlight the need for legislative reform.[81] Mance quotes an Estonian judge:

> Dissenting opinions of Supreme Court judges have promoted the internationalisation of justice, relying on the law of other countries as well as on international and European law. . . . When some opinions have been too progressive for their day . . . and considerably more liberal and far-reaching than the majority opinion, the dissenting opinions have also served not just to aid development of the law but also to provide limits to the role of the court and warn the majority against indirect, publicly undeclared alteration of earlier practice.[82]

It is interesting that sometimes it is in constitutional cases that unanimity is supposed to be important (as in Ireland), but sometimes it is precisely these cases that are seen to benefit from the possibility of dissent. In intermediate courts, dissents may help with final resolution by clarifying the issue that will be argued on a subsequent appeal.

---

[76] Alder, note 2 above, 223. See also Munday, note 45 above, 237.

[77] Alder, *ibid.*, 240. See also Lynch, note 32 above.

[78] Lipez, note 26 above, 316, attributing Linda Greenhouse, 'Ideas & Trends: Divided They Stand; The High Court and the Triumph of Discord', *N.Y. Times*, 15 July 2001, 4–1.

[79] 'Judicial Dissent' (address delivered at James Cook University, Cairns, 26 February 2005) quoted in Munday, 'Suppressing Dissent', *Criminal Law and Justice Weekly*, 27 December 2008, accessible at www.criminallawandjustice.co.uk/index.php?/Analysis/suppressing-dissent.html.

[80] Alder, note 2 above, 240.   [81] Lipez, note 26 above, 322.

[82] Mance, note 4 above, 11–12, quoting M. Julia Laffranque in *Juridica International*, IX/2004, 14.

Why do rates of dissent and concurrence vary?

Why do frequencies of these phenomena vary so much? Presumably, the personalities and views of presiding judges will have some impact.[83] So does workload. (Apparently, the Singapore Court of Appeal is so overloaded with work that it hears several cases a day, each occupying about one hour for argument.[84] Some have suggested that having computers and law clerks (to do research and sometimes even to contribute to the writing) might lead to more judgments.[85] But the latter does not seem to have affected multiple judgment rates in New Zealand.[86]

Presiding judges, perhaps with the support of their colleagues, may be more concerned to produce unanimity in certain types of cases – criminal cases, for example – or in cases that are likely to arouse special controversy. Munday suggests that the English Court of Appeal is more likely to give composite judgments when a new area of law is in issue,[87] when it wants to dispel obscurity,[88] or when the conduct of law enforcement officers or even judges is in question,[89] in particularly major or important cases,[90] or when the liberty of the subject is at stake.[91] It has been said that Chief Justice Warren worked very hard to get unanimity in *Brown* v. *Board of Education*.[92]

Some judges, it has been suggested, are better than others at building coalitions.[93] Some find it harder to shed the habit of arguing. Judges who dissent are often also those who give separate concurring judgments.[94] Very often, dissents – or even concurrences – will flow from different value systems. Perhaps human rights cases give more scope for values than other cases, which may partly explain why in New Zealand dissents were more common in Bill of Rights cases, in the Richardson court, but in other cases there was little variation.[95] And in Canada, dissents were notably more likely, under Lamer CJ at least, in Charter of Rights cases than in other cases.[96] Judges are less likely to dissent in statutory interpretation

---

[83] Munday, note 5 above, 330 suggests Slade LJ in the 1980s and Bingham, Woolf, and Phillips MR in the 1990s were important in this way in the CA. See also McCormick, note 30 above, 6.

[84] Personal information.   [85] Ginsburg, note 1 above, 148.

[86] Heine, note 23 above, 592.   [87] Munday, note 5 above, 329.   [88] *Ibid.*, 331.

[89] *Ibid.*, 333–5.   [90] *Ibid.*, 336.   [91] *Ibid.*, 341.   [92] McCormick, note 30 above, 3.

[93] *Ibid.*, 12.   [94] *Ibid.*, 10–11.   [95] Heine, note 23 above.

[96] McCormick, note 30 above, 8. And Alder, note 2 above, 227, says that human rights values are among those that may lead to disagreement.

cases,[97] although sometimes different values in interpretation may lead to dissent.[98]

Writing a separate judgment involves more work and may not always enhance relations with one's colleagues. Dissents are easier to explain. The judge may dissent because she cannot abide the result or even out of anger – 'blood in the neck'.[99] There may even be a desire not to waste work (also a possible motive for concurring).[100] And the judge may not only be convinced that she is right but also believe that future judges will agree with her and therefore wish her views to be recorded for posterity. So the audience is less the parties to the particular case than the public and the broader legal community.[101] Sometimes the judge may believe that highlighting the losing argument will soften the blow.[102] Douglas said: 'the right to dissent is the only thing that makes life tolerable for a judge of an appellate court',[103] and Wald that it is 'liberating'.[104]

The specificities of Hong Kong

What then might we expect from the CFA – directed to apply the common law (without restriction to the common law of England) and to apply the international Bill of Rights as it had been applied in Hong Kong?

Like the colonies in general, Hong Kong never quite had the 'common law of England'. It did not have legislative sovereignty. And it did not have a final court of appeal quite like the House of Lords. It did not have a bench drawn mainly from the practising bar. Its judges traditionally came from the Commonwealth/Colonial Judicial Service – men (only) who were very often promoted to the higher bench from the lower or had been colonial legal officers (prosecutors many of them), and the PC never had a practice of concurrences and dissents, as we have seen – certainly not at all before 1966 and even since then only one majority and one dissent.

The CFA was – is still – a new court, as controversial as the US Supreme Court was in its early years; controversial partly because the PRC had

---

[97] Lipez, note 26 above, 328, citing Antonin Scalia, *The Dissenting Opinion*, (1994) J. Sup. Ct. Hist. 33, 42.

[98] Alder, note 2 above, 227.   [99] Lipez, note 26 above, 328.   [100] *Ibid.*

[101] *Ibid.*, 319–20.   [102] *Ibid.*, 328.

[103] Quoted in Lipez, note 26 above, 340, from Scalia, note 97 above.   [104] *Ibid.*

not wanted it as a Hong Kong based court, partly because of its peculiar position as not quite the final court in cases to which Article 158 of the Basic Law (BL) could apply and controversial because of the debate over foreign judge(s).[105]

It would inevitably have been unusual by virtue of having foreign judges and perhaps was the more difficult to manage because it did not have a fixed component of such judges but a shifting group and not all of them from the same background. It was unusual for Hong Kong in that all its original local members came from private practice (directly or via the superior courts).

The CFA could have chosen to adopt a practice of composite judgments. That might have saved one foreign judge from this attack: 'What special line of reasoning did Lord Nicholls suddenly take in order to customise these innovative guidelines for Hong Kong while he never felt the need for it when presiding in British courts?'[106] But maybe Mr Ma would anyway have detected the hand of the foreigner in the decision.[107]

Concurring and dissenting in the Court of Final Appeal

Rates of concurrence and dissent in Hong Kong are lower than in many other common law courts, although naturally far higher than in the predecessor of the CFA, the PC, as pointed out elsewhere in this volume.[108]

The research team of the University of Hong Kong on the CFA has assigned 'degrees of dividedness' to each case, between 1 (single unanimous judgment) and 13 (a separate judgment from each judge, two of

---

[105] See Chapter 5 (Young, Da Roza, and Ghai) in this volume. See also the 2012 debate sparked by criticisms of the judiciary made by Ms Elsie Leung, former Secretary for Justice, and Tsinghua Law School academic Cheng Jie presenting the view that all CFA judges should be Chinese nationals. See Editorial, 'Overseas Judges Vital for Hong Kong's Common Law System', *South China Morning Post*, 14 November 2012.

[106] Ma Lik, 'A Judgment Found Wanting', *Hong Kong iMail*, 5 December 2000. It seems he made essentially the same statements in the *Hong Kong Economic Times* (a Chinese language journal), reported in an article by Albert Cheng, 'The Power of Final Judgment', *South China Morning Post*, 25 November 2000. The case is *Albert Cheng* v. *Tse Wai Chun Paul* (2000) 3 HKCFAR 339.

[107] The attack is, of course, nonsense, and the decision has subsequently been adopted by the English courts; see e.g. *Associated Newspapers Limited* v. *Burstein* [2007] 4 All ER 319.

[108] See Chapter 6 (Young and Da Roza) in this volume.

Table 12.1 *Degree of dividedness in the Court of Final Appeal, 1997–2010*

	Degrees of dividedness (civil/criminal)											
Decision date	1	2	3	4	5	6	7	8	10	11	12	13
1998	6/1		3/	3/	/1		1/	1/	/1			
1999	5/6		5/3	2/	2/					1/		1/
2000	13/7		6/	2/1	1/							
2001	10/6		6/1	1/								
2002	6/1	/1	2/4	3/			1/			1/		
2003	6/6	/1	4/		1/	1/	/1				1/	
2004	11/9		4/1			1/						
2005	6/6		5/1	1/1		1/	/1	1/				
2006	13/12	1/	10/1	/1								
2007	8/10	2/	4/2	1/	1/							
2008	13/7	3/	5/		1/		1/					
2009	9/9	4/	8/1						1/			
2010	3/5		1/1			/1			/1			
All civil	109	10	63	13	6	3	3	2	1	2	1	1
All criminal	85	2	15	3	1	1	2		2			
Total	194	12	78	16	7	4	5	2	3	2	1	1

which were dissents).[109] A 'concurring' opinion is one where something other than 'I agree with . . . ' was said.

Table 12.1 tries to show how this worked out, year by year, up until 2009, and considering civil and criminal appeals separately.

---

[109] The criteria for this are
  1. One opinion, one author
  2. One opinion, multiple authors (either one judgment with multiple authors or more than one judgment with multiple authors forming the opinion of the court)
  3. Majority opinion, one concurring opinion
  4. Majority opinion, two concurring opinions
  5. Majority opinion, three concurring opinions
  6. Majority opinion, four concurring opinions
  7. Majority opinion, one dissenting opinion
  8. Majority opinion, one concurring opinion, one dissenting opinion
  9. Majority opinion, two dissenting opinions [none fitted this pattern]
  10. Majority opinion, two concurring opinions, one dissenting opinion
  11. Majority opinion, three concurring opinion, one dissenting opinion
  12. Majority opinion, one concurring opinion, two dissenting opinions
  13. Majority opinion, two concurring opinions, two dissenting opinions

The majority of cases are decided unanimously. This is more marked
for criminal cases: of 111 criminal cases, 85 (76.6 per cent) were decided
without dissent or concurrence; this is true of 109 of the 214 civil appeals
(or 50.9 per cent). Other than unanimity, the most common pattern is one
majority with one concurring opinion. Only four of the cases with dissents
were criminal. And division is mostly a matter of concurrence rather than
dissent. Only in 14 cases in this period were there any dissents, and in
two of these cases, there were two dissents. But there were concurring
judgments in 114 cases.

Unanimity in different forms

Not all unanimous judgments take the form of a single judgment by a
single judge supported by a chorus of 'I agree with the judgment of ...',
although this is the most common pattern. At least 25 judgments were
delivered as the reasons of the court by a single judge when the court had
earlier stated its conclusions but had adjourned delivery of its reasons. This
suggests that the case gave rise to no difficulty or difference of emphasis,
and it was not necessary to have more than one judgment. These are very
often criminal cases and often involve a misdirection to the jury[110] or a
conviction reached on the basis of essentially no evidence.[111] It seems that
in only about seven cases did the court give judgment *ex tempore*; in two
of these, the judgment (very short) was that of the court.[112]

A few other judgments were introduced formally as 'the judgment of
the court'.[113] *Ng Ka Ling* itself was
'the unanimous judgment of the court',[114] as was, even less surprisingly,
the court's humiliating 'clarification' after the 'Interpretation'.[115] Another
in the sequence of abode cases had the added sensitivity that the court
declined to seek another 'interpretation' by the National People's Congress
(NPC) because the BL was so clear.[116] We might include here other abode
cases where Bokhary PJ dissented but the other judges delivered a joint

---

[110] E.g. *Chan Kar Leung* v. *HKSAR* (2006) 9 HKCFAR 827.
[111] E.g. *Chau Lin Su-E* v. *HKSAR* (2004) 7 HKCFAR 265.
[112] *Anderson Asphalt Ltd.* v. *The Secretary for Justice*, unreported, FACV19/2008, 19 Novem-
      ber 2008, CFA, per Li CJ and *HKSAR v Lam Pui Shan*, unreported, FACC8/1999, 27
      March 2000, CFA, per Bokhary PJ.
[113] See further Chapters 14 (Chen and Lo) and 15 (Young) in this volume.
[114] *Ng Ka Ling* v. *Director of Immigration* (1999) 2 HKCFAR 4.
[115] (1999) 2 HKCFAR 141.
[116] *Director of Immigration* v. *Chong Fung Yuen* (2001) 4 HKCFAR 211.

judgment.[117] In one case, the judgment was that of the court 'to which all of its members have contributed'.[118] Neither this, nor *Town Planning Board* v. *Society for the Protection of the Harbour Ltd.* was sensitive in terms of Hong Kong–Mainland relations, but the latter was in economic terms because it put a brake on reclamation of the iconic harbour.[119] In one case, the single judgment (elucidating an earlier CFA judgment delivered by Lord Millett) was introduced as that of Lord Millett, but 'it includes the contributions of other members of the Court'.[120]

Concurring judgments

Before moving on to real concurrences, we note a phenomenon in the CFA not necessarily found in other common law final courts: that of the joint judgment, usually written by two judges. The most common combination has been Justices Chan and Bokhary, but several others have occurred, including on at least two occasions a permanent judge (PJ) with a Law Lord.

Who are the concurrers?

Interestingly, and by way of contrast with the tradition in English appellate courts, it is rarely difficult to identify the 'majority opinion' and who wrote it. Those who wrote separate concurring judgments were mainly: Bokhary, 62 and several with Chan PJ; Litton, 33; Chan, 23 and several with Bokhary PJ; Ribeiro, 11; Mason, 7; Li, 7; Hoffmann, 8; and Millett, 4.

Length of concurrences

Some indication of the nature of concurring judgments can perhaps be obtained from word counts (kindly carried out by the research team). We can perhaps divide the judgments into length categories in an inevitably arbitrary way, counting less than 1000 words as 'short', 1000 to 2999 as 'medium', and 3000 or more as 'long'.

---

[117] *Tam Nga Yin* v. *Director of Immigration* (2001) 4 HKCFAR 251 and *Ng Siu Tung* v. *Director of Immigration* (2002) 5 HKCFAR 1.

[118] *Kung Ming Tak Tong Co. Ltd* v. *Park Solid Enterprises Ltd* (2008) 11 HKCFAR 403, a real property case.

[119] (2004) 7 HKCFAR 1.

[120] *Nam Chun Investment Co Ltd* v. *Director of Lands* (2005) 8 HKCFAR 668.

Among the significant concurrers, we find that Bokhary PJ has a definite tendency towards the short judgment, with 33 falling in that category (half under 550 words, in fact); in joint judgments with Chan PJ, their tendency is the same, with six short and one medium. However, Bokhary has also given 20 medium and 9 long concurrences. Chan PJ alone leans slightly less in the direction of brevity, and Litton (formerly PJ and now local non-permanent judge [NPJ]) fits into this middle category. Among the PJs, the less frequent concurrers also tend towards the middle group. The foreign NPJs generally fall more into the medium group but with the highest proportion of 'long' and even an average length of long. In fact, most never give short concurring judgments at all.

Concurring foreign non-permanent judges

The research team has produced the figures shown in Table 12.2 (omitting foreign NPJs who never gave concurring judgments[121]).

Table 12.2 seems to show that some NPJs are more enthusiastic concurrers. But it also shows that the NPJs give judgments less often than they probably would in their own jurisdictions. Only one, Lord Hoffmann, delivered any sort of judgment in more than half the cases in which he has been involved. Sir Anthony Mason came next in terms of proportion but top in terms of absolute number. The former's 20 of 36 equates to a judgment giving rate of 56 per cent and the latter's 32 of 91 to 35 per cent.

There are at least 19 instances of the majority judgment being given by a PJ and a concurring judgment of some length (over 1000 words) being given by a foreign NPJ. Some of the 'foreign concurrence' cases fell into the category in which neither judge referred to the other's judgment. Sometimes the other judges agreed with both.[122] Coming from jurisdictions where 'judgments of the court' or a chorus of 'I concurs' is relatively unusual in the apex court, it is likely that sometimes a foreign NPJ's delivering a concurring judgment is simply motivated by the fact of the case being interesting or one on which he has clear views. A number of NPJ concurring judgments are very short and restricted to making a specific point rather than being the classic 'parallel' concurrence.[123]

---

[121] Thus excluding Eichelbaum, Gault, Nicholls, Somers, Walker, and Woolf NPJJ.

[122] E.g. *Akai Holding* v. *Ernst and Young* (2009) 12 HKCFAR 649 (Bokhary PJ and Hoffmann NPJ) and *Chen Li Hung* v. *Ting Lei Miao* (2000) 3 HKCFAR 9.

[123] *Nation Group Development Ltd.* v. *New Pacific Properties Ltd.* (2000) 3 HKCFAR 427 (Lord Hoffmann NPJ 158 words).

Table 12.2 *Concurring foreign non-permanent judges,*
1997–2010

Non-permanent judge	Involved in	Majority	Concurred
Brennan	21	5	2
Cooke	16	2	2
Hoffmann	36	12	8
Mason	91	25 (6 joint)	7
McHugh	10	1	2
Millett	50	12	4
Richardson	10	1	1
Scott	22	7	3

But sometimes there is a specific reason. Lord Cooke explained why he was giving a concurring judgment, precisely because he was a foreign NPJ, in *Chen* v. *Ting*.[124] Having reviewed the history of the BL, he concluded:

> I think that it may be inferred that, in appropriate cases, a function of a judge from other common law jurisdictions is to give particular consideration to whether a proposed decision of this Court is in accord with generally accepted principles of the common law.[125]

He proceeded to emphasise that the enunciation by Lord Wilberforce[126] of the principle on which the decision was based, as was 'widely regarded as the leading modern expression of the principle in the common law' and 'supported by such other leading common law judges as Lord Scarman and Lord Donaldson M.R. (as they were respectively to become). I would add, too, Lord Denning M.R.'[127]

Lord Cooke, a New Zealander, cited English authorities in this case. But how far do the foreign NPJs use the chance to concur to bring in judgments from their home jurisdictions? In view of the very English traditions of Hong Kong and its courts, including that '[o]verseas counsel . . . are invariably English', as Sir Anthony Mason observed,[128] this is not an

---

[124] *Chen Li Hung* v. *Ting Lei Miao*, [47]. In another case, he observed, in a brief concurrence, 'The decision poses no new threat to the sanctity of written contracts in Hong Kong'; see *Bank of China (Hong Kong) Ltd* v. *Fung Chin Kan* (2002) 5 HKCFAR 515.

[125] *Chen Li Hung* v. *Ting Lei Miao*, [47].

[126] *Carl Zeiss Stiftung* v. *Rayner & Keeler Ltd (No. 2)* [1967] AC 853, 954.

[127] *Chen Li Hung* v. *Ting Lei Miao*, [49].

[128] 'The Hong Kong Court of Final Appeal' (2001) 2 *Melbourne Journal of International Law* 216, accessible at www.austlii.edu.au/au/journals/MelbJIL/2001/9.html.

interesting question when thinking about the role of English judges. The others have been Australian or New Zealanders.

In one case, McHugh NPJ (from Australia) had read the majority judgment, but while going along with the result, he introduced a number of antipodean, especially Australian, authorities – about 15 of them, none cited by the other members of the court[129] – although these were by no means the only authorities he cited. There are actually few other cases when a foreign NPJ cited a case from his 'home' jurisdiction not mentioned by any other judge in a concurrence.[130]

Sir Anthony Mason differed in his understanding not of Australian authority but of Canadian in *Koo Sze Yiu and Leung Kwok Hung* v. *Chief Executive of the Hong Kong Special Administrative Region*[131] but not in the result. Differences in reasoning, not all of them major, have motivated some other of Mason NPJ's concurrences.[132] Mason NPJ said:

> I agree with so much of the reasons of Mr Justice Litton PJ as relate to the conclusions that the second, but not the first, statement complained of conveyed a defamatory imputation and that it defamed the second, but not the first, respondent. I agree also with the conclusion that the defence of fair comment was made out.[133]

The gist of his concurrence was explaining the last point in terms somewhat different from those of Litton PJ. He said in *Lau Kong Yung*:

> In the light of the importance of the cases and the novelty of the issues, it is appropriate that I state in my own words the basis of my thinking on some issues. The comments which follow are not intended to qualify in any way my agreement with the Chief Justice's reasons.[134]

And in *Ho Choi Wan* v. *Housing Authority*,[135] Millett NPJ agreed with the Chief Justice but added a separate reason 'a logically prior' point, as he put it.

---

[129] *Lee Yee Shing* v. *CIR* (2008) 11 HKCFAR 212.

[130] In *The Tian Sheng No.8 (Owner of the Ship)* v. *Owners of Cargo* (2000) 3 HKCFAR 187. Mason NPJ cited two Australian authorities, and also one Canadian not cited by other judges.

[131] (2006) 9 HKCFAR 441.

[132] E.g. *Wu Wing Kuen* v. *Leung Kwai Lin Cindy* (CACV240/1999, 17 March 2000). In *Leung Sai Lun Robert* v. *Leung May Ling* (1999) 2 HKCFAR 94, he reached the same result while eschewing any comments on the state of Chinese customary law in Hong Kong, as ventured by Ching PJ.

[133] *Eastern Express* v. *Man Mo Ching* (1999) 2 HKCFAR 264.

[134] *Lau Kong Yung* v. *Director of Immigration* (1999) 2 HKCFAR 300, [156].

[135] *Ho Choi Wan* v. *Housing Authority* (2005) 8 HKCFAR 628. See also Lord Cooke in *Bank of China (Hong Kong) Ltd* v. *Fung Chin Kan* (suggesting a different analysis from that adopted by Litton NPJ).

Very occasionally, a case shows some significant degree of disagreement between the concurring NPJ and the other judges in the route taken even if not the result. In *Kensland Realty* v. *Tai, Tang and Chong*,[136] Ribeiro PJ and McHugh NPJ gave major judgments with little or no reference to each other. McHugh NPJ criticised members of the House of Lords in a previous case but said that he did not need to rely on it; Bokhary PJ and Power NPJ relied on that case. A difficult case for the *ratio* seeker! In *Frank Yu Yu Kai* v. *Chan Chi Keung,* Lord Hoffmann said:

> I have not found the answer to this case obvious. In fact, I have changed my mind more than once.... At first I thought that there was evidence upon which the judge could have reached this conclusion [on the facts]. But the careful analysis of Mr Justice Ribeiro PJ has persuaded me that the medical literature upon which the judge relied will not sustain it.[137]

The genuine multiple judgment cases

The next question that seems of interest is why do certain cases lead to a multiplicity of judgments, especially substantial judgments? We have seen that this is less likely in criminal cases. In fact, on a crude reckoning, only about eight criminal cases have generated significant concurrences (measured by length). Several of these were significant human rights decisions. One was the 'flag case' on whether legislation that criminalises desecration is violative of human rights.[138] There were strong suspicions at the time that the court was concerned not to ruffle any more Mainland feathers – this being not very long after the first right of abode cases. The court held that there was no human rights infringement, and although three judges concurred with the Chief Justice, Bokhary NPJ gave a separate concurrence (see later), with which none of his brethren said they concurred. Another human rights issue was whether penalising buggery (only homosexual) in otherwise than a private place was discriminatory. The court held that it was; all agreed with the Chief Justice on this. And the concurrence was not on this issue but on the question of what happens next when an offence has been declared unconstitutional – so not a 'true' concurrence.[139]

HKSAR v. *Yeung May Wan*[140] concerned the Falun Gong sect and rights of assembly or demonstration. The court held that the ingredients of the

---

[136] (2008) 11 HKCFAR 237.
[137] *Frank Yu Yu Kai* v. *Chan Chi Keung* (2009) 12 HKCFAR 705.
[138] *HKSAR* v. *Ng Kung Siu* (1999) 2 HKCFAR 442.
[139] *Secretary for Justice* v. *Yau Yuk Lung Zigo* (2007) 10 HKCFAR 335.
[140] (2005) 8 HKCFAR 137.

offence concerned (obstruction of a public place), had not, in a context where there is freedom of speech, been established. Four of the judges had a joint judgment (of 13,564 words); Bokhary PJ had his own of 5565 words. Two cases involved appropriate directions to the jury: in one, Bokhary PJ gave the lead judgment, and Sir Anthony Mason concurred at some length.[141] In the other, Bokhary dissented, and Sir Daryl Dawson and Li CJ (the latter very briefly) concurred.[142]

One involved the onus of proof in a forfeiture case, when the person whose goods were to be forfeit had not been convicted,[143] and one the nature of the reverse onus in a drugs case. In each case, there were judgments from both Bokhary PJ and Sir Anthony Mason.[144] And in another, there were three judgments, from Chan and Bokhary PJJ and Sir Alan Huggins NPJ, on the impact of the abolition of the common law offence of conspiracy on the liability of a person who committed an alleged conspiracy before the amendment came into force but was prosecuted after.[145]

Finally, there were two judgments in a case in which the issue was whether the conviction was safe because of incompetence of defence counsel.[146] Bokhary PJ explained his decision to give a concurring judgment:

> As Sir Thomas Eichelbaum NPJ has noted, this is the first time an appeal based on the incompetence of defence counsel has reached this Court. I propose therefore to say a few words as to why I agree with him that the crucial question is whether the appellant had a fair trial.[147]

Among the civil cases, a few generated several judgments of significant length. They are of very different types. One particularly interesting example is the *Nina Kung* case,[148] better known in Hong Kong as the Nina Wang case. The case depended essentially on facts, unusual enough in a final appeal court. It concerned whether the will of a disappeared, presumed dead, tycoon, was valid – and on that hinged whether his pig-tailed widow, 'the richest woman in Asia', or her father-in-law, benefited from the estate, valued at around $US128 million. In some courts, this might have been a

---

[141] *Tang Kwok Wah, Dixon* v. *HKSAR* (2002) 5 HKCFAR 209.
[142] *Tang Siu Man* v. *HKSAR* (1997–1998) 1 HKCFAR 107.
[143] *Wong Hon Sun* v. *HKSAR* (2009) 12 HKCFAR 877.
[144] *HKSAR* v. *Hung Chan Wa* (2006) 9 HKCFAR 614.
[145] *Chan Pun Chung* v. *HKSAR* (2000) 3 HKCFAR 392.
[146] *Chong Ching Yuen* v. *HKSAR* (2004) 7 HKCFAR 126.
[147] *Ibid.*, [2].   [148] *Nina Kung* v. *Wang Din Shin* (2005) 8 HKCFAR 387.

case for a composite judgment, but here every judge spoke. Possibly the very publicity, plus the fact that the court was not only reversing both the judge of first instance and the 2:1 judgment of the Court of Appeal, but also making some rather critical remarks about the first instance judge, may have led them to feel that a statement by each judge, making it clear that they all agreed, might be of value.

The only other case that produced five concurring judgments, none of which was 'small', was *Ying Ho Co. v. Secretary for Justice.*[149] Oddly enough, this also involved Nina Wang – here the consequence of the government's refusal to permit the construction of her planned 'Nina Tower', intended to be the highest in the world but curtailed because of airport height restrictions. This was a genuine case of different judges reaching the same conclusion for somewhat different reasons. Cons (local) NPJ said that because of the variety of approaches, he thought he should also explain his own views, and he added his 1000 words or so. One of the extensive judgments was that of Sir Ivor Richardson, who said that he agreed in the result but by a different route. None of the other judges agreed with him.

The *Financial Secretary* v. *Felix Wong*[150] was dealt with in four concurring judgments. In fact, however, the stimulus for much of the concurring activity was something close to a dissent. The issue was what to do about a 'disaster' caused by the mishandling of a case by the Insider Dealing Tribunal and the failure of the Financial Secretary to take any decision about what to do next. Bokhary PJ (writing the majority judgment) would have liked to develop the law in a particular direction to create a way out of the impasse but in the end decided that it was best for the court to speak, if not in one voice, at least in a 'harmonious voice'. Ribeiro PJ said he was initially attracted by Bokhary's preferred approach but decided it was not possible. Litton NPJ said he was initially inclined just to concur with Ribeiro PJ because he was in full agreement, but he wanted to explain why – on the same point. Millett NPJ simply concurred with Bokhary PJ.

Sometimes a concurring judgment can come close to a dissent; such was Bokhary PJ's concurring judgment in a case involving desecration of the Chinese and Hong Kong Special Administrative Region of the People's Republic of China (HKSAR) flags.[151] Apart from that there was a single majority judgment, by Li CJ. The case was of considerable sensitivity, coming on the heels of the Standing Committee of the National People's Congress (NPCSC) reprimand to the CFA arising from *Ng Ka Ling*. The

---

[149] (2004) 7 HKCFAR 333.   [150] (2003) 6 HKCFAR 476.
[151] *HKSAR* v. *Ng Kung Siu* (1999) HKCFAR 442.

defendants relied upon the constitutionally protected freedom of expression. The Li judgment relied heavily on the concept of *ordre public* as justification for limitation of the freedom. Bokhary PJ's view was that the court had not sufficiently analysed this concept and not appreciated its limits, saying, 'Where a concept is unclear the courts must clarify it before using it as a test by which to judge what, if any, restriction may constitutionally be placed on a fundamental right or freedom'.[152] His judgment was as close to a dissent as it can get while remaining a concurrence. Perhaps he was conscious of the need to show solidarity with his colleagues given the political context. But his remarks foreshadowed what was to become the defining characteristic of his approach to human rights cases.

It is not possible to say that sensitive cases necessarily give rise to single judgments. In one, Mason NPJ said: 'In the light of the importance of the cases and the novelty of the issues, it is appropriate that I state in my own words the basis of my thinking on some issues. The comments which follow are not intended to qualify in any way my agreement with the Chief Justice's reasons'.[153] This was one of the cases arising from the *Ng Ka Ling* (right of abode) case and the subsequent 'interpretation' by the NPCSC.[154] But *Lau Kong Yung* involved a dissent, which may have explained the existence of four separate concurring judgments.

The fact that the court is reversing the Court of Appeal may also generate multiple judgments, not necessarily long. In one case, Litton NPJ said, 'Since we are differing from a majority of the Court of Appeal I will add a few words of my own'; Lord Millett concurred.[155]

As with criminal cases, the novelty of an issue may generate a larger number of judgments. In *Waddington v. Chan Chung Hoo*,[156] the issue was whether a multiple derivative action was possible.[157] Apparently, there had 'never been a reasoned decision of a higher court in any common law jurisdiction outside the United States which [was] determinative of this question'.[158] Bokhary and Chan PJJ gave a short concurring judgment to emphasise that they took the view that the court should give a clear positive answer to the question.

---

[152] *Ibid.*, 464.   [153] *Lau Kong Yung* v. *Director of Immigration.*
[154] See further Chapters 14 (Chen and Lo) & 15 (Young) in this volume.
[155] *The Registrar of Births and Deaths* v. *Syed Haider Yahya Hussain* (2001) 4 HKCFAR 429.
[156] (2008) 11 HKCFAR 370.
[157] Defined as one 'brought by a person who is not a shareholder in the company in which the cause of action is vested and on behalf of which the action is brought but a shareholder in its parent or ultimate holding company' (*per* Lord Millett, *ibid.*, [33]).
[158] Lord Millett, *ibid.*, [51].

Shared judgments

In several cases, the concurring judges dealt essentially with different aspects of the case.[159] This approach was taken in an interesting way in *Ma So So, Josephine* v. *Chin Kuk Lung, Francis*,[160] concerning the discretion to make a 'wasted costs' order against a solicitor. Li CJ spoke on the principles to be applied, Ribeiro PJ applied them to the case, and the other judges agreed with both. Such division of labour raises none of the difficulties of searching for the *ratio decidendi* and really fits into a different class than the true 'concurring judgment'.

The micro-concurrence and other incidental points

Figures of concurring judgments are rather misleading, particularly because of the large number of concurring judgments that, although a little longer than a statement to the effect 'I agree', are shorter than 1000 words, many shorter than 500 or 600, perhaps what Baroness Hale referred to as 'footnotes or observations'. They have included what one might describe as airing of a bee in the judicial bonnet, as when Litton NPJ spoke in one case only about the excessive quantity of paper submitted in the case (536 words).[161] Judges of considerable experience like the PJs of the court have no doubt built up a considerable collection of views, gripes, and suggestions that they would like to share with the legal community. Examples include 473 words on a particular case[162] or suggesting that it was time for a review of the Board of Review (taxation) (431 words).[163]

There may be points that do arise from the case but that are matters of practice that have not arisen for decision – for example, that it is inappropriate for a bilingual judge to be expected to decide on whether a translation was accurate.[164] Not all micro-concurrences raise marginal issues. In a case about restraint of trade, decided unanimously on the basis of common law, Bokhary PJ added:

> All that I will say is a word on the position of any Hong Kong court asked to make an injunction excluding an employee from participation in any

---

[159] Including in *The Tian Sheng, A Solicitor* v. *Law Society of Hong Kong* (2008) 11 HKCFAR 117 and *Yau Yuk Lung Zigo.*

[160] (2004) 7 HKCFAR 300.   [161] *Re Ping An Securities Ltd.* (2009) 12 HKCFAR 808.

[162] *Kao, Lee and Yip* v. *Koo* (2009) 12 HKCFAR 830.

[163] *ING Baring Securities (Hong Kong) Ltd* v. *The Commissioner of Inland Revenue* (2007) 10 HKCFAR 417.

[164] *Eastern Express Publisher Ltd.* v. *Mo Man Ching* (1999) 2 HKCFAR 264 (Ching PJ at [36]).

given activity. The court would have to consider not only the common law policy... but also the 'freedom of choice of occupation' which everyone here has by virtue of arts 33 and 41 of our constitution the Basic Law.[165]

In fact, *obiter dicta* may well be part of a longer judgment that is mainly focussed on the issues to be decided. Thus, McHugh NPJ criticised at some length the Case Stated in a tax case and made the suggestion that 'the interests of justice [might] be better served by abandoning the Case Stated procedure and substituting an appeal on questions of law. The Case Stated procedure arose out of circumstances that have long gone'.[166] Bokhary, Chan, and Ribeiro PPJ agreed.

Does dissent generate more concurrence?

A reasonable hypothesis would be that if one judge dissents others would be persuaded to indicate their own views including why they agree with the majority. But among the dissent cases, the largest group (5 of the 14) fall into the category 'majority opinion, one dissenting opinion'. And most of the concurring opinions in others are short. However, in *Polyset* v. *Panhandat*,[167] Bokhary PJ said that he was giving a concurring judgment on the point on which Litton NPJ was dissenting, precisely because the court was deciding by a majority. And the fact of a dissent may have been one of several factors leading to several judgments in the *Lau Kong Yung* case.

Looking at the dissents

Fourteen cases in which dissent was entered during the period of the first 13 years covered by this book (of about 300 cases) is not a large number (4.3 per cent, in fact, as opposed to 7.3 per cent in the PC Hong Kong cases since dissent became possible). Any of the generalisations we venture in this section must be taken with caution; there are simply not enough cases to develop reliable hypotheses.

In the PC, 12 of their Lordships dissented at least once. By contrast, in the CFA, the majority of dissenting judgments are attributable to Bokhary PJ (12 in all); Justice Litton dissented once as a PJ and twice after he became a local NPJ);[168] and Ribeiro PJ, Cooke NPJ, and Nicholls NPJ dissented

---

[165] *PCCW – HKT Telephone Ltd* v. *Aitken* (2009) 12 HKCFAR 114.
[166] *Lee Yee Shing* v. *CIR* (2008) 11 HKCFAR 6, [109].   [167] (2002) 5 HKCFAR 234.
[168] *Bewise Motors Co. Ltd* v. *Hoi Kong Container Services Ltd* (1997–1998) 1 HKCFAR 256 and *Polyset Ltd* v. *Panhandat Ltd* (2002) 5 HKCFAR 234, respectively.

once each, the latter two being the only two NPJs to dissent in the period covered. Lord Nicholls wrote his own separate dissenting opinion but also agreed with Bokhary PJ's dissenting opinion,[169] and Bokhary PJ agreed with Lord Cooke's judgment without writing his own.[170]

And it seems unlikely that the future trend will be towards increasing dissents (only two additional dissents occurred in the three years after the period covered here), especially because the one major dissenter retired in October 2012.

Which issues have given rise to dissent

It is not easy to classify the broad category of the law within which cases with dissent fall because some may fall under more than one. The largest group of dissents occur in public, including criminal, law (11), most of which involve interpretation of the BL. There are several cases concerning the right of abode (in which case the scope for the interpretation by the CFA of the BL is limited by the Interpretations of the NPCSC), but the other cases are somewhat miscellaneous. Issues of human rights appear in a number of cases; these include presumption of innocence; freedom of expression, assembly, and procession; and liberty (in one or two cases, the majority treated an issue as one of statutory interpretation when Bokhary PJ analysed it in terms of the BL).

Procedural issues were divisive in three cases (as regards cross-examination of a prosecution witness regarding his conduct in another case, directions to the jury as to the 'good character' of the accused, and the time limit barring an action). Three cases dealt with contracts and one (or one and half) with torts, and two were concerned with broadly commercial law.

Studying the dissents

With most of the dissents coming from one judge, the most interesting question perhaps is: why does he dissent? But we begin with the other dissenters, namely Justice Litton three times, Ribeiro PJ once, and two foreign NPJs, once each.

One Litton dissent was in a tort case involving the relevance of *res ipsa loquitur* in view of the unsettled state of medical research.[171] During

---

[169]   *The Bank of East Asia Ltd* v. *Tsien Wui Marble Factory Ltd* (1999) 2 HKCFAR 349.
[170]   *Next Magazine Publishing Ltd* v. *Ma Ching Fat* (2003) 6 HKCFAR 63.
[171]   *Frank Yu Yu Kai* v. *Chan Chi Keung*.

prostate surgery, the plaintiff somehow sustained nerve injury, resulting in temporary paralysis of an arm. The lower courts had found the question hard: Suffiad J rejected *res ipsa*, and the Court of Appeal reversed him, although Rogers VP expressed some unease and at the application for leave to appeal to the CFA, more or less repudiated the CA's ruling; Litton NPJ described him as dissenting. In the CFA, Lord Hoffmann, too, found it hard to decide (see above) but joined the majority in favour of applying *res ipsa*.

Litton NPJ dissented, showing that Suffiad J did think that there could have been more than one cause of the injury, not all compatible with negligence of the defendant,[172] and observing: 'Surgery and its associated processes is not a perfect science'. And 'neuropathy arising from anaesthesia was complex, multi-factorial and incompletely understood: and it was so in this case'.[173]

Two commercial cases involved some tension between sanctity of contract and conceptions of reasonableness. In dissent, Justice Litton espoused the latter in one case and in the other the former. *Bewise Motors v. Hoi Kong Container Services*[174] concerned the validity and scope of a poorly drafted exemption clause in a contract of bailment and whether it applied to the theft of four very expensive cars from the defendant's care. The point of difference was whether theft was excluded from the exemption clause only if actually committed by the defendant or its employees or also if there was some other 'proven neglect or default'. Justices Ching and Litton were agreed that it would be surprising for a business person to agree to the former. Litton NPJ said: 'Thus, if on one view, clause 4(a) would lead to extreme results, and on another view it would conform with the reasonable expectations of honest men, the court would incline towards the latter unless the words used compel the opposite conclusion'.[175] But after a careful (and syntactically convincing) analysis of the exemption clause, Ching PJ did find himself so compelled, as did Nazareth NPJ, who was pretty scathing about the Litton approach, saying it 'would be destructive of the sanctity of contracts and of the certainty that commercial men seek to secure by their words deliberately used upon legal advice'.[176]

Polyset Ltd. v. Panhandet Ltd[177] raised 'fundamental questions under the law relating to deposits'[178] in land transactions. There is no clear rule as to what amount qualifies as a deposit; Bokhary PJ said the rationale

---

[172] *Ibid.*, [91].   [173] *Ibid.*, [107].
[174] *Bewise Motors Co. Ltd* v. *Hoi Kong Container Services Ltd.*   [175] *Ibid.*, [9].
[176] *Ibid.*, [60].   [177] *Polyset Ltd* v. *Panhandat Ltd.*   [178] *Ibid.*, [6] (Bokhary PJ).

for the traditional 10 per cent is obscure.[179] In this case, the deposit was 35 per cent. Having agreed that the purchaser was not entitled to rescind the contract, the court split on the issue of whether there were special circumstances justifying the payment made to the seller being forfeited in its entirety, a matter on which there seems to be not much learning.

In his characteristic manner, Ribeiro PJ sets out clearly the distinction between deposit, liquidated damages, and penalty, and all the judges were inclined to move away from the distinction between penalty and liquidated damages towards the concept of actual loss. The majority held that a deposit of 35 per cent was unreasonable, and there were no special circumstances allowing the seller to keep all.

Litton NPJ disagreed in what Malcolm Merry describes as a 'powerful judgment'.[180] Referring to the volatile land market in Hong Kong, especially at the time of the transaction, and the well-known propensity of purchasers to renege on land transactions plus what seems to be the understanding among the parties that 35 per cent was not unreasonable in the circumstances, he would have allowed the sellers to retain the 'deposit'. Unlike his position in *Bewise*, he stressed freedom of contract, including the considerations that both parties had equal bargaining capacity, as well as the fact that the 35 per cent was not too remote from the actual loss as assessed by the trial judge (29 per cent).

A scheme for the discharge of bankrupts provided for automatic discharge after a prescribed period unless the trustee in bankruptcy (generally the Official Receiver) sought from the court an extension of the time because of the bankrupt's non-compliance with the rules. In *Official Receiver* v. *Chan Wing Hing*,[181] the bankrupt had violated the rule requiring him to inform the trustee of absences from Hong Kong, on pain of having the prescribed period not run during those absences. The question was whether the provision was unconstitutional in the light of the freedom to travel, including to leave Hong Kong, under the BL (Article 31) and the Hong Kong Bill of Rights Ordinance (Article 8(2)). The action was brought by the Official Receiver to escape from the administrative burden of applying the rule.

Four justices held that the restriction to protect the rights of creditors, a valid purpose, was not proportional, being too draconian and inflexible and because there were other remedies open to the trustee and creditors. Justice Ribeiro disagreed with the majority only on

---

[179] *Ibid.*, [11].   [180] See Chapter 19 (Merry) in this volume.
[181] (2006) 9 HKCFAR 545.

proportionality, considering that the obligation to report on his departure and arrival was not onerous and easily discharged.[182]

Dissenting non-permanent judges

When the marble outer cladding of the Bank of East Asia's headquarters building had to be replaced, it sued everyone it could. In the CFA, two defendants remained, the subcontractors for the cladding, and the architects and engineers. The liability of the former hinged on whether they could delegate their duties and of both on whether the limitation period had expired. The point of disagreement was when the damage had occurred. The crux was whether to apply the House of Lords case of *Pirelli*,[183] under which the cause of action arose when the damage actually occurred even if not known about or discard that in the light of later developments in the House of Lords and elsewhere.

Justices Litton and Ching, Nazareth NPJ agreeing, took the view that they should apply *Pirelli*, largely because of (later) legislation intended to mitigate *Pirelli's* impact by extending the limitation period if the plaintiff could not have known of the damage. They also dismissed the PC decision from New Zealand in *Invercargill*,[184] which makes the cause of action arise when the damage is known. Ching PJ said:

> It is not for this Court to choose between conflicting decisions from different jurisdictions, especially not from one of those jurisdictions where the circumstances differ from those in Hong Kong and more especially when the legislation in Hong Kong precludes such an interpretation. Nor is it for this Court to impose what it considers to be the best solution or a solution better than that laid down by the House of Lords, at least when that solution runs contrary to logic and to other provisions in the relevant Ordinance.[185]

Lord Nicholls, the English judge, preferred *Invercargill* to *Pirelli*, finding support in Australia and in the approval of the Australian view in the House of Lords by Lord Keith and in the PC in *Invercargill*. And both Bokhary PJ and Nicholls NPJ strongly opposed the idea that a statute can somehow freeze the common law and prevent it moving on.

---

[182] *Ibid.*, [80].
[183] *Pirelli General Cable Works Ltd* v. *Oscar Faber & Partners* [1983] 2 AC 1.
[184] *Invercargill City Council* v. *Hamlin* [1996] AC 624.
[185] In *HKSAR* v. *Tang Siu Man* the majority including Justice Litton chose Australian authority over House of Lords authority.

In *Next Magazine* v. *Ma Ching Fat*[186] the principal complaint of the plaintiff was that he had been defamed by an allegation that he engaged in insider trading when selling his shares in a media company of which he was the director and substantial shareholder. The key question dividing the CFA was whether the case should be sent back for a new trial or determined in the CFA. The CFA appeal was lodged by the defendants who objected to the jury direction on malice on which, it was submitted, no evidence had been adduced by the plaintiff and to the ruling of the CA for a new trial. The Court of Appeal decided the case before the CFA had adopted the rule that malice did not nullify the defence of fair comment, so long as the defendant honestly believed in the comment.[187]

The court split (the majority Litton NPJ, with concurring, substantial judgments by Chan PJ and Mortimer NPJ, and the dissentients Cooke NPJ and Bokhary PJ and the last adding nothing to Lord Cooke's judgment, so completely did he agree with him) first over whether there had in fact been any allegation of insider dealing. The majority said there was none, but the minority was not convinced of this. On malice, the majority held that the issue should not have been referred to the jury because there was little convincing evidence of it (as Litton NPJ said, 'not even a scintilla'[188]). And now, under the principle of *Cheng* v. *Tse,* it would be difficult for the plaintiffs to prove that the defendants did not honestly believe their comments. Lord Cooke was not convinced that there was no evidence of malice. On the assumption that the plea of fair comment must succeed, the majority held for the plaintiffs and effectively disposed of the case.

Litton NPJ also spoke about the time litigation would take. Lord Cooke was concerned about the 'manifest lack of a factual foundation' in the trial.[189] A new trial would provide an opportunity for new facts and would provide an opportunity to present a case based in relation to malice solely on the *Cheng* test, which 'natural justice dictates'.[190]

The main dissenting voice

Although, as the chapters in this book show, the court's record on rights of the individuals is quite strong, it is interesting to note that many of Justice Bokhary's dissents come broadly within what might be described that category, especially against the state. Every one of his dissents has been in favour of the accused in criminal cases, of the individual against

---

[186] (2003) 6 HKCFAR 63.   [187] In *Albert Cheng* v. *Tse Wai Chun Paul.*   [188] *Ibid.,* [49].
[189] *Ibid.,* [130].   [190] *Ibid.,* [133].

the state in other public law cases, or of the plaintiff in tort cases (although in the *Bank of East Asia* case, that was hardly in favour of the individual).

His themes are consistent, especially the stress on the rights of the individual: 'The courts always interpret fundamental rights and freedoms generously so as to ensure their enjoyment in full measure' in *Leung Kwok Hung*,[191] 'The law should not – and in my view does not – dissipate its energies by fixing criminal liability on morally blameless people to no useful purpose' in *Hin Lin Yee*,[192] and 'Liberty of the person under the law is what this case is about' in *Thang Thieu Quyen* v. *Director of Immigration*.[193] Then there is an emphasis on purposive and contextual construction. In *Leung Kwok Hung*, he emphasised the need to 'read all of the relevant provisions together and in the context of the whole statute as a purposive unity in its appropriate legal and social setting'.[194] Finally, he would choose to rely on the BL when others might not (see later discussion of *Leung Kwok Hung* and *Tam Nga Yin* v. *Director of Immigration*).

Two of the criminal cases concerned essentially evidential issues and two more substantive. In *Tang Siu Man*, the immediate question was whether a trial judge who instructs the jury to treat a defendant as a person of good character must then give favourable directions on both credibility (i.e. whether the accused was likely to have told the truth) and propensity (i.e. whether the accused was likely to have committed the offence).[195] *Wong Sau-ming*[196] involved the issue of whether to allow evidence in the form of the transcript of a previous case in which the magistrate spoke of doubt about the evidence of a police witness (and acquitted the accused) as being relevant to assessing the credibility of the same police witness in the current case.

The nature of the divergence of opinion in the two cases was very different. In the first, it was whether the court should follow House of Lords authority that the judge must give the directions in question.[197] The majority thought such a direction unnecessary, so long as the evidence showed the accused to be of good character. Emphasising the high quality of Hong Kong juries and favouring the view that it is better to give the judge flexibility as to the conduct of the case, Litton PJ said that it is sufficient if the summing up is fair and balanced and relied on

---

[191] *Ibid.*, [101].   [192] *HKSAR* v. *Hin Lin Yee* (2010) 13 HKCFAR 142, [6].
[193] *Thang Thieu Quyen* v. *Director of Immigration* (1997–1998) 1 HKCFAR 167, [74]; see also *HKSAR* v. *Wong Sau-Ming* (2003) 6 HKCFAR 135.
[194] From *Medical Council* v. *Chow* (2000) 3 HKCFAR 144, 154 B-C.   [195] *Tang Siu Man.*
[196] *Wong Sau-ming*, note 193 above.   [197] In *Aziz* [1996] AC 41.

Australian decisions. Bokhary PJ, however, considered that the House of Lords' required directions were simple and moderate and 'represent the minimum due to any accused of good character'.[198] In *Wong*, there was no difference over the law or principles but over interpreting what the magistrate in the earlier case had actually said: had he really expressed disbelief in the witness? The majority said he had not, while Bokhary PJ considered that the magistrate had actually indicated that he did not believe the police witness in 'an observation redolent with disbelief of PW1's evidence on an important matter',[199] and the judge should have admitted the evidence from that previous case. His different interpretation of what the magistrate had said was influenced by the consideration that '[a] man's liberty is at stake, and he is entitled to a full and fair reading of such an observation made from the seat of justice'.[200]

In *Leung Kwok Hung*, Justice Bokhary had no disagreement with the rest of the court's holding that a provision restricting public assembly on grounds of '*ordre public*'[201] was unconstitutional for lack of clarity and reading it down to the more easily understood 'public order' or with their stress on the importance of freedom of assembly. But he disagreed when they held that the Commissioner of Police had a power to ban processions (albeit to be exercised on legitimate grounds and with regard to proportionality). After a close analysis of the powers of the Police Commissioner, a learned and wide-ranging discussion of the importance of freedoms, and an analysis of comparative jurisprudence on the freedom of assembly, he held that, although the requirement to give notice of planned processions is constitutional, it cannot be enforced by criminal sanctions, and any power of the Commissioner to ban in advance was unconstitutional.

In *Hin Lin Yee* v. *HKSAR*,[202] again the difference was essentially over a matter of fact. The important question was whether in a statutory offence a mistaken but honest belief is a defence. Ribeiro PJ's majority judgment treated the issue as one under common law because no constitutional issues were raised, and held the accused could not rely on a defence of absence of *mens rea* because the statute had provided defences (which in fact had not been invoked by the accused). Chan PJ ruled out a defence because of the consequences of the breach of statutory obligations.[203]

---

[198] *Ibid.*, [108].   [199] *Ibid.*, [70].   [200] *Ibid.*

[201] Taken from the International Covenant on Civil and Political Rights. See further on this case Chapter 15 (Young) in this volume.

[202] *Hin Lin Yee.*   [203] *Ibid.*, [17].

Bokhary PJ would have allowed the appeal of one accused on the basis of both common law and constitution: there were insufficient findings of primary fact to support a sure conclusion that the person had 'sold' goods within the meaning of the provision of the legislation. Additionally, the constitutional principle was that to impose absolute liability where it would have no deterrent effect is arbitrary.

Turning to the other public law cases, *Thang Thieu Quyen*[204] was a *habeas corpus* case. Bokhary PJ concluded that the applicants' detention was unlawful: had the applicants not been earlier detained for an excessively long time (because the Director of Immigration had refused to consider their case until she was told by the PC to do so), they would not now have been in detention at all.[205] Li CJ, with whom Litton and Ching PJJ and Mason NPJ concurred, although 'conscious that we are dealing with the liberty of the individual which is long cherished by the common law',[206] held that the previous detention could not be taken into account in determining the lawfulness of the present detention.

Bokhary's concern was with the context – to understand what principles are at stake. He reviewed the role of *habeas corpus* and its relationship with judicial review, stating: '*Habeas corpus* is so much a part of a culture of liberty that it must itself be studied as a culture should be: diachronically with full regard to its historical development as a continuous process'.[207] Because the law leans in favour of liberty, and reasonableness is a key element in assessing the legality of detention, the period of detention must be looked at as a whole. 'No power of detention can be exercised in a vacuum. It must be exercised against a background. And of course its impact is not felt once and for all at the moment of exercise. By its nature detention is a continuing thing. So its effect on any sentient being is a growing one'.[208]

The right of abode sage is recounted elsewhere in this volume.[209] After the initial decision and clarification, Bokhary consistently took a position as favourable as possible to the claimants. In *Lau Kong Yung* v. *Director of Immigration*,[210] he differed over whether in making removal orders the Director of Immigration was obliged to take humanitarian considerations into account. Li CJ, Litton PJ, Ching PJ, and Mason NPJ, in separate concurring judgments, held that he was not obliged to do so. Bokhary PJ placed the Director's obligation within 'classic judicial principles

---

[204] *Thang Thieu Quyen.*   [205] *Ibid.,* [83].   [206] *Ibid.,* 188.   [207] *Ibid.,* [116].
[208] *Ibid.,* [106].   [209] See Chapters 14 (Chen and Lo) and 15 (Young).
[210] *Lau Kong Yung* v. *Director of Immigration.*

fundamental to the preservation of the rule of law'[211] and concluded, 'In Hong Kong where we aspire to be humane as well as orderly, it is plain that the Director would have been duty-bound at least to read the applications to see if they or any one or more of them disclosed a strong and obvious case for a favourable exercise on humanitarian grounds of his discretion'.[212] In *Tam Nga Yin* v. *Director of Immigration*,[213] the issue was whether a child adopted by parents, one of whom was a permanent resident, acquired the status of permanent resident as a person 'of Chinese nationality born outside Hong Kong of' a resident. The position of the majority (in a composite judgment of Li CJ, Chan and Ribeiro PJJ, and Mason NPJ) was that 'born of' meant literally/biologically born to the parent. But Bokhary considered that it was also possible to read 'born' as referring to the place of birth, i.e. other than Hong Kong. Having thus found an ambiguity that the majority did not, he was able to take the interpretation that favoured 'family unity, which is valued at every level in our society including the constitutional level'.[214]

The most dramatic difference was in *Ng Siu Tung*, involving about 5000 people who argued that they ought to have the benefit of the CFA's original decision in the right of abode cases, before the Standing Committee's Interpretation.[215] They fell into various categories, and the majority, in a judgment of the court, approved the claims of only a few. Bokhary would have approved them all. The first area of difference involved interpretation of the BL, namely the provision that says 'previous judgments' of courts would be unaffected by an Interpretation. Although the majority said this meant the actual court order, Bokhary accepted the argument that it had a broader meaning and would encompass anyone whose situation fitted the law as laid down in the initial right of abode cases; on that basis, all would have had the right to remain in Hong Kong. Alternatively, he held that all the applicants had legitimate expectations – a doctrine that he explored at very great length – that they would be considered for grant of right of abode; their removal orders should be quashed, and the Director must consider their claims afresh. The majority had restricted such expectations to very small classes of applicants to whom very specific statements arousing such expectations had been made. Over the next few years, various subsequent cases reached the court. In each, Bokhary PJ

[211] *Ibid.*, [150] quoting Lord Diplock in *Council of Civil Service Unions* v. *Minister for the Civil Service* [1985] 1 AC 374, 410.

[212] *Ibid.*, [159].   [213] *Tam Nga Yin* v. *Director of Immigration*, note 115 above.

[214] *Ibid.*, [49].   [215] (2002) 5 HKCFAR 1.

sat but said he felt unable to participate in the decision. As the litigation drew to an end, he stated, 'With the last of these sad cases in sight, I cannot help wondering what could be more in keeping with the true spirit of reunification, now in its tenth year, than a humanitarian exercise of executive discretion in favour of the abode-seekers still here in this city of, after all, immigrants'.[216]

In *Ho Choi Wan* v. *Housing Authority*,[217] the plaintiff was a poor tenant of the Authority, seeking to compel it to review and revise the rent downwards. Under statute, the Authority could not determine the rent sooner than three years after the previous revision, but it had also the obligation to ensure that the median rent-to-income of tenants did not exceed 10 per cent. For nearly a decade, the Authority had deferred the review of rents (thus freezing them) at a time of economic deflation and the decreasing capacity of tenants to pay the rents, with the result that the average rent-to-income had reached 14 per cent. The question was whether the Authority was obliged to review the rent downwards. The outcome turned largely on questions of interpretation, with the majority and Bokhary PJ taking different approaches, although both sides claimed to be guided by purpose and policy.

The majority (in the judgment of Li CJ) decided four critical issues as follows: (1) deferring the rent was not determination of rent and therefore did not entail the obligation to review it for compatibility with the 10 per cent rule; (2) the Authority had no obligation to ensure compatibility with the 10 per cent rule, although it was obliged to review the rent as part of balancing its other obligations; (3) the plaintiff had no legitimate expectations that a determination would take place to adjust the rents; and (4) the adjustment of rent could only result in increase and not decrease of rents (because the amendment requiring three yearly adjustments was made at the time of inflation and was intended to put a brake on increases), a proposition advanced belatedly by Lord Pannick for the Authority and enthusiastically adopted by Millet NPJ.

In his dissent, Bokhary PJ emphasised the primary obligation of the Authority to provide housing at affordable prices, for which purpose it was to maintain rents at 10 per cent of income. Interpretation should be guided by the values inherent in the law, acknowledging that values cannot replace text but can shed light on it.[218] Also applying principles of interpretation, he disagreed that reviews could only lead to increases,

---

[216] *Ng Siu Tung* v. *Director of Immigration*, unreported, FACV1/2001, 25 July 2007, CFA, [23].

[217] *Ho Choi Wan* v. *Housing Authority*.   [218] *Ibid.*, [63].

not decreases (thus tying the text regardless of its language to a particular economic contingency in a changing situation). On the contrary, he held that the three-year rule restricted increases but not decreases in rent.

Yeung Chung Ming v. *Commissioner of Police*[219] involved a police officer charged with an offence and suspended with pay reductions, which were not made up when the officer was convicted. The issue was not the suspension but the docking of pay of a person as yet unconvicted. Although all the judges agreed that the presumption of innocence applied or had implications even outside the context of a trial (drawing upon decisions of the European Court of Human Rights), the majority (in a judgment by Li CJ) held that suspension or the withholding of salary did not imply guilt, and the bringing of criminal charges merely indicates that the accused *might* be guilty. Deduction of salary was therefore not unconstitutional. Bokhary PJ, in a judgment described by Johannes Chan as striking 'a better balance between the interest of the State and the right of the officer concerned',[220] held that withholding of any portion of salary was incompatible with the presumption of innocence. Unlike suspension, it could not be justified on the principle of proportionality, legitimate need, or rationality; the impact on the officer of suspension of part of his salary is 'inherently likely to be far in excess of any impact on the public purse of not withholding any of his pay'.[221]

As is his practice, he placed the issue in a broader framework:

> The presumption of innocence reflects the way in which the members of a free society generally approach each other unless and until there is good reason otherwise in any particular instance.... Many forms of treatment are recognised as arbitrary precisely because the persons subjected to it are presumed innocent. In a free society, persons are surrounded and protected by a network of interrelated rights and freedoms of a fundamental nature.... If a society is to remain truly free, the entirety of its network or continuum of fundamental rights and freedoms must be carefully kept in good repair. The thing to fear is too narrow an interpretation of the presumption of innocence, not too wide an interpretation of it.[222]

Reflections on Bokhary as dissenter

What Justice Bokhary offers us in his judgments, particularly his dissents, is erudition, drawing from philosophy, ethics, history, and wisdom from

---

[219] *Yeung Chung Ming* v. *Commissioner of Police* (2008) 11 HKCFAR 513.
[220] See Chapter 16 (Chan) in this volume.   [221] *Yeung Chung Ming*, [53].
[222] *Ibid.*, [42] and [44].

ancient and contemporary judges and scholars but not so often anthropology, which find expression in his lectures and articles. He offers us his conception of the law, and from this, doctrines are drawn and jurisprudence developed. He seldom starts with facts or texts but the principle at stake. In his recent decisions, justice has become his lodestar. Inevitably in this approach, buttressed by the general principles of the BL, the precise or literal meaning of words and phrases gives way to the higher purposes of the law. And his dissents, unconcerned with justification for an immediately binding ruling, enable him to expand on that, as setting beacons for the future.

Bokhary PJ's approach contrasts most markedly with the other dissenter, Justice Litton. Although Bokhary would emphasise the general purposes and objectives of legislation under the overarching objectives of the BL – 'our constitution' – as the starting point in interpretation, Litton would tend to stress the centrality of legislation at the apparent expense of the BL. In one of the right of abode cases, he said, 'Administrators function within the confines of their particular statutes. Hence, the question as to the factors which an administrator is bound to take into account in exercising a statutory power is determined generally by construing the statute which conferred the power'.[223] He went on to say that it would be rarely that the administrator would need to pay attention to the BL.[224]

But Justice Bokhary is no maverick. His major differences with colleagues generally are matters of emphasis, especially his views of the primacy of the BL and rights of the individual, particularly the underdog. As we have seen, the individual differences, motivated often by his personal degree of emphasis on these factors, have come down to different interpretations of what a judge said or of facts. But his judgments are closely argued, with many hypotheticals and with solid research on law.

Occasionally, Justice Bokhary has explicitly or by inference expressed his views about dissenting judicially and extra-judicially. In a lecture explaining why he dissents, he first drew attention to the many occasions of unanimity by the court. He said that he always considered the views of his colleagues and dissented when he felt 'driven'. He gave his philosophy of the progress of the law within which we can understand the role of dissents: 'One lifetime is not enough to do very much in the law. The contribution that each of us makes, if it is to amount to anything of lasting value, must be something on which others can build in future. Progress depends on that. And progress sometimes lies in the direction

---

[223] *Lau Kong Yung,* [130].   [224] *Ibid.*

pointed to by a dissent'.[225] To understand the orientation of the law that drives him to dissent, we turn to another statement:

> Overcoming all difficulties and obstacles including stagnation and even retrogression, the law eventually moves forward. And for this what matters the most must be the Court as a whole. It has been said – and I agree – that a legal system would have no meaning unless the law postulates 'a common denominator of just instinct in the community'. Reducing the distance between moral expectations and legal entitlements increases respect for the law.[226]

Reflections on dissents more generally

Sixteen cases with dissents in 13 years is not a lot. It may seem odd that there were so few commercial cases with dissent given the importance attached to the market economy in the BL. One explanation is that the area of public law is affected fundamentally by the transfer of sovereignty, the incorporation of human rights treaties, and generally the new constitutional order ushered in by the BL, whereas, as far as commerce and economy are concerned, the theme of the BL is continuity and stability. Over the years, critical legal issues were resolved by the courts (including the PC), giving that area of the law considerable clarity. Another explanation could be that in the field of public law, the failure of the political process, because of the lack of democracy and the dominance by Chinese authorities of the Hong Kong executive and to a lesser extent of the legislature, have pushed political and administrative issues to the courts, while in the commercial area, not only is the law more settled, but disputes can also be resolved in a number of ways that do not require resort to the courts, such as negotiations and arbitration – and are often of little concern to China.[227]

---

[225] 'Current State of Judicial Review in Hong Kong: An Address to the Peking University School of Transnational Law', 15 Sept 2009, accessible at www.docstoc.com/docs/19891156/new-current-state-of-judicial-review-in-hong-kong.

[226] *Ibid.*

[227] A major exception is *Democratic Republic of the Congo* v. *FG Hemisphere Associates LLC* (2011) 14 HKCFAR 95 (reference) and 395 (disposition) decided after the period under review in this volume. Chinese corporations were deeply implicated in the fortunes of the Congolese corporation (defendants in the case). The judiciary (and the executive) came under intense pressure from the Chinese government to hold that the defendants enjoyed state immunity (that being the Mainland rule). By a majority of three (Chan PJ, Mason NPJ, and Ribeiro PJ), the issue was referred to the NPCSC with advice in favour of immunity, which the NPCSC, to no one's surprise, accepted. Bokhary PJ and

In the major area of dissent (public law and human rights), there was unanimity on the importance of 'reasonable' exercise of state power in accordance with the BL and legislation and on the importance of human rights to Hong Kong and its identity. The differences often centred on striking the appropriate balance between the individual and the community.

One can only speculate on a few possible reasons for the limited use of dissent. The very nature of the CFA – a final court for Hong Kong but subject in critical ways to the Mainland, especially the NPCSC operating under Article 158 of the BL – possible Chinese sensitivity to the presence of foreign judges, delicate jurisdiction over human rights, keenness to modify the common law to signify the independence of the CFA from at least England, and the pervading sense that much depended on the judiciary for the success of 'one country, two systems' – all contributed to developing collegiality among its members. Some judges at least considered that collegiality was essential for the legitimacy of the CFA and public confidence in it. This is reflected in the BL cases when a composite judgment or unanimity was aimed at (as perhaps in Bokhary's holding back dissent in the flag case).

The collegiality was facilitated by the similarity in the background of most judges. They were the product of the common law and had achieved distinction in the understanding and use of its techniques, went to universities similar in their missions, most shared a liberal disposition, and came from broadly the same social class. The decision of the former Chief Justice to restrict foreign judges to three jurisdictions meant that all CFA judges have been, broadly speaking, of a like mind. Perhaps all this enabled them to tolerate the constant concern of the 'great dissenter', Bokhary, for social justice with equanimity. The inclusion of common law jurisdictions with more radical traditions on rights and justice such as India and Canada might have produced a different dynamic.

The concept of collegiality is not easy; if collegiality meant a constant search for consensus and composite judgments, it could hardly qualify as a virtue. So far as outsiders can tell, collegiality has not been sacrificed even in cases of dissent. The strength of the common law is dissent, which stimulates constant review of the purpose and fairness of its doctrines and rule, ever alert to the necessity of reform. So does the development of the constitution. Collegiality is based on mutual respect among judges,

Mortimer NPJ dissented. Bohkary's dissent is the most passionate and learned of all his judgments – and perhaps it cost him the extension of his term of office.

free discussion of differences, and opportunities to persuade others. An outsider gets the impression that this kind of collegiality does operate in the CFA. The very small number of dissents is testimony to this, as is the respectful manner in which dissent is expressed (save two or three instances of somewhat testy exchanges[228]). Bokhary's decision, as it seems, not to dissent in the flag case was taking an option for collegiality at a time when the court felt rather under siege from Beijing. And in another case, he decided not to make an issue of a point on which he disagreed with colleagues – although not such a sensitive issue – when it did not affect the outcome (in favour of the appellant).[229]

Final thoughts

We return briefly to our discussion in the first part of this chapter on the pros and cons of dissent and concurrence. There is little reason to think that the people of Hong Kong would lose confidence in the legal system if there were dissent (what the impact on the Mainland authorities might be is not known). In one sense, dissent has provided some comfort when the majority view might have upset some. Justice Bokhary's 'near dissent' in the flag case certainly brought some comfort to civil society activists in his response to Audrey Eu's anguished question – where is the line to be drawn in cases of the freedom of expression if not here?[230] The fact that judges can disagree reinforces the impression of judicial independence. When judges are free to express their individual views, there is less room for suspicion about who may not really agree with whom.

There is little reason to believe that dissents have created uncertainty about the law. For one, in most cases, four judges comprised the majority, indicating solid judicial support for the rule in question. Second, the majority probably made special efforts to clarify and defend their own position. The dissent and majority judgments have generally provided a high level of learning, explanation, and justification – and sometimes the exploration of cases from jurisdictions that might otherwise have not taken place – which are all critical to the understanding and developments

---

[228] See notes 168 and 174 above on Justices Nazareth and Litton in the *Bewise* case.

[229] *Prem Singh* v. *Director of Immigration* (2003) 6 HKCFAR 26, [25].

[230] He said, 'In the course of her powerful address, Counsel for the 2nd respondent posed a rhetorical question. If these restrictions are permissible, where does it stop? It is a perfectly legitimate question. And the answer, as I see it, is that it stops where these restrictions are located. For they lie just within the outer limits of constitutionality.' See *HKSAR* v. *Ng Kung Siu*, 468.

of the law. Justice Bokhary's dissents are evidence of great research and reflection. His approach to the law and its interpretation are of considerable value and may well shape future CFA judgments.

As to the impact of dissents on the development of the law, it is even more unlikely than on other issues that one can say much. But dissents can influence the development of the law not only by change in specific rules but also by the approach to the law, understanding of the role of precedents, the modes of interpretation of fundamental laws, and concern with rights and justice. The traces of influence in these respects may be harder to identity. But there is little doubt of the distinctiveness of Justice Bokhary's approach to the tasks and responsibilities of the judiciary and his passion for rights and justice – and the extraordinary range of sources that lawyers should draw upon.

There are no jokes, and few idiosyncrasies, in a composite judgment, but:[231]

> Single judgments of the court tend to be drab and lack individuality. Would we really be better off without Lord Bingham's historical accounts? Or Lord Hoffmann's references to Jane Austin? Or Lord Hope's accounts of what he sees in the London Underground on his journeys to and from the House?[232]

Similarly, the law of Hong Kong would be impoverished if the CFA judges were unable to express their views on bees in their bonnets, if the distinguished foreign NPJs were unable to make their distinguished individual contributions, and if Justice Bokhary could not constantly flag the importance of the BL and individual rights even when not in dissent. The first CFA has been a court of highly individual and highly intelligent judges whose long-term contributions, as individuals as well as collectively, have undoubtedly been enhanced by virtue of the fact they have been able to express individual views in concurrence as well as in dissent. This has been achieved while the results of cases have been unequivocally certain and a clear majority view of the law stated.

---

[231] Munday, note 45 above, 645.
[232] See Le Sueur, note 13 above, 31, summarising the views of an anonymous Law Lord.

PART IV

Jurisprudence of the court

13

The common law

SIR ANTHONY MASON

Although there may have been some doubts in 1997 about how the concept of 'one country, two systems' would work out, it has worked very well. From a legal perspective, the elements of the rule of law and an independent judiciary have been preserved, indeed reinforced, and the courts of Hong Kong have won a high reputation.

For that, much credit must go to the Chief Justice for his leadership, his judicial qualities, his dedication, and his abiding sense of justice. Over and above these qualities, the Chief Justice has qualities not often associated with lawyers, that is, strategic vision and a capacity for the long view. He achieved a large measure of consensus within the Court of Final Appeal (CFA) by instituting a system of judicial conferencing in which he led the discussion and ensured that all relevant questions were considered and resolved. The task that faced Hong Kong's first Chief Justice in 1997 presented an extraordinary challenge. The region was singularly fortunate that in the Chief Justice it found someone who responded so effectively to that challenge. For me, it has been a privilege and a pleasure to work with him and his colleagues on the CFA.

The aim of the chapter

The aim of this chapter is to examine the development of the common law in Hong Kong since 1 July 1997 and, in doing so, to view it from a general perspective rather than to simply identify cases in which advances have been made, although it will be necessary to look at them. The point of looking at the cases from a general perspective is to ascertain the main characteristics of the approach of the CFA to the common law in Hong Kong and, in so doing, to identify some questions that will arise in the future.

This chapter examines the CFA's application of the common rules of statutory and constitutional interpretation (noting their importance to

Hong Kong), the relationship between the Basic Law (BL) and the common law, the relationship between English authority and the jurisprudence of Hong Kong, the development of common law principles by the CFA, and the use of comparative law.

The point of commencement for any discussion of the place of the common law in the Hong Kong Special Administrative Region of the People's Republic of China (HKSAR) necessarily begins with the concept of 'one country, two systems', which is the central theme of the BL. This theme involves the maintenance of a capitalist system in Hong Kong within a national socialist system.[1] A capitalist system depends for its efficacy, among other things, on the existence of a sophisticated body of law regulating the rights and interests of its citizens and the powers and responsibilities of government. In Hong Kong, that sophisticated body of law consists of the common law and the other sources of law mentioned in Article 8 of the BL within the framework of the Constitution of the People's Republic of China (PRC) and laws applicable to the HKSAR enacted by the National People's Congress (NPC). That is why Article 8 is so important.[2]

The common law approach to statutory and constitutional interpretation

Article 8 provides:

> The laws previously in force in Hong Kong, that is, the common law, rules of equity, ordinances, subordinate legislation and customary law shall be maintained, except for any that contravene this Law, and subject to any amendment by the legislature of the [HKSAR].

The BL provides for the continuing operation of the laws to which it refers, including the common law, and in so doing, gives them constitutional backing, subject, of course, to legislative repeal or amendment.[3]

Article 8 picks up and endorses the common law rules of statutory interpretation. The operation of these rules has played a vital role in the important Hong Kong constitutional and public law cases in the past 12 years. I do not intend to discuss these cases in detail because they

---

[1] BL, Article 5 ('the previous capitalist system and way of life shall remain unchanged for 50 years').

[2] See also BL, Article 18.

[3] The vulnerability of the common law to legislative repeal and amendment means that the common law does not itself adequately protect human rights and fundamental freedoms.

are the subject of chapters by Albert Chen, P. Y. Lo, Simon Young, and Johannes Chan.

The common law rules of statutory interpretation are very different from those applied in the PRC. Subject to Article 158 of the BL, in Hong Kong, as in other common law jurisdictions, the courts are the final interpreters of statutes, but in the PRC, the Standing Committee of the NPC (NPCSC) is the authoritative adjudicator on questions of interpretation of statutes enacted by the NPC, the BL being such a statute. The NPCSC's approach to interpretation differs from the common law approach.[4] The power of final adjudication of the Hong Kong courts is subject to the important qualification that, under Article 158, the Hong Kong courts are bound to apply any interpretation of the BL issued by the NPCSC. A similar qualification arises in relation to a statute enacted by the NPC under Article 67(4) of the PRC Constitution.

The rule of law, as we know it, owes much to the common law approach to statutory interpretation. This approach supports and reinforces the rule of law with its emphasis on the primacy of the text of the statute. The rules of statutory interpretation ensure that the law as enacted will be interpreted and applied as it is expressed by the legislature, not by reference to the unexpressed intentions of others nor by reference to expedient political considerations. It is true the meaning of the text is to be ascertained in the light of its all-important context and its purpose:

> [T]he context, the general purpose and policy of a provision and its consistency and fairness are surer guides to its meaning than the logic with which it is constructed.[5]

But context and purpose are mainly ascertained, although by no means exclusively, from the provisions of the statute itself.

As I said in *HKSAR* v. *Lam Kwong Wai*[6]:

> [t]he modern approach to statutory interpretation insists that context and purpose be considered in the first instance, especially in the case of general words, and not merely at some later stage when ambiguity may be thought to arise.[7]

---

[4] As to which see *Director of Immigration* v. *Chong Fung Yuen* (2001) 4 HKCFAR 211.

[5] *Commissioner for Railways (NSW)* v. *Agalianos* (1955) 92 CLR 390, 397, per Dixon CJ.

[6] (2006) 9 HKCFAR 574 at 606E; cited in *HKSAR* v. *Cheung Kwun Lin* (2009) 12 HKCFAR 568, [12].

[7] In Australia, 'context' in this setting includes the existing state of the law and the mischief, identified by the reports of law reform bodies, that the statute is designed to remedy; see *CIC Insurance Ltd* v. *Bankstown Football Club Ltd* (1997) 187 CLR 384, 408.

A purposive interpretation is indeed mandated by section 19 of the Interpretation and General Clauses Ordinance.[8] The fundamental point is, however, that neither context, nor purpose, nor extrinsic materials for that matter, can justify an interpretation which the text is incapable of bearing. That is what is meant by the primacy of the text.

Extrinsic materials to which resort may be made are limited – for example, fundamental assumptions (such as the rule of law itself), the legislative history, the mischief rule, the reports of law reform bodies and public inquiries, legislative and expert committees and legislative materials (including Hansard and explanatory memoranda), subject in the case of legislative materials to the three conditions stipulated in *Pepper* v. *Hart*.[9] In that case, the House of Lords held (with Lord Mackay of Clashfern LC dissenting) that it was permissible to refer to parliamentary materials for the purpose of interpreting a statutory provision as long as (1) the legislation was ambiguous or obscure or led to an absurdity; (2) the material relied on consisted of one or more statements by a minister or other promoter of the bill together, if necessary, with such other parliamentary material as might be necessary to understand such statements and their effect; and (3) the effect of such statements was clear.

Subsequent decisions re-emphasized the importance of insisting on compliance with the three conditions, notably the first[10] and restricted the use of parliamentary materials for purposes other than statutory interpretation.[11] The House of Lords has made it clear that the proportionality of a measure, in the context of compatibility with the European Convention on Human Rights and Fundamental Freedoms (the European Convention), is not to be judged by the reasons advanced in support of it in the parliamentary debate or by the subjective state of mind of ministers or members.[12] Although this principle has been based on Article 9 of the Bill of Rights Act 1689, it is a principle that applies to legislatures generally and can be supported by reference to a general policy that it is not for the courts to question the sufficiency of reasons advanced by legislators in proceedings in the legislature. Neither the principle nor the policy is infringed if the courts point to those reasons as providing some

---

[8]   *Town Planning Board* v. *Society for the Protection of the Harbour Ltd* (2004) 7 HKCFAR 1, [29]; Interpretation and General Clauses Ordinance (Cap. 1).

[9]   *Pepper (Inspector of Taxes)* v. *Hart* [1993] AC 593 (HL).

[10]   *R* v. *Secretary of State for the Environment, Transport and the Regions Exp. Spath Holme Ltd* [2001] 2 AC 349, 392D-E, 408C-D and 413G-H (HL). *Robinson* v. *Secretary of State for Northern Ireland* [2002] NI 390, 405C (HL).

[11]   *Wilson* v. *First County Trust Ltd (No 2)* [2004] 1 AC 816 (HL).   [12]   *Ibid.*

measure of support for a favourable proportionality analysis because to do so does not involve the courts questioning proceedings in the legislature. *Lau Cheong* v. *HKSAR* is an example of a case in which the CFA had regard to the Legislative Council's consideration of legislation to support a proportionality or compatibility analysis.[13] In other respects, the Hong Kong reaction to *Pepper* v. *Hart* is a matter to which I shall refer shortly.

The second aspect of the rules of statutory interpretation to be mentioned is that they ensure that every statute will be interpreted in accordance with the principle of legality, so that its provisions will not be read as abrogating or curtailing rights and interests of individuals protected by the common law unless the statute expresses a clear and unmistakable intention so to do.[14] General words are not enough; specific words are required. Of the many rights and interests protected by the common law, it is sufficient here to mention personal liberty, freedom of expression, the right to a fair trial, freedom of assembly, and freedom of movement. The high importance of the protection of these rights by statutory interpretation has diminished to some extent because these and other rights and freedoms now have the constitutional protection provided by the BL and the Hong Kong Bill of Rights Ordinance (BORO).[15] But the spirit and values of the common law have informed the approach of courts in Hong Kong to the interpretation and the application of the guarantees of rights and freedoms in the BL and the BORO.

To return to *Pepper* v. *Hart* and its reception in Hong Kong, statements by government officials in relation to a bill in Hong Kong's Legislative Council have been used by the courts to ascertain the purpose of legislation. It is the use of these materials, in accordance with *Pepper* v. *Hart*, to ascertain meaning that remains to be resolved in Hong Kong. Although the CFA has applied *Pepper* v. *Hart* on occasions, on the assumption that it applies,[16] it has kept open the question whether and the extent to which

---

[13] (2002) 5 HKCFAR 415 (the imposition of mandatory life imprisonment for murder based on intention to cause grievous bodily harm).

[14] *Coco* v. *The Queen* (1994) 179 CLR 427, 437 (Austr HC); *R* v. *Secretary of State for the Home Department; Ex parte Simms* [2001] 2 AC 115, 131 (HL); *R (Daly)* v. *Secretary of State for the Home Department* [2001] 2 AC 532, [15,30] (HL); and *K-Generation Pty. Ltd* v. *Liquor Licensing Court* (2009) 83 ALJR 327, [47].

[15] Hong Kong Bill of Rights Ordinance (Cap. 383). Rights and freedoms in the BORO enjoy constitutional protection by virtue of BL, Article 39.

[16] *Commissioner of Rating & Valuation* v. *Agrila Ltd* (2001) 4 HKCFAR 83, 104A-B and *Registrar of Births & Deaths* v. *Syed Haider Yahya Hussein* (2001) 4 HKCFAR 429, 444A-C.

that approach is applicable in Hong Kong.[17] This statement of the Hong Kong reaction was made by Li CJ in *HKSAR* v. *Cheung Kwun Yin*.[18] In that case, Li CJ pointed out that when this question arises for consideration:

> the practical as well as the conceptual and constitutional implications in the Hong Kong context would have to be considered.[19]

In making this statement, the Chief Justice was reflecting an observation made by Lord Nicholls in his speech in *Wilson* v. *First County Trust*[20] in which he referred to the conceptual and constitutional difficulties in treating the intentions of the government revealed in debates as reflecting the will of Parliament as distinct from the possibility that they may give rise to an estoppel or the like against the government.[21]

Although there are differences in the constitutional and institutional arrangements in Hong Kong and the United Kingdom, they would not seem to support an approach that is *substantially* different from *Pepper* v. *Hart* as long as it is accepted, as it must be, that government statements cannot control the meaning of legislation, the courts alone having the authority to determine the weight to be given to a government statement, even if it transpires that it is necessary to clarify or vary the expression of the first condition prescribed by *Pepper* v. *Hart*. In Hong Kong, reference to legislative materials has not proved to be a practical problem for the courts.

The interpretation of the guarantees and the other provisions of the BL is a matter of constitutional interpretation. Subject to some qualifications, constitutional interpretation is similar to statutory interpretation. So, in the case of the BL, '[r]espect must be paid to the language which is used and to the traditions and usages which have given meaning to that language'.[22] One very important qualification is that a constitution is an instrument of government defining the powers of government and the rights of citizens, an instrument intended to make enduring provision for the future. A constitution is, as Chief Justice John Marshall once

---

[17] *Lam Pak Chiu* v. *Tsang Mei Ying* (2001) 4 HKCFAR 34, 44D-E; *PCCW-HKT Telephone Ltd* v. *Telecommunications Authority* (2005) 8 HKCFAR 337, 351F-J; and *Director of Lands* v. *Yin Shuen Enterprises Ltd* (2003) 6 HKCFAR 1, 15A-H.

[18] Note 6 above, 576B-D.   [19] *Ibid.*, 576D.   [20] Note 6 above.

[21] *Ibid.*, [59]; see also the criticism of *Pepper* v. *Hart* by Lord Phillips of Matravers, 'The Art of the Possible: Statutory Interpretation and Human Rights', Inaugural Alexander Lecture, Inner Temple Hall, London, 22 April 2010.

[22] *Minister for Home Affairs (Bermuda)* v. *Fisher* [1980] AC 319, 329E (PC), cited in *Director of Immigration* v. *Chong Fung Yuen* (2001) 4 HKCFAR 211, 224B.

famously said, 'intended to endure for ages to come'.[23] So a constitution is construed purposively, and the rights, freedoms, and powers that it confers are construed generously. The principle to be applied was stated in *Ng Ka Ling* v. *Director of Immigration*[24] by Li CJ in these terms:

> [I]n the interpretation of a constitution such as the Basic Law a purposive approach is to be applied. The adoption of a purposive approach is necessary because a constitution states general principles and expresses purposes without condescending to particularity and definition of terms. Gaps and ambiguities are bound to arise and, in resolving them, the courts are bound to give effect to the principles and purposes declared in, and to be ascertained from, the constitution and relevant extrinsic materials. So, in ascertaining the true meaning of the instrument, the courts must consider the purpose of the instrument and its relevant provisions as well as the language of its text in the light of the context, context being of particular importance in the interpretation of a constitutional instrument.[25]

A possible qualification is that the courts may adopt a more relaxed approach to the use of extrinsic materials in interpreting the BL than is mandated by *Pepper* v. *Hart* in relation to the use of parliamentary materials in interpreting statutes. In *Director of Immigration* v. *Chong Fung Yuen*,[26] the CFA did not decline *to have regard* to the pre-enactment materials in interpreting the BL on the ground that the provision was unambiguous or clear but concluded, after considering the materials, that they could not affect the meaning of language that was clear and unambiguous when read in context. In constitutional interpretation, there is a strong case for saying that pre-enactment legislative materials are part of the relevant context. This view has been adopted in Australia in relation to the Convention Debates leading up to the enactment of the Australian Constitution.[27]

A second possible qualification is whether post-enactment extrinsic materials can be called in aid. This possibility was left unresolved in *Director of Immigration* v. *Chong Fung Yuen*.[28]

The relationship between the Basic Law and the common law

The content of Article 8 and its presence in the BL highlight the importance of the relationship between Hong Kong's constitution and the

---

[23] *McCulloch* v. *Maryland* 17 US 315, [19] (1819).   [24] (1999) 2 HKCFAR 4.
[25] *Ibid.*, 28E-F, 29A-C.   [26] Note 22 above.
[27] *Cole* v. *Whitfield* (1988) 165 CLR 360.   [28] Note 22 above, 224H.

common law. If the common law is to develop, as it must, to meet changing conditions and circumstances, then it must develop in conformity with the BL. Indeed, of all the legitimate influences on the development of Hong Kong's common law, the BL is the most important. The implementation of this aspect of the relationship between the BL and the common law is an important matter for future consideration by the courts.

To illustrate what is involved I refer to the decision of the High Court of Australia in *Lange* v. *Australian Broadcasting Commission*[29] and compare it with the CFA decision in *Cheng and Another* v. *Tse Wai Chun.*[30] In *Lange,* the High Court said:

> Of necessity, the common law must conform with the Constitution. The development of the common law in Australia cannot run counter to constitutional imperatives. . . . The common law of libel and slander could not be developed inconsistently with the Constitution. . . .[31]

So, in *Lange,* the common law of qualified privilege required modification in order to comply with the Constitution's implied freedom of communication as to government and political matters. This was because the common law as then understood arguably provided no defence for a person who mistakenly but honestly publishes government or political matter to a large audience of unidentified persons. Qualified privilege was not available, even if the publication dealt with matters of general interest, because there was a lack of reciprocity of interest or duty, this being essential to the defence of qualified privilege at common law. Because this restraint was an unreasonable restriction on the constitutional freedom, the common law was modified by declaring that each member of the Australian community has an interest in the dissemination of information, opinions, and so on concerning government and political matters.

In *Cheng* v. *Tse,* the question was whether *the purpose* for which a defendant stated an honestly held opinion deprives him or her of the protection of the defence of fair comment – for instance, if the defendant's purpose was to inflict injury. The CFA held unanimously (with Lord Nicholls of Birkenhead delivering the leading judgment) that honesty was the touchstone and that actuation by spite, animosity, intent to injure, or other motivation, whatever it might be, even if it was the sole or dominant motive, did not defeat the defence of fair comment. The CFA might have deployed the guarantee of freedom of speech in Article 26 of the BL in

---

[29] (1997) 189 CLR 520.   [30] (2000) 3 HKCFAR 339.   [31] Note 29 above, 566.

order to support or to confirm the same result. Indeed, Li CJ seemingly had this in mind when he said:

> In a society which greatly values the freedom of speech and safeguards it by a constitutional guarantee, it is right that the courts, when considering and developing the common law, should not adopt a narrow approach to the defence of fair comment. See *Eastern Express Publisher Ltd. v Mo Man Ching* (1999) 2 HKCFAR 264 at 278. The courts should adopt a generous approach so that the right of fair comment on matters of public interest is maintained in its full vigour.[32]

Developing the common law in conformity with the BL, particularly provisions of the BL that guarantee rights and freedoms, is likely to become a matter of increasing importance in the future. There is an essential unity between the BL and the common law that is denied if they are treated as if each occupies a separate watertight compartment.

That said, the matter is by no means free from difficulty. We need to look no further than the United Kingdom to see how complex the topic of developing the common law by reference to the Human Rights Act and the European Convention on Human Rights and Fundamental Freedoms (the European Convention) has become.[33] There the difficulties arise from (1) the interrelationship between the European Convention and the Human Rights Act 1998, (2) the characterization of European Convention rights and freedoms as protecting individuals only as against government and public authorities and not against the acts of other individuals, and (3) the absence of any guarantee that there will be any particular rights or remedies in matters of private law.

Nevertheless, the United Kingdom courts, relying partly on section 6 of the Human Rights Act (which requires the court as a public authority not to act 'in a way which is incompatible with a Convention right'), have developed the action for breach of confidence by reference to Convention Article 8 (the right to respect for private life) and Article 10 (the right to freedom of expression). In the result, the plaintiff in such an action no longer needs to show an initial confidential relationship.[34]

To say this is not to suggest that the United Kingdom jurisprudence on this point is necessarily a sound guide as to the course that Hong Kong courts should follow. Hong Kong courts have to deal with constitutional

---

[32] Note 30 above, 345E.
[33] See the Rt Hon. Lady Justice Arden, 'Human Rights and Civil Wrongs: Tort Law Under the Spotlight', Hailsham Lecture 2009, 12 May 2009.
[34] *Campbell* v. *MGN Ltd* [2004] 2 AC 457 (HL).

provisions that take a different form. It is instructive, however, to refer to the dissenting judgment of Lord Bingham of Cornhill in *Chief Constable of The Hertfordshire Police* v. *Van Colle*, a case on duty of care in tort, in which his Lordship said:

> one would ordinarily be surprised if conduct which violated a fundamental right or freedom of the individual did not find a reflection in a body of law as sensitive to human needs as the common law, and it is demonstrable that the common law in some areas has evolved in a direction signalled by the Convention. . . . I agree . . . that "where a common law duty covers the same ground as a Convention right, it should, so far as practicable, develop in harmony with it".[35]

The defendant was, of course, a public authority.

On the other hand, the House of Lords has rejected the argument that English law should adopt a general cause of action for invasion of privacy despite the recognition of a right to privacy in the European Convention and the Human Rights Act.[36] The reasons for this conclusion are not material for present purposes.

The important point to be made is that if the BL recognizes a fundamental value, such as the right to freedom of speech, which is a central element in democratic government, there is much to commend the view that the value should be respected in the substantive private law regulating rights and obligations generally even if the value is embedded in a series of provisions directed to regulating rights and obligations as between citizens and government.

The relationship between English authority and the jurisprudence of Hong Kong

The authority of English case law constituted the common law foundation for Hong Kong before 1 July 1997. By section 3 of the Supreme Court Ordinance of 1844 and later section 5 of the Supreme Court Ordinance of 1873, the Hong Kong courts were required to apply English common law except where the same was 'inapplicable to the local circumstances of [Hong Kong] or of its inhabitants'.

This provision was in substance similar to the provision in other instruments, including British statutes, that provided for the common law

---

[35] [2009] 1 AC 225, [58] (HL), quoting Rimer LJ in *Smith* v. *Chief Constable of Sussex Police* [2008] EWCA Civ 39, [45] (CA).
[36] *Wainwright* v. *Home Office* [2004] 2 AC 406 (HL).

foundation of other British colonies.[37] In substance, they enacted that the English common law and statutes at a particular date should be the law of the particular colony unless conditions in the colony were such as to make them inapplicable. As Bokhary PJ has noted,[38] one consequence of the 1844 and 1870 provisions was that Hong Kong courts had to develop a common law of Hong Kong even though it was for the most part identical to English common law. This position was not altered by the Application of English Law Ordinance of 1966.[39]

The common law is not a fixed system of immutable rules. Rather, it has an inherent capacity to grow and develop by responding to changed circumstances even by correcting its own mistakes. If we look at the English common law through the lens of history, we perceive how its rules and principles have developed and changed over its long life of more than 800 years. We also perceive that the change has been slow, seemingly imperceptible in a short time span. So it is with Article 8, as it was in 1844, 1870, and 1966, that the common law to which it refers is a common law capable of development by the courts.

Because the Privy Council (PC) was the final court of appeal from the courts of Hong Kong before 1 July 1997, decisions of the PC on appeals brought from Hong Kong, by virtue of the doctrine of precedent, were binding on the courts of Hong Kong. Although decisions of the PC on appeals brought from other jurisdictions were not binding on the Hong Kong courts,[40] these decisions were so persuasive and influential that they would be invariably followed in Hong Kong unless local circumstances were materially different. The same comment may be made about decisions of the House of Lords. Again, although standing outside the hierarchy of appeals from Hong Kong courts, its decisions were also treated as if they were virtually binding.[41] Decisions of other English courts, particularly the English Court of Appeal, were very influential.

---

[37] See e.g. the Australian Courts Act 1828, 9 Geo IV, c.83, section 24, which provided that all laws and statutes in force in England on 25 July 1828 should be applied in the administration of justice in New South Wales and Van Diemen's land 'so far as the same can be applied within the said colonies'.

[38] *China Field Ltd* v. *Appeal Tribunal Buildings* (No 2) (2009) 12 HKCFAR 342.

[39] Application of English Law Ordinance (Cap. 88) was not adopted as the Laws of the HKSAR in accordance with BL, Article 160.

[40] *de Lasala* v. *de Lasala* [1980] AC 546 (PC); *Solicitor (24/07)* v. *Law Society of Hong Kong* (2008) 11 HKCFAR 117, 131E-F, 132H-133C.

[41] *Ibid.*, 133D-G.

All that changed on 1 July 1997. Because the PC ceased to be Hong Kong's final court of appeal and was replaced by the CFA as Hong Kong's final court of appeal, PC decisions given after that date are not binding on Hong Kong courts. PC decisions given before that date stand in a different position because they form part of the body of law in Hong Kong continued in force by Article 8 except in so far as they have been modified by statute. Although these decisions form part of the Hong Kong body of law, the CFA, being a final court of appeal, is entitled to depart from its own decisions and previous PC decisions as well, though the CFA will only do so with great circumspection.[42] Since 1 July 1997, as far as PC and House of Lords decisions are concerned, being in effect decisions of the final courts of appeal of other jurisdictions, which played such an important part in the creation of Hong Kong's common law, they are entitled to great respect. The extent of their influence and that of the decisions of the Supreme Court, the successor to the House of Lords, will depend upon the persuasiveness of their reasoning, not on the authority or status of the PC, the House of Lords or of the Supreme Court. Beyond that statement there is no principle governing adoption of, or departure from, such decisions.

English decisions have continued to be influential in Hong Kong since 1 July 1997 on common law questions. That this is so is hardly surprising in view of Hong Kong's English common law heritage which has endowed Hong Kong with a sophisticated and developed body of common law. It would be surprising, indeed, if Hong Kong courts failed to pay close attention to how that body of law continues to be developed by English courts. Further, the international standing of Hong Kong's legal system depends, to a significant extent, on the continuity of its English common law heritage. That does not mean that English authority should be followed by Hong Kong courts. Far from it, but it does mean that it will receive close attention.

The differences that distinguish the jurisprudence of the various common law jurisdictions are largely doctrinal. The variations in doctrine may be attributed, however, to different judicial responses to variations in the material circumstances and conditions of society in the various jurisdictions or to different judicial perceptions about particular societal values, e.g. sanctity of contract. Yet, at one time it was fashionable to think that the great virtue of the appeal to the PC from colonial courts was that

---

[42] Ibid., 134E-J.

it contributed to a uniform development of the common law,[43] at least in territories associated with Great Britain, even if decisions of the PC were strictly binding only on courts of the jurisdiction from which the appeal was brought. The assumption that informed this thinking was that differences in local circumstances were not significant in the formulation of common law principles.

Subsequently, the PC recognized that on matters of judicial policy, where the judicial policy judgment was related to an assessment of local sentiment or circumstances in the jurisdiction from which the appeal was brought, it was appropriate to leave the judgment on that policy issue with the colonial court.[44] There was, however, no instance of the PC taking this view in an appeal from Hong Kong.

How the Hong Kong courts have dealt with English decisions since 1 July 1997

Apart from the reservations about *Pepper* v. *Hart*, which have already been noted, there have been a number of cases in which the CFA either has declined to follow or has questioned the PC's or House of Lords's decisions since 1 July 1997. In *Solicitor (24/07)* v. *Law Society of Hong Kong*,[45] the CFA declined to follow the PC's decisions in *Campbell* v. *Hamlet*[46] and three earlier cases on the appropriate standard of proof in disciplinary proceedings before a tribunal. The PC held in *Campbell* v. *Hamlet* that the standard of proof in disciplinary proceedings is the criminal standard (i.e. proof beyond reasonable doubt). The CFA unanimously held that the applicable standard of proof was the civil standard of the preponderance of probability on the footing that the more serious the act or omission alleged, the more inherently improbable it must be regarded. And the more inherently improbable it was to be regarded, the more compelling would be the evidence needed to prove it on a

---

[43] *Trimble* v. *Hill* (1879) 5 App. Cas. 342, 345; *Robins* v. *National Trust Co. Ltd* [1927] AC 515, 519; *Waghorn* v. *Waghorn* (1942) 65 CLR 289, 297–8 (in which Dixon J stated: 'The common law is administered in many jurisdictions and unless each of them guards against needless divergences of decision its uniform development is imperilled'); and *Piro* v. *W. Foster & Co. Ltd* (1943) 68 CLR 313, 320.

[44] *Geelong Harbour Trust Commissioners* v. *Gibbs Bright & Co.* (1974) 129 CLR 576, 582–3; *Australian Consolidated Press Ltd* v. *Uren* [1969] 1 AC 590; and *Invercargill City Council* v. *Hamlin* [1996] AC 624.

[45] Note 40 above.   [46] [2005] 3 All ER 1116 (PC).

preponderance of probability.[47] The CFA thus endorsed the formulation of the standard of proof expressed by Lord Nicholls in a different context in *Re H & Others (Minors) Sexual Abuse: Standard of Proof*,[48] a formulation that had earlier been stated by the High Court of Australia in *Helton* v. *Allen*[49] and *Briginshaw* v. *Briginshaw*.[50]

In *Solicitor (24/07)* v. *Law Society of Hong Kong*, the CFA also declined to follow the House of Lords's decision in *Davis* v. *Johnson*[51] and the PC's decision in *A-G of St Christopher, Nevis and Anguilla* v. *Reynolds*,[52] each of which had affirmed the correctness of *Young* v. *Bristol Aeroplane Co. Ltd.*[53] That case had enunciated the controversial rule that the English Court of Appeal was bound by its previous decisions subject to three exceptions. The rule had been accepted and acted upon by the Hong Kong Court of Appeal. It was the rule as applied to that court that was considered by the CFA. After noting that in Australia, Canada, and New Zealand, the rule had not been adopted, the CFA concluded that the rule should no longer be applied in Hong Kong and that instead the Court of Appeal should regard itself as bound by its previous decisions unless a decision was 'plainly wrong'.[54] The CFA emphasized, however, that a departure from a previous decision should be 'wholly exceptional' and take place only when the Court of Appeal was convinced that the contentions against the previous decision were 'compelling'.[55]

Another decision of the House of Lords that the CFA declined to follow was *R* v. *Aziz*.[56] That case laid it down as an invariable rule of practice that once the trial judge determined a person to be of 'good character', he or she is entitled to a summing up in accordance with what have been called 'the *Vye* principles',[57] subject to a qualification. The *Vye* principles, as expressed in *Aziz*,[58] are:

> (1) A direction as to the relevance of his good character to a defendant's credibility is to be given where he has testified or made pretrial answers or statements. (2) A direction as to the relevance of his good character to the likelihood of his having committed the offence charged is to be given, whether or not he has testified, or made pretrial answers or statements. (3) Where defendant A of good character is jointly tried with defendant B of bad character, (1) and (2) still apply.

---

[47] Note 40 above, 157J-116F.   [48] [1996] AC 563, 586D-G, 587C-E (HL).
[49] (1940) 63 CLR 691.   [50] (1938) 60 CLR 336, 362.   [51] [1979] AC 264 (HL).
[52] [1980] AC 637 (PC).   [53] [1941] KB 718.   [54] Note 40 above, 135E-141G.
[55] *Ibid.*, 141H-143B.   [56] [1996] AC 41 (HL).
[57] *R* v. *Vye* (1993) 97 Cr App R 134 (CA).   [58] Note 56 above, 51D.

The qualification is that the judge has a residual discretion to decline to give any character directions in the case of a defendant without previous convictions if the judge considers it an insult to common sense to do so or to qualify the directions by adding appropriate words to deal with the defendant's criminal conduct revealed in the course of the trial.

In *Tang Sui Man* v. *HKSAR (No. 2)*,[59] the CFA declined to follow *Aziz*. The majority (with Bokhary PJ dissenting) regarded the *Vye* directions as presenting very considerable practical difficulties, as demonstrated by English experience, and as being discordant with the tendency in other jurisdictions to move away from rigid, prescribed directions in favour of a more flexible, discretionary approach that gives effect to the requirement to deliver a fair and balanced summing up. Litton PJ, who delivered the main majority judgment, drew support from the Australian and New Zealand experiences, particularly from the dissenting judgment of Thomas J in *R* v. *Falealili*.[60]

In *Swire Properties Ltd* v. *Secretary for Justice*,[61] the CFA unanimously declined to follow the House of Lords' decisions in *Pioneer Shipping Ltd* v. *BTP Tioxide Ltd (The Nema)*[62] and *Antaios Compania Naviera SA* v. *Salen Rederierna AB (The Antaios)*,[63] preferring instead the approach taken by the English Court of Appeal in *The Antaios*.[64] In the result, the CFA held that when a question of law of general public importance or the construction of a standard clause in a contract was involved, the courts should normally grant leave to appeal from an arbitral award when, but only when, there was a serious doubt as to its correctness. This test is less severe than the 'strong prima facie case' test that had been favoured by the House of Lords.

In *Swire Properties*, the CFA also held that a judge who refused leave to appeal to the High Court should give reasons for his or her refusal, pursuant to Article 10 of the Hong Kong Bill of Rights. In this respect also, the CFA departed from the House of Lords in *The Antaios*.

There have been occasions, apart from the *Pepper* v. *Hart* question, when the CFA has left open a question that has been considered by the House of Lords. On examination, however, some instances are cases in which the House of Lords has not given a final answer to the question. One such case was *Re Spectrum Plus Ltd*[65] in which it could be said that members of the House of Lords either tended to contemplate favourably

---

[59] (1998) 1 HKCFAR 107.   [60] [1996] 3 NZLR 664.   [61] (2003) 6 HKCFAR 236.

[62] [1982] AC 724 (HL).   [63] [1985] AC 191 (HL).   [64] [1983] 1 WLR 1362 (CA).

[65] [2005] 2 AC 680 (HL).

the possibility that the House might in the future engage in the technique of 'prospective overruling' in a suitable case or at least declined to rule it out altogether. In *Koo Sze Yiu* v. *Chief Executive*,[66] the CFA left the question open.

The question is one of very great importance both in matters of statute law and common law and, almost certainly, it will arise for determination in Hong Kong sooner rather than later. As the speeches in *Re Spectrum Plus* show, particularly that of Lord Nicholls, there are strong arguments for and against, involving the scope of judicial power that, in Hong Kong, is a relatively unexplored province. The case for prospective overruling is stronger in relation to the common law than statutes.

In Hong Kong, questions will arise for decision in relation to the scope of judicial power and its separation from legislative and executive power. One question is whether the separation of powers in Hong Kong mandates the principle accepted in Australia that an administrative function cannot be conferred on a court unless that function is incidental to the exercise of judicial power.[67] The principle has far-reaching consequences and, if adopted in Hong Kong, could affect the capacity of judges to undertake administrative functions (e.g. the conduct of administrative inquiries). Likewise, there is the question of whether Hong Kong should adopt, without qualification, the principle adopted elsewhere that the exercise of judicial power is confined to the adjudication of actual disputes.[68] This principle precludes a court from considering and deciding an important question that should be resolved as early as possible in the public interest.[69]

In *Koo Sze Yiu*, however, the CFA did take the innovative step of suspending for six months the coming into operation of declarations of the unconstitutionality of the Executive Order and section 33 of the Telecommunications Ordinance so far as it authorized access to or the disclosure of the contents of any message or class of message. The CFA substituted its order suspending the operation of the declarations for an order made by the Court of Appeal giving the Executive Order and the provisions of the Ordinance temporary validity for six months. In a concurring judgment, I pointed to the difficulties of making an order giving temporary

---

[66] (2006) 9 HKCFAR 441 at 495D-E.

[67] *Attorney-General (Cth)* v. *The Queen* (Boilermakers' Case) [1957] AC 288.

[68] In Australia, this principle turns in part, at least, on the definition of 'matter', an expression in Chapter III of the Australian Constitution to which there is no counterpart in the BL, but cf. the reference to 'all cases in the Region' in BL, Article 19(2).

[69] For an extreme application of this principle, see *North Ganalanja Aboriginal Corp.* v. *Queensland* (1996) 185 CLR 595, 612.

validity to legislation that a court holds to be invalid[70] despite the existence of Pakistan and Canadian authorities seemingly supporting such a course. The CFA has left open the question whether it could make such an order.[71] The judgments in *Koo Sze Yiu* make it very clear that suspending the operation of a declaration of invalidity of a statute does not entail, as some Canadian authority might seem to suggest, the valid operation of the statute in the period of suspension. Acts (including omissions) and transactions occurring in that period will ultimately be determined for legality by reference to the law as declared by the court. The suspension does not affect the rights of parties; indeed, its effect may be no more than cosmetic.

In another case, the CFA foreshadowed the possibility that it would adopt the minority opinion in *Westdeutsche* v. *Islington LBC*[72] in favour of awarding compound interest.[73] And in *Sze Kwan Lung* v. *HKSAR*,[74] the CFA left open the possibility that it would adopt the approach of the High Court of Australia in *R* v. *Wilson*[75] in preference to the approach of the House of Lords in *DPP* v. *Newbury*.[76] *Wilson* held that for a person to be guilty of manslaughter by an unlawful and dangerous act, the circumstances must be such that a reasonable person in the accused person's position would have realized that he or she was exposing another to an appreciable risk of serious injury. The *Newbury* formulation that there was a risk that some harm would result was not enough.

There have been cases in which the CFA has declined to follow the decisions of English courts below the level of the House of Lords, including decisions of the English Court of Appeal. One such case was *HKSAR* v. *Wong Sau Ming*[77] in which the CFA held that as a result of its decision as to the application of the finality rule to cross-examination as to credit, English authorities on the point should not be followed in Hong Kong.

Developing common law principles

Of much more importance than instances of disagreement (or possible disagreement) with the PC and the House of Lords is the record of the CFA in developing the common law. Of the decisions in this category,

---

[70] Note 66 above, 460H-461B; see also *HKSAR* v. *Hung Chan Wa* (2006) 9 HKCFAR 614, 633G-H.
[71] *Ibid.*, 455F; *Hung Chan Wa, ibid.*, 633A–634.   [72] [1996] AC 669 (HL).
[73] *China Everbright-IHD Pacific Ltd.* v. *Ch'ng Poh* (2002) 5 HKCFAR 630.
[74] (2004) 7 HKCFAR 475, 487E–488B.   [75] (1992) 174 CLR 313 (Austr HC).
[76] *DPP* v. *Newbury* [1977] AC 500 (HL).   [77] (2003) 6 HKCFAR 135.

there are some interesting examples. The best known decision is *Cheng v. Tse*,[78] the case on fair comment that has already been discussed and is regarded as a leading case in other jurisdictions, notably the United Kingdom.[79] The question that arose in *Cheng* was unresolved by existing Hong Kong and English authorities.

Another CFA decision on an unresolved question was *Unruh v. Seeberger*.[80] There the question was whether a memorandum of agreement, which provided for financial assistance by entities including Unruh, not being parties to an arbitration to be held in the Netherlands, to one of the parties in the arbitration, was a champertous agreement. The CFA held (with Ribeiro PJ delivering the main judgment) that it was not. This was because (1) Unruh had a genuine commercial interest in rendering assistance in the arbitration and receiving a share of the proceeds, and (2) it is not against public policy in Hong Kong to enforce an arbitration agreement, even if champertous, because it involved assistance in an arbitration taking place in a jurisdiction where maintenance and champerty are not contrary to public policy. The judgments provide a striking illustration of judicial development of the common law – in this case, applying the old principles of maintenance and champerty to modern commercial practices.

The CFA's judgment on ground (1) above should be compared with that of the PC in *Massai Aviation Services* v. *Attorney General*[81] delivered very shortly after *Unruh* v. *Seeberger*. There it was argued that an assignment of an interest in a lawsuit was void because it was champertous. The argument was rejected because the assignment of the bare chose in action to a company representing shareholders was an assignment to an entity having a genuine commercial interest in the outcome of the litigation. Both cases reflect a similar modern approach to the old law of maintenance and champerty. Both cases should be compared with *Campbells Cash & Carry Pty. Ltd* v. *Fostif Pty. Ltd*,[82] a decision of the High Court of Australia, where litigation instigated by a litigation funder who was to receive one-third of the amount recovered was held neither to involve champerty or maintenance nor to amount to an abuse of process.

---

[78] Note 30 above.
[79] See P. Milmo and W. V. H. Rogers (eds.), *Gatley on Libel and Slander*, 11th edn. (London: Sweet & Maxwell, 2008) index of cases. The decision is cited in 17 paragraphs. See also Chapter 22 (Lo) in this volume.
[80] (2007) 10 HKCFAR 31.   [81] [2007] UKPC 12 (26 February 2007).
[82] (2006) 229 CLR 386 (Austr HC).

Another instance of the development of common law principle is *Leung Tsang Hung* v. *Incorporated Owners of Kwok Wing House*.[83] There the question was whether the incorporated owners of a building could be liable in public nuisance, along with the individual owner, for a nuisance hazard encroaching upon or attached to a common part of the building, the individual owner having affixed an unauthorized concrete canopy to an external wall, the common part of which projected out over the street below. The extended canopy was 35 years old and of poor workmanship, and it fell into disrepair. A corner of the canopy broke off and killed a hawker below. Although the liability of an owner–occupier in public nuisance for failure to eliminate a nuisance hazard was well established where the owner–occupier knew or ought reasonably to have known that his or her act or omission would result in a nuisance hazard presenting a real risk of harm to the public, the potential liability of incorporated owners in relation to a common part of a building was free from authority. After a comprehensive review by Ribeiro PJ of the authorities dealing with liability in nuisance, the CFA concluded that the incorporated owners of the building, along with the individual owner, were liable on the basis that they had effective control of the common parts and they knew or ought to have known of the nuisance hazard.

Waddington Ltd v. *Chan Chun Hoo*[84] dealt with multiple derivative actions. The expression 'derivative action' denotes an action brought by a shareholder in right of a company to recover damages on its behalf. It is a form of relief permitted when the company is controlled by the alleged wrongdoers and their control prevents the company itself from bringing to redress the wrong that they have done. In *Waddington*, the question was whether a multiple derivative action could be brought. Such an action is the only means of redressing a situation when the wrongdoers, who, through their control of the parent company and consequential control of its subsidiaries, defraud a subsidiary or sub-subsidiary. Outside the United States and apart from the decision of a senior master of the state of Victoria, there was no direct authority upon the point, although there were dicta.

In *Waddington*, the plaintiff P was a minority shareholder of C. C wholly owned a subsidiary, S1. In turn, S1 wholly owned other subsidiaries, including S2 and S3. P alleged that X, the chairman and executive director of C, had concluded a series of transactions on behalf of S2 and S3 in breach of his duties. P sought to bring a derivative action in this respect.

---

[83]   (2007) 10 HKCFAR 480.   [84]   (2008) 11 HKCFAR 370.

The CFA held unanimously that a multiple derivative action was available at common law in Hong Kong. The justification for recognizing such an action was the same as that for a single derivative action.

It was also held that a single derivative action could not be brought when the relevant shareholder was suing for reflective loss. The principle against recovery for reflective loss is that a shareholder cannot recover loss that is merely reflective of the loss suffered by the company. *Giles* v. *Rhind*,[85] a decision of the English Court of Appeal, recognized a supposed exception to this rule. But the CFA declined to follow *Giles* v. *Rhind* and *Perry* v. *Day*,[86] a case that followed *Giles* v. *Rhind*. The CFA expressed the hope that the legislature might consider extending section 168BC of the Companies Ordinance, which preserved a derivative action at common law to cover multiple derivative actions and, in effecting this, also consider the undesirability of coexisting statutory and common law regimes.[87]

In administrative law, the CFA has signalled the possibility of adopting a general requirement that administrative decision-makers give reasons for their decisions[88] and that it could adopt a sliding scale of intensity of review in judicial review cases depending upon the nature of the administrative decision in question.[89] Likewise, in administrative law, *Ng Sui Tung* v. *Director of Immigration*[90] was a notable example of enforcement of a substantive legitimate expectation, a doctrine that is regarded as controversial in other jurisdictions.

The recent decision in *Tradepower (Holdings) Ltd* v. *Tradepower (Hong Kong) Ltd*,[91] although strictly speaking not an instance of common law development, should be mentioned. The question for decision related to the expression 'with intent to defraud creditors' in section 60 of the Conveyancing and Property Ordinance, a statutory descendant of the statute 13 Eliz1, c.5 that, similar to section 60, was aimed at fraudulent conveyances intended to defraud creditors.[92] The CFA, after considering many English, Australian, and New Zealand authorities, concluded that section 60 should be construed in accordance with the rule in *Freeman* v. *Pope*[93] and that in *Freeman* v. *Pope*–type cases, the circumstances are sufficient in themselves to justify drawing the inference of 'intent to

---

[85] [2003] Ch 618 (CA).   [86] [2005] 2 BCLC 405.

[87] Companies Ordinance (Cap. 32); note 84 above, [80].

[88] *Oriental Daily Publisher Ltd* v. *Commissioner for Television & Entertainment Licensing Authority* (1998) 1 HKCFAR 279.

[89] *Town Planning Board* v. *Society for the Protection of the Harbour Ltd* [2004] 7 HKCFAR 1.

[90] (2002) 5 HKCFAR 1.   [91] (2009) 12 HKCFAR 417.

[92] Conveyancing and Property Ordinance (Cap. 219).   [93] (1870) 5 Ch. App. 538.

defraud creditors' without more. In this respect, Ribeiro PJ, who delivered the judgment of the court, followed the reasoning of Blanchard and Wilson JJ in *Regal Castings Ltd* v. *Lightbody*[94] and the dissenting judgment of Kirby J in *Cannane* v. *J. Cannane Pty Ltd*.[95]

In matters of practice and procedure generally, particularly remedies, the CFA has been innovative, going beyond what has been established in other jurisdictions. Suspending the operation of a declaration of invalidity of a statute is one example. The emphasis placed on the wide power of remedial interpretation attributed to section 6(1) of the BORO and implied in the BL to make a provision BL and BORO compliant is another.[96] So also was the willingness of the CFA in *Koon Wing Yee* v. *Insider Dealing Tribunal*[97] to strike down a non-offending provision of a statute to enable the statute to conform to a constitutional requirement, even when unconstitutionality was the consequence of another provision, as long as what the court does results in giving effect to the legislative intention as far as it is possible to do so. *Koon Wing Yee* was an exceptional case in this respect because it was evident that the reformed statute represented the legislature's alternative choice in the event that its preferred choice was held to be unconstitutional.

The use of comparative law

The CFA has made extensive use of comparative law, particularly in cases that turn on the guarantees of human rights and fundamental freedoms in the BL and the BORO. That is because they are rights and freedoms which have generated a vast body of international and transnational jurisprudence. On common law questions, substantially more use has been made of English authorities than authorities from other jurisdictions, as was to be expected. Significant use has been made, however, of authorities from other common law jurisdictions, most notably Australia. Of the many examples that might be given of the use of Australian authority, it is enough to instance *HKSAR* v. *Lee Fuk Hing*[98] in which the CFA followed *Petty & Maiden* v. *The Queen*[99] in holding that previous silence about a defence subsequently raised at the trial provides no basis for inferring that the defence is a new invention or is rendered suspect or unacceptable.

---

[94] [2009] 2 NZLR 433.   [95] (1998) 192 CLR 557.
[96] See *Lam Kwong Wai*, note 6 above; *Koon Wing Yee* v. *Insider Dealing Tribunal* (2008) 11 HKCFAR 170.
[97] *Koon Wing Yee*, ibid.   [98] (2004) 7 HKCFAR 600.   [99] (1991) 173 CLR 95.

It has been suggested that the CFA should have done more to develop a distinctly Hong Kong jurisprudence.[100] The suggestion is easy to make as an abstract generalization. But it is difficult to execute without resorting to particular instances in which one can demonstrate that the adoption of different principles would have led to different outcomes. No one has yet done that. As the Australian experience shows, it takes time, after the elimination of the PC appeal, for a jurisdiction to develop its own coherent substantial body of jurisprudence. And in terms of developing its own autonomous jurisprudence, Australia had advantages over Hong Kong; Australia had long ceased to be a colony before the PC appeal from Australian State Supreme Courts finally was terminated by the Australia Act 1996,[101] and for a long time its judges had been appointed from the ranks of its own legal profession, which, with few exceptions, had been educated in Australia.

A criticism often made of the use of comparative law is that courts everywhere are selective in their use of it. How could it be otherwise? The volume of comparative law is immense, and the use of particular decisions in other jurisdictions can be hazardous unless a judge has an understanding of the doctrinal, political, and historical context that generated the decision under consideration. In the setting of argument in an oral hearing, even with the aid of written submissions, the available time frame does not allow for an exploration of that context in great depth. So courts such as the CFA tend to look more frequently at authorities in jurisdictions with which they are familiar.

The jurisprudence on human rights stands in a somewhat different position. Notwithstanding that it has a domestic as well as an international dimension, this jurisprudence, to a large extent, stands on its own foundations. Yet it, too, has its problems. The CFA has made extensive use of the jurisprudence of the Strasbourg Court, often mediated through the decisions of the House of Lords in a common law jurisdiction. In the interests of coherence and consistency, a court may be well advised to give emphasis to the comparative jurisprudence of particular jurisdictions. Now, however, a tide of criticism of the Strasbourg Court is rising. Lord Hoffmann's speech 'The Universality of Human Rights'[102] is perhaps the most prominent example of it. Two criticisms he makes are that (1)

---

[100] *Kensland Realty Ltd* v. *Tai, Tang & Chong* (2008) 11 HKCFAR 237 at [167].
[101] Australia Act 1996, s. 11.
[102] Judicial Studies Board Annual Lecture, 19 March 2009, published in (2009) 125 LQR 416.

the Strasbourg Court should allow a greater margin of appreciation for domestic courts to implement the general standards which it sets and (2) the Strasbourg Court's interpretation of the Convention is too liberal.

Lady Justice Arden has responded to these criticisms.[103] The response may not, however, allay criticism. The response, if acted upon, would lead to dialogue between the domestic courts and the Strasbourg Court in which domestic courts express their disagreement with the Strasbourg Court, thereby weakening the authority of its decisions. This is a matter that could be relevant to the use to be made by the CFA of the Strasbourg jurisprudence.

Another matter, by no means unrelated, is the possibility that the UK Supreme Court may retreat, to some extent, from its expansive interpretation of section 3 of the Human Rights Act 1998. Although the BL has no similar interpretive provision, the CFA has picked up the approach adopted by the House of Lords in *Ghaidan* v. *Godin-Mendoza*[104] to section 3. Since then the House of Lords in *R (Wilkinson)* v. *IRC*[105] emphasized the limitations attaching to the process of interpretation, limitations that had been emphasized earlier in *Re S (Minors)*.[106] A similar emphasis led the Supreme Court of New Zealand, in *R* v. *Hansen*,[107] to decline to follow *Ghaidan* in the context of section 6 of the New Zealand Bill of Rights Act. What this means, if anything, for Hong Kong remains to be seen.

In endeavouring to identify the boundary line between interpretation and amendment – that is, the point where interpretation ends and amendment begins – it is as well to remember that the problem is by no means new. As long ago as 1938, in *Sutherland Publishing Co. Ltd* v. *Caxton Publishing Co. Ltd*,[108] it was stated that:

> When the purpose of an enactment is clear, it is often legitimate, because it is necessary, to put a strained interpretation upon some words which have been inadvertently used, and of which plain meaning would obviously defeat the intention of the legislature.[109]

Lord Reid put the point more forcefully in *Luke* v. *IRC*[110] when he said:

---

[103] Note 33 above.   [104] [2004] 2 AC 557 (HL).   [105] [2006] 1 AII ER 529 (HL).

[106] [2002] 2 AC 291 at [39]; see Lord Hope at [108]; see also Lord Phillips of Worth Matravers, 'The Art of the Possible. Statutory Interpretation and Human Rights', Inaugural Alexander Lecture, Inner Temple Hall, London, 22 April 2010.

[107] [2007] 3 NZLR 1; see also *R* v. *Momcilovic* [2010] VSCA 50, 17 March 2010, [61] where the position in Hong Kong was distinguished from that arising under the Victorian Charter of Human Rights and Responsibilities Act 2006.

[108] [1938] 1 Ch. 174.   [109] *Ibid.*, 201.   [110] [1963] AC 557.

> The general principle is well settled. It is only where the words are absolutely incapable of a construction which will accord with the apparent intention of the provision and will avoid a wholly unreasonable result that the words of the enactment must prevail.[111]

Sutherland and *Luke* are cases in which, in the one statute, there was a tension between the text of the statute and its purpose or evident intention. In the context of interpretive provisions in human rights statutes, the tension is between two statutes with the result that there is scope for an argument that different considerations apply. Whether they should require a different outcome is a matter for debate. But this question is not critical to the interpretation of the BL. It is a constitution and must be interpreted as such, so the authorities on statutory interpretive provisions involving the interaction of two statutory provisions in other jurisdictions are by no means a reliable guide to questions arising under the BL. The interpretive force of the BL and of the principle that a court will adopt that interpretation that will ensure the constitutional validity of a statute[112] is necessarily stronger than the interpretive force of the principle of legality.

Conclusions

By way of conclusion, we can say of the CFA's first 13 years that, first, it has reinforced the rule of law and exhibited the strength of an independent judiciary in giving effect to the theme 'one country, two systems' under the BL. Second, it has achieved this outcome by applying the common law rules of statutory interpretation and constitutional interpretation and drawing upon the BL and the BORO, subject to applying interpretations of the BL issued under Article 158 of the BL. Third, the authority of the CFA's decisions has almost certainly been enhanced by its adoption of a collegiate approach to the delivery of judgments in preference to the individual approach formerly favoured in the High Court of Australia and the Supreme Court of the United States. Fourth, it has made extensive use of comparative law, not only from other common law jurisdictions but also from other jurisdictions, most notably in the area of human rights jurisprudence. Fifth, it has already developed the common law in a number of cases and may be called upon to develop the common law by reference to the BL. Sixth, although paying considerable respect to the

---

[111] *Ibid.*, 577.
[112] For an extreme example of a strained interpretation given to an ouster clause to ensure its validity, see *R* v. *Hickman; Ex parte Fox and Clinton* (1945) 70 CLR 598.

decisions of United Kingdom courts, particularly the PC and the House of Lords, the CFA has on occasions declined to follow them. Seventh, there are some substantial questions that will confront the CFA in the future, including questions relating to the BL's provisions concerning judicial power and the separation of powers and the *Pepper* v. *Hart* conditions on the use of legislative materials, and most importantly, there remains the possibility of conflict between NPCSC interpretations of the BL under Article 158 and common law interpretations of the BL, although the risk of conflict seems to have decreased if recent experience is a reliable guide.

14

The Basic Law jurisprudence of the Court of Final Appeal

ALBERT H. Y. CHEN AND P. Y. LO

Introduction

The establishment of the Hong Kong Special Administrative Region of the People's Republic of China (HKSAR) in July 1997 was accompanied by the introduction of a new constitutional order. On 1 July 1997, the Basic Law of the HKSAR (BL)[1] came into force. The Court of Final Appeal (CFA) replaced the Judicial Committee of the Privy Council (PC) as the highest appellate court in Hong Kong. Whereas the laws of Hong Kong in the domain of private law were little affected by the handover, the domain of public law with the BL at its core became the most rapidly developing area of Hong Kong law immediately after 1997 as new issues arising from the implementation of the BL came to be tackled. The development of the jurisprudence of the BL, including the jurisprudence of 'one country, two systems', thus became the most challenging task faced by the CFA when it came into existence in 1997.[2]

---

[1] *Basic Law of the Hong Kong Special Administrative Region of the People's Republic of China* (adopted at the Third Session of the Seventh National People's Congress on 4th April 1990; promulgated by Order No. 26 of the President of the People's Republic of China on 4th April 1990) (1990) 29 ILM 1511.

[2] Several recent academic and practitioners' texts have reviewed the jurisprudence of the BL at varying depths. Ramsden and Jones' annotations are organized in accordance with the articles of the BL: Michael Ramsden and Oliver Jones, *Hong Kong Basic Law: Annotations and Commentary* (Hong Kong: Sweet and Maxwell, 2010). Lo's effort seeks to map, following the structure of the BL, the relevant jurisprudence in the company of Mainland scholarship, Macanese constitutional and legal practice, Hong Kong executive–legislative interactions, comparative law, and other thematic studies, resulting in a product that is similar to a *Kommentar* in the German tradition: P. Y. Lo, *The Hong Kong Basic Law* (Hong Kong: LexisNexis, 2011). Chan and Lim coordinated a group of local and overseas scholars to weave together a textbook of Hong Kong constitutional law that discusses the subject matter in five parts: historical background, a new constitutional era, political structure,

This chapter reviews the history of the development of the CFA's jurisprudence relating to the BL. This review presents a narrative history of this aspect of the CFA's jurisprudence to enable readers to understand the evolving challenges the CFA faced and how it responded to them. In the concluding section, the overall record of the Andrew Li Court in the development of BL jurisprudence is evaluated.

The presentation of the narrative history is organized into three phases of development of the CFA's BL jurisprudence. During the first, *foundational*, phase between 1997 and 2002, the CFA laid out the parameters of its constitutional jurisdiction, including its approach in exercising the power of interpretation of the BL. In the second, *consolidation*, phase between 2002 and 2006, the CFA articulated the ingredients of its operative regime of rights protection. The third, *innovation*, phase between 2005 and 2009 saw the CFA making strides and breakthroughs in defining and exercising its judicial power in constitutional cases, as well as beginning to tackle questions of interpretation other than involving rights protection. Due to the limitation of space, it is not possible to encompass every case decided by the CFA that touched upon the BL, so only key constitutional cases, selected on the basis of the authors' assessment of their importance in the evolutionary process of the BL jurisprudence as a whole, are outlined and discussed.

The foundational phase (1997–2002)

Although the handover took place on 1 July 1997, the first major cases on the BL were decided by the CFA only on 29 January 1999 as they worked their way up the hierarchy of courts. *Ng Ka Ling* v. *Director of Immigration*[3] and *Chan Kam Nga* v. *Director of Immigration*[4] raised two questions on the interpretation of the BL that were litigated immediately on the establishment of the HKSAR: the legality of the establishment of the Provisional Legislative Council (PLC) in 1997 and the right of abode in Hong Kong of children born in Mainland China of Hong Kong permanent residents.

The applicants in *Ng Ka Ling* and *Chan Kam Nga* were children born in Mainland China of Hong Kong permanent residents who claimed the

---

economic and social policies, and fundamental rights and freedoms: Johannes Chan and C. L. Lim (eds.), *Law of the Hong Kong Constitution* (Hong Kong: Sweet & Maxwell, 2011).
[3] *Ng Ka Ling* v. *Director of Immigration* (1999) 2 HKCFAR 4.
[4] *Chan Kam Nga* v. *Director of Immigration* (1999) 2 HKCFAR 82.

right of abode in Hong Kong pursuant to Article 24(2)(3) of the BL. They sought to uphold this right in a piece of 'test case' litigation funded by legal aid challenging the constitutionality of immigration legislation passed by the PLC.[5] They argued that the immigration legislation contravened the BL and therefore was invalid. They claimed as contraventions the enactment of the immigration legislation by the PLC, which was said to be not lawfully established; the qualifications in the immigration legislation of their permanent resident status under Article 24(2)(3), properly interpreted, thereby seeking to exclude some Mainland children from being entitled to the right of abode in Hong Kong; and the restriction of the enjoyment of the right of abode through the provision of a procedural framework for their migration to Hong Kong for settlement based upon their obtaining first in Mainland China a one-way exit permit.

The CFA affirmed in *Ng Ka Ling* the legality of the PLC, but in doing so, it sought to overrule the judgment of the Court of Appeal in *HKSAR* v. *Ma Wai Kwan David and Others*,[6] which rejected a similar challenge earlier in 1997 by holding that the HKSAR courts had no jurisdiction to overturn acts of the National People's Congress (NPC) or the Standing Committee of the NPC (NPCSC).[7] The CFA stated in *Ng Ka Ling* that the HKSAR courts had the jurisdiction 'to examine whether any legislative acts of the National People's Congress or its Standing Committee are consistent with the BL and to declare them to be invalid if found to be inconsistent'.[8] This immediately sparked a strong reaction in Mainland China,[9] which

---

[5] Immigration (Amendment) (No 2) Ordinance 1997 (122 of 1997) and the Immigration (Amendment) (No 3) Ordinance 1997 (124 of 1997).

[6] *HKSAR* v. *Ma Wai Kwan David and Others* [1997] HKLRD 761, [1997] 2 HKC 315 (CA). This case was the first case in which a court of the HKSAR heard and determined a matter relating to the BL since the establishment of the HKSAR.

[7] It was necessary to consider the question of the validity of acts of the NPCSC in the context of the validity of the establishment of the PLC because the PLC was established by the Preparatory Committee for the HKSAR, a body appointed by the NPCSC.

[8] *Ng Ka Ling*, 26.

[9] In a highly publicized seminar reported in the Hong Kong and Mainland Chinese media on 7 February 1999, four leading Chinese law professors, who were also former members of the Drafting Committee for the BL and the Preparatory Committee for the HKSAR, attacked the statement. They suggested that it had the effect of placing Hong Kong courts above the NPC, which is the supreme organ of state power under the Chinese Constitution, and of turning Hong Kong into an 'independent political entity.' After the HKSAR's Secretary for Justice Elsie Leung's visit to Beijing on 12 and 13 February 1999 to discuss the matter, it was reported that Chinese officials had criticized the statement as unconstitutional and called for its 'rectification'. See generally Johannes Chan, Hualing Fu, and Yash Ghai (eds.), *Hong Kong's Constitutional Debate: Conflicts over Interpretation* (Hong Kong: Hong Kong University Press, 2000) 53–9, 73–4.

led to the HKSAR government's surprise and unprecedented application to the CFA on 26 February 1999 to request the court to 'clarify' that part of its judgment. The CFA acceded to the request and stated that (1) the HKSAR courts' power to interpret the BL is derived from the NPCSC under Article 158 of the BL, (2) any interpretation made by the NPCSC under Article 158 would be binding on the HKSAR courts, and (3) the judgment of 29 January 1999 did not question the authority of the NPC and its Standing Committee 'to do any act which is in accordance with the provisions of the Basic Law and the procedure therein'.[10]

Article 158 of the BL is the provision whereby the NPCSC authorizes the HKSAR courts under Article 158(2) to interpret 'on their own, in adjudicating cases, the provisions of this law which are within the limits of the autonomy of the Region' and in Article 158(3) requires the CFA to seek an interpretation of 'provisions of this law concerning affairs which are the responsibility of the Central People's Government, or concerning the relationship between the Central Authorities and the Region' relevant to and affecting the judgment of cases before making the final, non-appealable judgments. In *Ng Ka Ling*, the questions of interpretation involved interpreting Articles 24(2)(3) and 22(4) of the BL, and submissions were made before the CFA on whether it was bound to refer Article 22(4) to the NPCSC for interpretation. The CFA decided not to refer that provision to the NPCSC – even though it seems to be covered by Article 158(3) – on the ground that Article 22(4) was not the 'predominant provision' to be interpreted in the case.[11] The CFA adopted this 'predominant provision' test to retain the jurisdiction to interpret on its own a provision within the limits of the HKSAR's autonomy even when the context of the interpretation of that provision included another provision that was within the rubric of a provision 'concerning affairs which are the responsibility of the Central People's Government, or concerning the relationship between the Central Authorities and the [HKSAR]'.

The CFA proceeded to determine the questions of interpretation and declared the impugned parts of the immigration legislation null and void and excised therefrom. The judicial declarations were short-lived as the Chief Executive of the HKSAR, opining that consequent to the CFA's judgment, Hong Kong would need to absorb a migrant population of 1.67 million from Mainland China in the coming decade, reported the matter to the Central People's Government with the view that 'the HKSAR

---

[10] *Ng Ka Ling* v. *Director of Immigration (No 2)* (1999) 2 HKCFAR 141.
[11] *Ng Ka Ling*, 33.

is no longer capable of resolving the problem on its own' and requested assistance by proposing to the NPCSC for interpretation of the provisions of the BL that the CFA interpreted in both *Ng Ka Ling* and *Chan Kam Nga*.[12] The Central People's Government acceded to the request, and upon its proposal, the NPCSC issued an interpretation of Articles 22(4) and 24(2)(3) of the BL on 26 June 1999 ('the NPCSC Interpretation of 26 June 1999'),[13] which superseded the CFA's interpretation of Article 22(4) in *Ng Ka Ling* and of Article 24(2)(3) in *Chan Kam Nga*. The NPCSC also pointed out in the text of the interpretation that the litigation did involve BL provisions concerning the responsibility of the Central People's Government or the relationship between the Central Authorities and the HKSAR that ought to have been referred by the CFA to the NPCSC for interpretation in accordance with Article 158(3).

The effect of the NPCSC Interpretation of 26 June 1999 was considered by the CFA in the same year in *Lau Kong Yung and Others* v. *Director of Immigration*.[14] In a unanimous judgment, the CFA held that the NPCSC Interpretation of 26 June 1999 was binding on the HKSAR courts, notwithstanding that it was issued not in pursuance of a request for interpretation made by the CFA under Article 158(3) of the BL. The CFA pointed out that the NPCSC's power to interpret the BL under Article 158(1) is a 'free-standing' one[15] in the sense that it can be exercised at any time even in the absence of a reference by the CFA. Any interpretation issued by the NPCSC, whether on its own initiative or upon a reference by the CFA, is binding on the Hong Kong courts. Applying the common law approach and English case law, the CFA held that the NPCSC Interpretation of 26 June 1999 had retrospective effect in the sense that it stated what the legal position had been since the BL came into effect.[16] Three

---

[12] *The Chief Executive's Report to the State Council Concerning Right of Abode* (20 May 1999), in *Hong Kong's Constitutional Debate*, note 9 above, 474–7. It should be noted that Article 158 of the BL does not expressly provide that the Chief Executive of the HKSAR or the HKSAR government may request the NPCSC to interpret the BL. Article 158(1) does stipulate that the power of interpretation of the BL 'shall be vested in' the NPCSC.

[13] *Interpretation by the Standing Committee of the National People's Congress of Articles 22(4) and 24(2)(3) of the Basic Law of the Hong Kong Special Administrative Region of the People's Republic of China* (L.N. 167 of 1999).

[14] *Lau Kong Yung* v. *Director of Immigration* (1999) 2 HKCFAR 300.   [15] *Ibid.*, 345.

[16] It should be noted, however, that the NPCSC Interpretation of 26 June 1999 states in the final paragraph that '*[as] from the promulgation of this Interpretation*, the courts of the Hong Kong Special Administrative Region, when referring to the relevant provisions of the Basic Law of the Hong Kong Special Administrative Region of the People's Republic of China, shall adhere to this Interpretation' (emphasis added).

years later in *Ng Siu Tung and Others* v. *Director of Immigration*,[17] the CFA was asked by thousands of applicants who were in Hong Kong at the material time of the *Ng Ka Ling* and *Chan Kam Nga* litigation but had not been selected as a litigant to join in those proceedings whether they had acquired an accrued right under the two judgments 'previously rendered' and so were unaffected by the NPCSC Interpretation of 26 June 1999. The CFA, by a majority (Bokhary PJ dissenting), rejected this contention, holding that the two judgments bound the parties to the litigation but not strangers to the litigation, and accordingly, only the position of those parties was not affected by the NPCSC Interpretation of 26 June 1999.

The CFA also acknowledged in *Lau Kong Yung* that because the preamble to the NPCSC interpretation of 26 June 1999 suggested that a reference to the NPCSC for interpretation should have been made by the CFA, it might be necessary for the CFA to revisit in future the test (e.g. the 'predominant provision' test used in *Ng Ka Ling*) for determining when a reference should be made to the NPCSC. The CFA was asked to do so in 2001 in *Director of Immigration* v. *Chong Fung Yuen*.[18] The HKSAR government argued that Article 24(2)(1) of the BL, which was involved in the adjudication of the case, should be referred to the NPCSC for interpretation because the 'implementation' of the provision would have a 'substantive effect' on the relationship between the Central Authorities and the HKSAR or on affairs which are the responsibility of the Central People's Government. The CFA held that in determining whether a reference to the NPCSC should be made, it should look at the character of the BL provision concerned rather than the factual determination of the effect of its implementation. On this basis, the CFA declined to refer Article 24(2)(1) to the NPCSC for interpretation. The CFA considered it unnecessary in this case to revisit the 'predominant provision' test for reference, which would only be relevant when more than one BL provision is at issue in a case; *Chong Fung Yuen* concerned the interpretation of only one BL provision.

The *Na Ka Ling* judgment still stands despite the parts that have been touched by the interpretation; it has remained the foundational judgment of the constitutional jurisdiction of the HKSAR courts and their approach

---

[17] *Ng Siu Tung* v. *Director of Immigration* (2002) 5 HKCFAR 1. Other holdings of the CFA in *Ng Siu Tung* are discussed in Chapter 16 (Chan) in this volume.

[18] *Director of Immigration* v. *Chong Fung Yuen* (2001) 4 HKCFAR 211. See, generally, *The Hong Kong Basic Law*, note 2 above, 830–41 and *Law of the Hong Kong Constitution*, note 2 above, 60–5, 476–8.

in interpreting the BL. Notwithstanding the controversy surrounding the asserted jurisdiction of the HKSAR courts to review acts of the NPC or its Standing Committee that led to the 'clarification', the CFA's statement in *Ng Ka Ling* regarding the constitutional jurisdiction of the HKSAR courts to review legislation of the HKSAR on the basis of the BL still stands as the first clear statement by Hong Kong's highest court of the HKSAR courts' power of constitutional review of legislation, which power has not been expressly provided for in the BL.[19] The CFA exercised this constitutional jurisdiction in *Ng Ka Ling* to strike down that part of the Immigration (Amendment) (No 2) Ordinance 1997 that denied the right of abode in the HKSAR to children born out of wedlock in Mainland China whose fathers were Hong Kong permanent residents[20] as being inconsistent with the BL as interpreted in the light of the International Covenant on Civil and Political Rights (ICCPR),[21] which is applicable to Hong Kong under Article 39 of the BL. This ruling, which upheld the principles of equality and the fundamental nature of the family, remains valid, and the HKSAR government subsequently introduced an amendment to the legislation recognizing the right of abode of such children.[22]

Decided in the same year as *Ng Ka Ling* and after the NPCSC Interpretation of 26 June 1999, the flag desecration case of *HKSAR* v. *Ng Kung Siu and Another*[23] turned out to be the case that built upon *Ng Ka Ling* to settle the question as to what extent Hong Kong's pre-1997 regime of rights protection has survived the handover, given the decision of the NPCSC on 23 February 1997 on treatment of the laws previously in force in Hong Kong in accordance with Article 160 of the BL ('NPCSC Decision of 23 February 1997').[24] This decision declared the non-adoption, *inter alia*, of three interpretive provisions in the Hong Kong Bill of Rights Ordinance (HKBORO),[25] which together with an amendment to the Letters Patent,

---

[19] The power of constitutional review of HKSAR legislation was also asserted by the Court of Appeal in *Ma Wai Kwan* in 1997. See *The Hong Kong Basic Law*, note 2 above, 65–7, 791–806 and *Law of the Hong Kong Constitution*, note 2 above, 473–4.

[20] The amendment to the Immigration Ordinance (Cap. 115) Sch. 1, para. 1(2)(b) under the Immigration (Amendment) (No 2) Ordinance 1997 (122 of 1997) s. 5.

[21] International Covenant on Civil and Political Rights (16 December 1966) 999 UNTS 171.

[22] See *Resolution of the Legislative Council under section 59A of the Immigration Ordinance (Cap. 115)* (16 July 1999) (L.N. 192 of 1999).

[23] *HKSAR* v. *Ng Kung Siu* (1999) 2 HKCFAR 442.

[24] For an English translation of the NPCSC Decision of 23 February 1997, see (1997) 27 *HKLJ* 419.

[25] Sections 2(3), 3, and 4 of the Hong Kong Bill of Rights Ordinance (Cap. 383). The Hong Kong Bill of Rights that is set out in the ordinance reproduces the provisions of the ICCPR applicable to Hong Kong.

formed the basis on which the courts of Hong Kong exercised the power of judicial review of Hong Kong legislation for conformity with the ICCPR to protect international human rights applied to Hong Kong. The CFA's unanimous judgment in *Ng Kung Siu* furnished the answer to doubts this decision raised as to the continued robustness of the rights protection regime in Hong Kong.

Ng Kung Siu was a final appeal by the prosecution from a judgment of the Court of Appeal that set aside convictions for the offences of desecration of the national flag[26] and of desecration of the regional flag[27] by two protesters on the ground that the relevant offence-creating provisions were inconsistent with Article 19 of the ICCPR and therefore contravened the BL.[28] The CFA chose to uphold those provisions as constitutional and valid after applying well-established principles in international human rights jurisprudence on whether a restriction to the freedom of expression can be justified on the ground that it is necessary for the protection of public order (*ordre public*) and proportionate to the legitimate objective sought to be achieved (and thus not excessive).[29] Although the CFA's actual decision in this case was to affirm the flag desecration laws, the approach and mode of reasoning it adopted had far-reaching positive implications for the regime of rights protection in post-1997 Hong Kong. This case demonstrated that the operative force of the Hong Kong Bill of Rights (HKBOR) and the ICCPR, as well as the Hong Kong courts' power to review the constitutionality of Hong Kong legislation on human rights grounds, and, if necessary, to strike down such legislation, had survived the non-adoption (by the NPCSC) of the relevant provisions in the HKBORO. Article 39 has been interpreted to mean that the relevant provisions of the ICCPR or the corresponding provisions of the HKBOR[30] have the same constitutional force as the BL itself, thus overriding laws

---

[26] This offence is prescribed under section 7 of the National Flag and National Emblem Ordinance (116 of 1997) and implements by reproduction Article 19 of the Law of the People's Republic of China on the National Flag and Article 13 of the Law of the People's Republic of China on the National Emblem, two national laws that has since 1 July 1997 been listed in Annex III of the BL as applicable to the HKSAR under Article 18 of the BL.

[27] This offence is prescribed under section 7 of the Regional Flag and Regional Emblem Ordinance (117 of 1997).

[28] *HKSAR* v. *Ng Kung Siu and Another* [1999] 1 HKLRD 783 (CA).

[29] *Ng Kung Siu* (CFA), 456–61. The proportionality test applicable was subsequently clarified in *Leung Kwok Hung* v. *HKSAR* (2005) 8 HKCFAR 229; see also Chapter 15 (Young) in this volume.

[30] Later Sir Anthony Mason NPJ made explicit that the provisions of the Hong Kong Bill of Rights are the embodiment of the ICCPR as applied to Hong Kong; see *Shum Kwok Sher* v. *HKSAR* (2002) 5 HKCFAR 381, [53].

that are inconsistent with these provisions; the HKBOR was reintegrated into and anchored onto the BL.[31]

The CFA enunciated in *Ng Ka Ling* the general approach to the interpretation of the BL, namely the 'purposive approach', plus giving a 'generous interpretation' to those provisions in the BL that provide constitutional guarantees for fundamental rights and freedoms.[32] In *Chong Fung Yuen*, however, the CFA had to state its approach in greater details in light of purported NPCSC guidance on how HKSAR courts should interpret the BL. The issue in this case was whether, as a matter of interpretation of Article 24(2)(1) of the BL, the right of abode in Hong Kong vests in children born in Hong Kong to Chinese parents who are not Hong Kong residents but who are Mainlanders visiting Hong Kong temporarily or illegally staying in Hong Kong. On a literal interpretation of Article 24(2)(1), such children are Hong Kong permanent residents and enjoy the right of abode. However, the Preparatory Committee for the HKSAR in 1996 had opined otherwise in an opinion on the implementation of Article 24. In the NPCSC Interpretation of 26 June 1999, there was a statement that the Preparatory Committee's 1996 opinion 'reflected' the 'legislative intent' behind Article 24(2) of the BL. The question for the CFA therefore was whether it should follow the views of the Preparatory Committee in this regard.

The CFA's unanimous judgment in *Chong Fung Yuen* was an emphatic statement that when HKSAR courts interpret the BL, they should adopt the common law approach to interpretation and do not need to resort to or otherwise take into account any principle or norm of the Mainland Chinese legal system. Applying the common law approach to interpretation in this case, the CFA held that there was only one possible answer to the legal question raised: the child concerned was entitled to the right of abode in Hong Kong. The CFA did not attach *any* weight to the passage in the NPCSC Interpretation of 26 June 1999, suggesting that the Preparatory Committee's 1996 opinion reflected the legislative intent behind Article 24 of the BL. The CFA stressed that the NPCSC Interpretation of

---

[31] See *The Hong Kong Basic Law*, note 2 above, 260–6 and *Law of the Hong Kong Constitution*, note 2 above, 440–58. The next constitutional case in which the CFA applied the Hong Kong Bill of Rights and the ICCPR by virtue of Article 39 of the BL was *Secretary for Justice and Others* v. *Chan Wah* (2000) 3 HKCFAR 459, which turned on the right to take part in the conduct of public affairs and is discussed in Chapter 15 (Young) in this volume.

[32] *Ng Ka Ling*, 28–9. Later Sir Anthony Mason NPJ made explicit that the same approach is to be adopted to the provisions of the Hong Kong Bill of Rights; see *Shum Kwok Sher*, note 30 above [58].

26 June 1999 was an interpretation only of Articles 22(4) and 24(2)(3). It was not an interpretation of Article 24(2)(1), which was the provision being interpreted in this case. In the absence of any binding interpretation by the NPCSC of Article 24(2)(1), the CFA was free to interpret it on its own, applying the common law approach to interpretation. Thus, in relation to provisions of the BL that the CFA considered as within the autonomy of the HKSAR, the CFA, by this judgment, asserted also its autonomy in interpreting them.[33]

In a very unusual manner not seen since the constitutional crisis of February 1999, the Central Authorities reacted publicly to the *Chong Fung Yuen* judgment.[34] On 21 July 2001, the morning immediately after the day

---

[33] The CFA also took this opportunity to expound on the sources it may refer to in interpreting the BL under the common law approach, distinguishing between intrinsic and extrinsic sources, and in respect to the latter, accepting the relevance of the Sino-British Joint Declaration 1984 (1399 UNTS 33, (1984) 23 ILM 1366) and drafting history but downplaying the usefulness of post-enactment/implementation materials. See *The Hong Kong Basic Law*, note 2 above, 823–8 and *Law of the Hong Kong Constitution*, note 2 above, 60–5, 476–8.

[34] The CFA also handed down on the same date its judgments in two other 'right of abode' cases: *Tam Nga Yin* v. *Director of Immigration* (2001) 4 HKCFAR 251 (concerning adopted children) and *Fateh Muhammad* v. *Commissioner of Registration* (2001) 4 HKCFAR 278 (concerning the requirement of continuous ordinary residence in Article 24(2)(4) of the BL). After *Ng Siu Tung* (above), there were much fewer 'right of abode' cases because the majority of the problems associated with the matter had been resolved, save in *Prem Singh* v. *Director of Immigration* (2003) 6 HKCFAR 26. In this case, the CFA invalidated the requirement in immigration legislation that a non-Chinese national must first be granted 'unconditional stay' status before he or she may become a HKSAR permanent resident, holding that this constituted an additional hurdle not provided for in the BL. However, the litigation in 2011 of foreign domestic helpers (FDHs) relying on Article 24(2)(4) to challenge the validity of immigration legislation deeming their presence in Hong Kong 'while employed as [domestic helpers] who [are] from outside Hong Kong' not to be ordinarily resident in Hong Kong for the purpose of the Immigration Ordinance (Cap. 115) generated a new spate of 'right of abode' cases; see *Vallejos Evangeline Banao* v. *Commissioner of Registration* [2011] 6 HKC 469, in which Lam J, applying *Chong Fung Yuen*, note 18 above, ruled that the relevant provision in the Immigration Ordinance (i.e. section 2(4)(a)(iv)) was inconsistent with Article 24(2)(4); it was held that this provision, 'by excluding the FDHs as a class from the benefit of Article 24(2)(4), derogates instead of clarifies the meaning of that Article' (at [175]). But on 28 March 2012, the decision was reversed by the Court of Appeal on the basis that Article 24(2)(4) of the BL implicitly authorised the legislature of the HKSAR to define, refine, elaborate or adapt the expression 'have ordinarily resided' therein by legislation, subject to review by the courts of the HKSAR by reference to an essential or core meaning of that expression: [2012] 2 HKC 185. On appeal to the CFA, the Department of Justice urged the CFA to make a reference to the NPCSC of Article 158(1) of the BL to enable the NPCSC to 'clarify' the binding effect (if any) of the statement in the NPCSC Interpretation of 26 June 1999 that the Preparatory Committee's 1996 opinion 'reflected' the 'legislative intent' behind

of the CFA's decision, a spokesman of the Legislative Affairs Commission of the NPCSC in a widely reported press statement pointed out that the CFA's decision in *Chong Fung Yuen* was 'not consistent' with the NPCSC's interpretation and 'expressed concern' about the matter. However, apart from this terse statement, no further action on the matter was taken by the Central Authorities. In particular, no interpretation on the issue was issued by the NPCSC.[35] Rather the HKSAR government introduced a legislative amendment in compliance with the CFA's *Chong Fung Yuen* judgment.[36]

all categories in Article 24(2) of the BL. In the end, the CFA disposed of the case on 25 March 2013 on the basis of the proper interpretation of Article 24(2)(4) of the BL, holding that the highly restrictive conditions under which FDHs were allowed to enter and reside in Hong Kong meant that the nature and quality of the residence of them as a class in Hong Kong were such that they were 'qualitatively so far-removed from what would traditionally be recognised as "ordinary residence" as to justify concluding that they do not, as a class, come within the meaning of "ordinarily resident" as used in Article 24(2)(4)'; and that given the court had reached the above conclusion, it was not necessary to seek an interpretation of Article 158(1) from the NPCSC through invoking the mechanism in Article 158(3); and that there was no basis for implying a general power in the CFA to seek an interpretation from the NPCSC otherwise than in accordance with Article 158(3): see unreported, FACV19, 20/2012.

[35] See Albert Chen, 'Another Case of Conflict Between the CFA and the NPC Standing Committee?' (2001) 31 *HKLJ* 179–187.

[36] See the *Resolution of the Legislative Council made under section 59A of the Immigration Ordinance (Cap 115)* (15 May 2002) (L.N. 84 of 2002). The *Chong Fung Yuen* case aroused public concerns about pregnant women from Mainland China coming to Hong Kong to give birth to their babies. The concerns proved to be justified; in the next few years after the CFA's decision, increasing numbers of pregnant women from Mainland China (some of whom were spouses of HKSAR permanent residents) visited Hong Kong to give birth, thus constituting a great strain on Hong Kong's hospitals. In 2007, administrative measures were adopted to reduce the influx, which promptly became the subject of an application for judicial review that was dismissed (*Fok Chun Wa* v. *Hospital Authority* (unreported, HCAL94/2007, 17 December 2008, CFI) and ultimately upheld on appeal to the CFA ([2012] 2 HKC 413), affirming the Court of Appeal (unreported, CACV30/2009, 10 May 2010). Further administrative measures involving the imposition of an annual quota for nonlocal pregnant women giving birth in Hong Kong was put in place for 2012. At the same time, there have been repeated calls for 'legal solutions' of this problem to be initiated by the HKSAR government, including the Chief Executive seeking assistance of the Central People's Government in proposing an interpretation by the NPCSC of Article 24(2)(1) and the Department of Justice urging the CFA to make a reference of provision(s) of the BL for interpretation by the NPCSC in the course of incidentally relevant litigation, all sought for the purpose of procuring an NPCSC interpretation to supersede the interpretation of the CFA of Article 24(2)(1) of the BL in *Chong Fung Yuen*. The Department of Justice was unsuccessful in urging the CFA in the *Vallejos* case, note 34 above, to make a reference to the NPCSC for an interpretation of the BL that would *also* be helpful in resolving this problem.

Given the NPCSC Interpretation of 26 June 1999 and the CFA's decision in *Lau Kong Yung*, the concern is valid that if the NPCSC were to exercise its overriding power to interpret the BL frequently, the autonomy and authority of the HKSAR courts in deciding cases on their own (at least in cases that touch upon an interpretation of the BL) would be severely hampered.[37] Fortunately, this has not happened. The NPCSC has practised self-restraint in exercising its power of interpretation of the BL. Since its interpretation of 1999, only three other interpretations have been issued – one in 2004 on the issue of political reform and democratization in Hong Kong and the Central Authorities' role in the process; one in 2005 on the issue of the term of office of the successor (to be elected in Hong Kong and appointed by the Central Authorities) to Chief Executive Tung Chee-hwa, who resigned in March 2005 before completing his second term of office of 2002 to 2007; and one in 2011 on the issues of the power of the Central People's Government to determine the rule or policy on foreign sovereign state immunity in the HKSAR, the obligation of the courts of the HKSAR to apply or give effect to such rule or policy, whether such determination by the Central People's Government on foreign sovereign state immunity falls within 'acts of state such as defence and foreign affairs' over which the courts of the HKSAR have no jurisdiction, and whether the common law on foreign sovereign state immunity previously in force in Hong Kong before the handover should be applied subject to such modifications, adaptations, limitations, or exceptions as were necessary to ensure that such common law is consistent with the rule or policy on state immunity as determined by the Central People's Government. The 2004 interpretation was issued on the NPCSC's own initiative in the absence of any litigation on the matter or any request for interpretation by the HKSAR government. The 2005 interpretation was issued at the request of the HKSAR government at a time when litigation was afoot to seek to resolve that issue judicially in Hong Kong; those applications for judicial review were either withdrawn or dismissed after the NPCSC issued the interpretation.[38] The 2011 interpretation was issued at the request of the CFA referring the above issues for interpretation by the NPCSC before final adjudication, pursuant to Article 158(3) of the BL.[39]

---

[37] See Sir Anthony Mason, 'The Rule of Law in the Shadow of the Giant: The Hong Kong Experience' (2011) 33 *Sydney Law Review* 623-644.

[38] *Re Ching Lok Suen Carl* (HCAL 35/2005) and *Chan Wai Yip Albert* v. *Secretary for Justice* (HCAL 36/2005).

[39] *Interpretation of Paragraph 1, Article 13 and Article 19 of the Basic Law of the Hong Kong Special Administrative Region of the People's Republic of China by the Standing Committee*

The consolidation phase (2002–2006)

The constitutional cases that the CFA heard and determined in the period between 2002 and 2006 were mainly concerned with questions arising in the course of criminal and administrative litigation and calling for remedies under the BL's rights protection regime. The CFA expounded and sharpened its operative elements and their underlying principles in the related judgments.

In *Shum Kwok Sher* v. *HKSAR*,[40] a civil servant convicted of the common law offence of misconduct in public office complained on appeal that this common law offence was too vague and ill defined and therefore could not be the basis for restricting his liberty. This claim implicated the principle of legal certainty and its position in the BL. Sir Anthony Mason NPJ, giving the principal judgment in the case, explained that in interpreting the provisions guaranteeing fundamental rights under Chapter III of the BL and the provisions of the HKBOR, the CFA 'may consider it appropriate to take account of the established principles of international jurisprudence as well as decisions of international and national courts and tribunals on like or substantially similar provisions in the ICCPR, other international instruments and national constitutions'.[41] Sir Anthony

---

of the National People's Congress (L.N. 136 of 2011). The CFA, by a majority of three to two (Chan and Ribeiro PJJ and Sir Anthony Mason NPJ; Bokhary PJ and Mortimer NPJ dissenting) made the judicial reference in *Democratic Republic of the Congo* v. *FG Hemisphere Associates LLC* (2011) 14 HKCFAR 95 with the majority judges setting out in their joint judgment of 8 June 2011 their reasoning for their provisional conclusions on the referred questions. The CFA handed down its judgment in final adjudication of the *Congo* case on 8 September 2011, with the majority judges holding that the interpretation of the NPCSC adopted on 26 August 2011 was consistent with their provisional conclusions and the dissenting judges accepting the binding force of the interpretation of the NPCSC so as to concur with the disposition of the case in final adjudication; see *Democratic Republic of the Congo & Others* v. *FG Hemisphere Associates LLC (No 2)* (2011) 14 HKCFAR 395. For scholarly discussion of the *Congo* case, see Albert Chen, Benny Tai, P. Y. Lo, Po-jen Yap, Tony Carty, Eric Cheung, and Simon Young, 'Focus: The Congo Case' (2011) 41 *HKLJ* 369–430. See also *Law of the Hong Kong Constitution*, note 2 above, 314–18.

40　*Shum Kwok Sher*, note 30 above.

41　*Shum Kwok Sher*, note 30 above, [59]. The CFA has taken account of international and national human rights jurisprudence widely and liberally, citing at times judgments of the German Bundesverfassungsgericht and the Inter-American Court of Human Rights in addition to the usual fare of 'precedents of other common law jurisdictions' (following the language of Article 84 of the BL), views of the United Nations Human Rights Committee, and the European Court of Human Rights. The CFA had paid attention to the most recent developments, adopting the reasoning of any new judgments when appropriate; see *Lam Siu Po* v. *Commissioner of Police* (2009) 12 HKCFAR 237, in which the CFA agreed that the rules defining a criminal offence must be accessible and precise enough to satisfy the requirement of legal certainty in order to be constitutional. The phrase 'prescribed by law' in Article 39(2) of the BL[42] imported such requirement of certainty, the contours of which are illustrated in the jurisprudence of the PC, the Supreme Court of Canada, and the European Court of Human Rights. Sir Anthony pointed out that the offence of misconduct in public office covers a wide range of misconduct, and what constitutes misconduct in a particular case will depend upon the nature of the relevant power or duty of the public official who is said to have abused his powers or position.[43] Having re-formulated or clarified the common law offence on the basis of authorities from England and South Australia, Sir Anthony held that the offence thus found was not so imprecise as to fail to satisfy the requirement of legal certainty.[44] The CFA applied the principle of legal certainty in later cases.[45]

In *Lau Cheong and Another* v. *HKSAR*,[46] questions were raised by two adult defendants convicted of murder on the validity of the rule in the law of murder that an accused is guilty of murder if it is proved that he did an act resulting in death with only the intent to cause grievously bodily harm and on the validity of the mandatory sentence of life imprisonment for adult murderers. The CFA dismissed these challenges. On the first issue, the CFA considered that the prohibition of arbitrary detention or imprisonment under Article 28 of the BL is a principle that may be

---

preferred the latest decision of the Grand Chamber of the European Court of Human Rights in *Eskelinen* v. *Finland* (2007) 45 EHRR 43 (which Ribeiro PJ described as 'more principled' in [90]) over the views of the United Nations Human Rights Committee in General Comment No. 32 (23 August 2007) (which Ribeiro PJ considered to be 'piecemeal and necessarily disjointed') on the question of whether the fair hearing protection of Article 10 of the Hong Kong Bill of Rights (based on Article 14 of the ICCPR and in similar terms to Article 6 of the European Convention on Human Rights) was engaged in police disciplinary proceedings.

42 Article 39(2) of the BL provides, *inter alia*, that the rights and freedoms enjoyed by Hong Kong residents shall not be restricted unless as prescribed by law. See *The Hong Kong Basic Law*, note 2 above, 263–6 and *Law of the Hong Kong Constitution*, note 2 above, 487–9.

43 *Shum Kwok Sher*, note 30 above, [69].   44 *Ibid.*, [88].

45 The cases include, in respect to the general discretionary powers for immigration control in *Gurung Kesh Bahadur* v. *Director of Immigration* (2002) 5 HKCFAR 480; in respect to binding over orders in *Lau Wai Wo* v. *HKSAR* (2003) 6 HKCFAR 624; in respect to noise abatement notices in *Noise Control Authority* v. *Step In Ltd* (2005) 8 HKCFAR 113; in respect to the conferring of discretion to regulate public assemblies and processions in *Leung Kwok Hung*, note 29 above; and in respect to the offence of conspiracy to defraud in *Mo Yuk Ping* v. *HKSAR* (2007) 10 HKCFAR 386. As to these cases, see Chapter 15 (Young) in this volume.

46 *Lau Cheong* v. *HKSAR* (2002) 5 HKCFAR 415.

applied to review whether a particular rule of substantive criminal law is constitutionally invalid because of being arbitrary.[47]

On the second issue, which these appellants argued by reference not only to the prohibition of arbitrary imprisonment under Article 28 but also the prohibition of cruel, inhuman, or degrading punishment under Article 3 of the HKBOR and the right to contest or review the sentence under Articles 5(4) and 11(4) of the HKBOR, the CFA mainly addressed the point put that the mandatory life sentence for murder was manifestly or grossly disproportionate and for this purpose embarked upon a thorough examination of the history of the sentence for murder in Hong Kong, including the mandatory death penalty that originally existed; the practice since 1973 of the Governor commuting every death sentence to imprisonment; the debate in the community in the early 1990s on how the law governing the sentence for murder should be reformed; the legislative amendment in 1993 to abolish the mandatory death penalty for murder and to replace it with a mandatory life sentence; the fact that murder is the only offence that attracts the mandatory life sentence, thus showing that the legislature intended to mark out murder as a uniquely serious offence; and the eventual enactment, in fulfilment of an assurance given by the government to legislators in 1993, of the Long-term Prison Sentences Review Ordinance[48] which put on a statutory basis the existing scheme for the review of life sentences.[49]

The CFA held that given this legal history of the punishment for murder in Hong Kong and given that 'the question of the appropriate punishment for what society regards as the most serious crime is a controversial matter of policy involving different views on the moral and social issues

---

[47] The CFA addressed the concept of arbitrariness by reference to the questions of whether 'such rule is arbitrary in that it is capricious or unreasoned or without reasonable cause' and whether 'the imprisonment which followed [can] be said to have been imposed without reference to an adequate determining principle'; see *Lau Cheong*, note 46 above, [48]. These questions were formulated by reference to cases interpreting provisions in the New Zealand Bill of Rights and the ICCPR protecting individuals from arbitrary arrest or detention. They set a standard different from and arguably more stringent than that under a proportionality analysis. The CFA later considered in *So Wai Lun* v. *HKSAR* (2006) 9 HKCFAR 530 the contention that the imposition of absolute criminal liability for unlawful sexual intercourse with a girl younger than the age of 16 years may be unconstitutional for arbitrariness when the imposition of such liability would have no deterrent effect. See further Chapter 17 (Young) in this volume.

[48] Cap. 524.

[49] Under the Long-term Prison Sentences Review Ordinance (Cap. 524), persons sentenced to life imprisonment have opportunities for the sentence to be converted to fixed-term imprisonment and then to be given conditional release or early release under supervision.

involved',[50] it should attach weight to the legislature's views on the matter. Taking on board the English approach of deferring in 'some circumstances' to the opinion of the legislature when administering the Human Rights Act 1998, the CFA counterweighed its duty, articulated in *Ng Ka Ling*, to hold legislation invalid in exercise of its constitutional jurisdiction in holding that 'when deciding constitutional issues, the context in which such issues arise may make it appropriate for the courts to give particular weight to the views and policies adopted by the legislature',[51] a step it had conspicuously taken earlier in *Ng Kung Siu* as part of the evaluation of the necessity of the flag desecration legislation.[52] The CFA held that '[the] context and circumstances of the present case render this approach relevant.... The legislature has to make a difficult and collective judgment taking into account the rights of individuals as well as the interests of society. It has to strike a balance bearing in mind the conditions and needs of the society it serves, including its culture and traditions and the need to maintain public confidence in the criminal justice system',[53] and it was this 'legislative judgment which this Court should respect'.[54]

In response to the appellants' argument that the mandatory life sentence for murder was arbitrary and manifestly disproportionate in that it did not distinguish between degrees of culpability ranging from a mercy killer to a person who commits multiple sadistic murders, the CFA pointed out that sentencing is not purely based upon moral culpability but that there exist 'also other legitimate sentencing objectives (such as protection of the public, preventing repetition of the offence, deterring others from committing like offences and societal denunciation of the offence)'.[55] The CFA concluded that the mandatory life sentence for murder did not represent a manifestly or grossly disproportionate sentence such as to be regarded as arbitrary or to constitute cruel, inhuman, or degrading punishment and also rejected the other grounds.

Chapter III of the BL enumerates fundamental rights, including those not directly provided for in the two international human rights

---

[50] *Lau Cheong*, note 46 above, [105].   [51] *Ibid.*, [102].
[52] *Ng Kung Siu*, note 23 above, 460.   [53] *Lau Cheong*, note 46 above, [105].
[54] *Ibid.*, [123]. Later in *So Wai Lun*, note 47 above, the CFA, when holding that legislation criminalizing unlawful sexual intercourse with a girl younger than the age of 16 years, although departing from identical treatment, was justified and not in violation of the constitutional guarantee of equality, stated that in reaching this conclusion 'we are not deferring to the legislature. Rather are we acknowledging the legislature's proper role' (at [28]).
[55] *Lau Cheong*, note 46 above, [121].

covenants[56] referred to in Article 39. One of those is the 'freedom to travel' of 'Hong Kong residents' provided in Article 31. The precise meaning of this provision was tested in *Gurung Kesh Bahadur* v. *Director of Immigration*[57] in which a non-permanent resident of Nepalese nationality who had been permitted to stay in Hong Kong for considerable periods challenged the decision of the immigration authorities at the airport to refuse him permission to stay upon his return from a trip, notwithstanding that his limit of stay granted to him before the trip would not have expired by the time of his return, as well as the consequent action to remove him from Hong Kong, citing Article 31.

The CFA found in his favour. The CFA pointed out that the BL makes it clear that all the rights guaranteed by Chapter III (with the exception of the right of abode and the right to vote and to stand for election, which are enjoyed only by permanent residents) are the rights of all Hong Kong residents, including both 'permanent residents' and 'non-permanent residents' as defined by the BL.[58] Among these rights is the freedom to travel in Article 31, which includes as its essential element the right of a non-permanent resident to re-enter Hong Kong after travelling during the unexpired permitted limit of stay.[59] Noting that these rights are provided only in the BL and not in the HKBOR and therefore Article 39(2), which spells out requirements that any purported restriction to rights recognized by the ICCPR as applied to Hong Kong must satisfy, does not apply, the CFA declared that:

> [I]t does not follow that rights found only in the BL can be restricted without limitation provided the restrictions are prescribed by law. The

---

[56] They are the ICCPR and the International Covenant on Economic, Social and Cultural Rights. It should be noted that Article 12 of the ICCPR provides, *inter alia*, that 'Everyone shall be free to leave any country, including his own', and 'No one shall be arbitrarily deprived of the right to enter his own country.'

[57] *Gurung Kesh Bahadur*, note 45 above.

[58] The CFA indicated that there were approximately 1 million non-permanent residents among the population of nearly 7 million in Hong Kong.

[59] *Gurung Kesh Bahadur*, note 45 above, [41]. The CFA held that the application of a legislative provision that any permission to stay granted to a person automatically expires upon the person's departure from Hong Kong to a non-permanent resident with an unexpired permitted limit of stay would be 'totally inconsistent with his rights and indeed would have the effect of abrogating the rights in question' (at [38]) and directed a construction of the relevant legislative provisions consistent with Article 31 of the BL. In the later case of *Director of Immigration* v. *Lau Fong* (2004) 7 HKCFAR 56, the CFA again highlighted this constitutional right of a non-permanent resident of reentry in requiring the immigration authorities to follow a procedure with higher requirements of procedural fairness if they propose to revoke a person's non-permanent resident status.

question of whether rights found only in the BL can be restricted and if so the test for judging permissible restrictions would depend on the nature and subject matter of the rights in issue. This would turn on the proper interpretation of the BL and is ultimately a matter for the courts.[60]

The CFA took the view that it cannot be the intention of the BL for Chapter III rights to be capable of being 'swept away' by legislation and therefore much less secure than the rights in the HKBOR. These rights being 'essential to Hong Kong's separate system', they are intended to be constitutionally entrenched with the courts having the duty to safeguard and protect them by adopting a generous approach to their interpretation.[61] Thus, the CFA did not accept arguments that the BL mandated a dual tracked rights protection regime, with Chapter III rights being the lesser cousins. Accordingly, the structural components of the post-1997 regime of rights protection in Hong Kong include not only Article 39, the ICCPR, and the HKBOR but also the Chapter III rights on an equal footing, and a challenge may be launched on the basis of any of these provisions, with the appropriate standard of review to be determined by the HKSAR courts.[62]

The CFA summed up its approach in constitutional adjudication involving a fundamental right in *Leung Kwok Hung and Others* v. *HKSAR*[63] in these terms:

> It is well established in our jurisprudence that the courts must give . . . a fundamental right a generous interpretation so as to give individuals its full measure. . . . On the other hand, restrictions on . . . a fundamental right

---

[60] *Gurung Kesh Bahadur*, note 45 above, [28]. For a commentary on this aspect of the case and its significance (particularly in terms of the standards for reviewing restrictions to rights provided for in the BL), see Simon Young, 'Restricting Basic Law Rights in Hong Kong' (2004) 34 *HKLJ* 109–32.

[61] *Gurung Kesh Bahadur*, note 45 above, [29].

[62] See *The Hong Kong Basic Law*, note 2 above, 147–50 and *Law of the Hong Kong Constitution*, note 2 above, 436–60. In *Official Receiver & Trustee in Bankruptcy of Chan Wing Hing and Another* v. *Chan Wing Hing and Another (Secretary for Justice, Intervener)* (2006) 9 HKCFAR 545, the CFA applied the proportionality test in determining whether the right to leave Hong Kong guaranteed both under Article 31 of the BL and Article 8(2) of the Hong Kong Bill of Rights was justifiably restricted even though the Official Receiver turned rights protection on its head in launching the constitutional litigation on a purely hypothetical basis so as to achieve the removal of an operationally burdensome legislative provision. In *Koo Sze Yiu* v. *Chief Executive of the HKSAR* (2006) 9 HKCFAR 441, the CFA held that an executive order issued by the Chief Executive of the HKSAR seeking to regulate covert surveillance by government agents did not constitute a set of 'legal procedures' for the purposes of Article 30 of the BL, which guarantees the freedom and privacy of communications of Hong Kong residents.

[63] *Leung Kwok Hung*, note 29 above. See also Chapter 15 (Young) in this volume.

must be narrowly interpreted. . . . Plainly, the burden is on the Government to justify any restriction. This approach to constitutional review involving fundamental rights, which has been adopted by the Court, is consistent with that followed in many jurisdictions. Needless to say, in a society governed by the rule of law, the courts must be vigilant in the protection of fundamental rights and must rigorously examine any restriction that may be placed on them.[64]

The CFA further formulated, in the context of the right of peaceful assembly,[65] the terms of the proportionality test to be used in Hong Kong to examine whether a restriction of a fundamental right is necessary: (1) the restriction must be rationally connected with one or more legitimate purposes and (2) the means used to impair the fundamental right must be no more than is necessary to accomplish the legitimate purpose in question.[66]

The last case to be discussed in this section concerns the CFA's power of final adjudication and the temporal reach of judicial power. In *A Solicitor* v. *Law Society of Hong Kong*,[67] the validity of a finality provision

---

[64] *Leung Kwok Hung*, note 29 above, [16].

[65] The *Leung Kwok Hung* (note 29 above) litigation involved a challenge in the course of a prosecution under the Public Order Ordinance (Cap. 245) of the validity of the scheme it lay down for notification and control of public processions. It followed from the case of *Yeung May Wan* v. *HKSAR* (2005) 8 HKCFAR 137 in which the CFA upheld the rights of Falun Gong followers to hold a peaceful assembly and to demonstrate as a value to be given due weight in determining whether their activities constituted unreasonable use of the pavement or lawful excuse for obstruction of a public place and the right of Hong Kong residents to use reasonable force to resist an unlawful arrest and detention. Both of these cases can be said to have infused constitutional law considerations in the politically charged subject of the policing of protests. The HKSAR government introduced, subsequent to the CFA judgment, legislative amendments to the Public Order Ordinance and the Societies Ordinance (Cap. 151) to conform the text of the ordinances with the terms of the judgment; see the Statute Law (Miscellaneous Provisions) Ordinance 2008 (10 of 2008), Pt. 2.

[66] *Leung Kwok Hung*, note 29 above, [36]. Later, in 2007, the CFA formulated a 'justification test' for operating the guarantee of equality before the law under Article 25 of the BL and Article 22 of the Hong Kong Bill of Rights in *Secretary for Justice* v. *Yau Yuk Lung* (2007) 10 HKCFAR 335, to require the governmental authority to demonstrate the following: (1) the differential treatment pursues a legitimate aim (i.e. a genuine need for such difference must be established but the mere act of legislative enactment does not so demonstrate), (2) the differential treatment must be rationally connected to the legitimate aim, and (3) the differential treatment must be no more than is necessary to accomplish the legitimate aim. See *The Hong Kong Basic Law*, note 2 above, 182–5, 199–200 and *Law of the Hong Kong Constitution*, note 2 above, 489–95.

[67] *A Solicitor* v. *Law Society of Hong Kong (Secretary for Justice, Intervener)* (2003) 6 HKCFAR 570.

relating to solicitors' disciplinary proceedings was challenged. The impugned provision was section 13 of the Legal Practitioners Ordinance,[68] which provided that the Court of Appeal's decisions on appeals against the decisions of the Solicitors Disciplinary Tribunal 'shall be final', thus precluding the possibility of a further appeal to the CFA. The Chief Justice, in delivering the CFA's judgment on the jurisdictional issue, held that the provision was invalid on two independent grounds. First, it did not form part of 'the laws previously in force in Hong Kong' that were preserved by Articles 8 and 18 of the BL. This was because under the Colonial Laws Validity Act 1865, which was applicable to colonial Hong Kong, any Hong Kong law that was repugnant to an Act of Parliament applicable to Hong Kong would be invalid; the impugned provision, in precluding appeals to the PC, was contrary to the Judicial Committee Acts 1833 and 1844 and the related Orders in Council. In this regard, the CFA rejected the argument of counsel for the Secretary of Justice (intervener in this case) that as long as a pre-1997 statutory provision had not been repealed and had not been declared by a court to be invalid before 1 July 1997, it would form part of the pre-1997 laws preserved by the BL.[69] Thus, the CFA's decision on this point had far-reaching implications for the identification of the sources of law and the role of the courts in that continuing process.[70]

Second, the Chief Justice held that the impugned provision needed to be subject to scrutiny under a proportionality test[71] insofar as it purported to impose restrictions on the CFA's 'power of final adjudication' under Article 82 of the BL. The Chief Justice concluded that '[the] total ban imposed by the finality provision where questions of this order of importance arise cannot, in my view, be said to be reasonably proportionate to any legitimate purpose which may underlie the finality provision'.[72]

---

[68] Cap. 159.

[69] A Solicitor, note 67 above, [19] (per Li CJ). For counsel's alternative argument, see [21].

[70] Whether the HKSAR may have such a role is a lingering question; see Po-jen Yap, 'Constitutional Review Under the Basic Law: The Rise, Retreat and Resurgence of Judicial Power in Hong Kong' (2007) 37 HKLJ 449–74 and further, Sir Anthony Mason NPJ's effort in dispelling it in HKSAR v. Lam Kwong Wai (2006) 9 HKCFAR 574, [59]. See also The Hong Kong Basic Law, note 2 above, 47, 854.

[71] According to [31] of Li CJ's judgment: 'The limitation imposed [on the CFA's power of final adjudication] must pursue a legitimate purpose and there must be reasonable proportionality between the limitation and the purpose sought to be achieved. These dual requirements will be referred to collectively as "the proportionality test"'.

[72] A Solicitor, note 67 above, [40]. The finality provision in the Legal Practitioner Ordinance was struck down. The HKSAR government introduced, subsequent to the CFA judgment,

The CFA's decision on this point is significant in duplicating the rights protection regime in the BL to entrench its guardianship of independent judicial power (including power of final adjudication) vested with the courts under the BL against statutory limitations, applying for this purpose the proportionality analysis.[73]

The innovation phase (2005–2009)

Although a few provisions of the BL that concern matters other than right of abode and human rights had been considered before,[74] it was in 2005 that the CFA turned its attention to a major theme of the BL other than its rights protection regime, namely the continuation of existing systems, policies, and rights for the purpose of maintaining the pre-1997 social order. One set of such provisions enacted for this purpose concerned the civil service and was contained in section 6 of Chapter IV of the BL. For example, Article 100 provides that public servants serving in the Hong Kong government before the establishment of the HKSAR 'may all remain in employment and retain their seniority with pay, allowances, benefits and conditions of service no less favourable than before'. The constitutional issue raised in *Secretary for Justice* v. *Lau Kwok Fai*[75] turned on the proper interpretation of this provision in the context of a constitutional challenge[76] to legislation passed by the Legislative Council (LegCo) in 2002[77] and 2004[78] to give legislative effect to two

---

legislative amendments to a number of ordinances containing similar finality provisions to remove such provisions from the text of the ordinance in light of the judgment; see the Statute Law (Miscellaneous Provisions) Ordinance 2005 (10 of 2005) Pt. 3, Div. 8 and the Statute Law (Miscellaneous Provisions) Ordinance 2008 (10 of 2008) Pt. 7.

[73] For commentary, see P. Y. Lo, 'Master of One's Own Court' (2004) 34 *HKLJ* 47–65.

[74] See *Re Yung Kwan Lee* (1999) 2 HKCFAR 245, CFA (on Article 153 of the BL concerning implementation of international agreements in Hong Kong). See also *Commissioner of Rating and Valuation* v. *Agrila Ltd* (2001) 4 HKCFAR 83, CFA (on Article 121 of the BL concerning the charging of government rent on the basis of rateable value of landed property).

[75] *Secretary for Justice* v. *Lau Kwok Fai* (2005) 8 HKCFAR 304.

[76] The constitutional challenge by way of application for judicial review was mounted by several civil servants for contravention of Article 100 of the BL, as well as other provisions, including Articles 103 and 160, and of the International Covenant on Economic, Social and Cultural Rights and International Labour Conventions, which continues to apply in Hong Kong under Article 39.

[77] The Public Officers Pay Adjustment Ordinance 2002 (Cap. 574), which gave legislative effect to a pay cut (ranging from 1.58 to 4.42 per cent) for Hong Kong's 180,000 civil servants.

[78] The Public Officers Pay Adjustment (2004/2005) Ordinance (Cap. 580), which provided that civil service pay would be further reduced by 3 per cent on 1 January 2004 and by

reductions of civil service salaries to cope with the severe budget deficits and to align public sector salaries with those in the private sector. What was at stake in the litigation was savings in the region of HK$10 billion for the HKSAR government and thus the government's budgetary position.

On 13 July 2005, the CFA unanimously upheld the pay cut law, over-ruling the Court of Appeal below,[79] and decided that it violated neither Article 100 nor Article 103 of the BL.[80] Sir Anthony Mason NPJ, writing for the CFA, stressed that just as before 1997, the colonial legislature had power to enact legislation to effect a pay cut for civil servants (even though it had never exercised this power), the BL did not prohibit the legislature of the HKSAR from enacting such legislation as long as the pay cut introduced by it did not reduce civil service salaries to a level below that applicable at the time of the handover in 1997 (thus making their pay 'less favourable than before'). Such legislation overrides the terms of the civil servants' contract of employment. Sir Anthony's judgment demonstrates the methodology for interpreting provisions of the BL purposively by reference to the theme of continuity; it is necessary for the interpreting court to find and consider the corresponding setting in the pre-1997 colonial governmental regime for its capabilities to be understood against the HKSAR measure said to be contravening a continuity guarantee under the BL. Resolving controversial issues of public affairs in accordance with the rule of law, the 'Hong Kong way' requires more often than not a long memory or tireless examination of archival materials.

The CFA again interpreted the BL in *Stock Exchange of Hong Kong* v. *New World Development Co Ltd and Others*.[81] The case concerned the right to representation by lawyers at a disciplinary hearing conducted by the Disciplinary Committee of the Stock Exchange of Hong Kong. It was argued that the directions of the Chairman of the Disciplinary Committee limiting the role of lawyers at its hearing infringed both Article 35 (regarding the right to lawyers for representation in the courts) of the BL and Article 10 (regarding the right to a fair hearing) of the HKBOR. The Court of Appeal interpreted Article 35, a provision in rights protecting

---

[79] another 3 per cent on 1 January 2005. These reductions did not, however, reduce civil servants' salaries below their salary levels on 30 June 1997. When the last reduction came into effect on 1 January 2005, civil service salaries (for existing civil servants) were reduced to the relevant levels of 30 June 1997.

[79] *Lau Kwok Fai* v. *Secretary for Justice* [2004] 3 HKLRD 570 (CA).

[80] Article 103 of the BL provides for the maintenance of the pre-1997 system of recruitment, employment, assessment, discipline, training, and management for the public service.

[81] *Stock Exchange of Hong Kong Ltd* v. *New World Development Co. Ltd and Others* (2006) 9 HKCFAR 234.

Chapter III of the BL, generously and found that the right to legal representation under the Article was both engaged and infringed.[82] Ribeiro PJ, writing the principal judgment for an unanimous CFA, reversed the Court of Appeal's decision and held that Article 35 was not engaged because as a matter of interpretation of the BL, the committee was not a 'court' within the meaning of the article.[83]

Ribeiro PJ's judgment on this point is significant in that it is one of the few occasions when the CFA interpreted a BL provision differently from a similar provision in the HKBOR and the ICCPR.[84] According to Ribeiro PJ, the question of interpretation in this case was to be answered by considering the other provisions in the BL where the word 'court' also appeared, the purposes of the BL that underlie the BL provisions containing the word 'court', and the context of Article 35 itself.[85] In BL provisions other than Article 35 where the word 'court' appears, the word refers to courts of law exercising judicial power and does not include disciplinary tribunals.[86] There are two dimensions identified in relation to Article 35; it confers constitutional rights that need not have anything to do with court proceedings and entrenches the individual's rights in relation to the 'courts'. The latter dimension 'is a crucial additional feature of the constitutional architecture of the BL in relation to the judicial system of the Region'.[87] Ribeiro PJ thus held that given the context and purpose of Article 35,[88] 'court' in this article bears the same meaning as in those provisions. It would seem then that the principle of interpreting generously

---

[82] *New World Development Co. Ltd and Others* v. *Stock Exchange of Hong Kong Ltd* [2005] 2 HKLRD 612 (CA).

[83] Ribeiro PJ thus overruled on this point the Court of Appeal decisions in *Ip Kay Lo* v. *Medical Council of Hong Kong* (No. 2) [2003] 3 HKC 579 and *Solicitor (302/02)* v. *Law Society of Hong Kong* [2006] 2 HKC 40 and made clear that none of the professional disciplinary bodies such as the Medical Council, the Solicitors Disciplinary Tribunal, or the Disciplinary Committee of the Stock Exchange of Hong Kong is a 'court' for the purpose of Article 35. See critique of this in Chapter 15 (Young) in this volume.

[84] Ribeiro PJ expressly rejected in [61] the following line of reasoning of the Court of Appeal below: 'Because Art. 14 of the ICCPR applies to both courts and tribunals, Art. 35 should also be interpreted to extend to courts and tribunals, since its interpretation should be consistent with the Region's international obligations.' See *The Hong Kong Basic Law*, note 2 above, 23–7, 233; *Law of the Hong Kong Constitution*, note 2 above, 299–302.

[85] *New World Development*, note 81 above, [38] to [44].

[86] *Ibid.*, [45].   [87] *Ibid.*, [48] to [50].

[88] Ribeiro PJ considered the purpose of the 'court'-related rights in Article 35 in these terms: 'Art. 35 ensures that the fundamental rights conferred by the Basic Law as well as the legal rights and obligations previously in force and carried through to apply in the HKSAR are enforceable by individuals and justiciable in the courts'. See also *A Solicitor*, note 67 above, [45] (per Bokhary PJ, commenting that Article 35 was 'an arterial right, being the avenue

constitutionally entrenched rights applies only *after* establishing what the essential right or freedom in question consists of.[89]

After disposing of the Article 35 issue, Ribeiro PJ turned to Article 10 of the HKBOR (Article 14 of the ICCPR), which provides, *inter alia*, for a fair hearing by a tribunal in the determination of any criminal charge or an individual's rights and obligations in a suit at law. It was held that in this regard, Article 10 adds nothing to the common law rules of procedural fairness.[90] As the present case involved a challenge to directions given by the chairman of the Disciplinary Committee rather than legislation, it could thus be decided on the basis of the common law,[91] and it was not necessary to determine whether the disciplinary proceedings in the present case involved a determination of 'rights and obligations in a suit at law'.[92] Later in 2009, the CFA decided that question in the affirmative in *Lam Siu Po*[93] and applied, in the context of the Article 10 analysis, common law principles of procedural fairness to reach the conclusion that the blanket exclusion of legal representation in subsidiary legislation governing police disciplinary proceedings was constitutionally invalid in denying the disciplinary tribunal a discretion in deciding whether legal representation is to be allowed in the particular case.

From 2006 onwards, the CFA further constructed its constitutional jurisdiction, making strides and breakthroughs along the way. The first of these cases was *Koo Sze Yiu and Another* v. *Chief Executive of the HKSAR*.[94] This case arose out of the critical scrutiny by district court judges of the legal basis for law enforcement agencies to conduct covert surveillance in Hong Kong in two criminal trials. The existing practice, it was pointed out, was probably a violation of Article 30 of the BL, which protects the

---

through which all . . . other fundamental rights and freedoms [of persons in Hong Kong] are enforced by an independent judiciary giving effective remedies in real life cases').

[89] *New World Development*, note 81 above, [51].

[90] *Ibid.*, [94]. It was also pointed out that even if the Disciplinary Committee of the Stock Exchange of Hong Kong were a court for the purpose of Article 35 of the BL, the question would still arise as to 'whether it may be proportionate to restrict legal representation in given circumstances – an inquiry which mirrors the inquiry that is undertaken at common law' (at [91]).

[91] According to the common law, what fairness requires depends on the circumstances; there is no absolute entitlement to full legal representation in disciplinary hearings. In the circumstances of the present case, the CFA considered that it was premature to assess whether the disciplinary proceedings would involve procedural unfairness and declined to intervene at the stage in light of procedural directions of the chairman of the Disciplinary Committee of the Stock Exchange of Hong Kong; see *ibid.*, [95] to [109], [124] to [131].

[92] *Ibid.*, [94].   [93] See note 41 above.

[94] *Koo Sze Yiu* v. *Chief Executive of the HKSAR*, note 62 above.

freedom and privacy of communication of Hong Kong residents and permits only interception of communications by governmental authorities done in accordance with 'legal procedures to meet the needs of public security or of investigation into criminal offences'. Also relevant was Article 17 of the ICCPR, which prohibits 'arbitrary or unlawful interference with . . . privacy, family, home or correspondence'. The Chief Executive's response was to promulgate in August 2005 the Law Enforcement (Covert Surveillance Procedure) Order (the 2005 Order).[95]

Claiming that they had probably been targets of covert surveillance and asserting their right as members of the public to mount a facial challenge, two political activists applied for judicial review of the existing regime authorizing interception of communications and covert surveillance. The Court of First Instance granted the application and held that both section 33 of the Telecommunications Ordinance[96] (which dealt with interception of telecommunications) and the 2005 Order were unconstitutional: the former created a power of interception of communications without adequate legal safeguards against its abuse, and the latter failed to comply with the procedural requirements of Article 30 of the BL[97] but declined, as the litigants requested, to declare that the impugned legislative provision and order were invalid and null and void and of no effect, which is what would normally be the case when a law is determined by the court to be unconstitutional. Instead, the Court of First Instance assumed an inherent power and acted to suspend the effectiveness of the declarations of invalidity for six months and held that the impugned legislative provision and order may still be regarded as temporarily valid during this six-month period, so as to give the HKSAR government time to introduce and enact corrective legislation and avoiding 'the probability of danger to Hong Kong residents, disorder by way of a threat to the rule of law and deprivation to Hong Kong residents generally' were the law enforcement agencies to lose the power to lawfully conduct interception of communications and covert surveillance in the meantime.[98] On appeal, the CFA affirmed the outcome but drew a distinction between granting a

---

[95] The Law Enforcement (Covert Surveillance Procedures) Order (Executive Order No 1 of 2005); see *Gazette of the Government of the Hong Kong Special Administrative Region* No 31/2005 (5 August 2005) E57. The Chief Executive's order was an executive order promulgated under Article 48(4) of the BL.

[96] Cap. 106.

[97] *Leung Kwok Hung* v. *Chief Executive of the Hong Kong Special Administrative Region* (unreported, 9 February 2006, HCAL 107/2005), CFI.

[98] *Ibid.*, [165].

declaration of temporary validity (for six months) with regard to the impugned laws and suspending (for six months) the declaration of invalidity of such laws, agreeing only to grant the latter remedy.[99] In the event, the corrective legislation[100] was enacted within the six-month 'grace period'.

Because the courts refrained from immediately invalidating interception of communications law and covert surveillance practice and agreed to give the HKSAR government and the LegCo six months to rectify the legal situation in *Koo Sze Yiu*, one might suppose that this case reflected an attitude of judicial restraint. But the better view is to note the strands of judicial activism in this case in entertaining the application for judicial review with little demonstration on the part of the applicants of both underlying decision-making and their own standing and in the innovative and unprecedented fashioning of the remedy the courts granted. *Koo Sze Yiu* must be regarded as a breakthrough in judicial creativity in Hong Kong to deal with novel situations brought about by BL litigation.

The CFA further developed the approach of refraining from invalidating legislative provisions found to be constitutionally suspect in *HKSAR v. Lam Kwong Wai and Another*[101] and *HKSAR v. Hung Chan Wa*.[102] In both cases, 'reverse onus' provisions in the existing criminal law were challenged as unconstitutional infringements of the presumption of innocence and the right to a fair trial under Article 87(2) of the BL and Articles 11(1) and 10 of the HKBOR. In *Lam Kwong Wai*, the impugned provision was related to the offence of possession of an imitation firearm, prescribing that the defendant would not be liable if he satisfied the magistrate that he was not in possession of the imitation firearm for a purpose dangerous to public peace or of committing an offence.[103] Sir Anthony Mason NPJ, writing the principal judgment of the CFA, held that the impugned provision imposed a persuasive burden[104] (and not an evidential burden[105]) on the defendant. Such a transfer of the persuasive

---

[99] For commentary, see P. Y. Lo, 'Levitating Unconstitutional Law' (2006) 36 *HKLJ* 433–442.

[100] The Interception of Communications and Surveillance Ordinance (Cap. 589).

[101] *HKSAR v. Lam Kwong Wai*, note 70 above.

[102] *HKSAR v. Hung Chan Wa* (2006) 9 HKCFAR 614.

[103] Section 20(3)(c) of the Firearms and Ammunition Ordinance (Cap. 238).

[104] A persuasive burden means that the defendant needs, in order to escape liability, to prove, on a balance of probabilities, the existence of certain facts relating to elements of the offence.

[105] An evidential burden means the defendant only needs to adduce or point to evidence to 'raise an issue' regarding the existence of certain facts relating to elements of the offence, whereupon it will be the prosecution's duty to prove beyond reasonable doubt the facts

burden was, on a proportionality analysis informed by the jurisprudence of the European Court of Human Rights and of the English courts applying the decisions of that court, not justified; an evidential burden would have been sufficient to achieve the legislative objective.[106]

That the impugned legislative provision was held to be disproportionate excited the CFA on whether it was possible to construe the relevant legislative language of 'if he satisfies the [court]' to impose only an evidential burden. Disagreeing with the Court of Appeal, Sir Anthony held that this could and, in the circumstances of the case, should be done and in his reasoning towards this conclusion considered two possible sources of power to construe legislation '[so] as to preserve its validity, even if the interpretation is one which would go beyond ordinary common law interpretation because it may involve the use of judicial techniques such as reading down, reading in and striking out'.[107] One possible source of power, on which Sir Anthony in the event found it unnecessary to reach a conclusive view, was said to be sections 3 and 4 of the HKBORO, which had been operational before 1997 and therefore, notwithstanding that they had not been adopted by the NPCSC as part of the laws of the HKSAR, their 'previous operation' was 'untouched' by the NPCSC decision of 23 February 1997, and they could still be relied on in determining what were 'the laws previously in force in Hong Kong' that were preserved by the Basic Law.[108] Rather, Sir Anthony answered the requisite question relying on the other proposed source of such power of remedial interpretation, the BL, which, by establishing the courts of the HKSAR and granting them judicial power, impliedly grants them all powers that are necessary to enable them to exercise their judicial power effectively,

---

corresponding to the relevant elements of the offence; see *Lam Kwong Wai*, note 70 above, [26].

[106] *Ibid.*, [54].

[107] *Ibid.*, [57]. The CFA had applied the judicial technique of severance in *Ng Ka Ling* and *Leung Kwok Hung* without asking questions over the source of judicial power for its application, although it must be noted that the conditions for applying severance are exact and so 're-moulding' of the legislative provision is arguably not involved in the exercise; see *Attorney General for Alberta* v. *Attorney General for Canada* [1947] AC 503, 518 (PC). The use of the other, more controversial, techniques in BL litigation was envisaged earlier, albeit without much elaboration; see Daniel Fung and Peter Wong, 'Constitutional Law and Litigation in the First Year of the Hong Kong SAR: Past Trends and Future Developments' (1998) 28 *HKLJ* 336–355.

[108] The HKSAR Government's argument opposing this view drew on the correctness of the CFA's judgment in *A Solicitor*, note 67 above, and in this connection, Sir Anthony Mason NPJ sought to affirm the correctness of that judgment in *Lam Kwong Wai*, note 70 above, [59].

including the power to grant such remedies as appropriate and to engage in remedial interpretation (going beyond common law principles of statutory interpretation) to preserve the validity of statutory provisions that are otherwise unconstitutional.

Thus, the HKSAR courts enjoy the same powers as those expressly granted by statutes to the courts of the United Kingdom and New Zealand to use judicial techniques such as severance, reading in, reading down, and striking out.[109] In explanation, Sir Anthony highlighted that courts armed with such power of remedial interpretation actually

> interfere less with the exercise of legislative power than they would if they could not engage in remedial interpretation. . . . Indeed, it can be safely assumed that the legislature intends its legislative provision to have a valid, even if reduced, operation than to have no operation at all, so long as the valid operation is not fundamentally or essentially different from what it enacted.[110]

Hung Chan Wa was concerned with whether sections 47(1) and 47(2) of the Dangerous Drugs Ordinance, which created legal presumptions also 'reversing' the burden of persuasion,[111] provisions relating to offences of the possession of dangerous drugs. Adopting again the same proportionality analysis, Sir Anthony Mason NPJ reached for the unanimous CFA the conclusion that it had not been demonstrated that less intrusive means, such as an evidential onus, had been considered and discarded. A

---

[109] *Lam Kwong Wai*, note 70 above, [67] to [79]. Sir Anthony Mason NPJ touched upon the implication to judicial power of the HKSAR courts assuming a power to make a remedial interpretation and was of the view that the exercise of such a power was not anathema to the adjudicative interpretation of judicial power while noting developments in England that have departed from this conception; see [75], [76]. The CFA had overreached this conception of judicial power (which finds support in the language of Article 84 of the BL ('shall adjudicate cases') in *Leung Kwok Hung*, note 29 above, because its holding of constitutional invalidity of certain provisions of the Public Order Ordinance did not affect the legality of the convictions of the appellants. See also *Chan Wing Hing*, note 62 above. The CFA later applied *Lam Kwong Wai* in *HKSAR* v. *Ng Po On* (2008) 11 HKCFAR 91, in which Ribeiro PJ repeated the judicial recognition of the limits of remedial interpretation in *Lam Kwong Wai* that the CFA 'cannot take up a curative measure which is so fundamentally at odds with the intent of the legislation in question that adoption of such a measure properly calls for legislative deliberation' (at [47]).

[110] *Lam Kwong Wai*, note 70 above, [77].

[111] Section 47(1) of the Dangerous Drugs Ordinance (Cap. 134) presumed, until the contrary was proved, that the defendant was in possession of a dangerous drug if it was proved that he had in his possession anything containing a dangerous drug or the keys of a container with a dangerous drug. Section 47(2) presumed, until the contrary was proved, that the defendant knew the nature of the drug if the defendant was proved or presumed to be in possession of a dangerous drug.

remedial interpretation was given based upon implied powers conferred upon the HKSAR courts by the BL.[112]

The Chief Justice, however, wrote a separate concurring judgment addressing the submission of the prosecution that the CFA should make an order limiting the retrospective effect of its judgment in the case to limit the categories of persons who may benefit from it, so as to avoid the reopening of a large number of previously decided dangerous drugs cases. The Chief Justice rejected both of the bases put forward in support. Article 160 of the BL does not provide that a determination of the unconstitutionality of an existing law would only have prospective effect; it should be interpreted to be applicable only to the legislative procedure. If it were interpreted to cover judicial procedure, it would be according to judgments determining pre-1997 laws to be in contravention of the BL 'a treatment that represents a radical departure from the established common law position'.[113] On the other hand, it was not necessary in the case to determine whether the judicial power of the HKSAR courts would in itself include the power to engage in 'prospective overruling' because even if the CFA had such a power, the circumstances of the case and the discretion of the courts in deciding whether to grant extensions of time to appeal in previously decided cases would not justify the exercise of such an extraordinary power by a court that must approach the matter with the greatest circumspection.[114]

The last pair of cases in this narrative section involved the CFA engaging in innovative moves for the peculiar circumstances in Hong Kong. In *Solicitor (24/07)* v. *Law Society of Hong Kong*,[115] the Chief Justice set out the rules of stare decisis of the HKSAR courts in the post-1997 legal order. From the perspective of the BL, the most significant point was that Articles 8 and 18 of the BL, which provide for the maintenance of 'laws previously in force in Hong Kong', was interpreted to mean that

---

[112] *Hung Chan Wa*, note 102 above, [84] to [86].

[113] *Ibid.*, [11]. The established common law position is that a judgment determining a legal question operates retrospectively as well as prospectively; see [10].

[114] *Ibid.*, [16] to [33]. See also Andrew Li, 'Reflections on the Retrospective and Prospective Effect of Constitutional Judgments' in Jessica Young and Rebecca Lee (eds.), *The Common Law Lecture Series 2010* (Hong Kong: Faculty of Law, The University of Hong Kong, 2011) 21–55; *The Hong Kong Basic Law*, note 2 above, 798–802; and *Law of the Hong Kong Constitution*, note 2 above, 303, 603–4.

[115] *Solicitor (24/07)* v. *Law Society of Hong Kong* (2008) 11 HKCFAR 117. See generally Oliver Jones, 'After the Decennial: The New Doctrine of Precedent in the Hong Kong Court of Appeal' in Michelle Cheng, Julienne Jen and Jessica Young (eds.), *Law Lectures for Practitioners 2009* (Hong Kong: Hong Kong Law Journal Ltd, 2010) 107–62.

PC decisions on appeal from Hong Kong, which were binding on Hong Kong courts before 1997, continue to be binding on the Court of Appeal and lower courts after 1997.[116] The CFA itself, however, is not bound by previous PC decisions on appeal from Hong Kong and the CFA's own previous decisions,[117] although the power to depart from such decisions 'will be exercised most sparingly'.[118] As regards the extent to which the Court of Appeal is bound by its own previous decisions in civil cases, the CFA substituted a new test for the existing rule in *Young* v. *Bristol Aeroplane*.[119] The new test is that 'it may depart from a previous decision where it is satisfied that it is plainly wrong'.[120]

In *Koon Wing Yee* v. *Insider Dealing Tribunal*,[121] the respondents (Koon and another) were found to be insider dealers by the Insider Dealing Tribunal. Several orders were made against them by the tribunal, including orders for disqualification as director of any listed company, disgorgement of their gain from insider dealing, and payment of a monetary penalty. The respondents argued that the procedural and evidential rules governing the proceedings of the tribunal provided for in the relevant legislation infringed their privilege against self-incrimination or the right to silence and applied to them the wrong standard of proof – the standard of proof in civil proceedings had been applied, but the correct one should have been the higher standard of proof in criminal proceedings, thus violating Articles 10 and 11 of the HKBOR (Article 14 of the ICCPR). The determination of these complaints required the CFA to rule whether the proceedings before the tribunal involved the determination of a 'criminal charge' within the meaning of the two articles of the HKBOR so that the protection of them became applicable. Relying on case law of the European Court of Human Rights and General Comments of the United Nations Human Rights Committee, the CFA, Sir Anthony Mason NPJ penning the principal judgment, held that the proceedings before the tribunal did involve the determination of a 'criminal charge' by reason of the monetary penalty imposed but not of the tribunal's power to disqualify insider

---

[116] *Solicitor (24/07)*, note 115 above, [8].   [117] *Ibid.*, [18].   [118] *Ibid.*, [20].

[119] [1944] KB 718 (Eng CA). This rule as enunciated by the English Court of Appeal been adopted in Hong Kong in *Ng Yuen-shiu* v. *Attorney General* [1981] HKLR 352 and had been upheld by the Court of Appeal after 1997: see *Solicitor (24/07)*, note 115 above, [22].

[120] *Solicitor (24/07)*, note 115 above, [45]. The Chief Justice also laid down guidelines on how the test should be applied in [46] to [50]. See further Chapter 13 (Mason) in this volume.

[121] *Koon Wing Yee* v. *Insider Dealing Tribunal* (2008) 11 HKCFAR 170.

dealers from directorship of listed companies.[122] Applying the guarantees in Articles 10 and 11 with their contents informed by the Human Rights Committee's General Comments, Sir Anthony held that not only the privilege against self-incrimination recognized in these articles had been violated but also the standard of proof mandated under these articles of beyond a reasonable doubt was not followed in the proceedings before the tribunal.

The fortunes of the respondent took an interesting, but not unanticipated,[123] turn when the CFA considered what remedy should be granted. Unlike the remedies granted by the Court of Appeal below (i.e. quashing the Insider Dealing Tribunal's findings and orders against the respondents), the remedy granted by the CFA here was quite different. Sir Anthony Mason NPJ breathed new vigour into section 6 of the HKBORO when holding that the CFA may apply its power to strike down a provision of the impugned ordinance that did not itself infringe the HKBOR (but that may be said to have caused the violation of the HKBOR in the present case) so as to render the impugned ordinance constitutional as far as possible and to give it 'as effective an operation as it can be given consistently with the Bill of Rights'.[124] Thus, it was decided that section 23(1)(c) of the Securities (Insider Dealing) Ordinance[125] should be struck down. This was the provision that provided for a monetary penalty as one of the sanctions that the Insider Dealing Tribunal could impose on those found to be insider dealers. The judicial deletion of this provision meant that no 'criminal charge' against the respondents would need to be recognized in the present case, and it would have been lawful to admit the evidence objected to by reason of a claim of the privilege against self-incrimination and to apply the civil standard of proof in determining whether the respondents were insider dealers to be sanctioned by disqualification as directors and orders for disgorgement of gains from insider dealing.[126]

---

[122] The CFA subsequently applied this part of the reasoning in *Koon Wing Yee* in *Wong Hon Sun* v. *HKSAR* (2009) 12 HKCFAR 877 (which concerned forfeiture proceedings).

[123] The first occasion when counsel for the Insider Dealing Tribunal sought an order of this unusual nature was near the conclusion of the proceedings before the Court of Appeal; see *Koon Wing Yee*, note 121 above, [119].

[124] *Ibid.*, [113].

[125] Cap. 395, which had in fact been repealed in 2008, with its effect saved by Part 1 of Schedule 10 of the Securities and Futures Ordinance (Cap. 571) in respect to insider dealing inquiries not yet concluded at the time of its repeal in 2002. Accordingly, this provision is of nil prospectivity.

[126] *Koon Wing Yee*, note 121 above, [115].

The remedy granted by the CFA in this case was most innovative, unconventional, and unusual; actually, no authorities were cited in the judgment in support of this approach. In justification for dismembering this long repealed ordinance, 'bearing in mind that a declaration of invalidity operates retrospectively to the date of enactment of the relevant provision', Sir Anthony offered the same kind of reasoning he used in *Lam Kwong Wai*: 'The history of the matter demonstrates that the legislature would have preferred to sacrifice the power to impose a penalty and retain the other provisions in [the Ordinance] rather than lose the investigatory powers which have resulted in violations of the [HKBOR]'.[127] The CFA considered that it was just and appropriate to do so,[128] bringing the proceedings to final adjudication.

Conclusion: observations and challenges

After the establishment of the HKSAR, the new CFA had to find a place for the HKSAR courts in the new constitutional order of 'one country, two systems' and lead them forward as they participated in the legal and constitutional development of the HKSAR. Delicate issues of Hong Kong's constitutional relationship with the Central Authorities in Beijing had to be addressed. At the same time, the CFA also had to tackle the common constitutional problem of how to safeguard human rights and fundamental freedoms and to work out the appropriate balance between individuals' rights and community interests. In the first period (1997–2002) discussed in this chapter, the CFA laid down the foundation of its BL jurisprudence as it responded to this dual challenge of defining Hong Kong's constitutional relationship with Beijing and of defending rights while delineating the limits of these rights.

In its first BL decisions in *Ng Ka Ling* and *Chan Kam Nga*, the CFA attempted to assert its supreme judicial authority as the constitutional guardian of the BL, of Hong Kong's autonomy, and of the rights of the people of Hong Kong. Unfortunately, the decisions backfired and led to the 'clarification' and the NPCSC interpretation of 26 June 1999. The CFA's 'clarification' may be understood not as a retreat from its original position as stated in *Ng Ka Ling* but as a statement to render

---

[127] *Ibid.*, [117]. In addition, it is submitted that the CFA would draw comfort from the Chief Justice's statement in *Hung Chun Wa* on the discretion of the courts in deciding whether to grant extensions of time to appeal in previously decided cases in not expecting a revival of past insider dealing cases.

[128] This is the criterion for invoking section 6 of the HKBORO.

explicit what was implicit in the original judgment that had not denied or challenged the NPCSC's power to interpret the BL. Although the NPCSC interpretation overruled the CFA's interpretation of Articles 22(4) and 24(2)(3) of the BL, it did not, in retrospect, adversely affect the authority of the Chief Justice's judgment in *Ng Ka Ling* as a definitive statement of the methodology that the HKSAR courts should adopt in interpreting the BL, including the 'purposive approach' of constitutional interpretation and giving a 'generous interpretation' to BL provisions on fundamental rights and freedoms. The approach to the interpretation of the BL was further elaborated by the CFA in *Chong Fung Yuen*.

After the CFA's decisions in *Lau Kong Yung* and *Chong Fung Yuen*, the first problems of the constitutional relationship between Beijing and the HKSAR courts and of the relationship between NPCSC and Hong Kong judicial interpretations of the BL were essentially resolved. The basic principles of this jurisprudence of 'one country, two systems' may be summarized in this way. The NPCSC has supreme authority over the interpretation of the BL, including BL provisions governing both affairs that are the responsibility of the Central People's Government and the relationship between the Central Authorities and the HKSAR as well as provisions pertaining to HKSAR's domestic affairs, which it can exercise not by trying cases but by the legislative process of passing an instrument titled an interpretation.[129] Whether, when, and how it will exercise this power is not governed by law but is a matter of the accretion of choices made in the course of events, which will eventually evolve into practices that supplement the written text of the BL.[130] Fresh choices can always be made.[131]

---

[129] For commentary on these 'ground rules', see P. Y. Lo, 'Rethinking Judicial Reference: Barricades at the Gateway' in Hualing Fu, Lison Harris, and Simon Young (eds.), *Interpreting Hong Kong's Basic Law: The Struggle for Coherence* (New York: Palgrave Macmillan, 2007) 157–81. See also *The Hong Kong Basic Law*, note 2 above, 817–41; *Law of the Hong Kong Constitution*, note 2 above, 50–6, 60–5, 314–18.

[130] Such practices may be called constitutional conventions. Jennings pointed out that 'constitutional conventions . . . provide the flesh which clothes the dry bones of the law; they make the legal constitution work'; see Ivor Jennings, *The Law and the Constitution*, 5th edn. (London: University of London Press, 1965) 81–2. For constitutional conventions in colonial Hong Kong, see Peter Wesley-Smith, *Constitutional and Administrative Law in Hong Kong* (Hong Kong: Longman Asia, 1994) 6–8. For constitutional conventions in post-1997 Hong Kong, see Shiu-hing Lo, 'The Emergence of Constitutional Conventions in the Hong Kong Special Administrative Region' (2005) 35 *HKLJ* 103–28.

[131] See *Congo*, note 39 above, and *Vallejos*, note 34 above.

In the absence of any relevant interpretation by the NPCSC, the HKSAR courts are free to interpret the BL on their own when adjudicating cases. In doing this, they adhere to the common law approach and do not take account of any Mainland Chinese approach. This is evident from choices made in a continuous flow of cases beginning in *Ng Ka Ling* to *Lau Kong Yung*, *Chong Fung Yuen*, and *Ng Siu Tung* and more recently to *Hung Chan Wa*.[132] Interpretations of the BL by the NPCSC operate in practice as if they were legislative amendments to the BL that nevertheless may have the same retrospective effect as interpretations of the law contained in decisions by a common law court (*Lau Kong Yung*). The NPCSC's interpretations have the same force as legislation after they are issued, but they cannot overturn any court judgment as far as the rights and interests of the parties to the litigation are concerned (*Ng Siu Tung*). And it is for the Hong Kong courts to interpret the meaning, scope, and effect of any NPCSC interpretation of the BL and to apply it to concrete cases, just as they interpret any relevant law that is in force in Hong Kong and apply it to concrete cases. Any guidance to interpreting the BL that may be implicit in the interpretations issued by the NPCSC so far would not affect how Hong Kong courts interpret the BL (*Chong Fung Yuen*). A judicial determination of the unconstitutionality of a pre-1997 law would have both retrospective and prospective effects (*Hung Chan Wa*).

Another aspect of the work of the CFA during the first period (1997–2002) was to lay down the foundation for the legal protection of individuals' rights and fundamental freedoms in the new constitutional order. This work began with *Ng Ka Ling* and was further elaborated in *Ng Kung Siu*, a case not on the right of abode under the BL but on the core human right of freedom of expression guaranteed simultaneously by the BL, the ICCPR, and the HKBOR. It then became very clear that Article 39's effect is to ensure that the relevant provisions of the ICCPR or the corresponding provisions of the HKBOR have the same constitutional force as the BL itself and can be, in addition to other BL provisions, the basis of judicial review of the constitutionality of legislation and executive acts. In other words, the pre-1997 regime of judicial review on the basis on the ICCPR and the HKBOR has survived the non-adoption by the NPCSC in 1997 of the three interpretative provisions in the HKBORO.

The second period (2002–2006) discussed in this chapter was characterized by its consolidation of the regime of rights protection. Whereas in

---

[132] See also *Vallejos*, note 34 above. See also *The Hong Kong Basic Law*, note 2 above, 823–8; *Law of the Hong Kong Constitution*, note 2 above, 60–5, 476–8.

the first period, 'right of abode' cases seemed to dominate the BL jurisprudence of the CFA, in this second period, the CFA decided cases on several other rights, such as the freedom of the person (i.e. the certainty and nonarbitrariness of the criminal law) (*Shum Kwok Sher* and *Lau Cheong*), the freedom to travel (*Gurung Kesh Bahadur* and *Lau Fong*), and the freedom of assembly and demonstrations (*Yeung May Wan* and *Leung Kwok Hung*). In particular, the cases on the freedom to travel represented a significant development of the CFA's rights jurisprudence because this right is only expressly provided for in the BL and not in the ICCPR and is conferred on both permanent and non-permanent residents of the HKSAR. *Lau Cheong* involved the CFA experimenting with the doctrine of judicial deference, giving due weight in some circumstances to legislative decision-making.[133] The case of *A Solicitor* (2003) is singularly significant in that the CFA asserted its competence to review the constitutionality of legislative restrictions on its own jurisdiction to hear appeals by applying the proportionality analysis. In this case, the CFA also addressed the question of what exactly are the 'laws previously in force in Hong Kong' preserved by the BL upon the establishment of the HKSAR by following the interplay of colonial laws.

The third period (2006–2009) was characterized by the theme of 'further innovations and breakthroughs' or simply the words 'doing something else'. In *Lau Kwok Fai* and *New World Development*, the CFA was concerned with the theme of continuity and the constitutional architecture for the independent judicial power respectively in the interpretation of the BL, when the substantive cases were about civil service salaries reduction and right of legal representation in the courts. The approach to constitutional interpretation involved in these contexts had little connection with international and comparative human rights jurisprudence but was concerned much more with the drafting context and history of the BL,[134] as well as an introspective working out of the scheme, structure and underlying aims of the BL. In the foreseeable future, judicial and legal thinking may have to be better deployed along these fronts in light of

---

[133] See *The Hong Kong Basic Law*, note 2 above, 150–8 and *Law of the Hong Kong Constitution*, note 2 above, 495–9.

[134] For a study of admissibility and application of drafting history in the interpretation of the BL, see Simon Young, 'Legislative History, Original Intent, and the Interpretation of the Basic Law' in Hualing Fu, Lison Harris, and Simon Young (eds.), *Interpreting Hong Kong's Basic Law: The Struggle for Coherence* (New York: Palgrave Macmillan, 2007) 15–32.

the rising incidence of cases on the separation of powers,[135] the political provisions of the BL,[136] and the social and economic policy provisions of the BL.[137]

Remedial innovations and breakthroughs in the third period began with the case of *Koo Sze Yiu*, in which the CFA, after determining the impugned laws to be unconstitutional, decided to suspend for six months the declaration of invalidity so as to allow time for the HKSAR government and the LegCo to put in place a new legislative scheme for interception of communications and covert surveillance by law enforcement agencies. The *Koo Sze Yiu* decision was followed by the 'reverse onus' cases of *Lam Kwong Wai* and *Hung Chan Wa*; in both, the CFA adopted the approach of remedial interpretation in reading infringing 'persuasive burden'

---

[135] See *Luk Ka Cheung* v. *Market Misconduct Tribunal* [2009] 1 HKLRD 114 (CFI) (on whether the Market Misconduct Tribunal usurped the independent judicial power vested with the HKSAR courts). See also *The Hong Kong Basic Law*, note 2 above, 23–7, 286–7 and *Law of the Hong Kong Constitution*, note 2 above, 299–302.

[136] See *Leung Kwok Hung* v. *Clerk to the Legislative Council* (unreported, 6 October 2004, HCAL 112/2004), CFI (on the form of oath of office of a member of the Legislative Council); *Leung Kwok Hung* v. *President of the Legislative Council* [2008] 2 HKLRD 18 (CA) (on the validity of the Rules of Procedure of the Legislative Council restricting amendments with charging effect); *Cheng Kar Shun* v. *The Honourable Li Fung Ying* [2009] 4 HKC 204 (CFI) (on the power of Legislative Council select committees to summon witnesses and the application of the doctrine of parliamentary privilege); *Chan Yu Nam* v. *Secretary for Justice* [2010] 1 HKC 493, CFI (affirmed on appeal in *Chan Yu Nam* v. *Secretary for Justice* [2012] 3 HKC 38) (on the validity of corporate voting in functional constituency elections to return members of the Legislative Council); *Cheung Tak Wing* v. *Legislative Council* (unreported, 26 May 2010, CACV 61/2010), CA (on the validity of motions tabled for the censure of a member of the Legislative Council); and *Leung Kwok Hung v President of the Legislative Council of the Hong Kong Special Administrative Region* [2012] 3 HKLRD 470, CFI (affirmed on appeal in *Leung Kwok Hung* v. *President of the Legislative Council of the Hong Kong Special Administrative Region* (2013) 2 HKC 580, CA) (on the power of the President of the Legislative Council to end the debate on committee stage amendments to a Bill and thus a filibuster exercise against the Bill, in exercise of a power under the Rules of Procedure of the Legislative Council of the Hong Kong Special Administrative Region). See also *The Hong Kong Basic Law*, note 2 above, 273–553; *Law of the Hong Kong Constitution*, note 2 above, 181–318.

[137] See *Fok Chun Wa*, note 36 above (on the social welfare system); *The Catholic Diocese of Hong Kong* v. *Secretary for Justice* (unreported, 3 February 2010, CACV 18/2007 (CA); [2012] 1 HKC 301 (CFA)) (on the educational system and the rights of religious organizations); *Kong Yunming* v. *Director of Social Welfare* [2009] 4 HKLRD 382 (CFI), affirmed on appeal in [2012] 4 HKC 180 (CA) (on the social welfare system); and *Li Yiu Kee* v. *Chinese University of Hong Kong* (unreported, 23 July 2010, CACV 93/2009), CA (on the educational system). See *The Hong Kong Basic Law*, note 2 above, 555–693, 695–745 and *Law of the Hong Kong Constitution*, note 2 above, 321–422.

provisions as imposing on the defendants 'evidential burdens' only. In *Koon Wing Yee*, the CFA went even further and struck out a statutory provision that on its own did not infringe any constitutional right but the excision of which would avoid the problem of unconstitutionality and enable the statute to be given as effective an operation as possible. Although the CFA justified these remedies, suggesting that the legislature would have chosen to have a piece of operational legislation, these cases broadened the scope of remedies that the HKSAR courts may grant in respect of laws determined to be unconstitutional, revealed a deep well of judicial power implied in the BL, and blurred the conceptual divide between interpretation and legislation.[138]

Generally speaking, the development of BL jurisprudence by the CFA in the period from 1997 to 2009 may be understood as a learning experience in the course of adaptation to the new environment of the post-1997 constitutional order that nevertheless is closely linked to and maintains a high degree of continuity with the previous order under colonial rule. The learning curve was steep; the CFA had to work out the terms of accommodation to the new environment without jeopardizing its mission of safeguarding the judicial autonomy – and common law-based legal system of the HKSAR. By 2002, the place of NPCSC interpretations of the BL in the new constitutional order had been defined. The power and basis of judicial review of laws and governmental actions in the HKSAR had been clarified. As more constitutional cases reached the CFA, and as it acquired more experience, its analysis became more sophisticated and its reasoning more refined and more extensive use was made of international and comparative jurisprudence. New remedial techniques were developed. The creation of these remedies and the related self-reflection on the nature and scope of judicial power in the HKSAR were signs that the young BL jurisprudence of the CFA was approaching maturity, knowing that its duty to enforce the BL would have to be tempered by discretion in the choice of remedies, exercised with a keen understanding of the consequences.

Yet there exist inherent limits on the development of the BL jurisprudence of the CFA. Unlike the legislature, it is not possible for the CFA to engage in systematic and comprehensive development of the law. What the CFA can do depends on the accidents of litigation. If no case raising a

---

[138] Cf *R v. Momcilovic* [2010] VSCA 50, (2010) 25 VR 436 (Victorian Supreme Court, Court of Appeal, 17 March 2010); *Momcilovic v. R & Others* (2011) 245 CLR 1 (High Court of Australia, 8 September 2011) and Chapter 22 (Lo) in this volume.

particular constitutional issue is litigated before the courts, the CFA will not have the chance to pronounce upon it. Even if such a case does come before the courts, the CFA will not have the chance to pronounce upon it unless it is appealed all the way up. There thus remains many provisions of the BL that have yet to be interpreted by the CFA – the authoritative interpreter of the BL in the HKSAR[139] – including, for example, the economic provisions of the BL in Chapter V; the protection of private property and the right to compensation in real value for lawful deprivation of property under Articles 6, 7, and 105 of the BL;[140] the horizontal effect (if any) of the BL;[141] and the modalities for making a judicial reference under Article 158 of the BL.[142]

---

[139] Article 158(2) of the BL provides that the NPCSC authorizes the HKSAR courts to interpret on their own, in adjudicating cases, the provisions of the BL that are within the limits of the autonomy of the HKSAR. Article 158(3) of the BL provides that, subject to the requirement on the part of the CFA to make a reference of excluded provisions to the NPCSC for interpretation before final adjudication, the HKSAR courts may also interpret other provisions of the BL in adjudicating cases. Pursuant to *Lau Kong Yung* (note 14 above), an interpretation of the NPCSC under Article 158 of the BL is binding on the HKSAR courts irrespective of whether it is issued upon a reference by the CFA.

[140] Although the CFA has adjudicated a large number of cases on land resumption, town planning, and adverse possession, it has so far not given a definitive statement on the effect of Articles 6, 7, and 105 on the existing land management system (i.e. the private landlord model) of the HKSAR government and over restrictions to developments imposed by town planning, building, transport, and land management authorities; see, for examples, *Secretary for Justice* v. *To Kan Chi* (2000) 3 HKCFAR 481; *Director of Lands* v. *Yin Shuen Enterprises Ltd* (2003) 6 HKCFAR 1; *Chan Tin Shi* v. *Li Tin Sung and Others* (2006) 9 HKCFAR 29; *Fine Tower Associates Ltd* v. *Town Planning Board* (unreported, 8 September 2008, FAMV 20/2008); and *Rank Profit Industries Ltd* v. *Director of Lands* (unreported, 25 June 2009, FAMV 7/2009). See *The Hong Kong Basic Law*, note 2 above, 40–6, 561–7 and *Law of the Hong Kong Constitution*, note 2 above, 359–98.

[141] In *Chan Wah*, note 31 above, and *Leung Lai Fong* v. *Ho Sin Ying* (2009) 12 HKCFAR 581, the CFA addressed only the question of interpretation of Article 39 of the BL to hold that provisions of the ICCPR, to be applicable in Hong Kong, must be made to be so through the laws of Hong Kong, with the effect that the enactment of section 7 of the HKBORO provides that the law has expressly and unequivocally stated that the ICCPR binds only the HKSAR government and statutory bodies. See *The Hong Kong Basic Law*, note 2 above 260–2 and *Law of the Hong Kong Constitution*, note 2 above, 480–3.

[142] This will arise where the final adjudication before the CFA turns solely, partly, or predominantly on interpreting a provision of the BL concerning affairs that are the responsibility of the Central People's Government or concerning the relationship between the Central Authorities and the HKSAR; see again, P. Y. Lo, 'Rethinking Judicial Reference', note 129 above. The majority judges of the CFA proposed a modality in their joint provisional judgment in *Congo*, note 39 above, which turned out to be different from the modality actually used; see P. Y. Lo, 'The Gateway Opens Wide' (2011) 41 *HKLJ* 385–92.

In the final analysis, the BL jurisprudence of the CFA as recounted in this chapter is thus a product of the contingent history of litigation in the HKSAR. The CFA could have done more or less or done it differently if more or fewer or different cases came before it. We can only look at what it has actually done, and in the authors' necessarily subjective opinion, the work it has done is good work. It has served us well as the custodian of the constitution of the HKSAR. It deserves our salute. And given the nature of the challenges inherent in the enterprise of 'one country, two systems', it deserves our understanding were it to encounter stormy waters again under the captaincy of the new Chief Justice.

15

Human rights

SIMON N. M. YOUNG

Introduction

The human rights cases comprised only 17 per cent of the Court of Final Appeal (CFA) judgments but probably attracted the greatest attention in the local community. In the years following the 1989 violence in Tiananmen Square, there was extreme concern with the protection of rights and freedoms in Hong Kong after China resumed sovereignty in 1997. People watched closely to see if they could rely upon the courts to safeguard them from rights encroachments by the Hong Kong and Mainland governments. The CFA's first rights judgment in 1999 sent the inspiring message that rights were to be interpreted generously and purposively and courts were duty bound to strike down unconstitutional laws and actions.[1] However, the Standing Committee of the National People's Congress (NPCSC)'s reversal of part of that judgment in the same year sank public confidence and gave rise to a crisis over the future of rule of law in Hong Kong.[2] Fortunately, it was not until 2010 that the NPCSC would come to reinterpret Hong Kong's constitution again in a non–human rights case,[3] and in the interval the CFA by and large restored public confidence in the courts' independence and ability to protect human rights. This chapter analyses how that was done.

The human rights judgments can be analysed for both their jurisprudential importance and what they impart about decision-making and judgment writing in the CFA. The chapter begins with a study of the

---

[1] *Ng Ka Ling* v. *Director of Immigration* (1999) 2 HKCFAR 4, 25–8.
[2] The Interpretation by the Standing Committee of the National People's Congress of Articles 22(4) and 24(2)(3) of the Basic Law of the Hong Kong Special Administrative Region of the People's Republic of China, adopted by the Standing Committee of the Ninth National People's Congress at its Tenth Session on 26 June 1999 ('1999 Interpretation').
[3] See *FG Hemisphere Associates LLC* v. *Democratic Republic of the Congo* [2011] 4 HKC 151 and [2011] 5 HKC 395 (CFA) and commentary in (2011) 41(2) *HKLJ*.

court's decision-making and identifies characteristics in the rights judgments as a whole. This is followed by a critical review of decisions in different areas of human rights. Rights arguments most commonly arose in migration and criminal law cases and also found their way into disputes between private parties. The chapter concludes with a summary of the approach of the CFA to rights cases in its first 13 years and thereafter.

Decision-making

A quantitative study of the jurisprudence reveals a number of important characteristics of the court and its approach to decision making.[4] The CFA decided 55 human rights cases during the tenure of Li CJ. The court spent a relatively large proportion of its time hearing and writing judgments in these cases (25 per cent, respectively). About 45 per cent of the cases related to criminal law, 40 per cent were administrative law cases, and the remaining cases involved litigation between private parties. Twenty per cent of all cases related to immigration and asylum law. These figures indicate the special attention the court paid to rights cases as it developed a foundational body of case law that was generally protective of individual rights.

Rights and claimants

Although a large number of different rights and freedoms were considered, four rights were given relatively more attention: right of abode, presumption of innocence, arbitrary detention and imprisonment (including review for legal certainty), and right to a fair hearing. In one case, consideration was given to the right to adequate housing under the International Covenant on Economic, Social and Cultural Rights (ICESCR).[5]

Rights claimants had diverse backgrounds. Criminal defendants and immigration applicants together made up more than half of the claimants. Corporate and company director litigants were behind 10 cases, political activists were involved in four, medical and legal professionals also brought four, and four cases involved serving or former civil servants.

---

[4]   This updates the earlier analysis published in Simon N. M. Young, 'Constitutional Rights in Hong Kong's Court of Final Appeal' (2011) 27 *Chinese (Taiwan) Yearbook of International Law and Affairs* 67.

[5]   See *Ho Choi Wan* v. *Hong Kong Housing Authority* (2005) 8 HKCFAR 628, [65]–[68].

Just under half (47 per cent) of all rights claimants were legally aided. In one unusual case, a government entity brought a successful human rights challenge to legislation.[6]

International influence

A significant degree of international influence went into the rights jurisprudence. It came in three ways. First there was the overseas non-permanent judge (NPJ) sitting on every rights case. Of all the NPJs, Sir Anthony Mason had the most significant impact. He sat on 64 per cent of all rights case and authored (or co-authored) the majority opinion in 37 per cent of those cases. The other overseas NPJs, including Lord Millett, Lord Scott, and Lord Woolf, sat on fewer than 10 per cent of the rights cases and contributed in total no more than 13 per cent of all the majority judgments.[7] Overall, the overseas NPJs contributed 36 per cent of all the majority decisions. By contrast, local NPJs had very little involvement in the rights cases.

Second, there is the international influence of counsel. About 31 per cent of all rights cases had at least one party represented by an English Queen's Counsel (QC), who was admitted to practice on an ad hoc basis. Eighty-four per cent of all rights cases had a local Senior Counsel (SC) leading junior counsel for at least one party. Most of these SCs received their legal education outside of Hong Kong and may have practiced law in jurisdictions such as the United Kingdom, Australia, New Zealand, Canada, and Zimbabwe.

Finally, international influence is evident in the citation of authorities in judgments. The CFA has been quite receptive to international and comparative law influences. Although Hong Kong and UK authorities are still cited most frequently, about a quarter of all citations were to non-Hong Kong and non-UK authorities. Similarly, around 21 per cent of the citations to legislative authorities were to non-Hong Kong and non-UK authorities. Secondary literature was cited much less frequently; on average, a single item of secondary literature was cited for every nine cases cited.

---

[6] See *The Official Receiver and Trustee in Bankruptcy of Chan Wing Hing* v. *Chan Wing Hing* (2006) 9 HKCFAR 545.

[7] Sir Anthony Mason NPJ wrote (or contributed to) 13 majority opinions, Lord Scott NPJ two, Sir Gerard Brennan NPJ two, Lord Millett NPJ two, and Lord Nicholls NPJ one. Lord Hoffmann NPJ wrote only a separate concurring judgment in one case.

Judges and their decisions

Li CJ demonstrated leadership in the development of the rights jurisprudence. He presided over 82 per cent of all the rights cases and delivered the majority opinion in 42 per cent of those cases. He wrote separate concurring reasons in two other cases and never dissented. Bokhary PJ was the most prolific of all the judges, having sat on all the rights cases less one.[8] He authored (or co-authored) the majority opinion in 14 cases, a concurring opinion in 17 cases, and a dissenting opinion in six cases. Ribeiro PJ sat on 76 per cent of all the rights cases and contributed 12 majority opinions and one dissenting opinion. Chan PJ sat on 85 per cent of all the rights cases and contributed eight majority opinions and one separate concurring opinion.

Obtaining leave to appeal from the CFA Appeal Committee was no guarantee that the court was likely to accept the rights argument in the final appeal. The court accepted the rights argument in fewer than half (49 per cent) of the cases. In cases involving the government, the government party won 55 per cent of the time.[9] Not surprisingly, of the core team of judges hearing rights cases, the judge who accepted the rights argument most often was Bokhary PJ (56 per cent) followed by Sir Anthony Mason NPJ (54 per cent), Ribeiro PJ (52 per cent), Li CJ (51 per cent), and Chan PJ (47 per cent). Decision making was very much consensus driven, and the court usually spoke with one voice. Only Bokhary and Ribeiro PJJ dissented, in a total of seven cases.

The data tend to confirm that the CFA is more liberal than the court below, which is typically the Court of Appeal. In cases in which the CFA accepted the rights argument, there was a substantially greater tendency (63 per cent vs. 37 per cent) for the court below to be overturned than to be affirmed. Similarly, in cases in which the CFA rejected the rights argument, it tended to affirm the lower court more often than to overturn that court (57 per cent vs. 43 per cent).

Efficiency

The CFA also handled the rights cases efficiently. On average, each case was heard over 2.6 days and decided about 32 days after the hearing of

---

[8] Bokhary PJ did not sit in the case concerned with the challenge to the common law offence of murder; see *Lau Cheong* v. *HKSAR* (2002) 5 HKCFAR 415.

[9] These data exclude the unusual case in which the government party sought the constitutional relief (see *Chan Wing Hing*). The government tended to win more in criminal cases (57 per cent) than in noncriminal cases (52 per cent).

the appeal. Judgments were reasonable in length: majority judgments on average ran about 8200 words, and all judgments on average ran about 11,000 words.[10]

Jurisprudence

Migration

As an international city sharing a border with Mainland China, it is no surprise that there would be an abundant amount of cases on rights in migration. In general, the court was protective of these rights, notwithstanding strong government interests that weighed in the balance. The cases can be divided into three categories relating to the right of abode, the right of residents to enter and leave Hong Kong, and the right of nonresidents not to be returned to face torture.

Right of abode

The right of abode judgments, from 1999 to 2003, were the most important rights decisions in that period. The right was described as a 'core right' because without it, the full array of rights and freedoms guaranteed in the Basic Law (BL) could not be enjoyed.[11] The decisions demonstrated the CFA's approach to the interpretation of rights in the BL and how that approach evolved after the NPCSC's 1999 Interpretation.

In the landmark companion cases of *Ng Ka Ling* and *Chan Kam Nga*, the court held that the text of rights provisions should be interpreted purposively, generously, and in context.[12] The cases concerned Mainland-born children who sought to enjoy their right of abode on the basis that one of their parents was a Hong Kong permanent resident (category 3 in Article 24).[13] *Chan Kam Nga* (but not *Ng Ka Ling*) articulated the purpose

---

[10]   Decisions of 8200 and 11,000 words will generally run about 18 and 24 pages, respectively, of the authorized law reporter, the *Hong Kong Court of Final Appeal Reports* (Thomson Sweet and Maxwell).

[11]   *Ng Ka Ling*, 34.   [12]   *Ibid.*, 28–9; *Chan Kam Nga*, 89–90.

[13]   Only permanent residents enjoy the right of abode. Article 24 provides for six categories of permanent residents of the HKSAR. The cases considered the first four categories: '(1) Chinese citizens born in Hong Kong before or after the establishment of the [HKSAR]; (2) Chinese citizens who have ordinarily resided in Hong Kong for a continuous period of not less than seven years before or after the establishment of the [HKSAR]; (3) Persons of Chinese nationality born outside Hong Kong of those residents listed in categories (1) and (2); (4) Persons not of Chinese nationality who have entered Hong Kong with valid travel documents, have ordinarily resided in Hong Kong for a continuous period of not less than seven years and have taken Hong Kong as their place of permanent residence before or after the establishment of the [HKSAR] . . . .'

of the right as that of 'securing the unity of the family'.[14] The reasoning in *Ng Ka Ling* was animated not so much by a purposive approach but clearly by a generous approach to rights interpretation 'in order to give to Hong Kong residents the full measure of fundamental rights and freedoms so constitutionally guaranteed'.[15] The generous approach was used to reject the argument that another BL provision (Article 22(4)) supplied the legal basis for the impugned scheme requiring Mainland children who had the right of abode to obtain a one-way permit from Mainland authorities before they could enjoy the right.[16] Article 22(4), when read narrowly to exclude Hong Kong permanent residents, did not qualify the rights in Article 24.[17] Absent any constitutional basis, the scheme had to be struck down.[18]

The court also struck down a provision that limited a child who was born out of wedlock from enjoying the right of abode when the father was a Hong Kong permanent resident.[19] A contextual approach was applied, the context being the International Covenant on Civil and Political Rights (ICCPR), which remained in force by virtue of Article 39. The ICCPR principles of equality (i.e. treating illegitimate and legitimate children the same) and protection of the family were used to inform a generous interpretation, notwithstanding a reservation to the ICCPR precluding the direct application of those rights to immigration legislation.[20] In *Chan Kam Nga*, the court struck down the requirement that one of the parents be a Hong Kong permanent resident at the time of the child's birth.[21] Bokhary PJ, writing for the court, found that to admit such a restriction was contrary to both the natural meaning of the words in category (3) and the purpose of the right.[22]

The constitutional crisis that followed these two decisions is notorious.[23] In 2011, a WikiLeaks of a 2007 interview with Bokhary PJ revealed that the CFA judges had considered resigning after the 1999

---

[14] *Chan Kam Nga*, 89.   [15] *Ng Ka Ling*, 29.

[16] The salient part of Article 22 reads: 'For entry into the [HKSAR], people from other parts of China must apply for approval. Among them, the number of persons who enter the Region for the purpose of settlement shall be determined by the competent authorities of the Central People's Government after consulting the government of the Region'.

[17] *Ng Ka Ling*, 34–5.   [18] *Ibid.*, 36–7.   [19] *Ibid.*, 40–3.   [20] *Ibid.*, 41–2.

[21] *Chan Kam Nga*, 92–3.   [22] *Ibid.*, 89–90.

[23] See generally Chapters 1 (Ghai), 2 (Ghai), and 14 (Chen and Lo) in this volume; Johannes M. M. Chan, H. L. Fu, and Yash Ghai (eds.), *Hong Kong's Constitutional Debate: Conflict Over Interpretation* (Hong Kong: Hong Kong University Press, 2000).

Interpretation.[24] Instead they chose to stay because it was thought that this was the better way to serve the rule of law in Hong Kong.[25] Choosing to remain as judges meant that they had to show their respect for the NPCSC's interpretative authority and to legitimize it as part of Hong Kong's unique system of rule of law. This they did unanimously in *Lau Kong Yung*, in which the Interpretation was applied to reach opposite results from those in *Ng Ka Ling*.[26] More interesting is how the crisis also changed the approach of the judges in subsequent right of abode cases. It has been said that they became more pragmatic and conscious of the possible consequences of their decisions.[27] There were at least three signs of this change.

First, the court was less enthusiastic about giving a generous interpretation and more attuned to the textual meaning. This was seen in the two cases of *Tam Nga Yin* and *Chong Fung Yuen*, judgments rendered together in July 2001.[28] In *Tam Nga Yin*, the majority held it was not possible to read the category (3) words 'Persons of Chinese nationality *born* outside Hong Kong *of* those residents listed in categories (1) and (2)' (emphasis added) to include adopted children.[29] In *Chong Fung Yuen*, the court held that the category (1) words 'Chinese citizens born in Hong Kong' were clear and could not imply a requirement that one of the parents have permanent residency at the time of birth.[30] In both judgments, the court repeatedly emphasized the importance of giving primacy to the language of the provision and, unless there was ambiguity, purpose, context, generosity, and extrinsic materials would do little to alter the literal meaning.[31] This new approach was not designed to prefer one party to another because many abode seekers benefited from *Chong Fung Yuen*, which was thought by the executive at the time not to cause too great an influx to warrant another Interpretation and crisis.[32] The approach signified a move by the court, newly reconstituted in 2000 with new judges Ribeiro and Chan PJJ, to find firmer ground in traditional common law interpretative principles

[24] Gary Cheung and Chris Ip, 'All City's Top Judges "Considered Quitting"', *South China Morning Post*, 8 September 2011.
[25] Mary Ann Benitez, 'Abode Judges "Nearly Quit"', *The Standard*, 8 Sept 2011.
[26] *Director of Immigration* v. *Lau Kong Yung* (1999) 2 HKCFAR 300.
[27] See e.g. Pojen Yap, '10 Years of the Basic Law: The Rise, Retreat and Resurgence of Judicial Power in Hong Kong' (2007) 36 *Common Law World Review* 166.
[28] *Tam Nga Yin* v. *Director of Immigration* (2001) 4 HKCFAR 251; *Director of Immigration* v. *Chong Fung Yuen* (2001) 4 HKCFAR 211.
[29] *Tam Nga Yin*, 262–4.   [30] *Chong Fung Yuen*, 231–3.
[31] *Ibid.*, 221–5; *Tam Nga Yin*, 258.   [32] See Chapter 14 (Chen and Lo) in this volume.

instead of more value-laden substantive ones. From this standpoint, the court found sanctuary in the BL's promise of an autonomous common law system to more readily resist government entreaties to adopt Mainland evidence and interpretations. The court evolved not by retreating or surrendering to executive pressure but by becoming a more traditional common law court rather than a constitutional court.

The approach was seen also in *Fateh Muhammad*, which considered the meaning of the category (4) words 'have *ordinarily resided* in Hong Kong for a continuous period of not less than seven years' (emphasis added).[33] The court looked to the 'natural and ordinary' meaning of the expression 'ordinarily resident' and made reference to old English cases that considered the expression in ordinary legislation.[34] Finding utility in a 1928 tax case, the court held that Muhammad could not count periods of imprisonment as part of the seven years requirement because imprisonment was 'something out of the ordinary'.[35]

A second sign of change was in the court's application of the purposive approach. In *Chan Kam Nga*, the court identified the purpose of family unity for the *specific* category in Article 24 relevant in that case.[36] In *Tam Nga Yin* and *Chong Fung Yuen*, the court took a different approach by identifying a purpose for the whole of Article 24 in the following terms: 'the purpose ... can be said to be to limit the persons who are permanent residents of the HKSAR and hence its population'.[37] Put in these terms, the purpose had a limiting effect on the right in a manner inconsistent with the spirit of generous interpretation.

A third sign of change was the emergence of Bokhary PJ's minority opinions in the right of abode cases. His adherence to the purposive and generous approach of *Ng Ka Ling* made it apparent that the other judges had drifted. For example, in the adoption case, Bokhary PJ reasoned purposively that category (3) could be read to include adopted children because that was 'the reading which promotes family unity, which is valued at every level in our society including the constitutional level'.[38] In the important case of *Ng Siu Tung*, which considered whether thousands of similarly situated category (3) claimants could still be treated favourably as those in *Ng Ka Ling* even after the Interpretation, Bokhary PJ held that all 5000 claimants should benefit from *Ng Ka Ling* or from

---

[33] *Fateh Muhammad* v. *Commissioner of Registration* (2001) 4 HKCFAR 278.
[34] *Ibid.*, 283.   [35] *Ibid.*, 284, citing *IRC* v. *Lysaght* [1928] AC 234 (HL).
[36] *Chan Kam Nga*, 89.   [37] *Chong Fung Yuen*, 231; *Tam Nga Yin*, 258.
[38] *Tam Nga Yin*, 265.

legitimate expectations based on representations made by government.[39] By contrast, the majority only allowed a much smaller group, who had legitimate expectations based on specific representations, to benefit.[40] To give effect to the expectations of the larger group, according to the majority, undermined the legislative scheme; their expectations were overridden by the 'overwhelming force of immigration policy', which underlay the immigration legislation validated by the Interpretation.[41]

A third illustration is *Prem Singh* in which the court unanimously held that it was unconstitutional to require claimants to be free from all discretionary limits of stay before they could satisfy the category (4) requirement of having 'taken Hong Kong as their place of permanent residence'.[42] Bokhary PJ, writing for only himself, used overt constitutional reasoning holding that 'the notion of any legal right, let alone a constitutional right, being downgraded to something which can be granted or withheld as a matter of discretion is repugnant to the rule of law'.[43] The other judges confined their approach to text and context, reasoning that because it was inevitable for one to be subject to a limit of stay in building up the seven-year continuous period of ordinary residence, category (4) 'implicitly regards satisfaction of the permanence requirement as achievable at a time when an applicant is still subject to a limit of stay'.[44] But logically, it does not follow that because a limit of stay does not preclude continuous ordinary residence it also cannot preclude satisfaction of the permanence requirement, which obviously requires something more than mere ordinary residence. The best answer to this logical leap is Bokhary PJ's constitutional concerns with overriding executive powers.

Freedom to travel

The freedom to travel cases reflected the *Ng Ka Ling* generous and purposive approach to interpreting rights, probably because these cases had little, if any, impact on Mainland and Hong Kong relations. They also provided insights into the court's approach to restrictions on BL rights. Both *Bahadur* and *Lau Fong* concerned non-permanent residents who were denied permission to enter Hong Kong even though they had an unexpired permission to remain when they departed and attempted to re-enter.[45] Legislation provided that when such residents left Hong Kong,

---

[39] *Ng Siu Tung* v. *Director of Immigration* (2002) 5 HKCFAR 1, 120.   [40] *Ibid.*, 86–90.
[41] *Ibid.*, [134]–[137].   [42] *Prem Singh* v. *Director of Immigration* (2003) 6 HKCFAR 26.
[43] *Ibid.*, [7].   [44] *Ibid.*, [62].
[45] *Director of Immigration* v. *Gurung Kesh Bahadur* (2002) 5 HKCFAR 480; *Director of Immigration* v. *Lau Fong* (2004) 7 HKCFAR 56.

their permission to remain expired immediately after their departure. The court held that this rule when applied to such residents was unconstitutional, being inconsistent with the freedom to travel guaranteed under the BL.[46] In *Lau Fong*, the court went further and held that even if the residency status had been obtained by fraud or deception, these were not determinations that immigration officers could make as part of lower level decisions to refuse permission to enter, remove, and detain.[47] The legislation provided for a separate higher level decision-making process with stronger procedural safeguards in which an identity card was to be invalidated for being obtained by fraud.[48]

Bahadur also confirmed that any restriction on rights had to be construed narrowly and justified by government.[49] Article 39 was not a freestanding restrictions clause. Satisfying its 'prescribed by law' requirement alone was insufficient to justify a restriction; it was only the antechamber of restriction analysis.[50] Whether a BL right could be subject to restrictions and the test for determining permissible restrictions depended on the nature and subject matter of the right.[51] Signifying its robust approach, the court held it unnecessary to articulate a restrictions test because there could be no justification for the 'virtual abrogation' of the freedom to travel in this case.[52] Four years later in the bankruptcy case, *Chan Wing Hing*, the court held that the freedom to travel could be subject to restrictions and the test to apply was whether the restriction was rationally connected to the aim of protecting the rights of others and no more than necessary to achieve this aim.[53] This restriction test originated from the freedom of assembly case, *Leung Kwok Hung*, and was adopted again in several other cases, particularly in the criminal law context.[54] What made the case interesting is that the court was divided on how the restriction test should be applied, and Ribeiro PJ, writing for himself, penned his first and only dissenting judgment to date.

The case was concerned with a statutory rule that automatically extended a bankrupt's period of bankruptcy for the period of time he or she was outside of Hong Kong until he returned and notified his trustee in bankruptcy. Although all the judges agreed that the rule was

---

[46]   *Bahadur*, [36]–[42].   [47]   *Lau Fong*, [46].   [48]   *Ibid.*, [44].

[49]   *Bahadur*, [24]; Simon N. M. Young, 'Restricting Basic Law Rights in Hong Kong' (2004) 34 *HKLJ* 109.

[50]   *Ibid.*, [28]–[29].   [51]   *Ibid.*, [28].   [52]   *Ibid.*, [49].

[53]   *Chan Wing Hing*, [33]–[36]. The case concerned the right to leave Hong Kong, which is protected in both the BL (Article. 31) and BOR (Article 8(2)).

[54]   *Leung Kwok Hung* v. *HKSAR* (2005) 8 HKCFAR 229, [33]–[38].

rationally connected to the aim, they disagreed on whether it was no more than necessary. The majority described the suspension period as a sanction that was harsh, applying indiscriminately and unnecessarily because there were other mechanisms in the scheme to protect creditors.[55] It applied 'a generous approach to the interpretation of the right to travel' and concluded that the restriction on the right could 'not be regarded as no more than is necessary to protect primarily the rights of creditors'.[56] Ribeiro PJ differed in seeing that the rule imposed a burden on the right only insofar as it required that notice be given to the trustee before travelling, a burden he described as being 'not onerous'.[57] As to length of the suspension, this was something within the control of the bankrupt who could terminate the suspension by simply notifying the trustee. He concluded that the prior notice requirement was unobjectionable and constituted only a minimal impairment on the freedom.[58] Ribeiro PJ's analysis works fairly if all bankrupts were informed and rational actors, but the majority opinion is more in line with ordinary human behaviour and expectations. In this rare instance of finding Ribeiro PJ standing alone, it is telling that only the majority opinion had regard to the generous approach to interpreting constitutional rights. One might infer from this that the change seen in 2001 in the CFA's approach to rights was largely attributable to the influence of Ribeiro PJ after his appointment to the court in 2000.

Following the bankruptcy case, there is now the possibility that the right of abode might also be subject to an implied restrictions test. None of the right of abode cases addressed this question, probably because most were concerned with the question of having the status of permanent residency and not the exercise of the right of abode. *Ng Ka Ling*, however, was concerned with claimants who had the right of abode but were restricted from enjoying it because of a statutory requirement. Mention is made in the judgment to the argument that Article 24 should be interpreted 'as subject to implied restriction based on reasonableness that the Mainland laws regarding exit approval for coming to Hong Kong have to be complied with', but the argument was dismissed curtly because it would undermine Hong Kong's separate legal system.[59] It is not clear, however, why the argument was presented only as a restriction imposed by Mainland law when it was clear that the restriction came from prescribed domestic law. As the first rights case, the question of restrictions had not been settled,

---

[55] *Chan Wing Hing*, [46]–[49].   [56] *Ibid.*, [36] and [50].   [57] *Ibid.*, [84].
[58] *Ibid.*, [84]–[93].   [59] *Ng Ka Ling*, 35–6.

but now that the court has developed a general restrictions test, there is a real possibility that the test could be applied not to the categories of permanent residency but to the application of the right of abode in Article 24.

Torture *non-refoulement*

In a jurisdiction that has never been bound by the Refugee Convention[60] as a matter of treaty law, the 2004 decision in *Sakthevel Prabakar* was transformative in many ways.[61] Prabakar was a potential deportee who claimed that if returned to Sri Lanka, he would be subject to torture by those who had tortured him before. Hong Kong was bound by the Convention Against Torture but had yet to implement in domestic law the *non-refoulement* obligation in Article 3.[62] The government had a policy not to return individuals to torture and in practice applied this policy on the basis of the refugee status determination made by the local office of the United Nations High Commissioner for Refugees (UNHCR).[63] The court, assuming that the government had a legal duty to follow the *non-refoulement* policy, held that the screening process had to adhere to high standards of fairness because the decision was 'plainly one of momentous importance' as 'life and limb [were] in jeopardy and his fundamental human right not to be subjected to torture' was involved.[64] It held that the practice of relying upon the UNHCR's unexplained rejection of refugee status fell below the requisite standards of fairness for several reasons, including the important differences in the definitions of the *non-refoulement* obligations under the Refugee Convention and the Torture Convention, the absence of reasons given to the claimant for rejecting the claim, and the failure to conduct a proper independent assessment of the torture claim.[65]

The impact of *Prabakar* was significant. Together with the subsequent case law, it caused the government to transform the administrative torture screening mechanism and ultimately pass legislation in 2012 to put the

---

[60] See Kelley Loper, 'Human Rights, Non-refoulement and the Protection of Refugees in Hong Kong' (2010) 22 *International Journal of Refugee Law* 404; Oliver Jones, 'Customary Non-refoulement of Refugees and Automatic Incorporation into the Common Law: A Hong Kong Perspective' (2009) 58 *ICLQ* 443.

[61] *Secretary for Security* v. *Sakthevel Prabakar* (2004) 7 HKCFAR 187.

[62] The Crimes (Torture) Ordinance (Cap. 427) implements other aspects of the United Nations Convention Against Torture.

[63] *Prabakar*, [3].   [64] *Ibid.*, [44].   [65] *Ibid.*, [46]–[60].

scheme on a statutory basis.[66] The government had to invest millions of dollars to develop a workable and fair system that included the following features: a system of free legal representation to claimants, a team of trained legal advisors and frontline officers, a credible appeal mechanism handled by former judicial officers, and new guidelines and procedures comparable to asylum protection systems in overseas jurisdictions.

Criminal law

In this volume and elsewhere, much has been written on the CFA's rights cases in criminal law.[67] This chapter highlights and discusses five features of the rights jurisprudence in this area. The first feature is what could be called the court's common law approach to rights. This is the tendency to keep the common law robust but not to take the BL or Hong Kong Bill of Rights (BOR) too much beyond the common law position.[68] For example, it has been noted that the common law of prosecutorial disclosure as inherited from England and Wales does not go any further under the BL,[69] and the abuse of process doctrine continues to apply as only a common law doctrine.[70] In another case, it was found that the use of hearsay evidence to prove copyright does not infringe the right to examine witnesses because the witness who conveys the hearsay can be examined even though the declarant cannot.[71] There is also a tendency to borrow from the ever-growing body of comparative human rights law rather than to innovate an approach or theory specific to the Hong Kong criminal justice system.[72] As explained later in this chapter, European human rights law has tended to be more influential than North American sources.

---

[66] The Immigration (Amendment) Ordinance 2012, Ordinance 23 of 2012, was enacted in July 2012. Some notable post-Prabakar cases included *CH* v. *Director of Immigration* [2011] 3 HKLRD 101 (CA); *Iqbal Shahid* v. *Secretary for Justice* [2010] 4 HKLRD 12 (CA); *FB* v. *Director of Immigration* [2009] 2 HKLRD 346 (CFI); and *A (Torture Claimant)* v. *Director of Immigration* [2008] 4 HKLRD 752 (CA).

[67] See Simon N. M. Young, 'Human Rights in Hong Kong Criminal Trials' in Paul Roberts and Jill Hunter (eds.), *Criminal Evidence and Human Rights* (Oxford: Hart Publishing, 2012) 55; Simon N. M. Young and Sarah Cheng, 'Right to a Fair Trial and the Criminal Process' in Johannes Chan and C. L. Lim (eds.), *Law of the Hong Kong Constitution* (Hong Kong: Sweet and Maxwell, 2011) 529–604.

[68] Young, 'Human Rights in Hong Kong Criminal Trials', 66.

[69] *HKSAR* v. *Lee Ming Tee* (2003) 6 HKCFAR 336, [157].

[70] *HKSAR* v. *Lee Ming Tee* (2001) 4 HKCFAR 133.

[71] *Tse Mui Chun* v. *HKSAR* (2003) 6 HKCFAR 601.

[72] Young, 'Human Rights in Hong Kong Criminal Trials', note 67 above, 74–6.

When asked to accept more novel applications of rights, the court is usually reluctant to do so. Such was the fate of the submission to extend the right to silence (within the right to a fair trial) to prohibit the police from making derivative use of statements obtained by the compulsory powers of a company inspector.[73] The judges were also unmoved in the two arbitrary imprisonment cases calling for substantive review of the *mens rea* and mandatory life sentence for murder and absolute liability for the offence of sexual intercourse with a minor.[74] Unsurprisingly, the court has yet to strike down an offence for being in breach of the principle of legal certainty despite several worthy challenges to old common law offences.[75] In one interesting case, the majority interpreted the presumption of innocence right narrowly and rejected the submission that the withholding of a police officer's pay during suspension pending criminal charges infringed the officer's presumption of innocence in relation to those charges.[76] Bokhary PJ, dissenting, found a less intrusive means to meet the aim by having a power to obtain repayment of salaries received during suspension if and only if the officer was convicted.[77]

There are occasions, however, when the court is prepared to invoke BOR thinking to develop the common law or interpret legislation. For example, the right to the benefit of the lesser penalty helped shape a new rule to allow sentenced persons to enjoy the benefit of reduced sentencing guidelines set after they were sentenced.[78] And in the well-known Falun Gong case, the right against arbitrary arrest was invoked to find the arrests unlawful, thereby necessitating the convictions for assaulting police officers to be quashed.[79] This decision underlined the independence and impartiality of the court because not only did it overturn all the convictions entered and upheld in the courts below, but it also did so in the midst of strong Hong Kong and Mainland government concerns given the circumstances of the case (i.e. protests by members of Falun Gong, a banned organization on the Mainland) outside the Central Peoples' Government Liaison Office in Hong Kong, turning violent when police officers attempted to remove them. This decision reaffirmed that following the 1999 Interpretation,

---

[73]   *Lee Ming Tee* (2001).
[74]   *Lau Cheong; So Wai Lun* v. *HKSAR* (2006) 9 HKCFAR 530. See also Chapter 17 in this volume.
[75]   *Shum Kwok Sher* v. *HKSAR* (2002) 5 HKCFAR 381; *Mo Yuk Ping* v. *HKSAR* (2007) 10 HKCFAR 386; *B* v. *The Commissioner of the Independent Commission Against Corruption* (2010) 13 HKCFAR 1; and *Winnie Lo* v. *HKSAR* [2012] 1 HKC 537 (CFA).
[76]   *Yeung Chung Ming* v. *Commissioner of Police* (2008) 11 HKCFAR 513.
[77]   *Ibid.*, [50]–[62].   [78]   *Mark Anthony Seabrook* v. *HKSAR* (1999) 2 HKCFAR 184.
[79]   *Yeung May Wan* v. *HKSAR* (2005) 8 HKCFAR 137.

the court had not retreated from controversy or surrendered to Mainland interests and remained constant in its common law method even if the results displeased executive interests.

A second feature of the jurisprudence is its strong reliance on the case law of the European Convention on Human Rights.[80] It is a reflection of the influence that English law (as shaped by the Human Rights Act 1998) continues to have in Hong Kong. The court adopted the Strasbourg three-part test for when a process is considered 'criminal proceedings'.[81] Applying the test, it held that the old insider dealing proceedings, although considered civil in domestic law, were in fact criminal in nature given the serious and dishonest nature of the conduct and the potentially harsh penalty of paying three times the gain.[82] It also held that forfeiture proceedings (in relation to 42 silver bricks found as unmanifested cargo on a lorry) were not criminal proceedings because 'the character of the proceedings as civil proceedings *in rem* against the goods . . . denies them the character of criminal proceedings'.[83] The court also adopted the *Sunday Times* v. *United Kingdom* test for legal certainty as one of the principles within the expression 'prescribed by law' in Article 39 of the BL.[84] It applied this test in several cases, and notably, following European Court of Human Rights (ECtHR) and English authorities, to hold that bare conditions to 'keep the peace and be of good behavior' in binding over orders were too uncertain to be enforceable.[85] The principle was also used in *Leung Kwok Hung* to strike out the *ordre public* ground for police objections to public assemblies.[86] Although there is jurisprudential advantage to having Hong Kong's human rights law interlocked with European law, the disadvantage is when ECtHR law falls short of what is needed to maintain the *Ng Ka Ling* principle of ensuring that rights continue to lie at the heart of Hong Kong's separate system. Critics of ECtHR jurisprudence will know very well where those shortcomings lie.[87]

The third feature is the development of a restrictions test applied without a coherent approach to the issue of deference to the legislature

---

[80] See Young, 'Constitutional Rights in Hong Kong's Court of Final Appeal', note 4 above, 82.

[81] *Insider Dealing Tribunal* v. *Koon Wing Yee* (2008) 11 HKCFAR 170, [31]–[37].

[82] *Ibid.*, [45]–[53].

[83] *Wong Hon Sun* v. *Commissioner of Police* (2009) 12 HKCFAR 877, [72].

[84] *Shum Kwok Sher*, [60]–[65], [89]; *Mo Yuk Ping*, [60]; *Leung Kwok Hung*, [26]–[29]; and *Medical Council of Hong Kong* v. *Helen Chan* (2010) 13 HKCFAR 248, [77]–[78].

[85] *Lau Wai Wo* v. *HKSAR* (2003) 6 HKCFAR 624; *David Morter* v. *HKSAR* (2004) 7 HKCFAR 53.

[86] *Leung Kwok Hung*, [77]–[85].

[87] See e.g. chapters 5, 6, 10, and 12, in Roberts and Hunter (eds.), note 67 above.

and executive. The first occasion for the court to apply a restrictions test was in the 1999 freedom of expression case concerning flag desecration decided shortly after the first batch of right of abode cases.[88] The unanimous decision to uphold the national and regional flag desecration offences as being necessary for public order (*ordre public*) suggested the court would take a deferential approach to restrictions. The majority referred to deference as giving 'due weight to the view of the HKSAR's legislature' and noted the importance 'at the early stage of the new order' of implementing the one country, two systems principle and reinforcing national unity and territorial integrity.[89] Bokhary PJ, in his separate concurring opinion, did not believe that deference to the legislature was involved because it was more a test of whether the desecration laws were reconcilable with the freedom of expression.[90]

The next significant decision was the 2005 *Leung Kwok Hung* freedom of assembly case in which the court articulated for the first time the two-part rationality and proportionality tests for restrictions prescribed by law.[91] The majority's myopic approach was to focus solely on the constitutionality of the public order (*ordre public*) objection ground. In finding the first half of this ground unobjectionable, the majority believed that one of the features of the scheme that made it proportional was that the commissioner also had to apply a proportionality test before exercising the power.[92] Showing such trust in the police was surely a sign of deference, even if not so explicitly acknowledged. Bokhary PJ, dissenting, had more fundamental objections, finding that the commissioner's powers of prior restraint under the legislative scheme were insufficiently circumscribed and could not be saved by 'supplying the necessary safeguards through interpretation'.[93] He also offered a richer purposive analysis, perfectly capturing a reality of post-1997 Hong Kong when he wrote, 'In today's Hong Kong street demonstrations, both stationary and moving, form a significant and even potent element of public discourse. . . . A peaceful demonstration is a sign of freedom and can have a legitimate effect on policy'.[94]

With the reverse onus and presumption of innocence cases, however, the court appeared to signal a different approach to restrictions. In three decisions in which reverse onuses of proof were challenged, the court held that the provisions had derogated from the presumption of innocence and were not justified on the proportionality test (albeit the rationality test

[88] *HKSAR* v. *Ng Kung Siu* (1999) 2 HKCAR 442.   [89] *Ibid.*, 460–1.   [90] *Ibid.*, 467.
[91] *Leung Kwok Hung*, [33]–[37].   [92] *Ibid.*, [96].   [93] *Ibid.*, [202].   [94] *Ibid.*, [120].

was met).[95] On the issue of deference, Sir Anthony Mason NPJ wrote that the 'weight to be accorded to the legislative judgment by the Court will vary from case to case depending upon the nature of the problem, whether the executive and the legislature are better equipped than the courts to understand its ramifications and the means of dealing with it'.[96] In applying this to the case, he found that because 'the issue turns on matters of proof, onus and evidence... the Court is able to form its own judgment, without laboring under a disadvantage vis-a-vis the legislature'.[97] Under this functional approach, little, if any, deference was to be afforded. But this apparently less deferential approach may also be explained by the court's readiness in all three cases to accede to the government's remedial submission of reading down the burden to only an evidential one to save the legislation from being struck down.[98] Thus, one might say deference was only deferred and not denied.

Perhaps the lack of coherence on deference is largely attributable to Hong Kong's unusual and evolving political system under the BL. With only part of the legislature directly elected and the other part largely controlled by the executive through the system of functional constituencies,[99] the notion of deference to the legislature on democratic grounds does not have the same currency as in other common law jurisdictions.[100] It may be necessary to wait until Hong Kong becomes more democratic before the court will be able to invoke deference on more legitimate and explicit terms.[101]

The fourth feature is the use of innovative constitutional remedies, not so much to vindicate rights but to serve the greater good and minimize disruption incident to unconstitutionality. In the reverse onus cases, remedial interpretation (in contrast to common law interpretation) was invoked to read down the persuasive burden to an evidential burden and

---

[95]   *HKSAR* v. *Lam Kwong Wai* (2006) 9 HKCFAR 574; *HKSAR* v. *Hung Chan Wa* (2006) 9 HKCFAR 614; and *HKSAR* v. *Ng Po On* (2008) 11 HKCFAR 91.

[96]   *Lam Kwong Wai*, [45].   [97]   *Ibid.*

[98]   *Lam Kwong Wai*, [84]; *Hung Chan Wa*, [86]; and *Ng Po On*, [77].

[99]   On the political and social impact of functional constituencies, see generally Christine Loh and Civic Exchange (eds.), *Functional Constituencies: A Unique Feature of the Hong Kong Legislative Council* (Hong Kong: Hong Kong University Press, 2006).

[100]   See *R.* v. *DPP Ex p. Kebeline* [2000] 2 AC 326, 381 (HL), per Lord Hope and criticisms in Cora Chan, 'Judicial Deference at Work: Some Reflections on Chan Kin Sum and Kong Yun Ming' (2010) 40 *HKLJ* 1. See also Chan and Lim, note 67 above, [16.059].

[101]   For another insightful perspective, see Cora Chan, 'Deference and the Separation of Powers: An Assessment of the Court's Constitutional and Institutional Competences' (2011) 41 *HKLJ* 7.

thereby preserve the constitutionality of the offence. This still had some disruptive effect because persons convicted under the unconstitutional position had in theory a basis for complaint. In practice, however, if the time to appeal had expired, extensions of the deadline were not granted solely because the law had changed.[102]

Remedial interpretation was taken to a new level when in the insider dealing case the court fixed the unconstitutionality by rendering invalid the penalty power, which was not in itself unconstitutional.[103] This made the proceedings no longer criminal in nature and the complaints about rights violations in the criminal context went away. It was no surprise that the court was presented with no comparative constitutional law precedent for such a remedial order.[104] The cardinal rule in striking down legislation is that laws are invalid to the extent of unconstitutionality.[105] When a court decides to order a non-infringing provision invalid, it goes beyond this rule and begins to make choices on how best to deal with the unconstitutionality. Quite simply, it begins to legislate. In acceding to the government's request for an expedient solution that could best preserve past insider dealing proceedings, the court overstepped its judicial role.

A third example is the court's remedy to order the temporary suspension of a declaration of unconstitutionality. It made this order for a six-month period in the interception and covert surveillance case in which lower courts held that existing powers were unconstitutional.[106] Although the court was not prepared to order the temporary validity of those unconstitutional laws and executive orders, it believed that the operational needs of law enforcement to carry on such investigations without being in breach of the court's order pending the enactment of new legislation justified a temporary suspension order.[107] Again, the order had the effect of minimizing disruption and maintaining the status quo.

The final feature of the jurisprudence is the absence of any real dialogue between the court and the legislature over unconstitutional legislation. The closest to a dialogue is following the covert surveillance temporary suspension order the executive and legislative branches responded by passing corrective legislation within the six-month period.[108] In other instances, the court has declared laws unconstitutional without any

---

[102] *Hung Chan Wah*, [23]–[27].   [103] *Koon Wing Yee*, [109]–[120].   [104] *Ibid.*, [110].
[105] *Ng Ka Ling*, 25.   [106] *Koo Sze Yiu* v. *Chief Executive* (2006) 9 HKCFAR 441.
[107] *Ibid.*, [45]–[50].
[108] The Interception of Communications and Surveillance Ordinance (Cap. 589) was passed and brought into force on 9 August 2006, approximately one month after the CFA's judgment was handed down and almost exactly six months after the Court of First Instance's decision.

executive or legislative response. Take, for example, the offence of homosexual buggery committed otherwise than in private.[109] The CFA struck down this offence for being discriminatory.[110] Because the case was the first prosecution for this offence (since it was enacted in 1991), the government accepted the unconstitutionality and did not try to reintroduce the offence in amended form. One possible reason for the lack of dialogue is that most of the impugned provisions in the criminal law cases had little, if any, public interest concerns backing them.[111] The temporary suspension case (and others in the lowers courts that have followed) shows at least that the government is prepared to respond to temporary suspension orders and pass corrective legislation.

Administrative law

One of the most important 'access to justice' cases since 1997 was the challenge to the finality clause that purported to preclude appeals to the CFA from the Court of Appeal in solicitor disciplinary matters.[112] It was held that the clause, being an 'absolute one . . . a total ban', was a disproportionate limit on the Court's power of final adjudication under the BL.[113] In his separate concurring opinion, Bokhary PJ noted that 'access to the courts . . . is in practical terms the most important right conferred by the Basic Law' because it was an 'arterial right' necessary for enforcing all other rights.[114]

By contrast, other administrative law rights cases were less inspiring. In another solicitor's disciplinary case, the court upheld the inspector's power to order the production of the solicitor's files even if the files contained privileged documents.[115] The court held that this was a justifiable and proportionate restriction on the right to confidential legal advice in furtherance of maintaining high standards within the legal profession.[116] Counsel in the case would later criticize the court 'for having swung the pendulum too far by adopting a relatively loose standard to allow LPP to be abrogated'.[117] Also in 2006, the court decided *Stock Exchange* v. *New World Development,* which severely restricted the potential of the BL to

---

[109] Crimes Ordinance (Cap. 200), s. 118F.

[110] *Secretary for Justice* v. *Yau Yuk Lung Zigo* (2007) 10 HKCFAR 335.

[111] Young, note 67 above, 55–7, 76.

[112] *A Solicitor* v. *The Law Society of Hong Kong* (2003) 6 HKCFAR 570.

[113] *Ibid.,* [39]–[41].   [114] *Ibid.,* [45].

[115] *A Solicitor* v. *The Law Society of Hong Kong* (2006) 9 HKCFAR 175.

[116] *Ibid.,* [25]–[26].

[117] Johannes Chan, 'Legal Professional Privilege: Is it Absolute?' (2006) 36 *HKLJ* 462.

protect rights in tribunal proceedings.[118] It was argued that a restriction
on a party's lawyer from addressing the Disciplinary Committee of the
Stock Exchange violated Article 35, which provides the right of residents
to 'choice of lawyers for timely protection of their lawful rights and interests or for *representation in the courts*' (emphasis added).[119] To the surprise
of many, probably including the judges in the court below who had taken
a more liberal approach,[120] the court held that 'representation in the
courts' referred only to courts that were part of the judiciary exercising
judicial power, and not administrative tribunals.[121] The Court of Appeal
used a more inclusive approach to qualify tribunals if they were 'acting
judicially'.[122] Similar to the post-*Ng Ka Ling* decisions, *Stock Exchange*
allowed text and context to triumph over the purposive and generous
approaches to constitutional interpretation. Even on its approach, the
court's reasoning was unconvincing.

It should have begun by acknowledging that the BL contained no definition for 'courts', and the closest is Article 81, which states that 'The Court
of Final Appeal, the High Court, district courts, magistrates' courts and
other Special courts shall be established in the [HKSAR]'. The reference
to 'other Special courts' signifies that even under this article, the courts
to be established were left open ended. As in *Tam Nga Yin* and *Chong
Fung Yuen*, *Stock Exchange* subverted the purposive approach by looking
to more general purposes of the BL (i.e. separate legal system, continuity
of legal system, independence of the judiciary).[123] At this macro level,
the meaning of 'courts' is seen narrowly, in a more traditional sense.
But the purposive approach should have focused on the purpose of the
right in particular; had that been done, the focus would have been on
the importance of legal representation to protect rights and interests
and the fora in which such representation would be needed. The court's
reliance on *Attorney-General* v. *BBC* was misplaced because it concerned
a different context.[124] The issue of whether the contempt power with its
implications on freedoms applied to a local valuation court would naturally attract a narrow definition, but in *Stock Exchange*, following the
same concern for rights, one would have thought that a more generous
approach ought to have been taken. What is unexplained in the judgment

---

[118] *The Stock Exchange of Hong Kong* v. *New World Development Co Ltd* (2006) 9 HKCFAR
234.
[119] *Ibid.*, [37]–[38].
[120] [2005] 2 HKLRD 612 (CA); *Dr Ip Kay Lo Vincent* v. *Medical Council of Hong Kong
(No 2)* [2003] 3 HKC 579 (CA).
[121] *Stock Exchange* (CFA), [47]–[52].   [122] *Ibid.*, [65]–[66], [84].
[123] *Ibid.*, [39]–[46].   [124] *Attorney-General* v. *BBC* [1981] AC 303 (HL).

is why Article 35's discrete right to choice of lawyers for timely protection of lawful rights and interests was not engaged because this right, seen clearly from both the English and Chinese texts, is not limited to application in 'courts'.

Three years later, the court in *Lam Siu Po* appeared to take a 180-degree turn in striking down a statutory bar to legal representation in police disciplinary proceedings.[125] The outcome, however, was not the result of rediscovering the purposive and generous approaches to BL interpretation. Instead, what drove the result in the majority's judgment were two main factors. First, the focus moved from Article 35 of the BL to the right to a fair hearing under the BOR, which is more closely interconnected with international human rights law. The scope of Article 10 was broader, not being confined to application in 'courts', applying generally to the determination of 'rights and obligations in a suit at law'. The second main factor was the influence of the European Convention jurisprudence, which as noted earlier was already influential in the CFA criminal cases. Notwithstanding the ICCPR pedigree of the BOR, the court found the ECtHR cases on Article 6 to be highly persuasive in concluding that police disciplinary proceedings was a 'suit at law' under Article 10.[126] In contrast to *Stock Exchange*, the court in *Lam* canvassed rights cases from Europe and Canada and arrived at a generous interpretation of 'suit at law', thereby enabling more litigants to enjoy the important rights in Article 10.[127] However, when it came to the content of Article 10, the majority fell back on its common law approach to rights: 'An arrangement which satisfies the requirements of the common law will almost certainly conform with the fairness requirements of article 10'.[128] It was not prepared to rule categorically that fairness required a right to legal representation in all police disciplinary proceedings but only that it was to be left to the tribunal's common law discretion.

Helen Chan was another decision by which the court surprised many in reversing a more liberal Court of Appeal judgment.[129] This case challenged the practice of allowing the Medical Council's legal advisor

---

[125] *Lam Siu Po* v. *Commissioner of Police* (2009) 12 HKCFAR 237. See also Chapter 16 (Chan) in this volume.

[126] *Ibid.*, [62]–[65].

[127] As in other cases, Bokhary PJ wrote a separate concurring judgment making overt references to the generous approach to rights, see [16], [17], and [24]. Woolf NPJ was the only other judge who agreed with both the majority and Bokhary PJ's judgments.

[128] *Ibid.*, [137].

[129] *Medical Council of Hong Kong* v. *Helen Chan* (2010) 13 HKCFAR 248, rev'g [2009] 4 HKLRD 174 (CA).

to be present during disciplinary inquiry deliberations and, after deliberations, to prepare a draft of the council's decision. The court unanimously held that this practice did not violate the Article 10 right to a fair hearing by a 'competent, independent and impartial tribunal'.[130] The judgment can be criticized for its narrow approach to 'independent tribunal', conceiving the right as no more than formal independence from the parties, and failing to recognize the risk of the legal advisor joining the deliberations (e.g. inadvertently at the request of members) and the inability of the parties to know of such participation. Reference to the 'extremely far-reaching implications' of the challenge at the outset of the judgment because many administrative tribunals also had appointed legal advisors, suggests that pragmatism won over principle in this case.[131]

Social, political, and economic rights

The court decided only a small handful of cases concerned with social, political, and economic rights. *Chan Wah* was a progressive political rights case that had significant impact.[132] It concerned the system used by indigenous villagers to elect their representatives in the New Territories. Indigenous villager was a status that could only be acquired by descent through the male line; the two applicants, although they lived in the village all their lives, could not establish patrilineal descent and thus could not vote or stand in elections for village representatives. The court held that this restriction on the applicants' right to take part in the conduct of public affairs was unreasonable and was discriminatory on grounds of sex.[133] The decision had serious ramifications, forcing the government to introduce a new statutory scheme to regulate and legitimize the much-discredited previous system.[134]

Ho Choi Wan was a statutory interpretation case that divided the court on the issues of affordable rental housing and the duties of the Housing Authority in recessionary times.[135] The case revolved around a provision added to the Housing Ordinance in 1997 that limited the frequency (at least three years) and amount (median rent to income ratio not to exceed 10 per cent) of rent variation in public housing.[136] As a result of a recession and government's freeze in rents, the median rent to income

---

[130] *Ibid.*, [58]–[64].   [131] *Ibid.*, [13]–[15].
[132] *Secretary for Justice* v. *Chan Wah* (2000) 3 HKCFAR 459.   [133] *Ibid.*, 474.
[134] The Village Representative Election Ordinance (Cap. 576) came into force partially on 14 February 2003 and fully on 1 October 2003.
[135] *Ho Choi Wan.*   [136] *Ibid.*, [9].

ratio exceeded 10 per cent over a number of years and became as much as 14.7 per cent in the second half of 2004.[137] The appellant argued that there was a positive duty on the Housing Authority to reduce rents to keep within the 10 per cent cap. If correct, this point had significant implications because about 30 per cent of the population lived in public housing, and the reduction in rent would have resulted in an annual loss of rental income of HKD1.52 billion, money that would normally be used by the authority to provide housing for the many on the waiting list. The majority rejected the argument and held that the provision, enacted to protect tenants in inflationary times, served only to limit the frequency and quantum of rent increases.[138] Because there had only been rent freezes and no increases, it had no application. The decision was true to legislative intent and did not try to read more into the legislation, whether arising from comparative constitutional or international law. In another of his famous dissents, Bokhary PJ held that there was such a positive duty, beginning his judgment with the short sentence, 'Affordable housing is what this case is about'.[139] For him, the issue was very much a human rights matter, making express reference to the right to adequate housing in the ICESCR and its potential application under Article 39 of the BL.[140] Despite the rights-friendly approach, Bokhary PJ qualified that his decision was reached without taking the ICESCR into account, although it was relevant.[141] Unlike with the ICCPR, the CFA has yet to engage with the ICESCR in rights cases.[142]

Yin Shuen Enterprises was the first CFA decision to interpret the right to property under the BL.[143] It concerned the assessment of compensation payable by the government upon resumption of agricultural land for building public housing. The BL provides the right to compensation corresponding 'to the real value of the property concerned at the time', and the issue was whether 'real value' included a speculative value obtainable in the open market from buyers hoping the government will modify the terms of the lease to permit development.[144] Lord Millett NPJ, writing for the court, held that it did not and that the meaning of

---

[137] *Ibid.*, [34].   [138] *Ibid.*, [46]–[49].   [139] *Ibid.*, [60].

[140] *Ibid.*, [66]–[68].   [141] *Ibid.*, [65].

[142] See also criticisms in Carole J. Petersen, 'Embracing Universal Standards? The Role of International Human Rights Treaties in Hong Kong's Constitutional Jurisprudence' in Hualing Fu, Lison Harris, and Simon N. M. Young (eds.), *Interpreting Hong Kong's Basic Law: The Struggle for Coherence* (New York: Palgrave Macmillan, 2007) 33.

[143] *Director of Lands* v. *Yin Shuen Enterprises Ltd* (2003) 6 HKCFAR 1.

[144] BL, Article 105.

'real value' reflected the exceptions to open market value as contained in the Lands Resumption Ordinance.[145] The significance made of the words 'property concerned' and the reference to what the 'courts of Hong Kong have repeatedly emphasized' indicated a textual and contextual approach (including historical context) rather than an original purposive interpretation, let alone a generous one.[146]

Disputes between private parties

One of the major criticisms of the pre-1997 BOR case law was the Court of Appeal's failure to apply it to disputes between private parties, that is, to give it horizontal application (as contemplated in the ICCPR) in addition to vertical application as between the government and individuals.[147] Although the CFA maintained this aspect of the BOR jurisprudence,[148] it took a broader approach to BL rights giving them a degree of impact in private law disputes. It did this in two ways. First, in *Ng Ka Ling*, it was recognized that ICCPR rights (where inapplicable because of a reservation in respect of immigration legislation) formed part of the context for interpreting BL rights provisions.[149]

Second, BL rights themselves have been invoked directly usually as part of statutory interpretation or development of the common law. The most notable case was *Albert Cheng* v. *Tse Wai Chun Paul*, in which the court had regard to the freedom of expression in shaping a more robust defence of fair comment in a defamation action.[150] Other cases in which rights have been invoked concerned the freedom of conscience and forced apologies in a disability discrimination case,[151] orders against vexatious litigants and the right to access to the courts,[152] fair hearing and the admission of fresh evidence in a civil contempt

---

[145] Cap. 124, s. 12.   [146] *Director of Lands*, [55]–[58].

[147] *Tam Hing-yee* v. *Wu Tai-wai* [1992] 1 *HKLR* 185 (CA), criticised in Andrew Byrnes, 'The Hong Kong Bill of Rights and relations between private individuals' in Johannes Chan and Yash Ghai (eds.), *The Hong Kong Bill of Rights: A Comparative Approach* (Hong Kong: Butterworths Asia, 1993) 71.

[148] See *Chan Wah*, 470–1; *Ho Sin Ying* v. *Leung Lai Fong* (2009) 12 HKCFAR 581, [37]–[48].

[149] *Ng Ka Ling*, 40–3.

[150] *Albert Cheng* v. *Tse Wai Chun Paul* (2000) 3 HKCFAR 339, followed in *Sugar* v. *Associated Newspapers Ltd* [2002] QB 737; *Panday* v. *Gordon* [2005] UKPC 36; *Channel Seven Adelaide Pty Ltd* v. *Manock* [2007] HCA 60; and *WIC Radio* v. *Simpson* [2008] 2 SCR 420. See Chapter 20 (Glofcheski) in this volume.

[151] *Ma Bik Yung* v. *Ko Chuen* (2006) 9 HKCFAR 888.

[152] *Ng Yat Chi* v. *Max Share Ltd* (2005) 8 HKCFAR 1.

appeal,[153] civil non-disclosure of privileged documents obtained by private examination under the Companies Ordinance (Cap. 32),[154] and the duty of the court to provide reasons when leave to appeal an arbitral award is refused.[155]

Conclusion

In retrospect, *Ng Ka Ling* was a bold and daring judgment that exemplified the purposive and generous approaches to the interpretation of constitutional rights. The 1999 Interpretation and 2000 change in the court's permanent composition brought about a rethink in its approach. The response to the Interpretation was not to kowtow to executive interests and surrender its independence. Instead, it affirmed its independence by adopting a common law approach to interpretation that emphasized text and context before other considerations. By applying the approach consistently, it sometimes favoured the rights claimant, and other times it did not. The court could hardly be criticized for being deliberately confrontational or particularly creative, nor did it appear that individual judges were trying to pursue their own agendas. It was simply discharging its duty under the BL to maintain the separate common law system including methods of interpretation. The overseas NPJs gave their full support to the approach and thereby enhanced the credibility of the court, especially in international eyes. By this method, the court managed to avoid further Interpretations and to win over general support and respect from all corners.

Bokhary PJ's dissents spoke of a different world and vision, shining light on another path for the court to follow in the future.[156] In no way were these views radical or far-fetched. He was following the approach to interpretation set out and applied in the first two rights cases. Perhaps what set him apart was a greater tendency to see ambiguity in the text of constitutional rights, ambiguity that required resolution by resort to the purposive and generous approaches.

Post-2010, the European rights jurisprudence will likely continue to have great influence, not only in criminal cases. The court will need to

---

[153] *Donald Koo Hoi-Yan* v. *Kao, Lee & Yip* (2009) 12 HKCFAR 830.
[154] *Akai Holdings Limited* v. *Ernst & Young* (2009) 12 HKCFAR 649.
[155] *Swire Properties Ltd* v. *Secretary for Justice* (2003) 6 HKCFAR 236.
[156] For a discussion of Bokhary PJ's dissents, see Chapter 12 (Cottrell and Ghai) in this volume.

remain critical of this case law to see if it suitably affords the full measure of rights protection to persons in Hong Kong. The jury is still out on the influence of the ICESCR on the court's decision making. The development of a BL jurisprudence of tribunal justice will also need to await another period. Rights will continue to be invoked in private disputes, this having the effects of further relegating the BOR vertical restriction and forcing practitioners to open their eyes to the potential of constitutional argumentation. Future challenges to legislation and policies based on the current sentiments and aspirations of Hong Kong people will necessitate further reflection by the court on the issues of deference, remedies, and constitutional dialogue with other organs of government.

16

Administrative law

JOHANNES CHAN

The ideal of the rule of law is probably best exemplified by judicial review. It is a process whereby the exercise of public power is brought under scrutiny by an independent and impartial judiciary. Traditionally, in judicial review, the court is essentially concerned with the legality, procedural propriety, and rationality of the decision-making process, with limited scope of review of the merits of a decision.[1] This traditional scope of judicial review was significantly expanded by the introduction of the Hong Kong Bill of Rights Ordinance[2] in 1991 and more so by the coming into operation of the Basic Law (BL) on 1 July 1997 by bringing under judicial scrutiny not only the *vires* of administrative decisions but also the *vires* of the sources of power.

The court is now empowered to strike down legislative provisions that are inconsistent with the constitutional instruments.[3] As Chief Justice Li remarked:

> [I]t is not an exaggeration to say that the phenomenon of judicial review has redefined the legal landscape. Further, the availability and use of judicial review has had a significant impact on the conduct of the business of the government and has exercised considerable influence on public debate on many issues.[4]

I am grateful to the Judicial Administrator for kindly supplying me with the statistical information in this chapter.

[1] See e.g. the classic statement of Lord Diplock in *Council of Civil Service Unions* v. *Minister for the Civil Service* [1985] AC 374, 410 (HL).

[2] Cap. 383.

[3] The power of constitutional review existed even before the introduction of the BOR in 1991 because the court could always strike down a legislative provision that was repugnant to the Letters Patent; see e.g. *Rediffusion (HK) Ltd* v. *Attorney General* [1970] AC 1136 (PC).

[4] 'CJ's speech at Ceremonial Opening of the Legal Year 2007', 8 January 2007, accessible at www.info.gov.hk/gia/general/200701/08/P200701080120.htm.

Table 16.1 *Number of applications for
judicial review, 2001–2010*

Year	Number of applications	Year	Number of applications
2001	116	2006	132
2002	102	2007	143
2003	125	2008	147
2004	146	2009	144
2005	149	2010	134

The parallel development of constitutional law jurisprudence, particularly in relation to human rights, also means that the boundary between
administrative law and constitutional law is increasingly blurred. In fact,
development in one area reinforces and enriches the other. However, for
the sake of analysis, this chapter will concentrate on the traditional areas
of administrative law.

Statistics and threshold

Although there has been a steady increase in the number of judicial review
applications in the past decade, the number has remained more or less
at about 140 to 150 applications each year since 2004. In 2001 and 2002,
the number of applications for judicial review filed in the Court of First
Instance was, respectively, 116 and 102. Since 2004, the figure remains
relatively stable and stands close to around 150. Thus, the popular public
perception that there have been far too many judicial review applications and that the number of which has been escalating over the years is
untrue. Table 16.1 provides the number of applications between 2001 and
2010.

   Compared with the 1980s, there are many more judicial review applications these days.[5] The increase can be accounted for by many different

---

[5] Even as late as 1988, there were only 29 applications for judicial review; see *Re Sum Tat-
man* [1991] 2 *HKLR* 601, 613 (HC). For an interesting account of the rise of judicial
review in HK, see David Clark and Gerald McCoy, *Hong Kong Administrative Law*, 2nd
edn (Singapore: Butterworths Asia, 1993) ch. 1; Swati Jhaveri, Michael Ramsden, and
Anne Scully-Hill, *Hong Kong Administrative Law* (Hong Kong: LexisNexis, 2010) ch. 2; and
Johannes Chan, 'Administrative Law, Politics and Governance: The Hong Kong Experience'
in Tom Ginsberg and Albert Chen (eds.), *Administrative Law and Governance in Asia*
(London and New York: Routledge, 2009) 143–74.

Table 16.2 *Success rate in obtaining leave, 2008–2009*[a]

Year	Number of applications dealt with	Leave granted	Leave refused
2008	130	66 (51%)	64 (49%)
2009	119	63 (53%)	56 (47%)
2010	124	68 (54%)	56 (46%)

[a] See 'CJ's speech at Ceremonial Opening of the Legal Year 2010', 11 January 2010, accessible at www.info.gov. hk/gia/general/201001/11/P201001110174.htm., for the figures in 2008 and 2009; the figures in 2010 were kindly provided by the judiciary. For 2008 and 2009, the figures provided by the judiciary are slightly higher. Number of files in which leave was granted: 67 (2008), 67 (2009), and 68 (2010). Number of files in which leave was refused: 66 (2008), 73 (2009), and 56 (2010).

reasons, such as the increasing complexity of the government; better education of the public and increasing awareness of their rights; higher expectation of good and fair governance; availability of avenues to challenge government decisions through the Hong Kong Bill of Rights Ordinance (HKBORO) and the BL; willingness and innovation on the part of the legal profession to mount such challenges, sometimes on a *pro bono* basis; and frustration at the lack of progress on political reforms and the dominance of the pro-establishment forces in the Legislative Council, which has not been able to serve as a platform for discussions, negotiations, and resolution of conflicting interests in the community.[6]

A closer analysis of these figures reveals that in 2008, of the 147 applications, 17 applications were either not proceeded with or not yet dealt with (Table 16.2). Of the remaining 130, leave was granted in only 66 applications. That is, about 49 per cent of the leave applications were unsuccessful. The situation in 2009 and 2010 was similar. Of the leave applications that had been dealt with, slightly more than half of them (about 53 per cent) were successful in obtaining leave.

[6] For a more detailed discussion, see Chan, note 5 above.

Table 16.3 *Successful applications in 2008*[a]

Year	Number of applications dealt with	Leave granted	Number of cases proceeding to judgment	Relief granted
2008	130	66	41	19

[a] Of the 41 judgments, four were consolidated in one single hearing. The corresponding numbers of cases in which relief was granted in 2009 and 2010 are 14 and 9, respectively, but there is no information on the number of cases proceeding to judgment in these two years.

At the same time, in 2008, among the 41 cases in which judgment was given, relief was granted in 15 cases (Table 16.3). If one takes as the basis the total number of applications dealt with, the success rate is only about 12 per cent. Yet if one takes the total number of judgments, the success rate is as high as 37 per cent. Of the remaining 25 cases in which leave has been granted, it appears that a large majority of them did not proceed beyond the leave stage. A possible explanation is that the government was prepared to settle the claim after leave was granted. If so, the success rate is even higher.

Hence, an interesting picture emerges. On the one hand, about half of the applications were unable to get through the leave stage. Yet for cases that have successfully obtained leave, the success rate could be as high as 37 per cent, that is, nearly one-third. This could mean that the filtering process has been effective because most unmeritorious cases have been screened out. Yet given the high success rate, it could also mean that the filtering process might be too stringent, filtering cases that would otherwise have been successful.

This brings us to the threshold for granting leave. The threshold was raised at the end of 2007 in *Chan Po Fun* v. *Winnie Cheung*.[7] Previously, the test was known as the potential arguability test, namely whether the materials before the court disclose matters that on further consideration might demonstrate an arguable case for the relief sought.[8] In laying down this test, the Court of Appeal (CA) expressly rejected the approach of requiring an applicant to show an arguable case. Instead, the court had

[7] (2007) 10 HKCFAR 676.
[8] *Ho Ming Sai* v. *Director of Immigration* [1994] 1 *HKLR* 21 (CA).

merely to do a quick perusal of the materials available; otherwise, the purpose of subsequent judicial review would be pre-empted.[9] This is a sensible rule because an applicant may not be in possession of all relevant materials at the time of making an application, which must be made as soon as practicable and in any event within three months from the date when the grounds for application arose, usually the date of the decision impugned.[10] A concern of a low threshold is that it would invite busybodies, and the government and public bodies should be protected against unarguable challenges[11] – apparently a major factor in the Court of Final Appeal's (CFA's) decision to raise the threshold in *Chan Po Fun*. After considering the development in England, the CFA raised the threshold from potential arguability to reasonable arguability, requiring the applicant to show a reasonably arguable case. The court would need more than a 'quick perusal of materials' to decide the application. The court also rejected a flexible test of a higher standard when the issue involved only statutory construction with no factual dispute on the ground that such a test would be unworkable in practice.[12]

A high threshold may invite arguments, delaying the application, and even turn the leave argument into a preliminary hearing of the substantive application – in this way giving the government 'two bites at the cherry'. Since this decision, the success rate for applications for leave to apply for judicial review has remained at just above 50 per cent. Statistical information on the rate of success before this case is not available. Such information is necessary before any firm conclusion can be drawn on the impact of the higher threshold for leave application. It is also necessary to examine how far the new test has lengthened the leave application or whether it has resulted in more applications to oppose or set aside leave and more extensive arguments on leave applications. Although the higher threshold may deter frivolous or unmeritorious challenges affecting both the relevant public authorities and the public, a high success rate in judicial review may be a cause for concern about the practices of public authorities.

---

[9] *Ibid.* See also *Inland Revenue Commissioners* v. *National Federation of Self-Employed and Small Businesses Ltd* [1982] AC 617, 643–4, per Lord Diplock (HL).

[10] Rules of the High Court (Cap. 4, sub. leg. A), O. 54 r. 4.

[11] Li CJ warned against the proliferation of judicial review applications as a means to achieve political ends; see 'Chief Justice's Speech at Ceremonial Opening of the Legal Year 2006', 9 January 2006, accessible at www.info.gov.hk/gia/general/200601/09/P200601090137.htm.

[12] (2007) 10 HKCFAR 676, 686.

On the other hand, the court is prepared to grant leave if the case involves matters of public interest, even when the issue in the case has become academic. Thus, in *Secretary for Security* v. *Prabakar* in which the decision of the Director of Immigration refusing the applicant's claim for asylum was challenged, the court was prepared to consider the merits of the case, although the applicant had already left Hong Kong to resettle in Canada and no longer had any interest in the matter when the appeal was considered.[13] This liberal approach is a welcome move because 'very often in public or administrative law cases, the duties of public bodies fall to be exercised on a continuing basis not only in relation to the parties before the court but also perhaps to others in the future'.[14]

The CFA has engaged in a number of wide-ranging issues in administrative law and has delivered some major judgments that have far-reaching implications or that have steered the development of the common law. The following sections focus on how the court has facilitated access to justice and enhanced procedural due process in disciplinary proceedings followed by an examination of the vexed question of the delineation of judicial supervision and executive autonomy.

Access to justice

Costs

The right to a fair hearing has little significance if there is no access to a court in the first place. Access to justice can be impeded by a number of factors, an obvious one being the sheer cost of litigation. Indeed, the general principle of cost following the event is the singular deterrence to public interest litigation because most publicly spirited litigants have limited resources and are very concerned about costs if the case is lost. In this respect, the case of *Town Planning Board* v. *Society for Protection of the Harbour Ltd (No 2)* is a welcome development.[15]

The case involved an attempt on the part of the Society to stop the government from carrying out excessive reclamation of Victoria Harbour.

---

[13] (2004) 7 HKCFAR 187, 204. For further discussion on the grant of declaratory relief in matters that might have become academic, see J. Chan, 'Some Reflections on Remedies in Administrative Law' (2009) 39 *HKLJ* 321–37.

[14] *Chit Fai Motors Co. Ltd* v. *Commissioner for Transport* [2004] 1 HKC 465, [20] (CA).

[15] (2004) 7 HKCFAR 114. See also *Chu Hoi Dick* v. *Secretary for Home Affairs* [2007] HKEC 1640 (CFI) and *Leung Kwok Hung* v. *President of the Legislative Council of the HKSAR* [2007] HKEC 788 (CFI).

The Court of First Instance and the CFA found in favour of the plaintiff, and both awarded costs to the Society on an indemnity basis pursuant to O. 62 r 28(3) of the Rules of the High Court. Without limiting its general discretion to determine the appropriate cost order, the CFA took into account the attributes of the parties and the character of the proceedings. The case was brought not to assert a private right but to protect a public asset which was a central element in Hong Kong's heritage. There was manifest public interest in the matter. If legal proceedings had not been taken, the public interest in securing compliance with the law would not have prevailed, and the fundamental legal issues involved would not have been resolved. The plaintiff had limited finances and was dependent on public donations. These factors were relevant to the indemnity cost order, which, as opposed to a cost order on a party to party basis, provides a more generous basis for taxation and would allow the Society to recover most of its costs. Although the readiness of the court to make an indemnity cost order is a great encouragement to promoting public interest litigation, such an order is to be made only at the end of the litigation, which means that a public interest litigant would not be able to ascertain the financial position until after substantial cost has been incurred.

In contrast, a pre-emptive cost order made at the beginning of litigation would have considerably allayed the anxiety of a public interest litigant. Hong Kong courts have not been enthusiastic in making pre-emptive cost orders – understandably because such an order may put unjustifiable pressure on the other litigants.[16] At the end of the day, it should be a matter of balance; if the concern is with an extravagant manner of conducting litigation given a pre-emptive cost order, conditions can be attached to avoid abuse.

Jurisdiction

Another important decision of the CFA concerned a delineation of its own jurisdiction. It is a common design in disciplinary proceedings of many professional bodies that an appeal against the decision of a disciplinary tribunal lies to the CA, whose decision is final. Such a finality provision in the Legal Practitioners Ordinance was challenged in *Solicitor* v. *Law Society of Hong Kong* on the ground that it unjustifiably precluded the applicant

---

[16] *R* v. *Lord Chancellor, ex parte Child Poverty Action Group* [1991] 1 WLR 347 (QB); *Solicitor* v. *Law Society of Hong Kong and Secretary for Justice (No 2) (Intervener)* (2004) 7 HKCFAR 45.

from a further appeal to the CFA.[17] The court held the finality provision repugnant to the Judicial Committee Act 1833 and two applicable Orders in Council and hence not 'law previously in force in Hong Kong' within the meaning of Articles 8 and 18 of the BL. Although it was possible for the court to dispose of the appeal on this ground alone, it proceeded to decide the case on an alternative ground under the BL.

The court was prepared to accept that there is a right to have a dispute resolved by final adjudication by the court because Article 82 has vested the CFA with the power of final adjudication, albeit that this right to appeal could be subject to restrictions. The restrictions, however, have to comply with the proportionality test, namely a legitimate purpose and reasonable proportionality between the limitation and the purpose, involving a consideration of the subject matter of the dispute, the nature of the dispute (whether it involved law or fact, substantive rights or procedural matters), the need for speedy resolution, and the cost of dispute resolution (including any appeal). Because it is necessary to obtain leave to appeal to the CFA, and leave is in general only granted when the appeal involves a question of great, general, or public importance, the leave is a sufficient safeguard to ensure that the final court would only allow appeals the outcome of which would be of importance to the legal system. A blanket restriction of appeal to the CFA was therefore unconstitutional.

Although this decision reverses the conventional belief that the decision of the CA on disciplinary matters is final, the decision itself is not surprising because courts have traditionally jealously guarded their own jurisdiction, not lightly accepting any legislative attempt at restriction.[18] By contrast, in *Stock Exchange of Hong Kong Ltd* v. *New World Development Co. Ltd,* the CFA rejected the argument that restriction on the role of lawyers to a purely advisory role at disciplinary hearings violates the right of access to court under Article 35 of the BL on the narrow ground that Article 35 applied only to formal courts and not disciplinary tribunals.[19] It pointed to two dimensions of Article 35, the first being the protection of constitutional rights that had nothing to do with court proceedings

[17] *Solicitor* v. *Law Society of Hong Kong* (2003) 6 HKCFAR 570.
[18] This is best exemplified by the line of cases on ouster clauses cumulating in the leading judgment in *Anisminic Ltd* v. *Foreign Compensation Commission* [1969] 2 AC 147 (HL). In Geoffrey Ma CJ's first constitutional judgment, he followed *Solicitor, ibid.,* and struck down a similar finality clause in relation to election petitions; see *Mok Charles Peter* v. *Tam Wai Ho* (2010) 13 HKCFAR 762.
[19] (2006) 9 HKCFAR 234.

(including the right to confidential legal advice) and the second being the entrenchment of an individual's rights in relation to 'the courts'. The reference to 'choice of lawyers . . . for representation in the courts', 'judicial remedies', and 'the right to institute legal proceedings in the courts against the acts of the executive authorities and their personnel' suggested that the word 'courts' referred to a formal court of law, as also in other BL provisions referring to 'courts', in which the expression meant formal courts.

The reference to other provisions in the BL is at best unhelpful because all those provisions are found in Chapter IV, which prescribes the judicial system. It would not be surprising that the reference to 'courts' in that context is confined to a formal court of law. Yet this does not mean that a provision in Chapter III on fundamental rights should receive the same narrow construction. Moreover, if it is true that the other provisions in Article 35 point to the direction that the reference to 'court' means a formal court of law, these provisions are equally capable of being given a more liberal meaning as the CA did in several judgments.

It was also open to the court to construe Article 35 in light of Article 14 of the International Covenant on Civil and Political Rights (ICCPR) or Article 10 of the Bill of Rights (BOR), which clearly have a wider scope. Nor did the court give sufficient consideration to the fact that many decisions made by administrative tribunals could have far-reaching implications on the l⸺ of ordinary people, which on policy grounds should be included within the scope of Article 35. The Court was obviously influenced by the fact that this was a pre-emptive strike because the action was taken before the disciplinary hearing was held so that the court was put into a position to speculate what the effect of restricting the role of lawyers would have on the fairness of the proceeding.[20] Yet by adopting a narrow interpretation of the word 'court' in Article 35, the court deprived itself of a powerful avenue to consider the constitutionality of any statutory restriction on a fair hearing before disciplinary tribunals.

Fortunately, the gap was covered by Article 10 of the BOR, and this was confirmed in the subsequent case of *Lam Siu Po* v. *Commissioner of Police*.[21] In this case, the applicant was denied legal representation by Regulations 9(11) and (12) of the Police (Discipline) Regulations, which served as an absolute ban on legal representation in police disciplinary proceedings. He abandoned his argument on Article 35 of the BL before

---

[20] See, in particular, the judgment of Bokhary PJ at 243.

[21] *Lam Siu Po* v. *Commissioner of Police* (2009) 12 HKCFAR 237.

the CA because the CFA had by then handed down its judgment in *New World Development Co. Ltd*.[22]

The unsuccessful appeal before the CA focused solely on Article 14 of the ICCPR, which also formed the main argument before the CFA. After extensive reference to the jurisprudence of the Human Rights Committee and the European Court of Human Rights, the CFA concluded that Article 10 was engaged in relation to disciplinary proceeding that had a direct and highly adverse impact on one's livelihood and pension. The nature of the police force was insufficient to justify any departure from the protection of fair hearing in Article 10, and the effective functioning of the police would not be impaired by allowing its disciplinary tribunal a discretion to permit an officer to be legally represented where fairness so dictated. It is interesting to observe that in tracing the development of the right to a court in Article 14.1 of the ICCPR and Article 6 of the European Convention of Human Rights (the equivalent of Article 10 of the BOR), the court noted that these provisions were not originally intended to apply to decisions of administrative tribunals or to the legal relations between, for instance, civil servants and the state that employs them, but these restrictions were 'of no more than historical interest'.[23] This is in stark contrast to the approach adopted by the court in *New World Development Co. Ltd* in which the court largely confined itself to a literal analysis of the relevant provision.

The significance of *Lam Siu Po* is that it extends the court's constitutional jurisdiction to all kinds of disciplinary proceedings, a gap that has been left open by its decision in *New World Development Co. Ltd*. The decision has since then been applied to disciplinary proceedings of other law enforcement agencies, civil servants, and the medical profession, and the list is far from exhaustive. On the other hand, Article 10 does not apply to every administrative or disciplinary decision. It is necessary to show that the decisions determine some civil rights and obligations, but the court has not laid down any guidance to determine what constitutes 'civil rights and obligations', save that it is prepared to adopt a broad and common sense construction of this term. In these cases, the court took into account the terminal nature of the decision and the impact of the decision on the pension rights or reputation or the continuing practice as a member of a

---

[22] This case also highlights the importance and continued relevance of the BOR in constitutional review cases.

[23] *Lam Siu Po*, [74], per Riberio PJ, citing Lord Walker in *Runa Begum* v. *Tower Hamlets London Borough Council* [2003] 2 AC 430, [109] (HL).

professional body and accepted that the right to employment constituted a civil right for this purpose.

Retrospectivity and extension of time to appeal

As a result of the CFA judgment in *Lam Siu Po*, many police officers sought to overturn their disciplinary convictions on the ground that they had been denied legal representation. In most of these cases, the application for leave to apply for judicial review[24] or if leave had previously been granted, an application to include a new ground to take advantage of the decision in *Lam Siu Po*[25] or an application for an extension of time to appeal to the CA or CFA on the basis of *Lam Siu Po*[26] were lodged long out of time. The courts had not been entirely consistent in handling these applications.[27] The matter was eventually resolved by the CFA in *Clarence Chan* v. *Commissioner of Police* in favour of finality of litigation.[28] It was held that the mere fact that the law has been changed in favour of a litigant who had previously lost on that view of the law was not a sufficient reason to justify an extension of time for appeal. Such extension could only be justified on very rare occasions of exceptional circumstances.

Although the issue was resolved by a refusal to exercise discretion to grant an extension of time for appeal, the aftermath of *Lam Siu Po* highlights the problem of retrospective operation of the common law. It is an inherent feature of the common law that the court in deciding a case is necessarily applying the principle to some events in the past, and hence the common law, by necessity, operates retrospectively. This

---

[24] See *Tsui Kin Kwok Johnnie* v. *Commissioner of Police*, HCAL 50/2009; *Yiu Sung Chi & Lam Yau Tak Joseph* v. *Commissioner of Police*, HCAL 101 & 102/2009; *Tsui Chun Fai Danny* v. *Commissioner of Police*, HCAL 131/2009; *Li Kin Wah & Yung Kam Cheung*, HCAL 126/2009 & 6/2010; and *Wong Chi Keung* v. *Commissioner of Police*, HCAL 1/2010, HCAL 20/2010 & HCAL 21/2010.

[25] *Chiu Kin Ho* v. *Commissioner of Police*, HCAL 135/2004.

[26] *Ho Ho Chuen* v. *Commissioner of Police*, HCMP 2276/2009 and *Chan Kang Chau Clarence* v. *Commissioner of Police*, HCMP 2824/2004.

[27] Leave to make an application or appeal out of time was granted in *Chau Cheuk Yiu* v. *Poon Kit Sang*, HCMP 121/2010 but subsequently set aside by the CFA: FACV 7/2011; *Chan Ka Man* v. *Commissioner of Correctional Services*, HCAL 111/2009. The CJ explained these decisions as turning on the peculiar facts of these cases and did not decide any principles of law; see Andrew Li, 'Reflections on the Retrospective and Prospective Effect of Constitutional Judgments' in Rebecca Lee (ed.), *Common Law Lectures Series 2010* (Hong Kong: Faculty of Law, The University of Hong Kong, 2011) 21, 44.

[28] (2010) 13 HKCFAR 462; affirmed in *Lam Chi Pan* v. *Commissioner of Police*, FAMV35/2010, 11 February 2011.

poses a major challenge to our system of justice when a settled principle of law is reversed because there may be numerous past decisions or actions that were based on the previous erroneous view of the law and may potentially be open to challenge, sometimes long after the decisions had been made. In the normal course of events, the time limit for filing a case or lodging an appeal will take care of the situation, but the situation becomes more complex when the *vires* of the source of power is successfully challenged. In the *Lam Siu Po* aftermath, the question was whether the disciplinary conviction of a police officer should be upheld when the restriction of legal representation was subsequently found to be unconstitutional.

This gives rise to the controversial issue of how far the courts can limit the temporal effect of its judgments so as to avoid disturbing decisions that have been made in the past or to avoid a legal vacuum in the future before necessary remedial measures can be taken.[29] The CFA appeared to have accepted, without deciding, that it has an inherent power to engage in prospective overruling.[30] It has also recognized that this question might depend on the understanding and extent of separation of powers and the particular relations among the legislature, the executive, and the judiciary in different jurisdictions, and as a result, this was not a question that might yield to a common answer in different parts of the common law world. With such a rider, Li CJ provided a helpful summary of the exercise of such power if it existed. He held that (1) if such a power exists, it is an extraordinary power that the court would approach its exercise with the greatest circumspection; (2) whether this power exists depends on the particular constitutional framework of the jurisdiction concerned, and there may not be a common approach across the common law world; (3) the existence and scope of such power may vary in different situations because the same considerations do not apply to all situations in the different context of private law, criminal law, or public law; (4) the existence of the power may also be dependent on the range of remedies that may be available; and (5) common law is developed by an evolutionary process, and such development cannot be regarded as an application of the power to prospectively overrule.[31]

---

[29] For a more detailed discussion, see Chan, note 15 above; Li, note 29 above; and Kevin Zervos, 'Constitutional Remedies under the Basic Law' (2010) 40 *HKLJ* 687–718.

[30] *HKSAR* v. *Hung Chan Wa* (2006) 9 HKCFAR 614 and *Koo Sze Yiu* v. *Chief Executive* (2006) 9 HKCFAR 441.

[31] *Hung Chan Wa*, 634.

Disciplinary proceedings and due process

Standard of proof

For a long time in Hong Kong, it was believed that the standard of proof in disciplinary proceedings is a standard that is commensurate with the gravity of the disciplinary charge.[32] This flexible standard is an acknowledgement that disciplinary charges involve allegations ranging from nothing more than a technical breach to something closely akin to criminal charges. As Keith JA observed:

> [This approach] has the inestimable advantage of flexibility, and does not tie the hands of the disciplinary tribunal to a particular standard of proof, whatever the nature of the allegations and whatever the consequences for the person facing the disciplinary action. The more serious the complaint, and the more dire its consequences, the greater the degree of proof required to prove it, even though the degree of proof required falls short of proof beyond reasonable doubt.[33]

Thus, when the disciplinary charge was in essence one of indecent assault, it was held that the standard of proof has to be something similar or close to the criminal standard of proof beyond reasonable doubt;[34] however, if the charge was purely technical, such as a failure to comply with certain procedural requirements or standards, it was held that the appropriate standard should be the civil standard of a balance of probabilities.[35] Unfortunately, flexibility also means uncertainty; the strength of this flexible approach is also its weakness. In *Pirie* v. *Bar Council*, Le Pichon JA observed *obiter* that:

> a party who has to defend himself against serious allegations which are tantamount to the commission of a criminal offence and which have serious repercussions on his professional career should not be placed in a situation where the ground rules for defending himself are elastic and the boundaries imprecise.[36]

---

[32] The leading authorities are *Tse Lo Hong* v. *Attorney General* [1995] 3 HKC 428, 442A-B, per Litton VP (CA); *Wu Hin Ting* v. *The Medical Council of Hong Kong* [2004] 2 HKC 367, 378D-G, per Ma CJHC (CA) and *Lai King Shing* v. *Medical Council of Hong Kong* [1995] 2 HKLR 465 (CA).

[33] *Lai King Shing* v. *Medical Council of Hong Kong* [1995] 2 HKLR 465, 468 (CA).

[34] *Tse Lo Hong* v. *Attorney General* [1995] 3 HKC 428 (CA); *Dr Mu Lie Lian* v. *Medical Council of Hong Kong* [1995] 1 HKLR 29 (CA); *Wu Hin Ting* v. *Medical Council of Hong Kong* [2004] 2 HKC 367 (CA); and *Lai King Shing* v. *Medical Council of Hong Kong* [1995] 2 HKLR 465 (CA).

[35] *Solicitor* v. *Law Society of Hong Kong* [1997] HKLRD 63 (CA).

[36] [2001] 4 HKC 190, 204 (CA).

The issue was eventually revisited by the CFA in *Solicitor (24/07)* v. *Law Society of Hong Kong*.[37]

Having set out that there are only two standards of proof known to our law, being proof beyond reasonable doubt and proof on a preponderance of probabilities, Bokhary PJ first examined the standard of proof in civil cases with an allegation of criminal conduct. Having stated that the appropriate standard of proof was the civil standard and that the more serious the allegation, the more cogent the evidence required to overcome the unlikelihood of what was alleged, his Lordship turned to disciplinary proceedings. It was acknowledged that the standard of proof in disciplinary proceedings 'must be clear and, at the same time, capable of accommodating the variety of circumstances in which it has to be applied from case to case. It must lend itself to the just and proper disposal of all those cases.'[38] The court then turned the standard of proof into a question of cogency of evidence, and held that:

> the standard of proof for disciplinary proceedings in Hong Kong is a preponderance of probability under the *Re H* approach. The more serious the act or omission alleged, the more inherently improbable must it be regarded. And the more inherently improbable it is regarded, the more compelling will be the evidence needed to prove it on a preponderance of probability.[39]

Lord Morris provided a further explanation of this approach in *Re H*:

> When assessing the probabilities the court will have in mind as a factor, to whatever extent is appropriate in the particular case, that the more serious the allegation the less likely it is that the event occurred and, hence, the stronger should be the evidence before the court concludes that the allegation is established on the balance of probability. Fraud is usually less likely than negligence. Deliberate physical injury is usually less likely than accidental physical injury. A stepfather is usually less likely to have repeatedly raped and had nonconsensual oral sex with his under age stepdaughter than on some occasion to have lost his temper and slapped her. Built into the preponderance of probability standard is a generous degree of flexibility in respect of the seriousness of the allegation.[40]

This explanation is almost self-serving, if not circular, because it begs the question why fraud is more unlikely than negligence or why a stepfather is more unlikely to commit rape against his stepdaughter. It is almost suggesting that a 'normal' person is less likely to commit a crime. Besides, when the conduct alleged is criminal in nature, the heightened civil

---

[37] (2008) 11 HKCFAR 117.   [38] *Ibid.*, 166, [112].   [39] *Ibid.*, 167, [116].
[40] *Re H & Others (Minors) (Sexual Abuse: Standard of Proof)* [1996] AC 563, 586D-G (HL).

standard is hard to distinguish from the criminal standard in practice,[41] or as Lord Bingham remarked, the distinction 'is in truth, largely illusory'.[42] Although it is understandable that the court would like one single standard of proof in disciplinary proceedings, shifting attention from the standard of proof to cogency of evidence is largely semantic when the evidence required to discharge this single standard of proof is to be varied according to the probabilities of the allegations.

Presence of legal adviser in deliberation

In a series of cases, the CFA clarified a number of procedural matters pertaining to due process before disciplinary tribunals that are of far-reaching consequences. In *Medical Council of Hong Kong* v. *Helen Chan*, the issue was the role of the legal adviser in disciplinary proceedings.[43] There are many disciplinary bodies, statutory appeal boards, and tribunals for which a legal adviser may be appointed.[44] In the case of the Medical Council, the office of legal adviser is created by the Medical Registration Ordinance,[45] and by section 6(1) of the Medical Registration (Miscellaneous Provisions) Regulation,[46] the legal adviser shall be present at every inquiry held by the Medical Council. The legal adviser will give his or her advice on the legal issues in the presence of all parties after the Medical Council has heard all evidence and submissions but before it retires to consider its judgment. The legal adviser will, however, retire together with the Medical Council and be present at its deliberation so as to ensure that the Medical Council does not inadvertently take into account irrelevant matters and to prevent any misunderstanding of the legal issues. If necessary, he or she may tender additional legal advice and will inform all parties of such advice. The adviser will then prepare the first draft of the decision of the Medical Council in its presence. The draft judgment will be scrutinized thoroughly and modified, if necessary, by the Council to ensure that it is not the product of the legal adviser but the collective product of the Council. Given the increasing complexity of the issues confronting the Medical Council and the increasing expectation on procedural fairness, both the CA and the CFA were supportive of this practice and were satisfied that its practice was well intentioned and properly motivated. The issues, however, remained whether the presence

---

[41] As observed by Lord Phillips in *Gough* v. *Chief Constable of Derbyshire Constabulary* [2002] QB 1213, 1243A (CA).

[42] *B* v. *Chief Constable of Avon and Somerset Constabulary* [2001] 1 WLR 340, 354A.

[43] (2010) 13 HKCFAR 248.   [44] For a list of such bodies, see *ibid.*, 259–60, [13–14].

[45] Cap. 161.   [46] Cap. 161, sub. leg. D.

of the legal adviser at the deliberations of the Medical Council and the role in drafting the judgment were authorized by law and whether they would give rise to an apparent bias and injustice. The CA answered both questions against the Medical Council.

The CFA, however, reversed. First, it found no express or implied statutory provision that prohibited the presence of the legal adviser at the Medical Council's deliberations or permitted or prohibited his or her drafting the Council's decision, leaving the matter to be resolved according to the common law. Despite a long line of authorities that cast doubt on the presence of a non-member at the deliberative stage of a disciplinary or statutory appeal tribunal, the CFA drew a distinction between a non-member who acted as prosecuting counsel and a non-member who acted as legal adviser to the tribunal. The CFA held that the presence of the legal adviser at the deliberative stage did not compromise the competence, independence, and impartiality of the tribunal, the safeguard being the quality of the members of the tribunal. As for drafting the decision, the court found the practice acceptable as long as the legal adviser's role is confined to recording and reducing into writing the decision, finding, and reasoning of the tribunal.[47]

The court further proffered two pieces of advice.[48] First, the legal adviser should immediately, before retiring and in the presence of all parties, make a full and accurate statement of the practice that is to be followed, explaining clearly what he or she would or would not do, so as to allay the concern of all parties – as well as to remind him- or herself and members of the tribunal – of his or her role. Second, the legal adviser shall take great care to make his or her impartiality manifest at all times.

Although this decision displays great pragmatism and will no doubt be welcomed by many lay tribunals, it may underplay the perception of bias. The line between giving legal advice on the law or consequences of a particular application of the law on the one hand and the merit of the decision on the other is sometimes very difficult to draw. Moreover, legal advice on what is permissible can occasionally influence the outcome. The danger is even more obvious when the advice is on what is a relevant or

---

[47] The CFA emphasized that 'the tribunal must deliberate without any participation by the legal adviser apart from giving it legal advice. No drafting by the legal adviser may commence until after the tribunal – having so deliberated – has arrived at its decision and has made its decisions, findings and reasoning known to the legal adviser. What the legal adviser drafts must embody the tribunal's finding and reasoning. The tribunal must scrutinize the draft. If necessary, the tribunal must modify the draft to ensure that it is the tribunal's product, not the legal adviser's, and that it says what the tribunal means' [62].

[48] *Ibid.*, 275, [65–6].

irrelevant consideration. Thus, a reasonable person who does not know what goes on in the deliberation of the tribunal could have a legitimate grievance. It is not about whether the tribunal or the legal adviser would adhere to their roles, which was the court's concern when it posed the question of a reasonable fair-minded observer.[49]

Legality of interim measure

In *Yeung Chung Ming* v. *Commissioner of Police*,[50] the court had to deal with the vexed problem of the legality of interim action such as withholding part of the salary during the period of interdiction of a police officer pending criminal proceedings. The appellant, a police sergeant, was interdicted upon the laying of criminal charges against him, whereupon the commissioner directed that 10 per cent, which was subsequently reduced to 7 per cent, of his pay should be withheld during the interdiction. After his conviction and dismissal from the police force, the appellant argued that the withholding of his pay before his conviction was a violation of the presumption of innocence. The court, by a majority, rejected the suggestion that any action taken against him on the basis that he *might be* guilty constituted a violation of the presumption of innocence.[51] This must be correct because the very act of charging a person with criminal offences must involve a view by the prosecuting authority that he or she might be guilty.

The proper test, as pronounced by the court, is whether the commissioner's decision to withhold any proportion of the pay of an interdicted officer who has been charged with criminal offences implies a view that the person charged *is* guilty. The test is an objective one. The majority of the court found no violation of his right because he had been interdicted in the public interest, and during the period of interdiction, he was relieved from his duties and doing no work. The statute permits the commissioner to withhold up to half of the officer's pay, and the officer is entitled to the full amount of the pay withheld if he is acquitted after trial. This decision is important because there may be many situations when an interim action might have to be taken against those charged with a

---

[49] Bokhary PJ observed that 'fair-minded persons would, in the absence of evidence to the contrary, credit responsible bodies with adherence to the safeguards of their practices. Being taken to be fair-minded, the hypothetical observer must be taken to be someone who would credit the Medical Council with adherence to the safeguards of its stated practice unless there is evidence to the contrary' [65]. See also Chapter 15 (Young) in this volume.

[50] (2008) 11 HKCFAR 513.   [51] *Ibid.*, 527, [25–8].

disciplinary or a criminal offence. It is important to note that there was no challenge against the interdiction itself. Li CJ, writing for the majority, upheld the interdiction because a police officer who was to remain on duty pending a criminal trial would seriously erode public confidence in the police force.[52] The test used by the court would mean that most interim measures would probably pass muster. The test proposed by Bokhary PJ in his dissenting judgment strikes a better balance between the interest of the state and the right of the officer concerned, namely, that 'if a person is treated, by the conduct of the State, as if he is guilty or as if it does not matter whether he is guilty or not, this infringes the presumption of innocence'.[53] As Bokhary PJ observed, 'indifference to a fundamental right or freedom is more insidious – and in that sense can be even more dangerous – than any open derogation from that right or freedom'.[54]

Duty to give reasons

Another important issue is the duty to give reasons for decisions. As Lord Mustill stated in *R* v. *Secretary of State for the Home Department, ex p Doody*, the law at present does not recognize a general duty to give reasons.[55] Nonetheless, there is a clear trend towards an insistence on greater openness of decision-making, and the duty to give reasons has increasingly been imposed in various contexts. In *Oriental Daily Publisher* v. *Commissioner for Television and Entertainment Licensing Authority*, the CFA affirmed this trend.[56] Without deciding on this issue, the court indicated that it would, as a matter of statutory interpretation or common law principle of fairness, be prepared to assume a duty to give reasons unless there is contrary intention in the statute or it is otherwise inappropriate. Such a duty would promote intellectual discipline, bring sharper focus on and attention to relevant issues, provide guidance to the community, enable the parties to decide any further course of action, promote transparency, enhance consistency in decision making and law enforcement, and foster public confidence in the work of the tribunal.[57] The court held that not only is the Obscene Articles Tribunal obliged to give reasons, but the reasons must be adequate. The adequacy would depend upon the context in which the decision maker is operating and the circumstances of the case in question. In the case of obscenity and indecency, sometimes

---

[52] *Ibid.*, 532, [46–7]. The majority of the court did not address this issue.
[53] *Ibid.*, 531, [44].   [54] *Ibid.*, 531, [44].   [55] [1994] AC 531, 564E (HL).
[56] (1997–98) 1 HKCFAR 279, 288–90.   [57] *Ibid.*, 290.

the content of the articles in question may be self-explanatory, but when this is not the case, the tribunal would have to explain its decision.[58] This welcome development enhances transparency and accountability of the administrative decision-making process.[59]

From *Wednesbury* to proportionality

Another major contribution of the CFA is the introduction of the principle of proportionality to judicial review.[60] A perennial problem in administrative law is the extent of judicial scrutiny. For decades, the principle of *Wednesbury* unreasonableness represented the orthodox position of judicial review. This principle is heavily influenced by the doctrine of the separation of powers, under which the proper role of the judiciary is to ensure the legality of administrative decisions, not to substitute them by its own. As modern administration becomes increasingly complex and when administrative discretion encroaches on almost every aspect of daily life, it comes as no surprise that the courts are increasingly dissatisfied with the narrow scope of the *Wednesbury* test. The strongest attack probably came from Lord Cooke in *R (Daly)* v. *Secretary of State for the Home Department,* who prophesized that 'the day will come when it will be more widely recognized that the *Wednesbury* test was an unfortunately retrogressive decision in English administrative law, in so far as it suggested that there are degrees of unreasonableness and that only a very extreme degree can bring an administrative decision within the legitimate scope of judicial invalidation'.[61]

As a partial response to the narrow scope of *Wednesbury* unreasonableness, the court introduced a 'heightened scrutiny' test when fundamental rights or liberty are at stake, dealing not with the process of decision

---

[58] In that particular case, the pictures involved some photographs of semi-naked women, and the court found that if these photographs were considered indecent, the tribunal would be coming close to holding that photographs of semi-naked women were per se indecent according to community standards. This is not self-explanatory, and the tribunal has to explain its decision: *ibid.*, 292–3.

[59] See also *Prabakar, Re SJM Holdings Ltd* [2009] 1 HKLRD 321 (CA); *Wong Hin Hang* v. *Hong Kong Housing Authority* [2009] HKEC 1151 (CFI); *Ming Pao Newspaper Ltd* v. *Obscene Articles Tribunal* [2008] HKEC 1750 (CFI); and *Three Weekly Ltd* v. *Obscene Articles Tribunal* [2007] 3 HKLRD 673 (CA).

[60] For a more detailed discussion, see Johannes Chan, 'A Sliding Scale of Reasonableness in Judicial Review' [2006] *Acta Juridica* 233–56.

[61] [2001] 2 AC 532, 549 (HL).

making alone but also on the merits of the decision. Thus, in *R* v. *Lord Saville of Newdigate, ex p A*, Lord Woolf MR said:

> What is important to note is that when a fundamental right such as the right to life is engaged, the options available to the reasonable decision-maker are curtailed. They are curtailed because it is unreasonable to reach a decision which contravenes or could contravene human rights unless there are sufficiently significant countervailing considerations. In other words it is not open to the decision-maker to risk interfering with fundamental rights in the absence of compelling justification. Even the broadest discretion is constrained by the need for there to be countervailing circumstances justifying interference with human rights. *The courts will anxiously scrutinize the strength of the countervailing circumstances and the degree of the interference with the human right involved* and then apply the test accepted by Sir Thomas Bingham MR in *R* v. *Ministry of Defence, ex p Smith* [1996] QB 517, which is not in issue.[62] (emphasis supplied)

In a similar tone, the CFA held that when personal liberty is at stake, the court would demand the highest standard of fairness and subject the decision to the most rigorous scrutiny.[63]

The principle of proportionality, developed notably in international human rights jurisprudence, has quickly found its way into domestic law in human rights matters.[64] The proportionality test acknowledges the central role of the courts in ensuring that administrative discretion cannot be exercised in a way that undermines fundamental human rights. As Lord Steyn pointed out, '[T]he doctrine of proportionality may require the reviewing court to assess the balance which the decision maker has struck, not merely whether it is within the range of rational or reasonable decisions'.[65] It goes beyond the traditional grounds of review 'inasmuch as it may require attention to be directed to the relative weight accorded to interests and considerations'.[66]

With the introduction of the Human Rights Act 1998 in Britain, the proportionality test is now firmly rooted in English human rights law. Yet despite the increasing influence of the jurisprudence from the European Court of Human Rights (ECtHR) in the United Kingdom, an attempt

---

[62] [2000] 1 WLR 1855, 1867 [37] (CA).   [63] *Prabakar*, 204D-I.

[64] See e.g. *Handyside* v. *United Kingdom* (1980) 1 EHRR 737, [49]; *Sunday Times* v. *United Kingdom* (1980) 2 EHRR 245, [62]; *Norris* v. *Ireland* (1991) 13 EHRR 186, [41]; *R (Daly)* v. *Secretary of State for the Home Department* [2001] 2 AC 532, [27] (HL); *R* v. *Shayler* [2003] 1 AC 247, [60–1] (HL); *R* v. *Oakes* (1986) 26 DLR (4th) 200 (SCC); *De Freitas* v. *Permanent Secretary of Ministry of Agriculture, Fisheries, Lands and Housing* [1999] 1 AC 69 (PC); *S* v. *Makwanyane* (1995) 3 SA 391 (South Africa Constitutional Court); and *Leung Kwok Hung* v. *HKSAR* (2005) 8 HKCFAR 229, 252–3.

[65] *R (Daly)*, 547.   [66] *Ibid*.

to introduce proportionality as the fourth ground for judicial review has been unsuccessful.[67] This gives rise to a strange situation that in human rights cases, the court will adopt the proportionality test or a heightened scrutiny test; otherwise, the *Wednesbury* unreasonableness test remains the guiding principle. In the United Kingdom, upon the introduction of the Human Rights Act, it has been forcefully argued that it is only a matter of time that proportionality will be accepted in English administrative law.[68] In Hong Kong, after the BOR and the BL, the court has readily accepted the proportionality test in assessing the constitutionality of any restriction on fundamental rights.[69]

An attempt to bring together this parallel concept of proportionality and *Wednesbury* unreasonableness is the introduction of the so-called 'sliding scale of intensity of scrutiny test'. This concept of a sliding scale of intensity of scrutiny first appeared in the judgment of Laws LJ in *R (Mahmood)* v. *Secretary of State for the Home Department*:

> [I]n a case involving human rights the second approach which I outlined at paragraph 16 as to the intensity of review is generally to be followed, leaving aside incorporation of the Convention; but that approach and the basic *Wednesbury* rule are by no means hermetically sealed one from the other. *There is, rather, what may be called a sliding scale of review; the graver the impact of the decision in question upon the individual affected by it, the more substantial the justification that will be required.* It is in the nature of the human condition that cases where, objectively, the individual is most gravely affected will be those where we have come to call his fundamental rights are or are said to be put in jeopardy.[70] (italics supplied)

Although confined to human rights cases,[71] there is no rational principle why the test of sliding scale should not be applied to other types of

---

[67] An argument that proportionality constituted a fourth ground for judicial review alongside illegality, procedural irregularities, and impropriety was rejected by the House of Lords in *R* v. *Secretary of State for the Home Department, ex parte Brind* [1991] 1 AC 696 (HL).

[68] Wade and Forsyth, *Administrative Law*, 8th edn. (Oxford: Oxford University Press, 2000) 368–9; Jeffrey Jowell, 'Beyond the Rule of Law: Towards Constitutional Judicial Review' [2000] *Public Law* 671; David Feldman 'Proportionality and the Human Rights Act 1998' in Evelyn Ellis (ed.), *The Principle of Proportionality in the Laws of Europe* (Oxford: Hart, 1999) 117, 127 et seq.

[69] *Leung Kwok Hung* v. *HKSAR* (2005) 8 HKCFAR 229, 252–3, per Li CJ. See also *R* v. *Lord Saville of Newdigate, ex parte A* [2000] 1 WLR 1855, 1867 (CA). For a more detailed argument, see Chan, note 62 above.

[70] [2001] 1 WLR 840, [19] (CA).

[71] See also Sir Thomas Bingham MR in *R* v. *Ministry of Defence, ex p Smith* [1996] QB 517, 554 (CA).

judicial review.[72] The proportionality test itself embodies an inherent flexibility because the degree of cogency of justification would vary with the importance of the interest to be protected. Parliament could always be presumed to confer a power the exercise of which is confined to what is necessary for the statutory objectives, whether involving rights or other interests. In this sense, there is little difference between a proportionality test and a sliding scale of intensity of review. These cases merely illustrate a general principle that the intensity of review should be proportionate to the gravity of the subject matter at stake,[73] and a violation of human rights simply provides a context that enables the court to exercise a more rigorous standard of scrutiny. The proper issue would be what the intention of the legislature is when it confers the powers on the public officer or the public body. If the legislature has decided to attach specific weight to a particular factor, it is only right that the court should ensure that such a specific weight has been accorded in the decision-making process.[74]

This argument received some blessing by the CFA in *Town Planning Board* v. *The Society for the Protection of the Harbour*.[75] The issue was the appropriate test to displace the presumption against reclamation of the harbour, which was described as a natural heritage of the people of Hong Kong under section 3 of the Protection of the Harbour Ordinance.[76] The Town Planning Board argued that section 3 created a mandatory factor that must be taken into consideration in any reclamation, but the weight to be attached to this factor was a matter for the Planning Board, subject only to the *Wednesbury* test. The Society, on the other hand, argued that, given the importance of the statutory objective to protect the harbour, the Planning Board has to demonstrate a compelling need before the presumption against reclamation could be displaced, an argument that the CFA accepted. The need has to arise within a definite and reasonable time frame, taking into account the time scale of planning exercises, to be proved by cogent and convincing evidence. Because the need has to be overriding, the extent of reclamation cannot go beyond the minimum that is required by the overriding need, and each area of reclamation must be justified. In the course of argument, the possibility of introducing a

---

[72] See also *R* v. *Secretary of State for the Home Department, ex p Launder* [1997] 1 WLR 839, 867 per Lord Hope (HL); *Minister for Aboriginal Affairs* v. *Peko-Wallsend Ltd* (1985) 162 CLR 24, 41–2 per Mason J (Austr HC).

[73] See *Peko-Wallsend*, 41–2, per Mason J (Austr HC); *R* v. *Secretary of State for the Home Department, ex parte Launder* [1997] 1 WLR 839, 867, per Lord Hope (HL).

[74] *Peko-Wallsend Ltd*, 41.

[75] *Town Planning Board* v. *The Society for the Protection of the Harbour* (2004) 7 HKCFAR 1.

[76] Cap. 531.

sliding scale of intensity of review was raised by Sir Anthony Mason NPJ. The CFA noted that this issue deserved serious consideration and could well point to how common law should develop but eventually found it unnecessary to resolve this issue.[77]

This was the first time that the court suggested that the proportionality test, or a sliding scale of intensity of review, was appropriate in judicial review of administrative decisions concerning subject matters other than human rights. The test is flexible enough to encompass, as appropriate, a more rigorous review or the conventional *Wednesbury* unreasonableness. The sliding scale principle was eventually adopted in *Society for Protection of the Harbour Ltd* v. *Chief Executive in Council (No 2)* in light of the unique legal status of the Harbour.[78] Quietly, the notion of proportionality has crept into the general principle of administrative law.

Deference

A related issue is the question of deference. Notwithstanding stricter scrutiny, the court is prepared to pay due deference to the views of the executive government in some circumstances, especially when allocation of resources or formulation of major policies is concerned. A conventional justification for due deference is that the judiciary, being unelected, lacks the legitimacy to frustrate the will of the general public manifested through the elected legislature. This justification is more relevant to constitutional review than in the classic situation of judicial review of administrative decision. It can also be argued that the judiciary is entrusted with the duty to ensure that the executive government, and likewise the legislature, does not transgress the limits of the law, including the BL. This argument carries more weight in Hong Kong when the BL confers on the judiciary the role of constitutional review (or at least this role is assumed by the judiciary without much queries from the community), but in the United Kingdom or New Zealand, even upon the introduction of the Human Rights Act or the BOR, it was explicitly decided that the judiciary should not enjoy the power to strike down legislation.

The second justification for deference is institutional incompetence. The judiciary does not have the expertise or knowledge to encroach on

---

[77] *Society for the Protection of the Harbour* (CFA), 21–2, [67, 68].

[78] *Society for Protection of the Harbour Ltd* v. *Chief Executive in Council (No 2)* [2004] 2 HKLRD 902, 929–930 (CFI). Despite the rhetoric, the manner the court applied this sliding scale test was not much different from the *Wednesbury* unreasonableness test, highlighting the uneasiness of the court to interfere with the executive assessment of competing factors. For a detailed discussion, see Chan, note 71 above.

some executive decisions, for example, concerning the allocation of state resources, which is a basis to some extent for the *Wednesbury* principle. Yet there are also many judicial review decisions that have had major adverse impact on the operation of the government. The Harbour Reclamation case resulted in setting aside many years of planning for reclamation of the harbour and sending the reclamation plan (at least part of it) back to the drawing board;[79] likewise, the decision in the public housing case would potentially affect more than 2.4 million residents in public housing.[80] There are numerous examples of judicial review cases that have major public implications, and the court has not felt constrained in deciding these cases. The strength of the court is to analyse objectively the evidence and to weigh competing interests and arguments. This is a role that the court is well suited to discharge, regardless of consequences. This is not to say that the court should not give weight to the views of the executive government. Rather, such views should form part of the weighing process. Unfortunately, the doctrine of due deference has sometimes gone far beyond that and may result in an abdication of judicial duty.[81] The issue of deference has determined the outcome of a number of cases involving social and economic rights,[82] and these cases will soon reach the CFA.

Substantive legitimate expectation

In the landmark decision of *Ng Siu Tung* v. *Director of Immigration*,[83] the CFA extended the doctrine of legitimate expectation to cover substantive

---

[79] *Society for Protection of the Harbour* (CFA).
[80] *Ho Choi Wan* v. *Hong Kong Housing Authority* (2005) 8 HKCFAR 628.
[81] For an insightful discussion on deference, see J. Jowell, 'Judicial Deference: Servility, Civility or Institutional Capacity?' [2003] *Public Law* 592–601; T.R.S. Allan, 'Human Rights and Judicial Review: A Critique of "Due Deference"' (2006) 63 *Cambridge Law Journal* 671–95; and M. Hunt, 'Sovereignty's Blight: Why Public Law Needs "Due Deference"' in N. Bamforth and P. Leyland (eds.), *Public Law in a Multi-Layered Constitution* (Oxford: Hart, 2003) 337.
[82] *Kong Yunming* v. *Director of Social Welfare* [2009] 4 HKLRD 382 (CFI), [2012] 4 HKC 180 (CA); *Fok Chun Wa* v. *The Hospital Authority* [2011] 1 HKLRD A1 (CA), [2012] 2 HKC 413 (CFA); *Lau Cheong* v. *HKSAR* (2002) 5 HKCFAR 415; *George Yau* v. *Director of Social Welfare* [2011] 1 HKLRD A2 (CFI) but also see *Kwong Kwok Hay* v. *Medical Council of Hong Kong* [2008] 3 HKLRD 524 (CA) and *Kong Yunming* v. *Director of Social Welfare*, supra, where Stock VP suggested the avoidance of using the term 'deference'; Cora Chan, 'Judicial Deference at Work: Some Reflections on Chan Kin Sum and Kong Yun Ming' (2010) 40 *HKLJ* 1.
[83] (2002) 5 HKCFAR 1.

protection.[84] Indeed, it is notable that the very first landmark case on legitimate expectation also came from Hong Kong. In *Attorney General v. Ng Yuen Shiu*,[85] the Privy Council held that when a public authority charged with a duty of making a decision promised to follow certain procedures before reaching that decision, good administration required that it should act by implementing the promise if the implementation did not conflict with the authority's statutory duty. In that case, it was held that, having promised to consider each case on its merits upon the discontinuance of the 'touch base' policy, the Director of Immigration could not retract from that promise by removing an illegal immigrant without affording him an opportunity to be heard. This is sometimes referred to as procedural legitimate expectation. The court has for some years been hesitant to hold that the promise made in such circumstances is enforceable, as it may unnecessarily hamper the Government's ability to change a policy. Thus, only a decade ago, the doctrine of substantive legitimate expectation was still labelled by the English CA as 'wrong in principle' and 'heretical'.[86]

On the other hand, important as it may be, procedural legitimate expectation leaves an aggrieved person with little consolation and would not be conducive to good administration when he or she has relied on a promise made by the government, yet the promise could be withdrawn without any consequence.[87] The challenge is to delineate the scope of proper judicial intervention without unduly tying the hands of the government when a change of policy is called for. Over the years, the court has on various occasions held the government to its promise. In *Wong Pei Chun v. Hong Kong Housing Authority*,[88] the commissioner for resettlement assured in writing that the residents at Rennie's Mill could reside in the area indefinitely; many of them were nationalist soldiers of the

---

[84] For a detailed discussion of this doctrine, see Forsyth and Williams, 'Closing Chapter in the Immigration Children Saga: Substantive Legitimate Expectations and Administrative Justice in Hong Kong' (2002) 10 *Asia Pacific Law Review* 29–47; Li and Leung, 'The Doctrine of Substantive Legitimate Expectation: The Significance of Ng Siu Tung and Others v. Director of Immigration' (2002) 32 *HKLJ* 471–96; and Tai and Yam, 'The Advent of Substantive Legitimate Expectations in Hong Kong: Two Competing Visions' [2002] *Public Law* 688–702.

[85] [1983] 2 AC 629 (PC).

[86] *R v. Secretary of State for the Home Department, ex parte Hargreaves* [1997] 1 WLR 906, 924–5 (CA).

[87] See C. Forsyth, 'The Provenance and Protection of Legitimate Expectations' [1988] *Cambridge Law Journal* 238, 240.

[88] [1996] 2 HKLR 293 (HC).

Kuomintang government who came to settle in Hong Kong after 1949. Confining the principle of legitimate expectation to procedural protection, the court held that it was an abuse of power for the government to breach the promise some 35 years later when the government decided to remove the residents to carry out urban redevelopment.

The principle of substantive legitimate expectation received renewed interest in England in recent years[89] and was finally and authoritatively established in Hong Kong in *Ng Siu Tung*. Shortly after 1 July 1997, about 5000 Mainland-born children of Hong Kong permanent residents claimed to have a right of abode in Hong Kong pursuant to Article 24 of the BL, a status that they did not enjoy before the changeover. To make the litigation manageable, it was agreed that a few representative cases should be chosen. Some of the claimants were advised not to join the litigation but were assured that they would be treated in the same way as the applicants in *Ng Ka Ling*, which was intended to be a test case. In *Ng Ka Ling* v. *Director of Immigration*,[90] the CFA upheld the claims. Subsequently, *Ng Ka Ling* was reversed by the Standing Committee of the National People's Congress (NPCSC) pursuant to Article 158 of the BL, which provided that 'judgments previously rendered shall not be affected'. The applicants in *Ng Siu Tung* claimed that they were given the expectation that they would be treated in the same way as the applicants in *Ng Ka Ling* and demanded that they be granted a right of abode in Hong Kong. In this sense, they were claiming a substantive benefit. The CFA upheld the claims of some of them and held that when the conduct of a public officer, whether by way of promise, representation, practice, or policy, gave rise to a legitimate expectation of a substantive outcome or benefit, it would be an abuse of power to refuse to honour such legitimate expectation in the absence of any overriding reason of law or policy.[91]

Although the principle is formulated in rather general language, the court narrowed it down with a number of qualifications. First, whether an expectation is legitimate depends partly upon the conduct of the relevant public authority and what it has committed itself. Secondly, although the expectation may arise from representation or conduct, the representation or conduct has to be clear and unambiguous. The court accepted that many policy statements are necessarily couched in vague terms. Hence, the more general a statement is, the less likely that the court

---

[89] See also *R* v. *North and East Devon Health Authority, ex parte Coughlan* [2000] 2 WLR 622 (CA).
[90] (1999) 2 HKCFAR 4.   [91] (2002) 5 HKCFAR 1, 41, [92].

will infer from it a definite promise or representation. The requirement of a clear and unambiguous promise or representation may prove to be the most difficult hurdle for any substantive claim of legitimate expectation. Thus, the court held that a general statement that the government would respect the rule of law and abide by the court judgment was insufficient.[92] Likewise, the court has held that there was no legitimate expectation of a periodic rental review when the Housing Authority refused to conduct a rental review in a deflationary economy (leading presumably to a reduction in rent as a result of a statutory cap) despite a consistent previous practice of rental review of public housing every two years for more than 20 years on the ground that the previous rental review was non-statutory based and was conducted in an inflationary economy (which consistently resulted in a rental increase).[93] The court further held that if a representation was reasonably susceptible to a competing construction, it would be wrong to adopt the construction most favourable to the person asserting the legitimate expectation. Instead, the correct approach would be to accept the interpretation applied by the public authority, subject to the application of the *Wednesbury* unreasonableness test.[94] This was particularly apt in relation to the government's policy statements because, in general, no unfairness could arise when the government acted on a rational view of its policy statements.[95]

Third, for an expectation to be legitimate, the benefits to be accorded must be what the claimant is legally entitled to expect. It is not legitimate to expect a benefit that is unlawful to confer. Nor is it legitimate to expect the public authority to make a decision or exercise a discretion in a manner that is contrary to law, that is outside the power of the public authority, or that would undermine the statutory purpose.[96] In this case, the government argued that when the NPCSC had given the interpretation that had the effect of reversing *Ng Ka Ling*, the Director of Immigration had no power to exempt the applicants from the requirement of having a one-way exit permit from the Mainland authorities because such an exemption would be unlawful. The court accepted this argument but held that the director would nonetheless have a general discretion under the Immigration Ordinance to permit the eligible applicants to stay in Hong Kong. The director argued that this would still be an unlawful fettering of the discretion of the director, and if the director exercised his

---

[92] At 38, [82].

[93] *Ho Choi Wan* v. *Hong Kong Housing Authority* (2005) 8 HKCFAR 628, 648–50, [50–5].

[94] (2002) 5 HKCFAR 1, 44, [104].   [95] *Ibid.*, 44–5, [104].   [96] *Ibid.*, 47, [112].

discretion in favour of the entire class of claimants, it would undermine the statutory scheme.[97] The court responded:

> if the circumstances are such as to raise a legitimate expectation, the common law itself imposes a duty on the decision maker, grounded in the principle of good administration and the duty to act fairly, to take that legitimate expectation into account, so long as, and to the extent that, taking it into account is not inconsistent with the statutory provisions and does not undermine the statutory purpose.[98]

However, the court did reckon that to allow the entire class of claimants to stay in Hong Kong would be contrary to the statutory scheme that has been validated by the NPCSC's interpretation.[99] Those who relied on a specific representation of the director of legal aid or the Director of Immigration were treated separately from claimants who relied on general statements from the government. A crucial factor was that the former class was a determined class of people of a finite size. It was held that exercising discretion in favour of a small and finite class of claimants to stay in Hong Kong to mitigate the failure of the original legitimate expectation would be lawful – a pragmatic solution to a conflict between legitimate expectations and statutory obligations.[100] It is difficult, however, to see why, as a matter of principle, that legitimate expectation should be defeated by the sheer number of beneficiaries, as Bokhary PJ stated in his powerful dissent:

> I do not regard the fact that an abuse of executive power on a large scale as a reason for letting such abuse pass unremedied. Nor do I regard it as any part of the statutory purpose of the provisions in question that those provisions cannot be resorted to even when resorting to them would avoid an abuse of executive power.[101]

When an applicant succeeds in establishing a legitimate expectation, the expectation has to be properly taken into account in the decision-making process and is normally expected to be honoured. This is so even if the decision involves policy considerations. If effect is not given to the expectation, the decision maker should express its reasons so that they may be tested in court. In general, the failure to take account of the legitimate expectation would constitute an abuse of power.[102]

---

[97] *Ibid.*, 50–5, particularly [129, 134–8, and 143].
[98] *Ibid.*, 52, [129].   [99] *Ibid.*, 54, [136].
[100] *Ibid.*, 26–7. Although *Ng Ka Ling* and *Chan Kam Nga* were regarded as 'representative cases', neither case was constituted by a court order to make the applicants representative parties.
[101] *Ibid.*, 119, [399].   [102] *Ibid.*, 42–3, [94–8].

Formulated in this manner, there is close resemblance between the doctrine of legitimate expectation and estoppel. A major difference is that because legitimate expectation is grounded on fairness and good administration, it would not be essential to establish detrimental reliance.[103] The rationale is that it is unfair and contrary to good administration to allow the public authority to renege on a representation or a promise of benefits without good reasons and not, as in the estoppel, that an applicant has altered his or her position to their detriment by relying on a promise or a representation of the public authority. At the same time, it could be difficult to prove reliance in a legitimate expectation case when the representation is made by reference to a large and innominate class of applicants, and as Bokhary PJ pointed out, there was no good reason to deny a person of the benefit of a legitimate expectation of his or her class merely because he or she learned of the relevant representation after a decision disappointing it.[104] In practice, there may be little difference whichever route is adopted because there would be few cases of legitimate expectation when there is no detrimental reliance. In any event, if the claimant has suffered no detriment, this could always be a factor that the court could take into account in determining the appropriate relief.

The recognition of the doctrine of substantive legitimate expectation is a major development in the common law. Although the public authorities might become more cautious in making public statements, the various safeguards that the court has established suggest that the court would avoid unduly trespassing upon the policy preserve of the executive. The doctrine greatly enhances the role of judicial scrutiny of administrative actions and the accountability of public authorities. *Ng Siu Tung* soon became a landmark decision in the common law and has been followed both locally and overseas.[105]

---

[103] The majority of the court left open the issue whether detrimental reliance was necessary (*ibid.*, 46, [110]), but the issue was addressed at length by Bokhary PJ in his dissenting judgment (*ibid.*, 106–8, [354–9]).

[104] *Ibid.*, 106, [355].

[105] See *R* v. *Secretary of State for the Home Department, ex parte Zeqiri* [2002] UKHL 3 (HL). It has generated a large number of cases in Hong Kong; see e.g. *Cathay Pacific Airways Flight Attendants Union* v. *Director General of Civil Aviation* [2007] 2 HKC 393 (CA); and *Ho Choi Wan* v. *Hong Kong Housing Authority* (2005) 8 HKCFAR 628. For further discussion of this doctrine, see Forsyth and Williams, Li and Leung, Tai and Yam, all note 86 above; and Chapter 22 (Lo) in this volume.

Conclusion

Unlike constitutional law in which the court is charting into a completely new area and has to deal with the novel and difficult issue of delineation of powers between the central and the special administrative region government, in administrative law, the court is building on well-established principles and making incremental changes and sometimes novel advancement. That said, it is inevitable that the court, in exercising judicial scrutiny over administrative action, will be affected and guided by its perception of separation of powers between the judiciary and the executive. The development of administrative law is further complicated by the increasingly blurred distinction between administrative law and constitutional law. Under the BL, it is possible to challenge not just the *vires* of administrative decisions, which are the conventional purview of administrative law, but also the *vires* of the source of power of administrative decisions. In so doing, the CFA has shown great sensitivity towards the delicate delineation of powers between the executive and the judiciary. It has established itself as a reasonably liberal court, striking a good balance between achieving good administration and governance on the one hand and respecting the rights of individuals and the rule of law on the other. It has also been shown to be innovative and is ready to explore the uncharted areas, such as prospective overruling or substantive legitimate expectation.

Space constraint does not allow us to survey all the important decisions of the court in the area of administrative law. What has been shown in this chapter is how the court has contributed to enhancing good administration and accountability of public authority through liberal procedures facilitating access to justice; refinement of procedural due process; and review of substantive merits of administrative decisions using the doctrines of proportionality, a sliding scale of intensity of review, and substantive legitimate expectation. The court has also been confronted with issues that have grave political consequences. It has not shied away from such challenges and has tried to do its best to develop legal solutions without losing sight of the importance of pragmatism and flexibility, although one may question whether the court has on some occasions been too ready to achieve a pragmatic solution at the expense of a principled outcome.

17

Criminal law

SIMON N. M. YOUNG

Introduction

This chapter reviews the Court of Final Appeal's (CFA's) first 13 years of criminal law decisions. The CFA decided 111 criminal cases, about a third of the total caseload, during the tenure of Chief Justice Andrew Li. Such a large number of cases cannot be reviewed individually within the space of this chapter. Instead, general themes in the jurisprudence will be discussed to show how the CFA contributed to the development of Hong Kong criminal law and procedure from 1997 to 2010. The chapter begins with a discussion of its first criminal case as a point of reference for later developments.

The first case

The case of *Tang Siu Man* v. *HKSAR*, decided eight months after the court's establishment, was remarkable in many ways.[1] In a robust and independent manner, the court by majority chose not to follow the English *Vye* principles[2] for directing a jury on an accused's good character. Instead, it held that Hong Kong courts should have discretion to give either or both the credibility and propensity limbs of the direction if the accused was a person of good character in the opinion of the judge. Tang, only 23 years old at the time of conviction, had very little to impress about his character. Omitting the propensity limb of the *Vye* direction was not fatal to the conviction, and upon the CFA's dismissal of his appeal, he continued to serve his sentence of 25 years of imprisonment for drug trafficking and manufacturing. Justice Bokhary, dissenting, believed that the *Vye* direction was the 'minimum level of protection due to an accused'.[3] In

---

[1] *Tang Siu Man* v. *HKSAR (No 2)* (1998) 1 HKCFAR 107.
[2] *R* v. *Vye* (1993) 97 Cr App R 134 (CA), followed in *R* v. *Aziz* [1996] AC 41 (HL).
[3] *Tang Siu Man*, 134.

a brief judgment, the Chief Justice retorted that the majority's approach 'when properly understood and applied, [was] not, in any way, less protective of an accused person' compared with English law.[4]

Tang Siu Man set the tone for the court's approach to the development of the common law in criminal cases. Gone was the gut instinct to follow English authority. With the new influence of the sitting foreign judge, the judicial mind opened to a wider range of approaches in other common law jurisdictions. In *Tang*, Australian and New Zealand authorities were found to have greater persuasive force than the English ones. In later cases in which human rights points arose, reference to relevant international law from the European Court of Human Rights (ECtHR) or other courts and tribunals was commonplace. Pre-1997 Hong Kong authorities suggesting a distinctive local practice were sometimes cited to justify a unique Hong Kong common law, as was true in *Tang*,[5] but in appropriate cases, the CFA overruled pre-handover authorities.[6] In other cases, it would again decide not to follow English authorities.[7]

The judgments in *Tang* were also noticeably lengthy, in total about three times the length of the average criminal law judgment. There was a long majority opinion by Litton PJ (who remains a non-permanent judge [NPJ]), a long dissenting opinion by Bokhary PJ, and separate concurring opinions from Li CJ and the Australian judge, Sir Daryl Dawson NPJ. Such plurality of legal opinion in one criminal case was rarely seen again.[8] There were only three more cases with dissenting views, all from Bokhary PJ.[9] None of these dissents reflected any serious ideological disagreement with the majority but rather a different view of the particular issue or facts in the case. Indeed, Bokhary and Chan PJJ would go on to write the bulk of the criminal law majority opinions. The Chief Justice, who was not a criminal lawyer in his time at the bar, also took an active interest, particularly in cases concerning the rights of a defendant or

---

[4] *Ibid.*, 114.   [5] *Ibid.*, 120.

[6] E.g. *Secretary for Justice* v. *Lam Tat Ming* (2000) 3 HKCFAR 168; *Hin Lin Yee* v. *HKSAR* (2010) 13 HKCFAR 142; *Secretary for Justice* v. *Yau Yuk Lung* (2007) 10 HKCFAR 335; *P* v. *The Commissioner of the Independent Commission Against Corruption* (2007) 10 HKCFAR 293 ('*P* v. *ICAC*'); *Z* v. *HKSAR* (2007) 10 HKCFAR 183; and *HKSAR* v. *Tin's Label Factory Limited* (2008) 11 HKCFAR 637.

[7] E.g. *HKSAR* v. *Wong Sau Ming* (2003) 6 HKCFAR 135; *Hin Lin Yee, ibid.*

[8] The court gave four judgments in *Oriental Daily Publisher Ltd* v. *Commissioner for Television and Entertainment Licensing Authority* (1997–1998) 1 HKCFAR 279 and in *Hin Lin Yee*, and five judgments in *HKSAR* v. *Kevin Egan* (2010) 13 HKCFAR 314.

[9] *Hin Lin Yee, ibid.*; *Wong Sau Ming*; *Leung Kwok Hung* v. *HKSAR* (2005) 8 HKCFAR 229.

calling for jurisdictional clarification.[10] Ribeiro PJ wrote less than Bokhary and Chan PJJ but chose to write majority opinions in more cerebral cases requiring a thorough canvassing of the common law.[11]

The foreign judge would become a fixture in criminal cases, although Sir Daryl himself did not sit again in crime. Consistent with the overall average, there was a foreign judge in 96 per cent of all the criminal cases. They wrote 26 per cent of all the majority judgments in criminal cases. English and Australian judges had the most involvement; New Zealand judges sat on a few occasions. Of all the sitting foreign judges, Sir Anthony Mason NPJ had by far the most involvement and impact. He sat on 38 per cent of the cases and wrote majority opinions in 14 of them. He left his mark on the common law offences of misconduct in public office[12] and conspiracy to defraud,[13] the common law of prosecutorial disclosure,[14] and Basic Law (BL) principles such as the principle of legal certainty[15] and presumption of innocence.[16] But the cases that stood out were those in which convictions were quashed for serious offences, such as homicide,[17] child sexual abuse,[18] major bribery,[19] and assaults on police by Falun Gong members.[20]

When common law countries differed on a particular legal issue, the foreign judge appeared to influence the majority to adopt the legal position of his home jurisdiction. Two cases illustrate this phenomenon. In *Chim Hon Man* v. *HKSAR*, Sir Anthony, in his first case sitting as a Hong Kong judge, followed the strict Australian approach on the use of specimen counts in child sexual abuse cases rather than the more permissive

---

[10] E.g. *Oriental Daily Publisher Ltd*; *HKSAR* v. *Ng Kung Siu* (1999) 2 HKCFAR 442; *Lam Tat Ming*; *Lau Cheong* v. *HKSAR* (2002) 5 HKCFAR 415; *Wong Sau Ming*, *ibid*.; *Hau Kin* v. *HKSAR* (2005) 8 HKCFAR 63; *Leung Kwok Hung*, *ibid*.; *P* v. *ICAC*; *Secretary for Justice* v. *Yau Yuk Lung Zigo* (2004) 7 HKCFAR 335; and *Tin's Label Factory Limited*.

[11] E.g. *Hin Lin Yee*; *HKSAR* v. *Lee Ming Tee* (2001) 4 HKCFAR 133.

[12] *Shum Kwok Sher* v. *HKSAR* (2002) 5 HKCFAR 381; *Sin Kam Wah* v. *HKSAR* (2005) 8 HKCFAR 192.

[13] *Mo Yuk Ping* v. *HKSAR* (2007) 10 HKCFAR 386.

[14] *HKSAR* v. *Lee Ming Tee (No. 2)* (2003) 6 HKCFAR 336.

[15] *Shum Kwok Sher*; *Mo Yuk Ping*.

[16] E.g. *HKSAR* v. *Lam Kwong Wai* (2006) 9 HKCFAR 574; *HKSAR* v. *Hung Chan Wa* (2006) 9 HKCFAR 614.

[17] *Nancy Ann Kissel* v. *HKSAR* (2010) 13 HKCFAR 27; *HKSAR* v. *Zabed Ali* (2003) 6 HKCFAR 192.

[18] *Chim Hon Man* v. *HKSAR* (1999) 2 HKCFAR 145; *Leung Chi Keung* v. *HKSAR* (2004) 7 HKCFAR 526.

[19] *Ewan Quayle Launder* v. *HKSAR* (2001) 4 HKCFAR 457.

[20] *Yeung May Wan* v. *HKSAR* (2005) 8 HKCFAR 137.

approach taken by New Zealand authorities.[21] In *HKSAR* v. *Wong Kwok Wang Warren*, the CFA sitting with the New Zealand judge, Sir Thomas Gault NPJ, followed New Zealand and English authorities, and not the conflicting Canadian and Australian cases, in holding that the prosecution was allowed to ask the accused if he or she was aware of any reason to support the suggestion that the prosecution witness(es) were lying.[22] Aware of the potential influence of the foreign judge, it is now common for those who practice in the CFA to ensure that the relevant authorities from the jurisdiction of the foreign judge are fully and competently canvassed.

Some may have thought that the discretion recognised in *Tang* signalled an approach to afford trial judges greater leeway to direct juries as they saw fit. In *Tang*, Litton PJ famously remarked that 'the quality of the Hong Kong panel of jurors probably ranks among the highest in the common-law world' as a result of educational and language requirements.[23] Did this mean that the appellate courts would be less critical of questionable jury directions because the common sense of the Hong Kong jurors could be trusted to do justice? Fortunately, this attitude was not reflected in later CFA judgments when the court demonstrated an exacting approach to the review of jury directions. Nor did *Tang* foretell that the CFA was going to be especially tough on drug traffickers; indeed, the prosecution would go on to lose 13 of 15 CFA drug trafficking appeals up to 2010.

Themes in the jurisprudence

Before 1997 in the criminal jurisprudence of the Privy Council (PC), one can discern few, if any, specific themes in the Hong Kong cases. There were only 56 criminal judgments, spanning almost 90 years from 1909 to 1997. Given this long period and the disparate panels that decided the Hong Kong cases, it is difficult to say much more than that the PC adopted a 'humane and liberal approach' to criminal justice.[24]

With the establishment of a local final court manned by permanent judges under a new constitutional order comes the emergence of distinct themes in the jurisprudence. Three themes will be discussed in this chapter. As most of the fundamental rights provisions in the BL and Hong Kong Bill of Rights (BOR)[25] relate to the criminal process, it should come

---

[21] (1999) 2 HKCFAR 145.   [22] (2009) 12 HKCFAR 218.   [23] *Tang Siu Man*, 120.

[24] See Simon N. M. Young, 'Human Rights in Hong Kong Criminal Trials' in Paul Roberts and Jill Hunter (eds.), *Criminal Evidence and Human Rights* (Oxford: Hart Publishing, 2012) 55, 57.

[25] Part II of the Hong Kong Bill of Rights Ordinance (Cap. 383).

as no surprise that there was a human rights impact in the crime jurisprudence. The impact went beyond formal rights provisions and extended to the common law, which continues to have a significant influence in Hong Kong's criminal cases.

The CFA has absolute control over which criminal appeals it will hear. It grants leave on two possible limbs: points of law of great and general importance or where substantial and grave injustice has been done.[26] Although these were the same grounds upon which leave to the PC were previously obtained,[27] the difference after 1997 is that the CFA has granted leave on the second limb in a greater proportion of cases, from the most minor to the most serious. There emerges then the theme of the CFA working to undo injustice in the lower courts. It pursues this theme not only by example but also by widening the powers of courts to examine claims of injustice.

By having a core group of local permanent judges hearing and deciding cases, there is the greater potential for ideas and approaches to be repeated and developed in the jurisprudence. Li CJ and Bokhary PJ, both of whom were members of the court in its first 13 years, sat on 63 and 95 per cent, respectively, of the criminal appeals. Litton and Ching PJJ were permanent members of the court from 1997 to 2000 and both sat on all 16 criminal appeals decided during their tenure as PJs. Chan and Ribeiro PJJ sat on 100 and 87 per cent, respectively, of the criminal appeals from when they were appointed in 2000 to August 2010. These individuals, with their many decades of legal experience, came to the court with local knowledge of the prevalent forms of criminal activity and the difficulties faced by law enforcement in this jurisdiction. In several judgments, including those in which the appeal was allowed, the court made explicit reference to the importance of law enforcement goals and the difficulties that law enforcement faces. This is the theme of being responsive to the fight against serious crime, especially financial crime and corruption, in the Hong Kong context.

Human rights approach and values

The theme of human rights resonated strongly in the CFA's criminal law jurisprudence.[28] This came about primarily as a result of defendants making rights arguments based on guarantees in the BL and BOR either

---

[26] Hong Kong Court of Final Appeal Ordinance (Cap. 484), section 32(2).
[27] See Chapter 6 (Young and Da Roza) in this volume.
[28] See Young, note 24 above.

at trial or on appeal. The results in these rights cases were mixed and the direct impact was modest.[29] For example, in 2007 the court struck down the offence of male buggery otherwise than in private for discriminating on grounds of sexual orientation in violation of the BL's equality provision; however, there had never before been a prosecution of this offence.[30] The case's real significance was in recognising sexual orientation as a ground of discrimination.

Presumption of innocence

Probably the most notable cases were those concerning the constitutional presumption of innocence, where the court found reverse onus provisions in respect of offences of varying seriousness unjustified and amenable to being read down as evidential burdens.[31] The challenges were obviously inspired by developments in the UK courts under the Human Rights Act.[32] The CFA cases led to only a small number of other challenges in the lower courts. One reason was that the court applied a strict test for granting leave out of time with the effect that those convicted under the old unconstitutional position would not be granted an extension of time to appeal on the sole basis that the position had changed.[33] Another reason was that Hong Kong already cleaned up many of its problematic reverse onuses in the early 1990s when the BOR was enacted and had its initial impact.[34]

Also notable were a few statutory interpretation cases in which the court read the statutory element 'without reasonable excuse' as an essential ingredient of the offence rather than as a negative averment requiring the defendant to prove on balance of probabilities.[35] These decisions created

---

[29] See Simon N. M. Young, 'Constitutional Rights in Hong Kong's Court of Final Appeal' (2011) 27 *Chinese (Taiwan) Yearbook of International Law and Affairs* 67.

[30] *Yau Yuk Lung Zigo.*

[31] E.g. *Lam Kwong Wai* (possessing an imitation firearm); *Hung Chan Wa* (drug trafficking); *HKSAR* v. *Ng Po On* (2008) 11 HKCFAR 91 (failure to furnish information requested by the Commissioner of the Independent Commission Against Corruption), and since October 2010, see also *Lee To Nei* v. *HKSAR*, unreported, FACC5/2011, 30 March 2012; *Fu Kor Kuen Patrick* v. *HKSAR*, unreported, FACC4/2011, 24 May 2012.

[32] See e.g. *R* v. *Lambert* [2002] 2 AC 545 (HL); *Sheldrake* v. *DPP* [2005] 1 AC 264 (HL).

[33] *Hung Chan Wa*, [23]–[27].

[34] See *R* v. *Sin Yau Ming* (1991) 1 HKPLR 88 (CA); Andrew Bruce, 'The Bill of Rights and the Criminal Law' in George Edwards and Johannes Chan (eds.), *Hong Kong's Bill of Rights: Two Years Before 1997* (Hong Kong: Centre for Comparative and Public Law, University of Hong Kong, 1996) 77.

[35] See *Lam Yuk Fai Steve* v. *HKSAR* (2006) 9 HKCFAR 281; *Tong Yiu Wah* v. *HKSAR* (2007) 10 HKCFAR 324; Criminal Procedure Ordinance (Cap. 221), section 94A.

new complexities for prosecutors, who would have to prove these negative elements beyond reasonable doubt, but they averted constitutional challenge and kept the common law presumption of innocence robust.

Certainty review

Constitutional challenges to criminal legislation for being in breach of the principle of legal certainty generally failed.[36] But indirectly, these cases had a positive effect. The CFA borrowed the ECtHR's *Sunday Times* test for legal certainty, which required that prescribed laws purporting to restrict a fundamental right be sufficiently accessible and precise.[37] It became a standard used in legal drafting and legislative scrutiny to improve the clarity of new laws.[38]

Challenges to common law offences effectively brought greater clarity to the elements of the challenged offences even though at times it appeared the court restated the law to meet the certainty challenge. With the offence of misconduct in public office the court, showing itself to be as fallible as legislatures, needed two attempts and a critical comment from the English Court of Appeal before it could settle the *mens rea* elements of the offence.[39] Perhaps this showed that the common law was alive and well in Hong Kong, and judicial dialogue in judgments continued to occur between jurisdictions. Another view is that the common law offence is incapable of being made certain however hard the court tried (and tries), and by implication, the delimitation of the offence should be left to the executive and legislative branches. The court had reasonably better success in restating the elements of conspiracy to defraud, but even here it required a subsequent case to make clear following English authorities

---

[36] Failed in *Shum Kwok Sher; Mo Yuk Ping; B* v. *The Commissioner of the Independent Commission Against Corruption* (2010) 13 HKCFAR 1 ('*B* v. *ICAC*'), but succeeded in *Leung Kwok Hung; Lau Wai Wo* v. *HKSAR* (2003) 6 HKCFAR 624.

[37] *Sunday Times* v. *United Kingdom* (1979) 2 EHRR 245, applied in *Shum Kwok Sher, ibid.*; *Mo Yuk Ping, ibid.*

[38] See e.g. Legislative Council Secretariat, 'Review of Legislative Provisions Containing the Drafting Formula "to the Satisfaction" of an Enforcement Agency', Background Brief for Panel on Administration of Justice and Legal Services on 23 Oct 2006, LC Paper No CB(2)135/06–07(04), 20 Oct 2006; Law Drafting Division, Department of Justice, *Drafting Legislation in Hong Kong: A Guide to Styles & Practices* (Hong Kong: DOJ, 2012) ch 6.

[39] See *Shum Kwok Sher*, clarified in *Sin Kam Wah*, applying *Attorney General's Reference (No. 3 of 2003)* [2005] 4 All ER 303 (CA).

that price fixing was not dishonest and thus did not come within the common law offence.[40]

Substantive review

Certainty review, although a powerful force against arbitrariness, provides only a thin and formal review of laws. For constitutional courts, there is the question of whether they are empowered to review laws substantively, for example, to ensure consistency with fundamental principles and values of the constitution. Canadian courts are empowered under section 7 of the Charter of Rights and Freedoms to ensure that criminal laws are 'in accordance with the principles of fundamental justice' which has been interpreted to 'cover substantive as well as procedural justice'.[41] A principle of fundamental justice is a 'basic tenet of the legal system', more particularly a legal principle for which there is a 'significant societal consensus that it is fundamental to the way in which the legal system ought fairly to operate' and is capable of being 'identified with sufficient precision to yield a manageable standard'.[42]

In *Lau Cheong* v. *HKSAR*, the CFA accepted that Hong Kong courts had a power of substantive review under Article 28 of the BL, but to what depth the review should go remains unclear.[43] This case concerned whether 'arbitrary imprisonment' resulted from either (1) convicting someone of murder if only an intention to cause grievous bodily harm ('GBH rule') and not to kill was proven or (2) sentencing a person convicted of murder under the GBH rule to life imprisonment without discretion to impose a lighter sentence.

In discussing the meaning of 'arbitrary', the court held that it meant something different from merely unlawful.[44] It adopted the UN Human Rights Committee's approach in *Hugo van Alphen* v. *The Netherlands* to interpret arbitrariness 'more broadly to include elements of inappropriateness, injustice and lack of predictability'.[45] It also followed Lord Cooke's decision in *Fok Lai Ying* v. *Governor in Council* (a pre-1997 BOR decision), which held that 'the concept of arbitrariness is intended to guarantee that even interference provided for by law should be in accordance with the

---

[40] See *HKSAR* v. *Chan Wai Yip* (2010) 13 HKCFAR 842.
[41] Peter Hogg, *Constitutional Law of Canada*, 5th edn (Scarborough: Thomson Carswell, 2007) 47–21 citing *Re B.C. Motor Vehicles Act* [1985] 2 SCR 486.
[42] *R* v. *Malmo-Levine* [2003] 3 SCR 571, 628 and 634; Hogg, *ibid.*, 47–27.
[43] Note 10 above.   [44] *Ibid.*, 435.
[45] *Ibid.*, applying *Hugo van Alphen* v. *The Netherlands* (Comm. No. 305/1988, 15 Aug 1990, UNHRC).

provisions, aims and objectives of the Covenant and should be, in any event, reasonable in the particular circumstances'.[46] The New Zealand case of *Neilsen* v. *Attorney-General* was said to add 'flesh to the approach adopted in the *Hugo van Alphen . . .* opinion', and ultimately the first issue was framed as whether the rule was 'capricious or unreasoned or without reasonable cause' and whether the imprisonment was imposed without reference to an 'adequate determining principle'.[47] It is unclear whether 'adequate determining principle' is used in the same sense as 'principles of fundamental justice' in the jurisprudence of the Canadian Charter. The court reasoned simply that one who kills with intent to cause grievous bodily harm does an act that carries an inherent risk of death, so it would not be capricious or unreasonable as a matter of policy to treat that person in the same way as one who kills with intent to kill.[48] No reference was made to principle, and the court was not prepared to question the wisdom of decades of common law.

In analysing the second issue concerning mandatory imprisonment, the court was not prepared to question the wisdom of the legislature, which after a thorough debate in the early 1990s decided to replace the death penalty for murder with a sentence of mandatory life imprisonment.[49] In 1997, the legislature passed legislation to establish the Long-term Prison Sentences Review Board to review life sentences and order the release of persons originally serving an indeterminate sentence.[50] The court gave this legislative deliberation much weight in concluding that mandatory life imprisonment for murder, a crime of 'inherent and unique gravity', was not 'a manifestly disproportionate sentence' as to contravene the BL on grounds of arbitrariness.[51] The deference shown by the court in *Lau Cheong* was reasonable as legislators would have had to turn their minds to the dictates of the then recently enacted BOR. The facts of the case, involving the killing of a robbery victim bound by rope, were not at all compelling to drive a change in the law.

So Wai Lun v. *HKSAR* greatly disappointed hopes for a more robust approach to substantive review of criminal offences.[52] It concerned a constitutional challenge on equality and arbitrariness grounds to the absolute liability offence of unlawful sexual intercourse with a girl younger

---

[46] *Fok Lai Ying* v. *Governor in Council* [1997] HKLRD 810, 819 (PC).

[47] *Lau Cheong*, 436–7, applying *Neilsen* v. *Attorney-General* [2001] 3 NZLR 433 (CA).

[48] *Lau Cheong, ibid.*, 437.   [49] *Ibid.*, 449–50.

[50] *Ibid.*, 446. Long-term Prison Sentences Review Ordinance (Cap. 524).

[51] *Ibid.*, 453.   [52] *So Wai Lun* v. *HKSAR* (2006) 9 HKCFAR 530.

than 16 years of age. *Lau Cheong* left unclear whether arbitrariness review admitted a determining principle that the morally innocent should not be punished, which is a principle of fundamental justice recognised in section 7 of the Canadian Charter.[53] *So Wai Lun* suggests that no such principle exists under the BL. Justice Bokhary, who is typically known for his strong human rights decisions, showed unusual deference to the legislature, holding that '[w]here the legislature has enacted an absolute offence, the judiciary will not strike down the offence merely on the basis of a view that it would be preferable for the offence to admit of a defence of belief or reasonable belief'.[54] He found that the 'legislative possibilities and permutations are matters fit for public consultation and debate' and concluded that given the 'vital importance of protecting young girls', imposing absolute liability was 'a choice constitutionally open to the legislature'.[55]

The depth of reasoning in *So Wai Lun* contrasts starkly with the majority's principled approach in the Canadian case, *R v. Hess*; *R v. Nguyen*.[56] In finding absolute liability unconstitutional in that case, Justice Wilson stated that 'to imprison a "mentally innocent" person is to inflict a grave injury on that person's dignity and sense of worth'.[57] She also emphasised the need for 'concrete and persuasive evidence' to support any justification based on deterrence.[58] In *So Wai Lun*, the court found without reference to evidence that absolute liability for the offence would cause men to steer 'well away from the line between legality and illegality' and thereby materially protect young girls.[59] One hopes the court will revisit the issue, if not to uphold rights and human dignity than at least to provide a more convincing and principled decision.

Strict liability

In 2010, the court recognised that when the presumption of *mens rea* was displaced in respect of statutory offences, it was possible to read in a common law halfway house defence of honest and reasonable belief.[60] Although the Court of Appeal recognised this possibility in 1995, *Hin Lin Yee v. HKSAR* settled any doubt about the existence of the halfway house defence and in doing so departed from English authorities, chose not to follow Australian authorities, and found support in Canadian and New

---

[53] *Re B.C. Motor Vehicles Act*; *R v. Pontes* [1995] 3 SCR 44; *R v. Vaillancourt* [1987] 2 SCR 636, 652–3; *R v. Martineau* [1990] 2 SCR 663.
[54] *So Wai Lun*, 542.   [55] *Ibid.*, 542–3.   [56] [1990] 2 SCR 906.   [57] *Ibid.*, [14].
[58] *Ibid.*, [26].   [59] *So Wai Lun*, 543.   [60] *Hin Lin Yee*.

Zealand authorities.[61] Although not a constitutional case, the court made reference to human rights principles to justify having a halfway house: 'To convict a person regardless of the mental state accompanying his conduct, even if he can show that he acted in a reasonable, diligent and socially unblameworthy manner is contrary to the fundamental values of the common law'.[62] When explaining why the regulatory nature of an offence is an insufficient basis for finding absolute liability, the court stated, '[i]t remains in principle objectionable for someone who behaved honestly, reasonably and without social blameworthiness nevertheless to suffer conviction of a criminal offence'.[63] The court, however, was not backtracking from its decision in *So Wai Lun,* which was cited as an illustration of when absolute liability could legitimately be imposed, that is when persons engage in unacceptable societal conduct at one's peril.[64]

Criminal evidence and procedure

The weak approach to substantive constitutional review was compensated for by a robust approach to common law fair trial standards and police powers.[65] The human rights theme was clearly evident in the cases in which the common law right to silence was upheld,[66] admitted prejudicial evidence compromised the conviction (including several cases where murder convictions were quashed),[67] trial counsel was found to be incompetent,[68] trial judges misdirected the jury,[69] and the prosecution failed to disclose relevant information to the defence.[70]

The CFA held law enforcement agencies to an exacting standard and chipped away at coercive powers even without formal constitutional challenge. Three cases illustrate their approach. The first is the well-known Falun Gong case in which members of this organisation were prosecuted

---

[61] *Ibid.*   [62] *Ibid.*, 181.   [63] *Ibid.*, 192.   [64] *Ibid.*, 194, citing *So Wai Lun*, [39].

[65] See Young, note 24 above, 66–71; Simon N. M. Young and Sarah Cheng, 'Right to a Fair Trial and the Criminal Process' in Johannes Chan and C.L. Lim (eds.), *Law of the Hong Kong Constitution* (Hong Kong: Sweet & Maxwell, 2011) ch 18 (529–604).

[66] See e.g. *Lee Fuk Hing* v. *HKSAR* (2004) 7 HKCFAR 600 and, generally, Simon N. M. Young, 'A Decade of Self-Incrimination in the Hong Kong Special Administrative Region' (2007) 37 *HKLJ* 475.

[67] *Wong Wai Man* v. *HKSAR* (2000) 3 HKCFAR 322; *Zabed Ali*; *Nancy Ann Kissel.*

[68] *Chong Ching Yuen* v. *HKSAR* (2004) 7 HKCFAR 126.

[69] E.g. *Chan Chuen Ho* v. *HKSAR* (1999) 2 HKCFAR 198; *Lin Ping Keung* v. *HKSAR* (2005) 8 HKCFAR 52; *Tam King Hon* v. *HKSAR* (2006) 9 HKCFAR 206; *Chan Kar Leung* v. *HKSAR* (2006) 9 HKCFAR 827; *Cai Zong Gang* v. *HKSAR* (2009) 12 HKCFAR 494; and *Ho Hoi Shing* v. *HKSAR* (2008) 11 HKCFAR 354.

[70] *Ching Kwok Yin* v. *HKSAR* (2000) 3 HKCFAR 387; *Lee Ming Tee (No. 2)* (2003); and *Brian Alfred Hall* v. *HKSAR* (2009) 12 HKCFAR 562.

for obstructing a sidewalk without reasonable excuse and assaulting police officers who tried to remove them.[71] In the end, they were acquitted of all charges, and the CFA held that to arrest someone lawfully for public obstruction, it was necessary for arresting officers to have reasonable suspicion as to the absence of reasonable excuse, which required consideration of whether the individuals were exercising a fundamental right such as the freedom of demonstration.[72] The court also held that the statutory power to arrest a person who the officer 'reasonably believes will be charged with' an offence also requires the same officer to have reasonable suspicion that the person committed the offence, lest it 'open the door to arbitrary arrest'.[73]

Another well-known case, brought by the legislator, Mr Leung Kwok Hung, involved a challenge to the legislative scheme for regulating public assemblies.[74] Although the majority upheld the notification requirements of the scheme, it struck down the police power to refuse assemblies on the statutory ground of *ordre public*. This was significant because only a few years earlier, the court had used the reason of *ordre public* to justify the restriction on freedom of expression imposed by a law that prohibited the desecration of the national flag even in a public protest.[75] In the flag case, it was found that 'the legitimate societal interests in protecting the national flag and the legitimate community interests in the protection of the regional flag [were] interests within the concept of public order (*ordre public*)'.[76] But when police are allowed to use the 'imprecise and elusive' concept of *ordre public* to restrain peaceful assemblies then rights are at much greater jeopardy of violation and the CFA would not allow it.[77]

The third case on police powers concerned the power of the Independent Commission Against Corruption (ICAC) to obtain evidence from non-suspects.[78] The process involved making an *ex parte* application to a judge for an order authorising the commissioner by a notice in writing to require a non-suspect to provide relevant information to the investigating officer. The existing practice was for the judge, after being satisfied that the statutory criteria had been met, to make a general order, allowing the commissioner to set the precise terms of the notice without oversight by the judge.[79] The court did not approve of this practice because it 'would give carte blanche to the commissioner to decide the width of

---

[71] *Yeung May Wan.*   [72] *Ibid.,* 154.   [73] *Ibid.,* 162.   [74] *Leung Kwok Hung.*
[75] *Ng Kung Siu.*   [76] *Ibid.,* 460.   [77] *Ibid.,* 459.   [78] *P* v. *ICAC.*
[79] See *X* v. *Commissioner of the ICAC* [2004] 1 HKC 228 (CFI).

the notice'.[80] Instead, it fashioned a new practice that required the draft notice to be annexed to the order and put before the judge who 'acts as the safeguard in the process'.[81] The 'independent scrutiny by the courts' was said to provide 'protection for the citizen against the unjustified use of the special investigatory powers'.[82] This was a significant decision because it highlighted the importance of having an impartial judicial officer oversee the use of coercive powers by law enforcement in Hong Kong.

Sentencing

The CFA heard only a handful of sentencing cases because it is 'only in extremely rare and utterly exceptional circumstances' that leave will be granted in such appeals.[83] When it intervened, it generally showed a tendency to favour human liberty and keep restrictions to a minimum. In the case of the young man who was sentenced to detention for 18 months in a training school for participating in a lion dance without a permit, the CFA found the detention 'wholly disproportionate' to the offence, and a fine of HK$100 was substituted (noting that the defendant had already spent four months in detention).[84] In another case, it was held that when new sentencing guidelines that lower the sentence for an offence are set, an offender convicted of that offence whose sentencing process was still extant should normally be allowed to benefit from the new guidelines.[85] This was said to be consistent with the right to the benefit of a lighter penalty protected by Article 12(1) of the BOR.[86] In a third case, the CFA held that imposing a bind-over order with the bare conditions to 'keep the peace' and 'be of good behaviour' was inconsistent with the principle of legal certainty because it did not spell out with precision what the person should not do.[87] It also held that the failure to warn an acquitted defendant of the proposal to bind him over and to give him an opportunity to make representations would invalidate the order.[88]

Undoing injustice

When a case raises no points of law of great and general importance, the CFA can still grant leave when 'there has been to the appellant's disadvantage a departure from accepted norms . . . so serious as to constitute

---

[80] *P* v. *ICAC*, 308.   [81] *Ibid.*, 306.   [82] *Ibid.*, 301.

[83] *Tam Wa Lun* v. *HKSAR*, unreported, FAMC56/2010, 6 May 2011, CFAAC, [1].

[84] *Wong Chu Cheong* v. *HKSAR* (2001) 4 HKCFAR 12, [44].

[85] *Mark Anthony Seabrook* v. *HKSAR* (1999) 2 HKCFAR 184.

[86] *Ibid.*, 195.   [87] *Lau Wai Wo*, [49].   [88] *Ibid.*, [53].

a substantial and grave injustice'.[89] This limb provides 'a residual safe-guard to cater for rare and exceptional cases' because the CFA 'does not function as a court of criminal appeal in the ordinary way'.[90] Despite this high threshold, one finds an abundant number of cases in which the CFA intervened to correct what appeared to be obvious errors in the trial or appellate processes. The frequency of these cases, which probably constitute about 20 per cent of all criminal appeals, highlights the CFA's role in undoing injustice even if it means assuming the function of an intermediate appeal court. The cases show that the final court is prepared to take a fresh look at the facts of the case to ensure that justice is done.

Setting an example

The CFA's injustice cases do little to advance the law, but one should not treat them as isolated cases of little importance. These cases reinforce the 'accepted norms' of criminal law and procedure in Hong Kong and serve to illustrate how the trial fact-finding and appellate review processes should be conducted. In this way, they serve an important educative function for all judges and magistrates and for the other participants in the system. For defendants, these cases validate that there is still access to justice from the final court in even cases that some might regard as being trivial or minor.

To provide a sense of when the CFA intervened to undo an injustice, a few selected cases will be discussed. First, there was the HK$232 theft case that Bokhary PJ described as 'unique' and hoped 'there will never be another case like it'.[91] It was alleged the defendant, a salesperson, took this money from a customer because the amount did not appear in the till; however, the case was flawed because there was no evidence of how much money was in the till at the start of the day.[92] In a drug trafficking case, the District Court judge committed an obvious error by reversing the burden of proof when he stated the following in his reasons: 'I found that the Defendant's explanation, even according to the lower standard of proof in civil cases, was unbelievable'.[93] In *Chau Lin Su-E*, the defendant produced evidence to show that she was not in Hong Kong at the time when, according to the complainants, she carried out a fraud in Hong Kong.[94]

---

[89] *So Yiu Fung* v. *HKSAR* (1999) 2 HKCFAR 539, [13].
[90] *Ibid.*, [7]; *Ong Chun Ying* v. *HKSAR* (2007) 10 HKCFAR 318, [1].
[91] *Lam Pui Shan* v. *HKSAR*, unreported, FACC8/1999, 27 March 2000, [1], CFA.
[92] *Ibid.*   [93] *Tsang Wai Man* v. *HKSAR* (2003) 6 HKCFAR 109, [5].
[94] (2004) 7 HKCFAR 265.

The magistrate erred by finding that the complainants were mistaken on the time when there was no evidential basis for so finding.

There was also the case of the young traffic constable who allegedly conspired with a pop star to pervert the course of justice by withholding the identity of the true driver of a car involved in an accident.[95] In quashing the conviction, the CFA said that there had 'been a grievous failure of process in the trial court, not corrected on appeal' involving a 'hard working police officer of spotless character, in the discharge of his normal duties ... caught up in web of sycophancy and deceit, not of his own making'.[96] A final case to mention is *Ong Chun Ying* in which the defendant adduced alibi evidence that he was at a restaurant in Kowloon from 10 to 11 AM, about the same time when it was alleged he had assaulted the complainant in a flat 30 minutes away in Yuen Long.[97] The magistrate found the alibi to be incomplete because it was 'not possible to be sure as to exactly when' the assault took place and convicted the defendant.[98] In quashing the conviction, the CFA stated, 'Although the intermediate appellate court failed to appreciate it, the appellant's pivotal complaint is justified: he was convicted on a view of the facts which is unsupported by evidence and involves denying him the benefit of a reasonable doubt on a crucial matter'.[99]

In all of these cases and others, the trial court committed basic procedural errors, and the appeal court failed to catch these errors. They all raise serious questions about the quality of justice in the lower courts and highlight an important adjudicative role played by the CFA in addition to settling questions of law of great importance.

Widening the powers to rectify injustice

In several decisions, the CFA has made sure that the courts in Hong Kong have sufficient powers to carry out their functions.[100] This is also true of the CFA's function in undoing injustice. The CFA reviews evidence and facts in injustice cases to determine if there has been a departure from accepted norms, such as when findings are made without evidence or otherwise perversely. Even in the certified points of law cases, the CFA held that it has 'jurisdiction to review findings of fact in exceptional cases when those findings are related to the certified points', and discretionary

---

[95] *Lau Chi Wai* v. *HKSAR* (2004) 7 HKCFAR 460.   [96] *Ibid.*, 474.
[97] (2007) 10 HKCFAR 318.   [98] *Ibid.*, 320.   [99] *Ibid.*, 323.
[100] *Poon Chau Cheong* v. *Secretary for Justice* (2000) 3 HKCFAR 121; *Yeung Siu Keung* v. *HKSAR* (2006) 9 HKCFAR 144; *HKSAR* v. *Tse So So* (2007) 10 HKCFAR 368; *Yau Yuk Lung*; *Yeung Chun Pong* v. *Secretary for Justice* (2006) 9 HKCFAR 836.

orders to stay a proceeding will be reviewed if the judge mistakes the facts or fails to give weight or sufficient weight to considerations relevant to a central matter.[101]

The court has also taken a generous approach to its receipt of fresh evidence on appeal, which was said to be based on satisfying the following conditions: 'The fresh evidence is likely to be credible; it would have been admissible in the courts below; it is relevant to an issue in the appeal; there is a reasonable explanation for the failure to adduce it in the courts below; and the court is satisfied that it would afford a ground of appeal'.[102] The last condition of 'would afford a ground of appeal' appeared to be more relaxed than the condition applied by lower courts that the evidence 'might have led to a different verdict or verdicts so that it renders the conviction or convictions appealed against unsafe or unsatisfactory'.[103] After being admitted, however, the CFA still needs to assess the effect of the fresh evidence, including whether the intermediate appeal court would have found that the conviction was unsafe and unsatisfactory.[104]

Magistrates courts handle more than 90 per cent of all criminal cases in Hong Kong. A person convicted by a magistrate has a statutory right of appeal or a right to apply to appeal by way of case stated.[105] In *Chou Shih Bin* v. *HKSAR*, the CFA held that the statutory right of appeal signified an appeal by way of a rehearing on the papers.[106] Witnesses would not be reheard unless they were admitted as fresh evidence, but the appeal court would come to its own conclusions on the facts and evidence after reviewing them afresh. On the facts of this case concerning a man who tried to board a plane with a pistol in his bag, the CFA, in treating the appeal as a rehearing, was able to quash the conviction because the 'weight of evidence denies that he knew that the gun and cartridge were in his bag'.[107] In a later case, it was said that this right of appeal 'gives a judge entertaining the appeal considerable latitude to correct injustice . . . to the defendant'.[108] Widening the powers of the intermediate appeal court to correct injustice lightens the injustice caseload of the CFA. Whether it

---

[101] *Lee Ming Tee* (2001), [163]–[165].
[102] *Mohammad Mahabobur Rahman* v. *HKSAR* (2010) 13 HKCFAR 20, [13], applying section 83V of the Criminal Procedure Ordinance (Cap 221).
[103] See *Cheng Wui Yiu* v. *HKSAR*, unreported, CACC532/2004, 21 December 2007, [30], CA; *HKSAR* v. *Shortall*, unreported, HCMA801/2009, 2 June 2010, [12], CFI.
[104] *Rahman*, [16].   [105] Magistrates Ordinance (Cap. 227), section 105.
[106] (2005) 8 HKCFAR 70.   [107] *Ibid.*, 79.
[108] *Raymond Chen* v. *HKSAR* (2010) 13 HKCFAR 728, [55].

was the CFA's intention to effect this result is unclear, but *Chou Shih Bin* certainly had a significant impact in the lower courts. It is by far the most often cited CFA judgment in Hong Kong.[109] Whether it has – and if so, to what extent – increased the incidence of error correction at the intermediate stage are questions that require further research.

Responsive to the fight against financial crime and corruption

As a centre of international commerce, Hong Kong has its share of white collar crime cases involving fraud, corruption, and money laundering. The schemes perpetrated in these cases range in sophistication and often have an overseas or cross-border dimension, especially in recent years with the closer socioeconomic integration with Mainland China. Multiple law enforcement agencies may need to coordinate their efforts in the investigation of both the substantive offence and the asset trail. Covert operations were made more difficult in 2005 when the previous practice of conducting covert surveillance and electronic interception was found to be unconstitutional.[110] A new statutory regime was put in place requiring authorisation from a panel judge or a senior law enforcement officer.[111]

The CFA has not been unsympathetic to the challenges faced by the prosecution and law enforcement in tackling serious fraud and corruption. It has very much the public interest in mind in these cases. For example, when the covert surveillance practices were found to be unconstitutional, the CFA, following the lead of the lower courts, suspended the declarations of unconstitutionality to ensure that law enforcement could continue to conduct its operations without being in breach of the court's order.[112] In other cases, the CFA displayed an understanding of these challenges, making express reference to the importance of the law enforcement aims. These statements in CFA judgments are often quoted in other decisions, typically in support of prosecutorial positions. The sentiments contrast with and provide balance to the human rights inclinations of the court. Some of the more notable statements are discussed next.

---

[109] A Westlaw.HK search run in June 2012 produced more than 200 citations to the case.
[110] *Koo Sze Yiu* v. *Chief Executive of Hong Kong* (2006) 9 HKCFAR 441.
[111] Interception of Communications and Surveillance Ordinance (Cap. 589).
[112] *Koo Sze Yiu*, [63].

Financial crime

The Allied Group case, involving the prosecution of its chairman, Mr. Lee Ming Tee, illustrated the court's approach to prosecution appeals from trials aborted because of findings of abuse of process.[113] On two occasions, the trial of Lee Ming Tee was stayed on grounds of prosecutorial abuse of process, and on each occasion, the government's appeal to the CFA was allowed, and the matter was sent back to trial, ultimately ending in negotiated guilty pleas.[114] In the CFA's first *Lee Ming Tee* judgment, corporate fraud was referred to as a 'genuine social evil'.[115] In considering whether it was unfair to allow police to use evidence, which was compelled by a company inspector, in the police investigation, it was held:

> Corporate fraud is today a matter of major concern which calls for strong regulation of the kind found in ss 142 to 152F of the [Companies] Ordinance, particularly s 145(3A). Moreover, those who hold corporate office and are engaged in corporate activities, especially activities which impinge upon the public, are well aware of the existence of the legislative regulatory régime and that compliance with its provisions is a necessary condition of participation in those activities.

> No one could seriously argue that it is wrong or unfair for the legislature to empower an inspector to investigate the facts where circumstances suggest that a company's affairs may be conducted with intent to defraud others. As discussed above, where the investigation confirms such fears, the public interest in protecting the public from fraud strongly suggests in principle that the product of the investigation should be made available to the appropriate public authorities. Balancing against that public interest the important countervailing public interest in an accused being assured of a fair trial, the solution adopted by s 145(3A) appears to be entirely acceptable and consistent with the purposes of Articles 10 and 11(1). The Legislature has struck a balance which allows the Inspector to abrogate the privilege but subjects the elicited evidence to a direct use prohibition, inferentially permitting derivative use.[116]

The court rejected the human rights argument that the right to a fair trial required a derivative use immunity that would preclude the police from using the compelled evidence.

In rejecting another human rights argument, that the common law offence of conspiracy to defraud violated the principle of legal certainty,

---

[113]   See *Lee Ming Tee* (2001); *Lee Ming Tee (No. 2)* (2003).
[114]   See Simon N. M. Young, 'Defending White Collar Crime in Hong Kong: A Case Study of the *Lee Ming Tee* Case' (2006) 36 *HKLJ* 35.
[115]   *Lee Ming Tee* (2001), 176.   [116]   *Ibid.*, 176–7.

Sir Anthony Mason NPJ in the case of *Mo Yuk Ping* highlighted the need for the common law offence:

> Nevertheless it has been generally accepted that there is a need to have a general offence, even if some law reform agencies and commentators believe that a newly minted general offence would be preferable to conspiracy to defraud. It has been widely recognized that there is no limit to the ingenuity of fraudsters in engineering novel means of defrauding others. This ingenuity leads to the conclusion that the enactment of specific offences is not an adequate safeguard unless they are accompanied by a general offence. It is for this reason that s.16A(4) of the Theft Ordinance, Cap. 210 preserved the common law offence of conspiracy to defraud without any qualification of it. Section 159E(2) of the Crimes Ordinance, Cap. 200 contains a similar provision.[117]

In a third case, the court considered whether the 1996 abolition of the common law offence of conspiracy to obtain a pecuniary advantage by deception meant that it was abolished for good and could not be prosecuted after 1996 even though the facts arose before 1996.[118] In rejecting this argument, the court stated that there was no injustice to prosecute such offenders who would have been liable to prosecution had the offence been discovered before 1996; rather, 'it would be a grave injustice to allow such offenders to escape the criminal justice system'.[119]

Corruption

The CFA was well aware of Hong Kong's historical and evolving battle against corruption, especially since 1974 when the ICAC was established. In finding that certain statutory powers given to the ICAC abrogated the common law privilege against self-incrimination, the court made reference to the historical context:

> Corruption was widespread and the community was determined to tackle this evil and was prepared to give to the ICAC the necessary investigative tools. We would note that the community is today as determined as ever in its resolve to combat corruption vigorously.[120]

In a later case (*P* v. *ICAC*), reference was again made to the ICAC's need for having coercive powers of investigation:

> Corruption is an evil which cannot be tolerated. For the purpose of combating corruption, special powers of investigation have been conferred

---

[117] *Mo Yuk Ping*, 410.   [118] *Chan Pun Chung* v. *HKSAR* (2000) 3 HKCFAR 392.
[119] *Ibid.*, 408.   [120] *Chan Sze Ting* v. *HKSAR* (1997–98) 1 HKCFAR 46, 50.

by statute on the Independent Commission Against Corruption. . . . These powers are necessary as crimes of corruption are inherently difficult to investigate and prove. But as their exercise intrudes into the privacy of citizens, the statutory scheme provides that they are exercisable only after judicial authorization has been obtained. In this way, the scheme seeks to balance the public interest in fighting corruption and the public interest in the protection of the individual.[121]

Note how this quotation differs from the earlier one in that the court made specific reference to fundamental rights and, as discussed earlier, was seeking to construe the *ex parte* power in a manner compatible with rights but without emasculating its effectiveness. One questions, however, whether the court leaned too much on the side of the law enforcement aims when it ruled out material non-disclosure as a basis for quashing *ex parte* authorisations:

But material non-disclosure in the sense in which it is used as a ground of discharge of interlocutory orders obtained ex parte in civil cases cannot be entertained as a ground for the discharge of an ex parte order authorizing a s. 14(1)(d) notice as such a ground would be incompatible with the statutory scheme. The intent of the scheme is that the integrity and effectiveness of the investigation should not be affected.[122]

Provided that the powers stop when they become oppressive, the concurring judges said the powers were 'no more than the price that people can properly be called upon to pay for the benefit of living in a society that manages to keep corruption in check'.[123]

The CFA has also acknowledged the importance of undercover operations in the fight against corruption. In an important early case, the CFA upheld the discretion of the trial judge to exclude confession statements obtained by undercover agents who effectively interrogate suspects and thereby undermine their right of silence.[124] At the same time, the CFA made the following statement in support of the need for undercover operations:

The law recognises that the use of undercover operations is an essential weapon in the armoury of the law enforcement agencies; particularly their use when the criminal activities are ongoing but also their use after crimes are completed to obtain evidence to bring the criminal to book. The use of undercover operations plays an important part in society's struggle to

---

[121] *P* v. *ICAC*, 300. See also similar sentiments expressed in the separate concurring opinion at 317.
[122] *Ibid.*, 312–13.   [123] *Ibid.*, 317.   [124] *Lam Tat Ming.*

combat crime especially serious crime, whether it be corruption, trafficking in dangerous drugs or terrorism. But the success and indeed viability of such undercover operations depend upon the concealment of the true identity of the law enforcement officer in order to establish the appropriate relationship with the alleged wrongdoers. They therefore unavoidably involve elements of subterfuge, deceit and trickery. The law accepts that law enforcement agencies may find it necessary to resort to tactics of that kind.[125]

This passage has been cited by lower courts to support the admission of evidence obtained by undercover agents in breach of the right to privacy under the BL.[126]

The CFA also rejected challenges claiming that the bribery and corruption laws were being improperly applied extraterritorially in respect of evidence or events outside Hong Kong.[127] The court found sufficient proximity to Hong Kong, and on the facts of the case concerning the bribery of a foreign government official it was said that Hong Kong

> makes a positive and important contribution to the worldwide struggle against corruption, an endeavour inherently and highly dependent on cross-border cooperation. Acting cooperatively, each jurisdiction properly protects itself and other jurisdictions from the scourge of corruption and other serious criminal activity. For Hong Kong in particular, criminalising and prosecuting the bribery here of foreign officials deters corruption here and helps to avoid the growth here of a culture of corruption.[128]

The court appeared to be informed by international developments against corruption, including China's (and Hong Kong's) obligations as a party to the United Nations Convention Against Corruption.[129]

When statutory offences have fallen short, law enforcement has made increasing use of the common law offence of misconduct in public office to prosecute government officials.[130] Again, the CFA has been supportive of this practice and rejected constitutional challenges based on the principle of legal certainty. Similar to its treatment of conspiracy to defraud, the

---

[125] *Ibid.*, at 180–1.
[126] See, for example, *HKSAR* v. *Wong Kwok Hung* [2007] 2 HKLRD 621 (CA).
[127] *B* v. *ICAC.*   [128] *Ibid.*, 12.
[129] China decided that the treaty would apply to Hong Kong and Macau when it became a party to the United Nations Convention Against Corruption (UN Doc A/58/422, entry into force on 14 December 2005) on 13 January 2006. See United Nations Treaty Collection, accessible at treaties.un.org.
[130] See *Shum Kwok Sher*; *Sin Kam Wah*; *Chan Tak Ming* v. *HKSAR* (2010) 13 HKCFAR 745.

CFA highlighted the importance of having the common law defined in broad and general terms:

> The common law offence of misconduct in public office is necessarily cast in general terms because it is designed to cover many forms of misconduct on the part of public officers. An alternative way of dealing with misconduct by public officers would be to enact a statute formulating specific offences for particular categories of misconduct in public office. The adoption of that course would involve a loss of flexibility and run the risk that the net would fail to catch some forms of serious misconduct. To suggest that the offence requires further definition would be to pursue a degree of definition which is unattainable, having regard to the wide range of acts and omissions which are capable of amounting to misconduct by a public officer in or relating to his office. The offence serves an important purpose in providing a criminal sanction against misconduct by public officers.[131]

Conclusion

Tang Siu Man's break from the grasp of English authorities was an approach the CFA continued to adopt in its criminal law jurisprudence. But later cases were more distinctly in favour of protecting the rights and interests of defendants while recognising the importance of law enforcement aims in serious fraud and corruption cases. It remains to be seen whether the CFA will put more teeth to substantive review of criminal offences under the BL.

A significant portion of its criminal caseload consisted of error-correction cases in which a grave and substantial injustice had occurred. In an ideal world, these injustices would be avoided or, at least, caught in the first tier of appeals. The fact that they were not probably reflected a difference of approach or even values between the final court and the lower court judges. The overseas judge in the CFA may also have brought a fresh or different perspective from that taken in the lower courts.

It is difficult to say if the size of the injustice caseload will be a permanent feature of the court. Some believe that the court has become too interventionist and should give more deference to the findings of fact by lower courts.[132] Another view is that the injustice cases take time

---

[131]   *Shum Kwok Sher, ibid.*, 411–12.

[132]   Kevin Zervos, 'Practice before the Court of Final Appeal 1997–2010 – A Prosecutor's Perspective', presentation at conference on 6 March 2012, 'Hong Kong's Court of Final Appeal: The Andrew Li Court 1997–2010', Centre for Comparative and Public Law, University of Hong Kong.

away from determining important questions of law, which is the usual business of supreme courts. However, by statute, the CFA cannot ignore its injustice jurisdiction, and such cases demonstrated improved access to justice post-1997. Ultimately, the size of the caseload will likely depend on the alignment of approach and thinking between the CFA and the lower courts. Closer alignment might be achieved if the CFA made greater use of local NPJs instead of the overseas ones. But such a change would be undesirable. The CFA would lose its special international character and deviate from its original constitutional design.[133] Alignment should come from below, and matters such as quality appointments to the bench and appropriate training for new and serving judicial officers need closer attention. Complete alignment will never be achieved in the real world, and having a final court that provides a safety net to catch instances in which justice has miscarried is one of the strengths of the Hong Kong legal system after 1997.

[133] See Chapter 11 (Young and Da Roza) in this volume.

18

Commercial law

WILLIAM WAUNG

Scope of commercial law

The area covered by the term 'commercial law' is not defined but is potentially very large. In this chapter, I will limit myself to contract law, shipping law, arbitration, banking and money lending, confidence, and company law. Land law and transactions relating to land are topics dealt with separately in Chapter 19 by Malcolm Merry.

Nature of commercial appeals to the Court of Final Appeal

Commercial appeals to the Court of Final Appeal (CFA) inherited the legacy from the colonial days, when civil appeals on final judgments were brought as of right, from Hong Kong to the Privy Council (PC). After 1997, final judgments in civil matters (above HK$1 million) enjoyed the same special privilege of being appealable to the CFA, as of right and without leave. Because the monetary limit is really low (the same as the limit for first instance matters heard by the District Court), the CFA is burdened by having to hear a large number of final appeals of commercial disputes irrespective of whether there is any important point of law at issue. This easy access of commercial appeals to the CFA without leave can be considered somewhat special for a final court in the common law world. In mature jurisdictions such as the United Kingdom, Australia, New Zealand, and the United States, commercial appeals are generally subject to leave applications and are therefore limited to only a small number of appeals raising important questions of law.[1] In Hong Kong, the CFA as the final appellate court has to hear and dispose of many commercial appeals that are only of marginal legal value. In this chapter,

---

[1] For further criticisms of the 'as of right' civil appeal route, see Chapter 8 (Thomas) in this volume.

I will limit my discussion to a small number of significant cases in different areas of law relating to commerce and business.[2]

Special expertise of the Court of Final Appeal judges on commercial law

Under our system, the Chief Justice selects and decides on the particular non-permanent judge (NPJ) to sit in any particular appeal. There is much expertise and experience in commercial law in the CFA for the Chief Justice to draw upon, this is both by way of permanent judges (PJs) and NPJs. In the CFA, a working pattern has developed whereby a leading judgment is given by a member of the court, sometimes with a concurring judgment given by other members of the court. Interestingly, dissent is very rare in the CFA, especially in commercial appeals.

A glance at the leading judgments, the substantial concurring judgments, and the two dissents given in the more significant commercial appeals I will be referring to later demonstrates the range of expertise in the CFA given by judges with a commercial law background: Ching PJ (*Bewise*), Litton PJ (*Bewise* dissent, *Resource 1* concurring), Bokhary PJ (*Resource 1, Polyset, Swire Properties, Chime* concurring), Chan PJ (*Strong Offer*), Ribeiro PJ (*Polyset, Shanghai Tongji, Emperor Finance, Celestial Finance, Unruh, Nam Tai, Carewins, PCCW*), Litton NPJ (*Polyset* dissent, *BOC Fung, Carewins* concurring), Mason NPJ (*Hebei, Resource 1*), Hoffmann NPJ (*PCCW* concurring), Millet NPJ (*Akai*), and Scott NPJ (*BOC Li, Chime*).

---

[2] *Polyset Ltd* v. *Panhandat Ltd* (2002) 5 HKCFAR 234 ('*Polyset*'); *Shanghai Tongji Science & Technology Industrial Co. Ltd* v. *Casil Clearing* (2004) 7 HKCFAR 79 ('*Shanghai Tongji*'); *Siegfried Analbert Unruh* v. *Hans-Joerg Seeberger* (2007) 10 HKCFAR 31 ('*Unruh*'); *Bewise Motors Co. Ltd* v. *Hoi Kong Container Services Ltd* (1997–1998) 1 HKCFAR 256 ('*Bewise*'); *Re Resource 1* (2000) 3 HKCFAR 187 ('*Resource 1*'); *Carewins Development (China) Ltd* v. *Bright Fortune Shipping Ltd* (2009) 12 HKCFAR 185 ('*Carewins*'); *Hebei Import & Export Corp.* v. *Polytek Engineering Co. Ltd* (1999) 2 HKCFAR 111 ('*Hebei*'); *Swire Properties Ltd* v. *Secretary of Justice* (2003) 6 HKCFAR 236 ('*Swire Properties*'); *Emperor Finance Ltd* v. *La Belle Fashions Ltd* (2003) 6 HKCFAR 402 ('*Emperor Finance*'); *Celestial Finance Ltd* v. *Yu Man Hon* (2004) 7 HKCFAR 450 ('*Celestial Finance*'); *Strong Offer Investment Ltd* v. *Nyeu Ting Chuang* (2007) 10 HKCFAR 529 ('*Strong Offer*'); *Bank of China (Hong Kong) Ltd* v. *Fung Chin Kan* (2002) 5 HKCFAR 515 ('*BOC Fung*'); *Li Sau Ying* v. *Bank of China (Hong Kong) Ltd* (2004) 7 HKCFAR 579 ('*BOC Li*'); *Nam Tai Electronics Inc.* v. *PricewaterhouseCoopers* (2008) 11 HKCFAR 62 ('*Nam Tai*'); *PCCW-HKT Telephone Ltd* v. *David Matthew McDonald Aitken* (2009) 12 HKCFAR 114 ('*PCCW*'); *Nina Kung* v. *Tan Man Kou (Re Chime Corp. Ltd)* (2004) 7 HKCFAR 546 ('*Chime*'); *The Joint and Several Liquidators of Akai Holdings Ltd* v. *The Grande Holdings Ltd* (2006) 9 HKCFAR 766 ('*Akai*').

Role of the Chief Justice in commercial appeals to the Court of Final Appeal

Before he became Chief Justice, Andrew Li was a popular barrister and leading counsel with a large commercial practice (including appearing before the PC). But although the Chief Justice sat in a substantial number of the significant CFA commercial appeals, he did not give any of the leading judgments in these commercial appeals. At first blush, this is puzzling. But when considered further, it is logical and reflects the true and dedicated character of the Chief Justice. Andrew Li had very little exposure to public law when he was in private practice. But upon taking up the office of Chief Justice, he ensured that he took the leading role in the important public law cases and that he gave the important leading judgments in many of these significant cases. This is in contrast to his deliberately not taking up the primary position in commercial appeals in the CFA.

My interpretation is that this conscious decision stemmed from his perception that as Chief Justice, his primary duty was to ensure that paramount care be given to the full and open development of public law by the CFA. This is of fundamental importance to Hong Kong. Commercial law in Hong Kong is well developed, and as said earlier, in the CFA, there are many PJs and NPJs of commercial experience and learning who can be relied upon as safe hands over commercial appeals. It is a tribute to the Chief Justice that he had the strength of character and the confidence to leave the familiar work of commercial law in the safe hands of other PJs and NPJs, but he took on the difficult and sometimes treacherous public law appeals to ensure the proper development of public law for the long term good of Hong Kong. This is a clear example of what Sir Anthony Mason referred to as the Chief Justice's leadership with a strategic vision and a capacity for the long view.[3]

Categories of commercial appeals to the Court of Final Appeal

In this chapter on the work done by the CFA on commercial law, it is not possible to do justice to the work of the very high quality that was done as a matter of course by the CFA during the Andrew Li years. The work consists of a wide variety, and I will attempt to touch upon some of

---

[3] See Chapter 13 (Mason) in this volume.

the leading cases in each of the following categories: contract, shipping, arbitration, banking and money lending, confidence, and company.

Contract

Because contract law principles are generally the foundation of commercial law, I will start with the subject of contract law. *Polyset Ltd* v. *Panhandat Ltd*,[4] although a case on land transaction, raised an interesting question of contract law. After entering into the contract to purchase five shops, the purchaser refused to complete on the ground that it had the option to rescind under the agreement. This contention raised two issues: first as to whether the purchaser was entitled to rescind and second, if not, whether the purchaser was entitled to the return of some part of the large deposit paid. The CFA unanimously affirmed the decision in the courts below that the purchaser was not entitled to rescind and held that it had repudiated the contract. By a majority with Litton NPJ dissenting, the CFA held that the total deposit of HK$40.25 million (paid in four installments under the main agreement) could not be forfeited and ordered the return to the purchaser of the difference between the deposit sum of HK$40.25 million and the sum of HK$33 million assessed as damages suffered by the vendor on the repudiation of the purchaser. The rescission issue turned on its special facts and was of interest only to the parties. However, the deposit issue gave rise to different views in the CFA. This issue was of general importance and attracted the attention of the academic community.

Deposit was described by Ribeiro PJ in his leading judgment:

> The forfeitable deposit is tendered to encourage the vendor to make the necessary commercial act of faith. It is, as the authorities show, an "earnest", that is, a thing of value given to signify serious intent on the purchaser's part. It is also the *quid pro quo* for the vendor depriving himself of the ability to deal commercially with the property, and so of making any potentially greater profits, while awaiting completion.[5]

As pointed out by Lord Hailsham in *Linggi Plantations Ltd* v. *Jagatheesan*,[6] the uniqueness of forfeitable deposits was of ancient origin, and judges always held that the rule relating to relief against penalty (a disguised liquidated damages clause) did not apply to deposit and that the bargain of the parties was to be carried out.

---

[4] (2002) 5 HKCFAR 234.   [5] *Ibid.*, [69].   [6] [1972] 1 MLJ 89 (PC).

The sea change was brought about by *Workers Trust & Merchant Bank v. Dojap Invstments Ltd.*[7] It introduced for the first time a test of reasonableness on deposit as earnest money and set the reasonableness test by reference to the usual market deposit of 10 per cent, requiring a larger deposit to be justified by reference to special circumstances. So instead of the starting point being the bargain of the parties on the deposit as shown by the contractual intention set out in the contract and with no relief, the courts intervened by requiring the vendor to justify a deposit higher than the usual percentage in the market.

The CFA applied the *Workers* test and held that in the circumstances, the 35 per cent deposit was too excessive. Reference was made to the 35 per cent being 3.5 times the usual 10 per cent deposit. There was also reference to the deposit being higher than a genuine pre-estimate of potential loss.

There was a strong and reasoned dissent from Litton as a NPJ. After referring to a passage in *Photo Production Ltd* v. *Securicor Transport Ltd,*[8] Litton NPJ stated:

> By whatever yardstick one measures the proposition – unconscionability, unreasonableness, or that articulated by Lord Diplock as set out above – the threshold for the court's intervention is necessarily high. Where business people are dealing with each other at arm's length, their freedom to contract as they please is something the courts respect and protect. The court's "conscience" – a metaphorical term indicating a common standard of behavior rather than a judge's conscience – is not easily engaged.[9]

Polyset was not received with universal enthusiasm in Hong Kong. In an article by Lusina Ho, the correctness of *Polyset* was questioned, and the author proposed various other alternative solutions to the problem.[10] Malcolm Merry refers to the very special circumstances of the transaction in *Polyset* that should have provided strong and compelling reasons for the CFA to uphold the deposit.[11] He asked the rhetorical question that if the facts of this unique case could not justify a valid deposit, it would be difficult to envisage any case that would pass the *Polyset* test.

It is difficult to disagree with Merry on that statement. Was this a missed opportunity for the CFA to develop the law by reference to our local conditions, as asked by Merry? Only time will tell, but it is difficult to envisage any future litigant who will be brave enough to take a case to the CFA in the hope that the CFA will modify *Polyset*. It is more likely that if

---

[7] [1993] AC 573 (PC).   [8] [1980] AC 827 (HL).   [9] *Polyset*, [156].
[10] 'Deposit: The Importance of Being (an) Ernest' (2003) 114 LQR 34.
[11] See Chapter 19 in this volume.

there is enough strong commercial feeling in Hong Kong against *Polyset*, then legislation can provide a more satisfactory solution to this thorny and difficult question of forfeitable deposit in a way that will satisfy both the necessity for commercial certainty and for enforcement of commercial bargains. Hong Kong has a notorious volatile property market with ups and downs often of 50 per cent, which is probably unique in the world. Business people in Hong Kong on the basis of *Polyset* would not know, when entering into a large commercial contract, which side of an agreed deposit of 15 per cent, 25 per cent or 35 per cent they fall on as 'special circumstances', with or without the advice of their lawyers.

In *Shanghai Tongji* v. *Casil*,[12] the CFA affirmed the principle of strictness of inferring contract by conduct. Ribeiro PJ in the leading judgment confirmed the requirement of unequivocality established by *The Aramis*[13] and *The Gudermes*.[14] In particular, he referred to what was said in *The Gudermes* as the stringent test: 'What they do must be consistent only with there being a new contract implied, and inconsistent with there being no such contract'.[15]

Then after referring to the double questions in relation to each of the parties to the alleged implied contract, Ribeiro PJ said:

> It would not be sufficient to answer, 'It might' to these questions. The objective test would only be met if the conclusion is reached in each case that the parties' conduct is consistent only with there being a new contract implied, and inconsistent with there being no such contract.[16]

The CFA took the view that such a requirement was not met in the case. The restitution claim also failed on the facts.

Whether a contract is unenforceable because of champerty is the subject of the dramatic case of *Unruh* v. *Seeberger*.[17] The plaintiff sought to enforce his agreement with the defendant in which the plaintiff agreed to use his best endeavour in connection with an arbitration in Holland. The contract provided a special bonus be payable to the plaintiff if the arbitration award received exceed US$10 million. The arbitration resulted in a settlement in excess of US$10 million, but the plaintiff was not paid the special bonus, and he issued proceedings against the defendant for breach of contract and against the second defendant company for liability under an alleged oral agreement. The defence to the claim for the bonus was that the

---

[12] (2004) 7 HKCFAR 79.   [13] *The Aramis* [1989] 1 Lloyd's Rep 213 (Eng CA).
[14] *Mitsui & Co. Ltd* v. *Novorossiysk Shipping Co (The Gudermes)* [1993] 1 Lloyd's Rep 311 (Eng CA).
[15] *Shanghai Tongji*, [39].   [16] *Ibid.*, [51].   [17] (2007) 10 HKCFAR 31.

contract for payment of the special bonus was champertous and there was no estoppel by convention in relation to the second defendant company. The plaintiff was successful at first instance and in the Court of Appeal. The CFA upheld the lower court finding that there was no champerty but allowed the appeal of the second defendant.

The CFA examined and confirmed that one category of conduct excluded from the scope of champerty was the legitimate 'common interest' in the outcome of litigation category. The CFA held that the champerty defence failed because first, the plaintiff's interest and duty in the arbitration was his means of realizing the value of the assets sold by the plaintiff, and second, because in Holland where the arbitration took place and where the plaintiff was to perform his assistance, champerty was not prohibited by Dutch law.

The very learned analysis of the CFA on maintenance and champerty will be of permanent value in that it sought to identify the modern diverse strands that constitute the contemporary public policy of non-enforceable contracts. As said by Sir Anthony Mason, *Unruh* provides a striking example of judicial development of the common law.[18] Ribeiro PJ's exposition of commercial common interest will no doubt provide essential reading on the modern common law of maintenance and champerty.

Although the review of the law on estoppel by convention by Ribeiro PJ is of value because of its vigorous analysis, the reversal of the Court of Appeal on estoppel by convention turned on really a lack of evidence to support the required estoppel by convention.

Shipping

The shipping case of *Bewise Motors Co. Ltd* v. *Hoi Kong Container Services Ltd*[19] is one of the early cases that came up to the CFA with Ching PJ still sitting. It is a case of sub-bailment with the owner of the cars suing the defendant warehouse for the theft of the cars. Two sets of conditions were in play, the one of freight forwarder–bailee (containing a larger exemption) and the other of the warehouse–sub-bailee (containing smaller exemption). The freight forwarder's conditions contained a Himalaya clause. At issue before the CFA were two questions, which set of conditions should apply and if the warehouse–sub-bailee's conditions should apply, on its proper construction, would it be wide enough to exempt the sub-baileee–defendant from liability for the theft of the cars.

---

[18]　See Chapter 13 in this volume.　　[19]　(1997–1998) 1 HKCFAR 256.

The CFA held unanimously that the warehouse–sub-bailee's conditions applied and by a majority (with Litton PJ dissenting) that on the true construction of the warehouse–sub-bailee's conditions, the defendant was exempted from liability.

The construction of the warehouse–sub-bailee's conditions turned on the particular terms of such conditions. The question of general interest, especially for shipping law, was the choice of the conditions applicable to this sub-bailment.

Ching PJ in giving the leading judgment said:

> Both the Himalaya clause and the so-called doctrine of sub-bailment are mechanisms designed to extend the benefit of the terms between the original parties to the sub-contractor or sub-bailee. Neither, however, are mechanisms which can supervene over the actual terms of a sub-contract or a sub-bailment. So, in logic, where a sub-contractor or a sub-bailee expressly declines to enter into a transaction except upon his own terms alone there can be no room for the incorporation of the terms of the contractor or bailee, still less ratification of those terms after the event.[20]

This judgment of *Bewise* and the above passage were cited by the English Court of Appeal in *Lotus Cars Ltd* v. *Southampton Cargo Handling Plc.*[21] It was also a similar case of theft at the docks. Rix LJ was of the view that there was good sense in what Ching PJ said above and in the circumstances of this case the sub-bailee's own terms should apply in preference to the terms brought into play via the Himalaya clause, to the extent of any inconsistency between them.[22]

The next shipping case that came before the CFA was *The Resource 1*[23] in which the CFA considered two issues, one on the mode of challenge to admiralty jurisdiction and the other on the construction of the expression 'owner' in the High Court Ordinance.[24]

The leading judgment on mode of challenge to jurisdiction was given by Mason NPJ. The issue was whether Order 12, Rule 8 provided an exclusive code of challenge to jurisdiction, including challenge to admiralty jurisdiction. This issue was raised by the defendant as it was out of time under Order 12, Rule 8 to apply to the court to set aside the proceedings and the arrest. Mason NPJ said that Order 12, Rule 8 in its application to section 12B(4) of the High Court Ordinance (providing for the exercise of Admiralty jurisdiction) did not exceed the rule-making power and that Order 12, Rule 8 provided a comprehensive and exclusive code for the

---

[20] *Ibid.*, 271H.   [21] [2000] 2 Lloyd's Rep 532 (Eng CA).
[22] *Ibid.*, [51].   [23] (2000) 3 HKCFAR 187.   [24] Cap. 4, s. 12B(4).

taking of jurisdictional objections (including admiralty actions *in rem*) and excluded a challenge under Order 75, Rule 13. The CFA held that the time limit, provided in Order 12, Rule 8 for objections to jurisdictions, was not *ultra vires*, and thus the application made was out of time.

The second issue of the defendant was successful in the CFA. The issue raised was if 'owner' in section 12B(4)[25] of the High Court Ordinance (providing for actions *in rem*) meant registered owner of the ship, there could not be any proper action *in rem* in the circumstances of this case. Bokhary PJ, in giving the leading judgment, accepted the argument for the defendant and followed the English Court of Appeal decision of *Evpo Agnic*[26] confining the meaning of owner in that provision of the statute to registered owner. This restrictive construction of 'owner' is apparently not shared in Singapore or in Australia.[27]

In the 2009 decision of *Carewins Development* v. *Bright Fortune Shipping Ltd*,[28] the issue was raised as to the application of the presentation rule, in which the original bill of lading ('to order') must be presented to obtain delivery of the cargo, to straight bills. The CFA held by the leading judgment of Ribeiro PJ that the presentation rule applies to straight bills as much as it applies to ordered bills. In England, Wales, and Singapore, the authorities cited were in favour of strict requirement of production for taking delivery. The same rule also applied in many European countries. By this decision, the CFA clarified the law in Hong Kong on the necessity to present the original straight bill for delivery of the goods.

---

[25] 12B. Mode of Exercise of Admiralty Jurisdiction . . . :
> (4) In the case of any such claim as is mentioned in s. 12A(2)(e) to (q), where–

> (a) the claim arises in connection with a ship; and
> (b) the person who would be liable on the claim in an action in *personam* (the relevant person) was, when the cause of action arose, the owner or charterer of, or in possession or in control of, the ship,

> an action *in rem* may (whether or not the claim gives rise to a maritime lien on that ship) be brought in the Court of First Instance against–

> (i) that ship, if at the time when the action is brought the relevant person is either the beneficial owner of that ship as respects all the shares in it or the charterer of it under a charter by demise; . . .

[26] [1988] 1 WLR 1090 (Eng CA).
[27] See Notes to Paul Myburgh in 'Arresting the Right Ship: Procedural Theory: The In Personam Link and Conflict of Laws' in M. Davies (ed.), *Jurisdiction and Forum Selection in International Maritime Law: Essays in Honor of Robert Force* (The Hague: Kluwer International Press, 2005) 283–320.
[28] (2009) 12 HKCFAR 185.

The second issue in *Carewins* was whether the terms of the straight bill exempted the carrier from liability for release of the cargo without production of the bill. Although the CFA confirmed that the Court of Appeal had rightly construed the exemption clause as not covering the deliberate release of the goods without production of the straight bill, the judgment of Ribeiro PJ on this issue was more than a mere exercise in construing the particular terms of the bill. The statement of principle regarding the proper construction of exemption clauses will be of long-term importance in the common law world. The principle was stated as follows:

> It will often be the case that an exemption clause uses very broad words which, viewed simply as a matter of language, may be thought apt to exclude all conceivable liability. But the process of construction does not stop there. Wide words of exemption will often cover a whole range of possibilities, some of which will be consistent with maintaining the contractual obligations which reflect the main purpose of the parties' agreement, and some of which would negate those obligations and effectively deprive the contract of any compulsory content. In such cases, the clause is construed contra proferentum to ascribe the narrower meaning to it in order to sustain the purpose and legal effect of the parties' contract.

> . . . The exemption clause is given effect as excluding liability for the breach only where the words are "clear and fairly susceptible of one meaning only". If it is also fairly susceptible of a meaning which does not exclude liability for the breach in question, it is that narrower, contra proferentum meaning which will ascribe to the term.[29]

Arbitration

In recent years, arbitration as a means of resolving commercial disputes has taken much of the workload from courts, including those in Hong Kong. The New York Convention has further reduced the involvement of courts with enforcement of foreign arbitration awards.

Two arbitration award cases came before the CFA. The first in 1999 involved a Beijing Award, and the second in 2003 involved a Hong Kong Award. In the case of *Hebei Import & Export Corp* v. *Polyteck Engineering*,[30] the CFA affirmed Finlay J's judgment allowing enforcement of a CIETAC Award in favour of the Beijing buyer of machinery against the Hong Kong seller. At issue was whether there was a denial of natural justice and apparent bias and whether the conduct of the seller in the arbitration

---

[29] *Ibid.*, [51] and [53].   [30] (1999) 2 HKCFAR 111.

precluded the seller from raising these defences. Mason NPJ gave the
leading judgment and held that:

(1) Failure to raise public policy grounds in Beijing does not mean that
    the point cannot be raised in HK when a different consideration of
    public policy applies. Beijing and HK each has its own public policy.[31]
(2) The seller failed in the arbitration to raise the point of the arbitrator's
    communication with technicians and proceeded with the arbitration
    as if nothing untoward had happened. Therefore the communication
    complained of does not give rise to a case within section 44(3) of the
    Ordinance.[32]
(3) On the facts, the CFA was not satisfied that the seller was unable to
    present its case or that there was violation of the basic notions of
    justice and morality of HK.

Emphasis was placed both by Mason NPJ and by Bokhary PJ (who gave
a concurring judgment) on the importance of finality, comity, and non-
interference of courts with international commercial arbitration awards
except in the most exceptional circumstances. The CFA affirmed and
applied the international norm for enforcing international commercial
arbitration awards.

The interference with domestic arbitration awards was the subject of
the case of *Swire Properties* v. *Secretary for Justice.*[33] The clause said to be
wrongly construed by the domestic arbitrator was not a standard clause
but a 'one-off' clause, and the CFA gave guidance as to how discretion
under section 23 of the Arbitration Ordinance[34] of granting leave to
appeal should be exercised. Leave was given by the Court of Appeal to
take the appeal further to the CFA because it was the first time the proper
approach to the granting of leave to appeal from an arbitration award was
seriously tested. Bokhary PJ giving the important leading judgment, held
that:

(1) In the case of questions of law of general public importance or con-
    struction of a standard clause, a slightly less severe test than the guide-
    line in *Nema-Antaios* (strong prima facie case) should be applied.
    The less severe test is that there was at least a serious doubt as to its
    correctness.[35]

31 *Ibid.*, 136I–137A.   32 *Ibid.*, 139I–140F.   33 (2003) 6 HKCFAR 236.
34 Cap. 341.   35 *Swire Properties*, [43].

(2) In the case of a 'one-off' clause, the high burden must be satisfied that the arbitral tribunal appeared to be obviously wrong. Further it is hoped that, having regard to the speed and finality at which arbitration is aimed, a refusal by the High Court of leave would normally prove difficult to upset.[36]

(3) A Hong Kong judge who refuses leave to appeal to the High Court from an arbitral award should give his reasons, although only very briefly for such refusal.[37]

Money lending and banking

Money lending has been subjected to statutory control in Hong Kong for some years. The heady days of financial speculation in the period before the handover of sovereignty in 1997 generated a number of cases involving money lending. In a series of three judgments, the CFA provided guidance to the legal community on the proper approach to resolve disputes arising out of money lending. The first and most important of the three judgments is *Emperor Finance Ltd* v. *La Belle Fashions.*[38] This judgment is regarded as the fundamental judgment of the CFA on money lending.[39]

The case of *Emperor Finance* started as a straightforward enforcement by the plaintiff money lender for the contractual sums payable by the defendants, resulting from heavy losses suffered by the defendants on the Hang Seng Index Futures. At first instance, the judge ordered enforcement and dismissed all defences of the defendants. Most astonishingly, the Court of Appeal (Rogers VP giving the leading judgment) reversed the judge on the facts and held that the enforcement claim failed. The CFA, in a meticulous judgment by Ribeiro PJ, first analysed the errors of the Court of Appeal on facts and restored the original findings of the judge on the facts. Then the CFA went on to consider the law, and this is where this judgment is of great general and public importance.

The Court of Appeal in *Emperor Finance* held that the plaintiff was engaged in the business of banking and taking deposits and was in breach of sections 11(1) and 12(1) of the Banking Ordinance;[40] thus, the amount claimed was illegal and not enforceable. The CFA held that the Court of Appeal was wrong to regard the plaintiff as carrying on a banking business

---

[36] *Ibid.,* [46].   [37] *Ibid.,* [55].   [38] (2003) 6 HKCFAR 402.

[39] I notice that in the University of Hong Kong's 2009 Postgraduate Certificate in Laws (PCLL) Examiners Report, PCLL candidates are expected to demonstrate their knowledge of the *Emperor Finance* series of CFA judgments.

[40] Cap. 155.

when it was not a case of the receiving money having come from the general public and when the transfer in question was not a 'loan'.

The CFA was at its most restrained when it dealt with the defence of breaches under the Money Lenders Ordinance (MLO),[41] which was first raised by the Court of Appeal itself. The CFA started by holding that section 18 of the MLO applied to bodies corporate. It then went on to reverse, in detail, the breaches of the various provisions of the MLO said by the Court of Appeal to have occurred. Finally, the CFA, after holding that there were two breaches of section 18, said nevertheless there should have been an exercise of discretion under section 18(3) in favour of the lender. Ribeiro PJ said

> In exercising its discretion the court should examine the breach or breaches in question, their consequences for the parties to the transactions and any other circumstances which may make it inequitable to hold the agreements unenforceable.[42]

The second case of *Celestial Finance Ltd* v. *Yu Man Hon*[43] was also an appeal from the Court of Appeal (leading judgment of Rogers VP). The Court of Appeal struck out the claim of the lender on the basis that breach of section 20(1)(c) of the MLO renders the loan totally non-recoverable. The CFA reversed the Court of Appeal, restored the action, and in its judgment affirmed the obiter opinion in *Emperor Finance* that breach of section 20(1) was not always fatal and was capable of being cured by the lender by reason of section 20(4). Ribeiro PJ said:

> It follows that the fact that the appellant was in breach of s20(1)(c) does not mean that it has been permanently deprived of its security. Such a default is curable and if, as a matter of fact, it was cured by the eventual delivery of a s20(1)(c) statement . . . , suspension of the appellant's entitlement to enforce its security will have come to an end.[44]

In *Strong Offer Investment* v. *Nyeu Ting Chuang*,[45] the CFA had the occasion to further clarify the law. Although the appeal was dismissed and the CFA affirmed the enforcement of the loan, the amount recoverable was ordered to be reduced because of the compound interest included. Chan PJ writing the leading judgment said the following, which is now often quoted as a good summary of the essence of what the MLO seeks to achieve:

---

[41] Cap. 163.   [42] *Emperor Finance*, [119].   [43] (2004) 7 HKCFAR 450.
[44] *Ibid.*, [22].   [45] (2007) 10 HKCFAR 529.

Section 18 offers one of the key protections to uneducated, ignorant and unsophisticated borrowers who may not be aware of all the terms and conditions under which the loans are made to them. It seeks to impose certain requirements the compliance with which is a pre-requisite to the enforcement of the loan agreement against the borrower. Section 18(1) provides that no agreement and no security shall be enforceable unless the following conditions are satisfied : (1) there must be a note or memorandum of the agreement in writing; (2) the note or memorandum must contain all the terms as required under s.18(2); (3) the note or memorandum must have been signed personally by the borrower; (4) the borrower must have been given a copy of the note or memorandum including a summary of the prescribed provisions of the Ordinance at the time of signing; and (5) the note or memorandum must have been signed before money was lent or the security was given. . . . These conditions are imposed to ensure that a borrower is fully aware of and freely agrees to all the terms and conditions of the loan, and in particular knows exactly how much money he has borrowed and what interest he has to pay.

On the other hand, the statute is not intended to stifle genuine money-lending transactions or to let the money lender lose all the money he has lent out and all the security he has because of a failure to comply with all such requirements, however trivial or unintentional the breach may be. Hence, where it is not inequitable to do so, the court would enforce the loan agreement with suitable variations, modifications and exceptions. This is the discretion given to the court by s. 18(3).

In resolving any dispute between the money lender and the borrower, therefore, there should be no pre-conceptions either in favour of or against the money lender or the borrower. The statute has sought to strike a fair balance between the two parties. In applying the provisions of s.18, the court has to bear in mind, amongst other things, the parties' respective rights and obligations under the statute as well as the agreement made by them . . . .

The above three judgments of the CFA on money lending have clarified the law in Hong Kong on this subject. They have been applied in many subsequent cases by judges at first instance (Waung J in 2004,[46] Mayo J in 2005,[47] Muttrie J in 2006,[48] Patrick Fung J in 2007,[49] and Poon J in

[46] *Chow Tai Fook Jewellery Co. Ltd* v. *Wong Shun* (unreported, HCA 22168/1998, 31 December 2004, CFI) of Waung J.
[47] *Silverlink (Hong Kong) Finance Ltd* v. *Zhang Sabine Soi Fan* (unreported, HCA 2783/1998, 24 November 1998, CFI) of Deputy Judge Mayo.
[48] *China Everbright Finance Ltd* v. *Chan Yung* (unreported, HCA 18300/1999, 24 October 2006, CFI) of Deputy Judge Muttrie.
[49] *Treasure Spot Finance Co. Ltd* v. *Li Chik Ming* (unreported, HCA 5387/2001, 10 July 2007, CFI) of Recorder Patrick Fung SC.

2008[50]). But in the Court of Appeal, Waung J was in the minority in the case of *Huaxin (Hong Kong) Co. Ltd* v. *Cheerful Corp.*[51] when Waung J applied the CFA judgments. Rogers VP disagreed and was in the majority; the majority prevailed, but there was a follow-up.[52]

On 1 April 2003, the amendment made to the MLO by Part V of the Securities and Futures Ordinance[53] came into effect, thereby exempting securities margin-trading financing by registered lenders from the operation of section 18. It is hoped that the CFA will in the future be less vexed on money lending enforcements.

I now turn to the two unusual banking cases in the CFA. The first is *Bank of China* v. *Fung Chin Kan*[54] in which the CFA held in favour of the bank customers who alleged that there was a pre-contract representation of liability limited to HK$3.3 million and that they should not be liable for any excess under the all monies charge. The judgment of Litton NPJ was put on the basis that there was a collateral contract that existed alongside but independent of the main contract constituted by the legal charge. On the basis of that collateral contract, the CFA ordered that judgment against the Fungs be limited to HK$3.3 million and the bank be given possession of the property charged under the legal charge.

The other members of the CFA (Bokhary and Chan PJJ and Mortimer and Cooke NPJJ) agreed with the judgment of Litton NPJ but also expressed the view that the same decision could have been reached by way of analysis of one composite agreement with two parts, as advanced by Lord Cooke NPJ (without the support of Litton NPJ). The decision of the CFA might be considered as being decided on somewhat special facts because most collateral contract judgments fall into that category. But what is surprising is that in its attempt to do justice in the particular case, the CFA (as a final court, the primary duty of which is to lay down legal principle) seemed to have departed from the usual cautious approach towards collateral contracts.

Hong Kong courts, following the famous authority of *Heilbut, Symons & Co* v. *Buckleton*,[55] have always been reluctant to uphold collateral contracts. This surprising case therefore caused the Hong Kong academic community to examine the judgment carefully. In a critical article by

[50] *The New China Hong Kong Finance Ltd* v. *Shimada Ltd* (unreported, HCA 11030/1999, 5350/2000 & 565/2005, 14 November 2008, CFI) of Poon J.
[51] Unreported, CACV 343/2003, 1 March 2005 (CA).
[52] For subsequent steps, see *Huaxin (Hong Kong) Co. Ltd* v. *Cheerful Corporation* (unreported, HCA 621/2003, 18 July 2005, CFI) of Deputy Judge Carlson.
[53] Cap. 571.   [54] (2002) 5 HKCFAR 515.   [55] [1913] AC 30 (HL).

Jessica Young, she discussed the various areas such as misrepresenta-tion, partial rescission, or rectification that could have been considered by the CFA but were not and concluded by suggesting that the same result could have been reached by way of rectification.[56] The article ended with a concern as to how in future the Hong Kong courts would deal with similar cases of pre-contractual statements as to a person's liabil-ity and whether the Hong Kong courts will resort to the same proac-tive approach compared with the conservative approach of the English courts.

In *Li Sau Ying* v. *Bank of China*,[57] the CFA gave guidance (which is an important function of the final court) on the proper approach to banking cases involving an allegation by a customer of undue influence. In the leading judgment of Scott NPJ, he cautioned against overcomplicating the undue influence issue where the relationship in question was not one of presumed undue influence category of Class 2A. Lord Scott expressed the hope that in future cases, when it was not a Class 2A category relationship, concentration should be on whether the evidence justified the inference that the impugned transaction was procured by the trust and confidence reposed on the alleged dominant party. There should be no reference to or assistance from evidential presumptions of undue influence, which is likely to cause confusion.

Confidence

Hong Kong was one of the early jurisdictions in the world involved in the international *Spycatcher* litigation (United Kingdom, Australia, and New Zealand were other notable jurisdictions involved) in which breach of confidence was the successful ground invoked for the injunction granted. This was one of the early successes of Robert Ribeiro as a rising barrister. It came as no surprise that the CFA took up and granted special leave to appeal in the case of *Nam Tai Electronics Inc.* v. *PricewaterhouseCoopers*.[58] This was a most instructive case in which the CFA examined the scope of the duty of confidence owed by the accounting firm to its former client. The case of the accounting firm–defendant was that the disclosure was a defensive response to the plaintiff's allegation to the creditors of a company in liquidation that the defendant should not be appointed as liquidator of that company because the defendant had a conflict of

---

[56] 'Misrepresentation or Collateral Contracts' (2003) 33 *HKLJ* 9.
[57] (2004) 7 HKCFAR 579.   [58] (2008) 11 HKCFAR 62.

interest. In a carefully written leading judgment, Ribeiro PJ examined the scope of the various qualifications to the duty of confidence (consent qualification, self-interest qualification, and self-defence). Having regard to the opaque statement by the plaintiff, the CFA was of the view that the disclosure of the defendant in response did not fall into either the consent or self-interest qualification category,[59] and therefore there was a breach of the duty of confidence.

As no financial loss was suffered, the CFA awarded to the plaintiff nominal damages of HK$100. The long litigation was therefore only a Pyrrhic victory for the plaintiff. But in reality, it was much worse than that. It was a disaster financially for the plaintiff. On 7 April 2008, the CFA handed down its decision on costs. As the defendant had made a payment into court before Waung J, sometime in May 2001, long before the trial started, the CFA made the costs order that the plaintiff was to pay to the defendant all costs incurred after the date of payment in, which means all costs at all three levels: before Waung J, before the Court of Appeal, and before the CFA.

PCCW v. *Aitken*[60] was a case in which the employer failed to obtain a comprehensive and wide injunction against an ex-employee to prevent the ex-employee from working for the new employer engaged in a competing business. The plaintiff appealed against a limited injunction order granted by the judge restricting the injunction to identified confidential information. Ribeiro PJ stated that the law adopted a policy in favour of freedom of employment and against restraint of trade. Courts would not restrain a former employee from deploying his or her own skills and knowledge for the benefit of the new employer. Restraint as to the former employee's field of activity (which was what the plaintiff was effectively seeking to do) would not be permitted. This policy is to be distinguished from the other policy deriving from *Prince Jefri Bolkiah* v. *KPMG*,[61] in which the court will restrain a former lawyer from acting for a new client unless it is satisfied that there is no risk of misuse or disclosure of the former client's confidential information.

Lord Hoffmann NPJ stressed the important difference between privilege and confidence in a passage quoted in Gary Meggitt's chapter in this volume.[62] In his substantial concurring judgment, Lord Hoffmann concluded:

---

[59] *Ibid.*, [81].   [60] (2009) 12 HKCFAR 114.   [61] [1999] 2 AC 222 (HL).
[62] See Chapter 21 in this volume.

> There is a very considerable difference between the position of a solicitor and an employee, even though the confidential information which they have obtained may be the same. The solicitor will normally have many clients and will not be dependent upon one for his livelihood. Even if the new client is important to him, he does not have to act for him in a matter in which he previously acted for the other side. The employee can have only one employer at a time and, in the nature of things, his new employer is likely to be in the same line of business and therefore in competition with the previous one. I therefore see no reason of logic or policy which requires the special remedy against solicitors to be extended to employees who have information which would be protected by LPP.[63]

The defendant was neither a former in house lawyer nor a former lawyer of the plaintiff, and thus the CFA held that the *Bolkiah* principle did not apply. The CFA left open the question of relief against a former in-house lawyer who changes side and a former in-house lawyer who goes into private practice acting for the other side.

Company

Nina Kung v. *Tan Man Kou (Re Chime Corp. Ltd)*[64] was part of the huge litigation arising from the death of Teddy Wang and the ensuing disputes between the father of Teddy Wang (Senior Wang) and Nina Wang, Teddy's widow. While the probate litigation was raging in the probate court between the widow and the Senior Wang (eventually leading to the CFA judgment of *Nina Kung* v. *Wang Din Shin*[65] with five separate substantial judgments), the company court had to consider a section 168A[66] petition brought by the administrator of the estate of Teddy Wang against Nina Wang for alleged unfair prejudice conduct. An application to amend the petition included an allegation that Nina Wang had improperly procured the company to advance loans of some HK$4.5 billion to CAL, a company of Nina Wang, and to seek an order of repayment of the loan to the company. The judge refused the amendment sought, but the Court of Appeal allowed the amendment. The CFA allowed the appeal and said that the amendment containing the prayer should not be allowed, and amendments to the body of the petition relating to conduct also should not be allowed (except to the limited alleged mismanagement conduct).

---

[63] *PCCW*, [62].   [64] (2004) 7 HKCFAR 546.
[65] (2005) 8 HKCFAR 387.   [66] Companies Ordinance (Cap. 32).

The leading judgment was given by Scott NPJ. He first defined the issue of the appeal before the CFA as 'whether the court can, on a s.168A petition, deal with and dispose of a cause of action for damages or restitution that is vested in the company and, if it can do so, in what circumstances it should do so'. Lying at the heart of this issue was the distinction in law between a section 168A petition for unfair prejudice and a derivative action in the name of the company.

Lord Scott NPJ made the following important statement of law:

> As a general rule, in my opinion, the court should not in a s.168A petition make an order for payment to be made by a respondent director to the company unless the order corresponds with the order to which the company would have been entitled had the allegations in question been successfully prosecuted in an action by the company (or in a derivative action in the name of the company). If the order does not so correspond then, either the company will have received less than it is entitled to, in which case it will be entitled to relitigate the issue in an action against the director for the balance, or the company will have received more than it was entitled to, in which case, a clear injustice to the director will have been perpetrated . . . . . .
>
> Moreover, the use of a s.168A petition in order to circumvent the rule in Foss v Harbottle (1843) 2 Hare 461 in a case where the nature of the complaint is misconduct rather than mismanagement is, in my opinion, an abuse of process . . . .[67]

As P. Y. Lo notes, the CFA judgment in *Re Chime* has been adopted by the PC and in Australia.[68]

In *Liquidators of Akai Holdings v. Grande Holdings*,[69] the important question was the scope of the power of the liquidator of a company to seek information in relation to the affairs of the company under section 221 of the Companies Ordinance.[70] In dismissing the appeal, Millett NPJ clarified the law in this way:

> Section 221 and corresponding provisions overseas are designed to enable a liquidator to carry out his functions. These are twofold: (i) to collect the assets of the company, settle its liabilities and distribute its surplus funds amongst its creditors; and (ii) to investigate the causes of the company's failure and the conduct of those concerned in its dealings and affairs. . . . The first of these functions is primarily of concern to the company's creditors and shareholders; the second serves a wider public interest

---

[67] *Chime*, [62] and [63].   [68] See Chapter 22 in this volume.
[69] (2006) 9 HKCFAR 766.   [70] Cap. 32.

in enabling the authorities to take appropriate action against those guilty of misconduct in relation to the company . . . .

The section is a vital part of the statutory insolvency regime. It is designed to meet the difficulties faced by liquidators in finding out what has happened to the company's assets and what has caused the failure of the company. It has often been observed that a liquidator is usually a stranger to the affairs of the company. He relies on orders for examination and production to reconstitute the knowledge of the company, in circumstances where the records are often inadequate, in order to be able to perform his duties in recovering the company's assets and generally to enable him to carry out his functions effectively and with as little expense and as expediently as possible.

The section's purpose, however, is not limited to reconstituting the state of the company's knowledge, even though that may be one of the purposes most clearly justifying the making of an order. . . . It may be used to discover facts and documents relating to potential claims by the liquidator against third parties or to enable him to report to the authorities with a view to taking action against those responsible for the company's failure . . . where it was used to enable disqualification proceedings to be taken against former directors. There is an important public interest ensuring that the liquidator should obtain the information needed to understand the company's affairs and the reasons for its failure; and to report to the authorities to enable them to take appropriate action against those guilty of misconduct in relation to the company's affairs.

It has been repeatedly stated, and the legislative purpose demands, that the powers conferred on the court by the section or its overseas equivalents are wide, general and unlimited. The liquidator must satisfy the court that the information or documents sought are reasonably required to enable him to carry out his functions. In considering this question, the authorities establish that great weight should be given to the views of the liquidator, for he is an officer of the court and alone has the necessary knowledge of the problems facing him in understanding the affairs of the company and his reasons for seeking production of documents in the terms proposed; moreover, there are often great difficulties in seeing how the terms of the order can be cut down and remain effective . . . .[71]

Lord Millett NPJ acknowledged that the exercise of the power was capable of being severe but that it was tempered by the court's discretion. Summarizing the general principles governing the balancing exercise, Lord Millett gave a reminder that the court 'must take care not to cut down the width of the order sought by the liquidator in a way which would

---

[71] *Akai*, [23]–[27].

risk making it ineffective'.[72] This CFA judgment will no doubt be of fundamental importance in common law jurisdictions having the same or equivalent provisions.

Conclusion

It will be seen from the account given in this chapter that the development of commercial law has continued unabated since the handover in 1997. The vigour of that development has been truly remarkable. The geographical availability of the CFA is one factor. As noted, the high quality of the PJs and NPJs is a key factor. The cross-fertilization arising from NPJs from different jurisdictions who are familiar not only with their own laws but also with international common law is a special bonus. Then finally, it must not be forgotten that the presence of counsel of the highest calibre both locally and from the United Kingdom ensured that the CFA is given not only reliable but superior assistance. Michael Thomas QC and SC (appearing in no less than five of the cases I have discussed), who qualifies under both categories of counsel, is undoubtedly the star counsel in the CFA. There can be no doubt that the high reliability of the CFA in commercial appeals contributes to the high regard for Hong Kong held by the international business community.

Many of the chapters in this volume refer to the presence of the eminent NPJs in contributing to the jurisprudence of the CFA. In his chapter, Michael Thomas refers to the large contribution made by Sir Anthony Mason NPJ to the CFA and to Hong Kong.[73] A tribute must be paid to Sir Anthony Mason for his enormous contribution to the jurisprudence of Hong Kong and to the CFA standing high in the international world. Both his presentation at the University of Hong Kong's CFA conference in March 2010 and his chapter in this volume attest to his intellectual vigour and his love for Hong Kong.

The contribution in the past 13 years of Sir Anthony Mason and all others earlier referred to helped to ensure that after 1997, instead of Hong Kong being left in the backwaters of Asia, the CFA has grown into an internationally recognized final court of high standing, with its judgments respected and held in high esteem by the common law courts. This was largely because of the combination of the good fortune of our constitution (by way of the Basic Law) establishing a legal regime of

---

[72] *Ibid.*, [30(8)].   [73] See Chapter 8 in this volume.

overseas NPJs sitting in the CFA and Andrew Li's judicious selection of NPJs of the highest calibre from England, Australia, and New Zealand to sit regularly in the CFA. In this sense, without his voice being heard in the reported CFA commercial law judgments, the Chief Justice was our true hero, who has ensured that judgments on commercial law in Hong Kong will continue to be cited, followed, and applied in the courts of the common law world.

19

Land law

MALCOLM MERRY

Land has always been expensive in Hong Kong and vital to its economy, but the importance of land increased during the latter half of the 20th century as prosperity from trade, manufacturing, and investment led to the development of land into high-rise buildings and the sale of flats, offices, shops, and factories in those buildings to the rising middle classes, those sales being largely financed by mortgage loans from banks. During the same period, the government was determined to provide housing for the less well-off , building vast estates of low-cost, small apartments in tower blocks, mainly in new towns in the previously rural parts of the territory. The combination of wealth, order, common law, settled government, and encouragement of business to be found in the British colony made it an attractive place in which to invest, particularly for overseas and later Mainland Chinese. Purchase of property became a popular form of investment and speculation. The value of property provided security for business and personal loans. Income from property grew to be a great source of government revenue. Property and related activities turned into a major sector of employment.

Accordingly, the fortunes of the property market are a barometer for the economy generally. They are enthusiastically covered by Hong Kong's boisterous newspapers and avidly followed by their readers. Historically, prices have been not only high but also volatile. The market is extraordinarily sensitive to changes in confidence and is prone to sudden rises and falls. These tend to result in outbreaks of litigation. The amounts at stake usually justify pursuit of the litigation to the highest level.

During the first 13 years of its existence, the Court of Final Appeal (CFA) decided about 50 appeals that involved land law, using that term in the broadest sense. The subjects of these cases ranged from adverse possession to unauthorized structures. They embraced matters as abstruse as Chinese customary trusts over land and rights of way by prescription and as mundane as agreements for the sale of land and preliminary agreements for tenancy. The majority of the cases concerned agreements for sale and purchase, title, and conveyancing, but there were also disputes relating to government leases, land compensation, and building management.

In the course of its judgments in these cases, the court departed from English law at least twice and expanded (or newly discovered) the common law at least once. The court also confirmed and developed certain special features of Hong Kong conveyancing. In the main, though, it applied well-settled principles of law to facts, sometimes after the Court of Appeal failed to do so.

The CFA delivered judgments that both favoured and disappointed developers and judgments that both favoured and disappointed speculators. It found both for and against vendors and for and against purchasers. It found for two landlords and for one tenant. So the court has been pretty even-handed. If it has a favourite litigant, that would be the government.

The scope of land-related issues which have been dealt with by the CFA is so wide that, in order to keep this chapter within reasonable bounds, what follows concentrates upon the mainstream of land law. By 'the mainstream' is meant issues of landholding, interests in land, title, and conveyancing, with emphasis upon the aspects of these subjects that are special to Hong Kong.

Departure from English law

Adverse possession has been a recurrent subject of CFA land cases and was in fact the subject of the court's very first decision, *Wong Tak Yue v. Kung Kwok Wai David*.[1] It was not the most auspicious of starts, for the court departed from English law without meaning to do so. This was one of those battles between developer and squatter over land in the rural New Territories which kept Hong Kong courts busy during the 1990s. The issue was whether the squatter had had the requisite intention to possess the land adversely to the exclusion of the registered or legal owner. In the course of earlier proceedings, the squatter had made an affidavit in which he had asserted willingness to pay rent if asked. The CFA seized upon this as an admission of intent not to hold the land adversely to the owner, relying upon an English Court of Appeal case to that effect.[2] The trouble

---

[1] (1997–1998) 1 HKCFAR 55. See Harpum, 'Adverse Possession and Statements Against Interest' (1998) 28 *HKLJ* 329.

[2] *R v. Secretary of State for the Environment, ex parte Davies* (1990) 61 P&CR 487 (Eng CA). The squatter here actually offered to pay rent.

with this was that there was Privy Council (PC) authority to the contrary, which was apparently not drawn to the CFA's attention, in which Lord Devlin had observed on behalf of the board that such an admission was of no assistance in judging intent because it was the kind of thing that a candid squatter hoping in due course to acquire a possessory title was almost bound to make. The trouble was compounded later when in the *Pye* case the House of Lords preferred the PC approach to that of the Court of Appeal.[3]

Authority aside, the CFA's decision is doubtful because intent is to be judged objectively so that declarations of subjective intent should be discounted and because an occupier who is willing to become a tenant nonetheless possesses the land to the exclusion of the true owner and intends so to do. This is certainly so if the latter is unwilling to let the land to the occupier and is even the case if the true owner had been willing to so let the land. The occupier's intent is to possess the land, not to own it, and to possess it by whatever means are available, and those means include occupation against the wishes of the true owner. During the running of the limitation period, the squatter will know that the only practical way of retaining possession is to take a lease but that does not exclude having the intent to assert possessory title once occupation for the requisite period has been achieved.

Wong Tak Yue may be viewed as an illustration of judicial antipathy (not limited to the CFA) to adverse possession as 'land theft'. The judgment can be confined and distinguished from the PC and House of Lords decisions in that the admission was volunteered rather than extracted under cross-examination, but this is hardly satisfactory. The CFA's reasoning is couched in terms of the persuasiveness of admissions against interest in evidence. The making of the admission can be explained as a tactical move by the squatter in the course of the tortuous passage of the case through the lower courts during a period in which the law was in flux, but again this does not seem a convincing reason to distinguish the case. Furthermore, these circumstances undermine the genuineness and credibility of the admission (at the time that it was made it was decidedly in the squatter's interest to make the admission) and therefore suggest that the squatter did indeed intend to occupy the land adversely to the landlord. The upshot, however, is that the Hong Kong law on adverse possession differs from that in England and elsewhere.

---

[3] *J. A. Pye (Oxford) Ltd* v. *Graham* [2003] 1 AC 419 (HL). The PC case is *Ocean Estates Ltd* v. *Pinder* [1969] 2 AC 19, 24D-F.

Wong Tak Yue is procedurally extraordinary because the CFA allowed the appellant squatter to argue a point that had not been raised on first appeal and had seemingly been abandoned. In the Court of Appeal, the squatter had not relied upon adverse possession, having abandoned it because the law both at first instance and on appeal was such that at the time of the true owner's commencement of proceedings 20 years' possession had not elapsed. The law was that when after the squatter began to occupy the land but before 20 years had elapsed, the true owner had acquired an extension of his lease from the government by exercise of an option to renew, time began to run afresh. Four days after the Court of Appeal rejected the squatter's appeal on other grounds, in another squatter appeal, the PC decided that time began to run against the true owner not on lease extension but when the squatter in fact took possession during the original term.[4] The CFA allowed the appellant to reopen the issue of adverse possession because of the highly unusual course of events.

The other departure from English law occurred more recently and more deliberately. In late October 2009, the CFA rendered its decision in appeals by two developers who wished to redevelop separate sites at Wang Fung Terrace in the Tai Hang district of Hong Kong Island.[5] One of the sites included an area that had long been used by neighbouring occupiers to reach their buildings. The Building Authority treated them as enjoying a right of way over the area by prescription and accordingly excluded it from plot ratio calculations with the result that the site developer was not permitted to build as tall a building as it wished. The developer's counsel argued that the acquisition of a right of way by presumed grant from long and open usage was not possible because the land was leasehold, as is virtually all land in Hong Kong, relying upon the established rule of English law that prescriptive rights, being permanent, can be granted by the freeholder only and therefore cannot be granted by or to a leaseholder. It is in fact a restriction which has been roundly criticized as irrational, since a leaseholder may submit to a right of way over his or her land or enjoy such a right over another's leasehold land if expressly granted and also as being based on misunderstandings by the Victorian-era judges who had declared the restriction. Irish judges had refused to follow their English brethren, since agricultural land in Ireland was predominantly

4 *Chung Ping Kwan* v. *Lam Island Development Co. Ltd* [1997] AC 38 (PC).
5 *China Field Ltd and Sun Honest Development Ltd* v. *Appeal Tribunal (Buildings)* (2009) 12 HKCFAR 342.

leasehold, and farmers there often enjoyed long-established rights of way and to water.

Lower court decisions about the applicability of the restriction to Hong Kong had gone both ways, although the more recent decisions had been against following the English law. The main basis was that to do so would mean in practice that acquisition of rights of way by long usage, whether under common law prescription as amended by statute or under the doctrine of lost modern grant, would be impossible.

The point was accordingly ripe for consideration at the highest level, and it came as no surprise when the CFA announced that the English restriction was not part of Hong Kong law. What was a slight surprise was that the court said that lost modern grant was a source of common law acquisition of easements separate from that of prescription proper and that the restriction should never have been applied to the doctrine. A greater surprise was that the English law was denounced as flawed: a matter of authority and not of principle, said Lord Millett, who delivered the main judgment. He even went on to say that the restriction would not be upheld if considered by the House of Lords. For the time being, however, the restriction remains the law of England, having been upheld (somewhat wistfully) by the Court of Appeal there in the early 1990s.[6] So the law in Hong Kong is now definitely different.

And it is, Lord Millett was at pains to explain, the common law of Hong Kong. Since 1997, the Basic Law (BL) has directed the courts to apply the common law as part of the law previously in force without stipulating which common law. We know that it is no longer just the English common law since the reference to that in the Application of English Law Ordinance[7] (AELO) has gone. The implication is that Hong Kong courts can draw on authority from any common law jurisdiction as persuasive and of course in practice that is what happens, especially at the higher levels. But in rejecting the English restriction, the CFA did not explicitly adopt the Irish rule. Rather, it made – or found – the common law of Hong Kong. This was what the courts had been doing even before 1997, announced Bokhary PJ, somewhat contentiously, in his judgment in *China Field*: the power to do so before 1997 had been derived from the directive in the AELO and predecessor Supreme Court Ordinances to adapt the common law to local circumstances.

---

[6] *Simmons* v. *Dobson* [1991] 1 WLR 720 (Eng CA).
[7] Cap. 88, but not adopted as the Laws of the HKSAR.

Making common law

If the CFA has the power to make or reveal a common law for Hong Kong, has it ever done so in a land case before 2010? On one view, yes, at least once, if somewhat peripherally, because in *Polyset Ltd* v. *Panhandat Ltd*,[8] the court held that a defaulting purchaser who had paid a deposit in excess of the conventional 10 per cent of the price was entitled to the return of that money in the form of a credit against damages for failure to complete on the ground that the money was not a true or reasonable deposit. In doing so, the court was building upon PC authority in which a deposit in excess of 25 per cent paid upon signing an agreement for the sale and purchase of land in Jamaica was similarly held to be returnable in its entirety as not being a true deposit,[9] that is to say an amount paid as an earnest of the intent of the purchaser to complete the contract and as compensation for the vendor for keeping the property off the market during the completion period. However, the PC had also observed that the amount was penal, an unfortunate observation that had reinforced pre-existing confusion between a forfeitable deposit and liquidated damages, the latter of which might constitute a penalty. This had misled courts, including the Court of Appeal in the instant case, into eliding the test of whether an amount is a true deposit with that of whether an amount is a penalty. The contribution of the CFA was to correct this confusion so that now it is clear that an excessive initial payment is to be returned not because it is a penalty but because it is not really a deposit, that is to say a payment made as an earnest of the intent of the payer to complete the contract.

The CFA also adopted the approach of the PC that 10 per cent of the purchase price was more than enough to signify earnest intent and so would not have been a true deposit were it not the convention for a purchaser to pay that sum on signing the contract, that when the sum exceeded 10 per cent the whole of the sum and not just the amount by which it exceeded that percentage was returnable and that an amount in excess of 10 per cent might constitute a true deposit in exceptional circumstances. In this last regard, however, the court eschewed an opportunity to develop the law by reference to local circumstances.

The sale upon which the purchaser in *Polyset* had reneged had been negotiated in the middle of 1997 during the final phase of the mid-1990s

[8] (2002) 5 HKCFAR 234.
[9] *Workers Trust & Merchant Bank Ltd* v. *Dojap Investments Ltd* [1993] AC 573 (PC).

property boom, so the price (HK$115 million for five shops in Causeway Bay, a shopping and tourist district) was high, and the risk of a market collapse that would lead the purchaser to choose not to complete was acute. That risk was exacerbated by the uncertainties associated with the impending transfer of sovereignty and the fact that the purchaser was an assetless shelf company which had negotiated a completion period of more than nine months: classic signs of speculation. Consequently, the vendor had protected itself from the risk in the way that commercial vendors normally do, by demanding and receiving a deposit of such magnitude (35 per cent, or HK$40.25 million, payable in tranches) that its forfeiture would discourage the purchaser from defaulting and would provide the vendor with security for loss that would be suffered if the purchaser did default. Moreover, the purchaser acknowledged by a special clause in the sale and purchase agreement that it was important commercially that the vendor should be able to forfeit the deposit in the light of the long completion. One would have thought that here was an exceptional circumstance justifying such a deposit, and one that the CFA could explain by reference to conditions in the Hong Kong property market.

Yet, by a four to one majority, the CFA declared the amount to be not a true deposit and the circumstances not exceptional, so the vendor had to make do with common law damages. The majority seemed to accept that the circumstances justified a deposit greater than 10 per cent but believed that 35 per cent was just too great, although there is also reference to the payment serving purposes other than that of a true deposit.[10] The dissentient was Litton NPJ, whose powerful judgment relied upon sanctity of contract as much as local market conditions.

If the facts in *Polyset* were not exceptional enough to justify a deposit larger than 10 per cent, it is difficult to imagine circumstances that would do so. One cannot escape the feeling that this aspect of the case was an opportunity lost.

Polyset was unusual amongst land decisions by the CFA not only because there was a dissent but also because all five of the justices delivered reasoned decisions (perhaps because of the strength of the dissent) and because two of the judges were non-permanent members.

Opportunity to expound, explain, and even expand the common law – in this instance, the law of public nuisance – was not, however, spurned

---

[10] No reliance was placed on that fact that the amount was not payable entirely on the making of the sale agreement as deposits normally are, but was payable in four installments like stage payments of the price.

in *Leung Tsang Hung v. Incorporated Owners of Kwok Wing House.*[11] A large piece of concrete had fallen from a building in Mongkok and had killed a female hawker in the street below. The piece had been the corner of an extended concrete canopy over the enclosed balcony of a flat on the 11th floor. The enclosure and extension had been carried out with poor workmanship and without Building Authority permission, probably soon after the building was erected in the 1960s. Who was to blame? The tenant and the owners of the flat, but not the owners' corporation, accepted responsibility for negligence and public nuisance. Both the trial judge and the Court of Appeal[12] said that the corporation owed no duty because it had had no occupational control over the canopy. This reflected general judicial antipathy towards making owners' corporations answer for the acts of occupiers at and about the private areas of buildings.

The issue on further appeal was whether an owners' corporation had the degree of control over the external parts of their building sufficient to found liability in public nuisance, an area of the law in a state of development. The Incorporated Owners (IO) argued that it was analogous to a public authority and could not be liable for hazards of which it was unaware. The CFA was thus required to investigate the nature of an owners' corporation and its rights and duties. This involved a close analysis of the Building Management Ordinance (BMO)[13] under which such corporations are founded and regulated. This legislation of everyday importance had hitherto received little attention at the highest level. The result was, for those of us interested in the law of building management, a most impressive judgment from Ribeiro PJ setting out the juridical nature and legal attributes of an IO.

The analogy with public corporations was rejected. The owners owned the whole building as tenants-in-common, and there was a close identification between them and the corporation: the corporation was the corporate embodiment of the co-owners collectively, given separate personality not because it had rights separate from the owners but in order to facilitate the exercise and enforcement of those rights. The corporate veil was highly transparent in that individual owners can be made liable for the debts of the corporation for purposes of enforcement of judgments or of winding up the corporation. An IO had the power to act on the owners' behalf in matters of common interest, was funded by their contributions,

---

[11] *Leung Tsang Hung v. Incorporated Owners of Kwok Wing House* (2007) 10 HKCFAR 480.
[12] [2006] 4 HKLRD 714 (CA).   [13] Cap. 344.

had a statutory duty to maintain the common parts of their building, and had a statutory duty to enforce the DMC binding among the owners. The deed in this case, as is usual, required each owner to share the cost of keeping the external parts in good repair, not to make structural alterations, and not to place anything on the common parts. The deed was supplemented by the BMO, which gave the IO the right of entry and inspection of a flat and which prohibited conversion of common parts by anyone.

Once the court had determined that the exterior of the building was a common part (by application of the statutory definition) and thus the responsibility of the IO, liability for the hazard posed by the poor state of the canopy followed. From the building management point of view, the case underlines the importance of owners collectively (either through IOs or their managers) maintaining their building and carrying adequate insurance. From the point of view of public nuisance, the case shows the importance of control, rather than ownership, to liability and applies that to a particular Hong Kong institution, the owners' corporation. The judicial dissection of the owners' corporation is particularly valuable and is of application in other aspects of the law of building management. It also serves to show the limits of the comparison which is frequently made between a corporation formed under the Companies Ordinance[14] and an owners' corporation.

One should beware, however, of overstating the practical impact of the decision. Most of the buildings in Hong Kong and some of the largest estates of flats and houses have no owners' corporation, and so no statutory duty arises. Also, modern, giant estates have been well planned within their own land and do not overhang the street, thus posing little danger to the public, and tend to be better managed than older, smaller buildings. Moreover, liability of the owners' corporation for the state of the common parts is hardly new: Previously, that liability, whether it was to residents, visitors, or passers-by, tended to be in terms of negligence or occupiers' liability.

Leung Tsang Hung was principally an instance of established law – in that case, nuisance – being applied to particular local facts. In truth, the CFA has done little law creating in the land sphere. Its contribution, no less significant within the jurisdiction, has largely been the application of the common law to Hong Kong circumstances. This can be seen most clearly in the core land topics: the system of landholding, title, and conveyancing.

----

[14] Cap. 32.

Landholding

The economic and commercial background to the court's early years was the successive recessions set off by, respectively, the Asian financial crisis, the bursting of the dotcom bubble, and the outbreak of severe acute respiratory syndrome. These caused a prolonged slump in the property market, which provided the motivation for purchasers to withdraw from transactions or, as the Cantonese put it, 'kick the lease' away, by finding flaws in the vendor's title. One such incident was *Polyset* in which the sale had been agreed in May 1997 with completion in March 1998, after the market collapsed in the autumn of 1997. Another gave rise to the decision by the CFA on a land matter that had the greatest effect and that may well be the most important civil judgment by the court yet, *Jumbo King Ltd* v. *Faithful Properties Ltd*.[15] In this decision from December 1999, the court analysed the system of holding land by tenancy-in-common in undivided shares, which is invariably used for the ownership of flats and other units in buildings. In addition, Lord Hoffmann used the opportunity to explain and lay down for Hong Kong the contextual approach to interpretation of contracts on which he had earlier expounded in the House of Lords.[16]

The sale under consideration in *Jumbo King* was of ground floor shops, four utility rooms, and flat roofs at Hankow Centre, a large building in Tsimshatsui with commercial units at lower levels and residential flats on the upper floors. The sale, for HK$275.5 million, had been agreed on 14 October 1997, about a week before the property market collapsed. In the 1960s when the developer, Mr Hotung, as owner of the whole building, had divided the building into shares and sold the first domestic flat with one of the 720 shares in the building, he had reserved to himself all the other units, including shop spaces and offices in the commercial portion but with no express mention of the utility rooms and roofs. That was the basis upon which the purchaser claimed that the utility rooms and roofs were common parts of the building and thus were not the vendor's to sell. It seemed a reasonable argument, even if dubiously motivated, because one would expect utility rooms and roofs of their nature to be common parts. Consistent with this, they had not been allocated to shares. Moreover, the legal principle is that tenants-in-common have unity of possession so the whole of the building is owned by them and they have the right to use it all

---

[15] (1999) 2 HKCFAR 279.
[16] *Investors Compensation Scheme Ltd* v. *West Bromwich Building Society* [1998] 1 WLR 896 (HL).

except to the extent that any parts are specifically excluded from common enjoyment by agreement between them in the deed of mutual covenant (DMC) governing their relations. The trial judge agreed. However, the Court of Appeal did not, and neither did the CFA, though for rather different reasons.

The CFA confirmed the principle stated above but said that the overriding objective in construction of documents was to give effect to what a reasonable person would have understood the parties to mean. If the provisions of the DMC were read in context rather than literally, the court said, the utility rooms and roofs had been reserved to the developer and so later had been validly sold by the developer to the predecessor of the current vendor and therefore could not be common parts. One had to read not just the particular provisions of the deed but also the rest of the document, and documents, such as assignments, made contemporaneously with the DMC and do so with the factual and legal background and the practical objectives of the deed in mind. An important consideration was that the building was in two self-contained parts and the utility rooms were in the lower, commercial portion of the building, whereas the flat conveyed to the first purchaser of a unit was on the domestic upper floors: that purchaser would have no interest in occupying utility rooms in the commercial part.

That may have been so, but it does not follow that other owners, especially of units in the commercial portion, would have had no interest in using for communal purposes (rather than physically occupying) the utility rooms. Lord Hoffmann's analysis seems to overlook this and to leave aside the purpose of the rooms evidenced by their very description: utility rooms are ostensibly for the housing of or use in connection with utilities, such as electricity, for common use. Maybe the omission of reservation of use of the rooms by the developer (or rather, his solicitor, who drafted the DMC) was not inadvertent. One cannot help feeling that while the contextual approach is right, it has been applied here so as to reach the result desired by the court.

The contextual, or purposive, approach to interpretation was not new (the 'factual matrix' had been first referred to in the 1970s and thereafter used in commercial cases in Hong Kong), but it had previously not been set out so lucidly and with such authority. Lord Hoffmann's judgment, with its provocative references to games with words and pedantic lawyers, has become frequently cited. It has proved a gift to barristers faced with a contractual provision that seems to be all against their client's case. To others lawyers, especially drafters of contracts, conveyancers, and others whose trade is precision with words (or pedantry), but also one suspects many lower court judges bombarded with evidence and arguments about context, the judgment has been less welcome. Nevertheless, Lord Hoffmann was careful to provide something for everyone: he said that one does not readily accept that words in serious utterances such as legal documents do not mean what they say and that if their ordinary meaning makes sense in relation to the rest of the document and the factual background, the court will give effect to the words even if the consequences are harsh for one party or other.

Jumbo King has been relied upon by the CFA in subsequent cases, both as authority upon interpretation of contracts and for its guidance upon the system of co-ownership of land. That guidance arose from a second argument deployed by the purchaser. In the DMC, the utility rooms and roofs, unlike the shops, had not been allotted to shares in the land; in fact, there was no mention of them there at all. The purchaser argued that the rooms and roofs could not be sold without being attached to related shares. This would have been a good point had they been sold on their own, for the proprietary interest which is sold is the shares in the land, the use of particular units being ancillary or, as land lawyers put it, an incident of ownership of the land. But in this instance, other units, shops, were included in the sale, and the DMC had allotted them to shares that were to be conveyed with them and with the rooms and roofs. The CFA found that it was enough that the units were accompanied by some shares, not necessarily shares to which the units had been allocated by the developer.

One consequence of co-ownership of land in undivided shares and subject to covenants between the co-owners laid down by their DMC is, as Lord Hoffmann explained in *Jumbo King*, that there can be no easements between the owners. This is because there is but one piece of land and for easements to arise, separate pieces of land are required, a dominant and a servient tenement. So, for instance, the rights of passage to and support of her or his flat granted to each owner in the DMC are created by covenants in the deed, yet they look very much like easements. This led the court to describe them as quasi-easements.

The court returned to this theme in *Kung Ming Tak Tong Co. Ltd* v. *Park Solid Enterprises Ltd*[17] in which it confirmed that the grant of exclusive possession of a unit in a building is not an interest in land but, similar to the quasi-easements, is a product of the mutual covenants in the DMC:

---

[17] (2008) 11 HKCFAR 403.

each owner gives a separate contractual undertaking to all the others not to exercise the rights of occupation and enjoyment which he would otherwise be able to exercise as a co-owner of all the land. In that case, the owner of shops at a building in Tsuen Wan had sold one immediately next to a busy lobby area from which access could be had to a walkway to the MTR station. The long side of the shop abutted onto the lobby and served as a counter for the service of fast food to passing customers. However, the lobby was not legally a common area of the building; rather, it belonged to the vendor, who now proposed to erect another shop on part of the lobby, immediately next to and blocking the counter, thereby depriving the shop of its principal feature.

The main argument below for the purchaser was that it had a right of way over the lobby. This did not work because the lobby was not a common part under the DMC (so there could be no right to pass over the lobby derived from common ownership and the DMC) and because the shop and the lobby were in legal theory part of the same land and not separate tenements (so there could be no easement of way). Counsel for the shop owner had valiantly argued that they were separate tenements and that what an owner had was possession of his area of exclusive use, in effect a long lease of the unit granted by all the other co-owners. This raised the very nature of ownership of units in buildings in Hong Kong.

In a long and erudite judgment delivered by Li CJ, the CFA would not accept this argument, reiterating that an owner is a tenant-in-common holding shares in the land with no more than a contractual right to occupy and use (but not to possess) his unit. This preserved the view that had prevailed in the courts and been acted upon for a generation but hardly did justice in the instant case. The appellant had bought from the respondents a shop with a long counter fronting upon a busy lobby. That was the principal feature and attraction of the shop, reflected no doubt in the price that the respondents had received. The respondents now proposed to deprive the appellant of that. Surely there must be some means by which the law would not allow it? The answer of the CFA was that the erection of the new shop by the respondents would be derogation from grant. What they had assigned to the appellant was not just a shop but a shop abutting upon a lobby: an injunction would issue to prevent them derogating from that.

This is an example of a case taking on a life of its own as it progresses through the courts. The argument that the proposal to block the shop's counter amounted to derogation from grant had been relied upon in the courts below but not as the centrepiece of the appellant's case. The argument had been mentioned in the judgments of both the trial judge and the Court of Appeal but relatively briefly and only to dismiss it as untenable. Yet it became the sole basis of the CFA's decision, the court treating the point as obvious, as indeed it does seem to be in retrospect and with the benefit of assured exposition by judges of ultimate appeal.

The government (formerly Crown) lease is the grant of land upon which buildings are constructed and in which shares are issued to units in the buildings. This lease is preceded by a contract, called conditions of grant or similar, laying down terms with which the developer of the land must comply before the lease will be granted. In recent decades, the practice has grown up of not issuing the formal lease. Instead, the developer and subsequent purchasers rely on the conditions of grant for the root of their title. Conveyancers say that a contract for a lease is as good as a lease because equity looks on as done that which ought to be done and will grant specific performance of the contract (i.e. order the vendor to grant the lease) if the need arises. Since the grantor is the government, no one doubts that a lease would be forthcoming without such an order anyway.

But a conditional contract for a lease is enforceable and is therefore as good as a lease, only if the conditions have been complied with, or to put it another way, the government would not go through with the formal lease if there were obligations under the contract still to be performed by the developer or its successors. Accordingly, the practice grew up of the government issuing a certificate or letter stating that the positive conditions in the conditions of grant had been complied with. These documents became so commonplace that their role has been recognized in legislation which provides that there is deemed compliance with any conditions precedent to the grant upon the issue of a certificate of compliance and the registration of that certificate and deemed issuance of a government lease when this has happened.[18] The need for such confirmation of compliance was the subject of the first title dispute to be adjudicated upon by the CFA, *Paul Chen* v. *Lord Energy Ltd.*[19]

---

[18] Section 14 of the Conveyancing and Property Ordinance (Cap. 219), enacted in 1984. Section 14 also provides that compliance is deemed where government conditions have been issued before 1970, so no certificate is necessary. Compliance occurs upon the coming into effect of the ordinance: *Minchest Ltd* v. *Lau Tsui Kwai* (2008) 11 HKCFAR 551.

[19] (1997–1998) 1 HKCFAR 365.

Title

That case arose out of the sale and purchase during the early 1990s property boom of a flat and parking space at Baguio Villas, a large luxury residential development erected at the western end of Hong Kong Island in the late 1970s. The conditions, which had been executed between the developer and the government in July 1973, entitled the developer to a Crown lease on compliance with the conditions and gave the government right of re-entry in the event of any breach of condition. As is common in modern conditions of sale of land for residential development, the conditions contained detailed provisions about car parking. The vendor's solicitors had been unable to supply a certificate of compliance with those conditions; apparently, such a certificate had never been issued. In consequence, the vendor was able to give an equitable estate only. The court held that the certificate was a document of title because without it or other proof of compliance the vendor could not convey the legal estate promised in the contract.

The vendor in *Chen* v. *Lord Energy* had also declined to supply to the purchaser a certified copy of the car park layout plan, which had been required by the conditions to be prepared and registered and the existence of which was evident from a search of the land register. Although either party could have obtained a copy from the registry and so, as Li CJ coolly observed, 'The position of both parties over such a simple matter could be said to be unmeritorious', the burden of proving title was upon the vendor who should have supplied a copy of the plan. The Chief Justice went on to approve dicta by lower courts that prima facie documents properly registered in respect of the property and that had not apparently ceased to affect the property ought to be treated as part of the title deeds and made available to a purchaser.

Underlying the legal issues in *Chen* v. *Lord Energy* is judicial exasperation, manifested in the short judgments of Litton and Bokhary PJJ, with the conduct of the parties and their solicitors. The vendor's solicitors had refused to face the fact that the developer had failed to obtain a certificate of compliance and had stubbornly – and incorrectly – stuck to the position that a certificate did not affect title and was not necessary; the purchaser's solicitors had been right to insist on having proof of compliance, but their requisitions could have been more clearly expressed and, when the vendor announced that the sale was off, the purchaser had reversed its position and asked that the vendor perform the contract with such title as it had. The vendor then refused to complete and held on to the deposit. Seven years later, they ended up in the highest court, facing legal costs that no doubt rivalled the purchase price of HK$2.5 million.

A third argument had been made by the purchaser in *Jumbo King*, concerning a question of title. The purchaser said that there were cocklofts, which had not been authorized under the Buildings Ordinance,[20] at the shops. The objection that there are 'illegal structures', or as the Building Authority calls them, unauthorized building works, at a property is a very common means by which purchasers seek to escape a contract which has proved inopportune. The law, as evolved by the lower courts, is that the risk of enforcement action by the Building Authority is an incumbrance on title unless the risk is theoretical and the purchaser's solicitor can advise his or her client that it is safe to purchase the property. Of course, inveterately cautious conveyancing solicitors will never do this, especially when their client is anxious not to complete the purchase. The Building Authority has a statutory duty to enforce the law even though it does not have the means to do so and therefore has a policy of 'prioritized' enforcement – euphemism for saying that they will take immediate action only where there is a special reason for doing so (such as that the structure is dangerous) and may get around to acting against the rest one day. The consequence is that the mere presence of unauthorized building works (and such works are very widely defined) is a blot on title and turns the contract into an option to purchase.

The authorities concerning whether the possibility of action by public authorities constitutes a defect in title are by no means all one way, as Bokhary PJ and Mason NPJ pointed out in their joint judgment in *Chi Kit Co. Ltd* v. *Lucky Health International Enterprise Ltd*,[21] a case that will be examined in more detail later in this chapter. *Megarry & Wade*, the leading English land law text, is equivocal on the matter.[22] One would have hoped that the CFA might one day consider the point. Objection to title for the presence of unauthorized works is so common that whether such works constitute an incumbrance is surely a question of public importance. Yet the way has been obstructed by *obiter dicta* of the judges in *Chi Kit*. Having acknowledged the uncertainty and accepted that the point was not really in issue in the case before them, their lordships somewhat gratuitously added that the law was too entrenched to be disturbed. Yet what is a court of final appeal for if it is not to consider points of law that, although

---

[20] Cap. 123.   [21] (2000) 3 HKCFAR 268.
[22] Harpum, Bridge, and Dixon (eds.), *Megarry & Wade: The Law of Real Property*, 7th edn. (London: Sweet & Maxwell, 2008) [15–082].

entrenched at lower levels, may yet be wrong? The CFA did not find an accretion of authority that was far older than that concerning illegal structures an obstacle to returning to first principles in *China Field*.

During the property slump, many of the vendor and purchaser summonses that swamped the courts concerned requisitions about illegal structures. Judges eventually came to find ways to resist unmeritorious claims by purchasers but the fundamental damage had been done by the strict line taken during the 1980s. In *Jumbo King*, the means of resistance was easy: the objection had been raised too late, and anyway the agreement between vendor and purchaser excluded the purchaser from raising the objection. In *Polyset*, the purchaser, apart from arguing that the deposit was excessive, had relied upon an advisory letter received from the Building Authority about the presence of unauthorized structures as blighting title. The court rejected this as mere advice constituting no threat of action.

It was not long before the court was again confronted by a late requisition concerning breach of the building legislation. This was in March 2000 in *Mexon Holdings Ltd* v. *Silver Bay International Ltd*[23] concerning the sale of a unit at an upper floor of Lippo Centre, a commercial building. The unit had been created in 1992 by partitioning the floor. The agreement there had been made in May 1997 with completion in January 1998. It contained the usual clause giving a time limit on raising requisitions, seven working days in this instance, but there was no provision excluding requisitions about the legality of structures so the short answer given in *Jumbo King* was unavailable. The market collapse intervened, and in November 1997, the purchaser asserted that the partitioning breached a code of practice issued by the Building Authority on means of escape in case of fire and a provision in the Building (Planning) Regulations[24] stating that every building should be provided with a means of escape from fire. The vendor said that the objection was out of time. The purchaser's response was that this did not matter because equity would allow the requisition if it went to the root of title.

The court had no difficulty in disposing of the purchaser's contention. The planning regulations and the code were for proposed new buildings, not existing buildings approved long ago.[25] The code was not law and

---

[23] *Mexon Holdings* v. *Silver Bay International Ltd* (2000) 3 HKCFAR 109.
[24] Cap. 123, sub. leg. F.
[25] As regards the regulations, this has subsequently been contradicted by Cheung J in *Building Authority* v. *Appeal Tribunal (Buildings)* [2010] 3 HKC 368 (CFI).

went nowhere near the root of title. The purchaser had not said when it first noticed the supposed breach of the code and regulations. As Bokhary PJ put it, 'One cannot rule it out as a real possibility that the purchaser was watching the property market for a time before deciding to raise its requisition'.[26] If the purchaser had been genuinely concerned about the way the floor had been partitioned, there had been plenty of time for it to ask the Building Authority, but it had not done so. In these circumstances, equity would not come to the purchaser's aid to excuse the raising of a requisition out of time. There was thus no need to examine the equitable doctrine.

The lasting impact of *Mexon* lies in dicta of Litton PJ about the proper approach to take with objections on title. Delivering the lead judgment, he said that a good title was not a perfect title, free from all blemishes and that whenever 'a question like this arises, it must be approached from the stand-point of a willing purchaser and a willing vendor, both possessed of reasonably robust commonsense' and 'both intending to see the transaction through to completion in terms of their own bargain'.[27] These words have been cited many times in subsequent title requisition cases in which one or both of the parties is manifestly no longer willing, has evidently abandoned common sense, and patently is not intending to see the transaction through to completion.

There is one circumstance in which a householder in Hong Kong may carry out building work to property without the need for government permission: when the work is in the building and does not involve its structure or any breach of regulation. This exception is in section 41(3) of the Buildings Ordinance[28] and played a subsidiary role in the saga of the sale of the hotel beneath the Lantau bridge near Tsuen Wan, *Mariner International Hotels Ltd* v. *Atlas Ltd*.[29] One of the London counsel engaged by the warring conglomerates in this case achieved a brief fee of almost one million pounds for arguing this case before the CFA, a distinction that perhaps reflects the reputation of the court.

The dispute was decided on the issue of whether the hotel had been practically completed by the vendor in accordance with the sale contract (it had not), but the purchaser had, almost inevitably, a fall back objection that the title was bad because of the presence of unauthorized building works. This referred to structures on the roof of the building that were not shown on the approved plans. The vendor said that they did not need approval from the Building Authority because they were in the building

[26] *Mexon Holdings*, 119.   [27] *Ibid.*, at 117.   [28] Cap. 123.   [29] (2007) 10 HKCFAR 1.

and did not involve the building's structure. The lower courts had agreed. The CFA did not: a structure on the roof was not 'in' the building, because 'in' meant inside, so as to be protected from the elements. Whether works involved the structure was a matter of whether they served a structural function or were capable of affecting the structure in some way. Previous court decisions had suggested that 'involving the structure' was to be equated with 'structural' and therefore was not as wide as the CFA indicated.

Another title problem special to Hong Kong is that of breach of the government lease or conditions of grant. Defunct or long-overlooked provisions in old leases can give a purchaser a route out of the contract. As with unauthorized structures, the test applied by the courts is whether there is a real (in the sense of not merely theoretical or fanciful) risk of enforcement action being taken by the authorities – in the case of government leases, the Lands Department. The CFA has given its imprimatur to this test, which was initially laid down by the lower courts, but has proved considerably readier to find that a risk is not real. Perhaps this reflects the confidence of being an ultimate court and the personality of CFA judges during its early years and also their acquaintance through legal practice with the attitude of Hong Kong businessmen and investors.

Expensive older residential areas of Hong Kong have long been subject to restrictions upon the height of buildings imposed through the Crown lease. In respect of the south side of Hong Kong Island, this restriction has been 35 feet, enough for a four-storey building. This was so with the lease of Repulse Bay Mansions, a building erected in the mid 1950s, which was the subject of *Jumbo Gold Investment Ltd* v. *Warren Yuen Cheong Leung*.[30] The sale and purchase agreement of a flat there was made in mid 1997. The purchaser raised a requisition to the effect that the building exceeded the height restriction (which it did) and persisted with this after the market collapse despite detailed attempts by the vendor to assure the purchaser that the risk of enforcement was fanciful. The trial judge thought there was no real risk, the Court of Appeal said there was, and the CFA said there was not. The CFA thought that there had possibly been a waiver, if not a modification, of the Crown lease in the 1940s or 1950s by the predecessors of the Lands Department as government land agent because plans had been approved and an occupation permit issued for the building by the Building Authority, but the evidence did not establish this definitely. In any event, the height of the building was so obvious

---

[30] (2000) 3 HKCFAR 52.

that the government could not have been ignorant of it. Any enforcement action would take the form of re-entry (termination) for breach of the lease or demand of a premium from the current owners for toleration of the breach. Whilst the government might have done that against the developer who caused the breach, it would be a wholly different matter to do so against later owners who had purchased their flats on the faith of the occupation permit and had paid rent to the government throughout the years, opined Litton PJ in the lead judgement: 'Is the Government to make itself a laughing stock, in the eyes of the community, by averring that it had only recently become aware that [the building], as originally constructed, contravened the height restriction in the lease? And how is it to explain to the scores of property owners that their property has, by dint of something that happened many years ago, become forfeited to the Government, without compensation?' The court had to look not just at the documentary evidence but also at the larger picture, explained Litton PJ, which the Court of Appeal had not done.

Bokhary PJ added his own perspective on government conduct: 'It is simply not in the nature of good government to harm innocent people unnecessarily like that. Accordingly it is safe to proceed on the basis that the Government would never do so.' One might legitimately ask whether this assumption of government conduct is justified. No doubt civil servants would baulk at forfeiting the lease, either because to forfeit would not be good government or because of fear of the consequences in a climate where every controversial administrative act becomes a political cause, but they might not desist from extracting a premium for waiving the breach or modifying the lease, especially during times when the government is short of income. As we shall see later, the government has fought successfully in the CFA to protect its revenue. But the judicial rhetoric in *Jumbo Gold* at least served to facilitate the just result.

The court's realistic attitude towards a possible breach of the government grant may be contrasted with its earlier and stricter approach in *Chen* v. *Lord Energy*. The chances of the government depriving the owners of Baguio Villas of their land in the latter case for failure to comply in some unknown respect with the conditions of grant might be said to have been equally as remote as, or even more remote than, the chances of that happening in respect of an undoubted breach at Repulse Bay Mansions. Yet in the first case, the title was held good, and in the latter, it was held bad. Could the fact that the Baguio purchaser wanted to proceed with a deal negotiated long before the 1997 collapse while the Repulse Bay purchaser wanted to escape from a deal negotiated shortly before that collapse have had anything to do with the respective results?

Breaches of the government lease or of the Buildings Ordinance may also constitute a breach of the DMC attracting complaints from the owners' corporation (if there is one) or the manager of the building and a consequent requisition on title about the risk of enforcement by them. The CFA has yet to adjudicate upon such a requisition, but it has had to consider the impact on title of a damages claim against an owners corporation. This arose in *Chi Kit Co. Ltd* v. *Lucky Health International Enterprise Ltd*[31] in which the court gave the first consideration of the provisions of the BMO at the highest level.[32]

In 1991, the unfortunate Mr Ta Xuong, a worker engaged by the IO of Sun Hing Building in Mongkok, was rendered quadriplegic when disused bamboo scaffolding at the common parts of the building collapsed. He had climbed on the scaffolding at the invitation of an employee of the IO to search for a burst pipe. He sued the IO in 1994, claiming more than HK$30 million. In early 1997, the case was set down for trial and the management committee of the corporation (on which Chi Kit had a representative) started to raise funds for legal costs. Soon after, Chi Kit, which for many years had owned and rented out offices, flats, and parking spaces at, and had 11.5 per cent of the shares in, the building, decided to sell its interests by tender: at the height of the property boom, again. Tender documents were made available to those interested in bidding, but the documents did not mention the legal claim. The terms of tender required bidders to accept and to raise no requisitions upon the title. Lucky Health made the highest bid, HK$118 million, and signed a sale and purchase agreement in August 1997 with completion to be three months later. The trial of Ta Xuong's claim took place in October 1997; he was awarded HK$25.7 million, then a record for a single personal injury claim.

The purchaser's solicitors complained of material non-disclosure and that the judgment might be enforced against their client under section 17 of the BMO, which empowers the Lands Tribunal to allow execution to be levied against an individual owner to meet part or all of the liabilities of the IO; this they said constituted an incumbrance on title. They rejected

---

[31]   (2000) 3 HKCFAR 268.

[32]   The BMO (Cap. 344) was later considered by the CFA in *Jikan Development Ltd* v. *Incorporated Owners of Million Fortune Industrial Centre* (2003) 6 HKCFAR 446 and in *Leung Tsang Hung*.

proposals by the vendor's solicitors to set aside money, fortified by bank guarantee, to meet the judgment liability and a suggestion that since the purchaser would not have been an owner at the time of the accident, the purchaser could not be liable to contribute towards the award.

The dispute divided the courts below: the trial judge held that the liability was personal and did not go to title.[33] Chi Kit appealed. The Court of Appeal allowed the appeal by two to one.[34] The CFA unanimously agreed that there was a blot on the title.

The actual result was no surprise, for the vendor certainly should have warned the purchaser of the suit. This was not an ordinary sale of a single property by immediate provisional agreement with no time for preliminary enquiries but a sale by tender of a number of properties for a large sum. Moreover, the claim against the IO was extraordinarily large, greater than the normal amount saved by management for contingencies and almost certainly requiring an extraordinary levy on owners. The challenge for the CFA was how to reason the way to this result. Contributions to management funds, which would be used to meet a judgment against an IO, are an inevitable incident of the ownership of flats in multi-storey buildings. Therefore, care had to be taken to ensure that the very existence of a claim against the IO was not to render title bad and that the need to raise extra management funds for unusual expenditure or emergencies (e.g. when the IO decides to renovate the common parts or the government requires work to be done at the building urgently) would not give a purchaser an excuse to withdraw. The route which the CFA took to avoid this trap yet to ensure that the purchaser would not be bound in the instant case was to emphasise the scale of the claim. This was perhaps inevitable but is not altogether satisfying.

There was no difficulty in disposing of the vendor's argument that the purchaser would not be liable to contribute to the judgment sum because it had not been an owner at the time of the accident. The BMO defines an owner as a person who 'for the time being' appears from Land Registry records to be an owner of an undivided share in the land.[35] Section 16 of the Ordinance provides that liabilities in relation to the common parts rest upon the owners' corporation, an entity separate from individual owners that can raise contributions from owners. This must mean from those who are owners at the time that the IO has to pay the debt. If the position was otherwise, as Litton PJ, who again delivered the first judgment in a land matter, observed, management would be a highly complex affair,

---

[33] [1998] 4 HKC 656 (CFI).   [34] [1999] 4 HKC 21 (CA).   [35] BMO, s. 2.

particularly in large estates, given the turnover in owners and the differing times at which various liabilities might be incurred.

The worker's claim was of extraordinary magnitude and likely to succeed. It was certain that contributions would be demanded from owners. The liability was outside the reasonable contemplation of any purchaser and was not an ordinary incident of property ownership. As Bokhary PJ and Mason NPJ explained in a joint judgment (unusual, at least in CFA land cases), the liability to pay contributions binds successive owners, thus 'goes with the unit' and is a matter of title. Ultimately, an owner can be required to pay the debts of the corporation, by operation of section 17 and also the winding-up provisions for IOs in the BMO.

The joint judgment reasoned that the vendor's offer of indemnity did not dispose of all the risk for at the time of the sale and completion there might have been expenditure beyond the amount of the judgment debt: there might have been an appeal or proceedings for enforcement (apparently some of the owners were quoted in the press as saying that they could not or would not pay) or claims for contribution between owners. Nor would the indemnity deal with the problem that until the claim had been finally disposed of, the resale value of the property would be affected, and banks would not advance loans for its purchase.

What then about the term in the contract by which the purchaser agreed not to object to the vendor's title and to complete irrespective of whether that title was good or defective? Here the justices were content to rely on what Lord Hoffmann had said in *Jumbo King* about such clauses: the prima facie duty of the vendor was to convey a good title, and if he relied upon contractual terms to shift that burden, the language must clearly do so. General words, such as those in the clause in question, would not suffice for the purchaser must be aware of the risk which he is being asked to take and the clause must therefore identify the specific defect, especially if it is one of which the vendor is aware or which he or she could easily have discovered.

Another means by which a vendor may seek to be relieved of the burden of proving title is to say that the purchaser has accepted the title or has waived any objection and affirmed the contract. Such an argument succeeded at trial in *Flywin Co. Ltd.* v. *Strong & Associates Ltd*,[36] another instance of a purchaser using the presence of unauthorized alterations to the property to pull out of the purchase after the market collapse. The CFA permitted this, holding that there was nothing in the circumstances

---

[36] (2002) 5 HKCFAR 356.

enabling the court to conclude that the purchaser had waived its right to object to encumbrances or had affirmed a contract for, or accepted, an encumbered title.

Conveyancing

Conveyancing, in the broad sense of the process from initial agreement for sale and purchase to delivery of the formal transfer of the property, as practiced in Hong Kong, has several distinctive features. The process invariably starts with an initial deposit and an immediately binding but informal contract. This is the preliminary or provisional agreement usually brokered by an estate agent before the lawyers are involved: there are thus no inquiries before contract. The provisional agreement is followed by a formal agreement containing additional and more detailed terms, many in common form and nearly always including a provision that time is to be of the essence. Title deeds are not supplied until after the formal contract. An epitome of title of sorts is provided by the results of a land registry search. Requisitions on title and answers thereto follow; in most of the sale cases that the CFA has had to consider, that is as far as the process has gone because the parties have fallen out over whether good title has been shown.

If the purchaser is satisfied on title, completion of the sale usually takes place not at the office of the vendor's solicitors but by messenger and undertaking, that is to say that the purchaser delivers payment of the balance of the price to the vendor's solicitors who give in exchange the keys to the property and a professionally binding promise to supply an executed assignment of the property to the purchaser's solicitors within so many days. In preparation for this, the vendor's solicitors send information to the purchaser's solicitors as to the identity of the payees of and the proportions into which the cheques or cashier's orders for the balance are to be divided (the 'split cheque' directive), and the purchaser's solicitors send a draft of the undertaking to be given by the vendor's solicitors. This procedure is the 'Hong Kong style of completion'.

The processes of sale and completion become complicated where, as often happens in a booming market, the purchaser resells the property before completion. Matters become more complicated if the subpurchaser in turn resells before completion of the head contract; indeed, one can end up with a string of subsales, all dependent upon the head sale going through. In these circumstances, the purchaser becomes a confirmor, and the assignment of the property at completion is usually by the vendor directly to the end purchaser.

The CFA has had to consider several of these features. A preliminary agreement, although of an unusual nature, came under scrutiny in *Kwan Siu Man Joshua* v. *Yaacov Ozer*.[37] Mr Ozer, a tenant who wanted to buy his flat from the landlord Mr Kwan, encountered Mr Kwan in the lift lobby of the building (the landlord also lived there) and made an oral offer to purchase at a sum which Mr Kwan accepted; they agreed that the details would be left to their lawyers. The lawyers proceeded to correspondence, but then Mr Kwan changed his mind. Mr Ozer sued for specific performance. Contracts for the sale of land have to be evidenced by signed writing if they are to be enforced.[38] Was there such evidence?

Both the trial judge and the Court of Appeal were satisfied that there was, but the CFA was adamant that there was not – another illustration of the benefits of having a second level of appeal staffed by confident judges. Whilst the basic terms of the identity of the parties and of the property, intention to sell and price had been orally agreed and were recorded in the correspondence, two other essential matters that were raised in the correspondence, the date of completion and the payment of a deposit, had not been orally agreed. Hence, the signed writing did not accurately reflect the agreement, and so the statute had not been complied with. Furthermore, the fact that such important terms had not been finalized showed that the parties were still in negotiation. Litton PJ reflected that the date of completion is an essential term of any contract for the sale of land in Hong Kong because of the volatility of the market.

A similar issue arose in one of the few landlord and tenant disputes to reach the CFA, *World Food Fair Ltd* v. *Hong Kong Island Development Ltd*,[39] in which the landlord and prospective tenant entered into prolonged negotiations for the leasing of a restaurant and food court at a shopping mall then under construction. The rent and other basic terms were settled orally, and the tenant even paid a deposit and had gone into possession to fit the premises out before the landlord changed its mind about having a food court at the mall. But something was missing: a firm date for commencement of the tenancy. This, and absence of agreement on other

---

[37] (1997–1998) 1 HKCFAR 343.
[38] Conveyancing and Property Ordinance (Cap. 219), s. 3. This is the 'Statute of Frauds' provision.
[39] (2006) 9 HKCFAR 735.

cardinal terms such as the rent-free period, led the CFA to reverse the Court of Appeal's finding that there was a binding agreement.

When it comes to the terms of sale agreements, the CFA has had to consider a variety of matters. In one agreement, the verbal description of the property merely described the premises as a shop and gave its address without stipulating the extent of the property. When the question arose as to whether it included a small yard which was in fact a common part of the building, the CFA held that a plan defined the property sold. The plan had not been attached to the sale agreement but to a tenancy agreement to which the sale was subject and had been shown to the purchaser when first viewing the premises.[40] In another agreement, a purchaser's right to inspect the property before completion was considered,[41] and in a third, to what tenancy a sale expressed to be subject to tenancy was intended to be subject.[42] In the last case, the contextual approach to interpretation laid down in *Jumbo King*, particularly the commercial objectives of the agreement, provided the answer.

The court's interpretation and application of special terms of particular contracts are of limited guidance and interest. Contractual terms in wide usage are, however, a different matter. The purchaser's rights to rescind under the standard terms of sale and purchase required to be used by developers under the Land Authority Consent Scheme for uncompleted developments were considered by the Court in *Global Time Investments Ltd* v. *Super Keen Investments Ltd*.[43]

The procedures leading to completion of the contract were scrutinized in *Kensland Realty Ltd* v. *Whale View Investment Ltd*.[44] The vendor, Kensland, was a confirmor, having itself contracted to buy a shop in Mongkok for HK$53 million and to resell it to Whale View for HK$55 million. To facilitate this, completion of the sale to Whale View was to take place before 1 PM on 2 September 1997 and completion of the purchase by Kensland from the head vendor was to take place later, before 5 PM the same day. Whale View's solicitors delivered the eight cheques and two bank drafts requested for the balance of the purchase price to Kensland's solicitors a few minutes after 1 PM; in the usual ruthless way, Kensland declared the agreement rescinded and forfeited the deposit; time was of

[40] *Green Park Properties Ltd* v. *Dorku Ltd* (2001) 4 HKCFAR 448.
[41] *Twinkle Step Investment Ltd* v. *Smart International Industrial Ltd* (1999) 2 HKCFAR 255.
[42] *Marble Holding Ltd* v. *Yatin Development Ltd* (2008) 11 HKCFAR 222.
[43] (2000) 3 HKCFAR 440.
[44] *Kensland Realty Ltd* v. *Whale View Investments Ltd* (2001) 4 HKCFAR 381.

the essence. However, the reason that the payment was late was that Kensland had not given the 'split cheque' direction until 72 minutes before the completion deadline. When the dispute reached the CFA, everybody agreed that a term was to be implied on grounds of commercial necessity that the direction should be given a reasonable time before completion. The dispute was as to whether 72 minutes was reasonable.

The court held that it was not; time was required not just for the preparation of the cheques and drafts and travel time between the firms' offices but also for the procedures for drawdown of any loan from a mortgagee bank and for final checking of the documents by the purchaser's solicitors and their composition of a letter, listing the cheques and drafts and setting out the undertakings, to accompany the payments and the engrossed assignment for later execution and return by the vendor.

The case gave the CFA the opportunity to import the test for implication of terms laid down by the PC in *BP Refinery (Westernport) Pty Ltd* v. *President etc of the Shire of Hastings*.[45] It also gave the opportunity for Ribiero PJ to expound upon the 'prevention principle', the ancient and simple rule by which a party whose acts cause the other party to be in breach of contract is prevented from taking advantage of his own wrong by relying on the other's breach.[46]

The *Kensland* case had a postscript or after effect that is described by Gary Meggitt in his chapter in this volume on procedure in the CFA.[47] This is not the only case with a postscript. *Chen* v. *Lord Energy*, the 1998 case about the certificate of compliance for Baguio Villas, returned to the CFA in 2002 on a dispute about the damages.[48] This was despite the scolding that the court had given the parties in their earlier judgments. The postscript gave the CFA the opportunity to observe that, in the volatile Hong Kong market, purchase for resale is common and therefore within the contemplation of the parties.[49]

Protecting public revenue

The government has generally fared very well in land cases before the CFA. These cases usually involve government income or expenditure in some way such as compensation payable to owners whose land has been

---

[45] (1978) 52 ALJR 20 (PC) at 26.   [46] *Kensland Realty*, [91]–[93].
[47] See Chapter 21 in this volume.   [48] (2002) 5 HKCFAR 297.
[49] *Kensland Realty Limited (in compulsory liquidation)* v. *Tai, Tang Chong* (2008) 11 HKCFAR 237, [15]–[21], [24]–[25].

compulsorily acquired ('resumed') for public purposes, premiums payable to the government for modification or waiver of restrictions in government leases, and the rateable value of tenements.

One of the more surprising and controversial of these cases was *Director of Lands* v. *Yin Shuen Enterprises Ltd*,[50] one of two appeals concerning the proper approach to the valuation of land in the New Territories resumed for public housing and thus of the amount of compensation to be paid to the dispossessed former owners. Both lots of land were zoned under planning legislation for residential use, had road frontage, and were close to new towns, but they were held under early 20th century block Crown leases as agricultural land. Such leases contain a restriction on building without government permission. It had been the practice of the Lands Tribunal in such cases to include in the valuation of this sort of land an element of 'hope value', that is to say to reflect the possibility that if the land had not been resumed, the owner would have been allowed to redevelop it. This was despite the fact that development would have required permission or a relaxation of the restriction and the presence in the land resumption legislation of a provision stating that no compensation is to be given in respect of any expectancy or probability of the grant or renewal of any licence, permission, lease, or permit whatsoever.[51] The tribunal had regarded this as referring to administrative-type permissions to use the land for certain regulated purposes such as a restaurant only. Consequently, the compensation awarded had reflected the market value of the land with development potential.

The government challenged this approach, arguing that the wording covered development permission and lease modification. The Court of Appeal resisted, saying that the hope value was part of the intrinsic or market value of the land, thereby reflecting the consensus among land professionals in Hong Kong. Lord Millett NPJ, who gave the lead judgment on further appeal, thought otherwise. The mischief at which the provision had been aimed, according to the explanatory memorandum to the bill in which the provision first appeared in 1922 (a time of land speculation in fast-expanding Kowloon), was to ensure that no compensation was to be awarded for expectancies or probabilities by virtue of which speculators were prepared to pay more than the value of land as agricultural land. In this, the administration had thought that it was following the law of England but in fact that was based on a misunderstanding of the effect

---

[50] *Director of Lands* v. *Yin Shuen Enterprises Ltd* (2003) 6 HKCFAR 1.
[51] Lands Resumption Ordinance (Cap. 124), s. 12(c).

of a case there. The upshot was that Hong Kong law was different from other jurisdictions even though local valuation practice had glossed over this. What was payable by the government was not the market value but a 'fair value'.

As a result of the CFA's giving effect to this difference, the government no longer has to compensate an owner for the development potential of the land. This means that the compensation does not reflect the market value, a matter of joy for the taxpayer but not for Hong Kong's free market reputation.

The former owners had a second string to their bow, Article 105 of the BL (BL 105). This enshrines the right to property, a somewhat controversial right that is not found in all constitutions but which may be said to be well in tune with local attitudes. BL 105 says that the Hong Kong Special Administrative Region of the People's Republic of China shall, in accordance with law, protect the rights of people to the acquisition, use, disposal, and inheritance of property and their right to compensation for lawful deprivation of their property. Of course, the Lands Resumption Ordinance[52] is the law principally being referred to in the 'in accordance with law', and section 12(c) is part of that Ordinance, so there is no inconsistency between the subsection and BL 105 there. But the article adds: 'Such compensation shall correspond to the real value of the property concerned at the time': the real value, not a discounted or artificial value.

Basic Law 105 is essentially a guarantee against confiscation of land, but the reference to the 'real value' seems to indicate something extra, that the open market value must be paid. So whatever speculators were willing to pay was what the land would fetch in the open market and should be reflected in the real value. Lord Millett was having none of that. He circumvented the meaning of 'real value' by focusing on 'the property concerned'. The latter was the property that the government had granted and restrictions on building and user limited that property, or, to put it another way, the government had retained those aspects of the property so they were not part of what was being resumed and need not be compensated for. Moreover BL 105, he observed, does not require compensation to be based upon the open market value but on the real value; whilst in general, property is worth what it will fetch in the open market and this reflects its real value, this was not always the case, he

---

[52] Cap. 124.

asserted. 'Sometimes the market is prepared to pay a speculative price which exceeds the true value of the property'.[53]

So it seems that the 'real value' referred to in BL 105 is not a market value but something else. One has the uncomfortable feeling that the CFA was playing with words so as to deprive unsavoury speculators and assist government finances. Was it merely a coincidence that this case was heard at the end of 2002, when Hong Kong was in the pit of depression, with salaries being cut, the property market comatose, and (in consequence) government income squeezed?[54]

Fortunately, the CFA did not allow a similar argument to that which prevailed in *Yin Shuen Enterprises*, based on restrictions on use in the planning legislation rather than in the government lease, to prevail in *Secretary for Transport* v. *Delight World Ltd*.[55] Although government leases in the New Territories commonly restrict building without permission, they do not forbid other uses, including open storage, which has proved far more lucrative than agriculture. The Town Planning Ordinance[56] was extended to the New Territories in the early 1990s to curb the despoliation of the land by storage; in the future, owners would require permission before changing the use to storage. This extension is, however, not to be taken into account in assessing the value of the land when compensation is awarded for its resumption for public purposes.

The CFA demonstrated a conservative attitude in the interpretation of government leases and conditions. The movement of manufacturing out of Hong Kong during the final two decades of the past century left many factory buildings underused in the old industrial districts. The administration, keen to extract premia for any change to commercial or residential use, has been vigilant to stop any breach of user covenants such as that found in *Raider Ltd* v. *Secretary for Justice*.[57] The special conditions for the building in question at Kwun Tong required that the land be used only for industrial purposes and that no building should be erected on the lot except a factory. Raider used its floor of the building for the manufacture of pagers and to operate a paging service. The CFA said that this was not a use for industrial purposes. The CFA equated industrial

---

[53] *Yin Shuen Enterprises*, [56].

[54] Consistent with its attitude in *Yin Shuen Enterprises*, *ibid.*, the CFA has said that the best evidence of value in such cases is sales of comparable properties with no prospect of lease modification so as to allow development because this eliminates the 'hope value': *Dragon House Investment Ltd* v. *Secretary for Transport* (2005) 8 HKCFAR 668.

[55] (2006) 9 HKCFAR 720. BL 105 again featured in the decision.

[56] Cap. 131.   [57] (2000) 3 HKCFAR 309.

purposes with use as for manufacturing, relying upon the condition as to the type of building to be erected as an aid to interpretation.

This was very restrictive and contrary to the natural and modern meaning of industry. No doubt manufacturing was the principal use that the government had in mind for the building when the land was sold, but why should industry be confined to manufacturing industry? Such a narrow view hardly reflects the flexibility and imagination for which Hong Kong is famous, nor does it seem attuned to the modern world and the needs of Hong Kong. No manipulation of the meaning of words would have been involved in saying that light industry and service industries were allowed. The CFA referred to the Factories and Industrial Undertakings Ordinance[58] as to the meaning of 'factory', but if extrinsic sources are to be referred to, it would have been more relevant to use the list and classification of uses allowed by the Town Planning Board that are notably more liberal about what constitutes industry. The judgment seems to have saddled Hong Kong business with a burden that could have been avoided.[59]

Conclusion

One way to assess the achievements of the CFA in land matters is to imagine what the law would be if the CFA did not exist and Hong Kong had but one level of appeal, as is the case in some jurisdictions. Without the CFA, defunct height restrictions in government leases would blight title to a great many properties, unauthorized structures on roofs would be permitted provided they were within the building line and did not affect the building's structure, owners corporations would not be responsible in public nuisance for hazards caused by dilapidated common parts of their buildings, and a vendor could sell a shop and then build across its main access with impunity. But for the CFA, the law regarding informal land contracts would be considerably looser. An oral, or simple written, open contract for the sale of land that did not specify the date for completion of the sale would be effective, and an informal, oral agreement for a tenancy would be enforceable despite the lack of a firm commencement date and the absence of any signed record of its cardinal terms. Last, if there had

---

[58] Cap. 59.

[59] A similarly restrictive attitude was manifested by the CFA towards the terms of the government lease of the River Trade Terminal at Tuen Mun in *River Trade Terminal Co Ltd* v. *Secretary for Justice* (2005) 8 HKCFAR 95.

been no CFA, compensation for land resumed by the government would reflect its development potential.

This assumes that the personnel deciding those cases in the Court of Appeal would have been much the same or at least would have reached the same conclusions had there been no CFA. Such an assumption may not be justified because at least some of the Permanent Judges of the CFA would surely have become (or remained) Justices of Appeal in a Court of Appeal that served as a final court; their strong personalities and confident grasp of legal points based upon years of experience in practice might well have swayed the outcome in a different direction. It is possible that knowledge that their decision is to be final inspires judges of every description to heighten their performance so that the Court of Appeal might anyway have reached different conclusions had it been the ultimate court. On the other hand, the Court of Appeal sits in panels, and there can be no certainty that the judges who decided a particular appeal would have been different. One also has to remember that the Court of Appeal is a very busy court, so its judges do not have the time for deep contemplation of their decisions or close composition of their written judgments that judges of the CFA enjoy. Nor do they have the benefit of exchanging views with overseas colleagues. So there has to be considerable doubt as to whether the quality of final justice in land matters would have been the same had there been no CFA.

The consequences of the CFA land decisions which have reversed the Court of Appeal are for the most part narrow, affecting very particular circumstances if not confined to the case itself. The decision with the greatest practical impact has been the restriction upon compensation for development value that must have saved public coffers an enormous amount of money. The CFA's clarification of the law concerning rights of way has had some social impact, especially in the rural New Territories; although the CFA was there confirming the decisions of lower courts, the clarity and confidence of the CFA's views have brought additional certainty to this area and have paved the way for judicial reform of the law in other jurisdictions. The CFA's removal of any doubt as to the liability of owners corporations for injuries to the public stemming from defects in the common parts of their buildings even where those defects are the result of acts by a particular owner must also have had some effect upon management of buildings and has contributed to the understanding of the law of public nuisance in the common law world.

20

Tort law

RICK GLOFCHESKI

Introduction

Before the 1997 transfer of sovereignty, there was little prospect for the development and reform of tort law that might take into account local conditions and needs. The local courts dutifully followed the English precedents,[1] and the Privy Council (PC) heard tort appeals infrequently, only about once every two years. Although the few cases that reached the PC produced some gems, decisions that continue to be cited today, they are important more for their clarifications of sometimes ambiguous tort law principles than for the actual breaking of new ground.[2] With the possible exception of one of these cases, they could not be said to have contributed to the development of a local Hong Kong law.[3] Certainly, they do not in themselves comprise what might be considered a coherent body of tort case law.

The establishment of a new final appeal court in Hong Kong in 1997 heralded the possibility of tort law reform or at least the possibility of a tort law more closely tailored to local needs. With the transfer of sovereignty, the implementation of a new constitution,[4] and the creation of the new

---

I would like to thank Carrie Lam and Alvin Chan, BBA (Law) 3, for their research assistance.

[1] As they were obliged to do, except in so far as such law was shown to be inapplicable to local circumstances: see s. 3(1) of the Application of English Law Ordinance (Cap. 88), repealed in 1997.

[2] Among the 'gems' I would include *Edward Wong Finance Co. Ltd* v. *Johnson Stokes & Master* [1984] AC 296 (standard of care of solicitors in their duty to clients); *Yuen Kun Yeu* v. *A-G of Hong Kong* [1988] AC 175 (Government regulators duty of care to bank depositors); *Ng Chun-pui* v. *Lee Chuen-tat* [1988] 2 HKLR 425 (effect of the application of *res ipsa loquitur*); and *Lee Ting-sang* v. *Chung Chi-keung* [1990] 1 HKLR 764 (requirements for a contract of service under the Employees' Compensation Ordinance [Cap. 282]).

[3] I have in mind *Lee Ting-sang* v. *Chung Chi-keung*, in which the PC closely examined the ECO requirement for employee status and set pragmatic and flexible guidelines that implicitly recognized the problems by certain local hiring practices, to be discussed further later.

[4] The Basic Law (BL) took effect in Hong Kong on 1 July 1997.

appellate court,[5] the path was largely cleared for Hong Kong to develop the law, including tort law, without strict adherence to English precedents, in a way that was more responsive to local needs and circumstances.[6]

More than 13 years have now elapsed since the establishment of the new court. Has it made any difference in the development of tort law? Is it too early to judge? Given its disparate nature, is it even possible to assess tort law in any meaningful way? Tort law encompasses a diverse range of protected interests and an equally diverse range of wrongful activities and actions. Moreover, the Court of Final Appeal (CFA) exercises only limited control over the kinds of cases it hears.[7] To a large degree, what the CFA can do by way of tort reform depends on the 'accidents' of litigation.[8] Under these conditions, the search for thematic patterns, for coherence, and for an imprint made by the court through its tort law jurisprudence is difficult and cannot be expected to produce more than modest results. After all, the court has heard only 30 appeals in the field of tort law, many of limited consequence beyond the parties to the litigation.[9]

Nonetheless, there is potentially much to learn from an exercise such as this – about tort law, about the court itself, and about ourselves. If, as Brennan CJ once observed, the issues that arise in litigation broadly reflect contemporary social concerns,[10] the cases reaching the highest court can tell us something about what is most important to us as a community.

---

[5] See BL, Article 81. The court comprises permanent judges from Hong Kong, and by virtue of Article 82, includes a panel of non-permanent judges, some of whom have held high judicial office or practised in Hong Kong and some of whom are foreign judges who have neither held office nor lived in Hong Kong but who sit or have sat on courts of unlimited jurisdiction in other common law jurisdictions. See HKCFAO, section 12(3) for their eligibility requirements and Chapter 11 (Young and Da Roza) in this volume.

[6] Although Article 8 of the BL ensures the continued application of the common law, Article 84 expressly authorizes the court to refer to precedents of other common law jurisdictions. Thus, the CFA is not bound by House of Lords decisions in developing the common law of Hong Kong. See Chapter 13 (Mason) in this volume.

[7] Litigants in civil cases are entitled to appeal ('as of right') if the amount or the value of the property in dispute is at least $1 million (section 22(1)(a) of the HKCFAO). Otherwise, the court has a discretion to hear an appeal 'if the question involved in the appeal is one which, by reason of its great general or public importance, or otherwise, ought to be submitted to the Court for decision' (section 22(1)(b) of the HKCFAO).

[8] Pun intended. I am grateful to my colleague Albert Chen, who used this phrase in his conference presentation on constitutional law in the CFA. It seems more *à propos* in the tort context.

[9] This will be so given the low threshold for appeal entitlement under section 22(1)(a) of the HKCFAO.

[10] Brennan CJ, 'Foreword' in N. J. Mullany (ed.), *Torts in the Nineties* (North Ryde, NSW: LBC Information Services, 1997).

On a close examination of the case law, some patterns do emerge. For instance, the court's work in tort law falls into a surprisingly few subject areas. The typical plaintiff is an injured worker, who is just as likely to be the appellant as the respondent in the appeal. The worker–plaintiff is almost always successful at the end of the appeal process, usually because of the court's sympathetic interpretation of the facts or in some cases because of the court's flexible interpretation or incremental development of the law. Through its decisions in the work injury tort cases, the court has improved the lot of the worker–plaintiff in Hong Kong in two ways: in the development of more flexible conditions for the proof of employee status (and hence the law's coverage) and in the development of a more rigorous standard that employers must follow in providing safe working conditions for their employees.

In terms of the general body of tort case law, the court has made a few groundbreaking decisions – in particular in defamation, vicarious liability, and public nuisance. This is important in an environment in which the administration has shown little or no inclination for statutory tort reform.[11] Somewhat surprisingly – and disappointingly, I might add – the court has made little impact in the general law of negligence, tending to follow established authority in this tort, in particular in the area of duty of care, in both the general duty of care and the duty of care in cases of pure economic loss.

In the aggregate, through its decisions in vicarious liability, public nuisance, and in negligence as it applies to workers, the court has extended the reach of liability beyond that which existed in 1997, and this is by and large good news not only for personal injury plaintiffs but also for the

---

[11] This is not so much a reflection of the current administration as it is the historical position. There has been little statutory intervention in tort law, exceptions being the three discrimination ordinances passed into law shortly before the 1997 transfer of sovereignty and a fourth passed into law in 2008. These provide a tort law remedy for relevant discriminatory acts: the Sex Discrimination Ordinance (Cap. 480), the Disability Discrimination Ordinance (Cap. 487), the Family Status Discrimination Ordinance (Cap. 527), and the Race Discrimination Ordinance (Cap. 602). A plethora of Law Reform Commission Reports dating to the late 1990s, each containing a significant tort law dimension, continues to gather dust, with little prospect for implementation: 'Civil Liability for Unsafe Products' (1998), 'Stalking' (2000), 'Regulation of Debt Collection Practices' (2002), 'Civil Liability for Invasion of Privacy' (2004), and 'Privacy and Media Intrusion' (2004), all available at www.hkreform.gov.hk/en/index/index.htm. Moreover, there has not, in Hong Kong, been any suggestion that a wholesale review of accident compensation law is in order, as has happened in recent years in Australia and the United Kingdom.

community as a whole in an environment where safe conditions, whether at work or in public areas, cannot be presumed.

An overview of tort law in the Court of Final Appeal

As this review seeks to present an analysis of all of the tort law activity in the CFA over the period of its existence, numbers are unavoidable, and I will occasionally make use of them. I will, however, try to restrain myself in the statistical aspects, bearing in mind that numbers tell only part of the story and that they are equally likely to mislead as to illuminate.

By my count, 30[12] appeals in tort cases were heard by the CFA in its first 12 years,[13] a remarkable tally if one compares this figure with the number of tort appeals heard by the PC in the 12-year period preceding the establishment of the CFA, by my count 6.[14] If nothing else, these figures indicate significantly increased access to the final appellate court.[15]

An examination of the aggregate of the tort law decisions in the CFA reveals what might be called a clustering effect, groupings of cases within

---

[12] I am including in this survey four appeals arising from claims for compensation for work-related injuries made under the ECO. Although not formally part of tort law, given the absence of a fault requirement and a remedy sounding in damages, the case law under the ECO comprises the second largest body of personal injury litigation in the HK courts, second only to common law tort actions for work-related injuries. Moreover, the main area of contention in the case law decided under the ECO, the issue of contract of service, requires the court to refer to common law principles.

[13] Comprising almost 10 per cent of 325 CFA appeals. Of the 30 appeals, 27 were unanimous decisions, and the appeal was allowed in 16 of them. The CFA confirmed or restored the decision of the trial judge in 16 of the appeals and disagreed with the trial judge in 14. Bokhary PJ sat on 28 of the tort appeals, Chan PJ on 25, Ribeiro PJ on 20, and Li CJ on 17.

[14] In addition to the four cases mentioned in note 2 above, these are *Chan Wai Tong* v. *Li Ping Sum* [1985] HKLR 156 (assessment of personal injury damages); and *Tai Hing Cotton Mill* v. *Liu Chong Bank* [1986] AC 80 (bank's duty of care to customers). I exclude *Cheng Yuen* v. *Royal Hong Kong Golf Club* [1997] HKLRD 1132, like *Lee Ting Sang* concerning the requirements for a contract of service, but it was a breach of employment contract action brought under the Employment Ordinance for statutory terminal benefits. I include the important case of *Edward Wong Finance*, although it falls just outside of the 12 year period that preceded the establishment of the CFA.

[15] This increased final appeal court activity can obviously be accounted for at least in part by the convenient location of the CFA and the consequent reduced costs. Section 22 of the HKCFAO sets out the circumstances in which an appeal to the CFA can be brought, substantially the same as those which applied to the PC, except that, for appeals as of right (section 22(1)(a)) the monetary threshold is now much higher, although modest by Hong Kong standards; see note 7 above.

a surprisingly few subject areas. The reasons that might explain clustering, or a particular cluster, make for interesting speculation. However, it is not difficult to imagine how clustering within a subject area could provide the CFA with the opportunity for greater impact and possibly coherent reform within that subject area, and this requires further consideration.

The 30 appeals can be broken down into the following broad categories. (1) *Negligence*: 18 cases consisting of eight negligence cases involving personal injury sustained at work;[16] five cases of negligence involving personal injury sustained in other (non-work) activities; and five cases of professional negligence resulting in financial loss. (2) *Employees' compensation*: four cases. (3) *Defamation*: five cases. (4) *Public nuisance*: one case. (5) *Breach of confidence*: one case.[17] (6) *Conspiracy*: one case. From this, three clusters can be identified within the tort law appeals, accounting for all but two of the cases: negligence, employees' compensation, and defamation. Each will be considered in turn.

Negligence

It should come as no surprise that negligence is the most commonly argued tort action in the CFA. Hong Kong is after all one of the most crowded cities in the world, and with its fast-paced lifestyle, accidents on a large scale are inevitable, whether at the workplace, on the streets, in the management of the high-rise commercial and residential tower blocks for which Hong Kong is famous, or in the daily routines of its residents.[18] Moreover, negligence is an all-encompassing tort action,[19]

---

[16] Here I include one case of breach of statutory duty to provide a safe place and system of work, a common law action closely related to negligence, and normally argued as a supplement to the negligence action.

[17] *Nam Tai Electronics Inc* v. *Pricewaterhouse Coopers* (2008) 11 HKCFAR 62. Although the origins of the action for breach of confidence are in equity, it is in modern times treated as a tort action (see e.g. *Campbell* v. *MGN Ltd* [2004] 2 AC 457) and so is included in this count. It was referred to as a tort by the editors of the official report in HKLRD.

[18] For a more graphic depiction of the factors that make Hong Kong a risk-prone society, see R. Glofcheski, 'Where Principle Meets Pragmatism: Tort Law in Post-Colonial Hong Kong' in J. Neyers (ed.), *Emerging Issues in Tort Law* (Oxford: Hart Publishing, 2007) 560–1.

[19] I have elsewhere described it as open-ended and indeterminate; see R. Glofcheski, *Tort Law in Hong Kong*, 2nd edn. (Hong Kong: Sweet & Maxwell Asia, 2007) 15 ('*Tort Law in Hong Kong*'). To paraphrase Lord MacMillan in *Donoghue* v. *Stevenson* [1932] AC 562, not only are the categories of negligence not closed, but the tort is also blurred at the edges, allowing for the possibility of the development of new rules of liability in sensitive cases

providing the remedy for the most common form of wrongful conduct that people engage in – a failure to take reasonable care. Negligence runs the gamut of the major accident-causing activities, and the boundaries of this tort are sufficiently broad and imprecise as to be applicable in most cases of unintended harm, whether the harm is personal injury, property damage, or financial loss.[20] Given the large volume of trial litigation that is understandably generated by this wide range of harm-generating activities, it is inevitable that the tort of negligence comprises what is probably the biggest private law preoccupation of the CFA.

For reasons of its open-endedness and all-embracing character, negligence as a category is too broad for the purposes of meaningful analysis of tort law litigation and appeal patterns in the CFA. A more focused examination is required. Hence, it can be observed (for example) that the 18 negligence cases can be broken into two groups: those concerning personal injury (13), and those concerning errors in professional practice resulting in financial loss (5).[21]

Moreover, of the negligence claims involving personal injury, the majority (8) concerned injuries arising from work-related negligence, a specialized area of negligence law imposing a heavier duty of care on employers to provide for worker safety than is found in the general law of negligence. If one combines with this tally the appeals heard under the Employees' Compensation Ordinance (ECO)[22] concerning compensation claims for work-related injuries (4), an important statistic emerges. Injuries at work comprise by far the biggest volume of tort law appeals before the CFA – two-fifths of the tort law appeals heard by the court in its first 13 years. This phenomenon arguably reflects certain local realities: the huge volume of personal injury litigation arising in a workplace environment that continues to suffer a weak safety culture and regulatory regime,[23] inevitably leading to appeals; an employer mentality that resists taking responsibility

---

such as claims for psychiatric injury damage and pure economic loss. These kinds of cases will continue to test the appellate courts in Hong Kong and elsewhere for some decades to come.

[20] This circumstance is not unique to Hong Kong. It can safely be assumed that negligence accounts for by far the largest volume of tort litigation in all common law jurisdictions.

[21] In four of these cases, the defendants were solicitors.   [22] Cap. 282.

[23] By way of a convenient comparison, in England in 2008, there were 0.97 occupational injuries per 1000 workers and a total of 147 occupational deaths (0.006 per 1000 workers); see Health and Safety Executive at www.hse.gov.uk/statistics/regions/england/. In the same period in Hong Kong, there were 1.58 occupational injuries per 1000 workers and a total of 181 occupational deaths (0.068 per 1000 workers); see Occupational Safety and Health Statistics Bulletin (Issue 9) at www.labour.gov.hk/eng/osh/pdf/Bulletin2008.pdf.

for accidents at work; insurers prepared to back that resistance;[24] and the continuing prevalence of casual and even deceptive hiring practices by which employers try to wriggle out of their duties to workers and their obligations to compensate for injuries sustained.[25]

Within this category can be observed two important preoccupations inherited from the trial courts: the question of how much should be expected of an employer in the provision of safe conditions of work and the age-old question of who is an employee, a question relevant for the purposes of determining who qualifies for the employer's specialized duty of care in negligence and for determining who qualifies for coverage under the ECO.[26] The importance of these two issues in the law of tort and in employment law cannot be overstated.

Safety at work

An important issue in work-related negligence that the court has been required to address more than once is the degree of care required of an employer in ensuring safe working conditions (the standard of care). In *Cathay Pacific Airways Limited* v. *Wong Sau Lai*,[27] the court provided a strong statement of what is entailed in a 'safe system of work'. The plaintiff, a flight attendant, was injured while engaging in what was for her the fairly routine activity of opening the drawer of a drinks trolley. While acknowledging the fourfold nature of the general duty of safety owed by employers (of which 'safe system of work' is one[28]), the court clarified that the employer's duty is a single duty of care in negligence owed to all employees. Although there was no known attempt to provide anything like an exhaustive list of what that duty entailed, the court

---

[24] Workplace insurance for injury is compulsory: ECO, section 40. Moreover, in addition to the right to compensation from the employer, an injured worker has rights directly exercisable against the insurer: ECO, section 44.

[25] This is a controversial issue in the context of the Hong Kong work place, where a practice of 'labelling' has long persisted among some unscrupulous employers seeking to avoid employment law obligations. Moreover, workers are often amenable to signing an agreement designating their status as self-employed because they may be desperate for work under any terms or because an enticement has been offered, usually in the form of higher remuneration; see e.g. *Chan Siu Ming and Others* v. *Kwok Chung Motor Car Limited* [2008] 1 HKCLRT 13.

[26] Or, for that matter, as a precondition to the imposition of vicarious liability.

[27] (2006) 9 HKCFAR 371.

[28] The others require the employer to provide competent coworkers, safe equipment, and a safe place of work. There is naturally overlap. See generally *Tort Law in Hong Kong*, note 19 above, 349–60.

nonetheless proceeded to clarify some important characteristics of this duty. A system of work must be instituted even when the work is of a regular and uniform kind, and that system must be a safe one. In planning such a system, regard must be had to the fact that some workers have to function 'in circumstances in which the dangers are obscured by repetition' and under considerable pressure. An employer must always have in mind 'not only the careful man, but also the man who is inattentive to such a degree as can normally be expected'.[29] Although the onus lies upon a plaintiff who seeks to have condemned as unsafe a system that has been used for a long time, there was 'no warrant for insisting that [an employee cannot succeed] unless the plaintiff manages to propose an acceptable alternative system'. Thus, the court made clear that the duty owed by employers is a heavy one, an important statement of principle in a city where the 'time is money' attitude prevails and the urgency to get things done too often trumps concerns about safety in the workplace.[30]

Still on the subject of duty and standard of care applicable to employers, the CFA's decision in *Sanfield Building Contractors Ltd* v. *Li Kai Cheong*[31] not only demonstrates the court's readiness to find a remedy for an injured worker when it is possible to do so, but it also reveals the court's proclivity to widen the distributive reach of tort liability through a flexible interpretation of existing legal principles. The case did not concern the standard of care as such but a plea of *res ipsa loquitur* by a worker injured when he fell from mobile scaffolding. The worker, arguing that the accident was caused by his employer's failure to provide safe equipment and safe conditions of work, was unable to prove what went wrong on the available evidence, given that, by all accounts, the castors on the scaffolding on which he was working had been locked before his climbing onto the scaffolding. Bokhary PJ, speaking for a unanimous court, accepted the

---

[29] A sentiment reinforced in other CFA decisions, in which the court has insisted that the same or even higher degree of care is required for experienced workers who by virtue of their familiarity with the work may become inured to risks; see *Rainfield Design & Associates Limited* v. *Siu Chi Moon* (2000) 3 HKCFAR 134, 139–40; and *Poon Hau Kei* v. *Hsin Chong Construction Co Ltd, Taylor Woodrow International Ltd (Joint Venture)* (2004) 7 HKCFAR 148, 163.

[30] Other CFA decisions on this subject are *Wishing Long Hong* v. *Wong Kit Chun* (2001) 4 HKCFAR 289 (concerning provision of safety equipment in mountainous terrain at night), *Rainfield Design & Associates Limited* v. *Siu Chi Moon, ibid.* (concerning breach of statutory duty), and *Jerry Chen* v. *Whirlpool (Hong Kong) Limited* (2007) 10 HKCFAR 619 (concerning duty of care to employee posted overseas).

[31] (2003) 6 HKCFAR 207.

plea of *res ipsa loquitur* as having been satisfied despite ambiguities in the trial judgment suggesting that the castors may have contained a latent defect not reasonably discoverable by the employer, principal contractor, and scaffolding subcontractor, each of whom exercised some control over the scaffolding.

Bokhary PJ was able to navigate around this interpretive problem by reading the trial judge's ambiguous usage as meaning a *mere defect* as opposed to a *latent defect*, thereby overcoming the defendants' objection that the accident was consistent with reasonable care having been taken by them. Of further interest and significance was Bokhary PJ's ruling that *res ipsa loquitur* could apply even in circumstances that fell short of the usual *res ipsa loquitur* requirement that the 'thing' that caused the injury be in the sole control of the defendant.[32] He held that when, as here, there was more than one person in control of the thing causing damage, an inference of negligence arose against each of them. Without acknowledging it, Bokhary PJ arguably expanded the reach of the *res ipsa loquitur* principle beyond its previously understood boundaries, a ruling that is, to say the least, very pro-plaintiff, whether in the workplace or otherwise.[33]

Who is protected at work?

The question of who qualifies as an employee is a critical one in tort law as applied to the workplace. A finding of employee status is necessary for the fourfold common law duty of care, for ECO coverage, for protection under the extensive network of work safety legislation,[34] and for a finding of vicarious tort liability.[35] It is therefore an issue that requires careful

---

[32] See e.g. *Easson* v. *London & North Eastern Railway Co* [1944] KB 421.

[33] Bokhary PJ's generosity did not end there, as he took the occasion to state, albeit in *obiter*, that *res ipsa loquitur* had application beyond negligence cases, to cases of breach of statutory duty and occupiers' liability. For a brief commentary, see *Tort Law in Hong Kong*, note 19 above, 62–5. For another CFA decision concerning the application of *res ipsa loquitur* but in a medical context, see *Frank Yu Yu Kai* v. *Chan Chi Keung* (2009) 12 HKCFAR 705, discussed in text accompanying notes 45 and 46 below.

[34] Most of the major work safety ordinances and their regulations extend protection to employees only; see e.g. the Factories and Industrial Undertakings Ordinance (Cap. 59), section 6A, and the Occupational Safety and Health Ordinance (Cap. 509), section 6.

[35] It is also a vital requirement in employment law generally. For instance, the entitlements and protections under the Employment Ordinance (Cap. 57) are available only on proof of a contract of employment (section 4(1)).

consideration when litigated. The CFA has grappled with it on three occasions.[36]

The question of employee status is essentially one of fact, and hence a trial judge's finding is not lightly to be disturbed as the CFA has regularly and reassuringly acknowledged.[37] On the other hand, a principled approach must be followed, and the CFA in its most important decision interpreting the ECO requirement of employee status emphasized that form will not prevail over substance and that, regardless of the terminology used to describe the worker at the moment of employment or in any written document, regardless even of the apparent willingness of the worker to accept independent contractor status, a finding of employee status will be made if the realities of the work relationship, objectively assessed, point to such a conclusion. Importantly, this will be so even in the absence of mutuality of obligation. That is because the ECO, by its terms, and according to its purpose, applies to casual workers. What is important is the employment status at the moment of the accident causing injury.[38] On the basis of this emphatic pronouncement and the flexible approach it advocates, many more workers will be found to be employees and come within the greater protection afforded by the common law of tort as applied to work and by the ECO.[39]

---

[36] *Chan Sik Pan & Another* v. *Wylam's Services Ltd & Others* (2001) 4 HKCFAR 308; *Ting Kwok Keung* v. *Tam Dick Yuen and Others* (2002) 5 HKCFAR 336; and *Poon Chau Nam* v. *Yim Siu Cheung* (2007) 10 HKCFAR 156.

[37] For instance, in *Ting Kwok Keung* v. *Tam Dick Yuen & Others, ibid.*, a case concerning employment status in which the CA had reversed the trial judge, Bokhary PJ in the CFA restored the trial judge's determination of a contract of service and warned against appeal judges lightly substituting their views of the evidence for that of the trial judge, who after all has the 'advantage of having received the evidence at first-hand'. Later, in *Poon Chau Nam* v. *Yim Siu Cheung, ibid.*, in which the CFA did reverse the courts below, Ribeiro PJ put it thus: '[A] finding that an employer-employee relationship does or does not exist can only be interfered with on appeal if it can be shown that the tribunal misdirected itself in law or came to a decision which no tribunal, properly directing itself on the relevant facts, could reasonably have reached' (at 169).

[38] *Poon Chau Nam* v. *Yim Siu Cheung,* continuing and reinforcing the pragmatic approach of the PC in *Lee Ting-sang* v. *Chung Chi-keung.* Ribeiro PJ condemned the practice of some employers to coax workers into signing agreements as independent contractors because that would effectively permit employers to opt out of their obligations under the Ordinance (at 180–1).

[39] It will also have implications for vicarious liability, in which a contract of service is one of two conditions for its application. In its short life (less than three years), the *Poon Chau Nam* decision has been cited by lower courts in Hong Kong 25 times, almost invariably resulting in a finding of employee status (Westlaw search conducted 12 February 2010).

In *Rainfield Design & Associates Limited* v. *Siu Chi Moon*,[40] the issue was not whether the plaintiff injured on the work site was an employee; he plainly was not. The issue was the scope of the statutory duty of a contractor on a construction site to 'ensure that, so far as is reasonably practicable, suitable and adequate safe access to and egress from every place of work on the site is provided and properly maintained'.[41] The court interpreted the statutory provision in question to mean that the duty was not restricted to employees but extended to independent contractors such as the plaintiff. In the kind of admonitory language that has become associated with the court in its work safety decisions, Bokhary PJ said:

> Physical safety is plainly the paramount element of the law's policy in this sphere. The only concern is whether the person injured or killed as a result of non-compliance with a statutory duty was within the class of persons which such statutory duty was imposed to protect. As a person working on a construction site, Mr Siu was clearly within the class of persons which the statutory duty here in question was imposed to protect.[42]

Medical negligence

Leaving aside claims for work-related injuries, other subcategories within negligence also merit some comment. Two of the negligence appeals concerned cases of personal injury resulting from medical treatment. This category of negligence action has proved to be rather sensitive across common law jurisdictions, with approaches that vary according to differences in culture, political climate, strength of the medical profession lobby, the voice of the patients' rights lobby, and the degree of development of civil society. Historically, this has been an underdeveloped area of Hong Kong tort law, the colonial courts towing the conservative line set in the English precedents, resulting in few findings of liability against medical caregivers.[43] Thus, these two CFA decisions may offer a hint as to what can be expected from the courts in the way of change being demanded

---

[40] Note 29 above.

[41] Construction Sites (Safety) Regulations (Cap. 59I), section 38A (2).

[42] Note 29 above, 141.

[43] According to the longstanding position in English and Hong Kong law, the opinion of the medical profession holds sway in the standard to be applied by the court in the determination of negligence liability; see *Bolam* v. *Friern Hospital Management Committee* [1957] 2 All ER 118; *Lai Wing Cheung* v. *Yep Chau Chung* (unreported, 14 February 2006, HCPI 43/2005).

by an increasingly vocal patients' rights lobby. In point of fact, in neither of the cases were the bigger issues in this area directly addressed,[44] but in the second of the two,[45] a difficult case on the facts as to why a patient who underwent prostate surgery was left with paralysis in his arm, the court clarified that *res ipsa loquitur* can apply to actions for medical negligence.[46] As such, the doctor, not the patient, bore the evidentiary burden to explain what happened, which he had not been able to do, resulting in a dismissal of the doctor's appeal. Although not a transformational ruling by any means, this decision strengthens the position of patients who are often unable to explain or prove on the evidence what exactly went wrong in the medical procedure.

Employers' vicarious liability

Two of the appeals within the negligence category involve novel arguments in employers' vicarious liability, an important plank in an agenda that might seek to advance the goals of distributive justice.[47] The first is a landmark ruling that greatly expands the scope of vicarious liability for the torts of an employee. The Supreme Court of Canada in *Bazley*

---

[44] The first case was an application by the plaintiff to amend her pleadings to include breach of duty to warn of risks. The application was granted and a trial on the issue ordered: *Kong Wai Tsang* v. *Hospital Authority* (unreported, 20 March 2006, FACV 16/2005). Unfortunately, the reasons for the decision given by Bokhary PJ offer little clue as to the court's thinking about this important and sensitive issue, that he somewhat ambiguously describes as a developing area of the law: 'The availability of negligent failure to warn as a basis of claim is widely recognised. It was recognised by the Supreme Court of Canada in *Reibl* v. *Hughes* (1980) 114 DLR (3d) 1, the High Court of Australia in *Rogers* v. *Whitaker* (1992) 175 CLR 479 and the House of Lords in *Chester* v. *Afshar* [2005] 1 AC 134. Even so, it represents what is very much a developing area of the law. As such, it is an area in which it is somewhat more difficult than usual to form a confident pretrial view, one way or the other, of a claim's prospects of success'.

[45] *Frank Yu Yu Kai* v. *Chan Chi Keung*.

[46] Ribeiro PJ explained that although *res ipsa loquitur* would not be relevant in all medical cases, presumably because of the potential complexity of reasons for a bad medical outcome, 'in a significant number of such cases – particularly where the patient is unconscious when the injury is incurred – the *res ipsa loquitur* or prima facie case approach will be indispensable'.

[47] Distributive justice is one of the major theoretical explanations advanced for tort law and is to be distinguished from corrective justice. Briefly, corrective justice reflects the idea that the imposition of liability corrects the injustice inflicted on one party by another. Distributive justice has broader aims and seeks to distribute the burden of the infliction of loss across a wider spectrum of those who participate in the risk-creating activity or benefit from it. See e.g. E. Weinrib, 'Corrective Justice in a Nutshell' (2002) 52 *University of Toronto Law Journal* 349–56.

v. *Curry*[48] and the House of Lords in *Lister* v. *Hesley Hall Ltd*[49] crafted a new test for vicarious liability in the context of sexual assault. Those courts found that the traditional *Salmond* formulation for vicarious liability,[50] until now thought to be relevant to all torts, was inappropriate for trespassory torts. A sexual assault on a young inmate in a warden's charge hardly constitutes a wrongful and unauthorized mode of doing an authorized act. Thus, according to the top courts in Canada and England, it would be sufficient to show that the wrongful act in question was so closely connected with the employment that it would be fair and just to hold the employer liable.

The CFA, without the benefit of precedent anywhere, took the view that the new test (the 'close connection' test) was not restricted to trespassory torts and applied it to a case of ordinary employee negligence in *Ming An Insurance Co. (HK) Ltd* v. *Ritz-Carlton Ltd*.[51] The facts of the case would have evoked the court's sympathy. A hotel bellhop who drove off in one of the hotel's leased limousines to get food for himself and colleagues lost control of the vehicle, which mounted the pavement and knocked down and gravely injured two pedestrians. Despite the poor factual fit with the Supreme Court of Canada and House of Lords decisions and the appearance of what would in previous times have been treated as classic frolic, taking the worker out of his employment, the CFA in a unanimous decision reversed both courts below and found the tort (negligence) to have been committed in the course of employment.

To Bokhary PJ, who delivered the main judgment, the close connection criterion was 'inherently just and fair for all cases of tort committed by an employee while engaged in an act not authorised by his employer . . . the concept is a simple one which ought not to be complicated by reading other requirements into it'.[52] He endorsed the approach of McLachlin J in *Bazley* v. *Curry*, paraphrasing that 'the courts should openly confront the question of whether liability should lie against the employer, rather than obscuring the decision beneath semantic discussions of "scope of employment" and "mode of conduct"'.[53] However much a more open approach is always to be commended, it is unfortunate that the court did

---

[48] [1999] 2 SCR 534.   [49] [2002] 1 AC 215.

[50] According to this formulation, an employer will be liable not only for a wrongful act of an employee that he has authorized but also for 'a wrongful and unauthorized mode of doing some act authorized by the master' – R. F. V. Heuston and R. A. Buckley, *Salmond and Heuston on the Law of Torts*, 21st edn. (London: Sweet & Maxwell, 1996) 443.

[51] (2002) 5 HKCFAR 569.   [52] *Ibid.*, [24].   [53] *Ibid.*

not see fit to address the distributive effects of the new formulation and to justify its decision by reference to the increased reach of liability thereby created. Moreover, it is doubtful whether the new test, applicable across the board in all employee tort cases, is any clearer or more practical in setting the boundaries for vicarious liability than the traditional *Salmond* formula.[54] Judges are invited to 'openly confront' the question of vicarious liability having regard to what is just and fair, but it is an assessment that judges will have to make on a case-by-case basis according to their own perceptions of what is just and fair. Certainly, close connection is an easier threshold to overcome than the *Salmond* test. Thus, the scope of employers' liability has been greatly expanded, and the nets of distributive justice have been cast far indeed.[55]

Public nuisance

The unanimous decision in *Leung Tsang Hung* v. *Incorporated Owners of Kwok Wing House*[56] does not fit neatly within the negligence cluster but is best treated here given the negligence-related configuration introduced by the court to the law of public nuisance in Hong Kong. Space restrictions will not allow complete justice to be done to this important decision that arguably has potentially further reaching consequences for Hong Kong residents than any other tort law decision that the CFA has rendered. In this decision, the CFA placed on a firm footing the liability of owners' corporations[57] for injuries caused by poor maintenance of common parts

---

[54] See generally Glofcheski, 'A Frolic in the Law of Tort: Expanding the Scope of Employers' Liability' (2004) 12 *Tort Law Review* 18.

[55] In the other vicarious liability case heard by the CFA, *Jerry Chen* v. *Whirlpool (Hong Kong) Limited* (2007) 10 HKCFAR 619, the court was also asked to accept an argument that would expand the scope of employer's liability, this time in an even more dramatic way. The plaintiff, employed by the defendant in Hong Kong but posted to work in China, was injured in a traffic accident, caused, it was accepted, by the negligence of his driver, an employee not of the defendant but of a related company. Despite citations of case authorities from Australia, the court had little difficulty in turning down the plaintiff's argument based on 'enterprise liability', what the court considered would have constituted a major development in the law. Moreover, the point had not even been raised in the courts below. This ruling demonstrates that the CFA's taste for adventure and innovation in the field of distributive justice has limits.

[56] (2007) 10 HKCFAR 480.

[57] Incorporated owners comprise all of the individual flat owners in a residential building that has incorporated under the Building Management Ordinance (Cap. 344). Incorporation is not mandatory under the Ordinance.

of a residential building, whether legal or illegal structures. The case concerned a 35-year-old illegal extension to a canopy, a piece of which broke off because of poor workmanship or possibly wear and tear, killing a pedestrian in the street below. The owners of the flat in question admitted liability, and the owners' tenant was found liable at trial. The appeal to the CFA concerned the liability of the owners' corporation in the tort of public nuisance. The owners' corporation resisted liability successfully at trial and before the Court of Appeal on the basis that it was not under a duty to maintain unauthorized structures.

Ribeiro PJ, providing the main judgment of the unanimous CFA, allowed the appeal against the owners' corporation. He held firstly that the corporation was analogous to an owner–occupier by virtue of its control over the external wall conferred on it by law,[58] control conferred for the purpose of building maintenance and safety. However, according to Ribeiro PJ's view of the law of public nuisance, in cases of injury caused by omission rather than an activity, occupation or control was not sufficient in itself to impose liability; in such cases, liability was possible only on proof that the one in occupation or control knew or ought to have known of the danger arising from the defective state of the building. This answered the respondent counsel's objection that the owners' corporation did not know of the danger. On the evidence, the owners' corporation had access to the building plans; had conducted inspections; and should have known of the illegal structure, its age, and the danger it posed. This will be the case for virtually all owners' corporations in Hong Kong. Finally, according to Ribeiro PJ's view of the law, in cases of omission, liability would be imposed only if the occupier or the one in control possessed sufficient resources to be able to inspect and remove any dangers. Here, the condition was satisfied, given that such inspections were routinely undertaken and indeed had already been undertaken by the corporation.

Although this was not the first time that a court in Hong Kong found an owners' corporation liable for death to a pedestrian caused by collapsing common parts,[59] it was the first such pronouncement of the CFA, and

---

[58] By virtue of the Building Management Ordinance, section 18, the incorporated owners are under a duty to maintain the common parts, which includes the external walls, and by virtue of section 40, the incorporated owners are empowered to enter a flat for the purpose of inspection and maintenance.

[59] *Aberdeen Winner Investment Co. Ltd* v. *Incorporated Owners of Albert House and Another* [2004] 3 HKLRD 910.

importantly, it was the first to consider collective liability for *unautho-rized* attachments to common parts. It was also the first time that the court examined in detail the attributes of incorporated owners under the Building Management Ordinance[60] and deeds of mutual covenants and in the process fixed the liability rules of owners corporations in public nuisance with a view to ensuring public safety. It is noteworthy that the CFA differed with both of the courts below. Bokhary PJ, who gave a brief concurring judgment, was acutely aware of the ground being broken, citing Lord Reid's famous dictum from *Home Office* v. *Dorset Yacht Co. Ltd*[61] that 'when a new point of law emerges, one should not ask whether it is covered by authority but whether recognized principles apply to it'. Ribeiro PJ buttressed his decision with reference to the deterrence effects of the imposition of liability on owners' corporations, in particular that it is only the collectivity of owners in the form of the incorporated own-ers that can effectively monitor the state of the building and ensure its safety vis-à-vis the public.[62] The importance of such a ruling in Hong Kong should not be underestimated, given that multi-unit, high-rise res-idential buildings dominate all but the most exclusive neighbourhoods. By virtue of the Building Management Ordinance provisions holding all owners liable for judgments against the corporations,[63] individual owners are effectively placed with the responsibility to ensure proper maintenance of the building as whole.[64] It will not do to deny knowledge of a defect or responsibility for an illegal attachment to a common part. The reach of distributive liability extended by this decision should not be underestimated.

---

[60] Cap. 344.   [61] [1970] AC 1004.

[62] 'There are moreover, in my view, sound reasons for making the incorporated owners, and not merely the individual owners implicated, responsible. Where the hazard involves the external common parts of a high-rise building, effective inspection and maintenance works can really only be carried out if those parts (and any illegal accretions thereto) are dealt with as a whole, with the erection of scaffolding and the like and with all the owners contributing to the cost, subject to possible adjustment regarding the individual owners implicated. And where the nuisance hazard consists of some unauthorized structure encroaching upon or being attached to the common parts, the individual owners who may have erected or adopted the structure and benefit from its existence, may well be unwilling to take any steps to remove it. Compulsion from, or direct action by, the incorporated owners may well be required if the hazard is to be nullified'; see note 56 above, [102].

[63] Building Management Ordinance, section 17.

[64] Even when owners decide not to incorporate, they would arguably be liable as a collective under the same principle, that is, on proof of control, knowledge or presumed knowledge, and sufficient resources. For elaboration, see Chapter 19 (Merry) in this volume.

Professional negligence

Moving away from personal injuries but still within negligence, the appeals in the professional negligence category are of note in that four of the five appeals concern solicitors as defendants. A variety of issues arose in the solicitors' cases, ranging from the duty of care to non-clients and the standard of care in the provision of legal advice to the application of limitation periods, none of which required innovation or a break with established tort principles. The defendant solicitors were found liable in three of the four cases, but with such a wide range of issues, nothing much can be inferred from these figures. The rather disproportionately high number of solicitors' cases does invite speculation: are solicitors making that many more errors than other professionals, resulting in a disproportionate number of appeals? Is there that much more at stake financially? Is it something about the nature of the litigants? Having had occasion to consult solicitors in the first place, when things go wrong, this group is more likely to assert its rights. It is important to recognize that in this branch of the law, the court is particularly expert in the subject matter at hand (the allegedly negligent activity concerns legal practice, in which judges have obvious expertise), so a closer than usual scrutiny and a greater detail of analysis can be observed in these decisions. Little else can be concluded.

Employees' compensation claims

The second cluster of cases concerns appeals in claims for compensation made under the ECO. The proportionately significant number of appeals (4) can be attributed to factors similar to those for work-related negligence cases, including the frequency of work-related injuries and the resistance of employers and insurers to compensation claims. In addition, there is also the age of the statutory regime in question and a judicially perceived need to ensure that the compensation scheme functions in a meaningful way in the face of government reluctance to engage in wholesale reform. Workers are just as likely, if not more likely, than employers to pursue their cases to the highest court.[65] As discussed earlier in the context of work-related negligence cases, the most commonly contested issue is the question of who is an employee and thus who qualifies for compensation under the ECO.

---

[65] In three of the four cases, the worker was the appellant before the CFA.

In the leading case, the CFA emphasized the flexible and purposive approach to be taken in the interpretation and application of the provisions of the ECO, and importantly, that mutuality of obligation is not necessary for employee status for the purpose of an ECO claim.[66] In the one other appeal of note, concerning the issue of causation of injury in the context of an ECO claim,[67] the CFA ruled that in order to give effect to the ECO's purpose as an instrument of social reform, the ordinary principles of causation in negligence do not apply to the compensation scheme established under this ordinance.[68] As such, the fact of a pre-existing injury will not result in a reduction of compensation for the injury that the worker sustains from after a workplace accident. This decision, like most of the CFA decisions concerning workers' injuries, demonstrates the court's concern for the plight of injured workers and its recognition that those mechanisms in place, whether common law or statutory, will be interpreted robustly when necessary and be made to serve their intended purpose.[69]

Defamation

The third cluster concerns appeals in defamation cases.[70] This is an area of tort law in which there has been considerable pressure for reform for some time, pressure that intensified with the arrival of the internet and the host of new issues triggered by the unique characteristics of electronic publication, in particular, the ease with which ordinary people can publish across multiple jurisdictions. In recent years, reforms have taken place

---

[66] See discussion above at notes 37 and 38 and the accompanying text.

[67] *LKK Trans Ltd* v. *Wong Hoi Chung* (2006) 9 HKCFAR 103.

[68] Per Bokhary PJ (at 107): '[T]he obvious object of the Employees' Compensation Ordinance is speedily and with considerable certainty to provide urgently needed no-fault and compulsorily-insured compensation to injured employees or the families they leave behind ... that is not a context in which I see any warrant for resorting to that sort of reading down [contended for by the employer] in order to permit apportionment and thus introduce the delay and uncertainty which apportionment would generally entail.... It suffices for full employees' compensation that the injury was a cause (even if not the sole cause) of the death, permanent total incapacity, permanent partial incapacity or temporary incapacity whether total or partial'.

[69] Here there is a decidedly corrective justice approach to the statutory compensation scheme: 'The focus is, in other words, on insurance-based compensation aimed at alleviating the incapacitated employee's hardship rather than on compensation confined in a manner which reflects the employer's fault', per Ribeiro PJ in *LKK Trans Ltd* v. *Wong Hoi Chung*, [36].

[70] There were five such cases.

elsewhere in both the statutory framework[71] and in the common law, not necessarily brought on by the internet.[72] Despite or perhaps because of the absence of statutory reform in Hong Kong, the CFA has not been idle and has made its own contribution to the international common law of defamation.

The issue that has arisen most often in the defamation cases is that of the defence of fair comment.[73] Central among these decisions is that of *Cheng and Another* v. *Tse Wai Chun*.[74] This is easily the most controversial and possibly the most influential decision of the CFA thus far in the field of tort law. The disputing parties, two well-known Hong Kong personalities, had been working separately for the release of a Hong Kong tour guide convicted (wrongly, it is presumed) in the Philippines for drug trafficking. The defendant, a radio talk-show host, made an on-air remark to the effect that the plaintiff, a solicitor, had acted unethically, against the interests of the tour guide, in persuading the tour guide not to sue his Hong Kong employer for damages arising from his detention. The statement was accepted as defamatory in the courts, and the case turned on the defendant's plea of fair comment. The plaintiff argued that any fair comment was defeated by malice, in this case that the defendant had been motivated by a desire to advance his own name in the public eye at the expense of the plaintiff. The defence failed in the courts below because the jury and the Court of Appeal found that the defendant was so motivated when making the statement and that malice was established.

However, the CFA reversed that decision on the basis that motive was irrelevant in fair comment, that the only form of malice that would defeat a comment that otherwise satisfied the objective requirements of the defence[75] was dishonesty, namely that the speaker did not believe what

---

[71] E.g. the Defamation Act 1996 (United Kingdom), which, *inter alia*, introduced a summary remedy to facilitate a more expeditious resolution in defamation cases.

[72] As in the example of the developments in the case law in relation to the defence of qualified privilege for the media in the coverage of public interest information. See e.g. *Reynolds* v. *Times Newspapers Ltd* [2001] 2 AC 127; *Lange* v. *Australian Broadcasting Corporation* (1997) 189 CLR 520; and *Jameel* v. *Wall Street Journal Europe* [2007] 1 AC 359.

[73] It arose in four of the five defamation cases: *Eastern Express Publisher Ltd and Another* v. *Mo Man Ching Claudia & Another* (1999) 2 HKCFAR 264; *Next Magazine Publishing Ltd and Others* v. *Ma Ching Fat* (2003) 6 HKCFAR 63; *Cheng and Another* v. *Tse Wai Chun* (2000) 3 HKCFAR 339; and *Mak Shiu Tong* v. *Yue Kwok Ying and Another* (2004) 7 HKCFAR 228. It was also an alternative ground in the other case, *Next Magazine Publishing Ltd and Others* v. *Oriental Daily Publisher Limited* (2000) 3 HKCFAR 160.

[74] *Cheng and Another* v. *Tse Wai Chun, ibid.*

[75] These are that the comment must be on a matter of public interest; the statement must be recognizable as comment, as opposed to an imputation of fact; the comment must be

he said. In this one stroke, the CFA effectively shifted the balance between free speech and protection of reputation decidedly in favour of the former, at a time when basic rights and freedoms were the cause of considerable anxiety in post-handover Hong Kong.[76] The decision has implications for the wider common law world and has already been cited and accepted as the law by English courts.[77] Received with scepticism, even cynicism, in some local circles,[78] in part out of resentment that the main judgment in this unanimous decision was given by Lord Nicholls, the overseas member of the panel and thus eliciting charges of intermeddling, in truth, the decision did not completely fall out of the sky, but as explained by Jill Cottrell,[79] it can be viewed as the culmination of judicial developments that had been under way for some time. It was strongly supported in the concurring judgment of Chief Justice Andrew Li, who rejected a narrow approach as inappropriate in a society 'which greatly values the freedom of speech and safeguards it by a constitutional guarantee'.[80] The adoption of the ruling by the English courts has helped to dispel conspiracy theories that the decision was driven by ulterior political motives directed only at Hong Kong and would not be accepted by courts elsewhere.[81]

---

based on facts that are true or are protected by privilege; the comment must indicate the facts on which it is based; and the comment must be one that could have been made by an honest person, however prejudiced he or she might be, and however exaggerated or obstinate his views.

[76] It could be argued that the CFA had signalled its pro-speech stance even earlier in *Eastern Express Publisher Ltd and Another* v. *Mo Man Ching Claudia and Another*, in which the court gave a generous reading of the pre-*Cheng* v. *Tse* fair comment defence, finding that the somewhat loose statement made by a TV journalist satisfied the objective requirements of the defence.

[77] See e.g. *Branson* v. *Bower* [2002] QB 737 (QB) and *Lowe* v. *Associated Newspapers Ltd* [2006] 3 All ER 357 (QB). It was also cited in *Channel Seven Adelaide Pty Ltd* v. *Manock* [2007] HCA 60, *WIC Radio Ltd* v. *Simpson* [2008] 2 SCR 420, *Panday* v. *Gordon* [2005] UKPC 36 (Trinidad and Tobago) per Lord Nicholls, and *Oei Hon Leong* v. *Ban Song Long David and Others* [2005] 3 SLR 608. I am grateful to P. Y. Lo for providing the latter three citations.

[78] See e.g. Lik Ma, 'A Judgment Found Wanting', *Hong Kong iMail*, 5 December 2000, and Sin-por Shiu, 'Victims the Losers in Court Decision', *South China Morning Post*, 28 November 2000, both cited and discussed in Cottrell, note 79 below.

[79] J. Cottrell, 'Fair Comment, Judges and Politics in Hong Kong' (2003) 27 *Melbourne University Law Review* 33. For an insightful discussion of the role of Lord Nicholls as the overseas judge see Cottrell, 61–4.

[80] Note 73 above, 345.

[81] At any rate, there is no evidence, in the decade since the appeal was decided, that press freedoms are in any way abused or indeed are in any way practised differently than before this decision.

Unaddressed issue – duty of care and economic loss

Despite the initiatives discussed earlier, there was what I would consider to be at least one glaring missed opportunity. The CFA has never addressed the bigger issues in duty of care in negligence.[82] One has the impression that this is considered sacred ground by the Hong Kong courts and that House of Lords pronouncements should simply prevail in this area of tort law.[83] In defence, one might argue that the opportunity for review and reassessment has not yet arisen, but that is not entirely true. In *Bank of East Asia Ltd* v. *Tsien Wui Marble Factory Ltd and Others*,[84] a case ultimately decided on limitations issues rather than on the basis of tort law *per se*, the entire court appears to have accepted at face value the House of Lords ruling in *Murphy* v. *Brentwood District Council*[85] to the effect that building defects are to be treated as pure economic loss. Yet the characterization of building defects as pure economic loss begs the question of whether a duty of care by a builder to an owner can be owed, and this question was not addressed.[86] Given the reverence shown by all members of the court for the decision in *Murphy*, it is a safe assumption that the ruling of no duty[87] in that case would also be accepted by the CFA. Nothing was said to contradict that position. For future purposes, this means that the actions of flat owners for defective construction are doomed to fail. The CFA missed the opportunity to directly address this unfortunate aspect of Hong Kong law.[88] The court declined putting the law on the same

---

[82] It was addressed by the PC only once, in *Yuen Kun Yeu* v. *A-G of Hong Kong*, a negligence claim concerning investors' financial losses.

[83] See e.g. the CFA decision in *Desmond Yiu Chown Leung* v. *Chow Wai Lam William* (2005) 8 HKCFAR 592. See generally my observations in *Tort Law in Hong Kong*, 134.

[84] (1999) 2 HKCFAR 349.

[85] [1991] 1 AC 398. The House of Lords thereby overruled its own decision in *Anns* v. *Merton London Borough Council* [1978] AC 728.

[86] At trial, the defendant architects admitted a duty, permitting the court to avoid the duty question, but it is an issue that was and is in need of clarification, as being one of great public importance, determining the consumer rights of property owners in Hong Kong. In New Zealand, the PC ruled that a duty of care will generally be owed (see *Invercargill City Council* v. *Hamlin* [1996] AC 624), despite the contrary position in England as stated in *Murphy* v. *Brentwood District Council* [1991] 1 AC 398 (HL).

[87] Except for cases in which the plaintiff was in privity with the defendant builder or contractor, in which case he or she would have actions in breach of contract as well as tort. In such a case, the action in tort would be important only where the contract limitation period had run but the extended period for latent damage in tort had not yet run.

[88] The principle in question was first applied in Hong Kong in *Sunface International Ltd* v. *Meco Engineering Ltd* [1990] 2 HKLR 193.

consumer protection footing as in New Zealand,[89] Canada,[90] Australia,[91] Singapore,[92] and Malaysia,[93] where the highest courts have ruled that such building defects are within the duty of care in negligence. As I have argued elsewhere, this position is not only open to the courts in Hong Kong but is required by basic notions of community fairness.[94]

A further issue left in an unfinished state by the court was the precise nature of such pure economic loss. Accepting that building defects are pure economic loss and not physical damage, when does such loss occur for purposes of accrual of the cause of action? The court was divided as to the time of occurrence of damage and expressed distinctly different views as to the date of accrual.[95] This is a vital issue for rare cases when a duty of care is owed and one that should have been unequivocally resolved.

An incidental matter but one pertinent to this study was the ambivalence expressed by some members of the court regarding the status of House of Lords decisions in the Hong Kong courts. Nazareth NPJ observed that the CFA 'would not be bound by House of Lords decisions in identifying and developing the common law of Hong Kong'.[96] Beside this was his observation that 'it may be thought, however, that this court would not depart from the law as it applied immediately before July 1, 1997 without good reason'.[97] Ching PJ was even more reserved: 'Nor is it for this court to impose what it considers to be the best solution or a better solution than that laid down by the House of Lords'.[98] These observations cannot be taken to reflect the views of the entire court, but they are vaguely suggestive of a continued reverence for the decisions of the House of Lords that may have impeded a more forward-looking result in this case.[99]

---

[89] *Invercargill City Council* v. *Hamlin.*

[90] *Winnipeg Condominium Corporation No 36* v. *Bird Construction Co. Ltd* (1995) 121 DLR (4th) 193.

[91] *Bryan* v. *Maloney* (1995) 128 ALR 163.

[92] *RSP Architects, Planners and Engineers* v. *Ocean Front Pte Ltd* (1996) 1 SLR 113.

[93] *Dr Abdul Hamid Abdul Rashid* v. *Jurusan Malaysia Consultants* [1998] 14 PN 115.

[94] This is a position that I have argued is not only consistent with developments elsewhere in the Commonwealth (leaving aside England) but consonant with justice. Moreover, 'The imposition of a duty of care could provide the missing incentive for builders to do their work carefully, in adherence to appropriate industry standards and those imposed by law' ('Defective Buildings and Defective Law' (2000) 30 *HKLJ* 206, 220).

[95] For a convenient summary and analysis of the various views see R. Glofcheski, 'The Law of Limitations as Applied to Latent Building Defects' (2000) 16 *Construction Law Journal* 379, 386–92.

[96] *Bank of East Asia* v. *Tsien Wui Marble Factory*, 438.　　[97] *Ibid.*, 439.　　[98] *Ibid.*, 405.

[99] Of the other issues passed over by the CFA, despite the opportunity to say more, I would only mention the issue of informed consent to medical treatment. This is an area ripe for

The expansion of liability in tort law

It has been said that there are 'lies, damned lies, and statistics'.[100] With such a small survey sample can any trends – for instance, a pro-plaintiff sympathy – be discerned with any degree of reliability? Of the eight negligence cases concerning work-related personal injury, the plaintiff emerged the victor in seven.[101] Of the ECO appeals, the applicant received a favourable ruling in the CFA in all four of them. Thus, the injured worker succeeded in 11 of the 12 appeals heard in the CFA. This is an impressive number, but exactly what can be inferred from this figure is a matter of debate and disagreement.[102]

I prefer to think that it suggests a judicial recognition of the unsatisfactory state of industrial safety law and practice in Hong Kong – a weak inspectorate, a perilous state of onsite safety culture, casual and sometimes deceptive hiring practices, a general recognition of the weakness of the employment law – and a judicial urge to right the balance. This may be reading too much into it, but the judgments of the lower courts in work-related injury cases are so rich with expressions of judicial concern about the absence of a safety culture at work, about the cutting of corners, and about shoddy and deceptive hiring practices that the members of the CFA would know the situation all too

a ruling from the highest court that would move Hong Kong away from the conventional approach to informed consent practised in England, where the emphasis has been placed not on patient choice but doctor's wisdom, to the patients' rights position that has long been accepted in Canada, Australia, and the United States. It is true that the only occasion for the CFA to consider the issue was in an interlocutory application for a pleadings amendment to include negligent failure to warn as a cause of action, but the court's description of negligent failure to warn as a 'developing area of the law' is not particularly promising unless, of course, it is intended to mean that the law will be developed along more modern lines when the opportunity arises. See discussion in text accompanying note 44 above.

[100] Mark Twain, 'Chapters from my Autobiography', in the *North American Review*, No. DCXVIII, 5 July 1907. Twain attributed the aphorism to Benjamin Disraeli but without citation.

[101] The only failed case, *Jerry Chen* v. *Whirlpool (Hong Kong) Limited* concerned a desperate attempt by a worker posted in China and injured there in a traffic accident, to impose strict liability for the driver's negligence on his Hong Kong employer based on the novel concept of 'enterprise liability' (see discussion at note 55 above).

[102] While the success rate of appeals before the CFA is an obviously important statistic, I would argue, in tort law at least, that the success rate of the plaintiff after appeal has been finally decided by the highest appellate court is more important. Tort law is after all about an imbalance created by the defendant's activity, in which the victim seeks an order from the court to correct the imbalance.

well[103] even if they were more restrained in the language adopted in their own judgments. It may also, as mentioned earlier, suggest employer and insurer recalcitrance in accepting responsibility for work site injuries, a hard-headed attitude that carries them right to the highest appellate court despite the costs.

In the two medical negligence cases, the plaintiff emerged the victor in both. In the other three personal injury negligence cases on appeal,[104] the plaintiff was successful in each of them. In the public nuisance case resulting in death to a pedestrian,[105] the plaintiffs were successful. Thus, personal injury plaintiffs and applicants enjoyed a success rate of 17 out of 18 cases in the CFA,[106] an even more remarkable statistic than that for injured workers cases alone, again inviting speculation as to its meaning. Given such results, one could be forgiven for suggesting a blatant pro-plaintiff bias,[107] but this would be too simplistic, even unfair, given the care taken in the analysis and reasons for judgments in the more seminal of these cases, most of which did not require a break with precedent.[108]

The record is certainly consistent with a corrective justice view of the aims of tort as much as its distributive aims, as seen from the extension of liability beyond previous limits in the new configurations of the law in, for instance, vicarious liability and public nuisance. Evidence to support this conclusion derives not only from the high rate of imposing liability on defendants but also from the way in which the liability rules were reconfigured in some of these cases. The acceptance of the close connection test for vicarious liability and its extension to a case of ordinary negligence in *Ming An Insurance Co (HK) Ltd* v. *Ritz-Carlton Ltd*[109]

---

[103] In *Chan Sik Pan and Another* v. *Wylam's Services Ltd and Others*, Bokhary PJ expressly made the point about the need for care in the determination of the employee status issue in the context of hiring practices on Hong Kong construction sites (note 36 above, 317–18).

[104] *Cheng Kin Ping and Another* v. *Woo Cho Wing John and Cheung Ming Wo (Third Party)* (2000) 3 HKCFAR 333; *Ming An Insurance Co (HK) Ltd* v. *Ritz-Carlton Ltd*; and *Lam Pak Chiu* v. *Tsang Mei Ying* (2001) 4 HKCFAR 34.

[105] An action that is closely related to negligence, given the court's introduction of the requirement that for liability to attach the incorporated owners either knew or ought to have known of the dangerous building defect.

[106] Of the 17 plaintiff successes, the CFA differed with the trial judge in 8.

[107] Especially if one includes in the tally the solicitors' negligence cases, which had a plaintiff's success rate of three out of four.

[108] An exception is *Ming An Insurance Co (HK) Ltd* v. *Ritz-Carlton Ltd* and to a lesser degree, *Leung Tsang Hung* v. *Incorporated Owners of Kwok Wing House*.

[109] Note 51 above.

dramatically alter the playing field in vicarious liability. Then the flexible approach to the conditions for employee status in *Poon Chau Nam* v. *Yim Siu Cheung*[110] contributes to that expansion, bringing potentially more employed persons and hence more tort victims into the category of vicarious liability. Even more important, by virtue of the more liberal definition of 'employee' in *Poon Chau Nam*, statutory and common law workers' coverage was extended to a potentially larger portion of the labour force.[111] The liability rules in the case of injuries to the public in general have been liberalized and the field of responsibility expanded in the configuration of the liability of residential owners' corporations in the decision of *Leung Tsang Hung*.[112] As discussed earlier, in a city of high-rise tower blocks, we are all at risk of serious injury whenever we walk out onto a public thoroughfare. By the same token – and by virtue of the same decision – most of us are also undertaking obligations and at risk of incurring liabilities through ownership of flats in multi-storey buildings. It is a decision that for many of us cuts both ways, widening the boundaries of liability.

Corrective and distributive justice explanations of tort law functions offer a possible framework for analysis of tort jurisprudence, but the CFA has not felt inclined to explain its tort law decisions on this basis, making reference to these tort theories on only one occasion and then only in passing.[113] Rather, the court has in general eschewed theory, preferring to express itself in terms of pragmatic policy explanations.[114] Neither has the court found it appropriate or necessary to explain any of its negligence decisions on the basis of economic theory despite the emergence of such an approach elsewhere and in recent years in the lower courts of

---

[110] Note 36 above.

[111] I hesitate to remind the reader of the expansion of liability in the liberal application of *res ipsa loquitur* in *Sanfield Building Contractors Ltd* v. *Li Kai Cheong*, which extended this favourable liability rule to cases of multiple defendants.

[112] Note 56 above. So too in the assertion that *res ipsa loquitur* is applicable in medical negligence cases, facilitating the imposition of liability in such cases, see *Yu Yu Kai* v. *Chan Chi Keung*.

[113] In *Rainfield Design & Associates Limited* v. *Siu Chi Moon* but did not offer elaboration of its meaning: 'Neither in terms of corrective justice nor in terms of distributive justice does there appear to be any reason in situations of this kind for distinguishing between employees and independent contractors' (per Bokhary PJ at 141).

[114] As in its justifications for its generally purposive interpretations of the ECO in *LKK Trans Ltd* v. *Wong Hoi Chung* and accompanying text, or its explanation for its decision expanding public nuisance liability in *Leung Tsang Hung* v. *Incorporated Owners of Kwok Wing House*, note 56 above and accompanying text.

Hong Kong.[115] Still on the subject of the role of theory and policy in judicial decision making, it is worth noting that the court has demonstrated no taste for the increasingly popular practice in the highest courts elsewhere to cite or note the writings of academics in its tort law decisions,[116] and to that extent, it is out of step with the highest courts of other jurisdictions, including England and Australia.

Looking again at the defamation cluster, the plaintiff succeeded in only one in five of the cases, but this is saying nothing more than that the CFA ruled in favour of the exercise of free speech in four of the cases. There is a danger of reading too much into this and in particular into the decision in *Cheng* v. *Tse* – for instance, that it was intended to send a broader political message about the rule of law, fundamental freedoms, and the role of the courts and the common law. Yet there can be no doubt that it has had such effects, not least of which is a reassurance about freedom of expression to an understandably anxious press and public in the jittery post-handover environment. Moreover, no matter how the decision and its background and the reasoning supporting it are explained, that a decision of such far-reaching consequence in the common law world, bringing such a dramatic shift in the balance between reputation and free speech, was rendered by a Hong Kong court, at such an early stage of the court's history, is still cause for remark and reflection, if not admiration.

Before concluding, it is also important to note the commendably high degree of respect that the CFA has shown for first instance decision-making in tort law, for trial processes, and for the trial judge as a finder of fact. This might not be apparent from the statistics, which show that in only just over half of the appeals (16) the CFA restored or confirmed the trial judge's ruling. However, on a number of occasions, members of the court have gone to some length to emphasize that trial findings should not be lightly disturbed on appeal,[117] on two occasions reversing the Court of Appeal for that very reason.[118] Moreover, the court has on

---

[115]   Cost–benefit analysis and principles of economic efficiency have featured in a number of negligence cases. See e.g. *Wong Wai Ming* v. *Hospital Authority* [2000] 3 HKLRD 612, *Tam Sau Fong* v. *Sheng Kung Hui Diocesan Welfare Council* [2002] 3 HKLRD 431, *Wong Shek Hung* v. *Pentecostal Lam Hon Kwong School* [2001] 2 HKLRD G15, *Wong Sau Chun* v. *Ho Kam Chiu and Others* [2000] 2 HKLRD E12, and *Wong Kit Chun* v. *Wishing Long Hong*.

[116]   I know of no instances when it has done so.

[117]   *Wishing Long Hong* v. *Wong Kit Chun*; *Ting Kwok Keung* v. *Tam Dick Yuen and Others*; and *Poon Hau Kei* v. *Hsin Chong Construction Co. Ltd, Taylor Woodrow International Ltd (Joint Venture)*. See the observations of Bokhary PJ at note 36 above.

[118]   *Ting Kwok Keung* v. *Tam Dick Yuen and Others* and *Poon Hau Kei* v. *Hsin Chong Construction Co. Ltd, Taylor Woodrow International Ltd (Joint Venture)*.

another occasion insisted on the integrity of trial processes and ordered a new trial rather than deciding the appeal when it believed that natural justice so required.[119]

Conclusion

On balance then, the court can point to its record in tort law as broadly progressive, extending the distributive reach of some of the liability rules, much to the benefit of personal injury victims and the community at large, introducing flexibility in some of the existing rules to extend the boundaries of entitlement where it is most needed, in particular, for injured workers, while expanding freedoms in the case of defamation. One might argue that over its history, tort law has always been progressive,[120] given the passage of sufficient time, that liability rules everywhere are much more liberal and expansive today than they were 50 or 100 years ago, and that the CFA is merely keeping up. Certainly, there has not been any conscious attempt to break with previous traditions, including those of the PC. The presence of an overseas judge, often from the House of Lords, may have helped ensure that, but equally would have brought fresh ideas to the court. Given the short period since the establishment of the CFA, a more balanced assessment may be that in its tort law docket, the court has met the challenge of its historical mission as a new court conferred with final appellate power, has not been shy to make controversial decisions, and, with only a few exceptions, has taken the opportunities that were presented to further develop and improve Hong Kong tort law.[121]

---

[119] See e.g. *Chan Sik Pan and Another* v. *Wylam's Services Ltd and Others*.

[120] With only a few, short-lived breaks of reactionary dispositions, for instance, the 1980's duty of care jurisprudence responding to the expansionary effects of the decision in *Anns* v. *Merton*.

[121] The decision of *Luen Hing Fat Coating & Finishing Factory Ltd* v. *Waan Chuen Ming* [2011] 2 HKLRD 223 (CFA) provides an appropriate postscript as well as reinforcement of one of the author's main arguments, that the CFA will go the extra distance in developing negligence law where issues of worker safety are at stake. In this case, the defendant factory operator contracted with a company to repair one of its machines. As on previous occasions, the defendant lent its pallet jacks and related equipment to the contractor to do the work, equipment that was otherwise safe but that, as used by the contractor, created a risk of injury to the contractor's workers. This method of doing the work and the danger posed were known to the defendant. The plaintiff, a worker employed by the contractor, was injured as a result of the dangerous method used. The plaintiff sued his employer (now impecunious) and the defendant factory operator. The appeal concerned the somewhat novel argument that an entity that appoints an independent contractor to perform a task can owe a duty of care to an employee of

Footnote continued

that independent contractor in common law negligence (occupiers' liability was not an available basis for liability because the accident did not arise from any defect in the premises). It is well established that an employer may be liable for the negligence of its independent contractor in circumstances of 'nondelegable duty' when the independent contractor's negligence causes injury or damage to others (see e.g. Glofcheski, note 19 above, 439–42), but in this exceptional line of cases, the employer's duty has not been extended to the independent contractor's employees. It is assumed that responsibility for the independent contractor's employees resides with the independent contractor alone. At any rate, the court did not treat the facts of this case as fitting within any of the categories of nondelegable duty. The court proceeded on the basis of ordinary common law negligence and found that a duty of care was owed even though the defendant did not supervise or participate in the dangerous method used. Applying the threefold duty of care test enunciated by the House of Lords in *Caparo* v. *Dickman* [1990] 2 AC 605, the court found that the necessary proximity was established by virtue of the employee's presence in the defendant's factory and his use of the defendant's equipment for the purpose of repairing the defendant's machine and that it was fair, just, and reasonable to impose a duty because the defendant chose to lend the equipment to the contractor knowing it would be used in a dangerous way. Bokhary PJ reinforced this conclusion on the basis that when personal safety is at stake, as opposed to (for instance) pure economic loss, the standards required by fairness and justice are more demanding, all the more so in the case of a 'vulnerable plaintiff' such as a worker who, in the nature of things, is in no position to protest against the use of unsafe methods. With reference to note 101 above and the accompanying text, this case raises the tally of injured workers' victories in the CFA – 8 of the 9 work-related negligence cases and 12 of 13 worker injury cases (including ECO cases) have resulted in successful verdicts for the injured worker.

21

Civil procedure

GARY MEGGITT

Introduction

There are three factors to keep in mind when looking at the Court of Final Appeal's (CFA's) decisions on questions of civil procedure over the period 1997 to 2010. The first is the rather disparate nature of 'civil procedure' when compared to, say, the law of tort or contract. The Rules of the High Court (RHC) contain 121 separate Orders and four Appendices dealing with subjects ranging from interrogatories to security for costs. Albeit RHC Ord. 1A r. 1 lays down a set of 'underlying objectives',[1] there is no equivalent of the 'neighbour principle' from *Donoghue* v. *Stevenson*[2] or the necessity of a common intention to enter into legal obligations,[3] which are fundamental to an understanding of negligence or contract law respectively. There is no doctrine – including the underlying objectives – that demands that a defence should be served within 28, rather than 14 or 21, days from acknowledging service of a writ or that requires discovery to be performed by the parties' mutual exchange of lists of documents. Civil procedure, when compared with substantive law, is largely concerned with practicalities rather than principles.

The second factor is the 'Banquo's ghost' comprising the Civil Justice Reform (CJR). The CJR began in February 2000 when Chief Justice Li appointed a Working Party to review and recommend changes to the RHC (and Rules of the District Court [RDC]). The Working Party published

---

[1] These are '(a) to increase the cost-effectiveness of any practice and procedure to be followed in relation to proceedings before the Court; (b) to ensure that a case is dealt with as expeditiously as is reasonably practicable; (c) to promote a sense of reasonable proportion and procedural economy in the conduct of proceedings; (d) to ensure fairness between the parties; (e) to facilitate the settlement of disputes; and (f) to ensure that the resources of the Court are distributed fairly'.

[2] [1932] AC 562 (HL).

[3] *Rose and Frank Co.* v. *Crompton Bros.* [1923] 2 KB 261, 293 (Eng CA), per Atkin LJ: 'To create a contract there must be a common intention of the parties to enter into legal obligations, mutually communicated expressly or impliedly'.

an Interim Report and Consultation Paper in 2001 followed by a Final Report in 2004. In 2006, a separate Steering Committee published a draft amended RHC. In February 2008, the Civil Justice (Miscellaneous Amendments) Ordinance was enacted by the Legislative Council, and the amended RHC was approved by the same body in July that year. The amended RHC came into force on 2 April 2009, thus completing the CJR over nine years after its inception.[4]

Whilst it would be wrong to suggest that the CFA avoided any decisions on difficult procedural points in deference to the CJR (and there is certainly no evidence to that effect),[5] its importance to the CFA cannot be ignored. After all, it was the Chief Justice himself who started the CJR, and two other members of the CFA sat on its Working Party.[6] It could be argued that, in light of the first two factors, the CJR gave the CFA's members more scope to influence civil procedure than they had through the usual channels of litigation. Moreover, the changes inherent in the CJR – especially the introduction of the underlying objectives and greater case management – mean that pre–April 2009 decisions may not be a particularly useful guide to the CFA's and lower courts' approach to civil procedure in the future.

The third factor is the parties' almost ever-present need for leave to appeal. Most procedural disputes, such as those over the scope of discovery under RHC Ord. 24,[7] are raised and resolved at interlocutory hearings. Appeals to the CFA from the Court of Appeal require leave from either

---

[4] The Hong Kong judiciary's CJR website, www.civiljustice.gov.hk/eng/home.html, contains much valuable material on this subject. Also see G. Meggitt, 'Civil Justice Reform in Hong Kong – Its Progress and Its Future' (2008) 38 *HKLJ* 89.

[5] By way of illustration, Lord Phillips MR concluded his judgment in *Three Rivers District Council* v. *Governor and Company of the Bank of England (No 6)* [2004] QB 916 (Eng CA) with the remarks at 935, [39] that '[t]he justification for litigation privilege is readily understood. Where, however, litigation is not anticipated it is not easy to see why communications with a solicitor should be privileged. Legal advice privilege attaches to matters such as the conveyance of real property or the drawing up of a will. It is not clear why it should. There would seem little reason to fear that, if privilege were not available in such circumstances, communications between solicitor and client would be inhibited. Nearly 50 years have passed since the Law Reform Committee looked at this area. It is perhaps time for it to receive a further review.' The CFA did not express a desire for reform or review in respect of the issues before it in the cases examined in this chapter.

[6] Chan J (as Chairman of the Working Party) and Ribeiro J (as its Deputy Chairman). See Chief Justice's Working Party on Civil Justice Reform, *Civil Justice Reform: Interim Report and Consultative Paper* (Hong Kong: HKSAR Government, 2001) 1[2].

[7] Cap. 4, sub. leg. A.

the Court of Appeal or the CFA itself.[8] Leave to appeal the former's interlocutory judgments lies at the discretion of either court and may only be granted if, generally speaking, the question raised is one of great general or public importance.[9] As a consequence, all but the most profound procedural disputes are likely to go no further than the Court of First Instance (CFI) or, at best, the Court of Appeal.[10]

Despite these three factors, approximately 80 CFA judgments between 1997 and 2010 touched upon civil procedure.[11] About a quarter of those decisions concerned the CFA's own procedures (i.e. when leave to appeal will be granted), and almost as many dealt with costs. Far fewer addressed weightier matters such as pleadings or evidence. Thus, whilst the three factors may not have prevented the CFA from deliberating important procedural matters, there appears to have been a skewering of the subjects it did address. An examination of some of the CFA's decisions is, nevertheless, a worthwhile exercise given the significance to practitioners and their clients of what the court's members said from 1997 to 2010. This chapter will do so in the sequence that procedural issues are usually encountered by parties (i.e. pleadings followed by discovery and so on). It is not a review of every case considered by the CFA – or even of every case on a specific issue – but a 'snapshot' that, it is hoped, will illustrate how the CFA approached some potentially tricky procedural issues during this formative period of its history.

Commencement and pleadings

Limitation

One of the first issues that a solicitor needs to address when advising a prospective plaintiff on his claim is whether the relevant limitation period has expired or will soon do so. Such an eventuality will enable the prospective defendant to defeat the claim. Various limitation periods are provided for in the Limitation Ordinance.[12] The most familiar are those

---

[8] Hong Kong Court of Final Appeal Ordinance (Cap. 484), s. 23(1). See also Chapter 7 (Da Roza) in this volume.

[9] HKCFAO, s. 22(1)(b).

[10] In addition, whilst leave to appeal to the Court of Appeal from an interlocutory judgment by a District Court judge has long been required, such leave must also now be obtained for appeals from most interlocutory decisions by a CFI judge to the Court of Appeal. See High Court Ordinance (Cap. 4), s. 14AA(1) and RHC, Ord. 59 r. 21.

[11] The absence of a precise figure is due to the ambiguity of the term 'civil litigation'.

[12] Cap. 347.

for claims under simple contract and in tort, each being six years from the date of accrual of the cause of action, subject to certain qualifications in unusual situations.[13]

It is almost trite law that a contractual claim accrues upon breach and that a claim in tort accrues upon damage being sustained as a result of the tortious act. That did not, however, prevent the latter from being addressed at length by the CFA in *The Bank of East Asia, Ltd.* v. *Tsien Wui Marble Factory Ltd.*[14] In the early 1980s, the appellant bank redeveloped its head office. The work was completed and paid for in 1982. Unfortunately, the design was defective, and physical damage to the building first occurred in 1985. It was not until 1993, however, that the defect was discovered by the appellant. Rectification works began, and the appellant sued the various respondents for negligence between 1994 and 1996.

At issue was whether the cause of action in negligence accrued in 1982, when the design work was carried out; in 1985, when 'real' physical damage occurred; or in 1993, when the problem was discovered. The appellant asserted – not unsurprisingly – that the cause of action accrued when the damage was discovered and the respondents stood by the earlier dates. Litton PJ held, with Ching PJ and Nazareth NPJ agreeing, that the cause of action accrued in 1985 when the physical damage first occurred and, as a consequence, that the appellant's claims were time barred. In doing this, Litton PJ followed the English authority of *Pirelli General Cable Works Ltd* v. *Oscar Faber & Partners*,[15] in which it was held that the cause of action for the negligent design of a chimney accrued when cracking in its structure first developed and not when this was or could have been discovered.

Dissatisfaction with the consequences of *Pirelli* – in that it left the plaintiff with no remedy for the defendant's negligence – led to the Latent Damages Act 1986 in the United Kingdom and the Limitation (Amendment) Ordinance[16] in Hong Kong. Unfortunately for the appellant in *The Bank of East Asia*, the 'special time limit' (in the new section 31 of the amended Ordinance)[17] for negligence claims when the relevant facts were

---

[13] *Ibid.*, section 4(1)(a).   [14] (1999) 2 HKCFAR 349.   [15] [1983] 2 AC 1 (HL).

[16] Limitation (Amendment) Ordinance 1991 (31 of 1991).

[17] Section 31(1) to (4) reads: '(1) This section applies to any action for damages for negligence, other than one to which section 27 applies, where the earliest date on which the plaintiff or any person in whom the cause of action was vested before him first had both – (a) the knowledge required for bringing an action for damages in respect of the relevant damage; and (b) a right to bring such an action, (referred to in this section as the 'date of knowledge') falls after the date on which the cause of action accrued. (2) The period of

not known at accrual was not introduced until 1 July 1991, by which time the claim was already time barred as per *Pirelli*. In the absence of any legislation to the contrary, Litton PJ maintained that a cause of action in tort accrued when the 'real and substantial' damage occurred, and the appellant's attempt to introduce a 'discoverability test' outside of the provisions of section 31 was not permissible because it would render that legislation without meaning. The appellant's secondary argument, that the 'damage', in the form of economic loss, was suffered only when the property's market value was depreciated was also rejected by the CFA (despite support from Bokhary PJ and Lord Nicholls NPJ).[18]

The CFA returned to section 31 in *Kensland Realty Limited (in compulsory liquidation)* v. *Tai, Tang Chong*.[19] Kensland entered into an agreement to sell shop premises to Whale View Investment Ltd (Whale View), with completion fixed between 10:00 AM and 1:00 PM on 2 September 1997 and time being of the essence. Whale View did not pay the balance of the purchase price until 1:06 PM. Kensland treated this delay as a repudiatory breach, refused to complete, and forfeited Whale View's HK$8.25 million deposit. Kensland were told by Tai, Tang Chong (TTC) that Whale View might claim for the return of its deposit, although TTC advised that such a claim was unlikely to succeed.

On 3 September 1997, Whale View did indeed issue proceedings against Kensland for specific performance and damages. In November 1997, after the property market fell, Whale View dropped the claim for specific performance and sought merely the return of its deposit and damages. Whale View's claim failed in the CFI on 5 April 2000, but it succeeded in the Court of Appeal on 23 January 2001, and the CFA upheld this decision in its favour on 10 December 2001.[20] Kensland sued TTC on 13 January 2004 for damages for negligent legal advice.

---

limitation prescribed by section 4(1) in respect of actions founded on tort shall not apply to an action to which this section applies. (3) An action to which this section applies shall not be brought after the expiration of the period applicable in accordance with subsection (4). (4) That period is either – (a) 6 years from the date on which the cause of action accrued; or (b) 3 years from the date of knowledge, if that period expires later than the period mentioned in paragraph (a).'

[18] It is interesting to note that the dissenting members of the CFA also took the view that whilst section 31 was enacted in 1991 on the assumption that *Pirelli* was correct, this legislation had not 'set in stone' or 'frozen' the common law in its 1991 state. This relationship between statute and common law was addressed by the House of Lords in *Harding* v. *Wealands* [2006] 3 W.L.R. 83, 103 (HL), per Lord Rodger.

[19] (2008) 11 HKCFAR 237.   [20] (2001) 4 HKCFAR 381.

Both Ribeiro PJ and McHugh NPJ, each giving lengthy judgments in the CFA, held that Kensland suffered damage (being the liability to repay the deposit plus further monies to Whale View) on 2 September 1997. As a consequence, the primary limitation period under section 4(1)(a) expired before Kensland sued TTC. Both members of the CFA analysed the case law on the meaning of 'knowledge' of damage within section 31(5),[21] and each dismissed the assertion that Kensland lacked the required knowledge until the Court of Appeal's or CFA's judgments in 2001. Knowledge of 'liability' was not required, merely knowledge of the damage and that it was attributable to an identified party (TTC in this case).[22] As Ribeiro PJ put it:

> Kensland plainly had actual knowledge about the relevant damage with a sufficient degree of certainty for section 31 purposes commencing on 2 September 1997.... Kensland's case is that the damage flowed from its acting on TTC's advice when it refused to complete the contract. It obviously knew that it was acting on such advice. It therefore knew that such damage was attributable to TTC's acts and omissions representing the advice tendered. Kensland's claim is accordingly, in my view, statute-barred and the appeal must be dismissed.[23]

Thus, a further attempt to escape the rigours of section 31 failed.

The CFA also addressed the questions of 'knowledge' and 'discovery' in *Peconic Industrial Development Ltd* v. *Lau Kwok Fai*.[24] A bank was induced by false representations by a Macau businessman called Chio Ho Cheong to purchase land, through a joint venture company, for HK$515 million. This price was substantially in excess of the land's true value. Ultimately, Mr Chio made a HK$350 million secret profit whilst the bank lost HK$400 million. The fraud took place in 1991, but it was not until 1999 that the joint venture company, Peconic, sued Mr Chio (together

---

[21] Section 31(5) reads: 'In subsection (1) 'the knowledge required for bringing an action for damages in respect of the relevant damage' means knowledge- (a) of such facts about the damage in respect of which damages are claimed as would lead a reasonable person who had suffered such damage to consider it sufficiently serious to justify his instituting proceedings for damages against a defendant who did not dispute liability and was able to satisfy a judgment; (b) that the damage was attributable in whole or in part to the act or omission which is alleged to constitute negligence; (c) of the identity of the defendant; and (d) if it is alleged that the act or omission was that of a person other than the defendant, of the identity of that person and the additional facts supporting the bringing of an action against the defendant.'

[22] Section 31(6) reads: 'Knowledge that any acts or omissions did or did not, as a matter of law, involve negligence is irrelevant for the purposes of subsection (1).'

[23] *Kensland Realty*, [140].   [24] (2009) 12 HKCFAR 139.

with some of his accomplices) and then, in 2002, sued a solicitor, Danny Lau, for dishonestly assisting Mr Chio.

At issue before the CFA was, first, whether Mr Lau was entitled to a limitation defence given that section 20(1) provides that 'No period of limitation prescribed by this Ordinance shall apply to an action by a beneficiary under a trust, being an action . . . (a) in respect of any fraud or fraudulent breach of trust to which the trustee was a party or a privy . . . .' Second, even if Mr Lau was not covered by section 20 and therefore entitled to rely on the usual six-year limitation period, was the limitation period postponed until a date less than six years before the issue of Peconic's writ by virtue of section 26?[25]

Lord Hoffmann NPJ, giving the leading judgment, found for Mr Lau on both questions. First, on the true construction of section 20, the limitation defence was available to Mr Lau because he was not a 'constructive trustee' within the meaning of the Ordinance. As to section 26, the question of what the plaintiff could with reasonable diligence have discovered had to be answered 'dispassionately and without regard to what might be perceived as the merits'.[26] Peconic had sufficient 'clues' about Mr Lau's role in the fraud before the action was time barred. Finally, reiterating Ribeiro PJ's comments on irrelevance of certainty of liability in *Kensland*, Lord Hoffmann added:

> [I]t is not necessary that Peconic should have known facts which put Danny Lau's participation in the fraud beyond all reasonable doubt. The purpose of the inquiry into whether Peconic could with reasonable diligence have discovered his fraud is to establish when they could reasonably have been expected to commence proceedings. For that purpose, they needed only to know facts which amounted to a prima facie case.[27]

Pleadings

The function of pleadings is to give the opposing party sufficient notice of the case against it. They also define the issues upon which the court will

---

[25] Section 26(1) reads: 'Subject to subsection (4), where in the case of any action for which a period of limitation is prescribed by this Ordinance, either- (a) the action is based upon the fraud of the defendant; (b) any fact relevant to the plaintiff's right of action has been deliberately concealed from him by the defendant; or (c) the action is for relief from the consequences of a mistake, the period of limitation shall not begin to run until the plaintiff has discovered the fraud, concealment or mistake (as the case may be) or could with reasonable diligence have discovered it.'

[26] *Peconic Industrial Development*, [29].   [27] *Ibid.*, [56].

have to give judgment.[28] Consequently, a party's case is restricted to the issues raised within its pleadings unless and until they are amended. The nature, formulation, and use of pleadings did not escape the attentions of the CJR. The most significant changes were that a defendant who denies an allegation must now file a substantive defence stating his or her reasons for doing so. The defendant must also plead his or her own version of events when he or she intends to submit a different version from that given by the plaintiff.[29] Amendments are now only permitted if they are necessary for the fair disposal of the case or for saving costs.[30] Furthermore, all original and amended pleadings must now be verified by a statement of truth.[31]

These reforms were designed to address, among other things, 'sparse pleadings' because it was believed by the Working Party that 'a defence consisting of bare denials and non-admissions does nothing to advance the proper functions of pleadings'.[32] The extra procedural hurdles to amending pleadings are also designed to encourage precision in drafting. Similarly, statements of truth are intended to 'deter sloppy and speculative pleadings' and dissuade parties from 'advancing a downright dishonest case' on pain of contempt proceedings.[33]

The importance of, and necessity for, 'precise' pleadings has been stressed by the courts on numerous occasions, which may explain its prominence in the Working Party's deliberations. In *Mak Shiu Tong* v. *Yue Kwok Ying*,[34] the defendant in a libel claim had relied on the defences of justification and fair comment and, in one paragraph of his defence, asserted that his allegedly defamatory remarks had been about a third party and not the plaintiff. The judge held that this paragraph was merely a denial that the remarks were about the plaintiff (which he found to be a hopeless defence) and that the defendant was deemed to have admitted the pleaded – defamatory – meanings of those remarks. As the defences of justification and fair comment were directed at such meanings and no alternative meanings were pleaded by the defendant, his defence was therefore unsustainable.

The defendant appealed this decision to the Court of Appeal, which ruled in his favour. The Court of Appeal held that the defendant had not

---

[28] See *Aktieselskabet Dansk Skibsfinansiering* v. *Wheelock Marden & Co. Ltd* [1994] 2 HKC 264, 269–70 (CA), per Bokhary JA.

[29] RHC, Ord. 18 r.13.   [30] RHC, Ord. 20 r.8(1A).   [31] RHC, Ord. 41A r.2 .

[32] Chief Justice's Working Party on Civil Justice Reform, *Civil Justice Reform: Final Report* (Hong Kong: HKSAR Government, 2004) section 9: Pleadings, [207].

[33] *Ibid.*, [222].   [34] (2004) 7 HKCFAR 228.

admitted the pleaded meanings but was advancing his, as yet unpleaded, own or different meanings of the remarks and that it should be possible to formulate viable defences of justification and fair comment in relation to these.

The CFA was critical of the Court of Appeal's approach. Ribeiro PJ, giving the leading judgment, held that a defendant who sought to rely on the defences of justification and fair comment had to identify the defamatory meaning(s) 'sought to be justified or made the subject of fair comment'. This was necessary for the court to be able to assess the viability of those defences and, moreover, went beyond the content of the pleadings to the ambit of discovery. In perhaps the most critical part of the judgment, he added:

> It was therefore quite inappropriate for the Court of Appeal to take it upon itself to raise or to try to 'improve' a defence of justification on behalf of a defendant who has not himself put forward any pleaded basis for taking such a course.[35]

The CFA returned to the importance of the pleadings in determining the issues that a court may and may not consider in *Ming Shiu Chung* v. *Ming Shiu Sum*.[36] A dispute arose over the distribution of shareholdings in a prosperous family business. The first defendant claimed that he had been allocated a majority shareholding by his father. He relied on 10 share certificates and board meeting minutes purportedly recording the resolutions for such an allocation to him. His siblings, the plaintiffs, sought a declaration that this purported allocation was void.

The trial judge drew an inference that the minutes were forgeries. Furthermore, on the basis of expert evidence that four of the share certificates were genuine and the remaining six might be genuine, he held there had been a fraudulent scheme involving the first defendant to mislead his father into signing seven of the certificates in the belief that they distributed the shares equally between all the relevant family members. The Court of Appeal reversed the findings of forgery and fraud but still dismissed the first defendant's appeal because it was satisfied that the father had not known what he was signing.

On the first defendant's appeal to the CFA, Ribeiro PJ held:

> The fraud theory was simply not open to the Judge. It is nowhere pleaded. It was not explored in evidence and was never put to either [the first

---

[35] *Ibid.*, [45].   [36] (2006) 9 HKCFAR 334.

defendant and his alleged accomplice] when they gave evidence at the trial.[37]

He also referred to Lord Hoffmann's remarks in *Aktieselskabet Dansk Skibsfinansiering* v. *Brothers* that:

> It is well established that an allegation of fraud has to be pleaded with sufficient particularity to give the defendant fair notice of the case he has to meet . . . fairness requires that the adverse findings which the judge will be invited to make should have been put squarely to the witness in cross-examination, so that he can have the opportunity to offer an explanation.[38]

A finding of fraud could not be based on conjecture or even on the balance of probabilities but only by inference from proved facts. Just as the Court of Appeal could not raise a defence that had not been properly pleaded in *Mak Shiu Tong,* the judge in *Ming Shiu Chung* could not raise a claim that had not been properly pleaded.

Yet the fact that a court cannot raise or 'improve' a party's pleaded case does not prevent it from finding for that party on the basis of its opponent's pleadings. This was the outcome in *Poon Hau Kei* v. *Hsin Chong Construction Co. Ltd*[39] in which the plaintiff, a scaffolding worker, sued the principal contractor on a railway station site for negligence after he was injured when he fell onto the platform from an elevated height. His pleaded case was that he was not provided with any safe means of working at such a height. The defendant contended that the accident was caused solely, or contributed to, by the plaintiff's own negligence. The defendant alleged, first, that the plaintiff had been standing on a folding step ladder and, alternatively, that he had been standing on a fluorescent light trough above the platform. The trial judge found for the plaintiff on the basis of the 'light trough scenario' albeit this had been pleaded by the defendant.

Giving the only substantive judgment in the CFA, Bokhary PJ held that although it should be careful when doing so, a court was entitled to decide in favour of the plaintiff on the basis of a factual 'scenario' pleaded by the defendant, even if it differed from that pleaded by the plaintiff. There had been no unfairness in this case, given that (1) the defendant pleaded the 'light trough scenario', (2) succeeded in proving it, and (3) the plaintiff had not won on a 'scenario' not pleaded by either side. Moreover, the plaintiff had been cross-examined about the 'light trough scenario', and the defendant had addressed the trial judge on the issue in submissions.

---

[37] *Ibid.*, [54].   [38] (2000) 3 HKCFAR 70, 91–2.   [39] (2004) 7 HKCFAR 148.

Bokhary PJ arrived at this proposition 'on principle' and quoted Lord Guest in *John G Stein & Co. Ltd* v. *O'Hanlon,* in which His Lordship remarked 'I fail to see how [the defendants] can have been in any way prejudiced when the facts upon which liability was established are those averred in the defences and spoken to by their witnesses in evidence'.[40] The moral of this tale appears to be that not only should parties' counsel plead their own client's case with precision but that they should also take care to avoid pleading the other side's case!

Evidence and trial

Evidence – generally

Evidence, comprising discovery, witness statements, experts' reports and the like, is the proverbial 'muscle' of a case, which is laid upon the 'skeleton' of the pleadings. The Working Party took the view that there was often more 'fat' than muscle, with 'parties overloading the evidence and investing disproportionate effort and expenditure in the preparation of witness statements'.[41] The scope of discovery and its possible replacement by English style disclosure was mooted (albeit ultimately rejected) in the CJR process. The role of expert witnesses may, however, change over the coming years, with the CJR's introduction of a Code of Conduct for Expert Witnesses[42] and single joint experts.[43]

Left unchanged by the CJR was the civil standard of proof. It remains, as stressed by Bokhary PJ in *Solicitor (24/07)* v. *The Law Society of Hong Kong,*[44] the 'balance of probabilities' test in ordinary civil cases, with a heightened civil standard for disciplinary proceedings under the *Re H* approach.[45] Both of these tests remain distinct from that applied in criminal cases, in which a charge must be established beyond reasonable doubt. As Bokhary PJ made clear in *Solicitor (24/07)*, that difference is 'no mere matter of words'.

Discovery

Lord Woolf's Access to Justice interim report described 'discovery' in the following terms:

---

[40] [1965] AC 890, 910A (HL).
[41] *CJR Final Report*, note 32 above, section 19. Evidence, 304 [575].
[42] RHC, App. D.   [43] RHC, Ord. 38 r.4A.   [44] (2008) 11 HKCFAR 117.
[45] *Re H (Minors) (Sexual Abuse: Standard of Proof)* [1996] AC 563 (HL).

The result of the *Peruvian Guano* decision was to make virtually unlimited
the range of potentially relevant (and therefore discoverable) documents,
which parties and their lawyers are obliged to review and list, and which
the other side is obliged to read, against the knowledge that only a handful
of such documents will affect the outcome of the case. In that sense, it is a
monumentally inefficient process, especially in the larger cases. The more
conscientiously it is carried out, the more inefficient it is.[46]

The nature of discovery, and within it the nature of privilege, has also
been considered in Hong Kong in recent years. As noted earlier, the
CJR's Interim Report suggested replacing 'discovery' with English Civil
Procedure Rules (CPR)-style 'disclosure',[47] albeit this item was dropped
from the Final Report and did not make it into the amended RHC. The
CFA has also been called upon to consider the nature of discovery and
privilege.

In *Solicitor (23/2005)* v. *The Law Society of Hong Kong*,[48] a solicitor was
convicted of breaching section 8AA of the Legal Practitioners Ordinance[49]
for failing to produce documents required by the Law Society's inspectors.
On appeal to the CFA, the solicitor argued that the documents were covered by legal professional privilege (LPP) and that section 8B(2), which
provided for the production of documents for inspection, was incompatible with the right to confidential legal advice guaranteed by Article 35 of
the Basic Law.

The CFA dismissed the appeal. In his judgment, Bokhary PJ referred
to Lord Denning MR's words in *A-G* v. *Mulholland*[50] that privilege 'is
not the privilege of the lawyer but of his client'. Albeit the courts had
to ensure that any production of documents, under section 8B(2) or
otherwise, was compatible with the right to confidential legal advice,
Bokhary PJ observed that LPP was only one 'fundamental condition
on which the administration of justice' rests. Among others were the
existence of 'a legal profession of efficiency and integrity'. The Law Society
was responsible for maintaining proper standards among solicitors and,
in the CFA's view, its power under section 8AA was vital to this task.
Moreover, the CFA observed that (1) any 'privileged' documents could
only be used for the purposes of an inquiry under the Ordinance, (2) the

---

[46] See Access to Justice, ch 21, [17] accessible at www.dca.gov.uk/civil/interim/chap21.htm.
[47] Standard disclosure under CPR Pt. 31 r.6 requires a party to disclose only '(a) the documents on which he relies; and (b) the documents which – (i) adversely affect his own
case; (ii) adversely affect another party's case; or (iii) support another party's case; and
(c) the documents which he is required to disclose by a relevant practice direction'.
[48] (2006) 9 HKCFAR 175.   [49] Cap. 159.   [50] [1963] 2 QB 477, 489 (Eng CA).

inspectors could not act without the Law Society Council's direction, and (3) strict confidentiality would be given to any documents so produced. Hence, section 8B(2) disclosure was compatible with a client's right to confidential legal advice under Article 35.

In *PCCW-HKT Telephone Ltd* v. *David Matthew Mcdonald Aitken*,[51] the plaintiff had employed the first defendant, a solicitor admitted in Australia but not in Hong Kong, as its 'General Manager, Regulatory Compliance'. He subsequently joined the second defendant as its 'Head of Regulatory and Corporate Affairs'. The plaintiff claimed that the first defendant was privy to confidential and legally privileged information on the plaintiff's position vis-à-vis the second defendant. It therefore sought interim injunctions to restrain his work activities (the Restrictive Order) and to prevent him disclosing or using any of its confidential information (the Non-disclosure Order). The plaintiff argued that LPP provided a basis for the Restrictive Order and so *Bolkiah*-type[52] relief could be granted against its ex-employee.

The CFA rejected the plaintiff's attempts to extend the nature of LPP in this way. Ribeiro PJ observed that solicitors could be (and were) prevented from acting for new clients under their duty of confidentiality towards their former client, not under LPP. The latter was designed to limit or prevent the disclosure of client-lawyer communications to third parties in situations in which such disclosure could be compelled, as under RHC Ord. 24. Ribeiro PJ remarked:

> No one is suggesting that [the first defendant] is entitled or can be compelled to divulge or use for [the second defendant's] benefit [the plaintiff's] privileged information to which he is privy.[53]

As a consequence, Ribeiro PJ was 'unable to accept' the argument that LPP could be used to obtain a *Bolkiah*-type restriction against the first defendant.

In an important passage, Lord Hoffmann NPJ, agreeing with Ribeiro PJ, stressed the differences between privilege and confidentiality:

> LPP is a privilege, that is to say, a legal right, by way of exception to some general obligation to answer questions or provide documents, to withhold

---

[51] (2009) 12 HKCFAR 114.

[52] *Prince Jefri Bolkiah* v. *KPMG* [1999] 2 AC 222 (HL). In brief, the court would prevent a solicitor from acting for a new client unless it was satisfied there was no risk of misuse or disclosure of a former client's confidential information, whether deliberate or otherwise, to the new client.

[53] *PCCW*, [37].

information falling within a particular category, such as information tending to incriminate or communications for the purpose of obtaining legal advice. The question of privilege arises only when information is sought under compulsory powers. Confidentiality, on the other hand, gives rise to a right to prevent someone else from using or divulging information. The right is not confined, like privilege, to particular categories of information but applies to all information in which confidentiality can subsist (i.e. which is not in the public domain) and usually depends upon the information having been communicated in confidence: see *Coco* v. *AN Clark (Engineers) Ltd* [1968] FSR 415. Information may be both privileged and subject to rights of confidentiality, but the rights are not the same.[54]

The *Bolkiah* principle was a part of the law of confidence, not privilege, and provided 'a special remedy against solicitors'.[55] It was not possible, in His Lordship's view, to 'transfer features of the law of privilege into the law of confidence'.[56]

In *Akai Holdings Ltd (In Compulsory Liquidation)* v. *Ernst & Young,*[57] the CFA again considered the nature of privilege. Akai, which was incorporated in Bermuda and listed on the Hong Kong stock exchange, was wound up in August 2000. Its liquidators faced 'a massive insolvency [involving] the apparent disappearance of substantial assets in a relatively short time in suspicious circumstances'.[58] Akai claimed that, for three years following the liquidators' appointment, its former auditors, Ernst & Young, refused to provide documents relating to their audits. Eventually, Akai sued Ernst & Young for considerable damages for negligence in respect of the audits for the years ending 31 January 1997, 1998, and 1999.

Akai's writ was issued on 24 May 2004, and both it and the Points of Claim were served on 21 November 2005. In the interim, the liquidators investigated what claims could be brought against Ernst & Young and any other parties. These investigations were aided by applications to the Companies Court for the production of documents and for the examination of individuals under section 221 of the Companies Ordinance.[59] Ernst & Young sought specific discovery under RHC

---

[54] *Ibid.,* [59].   [55] *Ibid.,* [61].   [56] *Ibid.*

[57] (2009) 12 HKCFAR 649.

[58] In the words of Lord Millett NPJ in *Joint & Several Liquidators of Kong Wah Holdings Ltd* v. *Grande Holdings Ltd* (2006) 9 HKCFAR 766, 776F-G.

[59] Section 221(1)–(3) reads: '(1) The court may, at any time after the appointment of a provisional liquidator or the making of a winding-up order, summon before it any officer of the company or person known or suspected to have in his possession any property

Ord. 24 r.7 of the records of the various interviews conducted pursuant to section 221 and of any other documents produced by the interviewees.

Akai asserted that these section 221 documents were covered by both categories of LPP. Ernst & Young argued that the section 221 process was an 'inquisitorial' one and that, at the relevant time, no litigation was 'in reasonable prospect'. Hence, litigation privilege did not attach. Ernst & Young also argued that, under the English Court of Appeal's approach in *Three Rivers (No.5)*,[60] the documents were not protected by legal advice privilege because they were not communications between Akai and its legal advisers. In the Companies Court, Kwan J dismissed Akai's claim for legal advice privilege, basing her decision on *Three Rivers (No.5)*, and also agreed with Ernst & Young's arguments on litigation privilege. The Court of Appeal, oddly, made no comment on legal advice privilege and followed Kwan J's view on litigation privilege.

In the CFA, Bokhary PJ spent much of his judgment reviewing the parties' arguments and the lower court's findings on LPP. Ultimately, however, he found as a matter of fact that the liquidators used the section 221 process for the dominant purpose of obtaining the records and other documents so that these could be given to Akai's legal advisers, who would in turn provide legal advice on the anticipated litigation against Ernst & Young. Bokhary PJ went so far as to say: 'Indeed, there was, in my view, no evidence that any other purpose could have been the dominant one'.[61] Accordingly, the CFA reversed the concurrent findings of the CFI and

of the company or supposed to be indebted to the company, or any person whom the court deems capable of giving information concerning the promotion, formation, trade, dealings, affairs, or property of the company. (2) The court may examine him on oath concerning the matters aforesaid, either by word of mouth or on written interrogatories, and may reduce his answers to writing and require him to sign them. (3) The court may require him to produce any books and papers in his custody or power relating to the company, but, where be claims any lien on books or papers produced by him, the production shall be without prejudice to that lien, and the court shall have jurisdiction in the winding up to determine all questions relating to that lien.'

[60] The plaintiffs in *Three Rivers* brought two successive applications for the disclosure of documents. The first Court of Appeal decision is reported as *Three Rivers District Council v. Governor and Company of the Bank of England (No 5)* [2003] QB 1556 (Eng CA) and the second as *Three Rivers District Council v. Governor and Company of the Bank of England (No 6)* [2004] QB 916 (Eng CA). The House of Lords' decision followed *Three Rivers (No. 6)* and is reported as *Three Rivers District Council v. Governor and Company of the Bank of England (No 6)*. [2005] 1 AC 610 (HL).

[61] *Akai*, [100].

Court of Appeal. As a consequence, there was 'no need to decide the issue of legal advice privilege'. This 'non-decision' is unfortunate because it leaves Kwan J's reliance on *Three Rivers (No.5)* intact despite the reasoning in it and the subsequent Court of Appeal decision in *Three Rivers (No.6)* being disparaged as rendering the law on LPP 'as unsatisfactory as is possible to imagine'.[62] This criticism was noted by Bokhary PJ in his judgment, albeit he neglected to act upon it.

Witnesses and experts

In *Nina Kung* v. *Wang Din Shin*,[63] the father and wife of a businessman, who was kidnapped in April 1990 and never seen again, contested the validity of two separate wills purportedly made by him. The father claimed probate of a will dated 15 March 1968 (the '1968 Will') under which he was the sole beneficiary. The wife counterclaimed for probate of a Chinese will dated 12 March 1990, under which she was the sole beneficiary (the '1990 Will'). The father alleged that the 1990 Will was a forgery and, at trial, this argument was upheld. The Court of Appeal subsequently dismissed the wife's appeal.

The CFA allowed the wife's appeal and ordered that the 1990 Will be admitted to probate. Ribeiro PJ stated in his judgment that someone who propounded a will had to prove, on the balance of probabilities, that it was the deceased's will. In particular, he had to demonstrate that (1) there was due execution, (2) the deceased was of testamentary capacity, and (3) the deceased had known and approved of the will's contents. For Chinese wills, due execution was proved by showing merely that the deceased had signed the will.

Ribeiro PJ added that someone who disputed the validity of a will bore the evidential burden of putting the relevant ground of challenge in issue. Moreover, the court had to bear in mind the 'seriousness of the misconduct' that was alleged in such circumstances and that it carried 'an inherent degree of improbability'. In this case, the court had been asked to find that there had been forgery as an inference on the basis of circumstantial evidence. As in *Ming Shiu Chung*, it was stressed that

[62] See Charles Hollander, *Documentary Evidence*, 9th edn. (London: Sweet & Maxwell, 2006) [13–10] and [13–12]. Also see A. Zuckerman, 'A Colossal Wreck – the BCCI/Three Rivers Litigation' (2006) CJQ 287 for a history of the litigation.

[63] (2005) 8 HKCFAR 387.

any such inference must be properly grounded in the primary facts. Lord Scott NPJ reiterated Ribeiro PJ's comments on the evidential burden of proving the allegations of forgery and conspiracy. The lower courts had applied the wrong burden of proof when they required the wife to 'dispel suspicious circumstances' about the 1990 Will.

Finally, Chan PJ observed that the handwriting expert's evidence was not the 'only evidence' and went on to add:

> If, having considered all the evidence, the court is satisfied to the requisite standard of proof that [a lay witness] was telling the truth, then notwithstanding the handwriting evidence to the contrary, the court can still hold that the . . . documents are genuine. There are decided cases in which despite clear evidence from experts to the effect that the handwriting in question was forged, the court refused to accept it but favoured other pieces of direct evidence.[64]

Trial

The substantive issues in *Albert Cheng* v. *Tse Wai Chun Paul*[65] were concerned with defamation and need not be addressed here. The case is of interest, however, in that it concerns the use of written directions to the jury. This point is, of course, of greater importance in criminal proceedings but, nevertheless, it arose here in a civil case, and the Chief Justice's comments on the same were intended to 'assist trial judges' in both. It should, however, be noted that 'civil' jury trials are very rare in Hong Kong.

In this case, the judge had provided the jury with a 10-page 'handout' that consisted of notes on the law and the applicable burden of proof. The judge elaborated on its contents when he gave his verbal summing up. Not only had counsel not been consulted about the handout, but they also did not even know of its existence until it was given to the jury.

Whilst the Chief Justice did not object to such handouts being provided to juries as part of the summing up, they should 'normally be given to counsel for their consideration a reasonable time before they begin their closing speeches'.[66] This would give counsel the opportunity to make submissions to the judge on their contents (although it was up to the judge how he chose to deal with those submissions), and this would also

---

[64] *Ibid.*, [12].   [65] (2000) 3 HKCFAR 339.   [66] *Ibid.*, 423.

inform counsel 'how the judge proposes to approach the matters dealt with in the note in the summing up so that they can take this into account when delivering their closing addresses'.[67]

Case management

Perhaps the most significant changes introduced by the CJR were the introduction of the 'underlying objectives' in RHC Ord. 1A and the promotion of English CPR-style 'active case management' in RHC Ord. 1B. In addition, augmenting these changes, the summons for directions process in RHC Ord. 25 was replaced with case management directions and conferences similar to those in the English CPR.

It is intriguing, given the focus on case management in the CJR, that there is no CFA jurisprudence directly on the subject except, perhaps, for *Ng Yat Chi* v. *Max Share Ltd & Anor*,[68] which concerned the courts' inherent power to make orders restraining vexatious litigants. It was argued in this case that such powers were inconsistent with the constitutional guarantee of access to the courts under Article 35 of the Basic Law. This argument was rejected by the CFA with the Chief Justice remarking that 'it would be absurd to suggest that the right of access involved a right to abuse the court's process'.[69] It was held that the courts have inherent power to prevent vexatious litigants from abusing process by (1) making a *Grepe* v. *Loam* order[70] by which a vexatious litigant is required to obtain leave to issue any fresh application in an ongoing current action or (2) making an 'extended' *Grepe* v. *Loam* order by which leave of the court is necessary for a litigant to commence any fresh proceedings to re-litigate issues that have already concluded.

Following this decision, the Chief Justice issued Practice Direction 11.3 on the exercise of these inherent powers. The Practice Direction, which was amended when RHC Ord.32A – Vexatious Litigants came into force in April 2009, states that it is concerned with the courts' inherent power at common law, whilst their statutory power to control vexatious proceedings is under sections 27 and 27A of the High Court Ordinance and governed by both those provisions and RHC Ord. 32A itself. In fact, in light of the introduction of RHC Ord. 32A, it

---

[67] *Ibid.*   [68] (2005) 8 HKCFAR 1.   [69] *Ibid.*, [44].
[70] *Grepe* v. *Loam* [1887] Ch 168 (Eng Ch).

may well be that little use will be made in the future of the inherent powers.

Settlement and alternative dispute resolution

RHC Ord. 1A includes the underlying objective that the courts should 'facilitate the settlement of disputes'.[71] 'Facilitating settlement' is commonly understood to mean the use of alternative dispute resolution (ADR), of which the most common form is mediation. Indeed, under Ord. 1A r.4(2)(e), the court's active case management includes 'encouraging the parties to use an alternative dispute resolution procedure if the Court considers that appropriate, and facilitating the use of such a procedure', and Ord. 1A r.4(2)(f) adds 'helping the parties to settle the whole or part of the case'. These two provisions match those of the English CPR 1.4(2)(e) and (f) word for word. The post-CJR Practice Direction 5.2 on case management adds that the court will 'encourage parties to compromise their disputes',[72] and Practice Direction 31 on mediation contains detailed guidelines on, unsurprisingly, mediation. Finally, it is important to appreciate that, under RHC Ord. 62 r. 5(1)(aa), the court may impose cost sanctions if a party refuses to mediate.

As with case management, it is intriguing that there have been no significant CFA decisions on settlement or ADR in the past few years.[73] One of the few reported decisions in the Hong Kong courts on mediation, *Hyundai Engineering & Construction Co. Ltd* v. *Vigour Ltd*,[74] saw the Hong Kong Court of Appeal negatively distinguish the English Commercial Court's decision in *Cable & Wireless plc* v. *IBM United Kingdom Ltd*[75] and hold that a dispute resolution clause that stated 'failing an ultimate agreement [after negotiations] then both parties shall agree and submit to Third Party Mediation procedure' was unenforceable. Leave to appeal this decision was refused by the CFA. Subsequent decisions in the lower courts, following the enthusiastic endorsement of mediation in the CJR

---

[71] RHC, Ord. 1A r. 1(e).   [72] Practice Direction 5.2, [3].

[73] With the possible exception of *Nam Tai Electronics, Inc.* v. *Pricewaterhouse Coopers* referred to later and *Ming An Insurance Co. (HK) Ltd* v. *Ritz-Carlton Ltd* (No 2) (2009) 12 HKCFAR 745, which held that whilst *Calderbank* offers could not be considered when deciding on costs where a party could have protected its position by a payment into court (or sanctioned payment since April 2009), the same principle would not prevent consideration of open offers.

[74] [2005] 3 HKLRD 723 (CA).   [75] [2002] 2 All ER 1041 (Eng Comm Ct).

and by the judiciary, would suggest that such an approach is unlikely to be followed in the future.[76]

Costs

The high cost of litigation is commonly regarded as one of the greatest obstacles to widespread access to justice. Indeed, the terms of reference of the CJR Working Party were:

> To review the civil rules and procedures of the High Court and to recommend changes thereto with a view to ensuring and improving access to justice at reasonable cost and speed.[77]

Whilst the general principle that costs should 'follow the event' has been left untouched by the CJR, it is no longer accorded dominant status. Ord. 62, r.5(1) now states that, when awarding costs, the court 'shall' take into account a variety of factors, including the underlying objectives, the conduct of all the parties, and any offers of settlement (unless, in the case of such offers, the party could have made a sanctioned offer or payment under RHC Ord. 22 instead).[78]

As under the CPR, the court may make a summary assessment of the costs of interlocutory applications if it considers it appropriate to do so.[79] The 'new' RHC also enables the court to make a costs order against a non-party if it is satisfied that this is in the interests of justice. Finally, the wasted costs regime now covers barristers as well as solicitors.

Unlike case management and ADR, costs rulings have featured in a number of CFA decisions in recent years. Some of the more significant examples will now be examined.

Costs follow the event

In *Commissioner of Inland Revenue* v. *Hit Finance Ltd*,[80] the CFA dealt with appeals and cross-appeals related to the tax assessments of Hit Finance Ltd. The Commissioner was successful despite having had some of her arguments rejected by the CFA. As Bokhary PJ observed, however,

---

[76] See *Golden Eagle International (Group) Ltd* v. *GR Investment Holdings Ltd* [2010] 3 HKLRD 273 (CFI).
[77] *CJR Interim Report*, note 6 above, 1 [1].
[78] Sanctioned offers and payments are dealt with by RHC, Ord. 22, which is based on CPR Pt. 36.
[79] RHC, Ord. 62 r.9A.   [80] (2007) 10 HKCFAR 717.

'[T]here is nothing exceptional about a case being won on only some of the winner's points'.[81] Moreover, whereas there is a discretion to 'deprive a successful party of the whole or part of his costs because he had caused a significant increase in the length or costs of the proceedings by raising issues on which he did not succeed', the CFA did not consider it appropriate to deprive the Commissioner of any of her costs in this case.[82]

It would be incorrect, however, to assume that the CFA always takes a zero-sum approach to the question of costs. For example, in *Tripole Trading Ltd* v. *Prosperfield Ventures Ltd*,[83] the CFA made an order nisi that the trial judge's award of costs to the plaintiffs should stand but that all costs incurred in the proceedings after the date of the trial judge's judgment should be awarded to the defendants. The defendants subsequently sought to vary the order nisi in respect of the costs up to judgment and asked for all or most of those costs. The defendants relied on *Elpe International (Far East) Ltd* v. *Hewlett Packard Hong Kong Ltd*,[84] in which it was held that courts dealing with costs should begin by looking at the realities and asking themselves, 'Who really won?'.

Bokhary PJ stated: 'There is a problem with the defendants' approach. The costs now in question are those at first instance.'[85] The defendants were looking at the overall result of the proceedings, whilst Bokhary PJ observed, 'the costs now in question pertain to the part of the proceedings in which the plaintiffs won'.[86] Consequently, the plaintiffs would have their costs up to the trial judge's judgment, and the defendants would have theirs thereafter.

In *Nam Tai Electronics, Inc.* v. *PricewaterhouseCoopers*,[87] the defendant made a payment into court (under the pre-CJR version of RHC Ord. 22) before trial but after the plaintiff had indicated that it was not alleging any pecuniary loss for an alleged breach of confidence. The payment into court was not accepted by the plaintiff, and the matter proceeded to trial before Waung J, who found in favour of the defendant. The plaintiff appealed to the Court of Appeal, seeking aggravated or exemplary damages for defamation and breach of confidence. The defendant then wrote to the plaintiff on a 'without prejudice save as to costs' basis, indicating that

---

[81] *Ibid.*, [6].
[82] The CFA came to similar decisions in *Kung Ming Tak Tong Co. Ltd* v. *Park Solid Enterprises Ltd* (2008) 11 HKCFAR 403 and *China Field Ltd* v. *Appeal Tribunal (Buildings)* (2009) 12 HKCFAR 342.
[83] (2006) 9 HKCFAR 172.   [84] [1993] HKLY 467 (CA).
[85] *Tripole Trading Ltd*, [5].   [86] *Ibid.*
[87] Unreported, FACV1/2007, 7 April 2008, CFA, judgment on costs in (2008) 11 HKCFAR 62.

the payment into court remained 'available'. The plaintiff's appeal failed although it was given leave to appeal to the CFA in respect of the breach of confidence claim.

The plaintiff succeeded in the breach of confidence claim before the CFA and, despite the payment into court and the award of merely nominal damages, it sought all the costs of the appeal and asked that each party bear its own costs in the CFI and the Court of Appeal. The defendant contested that the plaintiff had always, despite assertions to the contrary, sought aggravated or exemplary damages and, accordingly, that the proper order was for the defendant to have all the costs in the CFA and below. Alternatively, the defendant sought all its costs from the date of the payment into court, with the plaintiff bearing two-thirds of its own costs up to that date. The CFA's sympathies lay with the defendant, and it was ordered to pay only one-third of the plaintiff's costs up to the date of the payment into court with the plaintiff paying the whole of the defendant's costs incurred thereafter.

Indemnity costs and wasted costs

Indemnity costs orders are often regarded as a way of penalizing parties who have conducted litigation in an improper manner.[88] In *Town Planning Board* v. *Society For The Protection Of The Harbour Ltd*,[89] the Chief Justice discussed the basis upon which indemnity costs would be awarded. He stressed that indemnity costs would not only be ordered 'where a case has been brought with an ulterior motive or for an improper purpose or where there is some deception or underhand conduct on the part of the losing party'.[90] Indeed, it was undesirable to attempt to 'define the circumstances in which orders for indemnity costs are to be made'. The Town Planning Board was wrong when it argued that that the attributes of the parties and the character of the proceedings were irrelevant to such an award. Accordingly, Chu J's award of indemnity costs to the Society in the CFI, which took into account the public importance of the case (i.e. the protection of Victoria Harbour) and the Society's limited finances, was justified.[91]

---

[88] See RHC, Ord. 62 r.28(4A). On taxation on the indemnity basis, all costs are allowed unless they are of an unreasonable amount or have been unreasonably incurred. Any doubts on these two points must be resolved in favour of the receiving party.

[89] (2004) 7 HKCFAR 1.　　[90] *Ibid.*, [16].

[91] In *Donald Koo Hoi Yan* v. *Kao Lee & Yip* (2009) 12 HKCFAR 904, the CFA reiterated that indemnity costs orders were a matter of judicial discretion involving 'the evaluation of all the relevant circumstances'.

Wasted costs are costs incurred by a party as a result of 'an improper or unreasonable act or omission' or 'any undue delay or other misconduct or default by a legal representative'.[92] In *Ma So So* v. *Chin Yuk Lun*,[93] a vendor agreed to sell a flat to the purchaser, which was represented by the appellant solicitor. The purchaser insisted upon formal completion but wrongfully refused to produce a cashier order for inspection by the vendor at completion. As a consequence, the purchaser sued for the return of the deposit, and the vendor counterclaimed for damages for breach of contract. The appellant solicitor acted for the purchaser at the start of the claim but came off the court record two months later. The purchaser's claim was ultimately dismissed, and judgment was awarded in favour of the vendor. The vendor was, however, unable to recover its damages from the purchaser and instead sought a wasted costs order under RHC Ord. 62 r.8[94] against the solicitor.

Ribeiro PJ explained that the required 'causal link between the solicitor's conduct and the incurring of the wasted costs in question' was the 'abuse of bringing the Writ Action on a basis known to be false'.[95] It was stressed that the solicitor, being an officer of the court, should not have assisted in a claim that she knew was both false and had no chance of success. Although the solicitor argued that she should not be responsible for costs incurred after she ceased to act, Ribeiro PJ countered:

> The fact that the Appellant only had charge of the proceedings for about two months does not mean that the wasted costs order must be limited to the costs incurred during that period. The causal potency of knowingly commencing the false claim was not exhausted at the end of that period.[96]

Hence, she was liable for all the costs of all aspects of the litigation. It is worth noting that Practice Direction 14.5, 'Application for Wasted Costs Order', makes it clear that the general principles laid down in *Ma So So* still apply despite the reforms to the wasted costs regime in the CJR.[97]

---

[92] High Court Ordinance, s. 52A(6).   [93] (2004) 7 HKCFAR 300.

[94] By RHC, Ord. 62 r.8(1), the court may make a wasted costs order against a legal representative, only if he, whether personally or through his employee or agent, has caused a party to incur wasted costs (as defined in section 52A(6) of the High Court Ordinance), and it is just in all the circumstances to order him to compensate the party for the whole or part of those costs.

[95] *Ma So So*, [89].   [96] *Ibid.*

[97] Practice Direction 14.5 [3] reads: 'Although *Ma So So* involved a wasted costs order against a solicitor, the introduction of s. 52A(4) to (7) to the High Court Ordinance means that wasted costs orders may now be made against a counsel or solicitor conducting litigation on behalf of a party. The general principles in *Ma So So* are likely to still be relevant'.

Contingency fees

One issue that has not been changed as a consequence of the CJR is the status of contingency (or conditional) fees. Whereas conditional fee agreements are permitted in England, they are still prohibited in Hong Kong. In *Siegfried Adalbert Unruh* v. *Hans-Joerg Seeberger and Anor*,[98] the CFA addressed the law of maintenance and champerty that underpins the approach to contingency fees. Four points were stressed: (1) an agreement to share the spoils of litigation encourages the perversion of justice; (2) it was necessary, however, to examine 'the totality of the facts' to determine whether justice was being undermined; (3) such an examination should take account of 'modern public policies', including ensuring 'access to justice'; and (4) maintenance and champerty should not be relied upon too readily because other public policies may be used to prevent misconduct. Thus, the Hong Kong courts will not be inflexible, but it is unlikely that the English approach will be adopted wholesale.[99]

Appeals

The rules governing the appeals procedure were left relatively untouched by the CJR compared with other areas such as case management. Nevertheless, RHC Ord. 59 r.2A introduced a fresh procedure on seeking leave to appeal to the Court of Appeal. The Court of Appeal now has the power to determine the application based on written submissions without the need for a separate oral hearing.

As indicated at the start of this chapter, approximately a quarter of the CFA cases ostensibly concerning civil procedure in the period 1997 to 2010 actually dealt with the CFA's own rules and principles relating, for example, to the issue of admitting new evidence on appeal. These are dealt with in Chapter 7 of this volume and are not addressed here.

---

[98] (2007) 10 HKCFAR 31.

[99] The Law Reform Commission (LRC) of Hong Kong published a report on conditional fees in July 2007 in which it was recommended that 'notwithstanding that conditional fees can enhance access to justice to a significant proportion of the community who are currently neither eligible for legal aid nor able to fund litigation themselves, conditions at this time are not appropriate for the introduction of conditional fees'. See the LRC's website at www.hkreform.gov.hk/en/publications/rconditional.htm.

Conclusion

There have been relatively few cases in the CFA that have dealt with issues of 'pure' civil procedure. It could be argued that this shows that the 'system' is working in that procedural disputes are dealt with at a lower level with less cost and delay being incurred as a consequence. It can be seen that on those occasions when a pure procedural matter has reached the CFA, the eventual decision has usually been a pragmatic one based on the facts of the case before it. On only a few occasions, such as in *Poon*, has the CFA produced a thought-provoking judgment. By contrast, as in *Akai*, on other occasions, the CFA has not taken the opportunity to clarify an area of the law. As a consequence, it is difficult to identify or analyse any 'philosophy' or 'policy' towards civil procedure other than, perhaps, the desire to 'do justice'.

By contrast, the CJR is pregnant with judicial philosophy. The introduction of the underlying objectives (albeit they are not as prescriptive as the CPR's 'overriding objective'), active case management, sanctioned offers and payments, and – most of all – an emphasis on ADR reflect a desire to control and even eliminate what is perceived to be a 'litigation culture'. It remains to be seen, however, if the CJR will result in more or fewer cases reaching the CFA and – when they do – whether the CFA takes a more 'creative' approach in the future.

PART V

Perspectives from beyond Hong Kong

22

Impact of jurisprudence beyond Hong Kong

P. Y. LO

Chief Justice Andrew Li emphasized time and again the role of comparative jurisprudence to the courts of the Hong Kong Special Administrative Region of the People's Republic of China (HKSAR). Hong Kong, being the only common law jurisdiction in the People's Republic of China (PRC), is obliged to consider the approaches that have been adopted by courts in other jurisdictions in similar situations. This was underlined in Article 84 of the Basic Law (BL),[1] and consideration of judgments of courts outside Hong Kong was, according to Li CJ, 'so much a part of one's everyday work'.[2]

This chapter takes the reverse view of the telescope and attempts to present how judgments of the Court of Final Appeal (CFA) have been making an impact in jurisdictions outside Hong Kong. As Li CJ remarked, '[There] is no universal common law and no single common law system', and there is no uniform pattern in the development of the common law by courts of different jurisdictions.[3] The contribution of the CFA's jurisprudence to the diverse and 'flourishing market place of ideas for dealing with the challenging legal issues of our times'[4] will be considered

---

[1] Article 84 of the BL provides that the HKSAR courts 'may refer to precedents of other common law jurisdictions'. The HKSAR courts have taken this provision permissively and have considered judgments from civilian jurisdictions such as the German Bundesverfassungsgericht and the Italian Corte Suprema di Cassazione and of supranational courts such as the European Court of Human Rights, the Court of Justice of the European Communities, and the Inter-American Court of Human Rights.

[2] See Andrew Li, 'CJ's Speech at Conference on Effective Judicial Review: A Cornerstone of Good Governance', 10 December 2008, accessible at www.info.gov.hk/gia/general/200812/10/P200812100125.htm.

[3] See Andrew Li, 'CJ's Speech at Opening Ceremony of the 16th Commonwealth Law Conference in Hong Kong', 6 April 2009, accessible at www.info.gov.hk/gia/general/200904/06/P200904060130.htm.

[4] *Ibid.*

both in terms of the ways in which contributions are made and the substance and extent of the contribution.[5] It is found that the multiple 'human' links that the CFA and the local legal community have with the major common law jurisdictions and Mainland China are vital to enable and enhance the impact of CFA jurisprudence beyond Hong Kong.

The overview

Judgments of the CFA are variously published in law reports and cited and discussed by courts and law reform commissions in common law-based legal systems, as well as by practitioners and law scholars in texts and journals published abroad and in Mainland China. Notwithstanding the cessation of the *Law Reports of the Commonwealth* to publish Hong Kong judgments from 1997 onwards, selected CFA judgments continue to be reported in thematic law reports published in England[6] and Interights' *Commonwealth Human Rights Law Digest*.

Courts and tribunals of the common law jurisdictions far and wide, from England and Wales, Scotland, Australia, Canada, and New Zealand to Malaysia, Singapore, the Eastern Caribbean territories, the Cayman Islands, Trinidad and Tobago, the Fiji Islands, and Tonga, have cited CFA judgments. These courts have included the Privy Council (PC), the House of Lords, the Supreme Court of the United Kingdom, the High Court of Australia, the Supreme Court of Canada, the Supreme Court of New Zealand, and the Singapore Court of Appeal. In terms of the quantity of citations up to the end of 2010, the following jurisdictions stand out: courts sitting in the United Kingdom (including the PC), 36 occasions;[7] the Australian courts (at both Commonwealth and State

---

[5] In preparing this chapter, reference was made to electronic resources, particularly the legal information institutes covering the 'common law world' and the Chinese journal database; the bibliographies of BL and human rights-related materials compiled under the auspices of the Centre for Comparative and Public Law, the University of Hong Kong; and the libraries of the High Court and The University of Hong Kong. Citations of CFA jurisprudence in judgments of overseas jurisdictions have generally been tracked up to the end of 2010.

[6] These thematic law reports include the *Bankruptcy and Personal Insolvency Reports, Butterworths Company Law Cases, Butterworths Human Rights Cases, Entertainment and Media Law Reports, Lloyd's Law Reports,* and *Tax Cases.*

[7] The breakdown of the citations is as follows: PC, 3; Supreme Court, 1; House of Lords, 3; English Court of Appeal, 8; Court of Session, Scotland, 1; Court of Appeal, Northern Ireland, 1; and High Court, England and Wales, 19.

levels), 18 occasions;[8] the New Zealand courts, 7 occasions;[9] and the Singaporean courts, 11 occasions.[10]

Practitioners' texts such as *Clerk & Lindsell on Torts, Gatley on Libel and Slander, Jackson & Powell on Professional Liability, Arlidge, Eady and Smith on Contempt of Court, Dicey, Morris and Collins on Conflicts of Laws, Palmer's Company Law, De Smith's Judicial Review, Clayton and Tomlinson on the Law of Human Rights*, and *Lester, Pannick and Herberg on Human Rights Law and Practice* have included CFA judgments. The English and Scottish Law Commissions have cited them.[11]

Journal articles published outside Hong Kong citing CFA jurisprudence are wide ranging. One finds speeches and talks on CFA jurisprudence by Hong Kong judges, including the CFA's non-permanent judges (NPJs);[12] case notes and analyses by Hong Kong law scholars;[13] overseas

---

[8] The breakdown of the citations is as follows: High Court of Australia, 2; Federal Court of Australia (including the Full Court), 7; New South Wales, 2; Victoria, 5; Queensland, 1; and West Australia, 2.

[9] The breakdown of the citations is as follows: Supreme Court, 3; Court of Appeal, 1; and High Court, 3.

[10] The breakdown of the citations is as follows: Court of Appeal, 8 and High Court, 3.

[11] See Law Commission of England and Wales, *Land Registration for the Twenty-first Century: A Conveyancing Revolution* (2001); Law Commission of England and Wales, *In the Public Interest: Publication of Local Authority Inquiry Reports* (2004); and Scottish Law Commission, *Report on Double Jeopardy* No 218 (2009).

[12] See Anthony Mason, 'The Hong Kong Court of Final Appeal' (2001) 2 *Melbourne Journal of International Law* 216; Anthony Mason, 'The Rule of Law in the Shadow of the Giant: The Hong Kong Experience' (2011) 33 *Sydney Law Review* 623; Robin Cooke, 'Human Rights in Hong Kong' (1999) 29 *Victoria University of Wellington Law Review* 45; Frank Stock, 'Human Rights Litigation in the Hong Kong Special Administrative Region' (2001) 1 *Oxford University Commonwealth Law Journal* 147; and Kemal Bokhary, 'The Rule of Law in Hong Kong Fifteen Years after the Handover' (2013) 51 *Columbia Journal of Transnational Law* 287.

[13] See e.g. Chengguang Wang and Guobin Zhu, 'A Tale of Two Legal Systems: The Interaction of Common Law and Civil Law in Hong Kong' (1999) (4) *Revue Internationale de Droit Comparé* 917 (on the right of abode cases); Feng Lin, 'The Constitutional Crisis in Hong Kong: Is it over?' (2000) 9 *Pacific Rim Law and Policy Journal* 291; Benny Tai and Kevin Yam, 'The advent of substantive legitimate expectations in Hong Kong: two competing visions' [2002] PL 688 (on *Ng Siu Tung* v. *Director of Immigration* (2002) 5 HKCFAR 1); Benny Tai, 'Hong Kong/China' (2003) 1 *International Journal of Constitutional Law* 147 (on the right of abode cases); Lusina Ho, 'Deposit: The Importance of Being (an) Earnest' (2003) 119 LQR 34 (on *Polyset Ltd* v. *Panhandat Ltd* (2002) 5 HKCFAR 234); Jill Cottrell, 'Fair Comment, Judges and Politics in Hong Kong' (2003) 27 *Melbourne University Law Review* 33 (on *Cheng* v. *Tse Wai Chun* (2000) 3 HKCFAR 339); Andrew Halkyard, 'Common Law and Tax Avoidance: Back to the Future?' (2004) 14 *Revenue Law Journal* 19 (on *Collector of Stamp Revenue* v. *Arrowtown Assets Ltd* (2003) 6 HKC-FAR 517); Albert Chen, 'Constitutional Adjudication in Post-1997 Hong Kong' (2006)

practitioners and scholars taking an interest in recent Hong Kong judicial developments;[14] Mainland scholars considering how CFA judgments and BL interpretations fit into 'one country, two systems';[15] and overseas students publishing dissertations and notes on Hong Kong's legal system.[16]

15 *Pacific Rim Law and Policy Journal* 627 (on constitutional adjudications up to 2006); Rebecca Lee and Lusina Ho, 'Disputes over Family Homes Owned Through Companies: Constructive Trust Or Promissory Estoppel' (2009) 125 LQR 25; Kelvin Low, 'Family Property and Interposed Companies' [2009] 73 *Conv* 524 (both on *Luo Xing Juan Angela* v. *Estate of Hui Shui See Willy, decd* (2009) 12 HKCFAR 1); Alex Lau and Angus Young, 'The 2008 Declaration of Independence by Hong Kong Courts and Anomalies in the Hong Kong Company Law' (2009) 32 *Company Lawyer* 189 (on *A Solicitor (24/07)* v. *Law Society of Hong Kong* (2008) 11 HKCFAR 117); Rebecca Lee, 'Restraining Ex-employees: Conflicting Policy Considerations and the Proper Scope of Bolkiah' (2010) 29 CJQ 155; Gary Meggitt, 'Privilege – a Hong Kong Perspective' (2011) 30 CJQ 429 (both on *PCCW-HKT Telephone Ltd* v. *Aitken* (2009) 12 HKCFAR 114); Kelvin Low, 'The Lost Modern Grant: Untwisting Tangled Tales in a Former Colony' (2011) 127 LQR 200 (on *China Field Ltd* v. *Appeal Tribunal (Buildings) (No 2)* (2009) 12 HKCFAR 342); Po-jen Yap, 'Negligence in Hong Kong: Turning Caparo on Its Head?' (2011) 127 LQR 358 (on *Luen Hing Fat Coating & Finishing Factory Ltd* v. *Waan Chuen Ming* (2011) 14 HKCFAR 4); Malcolm Merry, 'Adverse possession and the principle of encroachment' [2012] 76 *Conv* 333 (on *Secretary for Justice* v. *Chau Ka Chik Tso & Ors* [2013] 2 HKC 303); C. L. Lim, 'Absolute Immunity for Sovereign Debtors in Hong Kong' (2011) 127 LQR 495; C. L. Lim, 'Beijing's "Congo" Interpretation: Commercial Implications' (2012) 128 LQR 6; and Cora Chan, 'State immunity: reassessing the boundaries of judicial autonomy in Hong Kong' [2012] PL 601 (all on *Democratic Republic of the Congo & Ors* v. *FG Hemisphere Associates LLC* (2011) 14 HKCFAR 95, 395).

14 See e.g. Mark Elliott, 'The Hong Kong Immigrant Children Cases' (1999) 4 *Judicial Review* 182 (on the right of abode cases); Nicholas J. Mullany, 'Limitation and Latent Damage in Hong Kong' (2001) 117 LQR 20 (on *Bank of East Asia Ltd* v. *Tsien Wui Marble Factory Ltd* (1999) 2 HKCFAR 349); Arad Reisberg and D. D. Prentice, 'Multiple Derivative Actions' (2009) 125 LQR 209 (on *Waddington Ltd* v. *Chan Chun Hoo Thomas* (2008) 11 HKCFAR 370); and Richard Nolan, 'When Principles Collide' (2009) 125 LQR 374 (on *PCCW-HKT Telephone Ltd* v. *Aitken* (2009) 12 HKCFAR 114).

15 The Mainland Chinese journals publishing papers on the interpretation of the BL are numerous and include *China Legal Science, The CASS Journal of Law, Fudan Journal (Social Sciences), Guangdong Social Sciences, Journal of Political Science and Law, The Jurist, Legal Science, Modern Law Science, The Rule of Law Forum, Rule of Law Research, Shandong Social Sciences,* and *Wuhan University International Law Review.* See also Yongping Xiao, 'Comments on the Judgment on the Right of Abode by Hong Kong CFA' (2000) 48 *American Journal of Comparative Law* 471.

16 See e.g. E. J. Barton, 'Pricing Judicial Independence: An Empirical Study of Post-1997 Court of Final Appeal Decisions in Hong Kong' (2002) 43 *Harvard International Law Journal* 361; T. Clarke, 'One Basic Law, Two Interpretation' (1999) 23 *Melbourne University Law Review* 773; M. L. Estanislao, 'Right of Final Adjudication in Hong Kong: Establishing Procedures of Constitutional Interpretation' (2000) 1 *Asian-Pacific Law and Policy Journal* 10; A. R. Fokstuen, 'The Right of Abode Cases: Hong Kong's Constitutional

The focused view

Of the dozens of CFA judgments cited and discussed in judgments, texts, and articles, several judgments or groups of judgments stand out for more detailed study. Their impact on the common law world are revealed and assessed below. Some jurisdictions, as the survey also reveals, tend to cite CFA judgments more frequently. The author will then draw from these studies the circumstances that may lead to such impact.

The most positive impact: Cheng *v.* Tse Wai Chun

The defamation case of *Cheng* v. *Tse Wai Chun*[17] is undoubtedly the CFA judgment that has had the most positive impact in the common law world. Lord Nicholls NPJ's main judgment, restating the defence of fair comment in defamation and how that defence may be defeated by proof of 'malice' by distinguishing that issue from the issue of the same name in the context of the defence of qualified privilege,[18] was picked up quickly in England and applied.[19] The judgment was also expeditiously reported in the *Entertainment and Media Law Reports.*[20] Soon enough the following edition of *Gatley on Libel and Slander* made it 'a fact that the leading authority on malice and fair comment in English law is now a decision of the Hong Kong Court of Final Appeal',[21] demonstrating that the former belief about the idea of 'malice' as 'incorrect'.[22] The editors of *Clerk &*

Crisis' (2003) 26 *Hastings International and Comparative Law Review* 265; K. Kam, 'The Judicial Independence of the Hong Kong Special Administrative Region v. The Sovereign Interests of China' (2002) 27 *Brooklyn Journal of International Law* 611; T. V. Lee, '*Après Moi Le Deluge?* Judicial Review in Hong Kong Since Britain Relinquished Sovereignty' (2001) 11 *Indiana International & Comparative Law Review* 319; T. Martin, 'Hong Kong Right of Abode: Ng Siu Tung & Others v. Director of Immigration – Constitutional and Human Rights at the Mercy of China' (2004) 5 *San Diego International Law Journal* 465; K. Olley, 'Introduction to Judicial Review in Hong Kong' (2003) 8 *Judicial Review* 109; and T. Schneider, 'David v. Goliath?: The Hong Kong Courts and China's National People's Congress Standing Committee' (2002) 20 *Berkeley Journal of International Law* 575.

[17] *Cheng* v. *Tse Wai Chun* (2000) 3 HKCFAR 339 (13 November 2000).

[18] Lord Nicholls had earlier on 28 October 1999 restated the defence of qualified privilege in defamation in his opinion in *Reynolds* v. *Times Newspaper Ltd* [2001] 2 AC 127 (HL). His Lordship indicated: '[T]he purposes for which the two defences exist are not the same'.

[19] *Sugar* v. *Associated Newspapers Ltd* (6 February 2001) (per Eady J) (referred to in *Branson* v. *Bower* [2002] QB 737 (15 June 2001) (per Eady J)).

[20] [2001] EMLR 31.

[21] *Gatley on Libel and Slander*, 10th edn. (London: Sweet and Maxwell, 2003) vii.

[22] *Gatley on Libel and Slander*, 11th edn. (London: Sweet and Maxwell, 2008) [12.25]. Lord Phillips, President of the UK Supreme Court, later wrote that this comment of the editors

Lindsell on Torts also endorsed the judgment as 'the modern authoritative statement of the law of fair comment'.[23] The UK Supreme Court examined the defence of fair comment in defamation some years later in 2010 and decided to endorse Lord Nicholls' formulation of the elements of the defence, subject only to simplification of the requirement concerning the factual basis the comment must have identified, and renamed it 'honest comment'.[24]

In the meantime, Lord Nicholls NPJ's judgment was well received beyond England. The PC, hearing a case from Trinidad and Tobago, expressed the common law position of the availability of the defence of honest comment by reference to the judgment before turning to the constitutional guarantee of free expression in that jurisdiction.[25] The High Court of Australia discussed the judgment together with other English authorities in relation to the Australian rule that the facts on which the supposed comment is alleged to be based must be sufficiently identified.[26] The Supreme Court of Canada accorded a similar treatment.[27] The Court of Appeal of the Supreme Court of Victoria agreed with the NPJ's summary of the elements of the defence.[28] The Singapore Court of Appeal agreed with the NPJ, indicating that his reasoning had 'much force'.[29] The New Zealand High Court discussed the judgment as part of the common law background without disapproval when approaching the construction of the statutory defence of honest belief.[30] The Eastern Caribbean Supreme Court, relying on the *EMLR* report of the case, cited it with

---

of *Gatley on Libel and Slander* 'is a remarkable tribute to the standing of the Court of Final Appeal of Hong Kong and, more particularly, of Lord Nicholls': *Spiller* v. *Joseph* [2010] UKSC 53, [2011] 1 AC 852, [68] (1 December 2010).

23   *Clerk & Lindsell on Torts*, 19th edn. (London: Sweet and Maxwell, 2006) [23–168].

24   *Spiller* v. *Joseph*, [105], where Lord Phillips rewrote the fourth proposition in *Cheng* v. *Tse Wai Chun*, 347G-I as 'Next, the comment must explicitly or implicitly indicate, at least in general terms, the facts on which it is based'.

25   *Panday* v. *Gordon* [2005] UKPC 36. The Board was presided by Lord Nicholls, who also delivered its opinion.

26   *Channel Seven Adelaide Pty Ltd* v. *Manock* [2007] HCA 60, 241 ALR 468. The Australian rule was that held in *Pervan* v. *North Queensland Newspaper Co Ltd* (1993) 178 CLR 309 (Aust HC).

27   See *WIC Radio* v. *Simpson* [2008] 2 SCR 420 (Canada SC), in which Le Bel J, having referred to the statement in *Gatley on Libel and Slander*, declined to adopt the British test stated in Lord Nicholls NPJ's judgment.

28   *Herald & Weekly Times Ltd* v. *Popovic* [2003] VSCA 161 (Victoria CA).

29   *Oei Hon Leong* v. *Ban Song Long David* [2005] 3 SLR 608 (Sing CA). See also *Hytech Builders Pte Ltd* v. *Goh Teng Poh Karen* [2008] SGHC 52 (Sing CA).

30   *Simunovich Fisheries Ltd* v. *Television New Zealand* [2005] 3 NZLR 134 (NZ HC), relating to the Defamation Act 1992, ss. 9, 10.

approval on three occasions.[31] The Chief Justice of Tonga likewise relied on the statement of the case in *Clerk and Lindsell on Torts*.[32]

As Jill Cottrell reported, Lord Nicholls' judgment was not received with universal praise in Hong Kong; some local politicians questioned the revamping of the law on defamation by a 'parachute judge' who had no idea or no real idea of what Hong Kong society was like.[33] Nevertheless, the judgment has by now become established as the definitive statement of the common law on the defence of fair comment in the parts of the British Commonwealth that follow or refer closely to the developments of English common law.

The dialogue: Shum Kwok Sher *v.* HKSAR *and* Sin Kam Wah *v.* HKSAR

The common law offence of misconduct in public office was the focus of a constitutional challenge in *Shum Kwok Sher* v. *HKSAR*,[34] in which it was argued that the offence violated the principle of legal certainty under the constitutional requirement of 'prescribed by law'. Giving the principal judgment in the case, Sir Anthony Mason NPJ reviewed the previous English and Australian authorities and stated the elements of the offence.[35]

The English Court of Appeal, in considering an Attorney General's reference, subsequently found Sir Anthony Mason NPJ's statement 'valuable' but questioned the first qualification that the misconduct must be both 'wilful' and 'intentional'. Pill LJ sought to explain why[36] and indicated the court was bound to apply the recent House of Lords judgment of *R* v. *G*,[37] which clarified the concept of recklessness in English criminal law.[38]

---

[31] They include *Elwardo Lynch* v. *Ralph Gonsalves* Civ App 18/2005 (18 September 2006), sitting as the Court of Appeal of St Vincent and the Grenadines; *Kenny D Anthony* v. *Vaughn Lewis* Claim No SLUHCV/2000/0411 (11 January 2006), sitting as the High Court of Justice of Saint Lucia; and *Abraham Mansoor (t/a Town House Furnishing)* v. *Grenville Radio Ltd* Suit No ANUHCA/2004/0408 (12 October 2007), sitting as the High Court of Justice of Antigua and Barbuda.

[32] *Edwards* v. *Senituli* [2009] TOSC 2 (Tonga SC).

[33] Jill Cottrell, 'Fair Comment, Judges and Politics in Hong Kong' (2003) 27 *Melbourne University Law Review* 33.

[34] *Shum Kwok Sher* v. *HKSAR* (2002) 5 HKCFAR 381.   [35] *Ibid.*, [84]–[87].

[36] *AG's Reference (No 3 of 2003)* [2005] QB 73, [45]–[46] (Eng CA).

[37] *R* v. *G* [2004] 1 AC 1034 (HL).

[38] The Court of Appeal summarized the elements of the offence to include 'wilfully neglects to perform his duty and/or wilfully misconducts himself'; see *AG's Reference (No 3 of 2003)*, [30] and [61].

When the CFA next considered the offence of misconduct in public office in *Sin Kam Wah* v. *HKSAR*,[39] Sir Anthony Mason NPJ took the opportunity to consider both *R* v. *G* and *AG's Reference (No 3 of 2003)*, especially with respect to the detailed treatment in those cases of the relationship between recklessness and wilful misconduct. The elements of the offence were reformulated so that the requisite misconduct had to be committed wilfully, by act or omission, meaning that the official 'either knew that his conduct was unlawful or wilfully disregarded the risk that his conduct was unlawful'.[40]

Later, the Supreme Court of Canada, in elucidating the elements of the statutory offence of breach of trust by a public officer, made reference to the English Court of Appeal's adoption of the second qualification Sir Anthony Mason NPJ made in *Shum Kwok Sher* that the misconduct must be 'serious misconduct'.[41] Chief Justice McLachlin stated approvingly: 'The questions posed by Sir Anthony Mason of the Court of Final Appeal of Hong Kong in *Shum Kwok Sher* provide a sound definition of the parameters of the inquiry into whether the conduct constitutes a marked departure from accepted standards'.[42]

More recently, the Court of Appeal of the Supreme Court of Victoria stated the elements of the common law offence of misconduct in public office in terms substantially similar to those Sir Anthony Mason NPJ set out in *Sin Kam Wah* v. *HKSAR* but with amendments seeking to 'draw further attention to the nature of the necessary nexus between the conduct and the office and further emphasize the necessary seriousness of the offence'.[43]

However, in the later case of *Chan Tak Ming* v. *HKSAR*, the CFA applied Sir Anthony Mason NPJ's re-formulation of the elements in *Sin Kam Wah*. Bokhary PJ, without mentioning the above developments abroad, indicating that personal benefit played no part in the elements of the

---

[39] *Sin Kam Wah* v. *HKSAR* (2005) 8 HKCFAR 192.   [40] *Ibid.*, [45]–[46].

[41] Indeed, the English Court of Appeal again applied Sir Anthony Mason NPJ's second qualification in *R* v. *Ahmati* [2006] EWCA Crim 1826 (Eng CA) in determining what was or was not 'serious misconduct' under the Prosecution of Offences Act 1985 section 19B for the purpose of making a costs order against a third party.

[42] *R* v. *Boulanger* [2006] 2 SCR 49, [53] (Canada SC). Both *Boulanger* and *Shum Kwok Sher* were cited in argument before the PC in *Lawrence* v. *Attorney General of Grenada* [2007] 1 WLR 1474 (PC).

[43] *R* v. *Quach* [2010] VSCA 106, 27 VR 310 (7 May 2010) (Victoria CA). Redlich JA, writing the principal judgment of the Court of Appeal, added: 'It will generally be desirable that the trial judge emphasize the notion that the conduct must be so far below acceptable standards as to amount to an abuse of the public's trust in the office holder'.

offence and that the question of whether the offence was serious must be considered, as Sir Anthony had stated, with 'regard to the responsibilities of the office and the office-holder, the importance of the public objects which they serve and the extent of the departure from those responsibilities'.[44] The CFA's dialogue with courts abroad continues.

The paradox of suspending a declaration of invalidity before the UK Supreme Court: Koo Sze Yiu v. Chief Executive of the HKSAR

Courts of the highest appellate level in the United Kingdom have cited approvingly of CFA judgments, which, as it happened, often involved an NPJ citing his own CFA judgment in his opinion in the House of Lords[45] and the PC.[46] Thus, it would not be surprising that soon after the UK Supreme Court came into operation, a CFA judgment would be cited and discussed. When the occasion arose, the CFA case cited was one in which a non-English NPJ participated.

In *HM Treasury* v. *Ahmed*,[47] the UK Supreme Court held that two orders made by the Treasury in implementing United Nations Security Council resolutions for the combat of international terrorism were *ultra vires* the United Nations Act 1946. The restrictions imposed on individuals under the orders had been imposed without authority and had no effect in law. The Supreme Court proposed to make orders declaring the Treasury orders *ultra vires* and quashing them.

---

[44] *Chan Tak Ming* v. *HKSAR* (2010) 13 HKCFAR 745, [26]–[27] (CFA).

[45] See *Chartbrook Ltd* v. *Persimmon Homes Ltd* [2009] 1 AC 1101 (HL), where Lord Hoffmann cited at [14], his remark in *Jumbo King Ltd* v. *Faithful Properties Ltd* (1999) 2 HKCFAR 279, 296 on the interpretation of contracts: 'But the overriding objective in construction is to give effect to what a reasonable person rather than a pedantic lawyer would have understood the parties to mean. Therefore, if in spite of linguistic problems the meaning is clear, it is that meaning which must prevail'. Admittedly, this remark was picked up much earlier by the English Court of Appeal in *Holding & Barnes Plc* v. *Hill House Hammond Ltd* [2002] 2 P&CR 11 and considered with other statements of Lord Hoffmann on the topic, including those before the House of Lords in *Investment Compensation Scheme* v. *West Bromwich Building Society* [1998] 1 WLR 896 (HL).

[46] See *Gamlestaden Fastigheter AB* v. *Baltic Partners Ltd* [2007] 4 All ER 164 (PC) (in which Lord Scott cited *Re Chime Corp Ltd* [2004] 7 HKCFAR 546, concerning an application for remedies in companies legislation on the ground of unfairly prejudicial conduct) and *Strachan* v. *The Gleaner Company* (2005) 1 WLR 3204 (PC) (in which Lord Scott cited *Hip Hing Timber Co. Ltd* v. *Tang Man Kit* [2004] 7 HKCFAR 212, concerning the validity of an order of an inappropriately constituted Court of Appeal).

[47] *HM Treasury* v. *Ahmed* [2010] UKSC 2, [2010] 2 WLR 378 (27 January 2010).

The Treasury applied for suspension of the operation of the Supreme Court's orders. Parties were in agreement that the court had the power to suspend. Treasury counsel referred to the CFA judgment of *Koo Sze Yiu* v. *Chief Executive of the HKSAR*,[48] in which Bokhary PJ held for a unanimous court that the CFA has power, concomitant to the power to make a declaration of unconstitutionality, to suspend the operation of the declaration, and considering the danger to be averted as of sufficient magnitude, suspended the declarations of unconstitutionality so as to postpone their coming into operation for the duration of six months to afford the executive authorities the opportunity of the enactment of corrective legislation.[49]

Treasury counsel accepted in submission the position stated in *Koo Sze Yiu* that there is no shield from legal liability for functioning pursuant to what has been declared to be *ultra vires* during the period of the suspension.[50] All that the Treasury sought in the application was the delaying of taking effect of the Supreme Court's orders, so that the effects of the judgment could be addressed either by introducing primary legislation for consideration by Parliament or for an order to be made under the European Communities Act 1972 to implement the parallel European measure in the United Kingdom, steps sought to be taken to ensure that the United Kingdom remains in compliance with its international obligations under the UN Charter.[51]

By a majority of six to one, the Supreme Court declined the application.[52] Writing for the majority,[53] Lord Phillips, the President, was of the view that:

---

[48] *Koo Sze Yiu* v. *Chief Executive of the HKSAR* (2006) 9 HKCFAR 441. It is not known how Treasury counsel came upon the case though the judgments handed down by the Supreme Court refer to the unreported citation of the case. The edited report in the *Weekly Law Reports* refers to the HKCFAR report of the case.

[49] *Ibid.*, [35] and [49]. Sir Anthony Mason NPJ gave a concurring judgment, preferring the formulation of postponing the making of a declaration of invalidity; see *ibid.*, [60]. For a discussion of this case, see P. Y. Lo, 'Levitating Unconstitutional Law' (2006) 36 *HKLJ* 433.

[50] Reference was probably made to *Koo Sze Yiu*, [50] in which Bokhary PJ indicated that: 'The Government can, during that period of suspension, function pursuant to what has been declared unconstitutional, doing so without acting contrary to any declaration in operation. But, despite such suspension, the Government is not shielded from legal liability for functioning pursuant to what has been declared unconstitutional'.

[51] *HM Treasury* v. *Ahmed (No 2)* [2010] UKSC 5, [2010] 2 WLR 378, [12] (4 February 2010).

[52] *Ibid.*

[53] The majority consisted of Lord Phillips (President), Lord Rodger, Lord Walker, Baroness Hale, Lord Brown, and Lord Mance.

The problem with a suspension in this case is, however, that the court's order, whenever it is made, will not alter the position in law. It will declare what that position is.... The effect of suspending the operation of the order of the court would be, or might be, to give the opposite impression. It would suggest that, during the period of suspension of the quashing orders, the provisions to be quashed would remain in force. Mr. Swift acknowledged that it might give this impression. Indeed, he made it plain that this was the object of seeking the suspension.... The ends sought by Mr. Swift might well be thought desirable, but I do not consider that they justify the means that he proposes. This court should not lend itself to a procedure that is designed to obfuscate the effect of its judgment.[54]

Lord Hope, the Deputy President, was the lone dissenter. Lord Hope indicated that the application before the Supreme Court was 'not simply a matter of meeting international obligations. The national interest in resisting threats to our own security is just as important'.[55] Lord Hope, as Lord Phillips did, clarified that the application was neither for temporary validity nor for prospective overruling. What Treasury counsel sought was 'simply a delay in the date as from which [the consequence of the Court's orders (which will apply retroactively as usual)] will take effect'.[56] Lord Hope was reassured by reference to Bokhary PJ's statement in *Koo Sze Yiu* that the suspension proposed would not shield anyone from legal liability[57] and thus would have no effect whatever on remedies for what had happened in the past or during the period of suspension.[58] Lord Hope weighed the factors and considered that the balance of advantages was in favour of exercising the power of suspending the coming into effect of the court's orders for five weeks. The risk that suspension would tend to obfuscate the effect of the court's judgment was not the decisive factor. The short periods of suspension were accepted to be of practical value in view of the way financial institutions (holding frozen terrorist assets) could be expected to respond to the suspension. There might, however, be serious and irreversible damage to the effectiveness of the measures that the international obligations required were the court's orders not suspended. The likelihood of measures remedial of the breaches of fundamental law being approved by Parliament in the short time frame seemed to Lord Hope that 'there is everything to be said for not letting the cat – whose dimensions and capacity to inflict damage we can only guess at – out of the bag in the meantime'.[59]

---

[54] *HM Treasury* v. *Ahmed (No 2)*, [4]–[8].   [55] *Ibid.*, [15].   [56] *Ibid.*, [6] and [18].
[57] *Koo Sze Yiu*, [63].   [58] *HM Treasury* v. *Ahmed (No 2)*, [19].   [59] *Ibid.*, [22] and [24].

The hearing on the proposed orders took place the day after delivery of judgment by the Supreme Court. Although the court had provided to the parties a copy of its judgment and a draft of the proposed orders six days in advance pursuant to its practice directions, there is reason to believe that arguments both written and oral in relation to the Treasury's application were prepared at relatively short notice. Reading the court's judgments alone, it might have been thought that rather than taking on the detailed Canadian jurisprudence on 'delayed declarations of invalidity',[60] the more distilled discussion in *Koo Sze Yiu* was used to assist the court. This initial thought was dispelled by the information of additional cases cited in argument on the application included in the report of the court's judgments.[61] The references to *Koo Sze Yiu* only in the court's judgments might simply reflect a wish to refer to a more summarized form of the disputed issues in the course of writing judgments expeditiously.

The majority's decision was not well received by the British press.[62] Whether the majority or Lord Hope was correct in their respective understanding of the true effect of the application before the Supreme Court, judicial power and the doctrine of separation of powers will now be committed to academic debate.[63] It may be useful to note in the debate this possible point of departure in the constitutional frameworks of the HKSAR and the United Kingdom, namely whereas the CFA performs the function of a constitutional check against the executive and the legislature, the judiciary of the United Kingdom exercises supervisory jurisdiction under the doctrine of parliamentary supremacy.

The UK government rushed through in four days the Terrorist Asset-Freezing (Temporary Provisions) Bill through the Houses of Commons and Lords to reinstate the regime that the Supreme Court's orders had quashed for a period up to 31 December 2010. While this legislation did

---

[60] See Kent Roach, *Constitutional Remedies in Canada* (Aurora, Ontario: Canada Law Books, 2005).

[61] The following Canadian Supreme Court cases were cited in argument on the application: *Re Manitoba Language Rights* [1985] 1 SCR 721; *R v. Feeney* [1997] 2 SCR 117, [1997] 3 SCR 100; *R v. Swain* [1991] 1 SCR 933; and *Schachter v. Canada* [1992] 2 SCR 679.

[62] See e.g. Alasdair Palmer, 'The Supreme Court Has Sunk Very Low Indeed', *Daily Telegraph*, 6 February 2010, who stated: 'It takes a truly ludicrous sense of judicial self-importance to think that the critical issue is not dead bodies on the streets, but that the Supreme Court should "not lend itself to a procedure designed to obfuscate the effects of its judgment"'.

[63] A good starting point may be Philip A. Joseph, *Constitutional & Administrative Law in New Zealand*, 3rd edn. (Wellington: Thomson-Brookers, 2007) [26.3.1(2)] (on prospective-only relief and discussing New Zealand, UK, Canadian, and Hong Kong laws).

not affect any liability of the Treasury in respect of an act or omission that would be unlawful if it had not been enacted, thus preserving a consequence of the Supreme Court's judgment, it did provide protection to 'a person other than the Treasury' (e.g. the financial institutions) in relation to things done or omitted beginning with the date of the majority's decision and ending with its coming into force.[64] The Bill received Royal Assent on 10 February 2010. These temporary provisions were eventually superseded and repealed by the Terrorist Asset-Freezing Act 2010, commencing on 16 December 2010.

The comity of courts: Chen Li Hong *v.* Ting Lei Miao

The enforcement in Hong Kong of a bankruptcy order of the Taipei District Court by the trustees in bankruptcy was the action that gave rise to the question before the CFA in *Chen Li Hong* v. *Ting Lei Miao*:[65] To what extent is effect to be given by the HKSAR courts to orders made by courts sitting in Taiwan that is part of and under the de jure sovereignty of the PRC but is presently under the de facto albeit unlawful control of a usurper government?[66]

To this question, the CFA unanimously answered the question in affirmative terms. In Bokhary PJ's principal judgment, the criteria for recognizing the orders of non-recognized courts was thus formulated: (1) the rights covered by those orders are private rights; (2) giving effect to such orders accords with the interests of justice, the dictates of common sense, and the needs of law and order; and (3) giving them effect would

---

[64] See the Terrorist Asset-Freezing (Temporary Provisions) Act 2010 section 2. See, however, Joshua Rozenberg, *Law Gazette*, February 2010, reporting the speech of Lord Pannick QC in the House of Lords, pointing out that the new law would still leave the financial institutions with a week's exposure, namely the period of time between the date of the handing down of the substantive judgment and the date of the majority's decision refusing suspension.

[65] *Chen Li Hong* v. *Ting Lei Miao* (2000) 3 HKCFAR 9. The judgment is also reported as [2001] BPIR 34.

[66] *Ibid.*, [3]. The formulation of this question should not be taken as an official determination regarding the governmental authorities in Taiwan, bearing in mind that the Hong Kong courts were focusing on the matter of their giving effect in Hong Kong to Taiwanese judgments and orders and that the lower courts had not considered it necessary for the adjudication of the case to seek a certificate of fact from the Chief Executive of the HKSAR on the matter of recognition of government, proceeding on the presumptive basis of treating Taiwan as Chinese territory with a government that had no legal foundation but allowed to remain in effective control; see *Ku Chia Chun* v. *Ting Lei Miao* [1998] 3 HKC 119 (CA).

not be inimical to the sovereign's interests or otherwise contrary to public policy. Bokhary PJ emphasized that none of them involved recognizing the unrecognized entity. The purpose was to protect private rights.[67] The CFA thus applied the criteria and gave effect to the bankruptcy order of the Taipei District Court.[68]

The goodness of the CFA judgment was felt in 2004 when the Taiwan Supreme Court considered an appeal over the dismissal of divorce proceedings instituted in the Taiwanese court after the HKSAR family court had granted a decree absolute for the dissolution of the same marriage and made provision for custody and access of the child of the marriage after hearing the parties.[69] The Taiwan Supreme Court applied Article 402 of the Civil Procedure Law to consider whether the decree and order of the HKSAR court should be recognized. In considering the criterion in Article 402(1)(4) against recognition, namely 'where there is no international mutual recognition', the Taiwan Supreme Court indicated that the criterion was not a reference to recognition of states or governments in international law and was rather a reference to the comity of courts in mutually recognizing each other's judgments. The appropriate approach would be that if the court outside Taiwan has not expressly declined to recognize the effect of a Taiwanese judgment, the Taiwanese court should as far as possible take a tolerant and active stance on the basis of mutual benefit to recognize the effect of the other court's judgment.[70] The Taiwan Supreme Court then considered the *ratio* of *Chen Li Hong*[71] and held

---

67 *Chen Li Hong*, 21C–E.
68 *Ibid.*, 21E–J. Bokhary PJ noted the fact that the trustees in bankruptcy acted in accordance with the directions of the Taiwan bankruptcy court was 'unremarkable', recognizing and giving effect to the bankruptcy order would not be going further than giving effect to a Taiwanese divorce decree.
69 *Lin* v. *Lin* (九十三年度台上字第一九四三號) (Taiwan Appeal No 1943/93) (23 September 2004). The judgment is reported: 47(7) *Judicial Yuan Gazette* 105 (2005).
70 The original text in Chinese is reproduced here: '如該外國未明示拒絕承認我國判決之效力, 應盡量從寬及主動立於互惠觀點, 承認該判決之效力。'. Later the Taiwan Supreme Court added: '而司法上之相互承認, 基於國際間司法權相互尊重及禮讓之原則, 如外國法院已有具體承認我國判決之事實存在, 或客觀上可期待其將來承認我國法院之判決, 即可認有相互之承認。'. ('As to mutual recognition in judicial matters, on the basis of the principle of mutual respect and comity of judicial authorities internationally, if a foreign court has as a matter of fact recognized Taiwanese judgments, or could be objectively expected to recognize Taiwanese judgments in the future, the Taiwanese court may accept that there is mutual recognition.')
71 The Chinese translation of the *ratio*, taken from the judgment of the Taiwan Supreme Court, is as follows: '台灣法院之判決涉及私權, 且承認其效力符合正義之利益、一般通念及法治需求, 於主權利益並無妨害, 且未牴觸公共政策時, 應為香港法院承認之。'. ('Where a judgment of a Taiwanese court covers private rights, giving effect to

that since the courts in Hong Kong had recognized Taiwanese judgments, the Taiwanese courts may not refuse to recognize the effect of Hong Kong judgments on the ground that there was no relationship of comity on recognition of judgments. As no other criteria for non-recognition applied, the decree and order of the HKSAR family court was automatically treated as a recognized judgment, such that the institution of divorce proceedings in Taiwan lacked a cause of action and was dismissed.

Despite this delightful event, it should be noted that the citation above is the only one by the Taiwanese higher courts of a CFA judgment even though the two territories are close to each other geographically, culturally, socially, and commercially. A recent study by Chang Wen-chen and Yeh Jiunn-rong of foreign law citation by Justices of the Council of Grand Justices indicates that the Justices of Taiwan's constitutional court tended to cite American, German, and Japanese law and judgments, probably because of their respective educational backgrounds.[72] Although the legal systems of the two territories hail from different legal traditions, it is believed that there is much room for judicial reception or borrowing, bearing in mind that both jurisdictions often encounter similar social problems. Much depends on the legal communities on both sides to engage in exchange of ideas and information.[73]

Specialist areas: companies

Three groups of CFA cases, distinguished by the area of law in question, constitute the balance of the focused studies.[74] The first group are the

such a judgment accords with the interests of justice, common sense and the needs of legal order, and giving it effect would not be inimical to sovereign interests or otherwise contrary to public policy, the Hong Kong courts should give recognition to it.')

[72] See Wen-chen Chang and Jiunn-rong Yeh, 'Judges as Discursive Agent: The Use of Foreign Law and Its Relationship with Judges' Learning Backgrounds' in Tania Groppi and Marie-Claire Ponthoreau (eds.), *The Use of Foreign Precedents by Constitutional Judges* (Oxford and Portland, OR: Hart Publishing, 2013) pp 373–92. See also David S. Law and Wen-chen Chang, 'The Limits of Global Judicial Dialogue' (2011) 86 *Washington Law Review* 523.

[73] For recent efforts, see Albert Chen, 'A Tale of Two Islands: Comparative Reflections on Constitutionalism in Hong Kong and Taiwan' (2007) 37 *HKLJ* 647 and Xianchu Zhang, 'An Empirical Study on Judicial Assistance between Hong Kong and Taiwan in Civil and Commercial Matters' (2009) 5 *Academia Sinica Law Journal* 1 (which refers also to an earlier instance in 2000 of lower courts in Taiwan considering the effect of *Chen Li Hong* in the procedurally unclear context of enforcement of a default judgment of the High Court of the HKSAR).

[74] There are admittedly other specialized areas that deserve individual study but are not considered in this chapter in an extended way. They include (1) admiralty law (where the CFA's judgment in *The Resource 1* (2000) 3 HKCFAR 187 (also reported as *The Tian*

company law cases, which, given the English model of the Hong Kong Companies Ordinance,[75] are often cited not only in England but also in other common law jurisdictions that likewise adopt or evolve from the English model in companies and corporations law. Some were reported in specialist law reports and also taken into one of the major works on the subject, such as *Palmer's Company Law.*

Four CFA judgments in company law have been influential. In *Aktieselskabet Dansk Skibsfinanciering* v. *Brothers,*[76] Lord Hoffmann NPJ ruled on, *inter alia*, the standard of proof for fraudulent trading. Later, Patten J of the Companies Court in England applied Lord Hoffmann's approach for determining an allegation that the defendants knowingly assisted the perpetration of a fraud.[77] The Singaporean Court of Appeal also cited the ruling with approval in 2005.[78]

The CFA was asked to determine questions for sanctioning interlinking schemes of arrangement for a group of insolvent companies in *UDL Argos Engineering & Heavy Industries Ltd* v. *Li Oi Lin.*[79] Lord Millett NPJ's principal judgment considered a line of English authorities and took account of the then latest discussion on this aspect of company law by the English Court of Appeal[80] before setting out a number of principles for summoning meetings, including whether there be separate meetings for differing classes of creditors or members. The English Companies Court thereafter considered Lord Millett's judgment as part of the body of authorities on sanctioning schemes of arrangement.[81] One of those company judges, Warren J, noted in the *Sovereign Marine & General Insurance* case that the

---

Sheng No 8 [2000] 2 Lloyd's Rep 430) was cited in *The Able Lieutenant* [2002] 6 MLJ 433 (Malay HC); *The Cape Moreton (ex-The Freya)* (2005) 143 FCR 43 (Fed Ct Aust (FC); *The Global Peace* (2006) 232 ALR 694 (Fed Ct Aust)) and (2) arbitration (where the CFA's judgment in *Hebei Import & Export Corp* v. *Polytek Engineering Co. Ltd* (1999) 2 HKCFAR 111 was cited in *Aloe Vera of America Inc* v. *Asianic Food (S) Pte Ltd* [2006] 3 SLR 174 (Sing HC); *Lombard Commodities Ltd* v. *Alami Vegetable Oil Products Sdn Bhd* [2010] 2 MLJ 23 (Malay Fed Ct)).

[75] Cap. 32.

[76] *Aktieselskabet Dansk Skibsfinanciering* v. *Brothers* (2000) 3 HKCFAR 70, [2001] 2 BCLC 324. The case was noted in *Palmer's Company Law*, [15.722.1].

[77] *Morris* v. *Bank of India* [2004] EWHC 528 (Ch).

[78] *Tang Yoke Kheng (t/a Niklex Supply Co)* v. *Lek Benedict* [2005] 3 SLR 263 (Sing CA).

[79] *UDL Argos Engineering & Heavy Industries Ltd* v. *Li Oi Lin* (2001) 4 HKCFAR 358. The case was noted in *Palmer's Company Law*, [12.041].

[80] *Re Hawk Insurance Co Ltd* [2002] 1 WLR 1345 (Eng CA).

[81] See *Re Pan Atlantic Insurance Co. Ltd* [2003] 2 BCLC 678; *Re Telewest Communications Plc* [2004] EWHC 924 (Ch); *Re British Aviation Insurance Co. Ltd* [2005] EWHC 1621 (Ch); and *Re Sovereign Marine & General Insurance Co. Ltd* [2006] EWHC 1335 (Ch).

principles enunciated in the *UDL* case deserved great respect because it was a summary by Lord Millett. Yet, on closer study, Warren J detected a slight difference in emphasis with the English position. Since legislation in identical terms had been enacted in many parts of the British Commonwealth, it did not take long before the principles were applied in the Cayman Islands,[82] Singapore,[83] and Australia.[84]

One of the questions before the CFA in *Re Chime Corp Ltd*[85] was the type of relief the court may order in an application for remedies on the ground that the business of the company had been conducted in an unfairly prejudicial manner. Both Bokhary PJ and Lord Scott NPJ gave judgments to which all other members of the CFA agreed, holding, *inter alia*, that the court may order the directors of the company to pay compensation or make restitution to the company for a breach of duty. Later, sitting in the PC on an appeal from Jersey in respect of an application under the Companies (Jersey) Law 1991 for remedies on the unfairly prejudicial conduct ground, Lord Scott applied his judgment in the *Chime* case, stating that no reason had been advanced before the Board on the appeal why the decision in *Chime* should not be followed.[86] The New South Wales Court of Appeal subsequently applied both cases with respect to an application under sections 232 and 233 of the Corporations Act 2001 of the Australian Commonwealth.[87]

The latest of the four cases was *Waddington Ltd* v. *Chan Chun Hoo*.[88] The principal judgment of the CFA was given by Lord Millett NPJ,[89] who held that a multiple derivative action could be brought under the common law in Hong Kong and that the principle against a shareholder recovering for reflective loss applied in Hong Kong without the exception

---

[82] *Re Euro Bank Corporation (in liq)* [2003] CILR 205 (Cayman Islands Grand Court).

[83] *Chew Eu Hock Construction Co Pte Ltd (under judicial management)* v. *Central Provident Fund Board* [2003] 4 SLR 137 (Sing HC); *Hitachi Plant Engineering & Construction Co. Ltd* v. *Eltraco International Pte Ltd* [2003] 4 SLR 384 (Sing CA).

[84] *Re Opes Prime Stockbroking Ltd (in liq)* (2009) 258 ALR 362 (Fed Ct Aust) (cited by the Full Court of Federal Court of Australia in *Re CSR Ltd* [2010] FCAFC 34 [23 April 2010] and by the Supreme Court of Victoria in *Re Mitchell Communication Group* [2010] VSC 423 [Victoria SC] [17 September 2010]).

[85] *Re Chime Corp Ltd* (2004) 7 HKCFAR 546.

[86] *Gamlestaden Fastigheter AB* v. *Baltic Partners Ltd* [2007] 4 All ER 164 (PC) (in which particular reference was made to Lord Scott of Foscote NPJ's judgment in the *Chime* case at [39]–[49]).

[87] *Campbell* v. *BackOffice Investments Pty Ltd* [2008] NSWCA 95, 66 ACSR 359.

[88] *Waddington Ltd* v. *Chan Chun Hoo* (2008) 11 HKCFAR 370. The case was noted in *Palmer's Company Law*, [8.3705].

[89] Ribeiro PJ gave a concurring judgment.

recognized in England in *Giles* v. *Rhind*.[90] Shortly thereafter, Lord Millett's judgment was cited before the English Court of Appeal on the matter of reflective loss.[91] The Master of the Rolls, in giving the judgment of the Court of Appeal, noted Lord Millett's view that *Giles* v. *Rhind* was wrongly decided but indicated that that decision was binding on the court and there was no basis for departing from it. The New South Wales Court of Appeal also cited the CFA judgment, merely noting the development of the common law in Hong Kong on multiple derivative actions because the matter before it was based on statute.[92]

Specialist area: taxation

Although a studious observer of Hong Kong's system of taxation has described it as 'simple',[93] there have been enough tax cases going to the CFA for judgments in this area of law to be passed on to other jurisdictions. One topic of some intricacy has been the *Ramsay* principle in relation to tax-avoidance transactions. Two CFA judgments in relatively quick succession and incidentally concerning private and commercial businesses of the same family have provided much assistance to courts outside Hong Kong. The first was *Shiu Wing Ltd* v. *Commissioner of Estate Duty*.[94] Sir Anthony Mason NPJ's characterization of the principle as 'both a rule of statutory construction . . . and an approach to the analysis of the facts' assisted the English Court of Appeal in understanding and justifying the principle, stating that:

> [I]t can perhaps be justified as statutory interpretation in the broader sense. It recognises the underlying characteristic of all taxing statutes, as parasitic in nature. They draw their life-blood from real world transactions with real world economic effects, to which the Revenue is not a party. To allow tax treatment to be governed by transactions which have no real world purpose of any kind is inconsistent with that fundamental characteristic.[95]

---

90   *Giles* v. *Rhind* [2003] Ch 618.

91   *Webster* v. *Sandersons Solicitors* [2009] 2 BCLC 542 (Eng CA). Lord Clarke MR then stated the relevant principles at [37], after noting at [36] that Lord Millett 'was wrong to say that this court had followed that decision in *Day* v. *Cook* [2001] EWCA Civ 592 (Eng CA) (which in fact preceded it)'.

92   *Oates* v. *Consolidated Capital Services Ltd* [2009] NSWCA 183, 72 ACSR 506.

93   See Michael Littlewood, 'How Simple Can Tax Law Be? The Instructive Case of Hong Kong' (2005) 1 *Journal of the Australasian Tax Teachers Association* 259. See also Michael Littlewood, *Taxation Without Representation: The History of Hong Kong's Troublingly Successful Tax System* (Hong Kong: Hong Kong University Press, 2010).

94   *Shiu Wing Ltd* v. *Commissioner of Estate Duty* (2000) 3 HKCFAR 215.

95   *Barclays Mercantile Business Finance Ltd* v. *HM Inspector of Taxes* [2003] STC 66 (Eng CA).

Sir Anthony's emphasis that the *Ramsay* principle was concerned with the purpose of the transaction or the 'aim or end in view' of it also assisted the New Zealand Supreme Court.[96]

While the second case of *Collector of Stamp Revenue* v. *Arrowtown Assets Ltd*[97] was concerned with stamp duty, the CFA's discussion of the *Ramsay* approach attracted much academic interest.[98] There was also judicial interest, particularly with respect to Ribeiro PJ's statements that the *Ramsay* approach 'continues to assert the need to apply orthodox methods of purposive interpretation to the facts viewed realistically', with the ultimate question being 'whether the relevant statutory provisions, construed purposively, were intended to apply to the transaction, viewed realistically' (which were cited approvingly by both the House of Lords[99] and the New Zealand Supreme Court[100]).[101]

On the other hand, while the question decided in Lord Millett NPJ's judgment in *Commissioner of Inland Revenue* v. *Secan Ltd*,[102] namely whether capitalized interest payments amounted to deductions in assessment of profits tax, might appear simple at first sight, the application of the judgment in the United Kingdom had not been. The Revenue relied on the judgment both in an English case[103] and a Scottish case.[104] Lightman J, hearing the English case, felt unable to give full weight to Lord Millett's observations as there apparently had not been addressed in the judgment whether there was a change in the principles of commercial accountancy since 1975 and eventually did not find the judgment to be

---

[96] *Glenharrow Holdings Ltd* v. *Commissioner of Inland Revenue* [2008] NZSC 116 (NZ SC).
[97] *Collector of Stamp Revenue* v. *Arrowtown Assets Ltd* (2003) 6 HKCFAR 517 (with Lord Millett NPJ being a member of the CFA).
[98] Andrew Halkyard, 'Common Law and Tax Avoidance: Back to the Future?' (2004) 14 *Revenue Law Journal* 19; Bill Cannon and Peter Edmundson, 'Refocusing on Fundamental Principles of Stamp Duty' (2006) 4 (2) *eJournal of Tax Research* 101; Chris Evans, 'Barriers to Avoidance: Recent Legislative and Judicial Developments in Common Law Jurisdictions' [2007] *UNSWLRS* 12; and Chris Evans, 'Containing Tax Avoidance: Anti-Avoidance Strategies' [2008] *UNSWLRS* 40.
[99] *Barclays Mercantile Business Finance Ltd* v. *Mawson* [2005] 1 AC 684 (HL) (Lord Nicholls, Lord Steyn, Lord Hoffmann, Lord Hope, and Lord Walker).
[100] *Ben Nevis Forestry Ventures Ltd* v. *CIR* [2008] NZSC 15, [2009] 2 NZLR 289 (per Elias CJ and Anderson J).
[101] The West Australian Supreme Court also cited the case in *Worsley Timber 2000 Pty Ltd (in liq)* v. *Commissioner of State Revenue* [2007] WASC 155, a stamp duty matter.
[102] *Commissioner of Inland Revenue* v. *Secan Ltd* (2000) 3 HKCFAR 411. The case was also reported as (2000) 74 TC 1.
[103] *HM Inspector of Taxes* v. *Mars UK Ltd* [2005] STC 958 (UK Ch).
[104] *Revenue and Customs Commissioners* v. *William Grant & Sons Distillers Ltd* [2006] SC 17.

of substantial assistance on the basis that Lord Millett ruled against the taxpayer by holding it to its election in accounting practice. Both cases ended up in the House of Lords.[105] Lord Hoffmann, writing the principal opinion of the committee, found, upon analysis of Lord Millett's judgment, that the 'considerable reliance' by the Revenue was misplaced. This was because the taxpayer's argument in *Secan* could be answered in two alternative ways, and the taxpayer was not entitled to have it both ways. But Lord Millett had not indicated in the judgment which of the two was to be adopted. The Revenue may not rely upon the case as deciding that 'when a cost item like interest or depreciation is carried forward as part of the value of stock or work in progress, it has nevertheless in some sense been deducted in the year in which the cost was incurred', a proposition that appeared to Lord Hoffmann to be 'an impermissible and confusing mixture of two different systems of computation'.

Specialized area: constitutional and administrative law

The citations in constitutional and administrative law cases, both in judgments and in journals outside Hong Kong, tend to confirm the saying that 'each constitution is the child of its environment'.[106] And one needs not go too far outside to find the different environment of Mainland China.

The CFA's right of abode cases[107] and the CFA's interaction with the Standing Committee of the National People's Congress (NPCSC) shortly thereafter[108] spawned a host of journal articles. There is a signal difference in emphasis between journal articles or notes published in Mainland China and those published outside Mainland China. The academic interest in Mainland China was in studying the methodology and rationale behind the CFA's interpretations in contrast with the intentions and

---

[105] *Revenue and Customs Commissioners* v. *William Grant & Sons Distillers Ltd* [2007] 1 WLR 1448 (HL).

[106] See *Luk Ka Cheung* v. *Market Misconduct Tribunal* [2009] 1 HKLRD 114, [31] (CFI) (per Andrew Cheung J).

[107] *Ng Ka Ling* v. *Director of Immigration* (1999) 2 HKCFAR 4; *Chan Kam Nga* v. *Director of Immigration* (1999) 2 HKCFAR 82.

[108] *Ng Ka Ling* v. *Director of Immigration (No 2)* (1999) 2 HKCFAR 141; *The Interpretation by the Standing Committee of the National People's Congress of Articles 22(4) and 24(2)(3) of the Basic Law of the Hong Kong Special Administrative Region of the People's Republic of China* (Adopted by the Standing Committee of the Ninth National People's Congress at its Tenth Session on 26 June 1999) (LN 167 of 1999); *Lau Kong Yung* v. *Director of Immigration* (1999) 2 HKCFAR 300; and *Director of Immigration* v. *Chong Fung Yuen* (2001) 4 HKCFAR 211.

imputed design principles of the BL and the methodology and rationale of the NPCSC.[109] Mainland academics were concerned with explaining the reasons for conflicts between the NPCSC's legislative interpretation and the CFA's judicial interpretation from the standpoint of the CFA being the delegate interpreting agency.[110] More recently, there have been suggestions in Mainland academic circles for solutions to avoid conflicts and crises in practice, such as for better dialogue and integration in the two cultures of constitutionalism;[111] for the 'defective provisions' of the BL to be 'improved';[112] and for the NPCSC to interpret the BL of the HKSAR to 'confirm' that the courts of the HKSAR do not enjoy the power of judicial review of legislation of the HKSAR, to stipulate the circumstances and procedures for the exercise of the NPCSC's authority to review legislation of the HKSAR, and to authorize the courts of the HKSAR to exercise power of review of legislation enacted by the legislature of the HKSAR that are on matters within the autonomy of the HKSAR.[113]

On the other hand, articles and notes published abroad invariably highlight the CFA's judgments and the HKSAR's judicial independence having been eroded by NPCSC political interference through interpretation. Authors of these works disclosed not only a perception of the two entities being distinct but also a value-based preference towards the Hong Kong common law courts.[114] As these studies seem likely to be one-off efforts, readers might not have paid as much attention as they deserve when compared with the sustained current of Mainland papers.

---

[109] See Yongping Xiao, 'Comments on the Judgment on the Right of Abode by Hong Kong CFA' (2000) 48 *American Journal of Comparative Law* 471.

[110] See Jie Cheng, 'On Hong Kong's Judicial Power Under Dual-track Politics – A Rethink from the Perspective of Constitutionalism' (2006) (5) *China Legal Science* 47; Jie Cheng, 'The Central Authorities' Governing Power and Special Administrative Region's High Degree of Autonomy – Using the Delegation Relationship under the Basic Law as the Framework' (2007) (8) *Legal Science* 61; and Pingxue Zou, 'A Preliminary Thesis on the Basic Characteristics of the Mechanism for Interpreting the Hong Kong Basic Law' (2009) (5) *Legal Science* 119.

[111] See Hongchang Jiao, 'An Analysis of the Reasons for Conflicts in Interpretation of the Hong Kong Basic Law' (2008) (3) *Guangdong Social Science* 181.

[112] See Jinghua Ji, 'The Authority and Procedure to Interpret Hong Kong Basic Law' 31(4) *Modern Law Science* 3. Professor Ji suggested, *inter alia*, that a constitutional court be established to exercise the power of interpretation of the Constitution of the People's Republic of China and the two Basic Laws, with the power of final adjudication now vested with the CFA to be withdrawn thereafter.

[113] See Likun Dong and Shutian Zhang, 'Power to Review Legislation of the Hong Kong Special Administrative Region Inconsistent with the Basic Law' (2010) 32(3) *Chinese Journal of Law* 3.

[114] See note 16 above.

How the notable developments in constitutional and administrative law in Hong Kong in the past decade have been received beyond these shores will now be examined. The application of the doctrine of substantive legitimate expectation in *Ng Siu Tung* v. *Director of Immigration*[115] to protect right of abode claimants who received specific representations from the Director of Immigration was noted academically abroad as an incident in the development of the doctrine after the decisive English Court of Appeal case of *R* v. *North and East Devon Health Authority, Ex parte Coughlan*.[116] Two Australian courts noted the case, also as part of the discussion of the *Coughlan* case and its progeny.[117] The Australian courts considered the judgment in *Thang Thieu Quyen* v. *Director of Immigration*[118] in a similar manner, alongside the line of cases applying the *Hardial Singh* principles on the legality of continued detention.[119]

Sir Anthony Mason NPJ's statement in *HKSAR* v. *Lam Kwong Wai*[120] on remedial interpretation was at first preferred by the Victorian courts in their efforts to construe Victoria's Charter of Rights and Responsibilities,[121] although the Court of Appeal of the Supreme Court of

---

[115] *Ng Siu Tung* v. *Director of Immigration* (2002) 5 HKCFAR 1.

[116] [2001] QB 213. *De Smith's Judicial Review* cited the case in relation to the proposition that '[it] is more likely that the legitimate expectation should be respected where it arises from a representative to an individual or a class rather than the world at large', making the point that the 'numbers in the class may not be relevant' (*De Smith's Judicial Review*, 6th edn. (London: Sweet & Maxwell, 2007) [12–055]). Matthew Groves integrated the case in his article on whether the English doctrine of substantive legitimate expectation should be introduced into Australia; see Matthew Groves, 'Substantive Legitimate Expectations in Australian Administrative Law' (2008) 32 *Melbourne University Law Review* 470.

[117] *Re Minister for Immigration and Multicultural Affairs, Ex p Lam* [2003] HCA 6, (2003) 214 CLR 1 (Aust HC); *Rush* v. *Commissioner of Police* (2006) 229 ALR 383 (Fed Ct Aust) (in which Finn J declined to follow both *Ng Siu Tung* and *R* v. *Secretary of State for the Home Department, Ex parte Zeqiri* [2002] Imm AR 296 [HL], quoting Sir Anthony Mason's view that adopting the English approach to substantive protection of legitimate expectation would require a 'revolution in Australian judicial thinking').

[118] *Thang Thieu Quyen* v. *Director of Immigration* (1997–8) 1 HKCFAR 167.

[119] *Minister for Immigration and Multicultural and Indigenous Affairs* v. *Al Masri* (2003) 197 ALR 241 (Fed Ct Aust [FC]); *B&B* v. *Minister for Immigration and Multicultural and Indigenous Affairs* (2003) 199 ALR 604 (Fam Ct Aust).

[120] *HKSAR* v. *Lam Kwong Wai* (2006) 9 HKCFAR 574.

[121] See *RJE* v. *Secretary to the Department of Justice* [2008] VSCA 265, 21 VR 526, 192 A Crim R 156 at [116] (where the Victorian Court of Appeal preferred *Lam Kwong Wai*, *ibid.*, over *R* v. *Hansen* [2007] 3 NZLR 1 [NZ SC]); and *DAS* v. *Victorian Human Rights & Equal Opportunity Commission* [2009] VSC 381, 24 VR 415, 198 A Crim R 305, [53] (Victoria SC) (per Warren CJ).

Victoria came to a different conclusion upon further reflection.[122] Ribeiro PJ's judgment in *Lee Ming Tee* v. *HKSAR*,[123] dealing with the abrogation of the privilege against self-incrimination by legislation, received mixed treatment as well. It was relied upon by a judge of the Federal Court of Australia to hold that the Australian Crime Commission Act 2002 abrogated that common law privilege and the judge's view was upheld by the Full Court on appeal.[124] On the other hand, Chief Justice Warren of the Victorian Supreme Court read Ribeiro PJ's judgment in *Lee Ming Tee* closely, recognizing its importance, as the Hong Kong Bill of Rights has many similarities with the Victorian Charter. Warren CJ eventually decided that *Lee Ming Tee* had limited application to Victoria, where a test of a different nature, more akin to section 1 of the Canadian Charter of Rights and Freedoms, applied.[125] So, in Victoria, the path of reasoning to be adopted should begin with the judgment of the High Court of Australia in *Reid* v. *Howard*,[126] ascertaining first the scope of the common law right against self-incrimination. And it is only after the right that constitutes the subject of the minimum guarantee has been ascertained

---

[122] *R* v. *Momcilovic* [2010] VSCA 50, 265 ALR 751, 25 VR 436 (Victoria SC) (17 March 2010), which, like *Lam Kwong Wai*, was concerned with the limiting of the presumption of innocence by statutory reversal of the burden of proof of possession of dangerous drugs. The Victorian Court of Appeal declined to follow Sir Anthony Mason's approach to remedially interpret the statutory reversed onus provisions to impose only an evidential onus, stating that 'to do so would have been to cross the line from interpretation to legislation' (at [35]), noting that 'the most important difference between the position in Hong Kong and that which applies under the [Victorian] Charter is that a finding of inconsistency between a statutory provision and a Charter right has no effect on the validity of the provision' (at [61]). The High Court of Australia, by a majority of six to one, allowed the appeal, with four of the six judges in the majority (namely, French CJ, Gummow, Hayne, and Bell JJ) finding the *Lam Kwong Wai* approach of 'remedial interpretation' to be of limited or nil assistance in the determination of the validity and effect of the Charter: *Momcilovic* v. *R* [2011] HCA 34, (2011) 245 CLR 1 (8 September 2011).

[123] *Lee Ming Tee* v. *HKSAR* (2001) 4 HKCFAR 133.

[124] *A* v. *Boulton* [2004] FCAFC 101, 207 ALR 342, 146 A Crim R 395. See also *Witness C* v. *Crime and Misconduct Commission* [2008] QSC 196, 187 A Crim R 322 (Queensland SC).

[125] The Court of Appeal of the Supreme Court of Victoria later reached the same conclusion in *R* v. *Momcilovic* [2010] VSCA 50, agreeing in [109] and [110] with the views of Elias CJ of the New Zealand Supreme Court in *R* v. *Hansen* [2007] 3 NZLR 1, 15. See, further, the reasoning of the majority judges of the High Court of Australia in *Momcilovic* v. *R* [2011] HCA 34, (2011) 245 CLR 1.

[126] *Reid* v. *Howard* (1995) 184 CLR 1 (Aust HC).

that a party seeking to limit it may proceed to 'demonstrably justify' such a limitation.[127]

The CFA's judgment in the Flags case (*HKSAR* v. *Ng Kung Siu*)[128] was cited before France J of the New Zealand High Court as part of the 'smorgasbord' of judgments on the same subject matter in an appeal against a conviction of national flag desecration by burning. Adopting what under Hong Kong legal nomenclature would be described as 'a remedial interpretation', the judge narrowed the requisite mental element in the legislative text of 'intention to dishonour' to require proof of an 'intention to vilify' and held that an otherwise blanket ban at the pain of criminal sanction of national flag burning was a disproportionate response in restricting freedom of political expression to the legislative objective of preserving the national flag as a national symbol.[129] Reading *Ng Kung Siu* with *Texas* v. *Johnson*,[130] the judge noted the differing views on whether prohibition of flag burning was a justified limit and exercised a judgment on behalf of the society that she served, upon expressing her perception that 'New Zealand has reached a level of maturity in which staunch criticism is regarded as acceptable. There may well be strong reactions to such criticism but there is an acceptance of the ability to make it'.[131]

Factors for judicial assimilation and borrowing

Hong Kong cases that have had sustained impact in the common law world, including its far-flung corners, have been PC cases such as *Ng Yuen*

---

[127] *DAS* v. *Victorian Human Rights & Equal Opportunity Commission* [2009] VSC 381 (Victoria SC).

[128] *HKSAR* v. *Ng Kung Siu* (1999) 2 HKCFAR 442. The CFA unanimously held that the national flag and regional flag desecration offences in Hong Kong were necessary restrictions of the freedom of expression on the ground of public order (*ordre public*).

[129] *Hopkinson* v. *Police* [2004] 3 NZLR 704 (NZ HC). See also *Morse* v. *Police* [2011] NZSC 45, [2012] 2 NZLR 1 (NZ SC) (6 May 2011), in which the Supreme Court of New Zealand, acting unanimously, quashed the conviction of the appellant for offensive behaviour in a public place, namely setting fire to the New Zealand flag in the grounds of the Law School of Victoria University in Wellington and within the view of people assembled at the Wellington Cenotaph for the dawn service on Anzac Day 2007.

[130] *Texas* v. *Johnson* 491 US 397 (1989) (USSC).

[131] *Hopkinson* v. *Police*, [73]–[76]. The judge also found support in Jackson J's statement in *Board of Education* v. *Barnette* 319 US 624 at 642 (1943) that 'freedom to differ is not limited to things that do not matter much. That would be a mere shadow of freedom. The test of its substance is the right to differ as to things that touch the heart of the existing order'.

Shiu,[132] *Lee Kwong Kut*,[133] *Yuen Kun Yeu*,[134] and *Wong Muk Ping*.[135] They are now happily joined by CFA judgments such as *Tse Wai Chun, Shum Kwok Sher, Koo Sze Yiu, UDL,* and *Arrowtown*.

There is a material difference, though. While PC cases are recognized as opinions of their Lordships sitting in London on a case coming from Hong Kong, the CFA cases are recognized as judgments of the final appellate court of Hong Kong sitting in Hong Kong, China with a majority of local Hong Kong judges. The survey above illustrates a number of factors for CFA judgments to have an impact beyond Hong Kong.

The favourable treatment CFA judgments have received in England demonstrates two intermediating factors. The fact that a senior and on occasion serving English judge sits in a CFA case as an NPJ actually goes beyond the constitutional and beneficial function that Lord Cooke thought of in giving 'particular consideration to whether a proposed decision of this Court is in accord with generally accepted principles of the common law'.[136] They have, by reason of the familiarity of the legal system and common law methodology, as well as the similarity in the content of the applicable law or judicial precedents, been able to continue to develop and summarize the common law much in the same way it was done in England. Their participation not only led to their citation of the CFA case later on in London in the appropriate case when sitting in the House of Lords or the PC, but also attracted the attention of law reporters, text writers, and practitioners, who must have become more ready to report, include, and cite the CFA case in their work as part of the relevant corpus of judicial opinion deserving consideration and respect even though such work would have to be aimed at the domestic (or English) audience. Having made a good start, the profile of the CFA has been raised, and it now appears that CFA cases are being considered as a source of good-quality common law[137] and followed with interest,[138] probably more so in the future given the current complement

---

[132] *Attorney General of Hong Kong* v. *Ng Yuen Shiu* [1983] 2 AC 629 (PC).

[133] *Attorney General of Hong Kong* v. *Lee Kwong Kut* [1993] AC 951 (PC).

[134] *Yuen Kun Yeu* v. *Attorney General of Hong Kong* [1988] AC 175 (PC).

[135] *Attorney General of Hong Kong* v. *Wong Muk Ping* [1987] AC 501 (PC).

[136] See *Chen Li Hong*, 23B–C.

[137] See the UK Supreme Court's citation of *Koo Sze Yiu*, as well as Lewison J's citation of *Polyset Ltd* v. *Panhandat Ltd* (2002) 5 HKCFAR 234 alongside judgments of the High Court of Australia and the New South Wales Court of Appeal on the nature of deposits in *Ng* v. *Ashley King (Developments) Ltd* [2010] EWHC 456 (Ch) (11 March 2010).

[138] The latest developments in CFA jurisprudence are followed in the UKSCblog; see www.ukscblog.com/article.asp?id=578.

of three serving members of the UK Supreme Court appointed as NPJs.[139]

Another vital factor for the wide dissemination of CFA judgments not only in England but also elsewhere is the function that publishers and practitioners have served to make London continue as a hub of legal exchange and logistics. CFA judgments, as the survey has shown, often were first reported, noted, discussed, or cited in a specialist series of law reports, a practitioners' text, or a judgment before being referred to elsewhere in the common law world, including sometimes the physically closer jurisdictions in Australia. It seems therefore that CFA judgments have benefited from a process of assimilation back into the source as English common law before being disseminated as such to other parts of the British Commonwealth.

While the discussion above dealing with specific CFA cases has been mainly concerned with citation and analysis of them before courts sitting in the United Kingdom[140] and Australia,[141] the survey has uncovered a phenomenon, apparently independent of the process of assimilation and 're-export' through England, of regular citation of CFA cases by three common law jurisdictions in the Asian-Pacific region, namely Malaysia, Singapore, and New Zealand.

The Malaysian courts have, apart from admiralty and arbitration matters mentioned earlier, cited CFA judgments on constitutional

---

[139] Lord Walker and more recently Lord Collins and Lord Clarke are NPJs. Lord Neuberger is also a NPJ but since the NPJ appointment became Master of the Rolls and then in 2012 President of the UK Supreme Court; he sat in the CFA in October 2010 and September 2012. His predecessor as President of the UK Supreme Court, Lord Phillips, was the most recent NPJ appointment.

[140] Other occasions of citation by the English courts include *Southampton Cargo Handling Plc* v. *Lotus Cars Ltd* [2000] 2 Lloyd's Rep 532, (Eng CA) (of *Bewise Motors* v. *Hoi Kong Container Services Ltd* (1997–8) 1 HKCFAR 256, a case on sub-bailment); *Rother District Investment Ltd* v. *Corke* [2004] 2 P&CR 311 (Lightman J) (of *Kensland Realty Ltd* v. *Whale View Ltd* (2001) 4 HKCFAR 381 on the notion that a person should not take advantage of his own wrong); and *National Westminster Bank* v. *Ashe* [2008] 1 WLR 710, (Eng CA) (of *Common Luck Investment Ltd* v. *Cheung Kam Chuen* (1999) 2 HKCFAR 229, holding that the judgment was wrong in several respects, a view shared by Law Commission of England and Wales but attributing the errors to the CFA not having the benefit of the House of Lords' exposition in *JA Pye (Oxford) Ltd* v. *Graham* [2003] 1 AC 419 (HL)).

[141] The Court of Appeal of the West Australian Supreme Court also cited *Lau Ka Yee Michael* v. *HKSAR* (2004) 7 HKCFAR 510 in *AM* v. *Western Australia* [2008] WASCA 196 (West Australian SC).

interpretation.[142] The Singaporean courts have, apart from arbitration and company matters mentioned earlier, cited CFA judgments on judicial deference to legislative judgment,[143] right of termination of a contract,[144] defamation,[145] and the drawing of inferences in criminal cases.[146] The New Zealand courts have also cited CFA judgments on the standard of proof in disciplinary proceedings[147] and crime.[148] All of these citations are not dependent on activities in London; the CFA judgments were apparently cited through direct search of law reports published in Hong Kong or a Hong Kong sourced electronic database (e.g. the Legal Reference System of the Hong Kong Judiciary website[149] or the Hong Kong Legal Information Institute's website[150]) and not by virtue of their being reported or cited elsewhere.

It is not easy to fathom the contributing factors to this phenomenon of these three jurisdictions tracking keenly the judicial developments of Hong Kong. This is because only one of the three jurisdictions, namely New Zealand, provides NPJs to the CFA,[151] and all of these jurisdictions

---

[142] *Lee Kwan Woh* v. *Public Prosecutor* [2009] 5 MLJ 301 (Malay Fed Ct) (citing *Leung Kwok Hung* v. *HKSAR* (2005) 8 HKCFAR 229 in support of its prismatic approach when interpreting fundamental rights).

[143] *Nguyen Tuong Van* v. *Public Prosecutor* [2005] 1 SLR 103 (Sing CA) (citing *Lau Cheong* v. *HKSAR* (2002) 5 HKCFAR 415 in support of the proposition that 'a fundamental question in every such case is the proper weight that ought to be ascribed to the views of Parliament encapsulated in the impugned legislation').

[144] *Sports Connection Pte Ltd* v. *Deuter Sports GmBH* [2009] 3 SLR 883 (Sing CA) (citing *Mariner International Hotels Ltd* v. *Atlas Ltd* (2007) 10 HKCFAR 1).

[145] *Jeyasegaram David* v. *Ban Song Long David* [2005] 2 SLR 712 (Sing CA) (citing *Next Magazine Publishing Ltd* v. *Ma Ching Fat* (2003) 6 HKCFAR 63 on the proposition that there was nothing sinister in being business rivals); *Review Publishing Co Ltd* v. *Lee Hsien Loong* [2010] 1 SLR 52 (Sing CA) (citing *Cheng* v. *Tse Wai Chun* (2000) 3 HKCFAR 339 in relation to its treatment of the English authority of *Reynolds* v. *Times Newspapers Ltd* [2001] 2 AC 127 [HL]).

[146] *Public Prosecutor* v. *Chee Cheong Hin Constance* [2006] 2 SLR 24 (Sing CA) (citing *Tang Kwok Wah Dixon* v. *HKSAR* (2002) 5 HKCFAR 209).

[147] *Z* v. *Dental Complaints Assessment Committee* [2009] 1 NZLR 1 (NZ SC) (citing *A Solicitor (24/07)* v. *Law Society of Hong Kong* (2008) 11 HKCFAR 117).

[148] *R* v. *Tuiloma* (CA 222/99, 8 December 1999), [1999] NZCA 296 (NZ CA) (citing *Tang Siu Man* v. *HKSAR (No 2)* (1997–8) 1 HKCFAR 107).

[149] Accessible at legalref.judiciary.gov.hk/lrs/common/ju/judgment.jsp.

[150] Accessible at www.hklii.org. The Hong Kong Legal Information Institute is a project of the Law & Technology Centre jointly established by the Department of Computer Science and the Faculty of Law of the University of Hong Kong.

[151] Australia, like New Zealand, provides NPJs to the CFA. Both jurisdictions, however, have declined to make available serving members of their judiciaries for appointment as NPJs.

are relatively self-sufficient in indigenous legal resources.[152] There may be different reasons for each of the three jurisdictions to consider CFA authorities. The literature on judicial citations and transjudicial communication and borrowing may throw some light.[153]

Geographical proximity and cultural linkages between Hong Kong on the one hand and Malaysia and Singapore on the other may be more significant contributing factors, although the linkages New Zealand has with the Hong Kong legal profession should be noted. The more regular citation by New Zealand courts of CFA judgments appears to be consistent with the findings of a study of New Zealand Court of Appeal citations of judgments from jurisdictions other than New Zealand and England,[154] although geographical proximity and population size do not begin to provide as good an explanation as was the case for Australia, and it is debatable whether the experiences in Hong Kong are relevant to New Zealand. It may be that the Australasian tradition of providing judges to sit in final appellate courts in the South Pacific nations has been a contributing factor towards a more cosmopolitan outlook.[155] And Smyth and Fausten's account of how socioeconomic factors such as levels of urbanization and commercialization and diversification of economies 'created a milieu ripe for complex litigation and new claims for rights that are conducive to judicial innovation'[156] may assist one's understanding of the diffusion of precedents out of Hong Kong.

[152] The author has explored whether jurisdictions that have appointed former Hong Kong judges in their courts, such as Bermuda (where Nazareth NPJ sat on the Court of Appeal until retirement) and Brunei (where Mortimer NPJ and formerly, Sir Noel Power NPJ, sits on the Court of Appeal), have been citing CFA judgments. The search results have been inconclusive because of the limited electronic accessibility of judicial decisions of those jurisdictions. See in this connection, Simon N. M. Young, 'The Hong Kong Multinational Judge in Criminal Appeals' [2008] *Law in Context* 130.

[153] See Lawrence Friedman, Robert Kagan, Bliss Cartwright, and Stanton Wheeler, 'State Supreme Courts: A Century of Style and Citation' (1981) 33 *Stanford Law Review* 773; Gregory Caldeira, 'The Transmission of Legal Precedent: A Study of State Supreme Courts' (1985) 79 *American Political Science Review* 179; Anne-Marie Slaughter, 'A Typology of Trans-judicial Communication' (1994) 29 *University of Richmond Law Review* 99; and Russell Smyth and Dietrich Fausten, 'Coordinate Citations Between Australian State Supreme Courts over the 20th Century' (2008) 34 *Monash University Law Review* 53.

[154] Russell Smyth, 'Judicial Citations – an Empirical Study of Citation Practice in the New Zealand Court of Appeal' (2000) 31 *Victoria University of Wellington Law Review* 847.

[155] See e.g. *Matalulu* v. *Director of Public Prosecutions* [2003] 4 LRC 712 (Fiji Islands SC); *Ah Chong* v. *Legislative Assembly of Western Samoa* [2001] NZAR 418 (Western Samoa CA).

[156] Russell Smyth and Dietrich Fausten, 'Coordinate Citations Between Australian State Supreme Courts over the 20th Century' (2008) 34 *Monash University Law Review* 53, 67–9.

Slaughter suggested in 1994, regarding what she called the 'phenomenon of transjudicial communication', that

> evidence of foreign intellectual influences, through direct citation or comparison to a foreign decision, is likely to reflect something more than simple cross-fertilization. In such cases evidence that a foreign court has reached the same conclusion apparently has independent value, leading the listening court not only to borrow the ideas, but to publicize its source. Indeed the listening court may reach the same legal conclusion or formulate the same line of reasoning independently, yet nevertheless search for and cite evidence that foreign courts are like-minded.[157]

Although this chapter has only sifted through in a quick but not necessarily comprehensive manner the echoes from courts and other sources beyond Hong Kong of CFA judgments of the past decade and therefore cannot claim to have untangled the complex web of judicial cross-fertilization among courts of the various jurisdictions with a legal system based upon English common law, the tacit signs one can discern are that the CFA has by now been recognized as a 'regular supplier' of common law jurisprudence of good analytical quality for others to take constant and careful notice. This is testament not only to the contributions made by the NPJs from common law jurisdictions outside Hong Kong, an institution that must be maintained, but also to the maturing indigenous judicial and legal human resources. The Andrew Li Court has made and maintained a respectable reputation for the Hong Kong courts.

---

[157]   Slaughter, note 153 above, 118–19. Cf Law and Chang, 'The Limits of Global Judicial Dialogue', note 72 above.

23

Macau's Court of Final Appeal

JORGE GODINHO AND PAULO CARDINAL

Introduction

The theme of this chapter is the Macau Court of Final Appeal (*Tribunal de Última Instância* or TUI[1]) of the Macau Special Administrative Region (SAR) of the People's Republic of China (PRC). It provides an overview and discussion of its role, activity and impact on the legal system of Macau since its establishment on 20 December 1999 upon the transfer of sovereignty. In civil law legal systems, the primary focus of academic research is usually on the study of codes and legislation; as a result, there is almost no research on the activity of courts, a gap that this chapter tries to bridge. This discussion does not attempt direct comparisons with the Court of Final Appeal (CFA) of the Hong Kong SAR except when the differences are of considerable relevance.

Background: comparative law aspects

As is well known, Macau is a civil law legal system, in the Roman-German strand, regardless of whether this legal family is understood in a broad or

---

The opinions expressed here are solely those of the authors and do not reflect the views of any institution to which they are affiliated. Thanks are due to Luís Pessanha for his suggestions and to Jane Zhang Yihe for her help with translation.

[1] In accordance with practice in Macau regarding names of courts and other public institutions, the court is abbreviated by its Portuguese initials: TUI. Its decisions are cited as follows: Ac. TUI [date] [case number]. Decisions appear in the TUI's database ordered by date. If more than one decision has been issued on any given day, the case number differentiates them. It is not customary in Macau to cite cases using the name of the parties, which in fact is not possible because of the practice of replacing the real names by 'party A', 'party B', and so on to keep anonymity. The same system applies to the Second Instance Court (*Tribunal de Segunda Instância* or TSI).

narrow sense.[2] This means that court decisions do not have the degree
of importance as a source of law as in the common law. There is no
binding precedent,[3] and courts are not empowered to issue decisions that
are binding for all citizens; as a rule, only the single case before the court
is decided. In addition, case law is not the primary driving force of the
development of the legal system; the various codifications perform that
role, and jurists are trained especially on the need to interpret written
legal provisions drafted in a typically concise or condensed ('scientific')
style using precise language and analytic concepts, such as those found in
the Civil Code (2161 articles), the Commercial Code (1268 articles) or the
Penal Code (350 articles). However, the centrality of the codes certainly
does not mean that case law should be dismissed as irrelevant; it is widely
recognized that the activity of courts and their case law contributes to the
creation and redefinition of the legal system.[4]

  The role of courts is perhaps more important in Macau's case because
of having the smallest possible number of judges in the highest court –
three.[5] Therefore, an individual decision made by the TUI will most

---

[2] See e.g. J. Godinho, *Macau Business Law and Legal System* (Hong Kong: LexisNexis, 2007)
    8; P. Cardinal, 'A Panoramic View on Fundamental Rights in Macau: From Territory Under
    Portuguese Administration to Special Administrative Region of the P.R. of China' in Jorge
    Godinho (ed.), *Studies on Macau Civil, Commercial, Constitutional and Criminal Law*
    (Hong Kong: LexisNexis, 2010) 1. René David and C. Jauffret-Spinosi, *Los grandes sistemas
    jurídicos contemporáneos*, 11th edn. (Mexico: IIJ/UNAM, 2010), underline that Macau is
    part of the *'continental European Law (Portuguese Law)' family*, at 398. Macau is not a mixed
    legal system (e.g. Scotland, the Philippines, or South Africa). Within civil law legal systems,
    Macau is most strongly linked to the German strand (as opposed to the French strand) via
    the Portuguese legal system. The Macau Civil Code is a direct descendant of the German
    Civil Code (BGB), and the Macau Penal Code is indirectly based on the German model. In
    addition, most key academics are followers of the highly analytic German doctrine, such
    as Professors J. Figueiredo Dias and M. Costa Andrade (University of Coimbra, leading
    academics in the field of criminal law and procedure) and Professor A. Menezes Cordeiro
    (University of Lisbon, leading academic in the field of civil and commercial law), among
    many others.
[3] Except in the specific case of an appeal for 'fixation of jurisprudence' (Article 427(1),
    Code of Penal Procedure; Article 652, Code of Civil Procedure), which presupposes and is
    designed to eliminate a contradiction between previous decisions. See note 13 below.
[4] Paula Correia, 'O sistema jurídico de Macau: uma perspectiva de direito comparado' in
    Augusto Garcia (ed.), *Repertório do direito de Macau* (Macau: University of Macau, 2007)
    17, 26, and 33.
[5] In addition, from 1999 until 2009, there were five judges in the Second Instance Court;
    in 2010, they became formally nine, but only eight are actually exercising their func-
    tions because of the appointment of Judge Fong Man Chong as Commissioner against
    Corruption on 20 December 2009.

likely be followed by the same court in similar future cases for the simple reason that the same judges will decide them. This causes rigidity and entrenchment of legal interpretations, effectively granting case law a major role. In addition, lower courts follow the opinions of the TUI, with some exceptions in the case of the Second Instance Court; there have been a number of divergent decisions between these two courts, which are discussed in this chapter.

On the use of comparative law, the various legal systems around the world that share the Portuguese language and the Portuguese legal tradition are in close contact and have common traits and sources that are sometimes almost identical, namely the Civil Code and the Penal Code. Macau courts do quote the case law of Portuguese courts. The potential role of Macau in this context is discussed below.[6]

Evolution of the judicial organization of Macau

Evolution leading to the transfer of sovereignty

First as a colony and then as a territory under Portuguese administration in the 20th century, Macau did not have an autonomous judicial system. Only in the transition period, after the signing by China and Portugal of the Sino-Portuguese Joint Declaration, deposited at the United Nations in 1987,[7] were concrete steps taken to advance it, by stages.

Until 1993, the only area in which Macau did not have special autonomy from Portugal was the judicial. Macau was a county (*comarca*) in the Portuguese judicial system, and appeals from Macau courts were litigated in the second instance court in Lisbon, with possibility of appeals to the Portuguese Supreme Court of Justice. In preparation for the transfer of sovereignty, the link with the Portuguese courts was replaced by a three-level independent judicial system. The process took place in two stages.

The first stage occurred between 1991 and 1993. Law 112/91, of August 29, separated the judicial organization of Macau from that of Portugal and became the foundation of the judicial system of Macau.[8] A further

---

[6] See section XI, b.   [7] In Macau Official Bulletin no. 23, 3rd sup., 7 June 1988.

[8] On this previous system, an overview in J. Oliveira, P. Cardinal, and P. Vidal, 'Macau' in C. Saunders and G. Hassal (eds.), *Asia-Pacific Constitutional Yearbook*, (Melbourne: University of Melbourne Centre for Comparative and Constitutional Studies, 1995) 84. For an overview of the system of appeals in civil litigation during this stage, see

change was approved in 1992, under which a court of appeal or second instance – the *Tribunal Superior de Justiça* (TSJ or High Court of Justice) – was established in 1992 and began functioning as the highest court until 1999.

Civil and criminal jurisdiction thus became localized, made of a court of first instance (renamed *Tribunal Judicial de Base* in December 1999), including an administrative court and the TSJ.[9] Links to the Portuguese civil and criminal jurisdictions were severed, and the decisions of the TSJ became final. During these years, the judicial system had, in most cases, two levels of courts. However, a number of links to Portuguese courts continued up to 1999, such as the possibility of appeal to the Constitutional Court. All remaining links to Portuguese courts were severed as of 1 June 1999.[10] Administrative jurisdiction was the last to be 'localized', as some legal proceedings against administrative acts were still being heard before the Supreme Administrative Court in Lisbon. The final step, in 1999, was the creation of the third level of jurisdiction required by article 84 of the Macau Basic Law (BL). The Court of Final Appeal was established immediately after the transfer of sovereignty.

Present structure

The administration of justice in the Macau SAR is, in accordance with the concept of the separation of powers, conducted by independent courts. The independence of the courts – a basic requirement of the rule of law – is enshrined in the Macau BL (Article 89), according to which courts

Jorge Godinho, 'Recursos admitidos na jurisdição cível de Macau e seu campo de aplicação', *Revista Jurídica de Macau*, 1/1998, 97 (bilingual Portuguese/Chinese).

[9] By December 1999, when it ceased to exist, this court was made up of seven judges, all senior magistrates in the Portuguese career system. This court was not directly continued after the transfer of sovereignty; it was extinguished, and most of its competences were continued by the Court of Second Instance (for which a totally different batch of five judges was appointed), but other competences more appropriate to a supreme court were continued by the TUI.

[10] By a decree of the President of the Portuguese Republic published in DR no 67, I Series-A, supplement, 20 March 1999. After this presidential act, only the Portuguese Constitutional Court competences, plus the exceptional competence of Lisbon courts to decide civil and criminal matters involving the Governor and the Under-Secretaries, were kept until the very end of the period during which Macau was a territory under Portuguese administration.

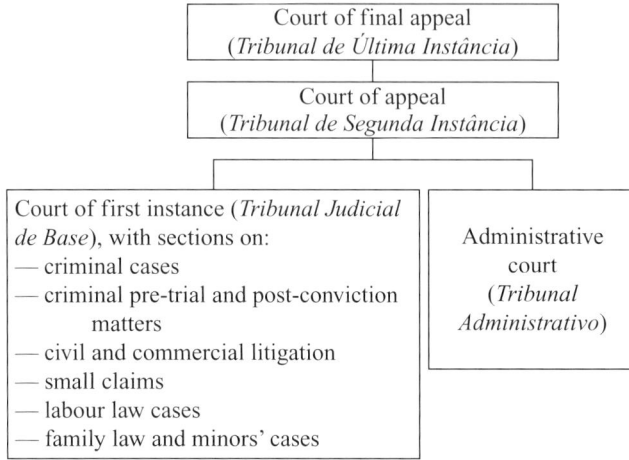

Figure 23.1 Judicial organization of the Macau Special Administrative Region.

should strictly apply the law and be free from instructions or pressures from other state powers, so as to enable a fair administration of justice.[11]

The law on judicial organization[12] sets out the current structure of the judicial system of Macau, which is made up of three levels, hierarchically organized for appeal purposes (see Figure 23.1).

First instance courts – normally where cases are initiated – are the *Tribunal Judicial de Base* and the *Tribunal Administrativo*. The *Tribunal Judicial de Base* is divided into a number of specialized sections, including a section on pretrial and postcriminal matters (which exercises competence over the preliminary phase of criminal proceedings, as well as competences over the execution of criminal penalties), a civil section, a small claims section, a criminal section, a labour law section, and a family law and minors' section. The Administrative Court is competent for litigation related to administrative, tax, and customs duties matters. The *Tribunal de Segunda Instância* (TSI) hears appeals from all first level courts; it is also the court in which certain proceedings should be initiated. The TUI is a supreme court composed of three judges, which is the

---

[11] For a discussion of the separation of powers from the point of view of the judiciary focusing on a similar legal structural design, see Peter Wesley-Smith, 'Judges and Judicial Power Under the Hong Kong Basic Law' (2004) 34 *HKLJ* 83.

[12] Law 9/1999 (*Lei de Bases da Organização Judiciária*), as amended by Law 9/2004, and by Law 9/2009.

top layer of the Macau judiciary. It hears appeals from lower level courts and is the court in which a very restricted number of proceedings should be initiated. It also performs one specific function: the uniformization of Macau courts' decisions.[13]

Regarding appeals in civil and commercial litigation, it should be noted that certain judicial decisions are immediately final and cannot be challenged. That is the case with the decisions of the *Tribunal Judicial de Base* and the *Tribunal Administrativo* in civil, labour, and administrative litigation if the amount involved is less than MOP$50,000 (around US$6,250).[14] In matters regarding taxation and customs duties, the limit is MOP$15,000 (around US$1,875). Similarly, the decisions of the TSI regarding cases of a value lower than MOP$1,000,000 (around US$125,000) are final.

After the transfer of sovereignty, no appeals from Macau courts are to be heard in Beijing courts, as the power of final adjudication rests with the Macau SAR.[15] However, Macau courts, similar to Hong Kong courts, do not have jurisdiction over acts of state such as defence and foreign affairs.[16] The interpretation power of the Standing Committee of the National People's Congress (NPCSC) in respect of the Macau Basic Law is similar to the situation of Hong Kong. Such power has been exercised only once.[17]

---

[13] It is possible to appeal a decision of the TUI if it contradicts a previous decision or when two decisions of the TSI are in contradiction, provided that the matter concerns the same legal issue and falls under the same legal provisions. This special type of appeal is aimed at clarifying the interpretation of a legal provision and shall function as a precedent for the courts in the ruling of future cases (Article 652-C, Civil Procedure Code). It is a special appeal to ensure the uniformity of the interpretation of the law or, in other words, the unity of the legal system; Viriato Lima, *Manual de direito processual civil* (Macau: CFJJ, 2005) 709.

[14] Article 18, Law 9/1999.   [15] Articles 19 and 84(2), Macau BL.

[16] If such issues arise in judicial proceedings, it is necessary for the courts of the Region to obtain a certificate on questions of fact concerning such acts of state from the Chief Executive, who, in turn, must previously obtain a certifying document from the Central People's Government. The certificate is binding on the courts: Article 19(3) BL. Another connection of local courts with nonjudicial Central Authorities is the mechanism of Article 143 of the BL.

[17] See section VI, b. See Chief Executive Notice 21/2012, in Official Bulletin 17/2012, 23 April 2012, pp. 430 f. According to this Interpretation, '1. The expression "should it be necessary to amend" in 2009 and subsequent years the Methodology for the Selection of the Chief Executive and the Methodology for the Formation of the Legislative Assembly under the two annexes [to the Basic Law] mentioned above means that it is possible to proceed with the amendment, and that it may also possible not to proceed with the amendment of such methodologies.'

Table 23.1 *Cases processed by the* Tribunal de Última Instância

Year	Cases decided	Left pending
2000	18	3
2001	18	4
2002	21	8
2003	36	6
2004	45	9
2005	36	9
2006	50	16
2007	41	39
2008	89	12
2009	53	9
2010	71	14
2011	84	6
2012	83	10

Number of cases in the *Tribunal de Última Instância*

As of the end of 2012, the number of cases decided by the TUI is 645. The annual number of cases processed is shown in Table 23.1.[18]

These figures show that, not surprisingly, there has been a gradual increase in the average number of cases decided by the TUI. It cannot be said that the TUI has been overloaded with cases; these are relatively small numbers, explained by the existence of somewhat restrictive rules on the admissibility of ordinary appeals, the elimination of judicial mechanisms that existed before 1999 such as the *amparo* appeal for the protection of fundamental rights, and the absence of a specific mechanism of constitutional review.[19]

[18] Source: Macau courts (www.court.gov.mo).
[19] Defending a formal (re)introduction of this mechanism, see Paulo Cardinal, 'Continuity and Autonomy – Leading Principles Shaping the Fundamental Rights Constitutional System' in F. MacGregor and Z. Larrea (coords.), *La ciencia del derecho procesal constitucional. Estudios en homenaje a Héctor Fix-Zamudio en sus cincuenta años como investigador del derecho*, vol. IV, *Derechos fundamentales y tutela constitucional*, Universidad Nacional Autónoma De México, Instituto Mexicano De Derecho Procesal Constitucional, Marcial Pons, 2008, 231; Zhao Guoqiang, 'O meio de tutela do processo executivo da Lei Básica' (2002) 57 *Administração* 922 (bilingual Chinese/Portuguese); Guo Tianwu and Chen Yan,

The Court of Final Appeal

The judges

Since its creation in 1999 and until 2011, the TUI has been composed of the same three judges: the President, Judge Sam Hou Fai (岑浩辉),[20] Judge Viriato Lima (Portuguese),[21] and Judge Chu Kin (朱健).[22] Unfortunately, Judge Chu Kin died at 42 years of age on 22 November 2011 following a car accident in Mainland China. To replace him, the first female Judge, Song Man Lei, was appointed to the TUI at the end of 2011.

The relatively young age of all judges in Macau is evident; the TUI judges are no exception. At the time of their nomination, they were respectively 40, 46, and 32 years old. Various factors relating to their training explain this. In addition, the three judges who have comprised the TUI for more than a decade had no more than a couple of years of experience as judges in Macau when appointed, except for Judge Lima. All three judges were recruited from the first instance court of the Macau territory; none came from the previous Superior Court of Justice of Macau. Judge Song Man Lei was formerly the deputy prosecutor of the Macau Public Prosecutions Office.

Number of judges

The number of judges of the TUI (three) has to be considered rather small, the smallest possible. This has the consequence of static or crystallized judicial doctrine and interpretation. Because of this, the need to enlarge

'As sugestões das Leis Básicas de Hong Kong e de Macau para o alargamento do regime jurídico da China' (2001) 51 *Administração* 222–3 (bilingual Chinese/Portuguese); Vitalino Canas, 'The general regime of fundamental rights in the BL and in the international instruments' in P Cardinal and J Oliveira (eds.), *One Country, Two Systems, Three Legal Orders – Perspectives of Evolution. Essays on Macau's Autonomy after the Resumption of Sovereignty by China* (Berlin: Springer-Verlag, 2009) 674.

[20] Born 1962. A short biography is available in China Vitae at www.chinavitae.com/biography/2452.

[21] Born 1954. Immediately before 1999, Judge Lima was a judge in the Court of First Instance and in this capacity tried one of the two highly visible cases of organized crime that marked the year 1999 just months before the transfer of sovereignty. Judge Lima has an academic interest in civil procedure and has published *Manual de direito processual civil* (Macau: CFJJ, 2005) (a comprehensive overview of civil procedure, 2nd edn., 2008).

[22] Judge Chu Kin graduated at the Catholic University of Lisbon, Portugal, and was also a part-time assistant professor at the Faculty of Law, University of Macau.

the number of judges has been suggested.[23] This need is more pressing if new competences are added to the TUI, as discussed later.

A 2009 law revised the number of judges in the first and second instance courts, enlarging the latter from five to nine judges,[24] but kept unchanged the number of judges in the TUI. It is clear that there is a need to considerably enlarge the number of judges that make up the TUI. The court should be composed of *seven* judges, therefore allowing it to judge in two sections of three and in plenary sitting (made of the two sections plus the president). This is needed for various reasons.

First, it would enable appeals in criminal cases against the members of the Macau government or other top leaders of the Macau SAR, a matter on which the TUI has original jurisdiction.[25] In these cases currently, the TUI acts as court of first and last resort as there can be no appeal; this breaches international law commitments binding on the Macau SAR, a situation evident since 2006. In such a case, the court in its present composition cannot even handle the standard first instance proceedings by itself in case the optional stage of *instruction* takes place, which makes it necessary to have four judges, one to preside over the instruction and three for the trial.[26] Second, it is necessary so that the court becomes self-sufficient to decide cases of uniformization of the jurisprudence of Macau courts. These are instances when the court is called upon to settle conflicting opinions of different courts. A larger court would no longer require calling additional judges from lower courts.[27] Third, it is necessary should a constitutional review mechanism be created, as it should happen. Given the importance of constitutional review, the matter should be decided in plenary sitting. Finally, the same reasoning applies in case the *amparo* mechanism is revived.[28]

---

[23] For example, by several lawyers and legislator Leonel Alves; see Isabel Castro, 'Advogados estão a favor do alargamento do quadro de magistrados mas sublinham necessidade de qualidade', in *Ponto Final*, 4 May 2009; Sónia Nunes, 'De regresso ao hemiciclo', in *Ponto Final*, 18 October 2010; and Cardinal, note 2 above, 28. The matter was also discussed during the 2009 elections for the Legislative Assembly.

[24] But see note 5 above.   [25] See note 63 below.

[26] Under Macau criminal procedure law, it is optional, after the accusation, to have a judicial review of the decision to accuse (*instrução*). This is presided by a judge and should not be seen as a sort of early trial but just as a review of the basis of the accusation. This was requested in the first *Ao Man Long* case, and it was presided by Judge Chu Kin, who then could not participate in the subsequent trial. The trial judges were the President, Judge Sam Hou Fai, Judge Viriato Lima, and Judge Lai Kin Hong (President of the Court of Second Instance).

[27] See note 13 above.

[28] As it should be, given its constitutional nature and *fundamentality*. In an *amparo* appeal, similar to that before 2000, it would also be possible to appeal from a decision of the TUI proper, judging in section.

Lack of dissenting opinions

It is necessary to mention that it was only in 2010 that the first dissenting opinion in TUI decisions was issued; around 350 decisions during more than a decade were taken by unanimity.[29] The first dissent came in a matter concerning administrative law.[30]

This has to be deemed unusual given the variety, legal complexity, and political sensitivity of the broad range of issues upon which the TUI is called to decide. Normally, three judges would sometimes disagree during the course of more than 10 years.

Origin of magistrates

Article 87(1) of the Macau Basic Law states that foreign magistrates may serve in the courts. Given the shortage of qualified jurists to fulfil the needs of the two bodies of magistrates (the judiciary and public prosecution), the recruitment of judges and public prosecutors from other Portuguese-speaking jurisdictions, such as Cape Verde or Brazil, aside from Portugal (from where limited recruitment takes place), should be considered.[31] This, of course, would require a political commitment, which has been lacking, despite repeated calls from the Macau Lawyers' Association.[32] In this regard, the situation of Macau is quite different from Hong Kong, where there is more openness.[33]

---

[29] The regulation on the functioning of the court clearly foresees the possibility of dissenting opinions. See *Regulamento do Tribunal de Última Instância da RAEM*, Article 12, in BO 5/2000, 2 Feb 2000.

[30] Ac TUI 10 May 2010, pr 14/2010 (Chu Kin; Viriato Lima dissenting). See Diana do Mar, 'TUI alinha com TSI no caso Finanças', in *Jornal Tribuna de Macau*, 14 May 2010.

[31] Even though Macau is not a common law system, thus making it more difficult to internationalized judges and prosecutors, the fact is that Macau has recruited judges from Portugal. Other non-common law systems do have external judges, including a Portuguese language legal system, East Timor, in which its current highest court is composed of an East Timorese, a Portuguese, and a Guinean Bissau judge. Besides, there are other judges and prosecutors from e.g. Brazil and Cape Verde.

[32] Jorge Neto Valente, Discurso do Presidente da Associação dos Advogados de Macau Dr. Jorge Neto Valente na sessão solene de abertura do ano judiciário, 2008, 10 (accessible at www.aam.org.mo/portuguese/DAJ2008_PT.pdf); Jorge Neto Valente, Discurso do Presidente da Associação dos Advogados de Macau Dr. Jorge Neto Valente na sessão solene de abertura do ano judiciário, 2010, 6 (accessible at www.aam.org.mo/portuguese/AJ_2010%20_PT.pdf).

[33] At the CFA, there have been non-permanent judges from Australia, the United Kingdom, New Zealand, Brunei, and South Africa. The same trend is present in other Hong Kong courts. Such judges improve the quality of judicial decisions, keep pace with international

Having foreign judges would allow new ideas to be brought into the court, as well as different judicial trends and even dissenting judgments, as is the pattern in any supreme or constitutional court. Finally, one area where there is sustained critique is the extent, quality, and detail of the justification of the decisions.[34] This is a more general problem in Macau.

Tribunal de Última Instância on fundamental rights and constitutional issues

Some specific mechanisms of constitutional review and for safeguarding fundamental rights that existed in the Portuguese tradition were abrogated upon the establishment of the Macau SAR.[35] However, the BL ranks as the highest law in the domestic legal system and states that 'no law, decree, administrative regulations and normative acts of the Macau SAR shall contravene this Law'.[36] It also states that 'Macau shall safeguard the rights and freedoms of the residents of the SAR and of other persons in the Region in accordance with law'.[37] Despite this, the TUI has adopted a timid role in protecting fundamental rights or engaging in constitutional review, especially in the early years of the MSAR.

Fundamental rights

It has been observed that while the TUI is not the *executioner* of fundamental rights, it is also not its *guardian*.[38] An overly formalistic approach

---

trends, and contribute to support the 'second system'. On this and other advantages brought by *external* judges e.g. Simon N. M. Young, 'Developing Constitutional Rights Jurisprudence in the Hong Kong Court of Final Appeal', paper delivered at the Macau Legislative Assembly second conference on Law and Citizenship, October 2008, later published as 'Constitutional Rights in Hong Kong's Court of Final Appeal' (2011) 27 *Chinese (Taiwan) Yearbook of International Law and Affairs* 67; Albert Chen, 'International Human Rights Law and Constitutional Law: Internationalization of Constitutional Law in Hong Kong', 2009, available at SSRN (ssrn.com/abstract=1527076). See also Chapter 24 (Marko) in this volume.

[34] See, in general, João Gil Oliveira, 'O juiz e o processo penal. Contributo para um reforço da legitimação' in Leonel Alves and Paulo Cardinal (eds.), *Primeiras jornadas de direito e cidadania da Assembleia Legislativa de Macau* (bilingual) (Coimbra: Coimbra Editora, 2009) 251.

[35] The constitutional review, in several modalities, and the *amparo*.

[36] Article 11.   [37] Article 4.

[38] Paulo Cardinal, 'Algumas notas sobre consolidação e vias de evolução dos direitos fundamentais na RAEM', paper delivered at the Macau Legislative Assembly second conference on Law and Citizenship, October 2008.

of the court to these issues can be detected, as well as a lack of deep-ening of important general principles and concepts (e.g. proportionality and other prominent principles) established in the Macau BL and the Sino-Portuguese Joint Declaration, including the principle of effective judicial protection[39] or the principle of continuity. These are usually sim-ply acknowledged in an administrative law context[40] – in contrast to what the Second Instance Court has already upheld.[41]

This timid approach is also reflected in the absence of specific mecha-nisms or in apparent loopholes in the legal regime, for example, regarding the freedom of demonstration, in which the TUI declared itself incom-petent to adjudicate a case that, by its own nature, demanded a swift response.[42] Another instance of a rigid, detached, or insensitive approach concerns family reunification, a right internationally established, which was dismissed with the court insensitively advocating that if a parent wishes to be reunited with his child, then instead of bringing the child to Macau, the parent – a legal immigrant worker – could simply cease to work in Macau and move back to his Southeast Asian homeland.[43] Finally, one more example is the *Ao Man Long* case and the dismissal of his right of appeal, also internationally guaranteed.[44]

---

[39] The Second Instance Court (Ac. TSI 26 February 2004, pr. 166/2003) stated that it is not difficult to see in Article 36 of the BL the establishment of a general principle of effective judicial protection to safeguard all subjective juridical positions as well as a special principle that guarantees fully access to administrative justice.

[40] For example, Ac. TUI 15 October 2003, pr. 26/2003 or Ac. TUI, 6, July 2007, pr. 14/2005, in which a matter of fundamental rights was decided solely from an administrative law perspective.

[41] Ac. TSI 11 April 2002, pr. 1284/2002, mentioning that the principle of proportionality is a necessary tool of analysis of admissible restrictions to fundamental rights and elevating proportionality to the realm of constitutional law.

[42] This gave rise to an amendment of the law on freedom of demonstration (see note 74 below and respective text). At the time of writing, the TUI had the chance to produce two rulings (Ac. TUI 29 April 2010, pr. 16/2010 and Ac. TUI 4 May 2010, pr. 21/2010) in which, in line with the spirit of legislative changes, demonstrated a more *pro libertate* and less formalistic approach and, more relevantly in this context, managed to produce timely decisions.

[43] Ac. TUI 30 January 2008, pr. 36/2007, regarding Article 9 of the United Nations Convention on the Rights of the Child, 'The Macau SAR does not impose the separation of the appellant from his son. This (the child) solely does not have the right to reside in Macau. The appellant can keep living with his son. He can simply stop working in Macau and return to his country of origin.' This sort of icy remark should be avoided in a formal judicial decision of a supreme court; it does not bring any legal argument to the discussion.

[44] The right of appeal arose from the ICCPR, Article 14(5), which is in force in Macau and was not subjected to any reservation or *similar* act. This right has been con-stantly reaffirmed in formal *reports* of competent international institutions, see e.g.

In the field of fundamental rights, in which there are relatively few cases, the tentative conclusion is that the court usually opts for a narrow or limited approach, with little elaboration of the fundamental rights enshrined in the BL and in international law.[45] The court does not engage an in-depth, proactive, and liberal stance, although it should be recognized that it does not present itself as being against human rights.

In a number of cases, most notably in *habeas corpus* matters, as shall be seen, and in recent cases of freedom of demonstration, the TUI has clearly assumed a guarantor role. In some others, for instance, relating to family rights as mentioned or in a case related to a fundamental right stated in Article 98 of the Macau BL,[46] it gave the appearance of a grey, distant, or shy court that does not give much room to recognize and emphasize certain fundamental rights.

In general, whereas one can see clearly active and widely respected *pro libertate* judicial activity in Hong Kong,[47] one fails to see such enthusiasm

---

Natalia Alvarez Molinero, 'Implementation of the Views of the UN Human Rights Committee in Spain: new challenges' unpublished (accessible at web.abo.fi/instut/imr/ research/seminars/ILA/Alvarez.doc) and documents mentioned therein. The matter is discussed in more detail below; see note 69 and respective text.

[45] When it does so, in some cases, is to reduce the scope of a right, such as in the right of appeal regarding criminal cases, in the *Ao Mao Long* case.

[46] Ac. TUI 25 October 2006, pr. 9/2006, in which it was argued that the application of professional tax to public servants was in violation of the guarantee established in Article 98 of the BL (similar to Article 100 of the Hong Kong BL), which states that upon the establishment of the Macau SAR, public servants previously serving in Macau may all remain in employment; continue service; and retain their seniority with pay, allowances, benefits, and conditions of service no less favourable than before. The court did not accept jurisdiction in view of the amount at stake: 'In litigations of tax matters, when the value of the case is lower than the appeal ceiling of the Court of Second Instance, an appeal cannot be lodged to the Court of Final Appeal against the ruling made by the Court of Second Instance. In the legal system of Macau SAR, courts in adjudicating cases can determine the conformity of laws with the Basic Law, in accordance with Article 11 of the Basic Law, and cannot apply norms which infringe the Basic Law or its principles, without prejudice to Article 143 of the Basic Law. In the legal system of Macau, because there is no specific proceedings to review the conformity of laws with the Basic Law, courts can only address such issues in the proceedings of concrete cases'. As a result, the complaint against a ruling not allowing the appeal was dismissed. In Hong Kong, a similar issue was dealt with e.g. by the CFA at (2005) 8 HKCFAR 304, stating that the conditions of the public servants cannot be less than before the handover. See also the dissenting vote of Judge João Gil Oliveira in Ac. TSI 24 November 2005, pr. 106/2004.

[47] J. Chan, 'Basic Law and Constitutional Review: The First Decade' (2007) 37 *HKLJ* 407, 419, states that the CFA has readily and consciously assumed a role of guardian of fundamental rights.

in Macau,[48] at least in the same dimension that can be seen on the other side of the estuary of the Pearl River.

Constitutional review

It is well known that a specific procedural avenue for issues of constitutionality does not exist in Macau. One must also bear in mind Articles 17 and 143 of the Macau BL, which may provide some review of constitutionality; but these mechanisms are of a political nature. The former article provides that if the NPCSC after consulting the Committee for the BL of the Macau SAR, considers that any law enacted by the legislature of the Region (thus not covering the control vis-à-vis administrative regulations) is not in conformity with the provisions of the BL regarding affairs within the responsibility of the Central Authorities or regarding the relationship between the Central Authorities and the Region, the Standing Committee may return the law in question but shall not amend it. The law returned shall immediately be invalidated. The latter article establishes that the power of interpretation of the Macau BL is vested in the NPCSC and when the Standing Committee makes an interpretation of a provision, the courts shall follow the interpretation of the Standing Committee.

However, these provisions do not obstruct the courts' competence to implement the constitutionality principle and safeguard the BL. The political mechanisms can coexist with normal judicial avenues, as in Hong Kong, which has to follow, in this aspect, the same type of rules in its BL.

Procedural institutions that existed before included the (general) *amparo* for fundamental rights and the constitutionality appeal, in several modalities. 'However, the year of 2000 revealed itself as the *annus horribilis*... on both fields. In fact, with a few and short rulings, the Court of Final Appeal, in the aftermath of the transfer of sovereignty, delivered a deadly blow to both institutions'.[49] This affected its mandatory

---

[48] See e.g. Pinheiro Torres, 'Comments' in *One Country, Two Systems, Three Legal Orders*, note 19 above, 318, stating; 'There is a particular need for a permanent rethinking for judicial decisions, especially (but not only) when human rights are involved and this should start at the highest level'.

[49] Basically, Ac. TUI 29 March 2000, pr. 8/2000 and Ac. TUI 2 February 2000, pr. 4/2000, for the constitutional review and Ac. TUI 16 February 2000, pr. 1/2000 and Ac. TUI 23 February 2000, pr. 2/2000 for the *amparo*. It was the understanding of the court that neither the *amparo* nor the compatibility of norms with the constitutional order could be exercised; in this last situation, there was even a case in which a given norm was allegedly

role of safeguarding the constitutionality principle and effective judicial protection because it was the understanding of the court at that time that the compatibility of norms with the constitutional order could not be reviewed in those cases. The provisions mentioned earlier, namely Articles 11 and 145 on the supremacy of the Macau BL over any ordinary norm[50] and the principles of justice and of the effective protection proclaimed in Article 36 demanded a different attitude – one that could easily be reached in Hong Kong – even in the absence of an expressly established judicial procedure. Besides, as stated in Article 83, the courts shall be subordinated to nothing but law, and the first law is the BL of Macau. This view changed only gradually.

It is worth taking a close look at the exact words of the Hong Kong CFA in *Ng Ka Ling*:[51]

both in violation of the previous constitutional order and the present one, as in Ac. TUI 16 February 2000, pr. 1/2000, 'After the appeal proceedings of the court judgments based on the application of rules in violation of the Constitution of the Portuguese Republic have been concluded according to Article 70(2) subparagraph 3 of Law No. 9/1999 of Macau SAR, a new proceeding cannot be recommenced to review the validity of the law against the Basic Law'. The quotation is from P. Cardinal, 'The Judicial Guarantees of Fundamental Rights in the Macau Legal System – A Parcours Under the Focus of Continuity and of Autonomy' in *One Country, Two Systems, Three Legal Orders,* note 19 above, 261.

50   For quite some time and despite a less than perfect clarity in the BL, many commentators have been claiming the necessity and adequacy of judicial review of the constitutionality of laws and administrative regulations (the latter are not even subject to the political control established in Article 17 of the BL) even if it would be better if there was an enactment of specific legislation. See e.g. Zhao Guoqiang, 'O meio de tutela do processo executivo da Lei Básica' (2002) 57 *Administração*, 922, affirming 'In my opinion, there should be someone with the competence to review, in the perspective of guaranteeing the correct implementation of the Basic Law and the perfection of the legal system. Given it is regarding the internal affair of the Macau SAR, the power to review belongs to the SAR not the Central Government, which means that there should be an organ of the Macau SAR to review. But which organ? In my opinion, this power to review can be given to the Court of Final Appeal of the Macau SAR.... Therefore, in the law stipulating its competence the Court of Final Appeal can be endowed with the power to determine whether all the laws, decrees, administrative regulations and other normative documents are in compliance with the Basic Law. Such does not contravene the Basic Law, as it is within the scope of internal affairs of the Macau SAR, and may also fill in the lacuna mentioned above'. See also A. M. Magalhães, 'O princípio da separação dos poderes na Lei Básica da futura Região Administrativa Especial de Macau' (1998) 41 *Administração*, at 721. G. Tianwu and C. Yan, 'As sugestões das Leis Básicas de Hong Kong e de Macau para o alargamento do regime jurídico da China' (2001) 51 *Administração* 22–3.

51   (1999) 2 HKCFAR 4. See also Chapters 13 (Mason) and 14 (Chen and Lo) in this volume.

In exercising their judicial power conferred by the Basic Law, the courts of the Region have a duty to enforce and interpret that Law. They undoubtedly have the jurisdiction to examine whether legislation enacted by the legislature of the Region or acts of the executive authorities of the Region are consistent with the Basic Law and, if found to be inconsistent, to hold them to be invalid. The exercise of this jurisdiction is a matter of obligation, not of discretion so that if inconsistency is established, the courts are bound to hold that a law or executive act is invalid at least to the extent of the inconsistency.[52]

The considerable success of constitutional justice in Hong Kong and its dozen or so rulings of unconstitutionality *erga omnes* of legal norms has been of such a sort that:

[m]any of these cases have involved government playing a more sophisticated role in presenting constitutional arguments. It is no longer the case that a constitutional remedy is a measure sought by the applicant party upon a successful rights violation being shown. Nowadays, government may seek a constitutional remedy (such as remedial interpretation) to save legislation from being declared unconstitutional or to suspend temporarily the declaration of unconstitutional in order to allow the legislature time to pass corrective legislation.[53]

As mentioned, there were initially refusals in Macau regarding the constitutional review. However, since 2007, various TUI rulings promisingly and clearly affirm that it has the competence to scrutinize the conformity of any rule with the Macau BL, further stating that in the cases adjudicated, the courts cannot apply norms stated in either laws or administrative regulations that are in violation of the BL or its settled principles.[54] These

---

[52] Also: 'We consider that the unconstitutional parts of the No 3 Ordinance can be appropriately severed from the rest which is constitutional. The test is whether the constitutional parts are distinct from the unconstitutional parts so that what is unconstitutional may be severed from what is constitutional leaving what is constitutional intact. In our view, that question must be answered in the affirmative. The following parts are unconstitutional and should be excised. . . . [W]e grant the following declarations and relief. . . . A declaration that the following parts of the Immigration Ordinance and Regulations are null and void and are excised therefrom'.

[53] Young, note 33 above.

[54] Ac. TUI 18 July 2007, pr. 28/2006, 'In the case submitted to the court, although no party raised the issue of illegality, the court cannot apply the provisions of laws or administrative regulations which infringe the Basic Law or principles it establishes, without prejudice to Article 143 of the Basic Law'. In Ac. TUI 14 May 2008, proc. 21/2007, the court stated: 'The violation of the principle of hierarchy of laws is within the scope of jurisdiction of the courts, therefore it is the matter that should be considered in the appeal, although it has not been raised by the parties in the case contended'.

are, from several angles, key decisions that merit further study and may indicate a deviation from a previously *conservative stance* by the court. Time will tell.

It is of relevance to take a closer look at more recent judicial decisions from TUI on this subject and note its nuanced position. For example, in Ac. TUI 30 April 2008, proc. 8/2007, it is said that:

> When courts adjudicate cases, they are subject to law only. Consequently, if the court deems that the law applied is against a law of higher hierarchy, the court shall apply the law of superior hierarchy or other legal norms, not the illegal norm of lower hierarchy. Unless the law provides otherwise, and regardless of the type of case, instance and procedural phase, the court applying the law can review its validity on its own initiative or upon request of a party, particularly if there is a violation of a higher law, provided the case is within its jurisdiction. If it confirms this breach of law, the court cannot apply the rule which should be applied otherwise but was deemed illegal, and shall apply other legal rules in order to pass a ruling within the scope of the plaintiff's petition. However, it shall be emphasized that the conclusion that a norm is in violation of law of superior hierarchy is merely an integral part of the courts' reasoning, or one step on the logical process leading to the final decision, and it does not constitute the content of the ruling. The court cannot pass a ruling that a norm is illegal with a general binding force. The sentence is only valid in the case itself, and does not produce any effect toward other cases and other courts. The norm considered illegal does not become invalid because of this particular ruling.[55] It shall be noticed that a preliminary issue is one question, and the issue of unconstitutionality (at another level) is another question. Unconstitutionality is not an incidental issue or issue of procedural law, but a preliminary issue or issue of substantive constitutional law. But it is brought incidentally in proceeding which has other different issues as object.[56]

The evolution is positive and appears to be consolidating a positive approach to constitutionality, although with justifiable doubts and

---

[55] Thus, in the opinion of the TUI, a declaration such as the one in (1999) 2 HKCFAR 4, of a certain regulation being null and void and therefore no longer exists in the legal system, is not possible in Macau.

[56] See also Ac. TUI 25 October 2006, proc. 9/2006, 'In the legal system of Macau SAR, the courts in hearing cases can consider the conformity of laws with the Basic Law. And in compliance with Article 11 of the Basic Law, the courts cannot apply norms which infringe the Basic Law or principles it establishes, without prejudice to Article 143 of the Basic law. In the legal system of Macau SAR, there is no specific procedure to review the conformity of laws with the Basic Law, therefore courts can consider this issue only in the proceedings of specific cases'.

caution. It seems, however, still insufficient,[57] namely because of the refusal to assume the power to declare *erga omnes* the unconstitutionality of norms by violation of the BL, in sharp contrast to the Hong Kong CFA.

This trend culminated in 2010 in the first TUI decision holding a norm to be in breach of the Macau BL and thus inapplicable, Ac. TUI 12 May 2010, pr. 5/2010 (Viriato Lima), which found a breach of the principle of equality. The TUI considered that:

> without prejudice to the legislative discretion that should be recognized as vested in the legislature, the existence of contradictory legal regulation applicable to civil servants, without any reasonable justification, breaches the principle of equality.[58]

The dispute revolved around a norm on the effects of absences from work of teachers. The court compared the rules in the University of Macau, the Macau Polytechnic Institute and secondary schools dependent upon the Education Department, and detected contradictory legal regulation, which was considered unacceptable.

Use of international and comparative law

The number of citations of foreign judgments in the decisions of the TUI is not very significant. However, it should be recalled that Macau is not a common law jurisdiction and therefore, by nature, the citation of foreign judgments would be less usual than in Hong Kong. But several citations do occur, for instance, in civil law (i.e. the law of obligations, property law, family law, inheritance law), commercial law, criminal law, and some public law areas. All citations are, as far as we are aware, of Portuguese courts.

As for foreign doctrine, there is ample use of Portuguese academic treaties, journal articles, and legal opinions, with a special emphasis on civil and commercial law matters but also in, for example, administrative law and criminal law.

---

[57] For example, in Ac. TUI 14 May 2008, proc. 21/2007, the TUI stated that, although the violation of the principle of hierarchy of laws is within the scope of its jurisdiction and therefore it is a matter that should be considered in the appeal, even if it has not been raised by the parties, however, it was stated that '[i]n proc. 38/2006, 2006/11/15, the court decided not to consider this issue. But in this case the appellant did not emphasize properly the violation of legal principle mentioned'.

[58] Ac TUI 12 May 2010, pr. 5/2010.

Citations of Chinese sources are fewer than Portuguese sources and occur especially in public law issues. Apart from Portuguese and Chinese citations, occasionally foreign texts citations, such as from France or Spain, appear, but this is rare. We are not aware of references to the European Court of Human Rights or to the European Court of Justice; such would be normal in discussions arising out of the interpretation of the International Covenant on Civil and Political Rights (ICCPR), which is applicable in Macau.[59]

There is a certain trend to use Chinese doctrine and concepts in Macau courts to justify decisions even in cases when the subject clearly at stake is well inside the boundaries of Macau's autonomy. This is not merely a comparative law contextualization exercise. This trend, if augmented and broadened, may well bring a new plane of intersection (indirectly, because of the relatively low importance of case law in a civil law legal system) between Macau law and Chinese law and, eventually, contribute to a dilution of Macau's own legal system identity and, at the end of the day, its own autonomy.

When adjudicating cases in which the issues are exclusively regulated by Macau law and have no connection with the Chinese legal system, such as fundamental rights, it is not in line with the principle of continuity and the Macau autonomy to elect Chinese law (and Mainland Chinese doctrine) as its main reference; instead, the main reference should be its European roots, especially Portuguese law.[60] This may look as being politically incorrect and may seem strange;[61] it may even have the potential to resemble some sort of neocolonialism (which clearly is not the case), but that is dictated until 2049 by the status of Macau under the paramount principle of 'one country, two systems'.

One point worth mentioning is the important contribution of the TUI in the field of the consolidation of the principle of primacy of international

---

[59] According to Chen, note 34 above, a review of relevant cases in Hong Kong from 1991 to mid-2009, presents the following panorama: cases citing the ICCPR – 255; cases citing documents of the UN Human Rights Committee under the ICCPR – 46; cases citing the Universal Declaration of Human Rights – 13; cases citing the ICCPR – 41; and cases citing the European Convention on Human Rights – 150.

[60] A quick overview of Hong Kong judicial decisions points towards the use of common law jurisdictions and not Mainland Chinese law (including in adjudicating cases involving BL norms). See e.g. A. Mason, 'The Place of Comparative Law in Developing the Jurisprudence on the Rule of Law and Human Rights in Hong Kong' (2007) 37 *HKLJ* 299; J. Chan, 'Basic Law and Constitutional Review: The First Decade' (2007) 37 *HKLJ* 407, 410.

[61] See Zhu Lin, 'A situação da língua chinesa nas sentenças judiciais de Macau – duma perspectiva dos direitos fundamentais' (2007) 75 *Administração* 173.

law. This is a traditional principle of law that implies that states and regions must conform their domestic legislation with the international treaties and international obligations. This implies, it is understood, that in case of conflict between international treaties and domestic regulation, the former shall prevail. It should be noted that the primacy of international law was enshrined in Article 1(3) of the Civil Code as a general principle of law that happens to be inserted in the Civil Code and not merely as a civil law principle. This primacy has been upheld by the TUI and the TSI,[62] although with variations in the *ratio decidendi.*

Tribunal de Última Instância and criminal law: the cases of the former Secretary Ao Man Long

The TUI was called upon to play a major and highly unusual role in what is by far its most well-known and debated case: the trial – in first, single and last instance – of the former Secretary for Transport and Public Works, Ao Man Long.[63] This case provided a most rare glimpse into the TUI working as a first instance trial court, which is quite useful to understand the attitudes of the TUI in the field of criminal law and procedure.

Because of the complexity of the facts, two different criminal cases were initiated against the former Secretary.[64] In addition, a procedural interim decision by Judge Viriato Lima also became of great visibility: the dispatch of 12 December 2007, issued in the first case.

---

[62] E.g. Ac. TUI 2 June 2004, pr. 2/2004; Ac. TSI 1 April 2004, pr. 301/2003; Ac. TSI 4 December 2003, pr. 221/2003.

[63] Following the Portuguese tradition, the highest ranking public officers are tried before the CFA for crimes committed in the exercise of their functions. This rule exists in a number of other countries, and there are various justifications for it, some more convincing than others such as senior judges would be better prepared for high-profile cases and less prone to political interference and the institutional setting would also be more adequate.

[64] The first was decided by Ac. TUI 30 Jan 2008, pr. 36/2007. In these proceedings, the trial in the TUI opened in October 2007 and concluded on 12 December 2007. Ao Man Long was found guilty of: 2 crimes of abuse of power; 20 crimes of corruption for an unlawful fact; 20 crimes of corruption for a lawful fact; 14 crimes of money laundering; 1 crime of intentional wrongful declaration of assets; and 1 crime of illicit enrichment. The outcome was 27 years imprisonment plus confiscation of MOP$800 million. The second case was decided by Ac. TUI 22 April 2009, pr. 53/2008, and increased the sentence to 28 and a half years. Other linked cases were started and have concluded or are still pending in the first instance court against various business persons and family members, but these are beyond the scope of the current discussion.

Right of appeal

An issue of particular interest and one that generated much discussion was that of the right of appeal. Should Ao Man Long, being tried directly in the top court, not have a right of appeal?

The matter was addressed in an interim admissibility decision (which considered an appeal that had been lodged regarding issues of evidence) by Judge Viriato Lima on 12 December 2007. Judge Lima held that there was no right of appeal regarding the evidential issues; that there would be no right of appeal of the final decision; and, furthermore, that the laws could not be changed in order to create a right of appeal while the case was pending. It was stated:

> It is not possible to lodge an appeal from the decisions issued by the TUI as a result of an obvious principle of procedural law, according to which it is not possible to appeal the decisions of the supreme body of a judicial organization, given that there is nowhere to appeal to.... Therefore, the TUI has the final word in the cases submitted to it, and its decision closes the case.[65]

However, this is debatable. Under the ICCPR, Article 14(5), 'Everyone convicted of a crime shall have the right to his conviction and sentence being reviewed by a higher tribunal according to law'. The ICCPR guarantees a right to judicial review in relation to decisions that affirm guilt and impose penalties. That is not what was at issue in the interim admissibility decision, which dealt with a matter of evidence, so the decision of 12 December 2007 needed not to have considered the matter. However, as mentioned, Judge Lima went on to consider and answer other issues that were not before the TUI. Specifically, Judge Lima affirmed that even if it was an appeal from the final decision, still there would be no right of appeal:

> Anyway, we can add straight away that even if the decision of the TUI was a decision considering the accused guilty of having committed a crime, it would also not be possible to appeal.

This is due to an understanding according to which:

> The legislator, by stating that in some cases the TUI is the Court competent for [a very restricted number of cases foreseen in Macau law] surely has taken into account that this Court, being the highest in the Macau SAR, has

---

[65]   Ac. TUI 12 Dec 2007, pr. 36/2007.

the best prepared and more experienced judges, as should be presumed. Therefore, the legislator has accepted that it decides in first instance and in last instance.[66]

This was a less than modest statement that the judges of the TUI are to be presumed the best and more experienced ones *ipso facto*.

On the interpretation of the ICCPR, Judge Viriato Lima drew attention to the parallel case of the European Convention on Human Rights (ECvHR) and, on this basis, stated that it was possible to have exceptions to the rule in Article 14(5) of the ICCPR. The ECvHR, Protocol 7,[67] Article 2, was cited as an instance of the general principle according to which there can be no appeal from a supreme court. He went on to conclude:

> It is a fact that in art. 14(5) ICCPR this exception is not expressly foreseen, which is probably due to the fact that the ICCPR is from 1966, while the said Protocol is much more recent, from 1984, and therefore more updated. But this does not mean that art. 14(5) should not be interpreted as we stated, that is, there is no breach of art. 14(5) ICCPR when the court that tries the case in first instance is the TUI.[68]

This interpretation missed a key point: in order to have an exception to Article 14(5) in the domestic legal order, it would have been necessary to formulate a reservation to the ICCPR. Macau, China, could have formulated a reservation but chose not to do it. Various states, including Belgium, Italy, Holland, and Switzerland, have done so. Therefore, Article 14(5) of the ICCPR is in force without limitations in the Macau SAR.

The Human Rights Committee has already considered this issue at least twice.[69] In both cases, Spain was held to be in breach of the ICCPR for not allowing an appeal. The ICCPR commentary states:

> Where the highest court of a country acts as first and only instance, the absence of any right to review by a higher tribunal is not offset by the fact of being tried by the supreme tribunal of the State party concerned; rather,

---

[66] *Ibid.*
[67] It should be recalled that this protocol is part of the regional European system of protection of fundamental rights and therefore was never in force in Macau.
[68] See note 65 above.
[69] *Jesús Terrón* v. *Spain* (Com. no. 1073/2002, CCPR/C/82/D/1073/2002, November 2004) in which a member of the regional parliament of Castilla-La Mancha was sentenced for forgery of documents in the Spanish supreme court and *Luis Oliveró Capellades* v. *Spain* (Com. no. 1211/2003, CCPR/C/87/D/1211/2003, August 2006) in which a member of the national parliament was convicted of forgery, organized crime, and tax crimes in connection with unlawful financing of the Socialist Party.

such a system is incompatible with the Covenant, unless the State party concerned has made a reservation to this effect.[70]

However, the issue was never argued. Just days after being convicted, Ao's lawyer announced that his client had instructed him that he would not appeal the decision. As a result, no attempt to file an appeal ever took place.

As a final observation on this point, it may be said that the issue is primarily a problem of law: Judge Viriato Lima was right in observing that no other court exists above the TUI, and a court cannot create another court. However, with due respect, Judge Lima was wrong on the content of the ICCPR; as mentioned, it grants a right of appeal to everyone in Macau. If Ao Man Long had appealed from the final decision, the appeal should have been allowed, to comply with the ICCPR. It would then be for the Macau SAR to solve the problem, which indeed has not yet disappeared; it is created by the law on judicial organization. In the final analysis, it is for the legislator to solve the matter. The law should be amended, either by having more judges in the TUI or by eliminating the criminal cases that are heard in first instance by the TUI, moving them to the TSI. However, the manner in which the issue was discussed showed poor handling of international law concepts and low sensitivity to an issue of fundamental rights.

Trend towards a harsher criminal law

The decision of the TUI in the first *Ao Man Long* case is quite significant as to the interpretation on various points of anti-money laundering law and on sentencing. In fact, the TUI has consistently dismissed nearly all of the restrictive or narrow interpretations that have been in the centre of academic debates regarding the crime of money laundering. It is not possible to engage here on an extended debate of the various issues; only some points shall be highlighted. The overall purpose is to illustrate the broad trend towards a harsher stance in dealing with criminal law and sentencing issues that Macau courts have been following.

One issue was the question of whether a link with organized crime under the law of 1997 was necessary, raising the scope of the crime of money laundering under the law that applied from 1997 until April 2007. The issue has been questioned in Macau over the years. The court found

---

[70] Human Rights Committee, General Comment No. 32. Article 14: Right to equality before courts and tribunals and to a fair trial, doc. CCPR/C/GC/32, 2007, point 47.

that it did not require a connection to organized crime. It should be recalled that Ao was not charged with organized crime. The implication was that the money laundering charges could stand.

Another matter was the relation between the predicate offence and the crime of money laundering; the question arises as to whether a person can be prosecuted for the crime that generated the proceeds and for the laundering of the same proceeds, therefore being punishable for both. The TUI stated that this is possible, with various arguments, observing that the legally protected interests are different.[71]

On the crime of 'illicit enrichment', the TUI held that there is no breach of the presumption of innocence. It held that the possibility to demonstrate the lawful origin is a defence (similar to self-defence or necessity) and considered that the presumption of innocence only refers to the objective or subjective elements of the crime but not to the defences.[72] This amounts to a restrictive reading of the scope of the presumption of innocence.

The overall message coming from the case was of a heavy-handed court, an impression reinforced by the extremely severe penalty applied: 27 years of imprisonment, which then became 28 and a half years in the second case. This sentence, which was received as a bit of a shock when it was issued, confirms and endorses a trend towards a harsher enforcement of criminal law. Coming from the highest court, the message is clearly heard across the entire legal system. Another aspect of this trend seems to be that the courts of Macau are now less prone to allow the early or conditional release from prison of convicts after having served two-thirds of the prison time.[73]

---

[71] For criticism of this interpretation, see Jorge Godinho, 'Sobre a punibilidade do autor de um crime pelo branqueamento das vantagens dele resultantes' in Manuel da Costa Andrade, Maria João Antunes, e Susana Aires de Sousa (orgs.), *Estudos em Homenagem ao Prof. Doutor Jorge de Figueiredo Dias*, vol. III (Coimbra: Coimbra Editora, 2010) 363.

[72] On this matter, see J. Godinho, 'Financial Strategies of Crime Control in the Macau SAR' in *Studies on Macau civil, commercial, constitutional and criminal law*, note 2 above, 249, 269–70; in more detail, J. Godinho, 'Do crime de «riqueza injustificada» (Artigo 28.° da Lei n.° 11/2003, de 28 de Julho)' (2007) 11(24) *Boletim da Faculdade de Direito da Universidade de Macau* 17, accessible at SSRN: ssrn.com/abstract=1097243.

[73] A number of petitions have been sent to the Legislative Assembly in this respect; reacting to this, the third Committee of the Assembly announced in January 2011 that it was conducting a study and raising the issue with the Macau government, with a view to possible law reform. See Joana Freitas, 'Liberdade condicional em fase de revisão', *HojeMacau*, 26 January 2011. The case of Ao Man Fu, the brother of Ao Man Long, who died in November 2010 in prison because of poor health, is striking in this regard. Ao had a leg amputated in February 2010 because of diabetes complications and applied for release,

The 'dialogues' between the Legislative Assembly and the courts

In the relations between the legislative branch and the judiciary, legislation clearly aimed at correcting judicial interpretations that were perceived as not ideal was approved twice in the field of fundamental rights: freedom of demonstration[74] and access to justice. There have been problems in the past with the judicial review of administrative decisions that restricted the right to hold political rallies, and these issues must be decided swiftly to ensure that freedom of demonstration can be exercised. One problem was the uncertainty over the competence of courts to hear the case; another problem was whether judicial representation by a lawyer was mandatory or not. The other issue was related to alleged denials of the right to have a lawyer present when investigated by public authorities, regardless of whether the person is a suspect or a witness.[75]

Another area of dialogue is the politically sensitive matter of the boundaries and correlations between laws of the Legislative Assembly and administrative regulations of the Chief Executive.[76] Important

---

but this was rejected by the first instance court and then by the TSI in July 2010. See Ac. TSI 15 July 2010, pr. 485/2010; 'Ao Man Fu Dies at Hospital', *Macau Daily Times*, 30 Nov 2010.

[74] Law 16/2008 and Law 1/2009, respectively. On freedom of demonstration, see the formal *Parecer of the 3.ª Comissão Permanente 2/III/2008* (Opinion of the 3rd Permanent Committee of the Legislative Assembly), accessible at www.al.gov.mo/lei/leis/2008/16-2008/po.htm, available in both official languages of the Macau SAR in which it is stated specifically that although some doubts arise since the law passed in 1993, Law 2/93/M stated that the competent court was the TSJ, which was then the top court, but after 1999, the doubt arose as to which court would be competent to deal with this special appeal on fundamental rights, the TUI having decided that such court would be the TSI; see Ac. TUI pr. 43/2006 (not available in the online database). Hence, the parliament introduced changes in the law in order to make it clear that the competent court is the TUI regarding this fundamental rights appeal and not the second instance, thus clarifying and opting for the solution that, in the eyes of the Legislative Assembly, is more coherent. It also concluded that in these cases, there is no mandatory need for a lawyer.

[75] In view of these allegations, the Legislative Assembly passed Law 1/2009, which has established the right of having the assistance of a lawyer in all acts conducted before any public authority, including judicial ones and criminal investigation ones, in any phase of the process regardless of the status (e.g. suspect or witness). In the *Parecer 1.ª Comissão Permanente* 1/III/2009, accessible at www.al.gov.mo/lei/leis/2009/01-2009/parecer.pdf (date accessed: 6 August 2011), it is stated the importance of the fundamental right of access to law, in its several corollaries, being guaranteed both by the BL and international instruments such as the Joint Declaration and the ICCPR. Law 1/2009 clarified the matter and reinforced this fundamental right.

[76] The matter was addressed by Law 13/2009. See *Parecer 1.ª Comissão Permanente 3/III/2009*, accessible at www.al.gov.mo/lei/leis/2009/13-2009/po.htm, in which it is mentioned that the need for a new law derives from the uncertainties in the courts decisions. In this case, the solutions of the new law can be seen as closer to the solutions pointed out by the

principles were affirmed in the ruling by the TUI, such as only the Legislative Assembly has legislative power; there is primacy of law; there are areas reserved to law, namely in fundamental rights; there may be independent administrative regulations, enacted without a previous authorizing law, in fields not reserved to law and directly based on the BL; a reinforcement of the principle that no court adjudicating a specific case can apply laws or administrative regulations that are not in conformity with the BL; and that courts should deal with the matter *ex officio* (Ac. TUI, 18 July 2007, pr. 28/2006). It should be noted that because of the restrictions set by Article 75 of the Macau BL on the power of the legislators to initiate legislative proposals, issues that might deserve legislative intervention may not be dealt with via an initiative of the Macau Legislative Assembly and have to depend on a possible impulse of the Government.

Habeas corpus

One area where the TUI was seen very positively was in its treatment of two habeas corpus cases.[77] Both were cases in which Hong Kong permanent residents were detained upon arrival in Macau at the ferry terminal. The arrests related to crimes allegedly committed in Mainland China, for which Interpol 'red notes' had been issued. The TUI concluded that in the absence of specific agreements for cooperation in criminal matters between Macau and Mainland China, it was not possible to simply arrest the suspects and just hand them to the Mainland authorities. It has proved so far impossible to conclude such agreement.[78] Therefore, while this legal status lasts, no person can be arrested and handed over, as actually happened in the second case. The TUI, perhaps somewhat shocked by the repetition of such incident shortly after a previous one, had harsh words, in the second case, for the authorities who rendered the person: 'Such acts

---

TUI rather than those of the lower courts, especially the TSI. In fact, the TUI position can be seen, in general, as more adequate to the Macau SAR constitutional system that, in this respect, bears little resemblance to the previous system in force or with Portugal. This TUI ruling is balanced and reasoned in depth. It was generally well received and has contributed to the pacification of the issue, which culminated with the approval of Law 13/2009.

[77] Ac. TUI 20 March 2007, pr. 12/2007, and Ac. TUI 12 February 2008, pr. 3/2008. The second case occurred during the lunar new year holiday and was decided by a court made of a judge of the TUI, a judge of the second instance courts, and a judge from the first instance courts.

[78] For a discussion of the pending issues, see Jorge Costa Oliveira, 'Macau SAR Inter-Regional Mutual Legal Assistance in Criminal Matters' in *One Country, Two Systems, Three Legal Orders*, note 19 above, 565.

affect the credibility of the justice system, undermine the rule of law and do not give prestige to the Macau SAR'.[79]

Conclusions

General observations

The TUI has several times become involved in controversial political and legal decisions, which have attracted critique from the legal community on technical grounds. The TUI did not manage to impose an aura of natural authority and be regarded as a highly qualified house of law where justice is administered in a way that *inevitably* commands the general respect by the legal community and acceptance of its technical solutions. It has not been seen as a significant beacon in areas such as constitutional review and fundamental rights, much in contrast to the Hong Kong CFA. It is viewed sometimes as engaging in an overly formalistic approach at the expense of a more *pro homine* stance. It has a deficit of its role in guaranteeing fundamental rights and 'constitutional review'.

In the field of criminal law, the TUI handed, in the Ao Man Long case, the harshest sentence in living memory for white collar crimes. While it was clear that the crimes committed by the former Secretary were many and serious, this prison sentence was received with surprise in many circles, signalling a clear departure from a certain tradition of leniency that existed under Portuguese rule. This illustrates a post-handover trend for harsher enforcement of criminal law, which was promoted and stimulated by the TUI in the highly visible Ao case – but this is hardly compatible with the concept of continuity of the pre-handover lifestyle. However, in a number of areas, it is possible to detect some signs of a positive evolution, such as in constitutional review issues and habeas corpus cases.

It seems clear that reform should take place in order to help and reinforce the TUI by enlarging considerably the number of judges; the recruitment of foreign non-permanent judges, as happens in Hong Kong and in East Timor; revising the legal regulation appeals; and introducing formal mechanisms of fundamental rights procedures and of constitutional review. The relevance of international law instruments as well as that of the Macau BL should also be recognized and promoted, and their implementation by the judiciary should be strengthened.

---

[79] Ac. TUI 12 February 2008, pr. 3/2008.

Prospects

In general, the legal system of Macau faces various different possibilities of evolution. One is to keep its proximity and dialogue with the lusophone legal systems, from which Macau and China can benefit. Another is a gradual loss of this link. No vision has been articulated so far, and the key operators of the system do not seem to have a clear perspective of the future direction or at least have not made it explicit.

The many linkages with the family of legal systems marked by the Portuguese language should be kept and developed. There are various lusophone legal systems,[80] originated from Portugal, first imposed and then adopted by Portuguese-speaking countries and jurisdictions. Macau should continue to be a full member of this group.

The similarities between these legal systems vary from, for example, Brazil (probably the less common because of historic reasons and the size of the country) to Cape Verde. The latter shares much legislation, doctrine, and other features, with the point of reference of this 'subfamily' that is Portugal. The similarity also varies among branches of law. For instance, in the field of fundamental rights, there is a sharing among several lusophony jurisdictions[81] caused by the irradiating force of the Portuguese constitutional system of fundamental rights.

In all fields, from criminal law to private law, the accomplished Portuguese doctrinal elaboration, produced in many universities, provides a safe and solid conceptual basis for both legal education and legal practice and a continuing link to the broader and highly sophisticated Roman-German family of legal systems.

This aspect is of great importance on several planes.[82] For example, there is a common academic doctrine even though specific laws may

---

[80] Various *lusophone* legal systems might even constitute a subfamily of the civil law family. On this hypothesis, see P. Cardinal, 'La institución del recurso de amparo de los derechos fundamentales y la juslusofonia – los casos de Macau y Cabo Verde' in Fix-Zamudio and Ferrer-Macgregor, *El Derecho de Amparo en el Mundo Hector* (México: UNAM, Editorial Porrúa, 2006) 897–8.

[81] Carlos Blanco de Morais highlights important common characteristics in the fundamental rights topic, C. Blanco de Morais, 'Tópicos sobre a formação de uma comunidade constitucional lusófona' in *Ab Uno ad Omnes* (Coimbra: Coimbra Editora, 1998) 69.

[82] Zhu Lin, 'A situação da língua chinesa nas sentenças judiciais de Macau – duma perspectiva dos direitos fundamentais' (2007) 75 *Administração* 159, states that the use of Portuguese as a technical-juridical language is one of the characteristics of Macau, revealing the origins of the system previously in force and maintaining the unity of the judiciary language and thus assuring, both from the doctrinal and the jurisprudential stance, the intrinsic relationship with the original system.

vary. For a small place such as Macau, which has a tiny legal community, this aspect is of high relevance – one can also have access to a 'certain common law of academic works and judicial decisions'.[83] Currently, the courts of Macau only quote doctrine and case law from Portugal, not from other Portuguese-speaking jurisdictions. Macau can only gain by exploring and deepening the linkages with Portuguese-speaking legal systems. This requires political commitment, which is already quite solid in the economic field,[84] and should be fully extended to the legal area.

A fifth of the so-called transition period (1999–2049) has elapsed. The second system is, as expected, surviving and developing. However, more should be done to maintain, enrich, and develop it further, anchoring it firmly in the institutions and society of Macau thus fully fulfilling the one country, two systems paramount maxim in all of its dimensions and corollaries. In this mission, the TUI in particular – and the courts in general – is not alone, but undoubtedly part of the success depends upon it.

---

[83] For example, the case of Cape Verde illustrates the advantages of maintaining a point of reference even after independence and after a reform of the legal system. 'All these projects follow openly in many (albeit not all) respects legal developments in Portugal. Rather than deviating from Portuguese law, they tend to re-create the similarity or even identify of the rules of the two legal systems'; see M. Bogdan, 'The Law of the Republic of Cape Verde after 25 Years of Independence' (2000) 44 *Journal of African Law* 94. All is done by, of course, exercising full sovereign powers and without prejudice or sense of a lesser capacity. No drama, political or other, is needed to cloud normal juridical communications and interfaces of legal systems.

[84] See José Carlos Matias, 'The Macau Forum: China's Charm Offensive for Lusophone Countries', in *IPRIS Lusophone Countries Bulletin*, November 2010, 5.

24

Foreign judges: a European perspective

JOSEPH MARKO

A structural framework of comparison

From the very beginning I must make clear that there are two important caveats with regard to this topic, which are also challenges for a scientifically sound comparison. Because of the doctrine of state sovereignty, it sounds almost inconceivable that a foreign citizen should serve on the bench of a national supreme court or a separate constitutional court of another country with the power to review the legislation, passed as an exercise of popular sovereignty, for conformity with the national constitution. Judicial review is a highly sensitive issue of legitimacy with regard to the 'right' balance between the two guiding principles of democracy and the rule of law. Switzerland, in this regard, must serve as an example of one of the two possible solutions, regardless of whether this is a civil law or common law system. The Swiss Constitution of 2000, in particular Article 188, still prohibits the Swiss Supreme Court to review federal law, begging the question whether the 'law' – that is, in Rousseauian terms, the 'people' – can do no wrong, for instance by violating basic principles of the rule of law. On the other hand, the US Supreme Court, having 'invented' judicial review of legislation in *Marbury* v. *Madison* (1803) under a common law system,[1] is perennially challenged to find the balance between judicial activism and judicial self-restraint, which follows

---

[1] The doctrine of parliamentary sovereignty under British constitutional law, which prohibits judicial review of legislation by judges must be seen as a singular exception in this respect, although the membership of the European Union and the incorporation of a bill of rights have led effectively to a measure of judicial scrutiny. Cf. Gernot Sydow, *Parlamentssuprematie und Rule of Law. Britische Verfassungsreformen im Spannungsfeld von Westminster Parliament, Common-Law-Gerichten und europäischen Einflüssen* (Tübingen: Mohr Siebeck, 2005) and Elliot Kay, 'To What Extent Do Traditional Propositions on Parliamentary Sovereignty Survive in a Modern Context?' (2010) *Durham Law Review*, accessible at www.scribd.com/doc/95035508/To-What-Extent-Do-the-Traditional-Propositions-on-Parliamentary-Sovereignty-Survive-in-a-Modern-Day-Context.

from the doctrine of separation of powers as the basic element of rule of law.

However, the same also holds true for constitutional courts in all civil law systems, which were initially established in Central Europe in the Germanic legal family as courts of final instance for adjudication in civil and criminal matters. Following the model of the Austrian Constitutional Court, established in 1920 according to the theories of the Viennese school of legal positivism, constitutional courts enjoy the sole power of judicial review of legislation.[2] They also provide the final institutional guarantee for the protection of human rights, in particular through a special individual complaint mechanism. Constitutional courts in the Romanistic civil law tradition in Western and Southern Europe (i.e. Italy, Spain, and Portugal)[3] were established only after World War II – in Italy in 1956, Spain in 1980, and Portugal in 1983, although at first without powers to review legislation or protect rights. The French Conseil constitutionnel, established according to the French Constitution of 1958, is ideologically still based on the Rousseauian concept, expressed in Article 6 of the French Declaration of the Rights of Men and Citizens,[4] that 'the' law expresses the will of the sovereign people. Hence the idea of judicial review of legislation by judges not enjoying direct democratic credentials militates, even now, against *ex-post* control of the validity of the law. Therefore, the Conseil constitutionnel could only be addressed before the adoption of the law until 2010.[5] At the same time, a claim against human rights violations can be submitted and adjudicated only before 'ordinary' courts. Since 2010, the Conseil d'Etat and the Cour de Cassation may refer a legal provision to the Conseil constitutionnel, if this provision is deemed to violate the rights and freedom guaranteed by the Constitution. Even this form of ex-post judicial review is seen as a revolution in the French system.

---

[2] Cf. Hans Kelsen, *Wesen und Entwicklung der Staatsgerichtsbarkeit* (*The Essence and Devel-opment of Judicial Review*), in Veröffentlichungen der Vereinigung der Deutschen Staat-srechtslehrer (Publications of the Association of German Staatsrechtslehrer), Wesen und Entwicklung der Staatsgerichtsbarkeit. Überprüfung von Verwaltungsakten durch die ordentlichen Gerichte (The Essence and Development of Judicial Review. The Review of Administrative Acts by Ordinary Courts), Nr. 5, W. de Gruyter, 1929, 53–73.

[3] For a short overview, see Louis Favoreu, *Les Cours Constitutionnelles* (Paris : Presses Universitaires de France, 1986).

[4] Article 6, first sentence, simply reads: 'La loi est l'expression de la volonté générale....', reprinted in Stéphane Rials, *Textes Constitutionnels Français*, 19th edn. (Paris: Presses Universitaires de France, 2006) 6.

[5] See Article 61 of the French Constitution.

After the collapse of communist regimes in Central and Eastern Europe in 1989, which had not – in the tradition of socialist law – established specialized constitutional courts, all new democratic constitutions in those countries saw the German Constitutional Court, established in 1951, as a model for an all-encompassing *ex-post* judicial review mechanism without, however, also taking over the all-encompassing individual 'constitutional complaint' mechanism (Verfassungsbeschwerde) against human rights violations.[6]

It goes without saying that because of the reasons discussed, nowhere in Europe had foreigners been invited to sit on the bench of a supreme court or a constitutional court until 1995. The only exception was Cyprus, where after the conflict between Greek and Turkish Cypriot leaderships and ethnic riots before and after independence in 1960, the newly adopted constitution had foreseen that the Presidents of the High Court (Article 153) and the 'Supreme Constitutional Court' (Article 133) could not be citizens of Cyprus, Greek, Turkey, or Great Britain, the former two being the warring parties and the latter two as protectors of the treaties underlying the declaration of independence. Hence, the prominent German scholar of public law, Ernst Forsthoff, served as President of the Supreme Constitutional Court from 1960 until 1963, when he resigned because of the ongoing conflict.[7]

The second, hypothetical exception would be Croatia, where – in the course of violent conflict in the second half of 1991 between the legitimate Croat government and the rebellious political leadership of the Serb minority population over the territory later called 'Srpska Krajina', encompassing approximately one third of the Croatian territory in the south and southwest of the country – the idea of a specialized Human Rights Court was promoted by international mediators. Hence, Article 60 of the constitutional law on the protection of national minorities, adopted in December 1991, provided for such a court under the leadership of a Chief Justice and with two of five members to be appointed from

---

[6] A comprehensive overview is given by Wojciech Sadurski, *Rights Before Courts: A Study of Constitutional Courts in Postcommunist States of Central and Eastern Europe* (Dordrecht: Springer, 2005). Only half of the postcommunist Central and East European constitutions have taken over the individual 'constitutional complaint' mechanism for the protection of human rights, that is, the Albanian, Croatian, Czech, Hungarian, Latvian, Macedonian, Polish, Slovene, and Slovak constitutions.

[7] See Cevalet Gürle, 'Die ungeliebte Republik (1960–1963)' (The 'Unloved Republic (1960–1963)'), accessible at miami.uni-münster.de/servlets/DerivateServlet/Derivate-2735/diss_guerle/05_diss_guerle.ptf.ptf.

member states of the European Union. However, this court, in fact, was not established.[8]

Both examples, Cyprus and Croatia, make clear that foreign judges as 'neutral' mediators on the bench of national courts come into play in situations after conflict over statehood when courts are seen as important instruments for peace-building. This was also the case in Bosnia-Herzegovina (BiH), where the bloody war between 1992 and 1995, including a genocide in Srebrenica by the military and paramilitary forces of the so-called 'Republika Srpska' under the political leadership of Radovan Karadzic and the military leadership of General Ratko Mladic, was ended only by NATO intervention in the fall of 1995 and with the conclusion of a peace treaty, the Dayton–Paris General Framework Agreement for Peace (GFAP) on 14 December 1995.[9] Karadzic was indicted and tried before the International Criminal Tribunal in the Hague, and Mladic was surrendered to the Tribunal only in May 2011.

The GFAP is composed of the Framework Agreement and 11 annexes. Annex 4 in the form of an international treaty, concluded between the warring parties, can be seen as 'the' Constitution of BiH. Article I, para 3 regulates the territorial division of the country, subdivided into two so-called 'Entities', namely the 'Federation of Bosnia and Herzegovina', which came into being by another international treaty, the Washington Agreement, concluded in April 1994, and 'Republika Srpska', which had seceded from the internationally recognized 'Republic of Bosnia-Herzegovina' in April 1992 and started the war. Annex 4 also contains a catalogue of human rights in Article II and regulates the allocation of powers between the Entities on the one hand and the so-called 'Institutions of Bosnia and Herzegovina' in Article III on the other. What is of additional relevance are Articles IV, V, and VI, regulating these institutions, namely the legislative, the executive and the judicial power. Article VI provides for a Constitutional Court as the sole judicial institution on state level. There is no supreme court of BiH[10] nor any other court because the judicial power rests within the residual competence of the Entities. Hence, both Entities have a fully fledged court system including supreme courts and separate constitutional courts.

---

[8]   See Joseph Marko, *Der Minderheitenschutz in den jugoslawischen Nachfolgestaaten* (Minority Protection in the Yugoslav Successor States) (Bonn: Kulturstiftung der deutschen Vertriebenen, 1996) 102.

[9]   General Framework Agreement for Peace in Bosnia and Herzegovina, 14 Dec 1995, 35 I.L.M. 75, 89.

[10] In 2002 a so-called 'State Court' was established to adjudicate on all civil and criminal matters arising out of the application of state laws.

A closer look into the jurisdiction of the Constitutional Court makes clear that this institution is a hybrid mix of the American and the Austrian–German model. Article VI, paragraph 3 (a) *inter alia* provides for the system of 'abstract' review of legislation through the Constitutional Court as a specialized court. Hence, without the necessity of a lawsuit before an ordinary court, a number of state authorities may submit a request to the Constitutional Court, in particular in order to decide 'whether any provision of an Entity's constitution or laws is consistent with this Constitution'. Such a 'dispute' over conflicts of norms can be referred only by a member of the three-member Presidency, composed of one Bosniak, one Serb, and one Croat (Article V), by the Chair of the Council of Ministers, by the Chair or a Deputy Chair of either chamber of the Parliamentary Assembly, namely the House of Representatives and the House of Peoples, again to be composed of five Bosniaks, five Serbs, and five Croats or by one fourth of either chamber of a legislature of an Entity.

Article VI, paragraph 3 (c) provides for the system of 'concrete' review of legislation – that is, any court in Bosnia and Herzegovina may address the Constitutional Court on 'whether a law, on whose validity its decision depends, is compatible with this Constitution, with the European Convention on Human Rights and Fundamental Freedoms and its Protocols, or with the laws of Bosnia and Herzegovina'. Finally, Article VI, paragraph 3 (b) provides for an 'appellate jurisdiction over issues under this Constitution arising out of a judgment of any other court in Bosnia and Herzegovina'. All of the legal-dogmatic problems arising out of this hybrid mix of the two models for judicial review are discussed in detail in this chapter with regard to the case law of the court.

Since there are no publicly accessible *travaux préparatoires* of the negotiations in Dayton, it remains unclear why the parties in Dayton agreed to include three foreign judges in the composition of the Constitutional Court as a 'national' court. This might even be more astonishing with regard to the fact that also 'international' judicial bodies were created under other annexes. In particular, annex 6 provided for a Human Rights Commission, composed of an Ombudsperson as first instance and a Human Rights Chamber as second instance. This institutional structure closely resembled the supranational human rights protection mechanism of the European Convention on Human Rights (ECHR) of the Council of Europe with a Commission as first instance and the European Court of Human Rights as second instance. In contrast to the Constitutional Court, whose entire composition followed the model of the US Supreme Court with all together nine judges, so that the three foreign judges were in a minority position, both the Ombudsperson and the majority of the members of the Human Rights Court, including its President, had to be foreign citizens. In addition, a Real Property Claims Commission was established under annex 7, again with a foreigner as chairperson. Finally, annex 10 established an International High Representative responsible for the entire civilian coordination of the implementation of the GFAP, and annex 11 provided for an International Police Task Force under UN auspices. Moreover, the Governor of the Central Bank had to be a foreigner.[11] Taken all together, it becomes clear that this strong international presence in BiH was seen as a necessary element to support the institutional, political, and economic reconstruction of the country after four years of terrible warfare.

The entire selection procedure for the three foreign judges must therefore be seen within this context. Article VI, paragraph 2 (a) of annex 4 provides that 'four members shall be selected by the House of Representatives of the Federation, and two members by the Assembly of the Republika Srpska. The remaining three members shall be selected by the President of the European Court of Human Rights after consultation with the Presidency'. Despite this seemingly ethnically 'neutral' language for the composition of the Constitutional Court, it must have been clear from the very beginning that the binational Federation parliament and the Republika Srpska (RS) parliament would appoint only members of the respective 'constituent peoples', namely Bosniaks, Croats, and Serbs, as they are labelled in the Preamble of the Dayton Constitution (annex 4). And that is how it came about. The Federation parliament elected two Bosniak and two Croat and the RS parliament two Serb jurists. Thus, the number of three foreign judges was obviously thought to counterbalance the *de facto* rigid ethnic representation so that the international judges could always prevent the 'outvoting' of one or even two of the 'members of constituent peoples' but remained themselves in a minority if all three ethnic groups were unanimous, thereby providing for a strong incentive to overcome the serious ethnic divide in the country and its institutions.

Finally, in the selection procedure for the foreign judges, the member states of the Council of Europe were asked to nominate appropriate candidates in 1996. All together 22 candidates were nominated this way. After the consultation procedure with the Presidency of Bosnia and Herzegovina as foreseen in the Dayton constitution, the President of the European

---

[11] Annexes 1 and 2 regulated military matters for the multinational military force deployed in Bosnia-Herzegovina under NATO leadership, initially called IFOR (International Force) and then renamed Stabilization Force or SFOR.

Court of Human Rights – at that time the distinguished Norwegian jurist Ralf Ryssdal – appointed the three foreign judges. One of them was Hans Danelius, a practising judge of the Swedish Supreme Court and member of the European Commission of Human Rights. Another was Louis Favoreu, Professor and 'doyen' of French constitutional law at the University at Aix-en-Provence. I was the third member, 42 years old at the time I was chosen, and had been Associate Professor of Comparative Constitutional Law and Political Sciences at the University of Graz. I was known to the Council of Europe because of my involvement as a constitutional expert and comparative lawyer in the Council's Commission for Democracy Through Law, commonly called the 'Venice Commission'. Moreover, what I see as an important added value for the position, elaborated in more detail later, I was the only one who spoke the – commonly called – 'domestic' language, that is, the Bosnian-Croat-Serbian (BCS) language.

After having outlined this context, I will come to my second caveat, the challenge in avoiding comparative fallacies. I discovered, to my astonishment, many more similarities between the situation of BiH and Hong Kong than the topic 'foreign judges' and the two institutions, the Bosnian Constitutional Court and Hong Kong's Court of Final Appeal (CFA), would suggest:

- Both 'constitutions' are strongly anchored in treaty-based international law.
- In both cases, an international human rights treaty is incorporated – in Hong Kong, the International Covenant on Civil and Political Rights (ICCPR), and in BiH, the ECHR, which, according to Article II (2) of the Dayton Constitution, 'shall have priority over all other law'.
- There are no publicly available official *travaux préparatoires* in BiH or Hong Kong.[12]
- With regard to linguistic questions, two languages, English and BCS, as well as English and Chinese, play an important role for interpretation.
- Last, but not least, in both cases, a communist system with its consequences for the understanding of rule of law and judicial review was or is involved.

---

[12] Yash Ghai, 'The Intersection of Chinese Law and the Common Law' in Jorge Oliveira and Paulo Cardinal (eds.), *One Country, Two Systems, Three Legal Orders – Perspectives of Evolution. Essays on Macau´s Autonomy after the Resumption of Sovereignty by China* (Berlin: Springer, 2009) 33. Some drafting material for the Basic Law is available on Basic Law Drafting History Online, accessible at sunzi.lib.hku.hk/bldho/home.action.

The most striking difference, of course, seems to be the fact that the GFAP serves to hold BiH together and to overcome the territorial and ethnic divide by 'integration' of the two Entities and their institutions into a 'common' state, whereas the autonomy of Hong Kong and the purpose of the Basic Law (BL) after the resumption of sovereignty by China is 'not to integrate the legal systems of Hong Kong and China, but rather to keep them apart' under the political formula of 'one country, two systems'.[13] Seen from another perspective, however, this is – despite formal political party pluralism – exactly the same purpose and motivation of the entire Serb political leadership in their view and interpretation of the legal system developed by the GFAP. They see the RS until now as a 'sovereign' national state of the Serb people that is linked to BiH in some sort of confederation, if at all, and with a 'natural' right to national self-determination to break away from BiH whenever it suits them. Hence, there is no interest in constitutional reform by de-ethnification of institutions and the transfer of powers from the Entities to the state level or even a new territorial division in terms of regionalism or federalism to make state institutions more effective for further integration into the European Union.[14]

These considerations must suffice to make clear that the observation of similarities and differences depends on the respective perspective so that – unlike the central perspective in Western painting developed in Renaissance Italy and its belief that this is the only one, 'true' perspective – politics and law are always multiperspective because of underlying basic values and functions. Hence, similarities and differences are always relative descriptions of social, political, and legal 'realities', which, depending on the perspective, can even change their positions. The comparative method, however, needs a 'firm' *tertium comparationis*, which can never be offered only by institutions 'as such'. It makes no sense to compare the Chinese National People's Congress (NPC) with the Westminster Parliament as a 'representative' institution. Seen from this perspective, both would simply seem to be the same, namely a 'parliamentary' institution.

---

[13] I hereby follow Ghai, 'Intersection', *ibid.*, 16. Strikingly, also Bosnia-Herzegovina was and is metaphorically characterized by numbering: one country, two Entities, and three peoples (or religions!).

[14] Cf. Joseph Marko, 'Defective Democracy in a Failed State? Bridging Constitutional Design, Politics and Ethnic Division in Bosnia-Herzegovina' in Yash Ghai and Sophia Woodman (ed.), *Practising Self-Government: A Comparative Study of Autonomous Regions* (Cambridge University Press, 2013).

Hence, it is not the comparison of institutions according to a description of similarities and differences at first sight, but the analysis of functions and structures[15] that will provide us with the necessary framework for the following comparative analysis of the jurisprudence of the Bosnian Constitutional Court.

The case law of the Constitutional Court of Bosnia and Herzegovina in comparative perspective

The starting point for analysis must thus be the function of any court of final appeal, supreme court, or constitutional court, namely to serve the value and purpose of rule of law through a politically independent body of judges who settle all sorts of disputes in an impartial and fair procedure on the basis of foreseeable rules. The lack of independence of such a body in a non-democratic system is thus not only a fact to be recognized as a 'difference' but becomes a problem in itself to be analysed. The same holds true for a structural perspective into which both Hong Kong and BiH can be put: the relationship – or 'interface'[16] created – between the 'two systems' of the People's Republic of China and Hong Kong and how the CFA, committed to the BL as 'the' constitution and basis for rule of law, and the Chinese NPC and its Standing Committee (NPCSC) with the competence to interpret provisions of the BL according to Article 158 BL interact. Thereby the following questions are raised: as a court of final instance, does the CFA have to follow any 'interpretation' of the BL by the NPCSC, and what is the meaning of interpretation? Is the CFA thereby subordinated to the NPCSC, which would, of course, seriously endanger Hong Kong's autonomy? And finally, to what extent 'are the Central Authorities, particularly the NPC, bound by the Basic Law?'[17]

The same structural problem of institutional relationships was created in BiH through the creation of the Human Rights Chamber and the Real Property Claims Commission, both bodies with international participation as elaborated above and that were given the power to hand down 'final and binding decisions' (Article 11 paragraph 2 annex VI, and Article 12.7 annex VII of the GFAP). Moreover, according to Article V of

---

[15] I have elaborated the functional-structural approach, that is, the turn from Parsons to Luhmann, for comparative constitutional law in some detail in Joseph Marko, *Autonomie und Integration. Rechtsinstitute des Nationalitätenrechts im funktionalen Vergleich (Autonomy and Integration. Legal Instruments of Minority Protection from a Functional Comparative Perspective)* (Wien-Graz-Köln: Böhlau Publisher, 1995) 25–36.

[16] See Ghai, note 12 above, 20.   [17] *Ibid.*

annex X, establishing the Office of the High Representative, he or she 'is the final authority in theater regarding interpretation of this Agreement on the civilian implementation of the peace settlement'. Again, this raised the following 'structural' questions: What are the position and role of the Constitutional Court vis-à-vis the Human Rights Chamber and the Real Property Claims Commission? Because they have an overlapping jurisdiction with regard to human rights protection, do they all stand on an equal footing, or is there a relationship of subordination of the latter bodies to the Constitutional Court or – if they are seen as 'international protection' mechanisms – the other way round? Even more important became the question of the scope of the mandate of the High Representative (HR) after two years in office, when this mandate was extended by the so-called Bonn Powers (i.e. the right to dismiss public functionaries from office because of their obstruction of the implementation of the Dayton Agreement and to adopt laws instead of the parliaments of Bosnia and Herzegovina).[18]

Thus, when HRs Carlos Westendorp from Spain and Wolfgang Petritsch from Austria started to interfere more and more into domestic politics by 'decreeing' necessary laws for the proper functioning of state institutions as long as the Parliamentary Assembly was blocked because of the use of veto powers along ethnic lines and to dismiss elected officials from their posts, including the Serb and Croat members of the Presidency, the question was raised to what extent is the HR bound by the Dayton Constitution and, in particular, the ECHR so that the Constitutional Court would enjoy the right to review also the decisions of the HR with regard to their conformity with the Constitution and the ECHR?

Below I present the case law of the Bosnian Constitutional Court with regard to these questions, critically analyse it, and discuss the role of the foreign judges in constitutional adjudication.

The scope of judicial review

As a preliminary question for the clarification of the institutional position of the Constitutional Court vis-à-vis international and national bodies, the Constitutional Court had early to address the meaning of the first sentence in Article VI. 3: 'The Constitutional Court shall uphold this Constitution'. This sentence included two problems, namely what is

---

[18]   The text of the Bonn powers can be found in OHR (ed.), *Bosnia and Herzegovina. Essential Texts*, Bonn Peace Implementation Conference 1997, Point XI.2, 199.

specifically meant by 'this Constitution' and what role is conferred on the Constitutional Court in order to 'uphold' the Constitution?[19]

Because the wording 'this Constitution' obviously referred to annex 4 of the GFAP, the first question raised the problem of the rank of the other annexes of the GFAP within a hierarchy of norms and thereby the question whether the other annexes might also serve as a normative standard for judicial review by the Constitutional Court. As for the first part of the problem, case U 7/97[20] contained a somewhat confusing *obiter dictum* insofar as the court stated that 'the' Constitution was part of the entire Dayton Agreement with the conclusion that there can be no conflict between these annexes. In contrast to scholarly opinion,[21] the court relied upon a theory of a 'legal unity' of the Dayton Agreement with the consequence that the text of the Framework Agreement and of all the other annexes were assigned constitutional rank, assuming that in the event of a nevertheless possible conflict of norms between the annexes, such a conflict cannot be resolved with recourse to the argument that annex 4

---

[19] Article VI. 3 reads:

The Constitutional Court shall uphold this Constitution.

   a) The Constitutional Court shall have exclusive jurisdiction to decide any dispute that arises under this Constitution between the Entities or between Bosnia and Herzegovina and an Entity or Entities, or between institutions of Bosnia and Herzegovina, including but not limited to:
     – Whether an Entity's decision to establish a special parallel relationship with a neighboring state is consistent with this Constitution, including provisions concerning the sovereignty and territorial integrity of Bosnia and Herzegovina.
     – Whether any provision of an Entity's constitution or law is consistent with this Constitution. Disputes may be referred only by a member of the Presidency, by the Chair of the Council of Ministers, by the Chair or a Deputy Chair of either chamber of the Parliamentary Assembly, by one-fourth of the members of either chamber of the Parliamentary Assembly, or by one-fourth of either chamber of a legislature of an Entity.
   b) The Constitutional Court shall also have appellate jurisdiction over issues under this Constitution arising out of a judgment of any other court in Bosnia and Herzegovina.
   c) The Constitutional Court shall have jurisdiction over issues referred by any court in Bosnia and Herzegovina concerning whether a law, on whose validity its decision depends, is compatible with this Constitution, with the European Convention for Human Rights and Fundamental Freedoms and its Protocols, or with the laws of Bosnia and Herzegovina; or concerning the existence of or the scope of a general rule of public international law pertinent to the court's decision.

[20] The case law of the Constitutional Court of BiH is accessible also in English at www.ustavnisud.ba.

[21] Cf. Oliver Dörr, 'Die Vereinbarungen von Dayton/Ohio' ('The Dayton/Ohio Agreements') (1997) 35 *Archiv des Völkerrechts* 129–80, esp. 130.

is 'the supreme law' but only through a harmonizing interpretation. In conclusion, whereas annex 4 was seen as the 'constitutional document' of BiH, the list of 15 international treaties for the protection of human and minority rights in annex 1 to annex 4 as well as the other annexes of the GFAP form the bulk of 'constitutional law' with the same purpose to serve as a standard of judicial review for the Constitutional Court.

This position of the first[22] court obviously served the purpose to gain a broad scope for judicial review in order to achieve as much legal ground as possible in terms of protection of 'the' Constitution and the protection of human and minority rights. Despite this 'benign' purposive intent, the majority of the court remained cautious in the beginning of its jurisprudence, insofar as provisions of the Framework Agreement and of other annexes were applied as standards of review only on a clear textual basis in annex 4 itself.[23]

As concerns the second problem of interpretation of the first sentence of Article VI. 3 of the Dayton Constitution, the court was also guided by the theory of 'legal unity' in order to close all possible gaps in the protection of, in particular, individual rights of citizens. Hence, reminiscent of the famous controversy between Hans Kelsen and Carl Schmitt,[24] the majority of the court understood its role to be the 'guardian of the constitution' and thereby constructed its own power of judicial review in a broad sense

---

[22] The mandate of the judges selected in 1997 was restricted to five years, according to Article VI.1(c) of the Dayton constitution. Hence, in the course of 2002 and 2003, an entirely new bench was selected. I therefore distinguish in the following between the 'first' and the 'second' court.

[23] Cf. The first, third and fourth partial decisions in case U 5/98 in Official Gazette (OG) BiH, nr. 11/00, [15]; OG nr. 23/00, [73], [79] et sequ. and OG nr. 36/00, [18], [20], [29], [31].

[24] Cf. the controversy between Carl Schmitt, *Der Hüter der Verfassung (The Guardian of the Constitution)* (Tübingen: Mohr, 1931) and Hans Kelsen, *Wer soll der Hüter der Verfassung sein? (Who Shall Be Guardian of the Constitution?)* (Berlin-Grünewald: W. Rothschild, 1931). Carl Schmitt had argued that the president of the republic as a *pouvoir neutre* above the political parties represented in parliament should be the 'guardian of the constitution', competent to review the conformity of legislation with the constitution. Hans Kelsen responded to this proposal by referring to his theoretical conception for the necessity of a separate judicial body having a monopoly for judicial review thereby following the tradition established by the US Supreme Court and the Imperial Court of the Habsburg Empire. It is interesting to note in this respect that Judge Snjezana Savic, elected by the Parliament of Republika Srpska, was appointed Professor at the Law Faculty of Banja Luka in the field of Theory of Law and State on the basis of her thesis on the legal theory of Hans Kelsen titled: 'Pojam prava kao normativnog poretka – prilog kritici Kelsenove normativne doctrine' ('The Concept of Law as Legal Order – A Contribution to the Critique of Kelsen's Doctrine'), published in Banja Luka in 1993.

by declaring that the phrase 'to uphold this Constitution' can only be given effect when there is a comprehensive and all-encompassing system of legal protection with the Constitutional Court as final institutional guarantee on top of the entire court system.

As a matter of principle, this would not have been contested with reference to the programmatic provision of Article I, paragraph 2 of the Dayton Constitution, declaring that 'Bosnia and Herzegovina shall be a democratic state, which shall operate under the rule of law . . . .' However, all of the 'domestic' judges of the first court had been trained under the communist system and were thus inclined to stick to the text of normative provisions in a rather literal and formalistic way. Moreover, the Swedish judge had no experience in judicial review of legislation because the Swedish Supreme Court declared a law unconstitutional only twice over the past 60 years. For him, there was therefore a strict dividing line between law and politics following from the priority of the text of constitutional provisions.

The strictly formal, positivistic approach could be seen from the very beginning in the interpretation of the provisions of Article VI. 3 (a) and (c) providing for the 'abstract' and 'concrete' review procedure. Nowhere does the Constitution mention administrative general regulations or individual decisions, let alone in the wording of Article VI. The majority of the domestic judges were therefore of the opinion that administrative decisions cannot at all be reviewed by the Constitutional Court. Because this interpretation would have created a big gap in the legal protection mechanism, exaggerated by the fact that no specialized administrative courts exist in BiH, two of the foreign judges vehemently argued that the text in Article VI. 3 (a): 'Whether any provision of an Entity's constitution or law is consistent with this Constitution' also covers administrative regulations and decisions because the English term 'law' in the singular is not restricted to the meaning of 'parliamentary statute'.[25] However, the court

---

[25] This was, in addition, also a linguistic problem of translation because most unofficial translations into Bosnian, Croatian, and Serbian use the term 'zakon', which is indeed a parliamentary statute. Despite the fact that according to the closing provisions the text of the GFAP is deemed equally authentic in Bosnian, Croatian, Serbian, and English, there is no 'official' translation adopted by the Parliamentary Assembly so that the foreign, but not domestic, judges considered only the English text as 'authentic' text. Another, even more important example can be found in Article II, [2], last sentence of the Constitution, which reads in English: 'These [i.e. the ECHR and its Protocols] shall have priority over all other law.' All translations of this phrase into Bosnian, Croatian, and Serbian translate the term 'law' into 'zakon' (i.e. parliamentary statute) with the consequence that the ECHR would – in the legal hierarchy – not be above the Constitution but below it so that

rejected this view in a series of cases and declared the review of general administrative regulations or individual acts under the 'abstract' review procedure simply inadmissible.[26] There were, of course, other arguments in favour of this decision because Article VI. 3 (a) definitively restricts the right to submit a request to the Constitutional Court to the state authorities enumerated there. Because under the former republican constitution of Bosnia and Herzegovina within the framework of the entire communist constitutional system of the Socialist Federal Republic of Yugoslavia, the Constitutional Court had the competence to decide on any submission by anybody against a law – that is, an *actio popularis*, it was, of course, quite understandable that the court rejected submissions by individual citizens and private companies but also political parties, the bar association, and associations of retired persons under Article VI. 3 (a). Otherwise the docket of the court would have exploded.[27]

As far as the relationship between Article VI. 3 (b) and (c), the appellate jurisdiction and the 'concrete review' procedure, is concerned, the hybrid mix of the American system of a 'diffuse' judicial review and the Austrian–German system of a monopoly of judicial review by a specialized constitutional court created several problems. Strictly in line with the text of Article VI. 3 (c), the first court was of the opinion that it is up to the district, appeals, and supreme courts of the Entities, whether they will refer to the Constitutional Court 'an issue . . . concerning whether a law, on whose validity its decision depends, is compatible with this Constitution', the ECHR or with the laws of Bosnia and Herzegovina. Because this never happened during the mandate of the first court, it did not have to decide on the issue whether this text would implicitly require at least the Supreme Courts and the Constitutional Courts of the Entities to submit the case to the Constitutional Court at state level for a 'preliminary ruling' – as this is by analogy the case in the relationship between national

provisions of the Constitution, which are not in conformity with the ECHR, cannot be reviewed by the Constitutional Court.

[26] Cf. Christian Steiner and Nedim Ademovic, *Constitution of Bosnia and Herzegovina. Commentary* (Sarajevo: Konrad-Adenauer-Stiftung, 2010) 691. But there is one exemption in the case law, namely case U 22/02, in which the review of the statute of an administrative district (i.e. a general administrative regulation) was declared admissible with reference not to the 'legal form' but to its function as a general normative regulation.

[27] The only post-communist constitution that granted the instrument of *actio popularis* was the Hungarian constitution. Because this led to an almost unmanageable workload for the Constitutional Court, it was abolished again. See Sadurski, note 6 above, 6.

supreme courts of the member states of the European Union and the European Court of Justice under EU law.

The fact that Entity supreme courts and constitutional courts never referred a case to the Bosnian Constitutional Court cannot be explained only by the fact that even among Bosnian attorneys there was almost no professional knowledge how to make use of the Dayton Constitution. This has to be seen much more as political resistance not to voluntarily subject themselves to the jurisdiction of the Constitutional Court, after it had rather bluntly decided that appeals against decisions of the Entity's constitutional courts were admissible,[28] whereas the judges of the Constitutional Court of RS had publicly declared their opinion to the contrary.[29] Hence, I do not agree with the scholarly opinion[30] that the first Constitutional Court supported the opinion that all state authorities were supposed to set aside unconstitutional law because of the supremacy of the Dayton Constitution and the direct applicability of the ECHR. Moreover, there is no empirical analysis available about whether this American way of 'diffuse' judicial review was ever practised. Anyhow, in the end, the Constitutional Court made clear in case AP 1603/05 that the courts of the Entities are not allowed to set aside unconstitutional law but must refer the question of constitutionality to the Bosnian Constitutional Court according to the 'concrete review' procedure of Article VI.3 (c).

However, this is not the end of the story of the development of legal protection mechanisms, but it brings me to the next problem, namely the differentiation between the notion of 'constitutionality' and 'legality' as a structural normative element of civil law systems. Article III.3 (b) of the Dayton Constitution provides for a 'supremacy clause' insofar as all authorities of the Entities have 'to comply fully with this Constitution, which supersedes inconsistent provisions of the law of Bosnia and Herzegovina and of the constitutions and law of the Entities'. Furthermore,

---

[28]   See cases U 5/99 and U 39/00.
[29]   Cf. Rajko Kuzmanovic and Miodrag Simovic, *Ustavni sud Republike Srpske i zastita ustavnosti i zakonitosti* (The Constitutional Court of Republika Srpska and the Protection of Constitutionality and Legality), Banja Luka 1999, 58. See also the contributions of the judges of the Constitutional Court of Republika Srpska, Rajko Kuzmanovic, Miodrag Simovic, and Marko Rajcevic as part of the Round Table in Sarajevo on 29 November 1999 and in Teslic on 8–9 December 2000 on the jurisdiction of the Constitutional Court and the provisions of Article VI.3 (b) of the Constitution, in *Okrugli stolovi Ustavnog suda BiH* (Round Tables of the Constitutional Court of BiH), Sarajevo 2001, 64–8, 164–76, and 182–90.
[30]   Steiner and Ademovic, note 26 above, 868.

the 'appellate jurisdiction' of Article VI.3 (b) speaks of 'issues under this Constitution arising out of a judgment of any other court . . . .' This again raises the question about general administrative regulations and individual decisions either of administrative or judicial authorities when the claim is made that these normative acts violate rights granted only by law but not explicitly guaranteed by the Constitution! Again, the majority of the domestic judges and one of the foreign judges of the first court were inclined, from a strictly literal reading of the text of the Constitution, to reject such appeals as inadmissible *rationae materiae*. The opposite view was taken by a minority of domestic and foreign judges, arguing from a common law perspective that the 'supremacy' of the constitution must encompass the entire normative hierarchy so that either implicitly or even following from the rule of law principle the violation of legal rules by administrative or judicial decisions amounts to a 'constitutional issue' as such. This argument was, however, never accepted by the majority of the court.

In the beginning of the first court, the majority of the domestic judges and one of the foreign judges also opposed the need for the Constitutional Court to review the constitutionality of laws in an appellate procedure under Article VI.3 (b), again with the literal reading but also following from the systematic interpretation that the court has simply to review whether the judgment of the respective court violates the Constitution or the ECHR, whereas the abstract or concrete reviews of legislation are reserved to the procedures under Article VI.3 (a) and (c). In addition, there was also a technical problem because the wording of the Rules of Procedure of the Constitutional Court for the proceedings under the appellate jurisdiction did not provide for the case that not the judgment directly, but the law on which the judgment was based violated the Constitution or the ECHR. Thus, in deliberations of the Constitutional Court, I referred to the possibility foreseen under Austrian constitutional law for such a case, namely to adjourn the proceedings before the Constitutional Court and to initiate a separate procedure in order to review the piece of legislation at stake, which would then end by either declaring the law constitutional with the following dismissal of the constitutional complaint or by declaring the law null and void and refer the case then back to the respective authorities. However, this approach was rejected by the majority of the judges with the argument that the court is not entitled to review legislation '*ex officio*' – that is, in a separate proceeding because this possibility had been given under the communist system and (mis)used as a political tool.

As can be seen, the problems of protection outlined came to the fore only case by case over time and can be summarized as follows. If an individual administrative or judicial act simply violates legal provisions but does not amount to a violation of 'constitutionally guaranteed subjective rights',[31] this violation can – as a consequence of the doctrinal distinction between legality and constitutionality – only be addressed through appeals to the Supreme Courts of the Entities without any possibility to make a further appeal to any of the constitutional courts. On the other hand, the Bosnian Constitutional Court recognized very soon the logic of the Bosnian system of administrative judicial review and accepted under both Article VI.3 (b) and (c) that individual administrative decisions might be overturned by an appeal to the court system, so that the Constitutional Court has also to decide an issue if the dispute determined by an Entity Supreme Court had started with an individual decision before an administrative authority.[32] But an important legal gap seems to remain. If a general administrative regulation is violating the law, only the public attorney has a subjective right to claim the 'illegality' of the general regulation as long as it does not amount to a violation of either the Entity or the Dayton Constitution.

Second, if a person considers that it is not the individual administrative or judicial decision but the law on which the decision is based, which is not in conformity with the Constitution or the ECHR, it follows from the more recent case law of the second court that a review of legal provisions will be accepted not under the 'abstract' review procedure but under its appellate jurisdiction and only if all legal remedies are exhausted.[33]

Hence, third, if a legal provision or the entire law directly affects the legal interests or subjective rights of a person – that is, without having clarified this through an individual administrative or judicial decision *and* if a legal interest or right might be violated for which evidence has to be given – there is no possibility to address the Constitutional Court unlike in Austria according to Articles 139 and 140 of the Austrian Constitution.

---

[31] I hereby intentionally use the Austrian legal terminology, which is in this context basically synonymous with the notion of human rights. But in contrast to a common law system, the notion of 'subjective rights' should make clear that civil law systems construct a basic doctrinal distinction between 'objective law' and 'subjective' rights, in particular rights of individuals. Only subjective rights are justiciable before administrative authorities and courts. In contrast, 'objective law', such as the principle of separation of powers, can never be made an individual legal interest to be enforced by courts.

[32] Cf. Cases U 15/00 and U 23/00.

[33] Cf. Steiner and Ademovic, note 26 above, 744.

The court has – in an *obiter dictum* – stated several times when it rejected the request to review a law under the 'abstract' review procedure that it might act in a similar situation under its appellate jurisdiction but only if the disputed issue had been addressed in another court proceeding and if all legal remedies are exhausted. Moreover, the Austrian mechanism comes close to an *actio popularis*, which was rejected by the Bosnian Court. Hence, there is still an important legal gap.

Finally, a problem is raised by decisions of lower courts when they declare a case inadmissible and the appellate courts confirm this decision. But a court's failure to decide on the merits might affect Article 6 of the ECHR, which guarantees access to a court. Hence, already the first court, by giving effect to Article 6 of the ECHR, accepted claims within its substantive scope and even took a decision on the merits of the case itself.[34]

The relation of the Constitutional Court vis-à-vis other judicial bodies and the High Representative

Due to the overlapping competences of the Constitutional Court and the Human Rights Chamber with regard to human rights protection and the possible, but confusing, parallel procedural protection mechanism with advantages or disadvantages for claimants before both judicial bodies,[35] it became clear from the very beginning that – without the possibility to rely on any rule in this respect in the GFAP – the jurisdiction of the Constitutional Court in relation to the other bodies established through the other annexes of the GFAP had to be clarified by case law.

Even before an appeal against a decision of the Human Rights Chamber was brought before the Constitutional Court, informal negotiations between the two bodies revealed that – because of 'institutional jealousy' – both parties claimed to be the superior judicial body. Hence, in the beginning, the Constitutional Court circumvented the problem in cases U 3/98 and U 4/98 by declaring the appeals inadmissible for other procedural reasons. However, in cases U 7/98 and U 11/98, the Court finally declared that it would not accept an appeal against a decision of the Human Rights Chamber, thereby following the position taken with

---

[34] *Ibid.*, 742.
[35] I have outlined this in more detail in Joseph Marko, 'Five Years of Constitutional Jurisprudence in Bosnia and Herzegovina: A First Balance' in *European Diversity and Autonomy Papers 7/2004*, accessible at www.eurac.edu/edap, 13–16.

regard to the same constitutional rank of all the annexes of the GFAP elaborated earlier so that the Constitutional Court could consequently not construct a superior rank for itself from a theoretical 'superior' rank of annex 4. Moreover, in an informal agreement, both bodies decided to reject claims as inadmissible if the party had already started proceedings before the other body. Following from this position, in cases U 21/01 and U 32/01, the Constitutional Court also declared appeals against decisions of the Real Property Claims Commission under annex 7 inadmissible. In those cases, the court opened, however, a back door, by declaring that for the clarification of specific matters excluded by the Commission, it would, according to Article 6 of the ECHR, be necessary to ensure access to the courts and thereby to the Constitutional Court under its appellate jurisdiction.

What functionally and structurally resembles the problem of jurisdiction of the CFA with regard to the question whether it can also review Mainland laws, came to the fore in BiH when – as elaborated earlier – the HRs started to 'decree' laws instead of the competent Parliamentary Assembly, being blocked by the so-called Entity veto mechanism.[36] Hence, it was only a matter of time before laws decreed by the HR and published in the Official Gazette would be contested before the Constitutional Court under the 'abstract' review mechanism.

In case U 9/00, in which the constitutionality of the law on the newly created State Border Service was contested, the Constitutional Court attempted to solve the constitutional and the political dilemma that the interventions of the HR into the Bosnian law-making process were in fact necessary in the interest of political effectiveness and in order to counterbalance the obstructionist policies of the ethnonational party leaders but that the judicial review of his decisions by the Constitutional Court might undermine at the same time his political authority necessary for the peace-building process. The attempt to square the circle is evident from the reasoning of the judgment. On the one hand, the court declared that the international law foundations of the powers of the HR *and their exercise* are not subject to review, but at the same time, the court developed a theory of 'functional duality', taken from French constitutional law, to construct the competence to review legislation decreed by the HR. More

---

[36] Article IV.3 (d) of the Dayton Constitution in a relatively complicated language regulates what is commonly called 'entity veto'. This means in practice that nine representatives in the House of Representatives elected from the Republika Srpska have an absolute veto right against any bill.

specifically, the court declared that the HR would only 'substitute' the competent Bosnian authority so that the law being published in the Official Gazette must formally be regarded as part of the Bosnian legal system. Hence, the court declared: 'The competence of the Constitutional Court to examine the constitutional conformity of the Law on State Border Service enacted by the HR *acting as an institution of Bosnia and Herzegovina* is thus based on article VI.3a of the Constitution. Consequently, the request is admissible' (emphasis added).

There is, of course, a contradictory logic in the reasoning in which first, not only the international law foundations but also the exercise of the competences of the HR was declared non-reviewable and second, that the legislative acts as part of the exercise of his Bonn powers would be subject to review. Nevertheless, this decision was accepted by the HR and the so-called 'international community' represented in the Peace Implementation Conference – to which the HR is politically responsible. This position was upheld in further cases U 16/00, U 25/00, and U 26/01 and established an important system of checks and balances not only between state powers but also between international supervisory mechanisms and national institutions in the newly established systems of international territorial administration for the purpose of peace building.[37]

Obviously, as some sort of political compromise in the balance of powers between the Bosnian Constitutional Court and the HR, the same court rejected the claims of individual persons. They had been dismissed from public office by the HR in – from the perspective of rule of law enforcement – a problematic approach. However, the courts had declared their complaints against the dismissal as inadmissible. In the first such case brought before the court in U 37/01, this was confirmed by the Constitutional Court. In a bluntly formalistic and literal reading of Article VI of the Dayton Constitution, the reasoning in this case – which has never been published – declared the lack of jurisdiction of the court with the simple argument that such a decision of the HR does not represent a 'judgment' in the sense of Article VI.3 (b) even though, on the basis of the theory of functional dualism, such a decision of the HR could

---

[37] From the perspective of rule of law enforcement and therefore the criticism already raised against international organizations that claim immunity for their actions in such a context it is, however, revealing that Article 147 of the new Kosovo Constitution of 2008 excludes the possibility that the newly established Constitutional Court of Kosovo may review any, including possible legislative, acts of the International Civilian Representative who is comparable to the High Representative in Bosnia and Herzegovina with the Bonn Powers.

simply have 'substituted' the management board of the public enterprise or even the Supreme Court of the Federation. In so doing, the court would nevertheless have been able to reject the appeal because of the non-exhaustion of legal remedies and could have avoided thereby the possible conflict with the HR at least for some time.

However, in a turnaround of the case law, the second court took exactly this road and declared in a series of cases all the appeals inadmissible in 2004 because of not having exhausted all possible legal remedies but referred to the possibility that the decisions of the HR might grossly violate human rights, arguing that there is no effective remedy foreseen as required under Article 13 of the ECHR and the HR's decisions might violate the non-discrimination provision under Article II of the Dayton Constitution.[38] Hence, it was only a matter of time before a case would reach the Constitutional Court having exhausted all legal remedies. This was finally the case in 2006 with the appeal Nr. AP 953/05. Because there is no effective legal remedy foreseen either under international law or the Dayton constitutional framework, the Constitutional Court not only declared the appeal admissible but also took a decision on the merits declaring that not the HR but the state Bosnia and Herzegovina had violated the human rights of the appellants for not having taken any steps in international fora[39] to ensure effective legal protection against decisions of the HR against individual persons.

However, this time the HR did not accept this decision and issued a strong statement in an 'Order on the Implementation of the Decision of the Constitutional Court of Bosnia and Herzegovina in the Appeal of Milorad Bilbija and Others, No. AP 953/05 of 23 March 2007'.[40] In this order, the HR stated his concern that the Bosnian institutions might misunderstand the position of the Constitutional Court and the fact that the HR had agreed to judicial review by the Constitutional Court of legislation decreed by him. He argued therefore that his decisions on removal from office would not be covered by the theory of functional duality because they would be 'exercised solely under Annex 10' not subject to any review by Bosnian authorities. Hence, Article 2 of the order warns:

---

[38] Cf. Steiner and Ademovic, Constitution, note 26 above, 802–6.
[39] The Venice Commission of the Council of Europe had already argued that such decisions should be reviewed by the United Nations itself and that the Security Council should set up a special body for this purpose.
[40] This order can be accessed on the webpage of the OHR, at www.ohr.int.

> Any step taken by any institution or authority in Bosnia and Herzegovina in order to establish any domestic mechanism to review the Decisions of the HR issued pursuant to his international mandate shall be considered by the High Representative as an attempt to undermine the implementation of the civilian aspects of the General Framework Agreement for Peace in Bosnia and Herzegovina and shall be treated in itself as conduct undermining such implementation.[41]

The prohibition, implicit in this 'warning' of the Order of the HR, for the Constitutional Court to declare other cases admissible was finally contested before the European Court of Human Rights in Strasbourg. In the decision *Berić and Others* v. *Bosnia and Herzegovina* of 16 October 2007, the European Court, however, confirmed the position of the HR and declared the applications inadmissible because:

> operations established by UN [Security Council (UNSC)] Resolutions under Chapter VII of the UN Charter are fundamental to the mission of the UN to secure international peace and security and since they rely for their effectiveness on support from member states, the Convention cannot be interpreted in a manner which would subject the acts and omissions of Contracting Parties which are covered by UNSC Resolutions and occur prior to or in the course of such missions, to the scrutiny of the Court. To do so would be to interfere with the fulfilment of the UN's key mission in this field including, as argued by certain parties, with the effective conduct of its operations.[42]

This authoritative decision from a supranational European court has therefore killed an innovative idea on the development of checks and balances for international organizations in order to limit their immunities through the rule of law principle.[43]

---

[41] *Ibid.*   [42] *Beric* v. *Bosnia and Herzegovina* (2008) 46 EHRR SE6 at [29].

[43] The Constitutional Court had, in the same spirit, also declared appeals against arrests by the multinational military force SFOR admissible. In case AP 696/04, the court argued in the same way as the German Constitutional Court had done in the famous 'Solange' decisions with regard to the transfer of powers to the European Community in the 1970s, namely that it would refrain from judicial review of European Community law 'as long as' (in German, *Solange*) the European institutions respected the human rights guaranteed under the German constitution. Hence, the Bosnian Constitutional Court declared to respect the special authority of SFOR under annex 1-A of the GFAP and the 'transfer of sovereign authority to international organisations' provided that the rights following from the ECHR are protected. However, the Bosnian authorities had failed to initiate any investigation in the case of possibly unlawful deprivation of liberty by SFOR so that the court concluded from Article 1 ECHR that the immunity of international military forces does not release the state of its positive obligation to protect individual rights. Cf. Steiner and Ademovic, Constitution; note 26 above, 849–51.

Means of interpretation and metaphors of constitutional doctrine

Finally, it may be worthwhile to see whether there are major differences in the methods of interpretation in a common or civil law system.

Shortly after the court commenced its judicial functions in September 1997, in case U 1/98, the problem was raised whether one of the 'co-chairs' of the Council of Ministers has a right to submit a request for an 'abstract' review procedure by the Constitutional Court or whether the co-chair has to act unanimously. The Constitution speaks of a 'chair' in Article V.4 but not of co-chairs as did the respective law on the Council of Ministers for ethnic purposes. The first draft by the judge rapporteur interpreted the Constitution in light of the subconstitutional law and did not see any problem with the rejection of the request. However, this simplistic approach was challenged by one of the foreign judges and finally decided in a narrow 5:4 decision. Because this case firmly established a functional approach of interpretation, a significant proportion of the court's reasoning is cited here in full:

> Interpreting the Constitution on the basis of subconstitutional provisions can be seen as a variant of the principle of interpretation which requires conformity of all subconstitutional norms with the Constitution insofar as there is a legal hierarchy based on the supremacy clause of article III.3(b) of the Constitution of Bosnia and Herzegovina. From that follows the general principle of interpretation that all statutes under review are supposed to be in conformity with the Constitution as long as possible. However, this general principle of interpretation in reviewing the constitutional conformity of statutes has to be distinguished from the case before us insofar as there is no request to review the conformity of the Law of the Council of Ministers with the Constitution! On the contrary, the problem raised concerns the interpretation of the Constitution in light of the sub-constitutional statute which, however, in itself would reverse the legal hierarchy that has to be derived from article III.3(b) of the Constitution.

> Moreover, from an interpretation that the two Co-Chairs must act jointly, it could follow that any access to the Constitutional Court by the Chair of the Council of Ministers may effectively be excluded if they block each other. Such an interpretation could thus have the effect that none of the two Co-Chairs can exercise this responsibility. This would violate the principle of effectiveness which is to be derived from the first sentence of article VI.3 of the Constitution of BiH that "the Constitutional Court shall uphold this Constitution."

> Hence, if the principle of interpretation supposing conformity of sub-constitutional norms with the constitution leads to unreasonable results

or, in the case of this admissibility question, raises serious doubts about the conformity of the Law on the Council of Ministers with the Constitution of BiH – the review of which was, however, not requested by the applicant – another principle, namely that of constitutional interpretation requiring functional conformity has to gain priority. The function of constitutional law is to provide a basic legal framework for living together in state and society. According to this function, constitutional law is formally characterized by its supremacy vis-à-vis statutes and other general legal norms and, usually, has to be amended in parliament by a qualified majority. It can be derived thus as a principle of interpretation that the function of the constitution must not be undermined by way of interpretation. In case of doubts, therefore, constitutional law must not be interpreted in such a way as to allow the "ordinary" legislature in actual effect to reach its goals without amendment of the constitution.[44]

Although the request of the respective person acting as co-chair was eventually withdrawn with the result that the court could no longer adopt a decision on the merits, one consequence of the doubt voiced in case U 1/98 as to the constitutionality of the Law on the Council of Minsters was that this very item of legislation was promptly challenged by others. The Court declared in case U 1/99 that not only the post of co-chair as introduced on the basis of ethnic considerations but also the post of Vice Prime Minister, who would have the power to nominate ministers from 'his' own ethnic group – a situation clearly contrary to the wording and principles of the Constitution – was indeed unconstitutional.

The court's decision in U 5/98[45] is one of the most significant cases for not only political reasons but also for an understanding of the development of constitutional doctrine. The starting point for the case was the application by the then Chair of the Presidency, Alija Izetbegovic, who requested the review of more than twenty provisions of the Entity constitutions. In his opinion, the Entities had not sufficiently fulfilled their obligations under Article XII. 2. of the Constitution to bring their constitutions into line with the Dayton Constitution. Perhaps the most politically sensitive issue was the allegation of the applicant that both Articles 1 of the Entity constitutions were not in conformity with the text of the Preamble of the Dayton Constitution, designating Bosniaks, Croats, and Serbs as 'constituent peoples' with an alleged right to equality

---

[44] Cf. U 1/98, [10]–[14].
[45] The court's entire decision of the case was published in four so-called Partial Decisions of U 5/98.

'on the entire territory of Bosnia and Herzegovina' – that is, not only on the Entity level.[46]

The first problem with regard to constitutional doctrine, which had to be clarified, was the question whether the Preamble had any normative meaning so that it can serve as a standard of review for the Constitutional Court because the representatives of the Parliament of RS in the procedure – by referring to the theories of Hans Kelsen – argued that a preamble has no normative content but is only of a political, declaratory nature. In contrast, the majority of the court held with reference to case law of the Canadian Supreme Court[47] that the Preamble of the Dayton Constitution contains:

> constitutional principles delineating... spheres of jurisdiction, the scope of rights and obligations, or the role of the political institutions. The provisions of the preamble are therefore not merely descriptive, but are also invested with a powerful normative force thereby serving as a sound standard of judicial review for the Constitutional Court.[48]

As such, the wording of the Preamble '... to promote the general welfare and economic growth through the protection of private property and the promotion of a market economy' was applied in conjunction with the provisions of Article I.4 of the Constitution, which laid down the 'full freedom of movement of persons, goods, services and capital throughout Bosnia and Herzegovina'. In conclusion, the provisions of the RS constitution relating to 'socially owned property', which had been taken over as a legacy from the Yugoslav communist system, were declared unconstitutional with the justification that in the process of privatization, such provisions hindered the development of a market economy as expressly referred to in the preamble of the Constitution.

Another issue was raised in relation to the interpretation of human rights and the extent to which they were to be regarded not only as

---

[46] A much more detailed review of this decision is given by Joseph Marko, '"United in Diversity"? Problems of State- and Nation-Building in Post-Conflict Situations: The Case of Bosnia and Herzegovina' (2006) 30 *Vermont Law Review* 503–50.

[47] In particular, in *Reference re Remuneration of Judges of the Provincial Court of Prince Edward Island* [1997] 3 SCR 3, [95], the Canadian Supreme Court stated: 'As such, the preamble is not only a key to construing the express provision of the Constitution Act, 1867, but also invites the use of those organizing principles to fill out gaps in the express terms of the constitutional scheme. It is the means by which the underlying logic of the Act can be given the force of law.'

[48] U 5/98, Partial Decision III, [26].

individual rights in the classic liberal tradition but could also be given a 'systemic' character. The Swedish judge and member of the European Commission on Human Rights insisted on the jurisprudence of the European Court of Human Rights, which protects only the possession of private property rather than the possibility of its acquisition in the context of Article 1 of the First Optional Protocol to the ECHR, but the two other foreign judges were inclined to follow the well-established doctrines of the German and Austrian Constitutional Courts that the 'individual' right to property in the human rights catalogues of the constitutions of these countries can also have a 'systemic' meaning for the protection of a market economy, what is called an 'institutional guarantee' by these courts. The Swedish judge, however, could not accept this doctrine and dissented with the argument that such an interpretation would transgress the borderline between law and politics.

Moreover and in accordance with the opinion of the majority of the court, the human rights provisions were interpreted as a source of positive legal obligations. With regard to the reconstruction of the economy, the interpretation of the term 'framework legislation' became particularly relevant in this context. The Dayton Constitution itself contains no reference to this term. The expression was used for the first time in a decision by the HR Carlos Westendorp in the context of privatization[49] but was given a clear constitutional basis by the Constitutional Court for the purpose of economic integration and thereby the integration of the state. This appears in both the second and fourth partial decision in case U 5/98. Against the argument of the RS representatives, that all matters not expressly enumerated in Article III.1 of the Constitution automatically fall into the exclusive competence of the Entities, the court first determined through systematic interpretation that the organs of the state as a whole are indeed endowed with other powers and in doing so relied upon the catalogue of human rights:

> Article II.3 therefore gives a general competence to the common institutions of Bosnia and Herzegovina to regulate all matters enumerated in the catalogue of human rights which cannot exclusively be left to the Entities since the protection has to be guaranteed to 'all persons within the territory of BiH'.

---

[49] Cf. Framework Law on Privatisation of Enterprises and Banks in Bosnia and Herzegovina, Official Gazette, Nr. 14/98.

The same holds true, the court went on to hold, for the text of Article I.4 of the Constitution, which provides for the freedoms of persons, goods, services, and capital for the whole of BiH. The court then concluded on the basis of such provisions that it is necessary for a functioning market economy based on these four fundamental freedoms and for the institutional guarantee of private property that not only the state as a whole but also the Entities are responsible for the maintenance of the relevant legal framework, which will reflect such constitutional principles. Hence, it is up to the state to adopt the necessary framework legislation to be specified then by implementing legislation of the Entities. The court also gave an explicit example for this positive obligation to adopt framework legislation: the Parliamentary Assembly is obliged to establish through the means of framework legislation the minimum standards for a uniform civil law code, in particular a law of property and a law of obligations.

Conclusion

Let me come to an end. I hope I have demonstrated throughout this chapter that foreign judges and the comparative law perspective that they bring with them are eye openers against cultural–national limitations in terms of interpretative approach or traditional constitutional doctrines. At the same time, I hope it demonstrates that there is no rigid, dichotomic distinction between common law and civil law, let alone that 'civil law' is by no means a uniform system. I am glad that I had – as a comparative law scholar – the unique experience on the bench of the Bosnian Constitutional Court to learn from my Bosnian colleagues irrespective of their ethnic belonging about the problems of a country not only in transition from communism to democracy and market economy but also from trying to recover from a terrible war and to reconstruct state and society. At the same time, I learned as much from my colleagues from France and Sweden and the hottest debates on matters of interpretation and constitutional doctrine that happened between the three of us as 'foreign' judges coming from different civil law traditions.

With all due respect, I therefore believe that we as foreign judges were also successful in playing the 'neutral' mediator, not the least by transferring our knowledge of how to apply the ECHR in our countries and the methods of interpretation of the European Court of Human Rights to our Bosnian colleagues so that – in the end – the principle of an effective enforcement of rule of law, in particular the protection of human rights, became the most important part of a *corps d'esprit* of the court.

When comparing the case law of the CFA and the methods of interpretation developed by this court, I can hardly find any difference between common law methods of interpretation and civil law interpretation. In *Leung TC William Roy* v. *Secretary of Justice* and *Leung Kwok Hung* v. *Chief Executive*,[50] the Hong Kong courts established a 'sufficient interest' requirement for judicial review of legislation even without specific state action, what I have identified in this chapter as necessary 'legal interest' to be demonstrated under Austrian constitutional law but still an important gap in the legal protection mechanism of the Bosnian Constitutional Court. Or with regard to possible restrictions of the exercise of fundamental rights, where the CFA has developed in a number of cases since 2002 a 'standard three-part test' for determining valid restrictions of the BL rights:[51] the first part, whether the restriction is prescribed by law, and the second and third part, labelled the 'rationality test' and the 'proportionality test', are exactly the same standards developed by the jurisprudence of the European Court of Human Rights and, following and refining this model, by the German and Austrian constitutional courts. It is thus no surprise that the foreign judges also introduced this test, generally labelled the 'proportionality test' in Central Europe, into the jurisprudence of the Bosnian Constitutional Court. Case U 19/01 of the Bosnian Court may again serve as a demonstration of the application of the proportionality test in which I disagreed with the majority opinion written by the Swedish judge and published a dissenting opinion. Last but not least, the principle that courts have to read unconstitutional laws in line with the requirements of the BL developed in *HKSAR* v. *Hung Chan Wa* and *HKSAR* v. *Lam Kwong Wai*[52] was also applied in one of the first cases of the court– that is, U 1/98 elaborated above, as a form of functional interpretation for the purpose of judicial restraint.

Finally, it seems to me that the functional approach in matters of interpretation has obviously become an important tool not only for comparative legal analysis but also for judicial review in order to put the case at hand into the proper factual context and thereby to avoid the pitfalls or

---

[50] Cf. the discussion of these cases by Simon N. M. Young, 'Fundamental Rights and the Basic Laws of the Hong Kong and Macau Special Administrative Regions' in Oliveira and Cardenal, note 12 above, 689–91.

[51] *Ibid.*, 691.   [52] *Ibid.*, 692.

even ideological misuse of the strictly literal reading so common in continental European legal positivism. Insofar, law and political sciences are no longer separated by a firewall, as this was established by Hans Kelsen, but interrelated requiring new ideas or even research agendas.[53]

---

[53] I have elaborated this topic in more detail together with my colleague M. Handstanger, a judge at the Austrian High Administrative Court, in an article on 'The Interdependence of Law and Political Sciences: About the "Essence and Value" of a "Juristenpolitologie-Approach", Wolfgang Mantl to his 70th Birthday' (2009) 3 *ICL Online Journal* 66–79. See also from an American perspective Keith Wittington, 'Constitutional Theory as Political Science' in Michael Gerhardt, Stephen Griffin, and Thomas D. Rowe, Jr. (eds.), *Constitutional Theory: Arguments and Perspectives*, 3rd edn. (Newark, NJ: LexisNexis, 2007) 690–703.